MORNING & EVENING

CHARLES SPURGEON

Whitaker House

All Scripture quotations are taken from the *King James Version* (KJV) of the Bible.

MORNING AND EVENING

ISBN: 0-88368-410-1
Printed in the United States of America
Copyright © 1997 by Whitaker House

Whitaker House
30 Hunt Valley Circle
New Kensington, PA 15068

Library of Congress Cataloging-in-Publication Data

Spurgeon, C. H. (Charles Haddon), 1834–1892.
    [Morning and evening daily devotions]
    Morning & evening / Charles Spurgeon.
       p.   cm.
    ISBN 0-88368-410-1 (trade paper : alk. paper)
    1. Devotional calendars—Baptists. I. Title.
BV4811.S6669 1997
242'.2—dc21   97-18623

4 5 6 7 8 9 10 11 12 / 06 05 04 03 02 01 00 99

MORNING
&
EVENING

January 1
Morning

"They did eat of the fruit of the land of Canaan that year" (Joshua 5:11).

Israel's weary wanderings were all over, and the promised rest was attained. No more moving tents, fiery serpents, fierce Amalekites, and howling wilderness. They came to the land which flowed with milk and honey, and they ate the old corn of the land. Perhaps this year, beloved Christian reader, this may be your case or mine. Rest assured that we have already experienced more ills than death at its worst can cause us. Let us banish every fearful thought and rejoice with exceeding great joy in the prospect that this year we will begin to be forever with the Lord. A part of the host will tarry on earth to do service for their Lord. If this is our lot, the New Year's text is still true. "We who have believed do enter into rest" (Hebrews 4:3). The Holy Spirit is the foretaste of our inheritance. Those who are in heaven are secure, and so are we preserved in Christ Jesus; there they triumph over their enemies, and we have victories too. Celestial spirits enjoy communion with their Lord, and this is not denied to us either; they rest in His love, and we have perfect peace in Him; they sing His praise, and it is our privilege to bless Him too. We will this year gather celestial fruits on earthly ground, where faith and hope have made the desert like the garden of the Lord. Man ate angel's food of old, and why not now? Oh for grace to feed on Jesus and to eat of the fruit of the land of Canaan this year.

January 1
Evening

"We will be glad and rejoice in thee" (Song of Solomon 1:4).

We will be glad and rejoice in God. We will not open the gates and begin the new year on a note of sadness. Rather, we will sing to the sweet strains of the harp of joy and the high sounding cymbals of gladness. "O come, let us sing unto the Lord: let us make a joyful noise unto the rock of our salvation" (Psalm 95:1). We, the called and faithful and chosen, *we* will drive away our griefs and set up our banners of confidence in the name of God. Let others lament over their troubles. We who have the sweetening tree to cast into Marah's bitter pool will magnify the Lord with joy. Eternal Spirit, our perfect Comforter, we will never cease from adoring and blessing the name of Jesus. Jesus must have the crown of our heart's delight. We will not dishonor our Bridegroom by mourning in His presence. We are ordained to be the minstrels of the skies. Let us rehearse our everlasting song before we sing it in the halls of the New Jerusalem. *We will be glad and rejoice*—two words with one meaning—double joy, blessing upon blessing. Should there be any limit to our rejoicing in the Lord even now? What riches are laid up in Jesus! What rivers of infinite bliss have their source and every drop of their fullness in Him! Sweet Lord Jesus, You are the present inheritance of Your people. Favor us this year with such a sense of Your preciousness that from its first to its last day, we may be glad and rejoice in You. Let January open with joy in the Lord and December close with gladness in Jesus.

January 2
Morning

"Continue in prayer" (Colossians 4:2).

It is interesting to notice how large a portion of the Word is occupied with the subject of prayer. We scarcely open the Bible before we read, "Then began men to call upon the name of the Lord" (Genesis 4:26); and just as we are about to close the volume, the "Amen" of an earnest supplication meets our ear. Instances are plentiful. Here we find a wrestling Jacob—there a Daniel who prayed three times a day—and a David who with all his heart called on his God. On the mountain we see Elias; in the dungeon Paul and Silas. We have multitudes of commands and myriads of promises. What does this teach us, but the sacred importance and necessity of prayer? We may be certain that whatever God has made prominent in His Word, He intended to be conspicuous in our lives. If He has said much about prayer, it is because He knows we have much need of it. So deep are our necessities that until we are in heaven we must not cease to pray. A prayerless soul is a Christless soul. If you are a child of God, you will seek your Father's face and live in your Father's love. Pray that this year you may be holy, humble, zealous, and patient. Pray for a closer communion with Christ. Enter into His banqueting-house of love more often. Pray that you may be an example and a blessing to others and that you may live more to the glory of your Master.

January 2
Evening

"Let the people renew their strength" (Isaiah 41:1).

All things on earth need to be renewed. No created thing continues on by itself. The psalmist recognized God's part when he said, "Thou renewest the face of the earth" (Psalm 104:30). Even the trees which do not wear themselves out with worry or shorten their lives with labor must drink the rain of heaven and consume the hidden treasures of the soul. A man's life cannot be sustained without renewal from God. As it is necessary to repair the body by the frequent meal, so we must repair the soul by feeding upon the Book of God or by listening to the preached Word or by the soul-fattening table of worship and praise. How depressed are our Christian lives when spiritual food is neglected! How poor and starving are some saints who live without the diligent use of the Word of God and secret prayer! If our faith can live without God, it is not divinely created. If God had begotten it, it would wait upon Him as the flowers wait upon the dew. Without constant restoration, we are not ready for the assaults of hell or even for the strife within. When the whirlwind is loosed, woe to the tree that has not grasped the rock with many intertwined roots. If we permit the good to grow weaker, the evil will surely gather strength and struggle desperately to master us. Let us draw near to the footstool of divine mercy in humble prayer. There we will realize the fulfillment of the promise, "They that wait upon the Lord shall renew their strength" (Isaiah 40:31).

January 3
Morning

"I will give thee for a covenant of the people" (Isaiah 49:8).

Jesus Christ is Himself the sum and substance of the covenant. As one of its gifts, He is the property of every believer. Believer, can you estimate what you have received in Christ? "In him dwelleth all the fulness of the Godhead bodily" (Colossians 2:9). Consider that word "God" and its infinity, and then meditate upon "perfect man" and all his beauty; for all that Christ, as God and man, ever had is yours. Our blessed Jesus, as God, is omniscient, omnipresent, omnipotent. Has He power? That power is yours to support and strengthen you, to overcome your enemies, and to preserve you even to the end. Has He love? There is not a drop of love in His heart which is not yours. Has He justice? It may seem a stern attribute, but even that is yours; for He will, by His justice, see to it that all which is promised to you in the covenant of grace will be secured to you. And all that He has as perfect man is yours. As a perfect man the Father's delight was upon Him. He stood accepted by the Most High. O believer, God's acceptance of Christ is your acceptance. Do you know that the love which the Father set on a perfect Christ, He sets on you *now?* That perfect righteousness which Jesus carefully formed through His stainless life is yours and is imputed to you. Christ is in the covenant.

January 3
Evening

"The voice of one crying in the wilderness, Prepare ye the way of the Lord, make his paths straight" (Luke 3:4).

The voice crying in the wilderness demanded *a way for the Lord to be prepared.* We must be attentive to the Master's proclamation and give Him a road into our heart, paved with His grace through the desert of our nature. *Every valley must be exalted.* Low and groveling thoughts of God must be given up. Doubting and despairing must be removed. Self-seeking and carnal delights must be forsaken. Across these deep valleys, a glorious highway of grace must be raised. *Every mountain and hill shall be laid low.* Proud self-sufficiency and boastful self-righteousness must be leveled to make a highway for the King of kings. Divine fellowship is never granted to haughty, high-minded sinners. The Lord cares for the lowly and visits the contrite in heart, but the proud are an abomination to Him. *The crooked shall be made straight.* The wavering heart must have a straight path of decision for God and holiness marked out for it. Double-minded men are strangers to the God of truth. Make sure that you are always honest and true before God, who searches all men's hearts. *The rough places shall be made smooth.* Stumbling-blocks of sin must be removed, and thorns and briers of rebellion must be uprooted. Such a great Visitor must not find miry ways and stony places when He comes to honor His favored ones with His company. This evening may the Lord find in your heart a highway made ready by His grace.

January 4
Morning

"Grow in grace, and in the knowledge of our Lord and Saviour Jesus Christ" (2 Peter 3:18).

Grow in grace. Grow in that root-grace, *faith*. Believe the promises more firmly than you have done. Let faith increase in fullness, constancy, and simplicity. Grow also in *love*. Ask that your love become extended, more intense, more practical, influencing every thought, word, and deed. Grow likewise in *humility*. As you grow in humility, seek also to grow nearer to God in prayer and experience more intimate fellowship with Jesus. May God the Holy Spirit enable you to *"grow in the knowledge of our Lord and Saviour."* He who does not grow in the knowledge of Jesus, refuses to be blessed. To know Him is "life eternal," and to advance in the knowledge of Him is to increase in happiness. Absence from Christ is hell; but the presence of Jesus is heaven. Seek to know more of Him in His divine nature, in His human relationship, in His finished work, in His death, in His resurrection, in His present glorious intercession, and in His future royal advent. An increase of love for Jesus and a more perfect understanding of His love for us is one of the best tests of growth in grace.

January 4
Evening

"Joseph knew his brethren, but they knew not him" (Genesis 42:8).

We all desire to grow in our relationship with the Lord Jesus and in our knowledge of His will. Tonight, let us consider *His knowledge of us* which was most blessedly perfect long before we had the slightest knowledge of Him. "Thine eyes did see my substance, yet being unperfect, and in thy book all my members were written. . .when as yet there was none of them" (Psalm 139:16). Before we existed in the world, we existed in His heart. When we were enemies to Him, He knew us, our misery, our madness, and our wickedness. When we wept bitterly in repentance and viewed Him only as a judge and a ruler, He viewed us as His beloved brethren, and His heart yearned for us. He never forgot His chosen, but always beheld them as objects of His infinite affection. "The Lord knoweth them that are his"(2 Tim 2:19) is as true of the prodigals who are feeding with the swine as of the children who sit at the table. But *we knew not our royal Brother* and, out of this ignorance, grew a host of sins. We withheld our hearts from Him and allowed Him no entrance to our love. We mistrusted Him and gave no credit to His words. We rebelled against Him and paid Him no loving homage. The Sun of Righteousness shone forth, and we could not see Him. Heaven came down to earth, and earth did not know it. Let God be praised, those days are over with us! Yet, even now, there is little that we know of Jesus compared with what He knows of us. We have only begun to study Him, but He knows us completely. When He returns to judge the earth, He will not say to us, "I never knew you," but He will confess our names before His Father.

January 5
Morning

"And God saw the light, that it was good: and God divided the light from the darkness" (Genesis 1:4).

Light might well be good, since it sprang from that command of goodness, "Let there be light." *Physical* light is said by Solomon to be sweet, but *gospel* light is infinitely more precious because it reveals eternal things. It also ministers to our immortal natures. When the Holy Spirit gives us *spiritual* light and opens our eyes to behold the glory of God in the face of Jesus Christ, we behold sin in its true colors and ourselves in our real position. We see the Most Holy God as He reveals Himself, the plan of mercy as He proposed it, and the world to come as the Word describes it. Spiritual light has many beams and prismatic colors. Whether they are knowledge, joy, holiness, or life, they are all divinely good. O Lord, give us more of Yourself, the true light. No sooner is there a good thing in the world, than a division is necessary. Light and darkness have no communion. God has divided them; let us not change them. Sons of light must not have fellowship with deeds, doctrines, or deceits of darkness. The children of the day must be sober, honest, and bold in their Lord's work, leaving the works of darkness to those who will dwell in it forever. Our churches should, by discipline, divide the light from the darkness. We, by our distinct separation from the world, should do the same. O Lord Jesus, be our light throughout this day, for Your light is the light of men.

January 5
Evening

"And God saw the light" (Genesis 1:4).

Notice the special attention which the Lord gave for the light. "God saw the light"—He looked at it carefully, gazed upon it with pleasure, and saw that it was good. If the Lord has given you light, He looks on that light with special interest. Not only is it dear to Him as His own handiwork, but it is *like* Himself, for He is light. It is pleasant to the believer to know that God's eye is tenderly observant of that work of grace which He has begun. He never loses sight of the treasure which He has placed in our earthen vessels. Sometimes *we* cannot see the light, but *God* always sees the light. It is very comforting for me to know that I am one of God's people—but it matters little whether I know it or not. If the Lord knows it, I am still safe. This is the foundation, "The Lord knoweth them that are His" (2 Tim 2:19). You may be sighing and groaning because of your sin and mourning over your darkness, yet the Lord sees light in your heart. He has put it there, and all the cloudiness and gloom of your soul cannot conceal your light from His gracious eye. You may have sunk low in despondency and even despair. But if your soul has any longing toward Christ and if you are seeking to rest in His finished work, God sees the light. He not only *sees* it, but He also *preserves* it in you. This is a precious thought to those who, after anxious watching and guarding of themselves, feel their own powerlessness to do so. The light preserved by His grace will one day be developed into the splendor of noonday and the fullness of glory. The light within is the dawn of the eternal day.

January 6
Morning

"Casting all your cares upon him; for he careth for you" (1 Peter 5:7).

It is a happy way of soothing sorrow when we can feel—"He careth for *me*." Christian, do not dishonor your Savior by always wearing a brow of care. Cast your burden upon your Lord. You are staggering beneath a weight which your Father would not feel. What seems to you a crushing burden would be to Him as the small dust of the balance. Oh, child of suffering, be patient. God has not passed you over in His providence. He who is the feeder of sparrows will also furnish you with what you need. Take up the arms of faith against a sea of trouble. There is One who cares for you. His eye is fixed on you, His heart beats with pity for your woe, and His omnipotent hand will bring you the needed help. The darkest cloud will scatter itself in showers of mercy. The blackest gloom will give place to the morning. He, if you are one of His family, will bind up your wounds and heal your broken heart. Do not doubt His grace because of your tribulation, but believe that He loves you as much in seasons of trouble as in times of happiness. What a serene and quiet life you might lead if you would leave providing to the God of Providence! With a little oil in the cruse and a handful of meal in the barrel, Elijah outlived the famine, and you will do the same. If God cares for you, why must you care too? Can you trust Him for your soul, and not for your body? He has never refused to bear your burdens, He has never fainted under their weight. Precious child, leave all your concerns in the hand of a gracious God.

January 6
Evening

"Now the hand of the Lord was upon me in the evening" (Ezekiel 33:22).

You are not the only one who is chastened in the night season. Cheerfully submit to the discipline of the Lord and carefully endeavor to profit by it. The hand of the Lord *strengthens* the soul and lifts the spirit upward toward eternal things. Oh, that I may feel the Lord dealing with me! A sense of the divine presence and indwelling lifts the soul to heaven upon the wings of eagles. At such times we are filled with spiritual joy and forget the cares and sorrows of earth. The invisible is near, and the visible loses its power over us. The servant-body waits at the foot of the hill, and the master-spirit worships upon the summit in the presence of the Lord. Oh, that a holy season of divine communion may be granted to me this evening! The Lord knows that I need it. My heart languishes, my faith is weak, my devotion is cold. All these are reasons why His healing hand should be laid upon me. His hand can cool the heat of my burning brow and quiet the tumult of my trembling heart. That glorious hand which made the world can renew my mind. The tireless hand which bears the earth's huge pillars up can sustain my spirit. The loving hand which encloses all the saints can cherish me. The mighty hand which defeats the enemy can subdue my sins. Jesus' hands were pierced for my redemption. I will surely feel that same hand upon me which once touched Daniel and set him upon his knees that he might see visions of God.

January 7
Morning

"For me to live is Christ, and to die is gain"
(Philippians 1:21).

The believer did not always live for Christ. He only began to after the Holy Spirit convinced him of sin and when, by grace, he was brought to see the dying Savior making a propitiation for his guilt. From the moment of the new and celestial birth, the man began to live for Christ. Jesus is to believers the one pearl of great price for whom we are willing to part with all that we have. He has subsequently won our heart, and it beats alone for Him. To His glory, we would live. In defense of His gospel, we would die. He is the pattern of our life and the model after which we would sculpture our character. Paul's words mean more than most men think. They imply that the aim and end of his life was Christ. In the words of an ancient saint, he did eat, drink, and sleep eternal life. Jesus was his very breath, the soul of his soul, the heart of his heart, the life of his life. Can you say, as a professing Christian, that you live up to this idea? Can you honestly say that for you to live is Christ? Are you, in your business, living for Christ? If a Christian professes to live for Christ, how can he live for another object without committing spiritual adultery? Who would dare say that he has lived wholly for Christ as the apostle did? Yet, this alone is the true life of a Christian. Lord, accept me; I present myself, praying to live only in You and for You.

January 7
Evening

"My sister, my spouse" (Song of Solomon 4:12).

Observe the sweet titles with which the heavenly Solomon, with intense affection, addresses His bride, the Church. *My sister,* one near to Me by ties of nature, partaker of the same grace. *My spouse,* nearest and dearest, united to Me by the tenderest bonds of love. She is My sweet companion and part of My own self. *My sister* by birth is bone of My bone and flesh of My flesh. *My spouse* by heavenly betrothal is espoused to Me in righteousness. *My sister*—I have known her since birth, and I have watched over her from earliest infancy. *My spouse* was taken from among the daughters, embraced by arms of love, and promised to Me forever. See how true it is that our royal Kinsman is not ashamed of us. He dwells with obvious delight upon this twofold relationship. We have the word *My* repeated twice in our text. It is as if Christ is filled with rapture by His possession of His Church. The Shepherd sought the sheep because they were *His* sheep. He has gone about "to seek and to save that which was lost" (Luke 19:10) because that which was lost was *His* long before it was lost. The Church is the exclusive possession of her Lord. No one else may claim a partnership or pretend to share her love. Christ is near through the ties of relationship. Christ is dear to you in bonds of marriage, and you are dear to Him. Behold, He grasps both of your hands with both of His own, saying, *"My* sister, *my* spouse." He neither can nor will ever let you go. Do not be slow to return the holy flame of His love.

January 8
Morning

"The iniquity of the holy things" (Exodus 28:38).

What a veil is lifted up by these words, and what a disclosure is made! It will be humbling and profitable for us to pause a while and see this sad sight. The iniquities of our public worship, its formality, lukewarmness, and wandering of heart! Our work for the Lord, its selfishness, carelessness, and slackness! Our private devotions, their laxity, coldness, neglect, sleepiness, and vanity! Dr. Payson, writing to his brother, says, "My parish, as well as my heart, resembles the garden of the sluggard; and what is worse, I find that many of my desires for the improvement of both, proceed either from pride, vanity, or laziness. I look at the weeds which overrun my garden and breathe out an earnest wish that they were uprooted. But why? What prompts the wish? It may be that I may walk out and say to myself, 'In what fine order my garden is kept!' This is *pride.* Or it may be that my neigbors may look over the wall and say, 'My, how your garden flourishes!' This is *vanity.* Or I may wish for the destruction of the weeds, because I am weary of pulling them up. This is *indolence.*" Even our desire after holiness may be polluted by ill motives. How cheering is the thought that, when the High Priest bore the iniquity of the holy things, he wore upon his brow the words, "Holiness to the Lord." Even while Jesus bears our sin, He presents before His Father's face not our unholiness, but His own holiness.

January 8
Evening

"Thy love is better than wine" (Song of Solomon 1:2).

Nothing gives the believer so much joy as fellowship with Christ. He has enjoyment as others have in the common pleasures of life. He can be glad in God's gifts and God's works. But in all these, he does not find as much true delight as in the matchless person of his Lord Jesus. He has wine which no vineyard on earth ever yielded. He has bread which all the cornfields of Egypt could never bring forth. The joys of earth are little better than husks for swine compared with Jesus, the heavenly manna. We would rather have one taste of Christ's love and a sip of His fellowship, than a whole world full of carnal delights. What is the chaff to the wheat? What is the sparkling glass to the true diamond? What is a dream to the glorious reality? What is time's greatest enjoyment compared to our Lord Jesus? If you know anything of the inner life, you will agree that our highest, purest, and most enduring joy must be the fruit of the tree of life which is in the midst of the Paradise of God. All earthly bliss is simply earthy, but the comforts of Christ's presence are heavenly. We can review our communion with Jesus and find no regrets of emptiness within. The joy of the Lord is solid and enduring. Pride does not look upon it, but it withstands the test of years. It is in time and in eternity worthy to be called *the only true delight.* For nourishment, consolation, exhilaration, and refreshment, no wine can rival the love of Jesus. Let us drink to the full this evening.

"I will be their God" (Jeremiah 31:33).

Christian, here is all you can require. If you can pour this promise into your cup, you can say, "My cup runneth over; I have more than anyone's heart can wish." When this is fulfilled, "I am thy God," are you not a possessor of all things? Desire is insatiable as death, but He who fills all in all can fill it. Who can measure the capacity of our wishes? But the immeasurable wealth of God can more than overflow it. But you want more than quiet satisfaction; you desire rapturous delight. Here is music fit for heaven in this your portion, for God is the maker of heaven. Not all the music blown from sweet instruments or drawn from living strings can yield such melody as this sweet promise, "I will be their God" (Genesis 17:8). Here is a deep sea of bliss, a shoreless ocean of delight. Bathe your spirit in it. Swim forever and you will find no shore. Dive throughout eternity and you will find no bottom. If this does not make your eyes sparkle and your heart beat high with bliss, then your soul is not in a healthy state. This is the masterpiece of all the promises. Its enjoyment makes a heaven below and will make a heaven above. Dwell in the light of your Lord, and let your soul be saturated with His love. Get out the marrow and fatness which this portion yields you. Live up to your privileges and rejoice with unspeakable joy.

January 9
Evening

"Serve the Lord with gladness" (Psalm 100:2).

Delight in divine service is a token of acceptance. Those who serve God with a sad countenance because they are doing something that is unpleasant to them are not serving Him at all. They bring the form of homage, but the life is absent. Our God requires no slaves to grace His throne. He is the Lord of the empire of love and desires His servants to be dressed in garments of joy. The angels of God serve Him with songs, not with groans. A murmur or a sigh would be a mutiny in their ranks. Obedience which is not voluntary is disobedience. The Lord looks at the heart, and if He sees that we serve Him from force and not because we love Him, He will reject our offering. Take away joyful willingness from the Christian, and you have removed the test of his sincerity. If a man must be driven to battle, he is no patriot. But he who marches into the fight with a flashing eye, singing, "It is sweet for one's country to die," proves himself to be sincere in his patriotism. Cheerfulness is the support of our strength. In the joy of the Lord, we are strong. It acts as the remover of difficulties. It is to our service what oil is to the wheels of a vehicle. Without oil, the axle soon grows hot, and accidents occur. If there is not a holy cheerfulness to oil our wheels, our spirits will be clogged with weariness. The man who is cheerful in his service of God proves that obedience is his life. Do *you* serve the Lord *with gladness?* Let us show the people of the world who think our religion is slavery that it is to us a delight and a joy. Let our gladness proclaim that we serve a good Master.

January 10
Morning

"There is laid up for me a crown of righteousness" (2 Timothy 4:8).

Doubting one, you have often said, "I fear I will never enter heaven." Fear not! all the people of God will enter there. I love the quaint saying of a dying man who exclaimed, "I have no fear of going home; I have sent all before; God's finger is on the latch of my door, and I am ready for Him to enter." "But," said one, "are you not afraid lest you miss your inheritance?" "No," said he, "There is one crown in heaven which the angel Gabriel could not wear. It will fit no head but mine. There is one throne in heaven which Paul the apostle could not fill. It was made for me, and I will have it." Oh Christian, what a joyous thought! *Your* portion is secure. "But can I forfeit it?" No, it is assigned. If I am a child of God, I will not lose it. It is mine as securely as if I were there. Come with me, believer, and let us sit on the top of Nebo and view the goodly land, even Canaan. See that little river of death glistening in the sunlight, and across it do you see the pinnacles of the eternal city? Do you mark the pleasant country and all its joyous inhabitants? Know then that if you could fly across you would see written on one of its many mansions, "This remaineth for such a one, preserved for him only. He will be caught up to dwell forever with God." Poor doubting one, see the fair inheritance. It is *yours*. If you believe in the Lord Jesus, if you have repented of sin, if you have been renewed in heart, you are one of the Lord's people. There is a place reserved for you, a crown laid up for you. There will be no vacant thrones in glory when all the chosen are gathered in.

January 10
Evening

"In my flesh shall I see God" (Job 19:26).

Notice the subject of Job's devout anticipation—"I shall see God." He does not say, "I shall see the saints"—though doubtless that will bring great joy. But he says, "I shall see *God.*" It is not, "I shall see the pearly gates, I shall behold the walls of jasper, I shall gaze upon the crowns of gold," but, "I shall see God." This is the substance of heaven and the joyful hope of all believers. It is their delight to see Him now in the worship service by faith. They love to behold Him in communion and in prayer. But in heaven they will have open and unclouded vision. By seeing Him as He is, they will be made completely like Him. *Likeness to God*—what more can we wish for? Some read the passage, "Yet, I shall see God in my flesh" and believe that it refers to Christ. He is the Word made flesh and the glorious beholding of Him will be the splendor of the latter days. Christ will be the object of our eternal vision. We will never want any joy beyond that of seeing Him. He is only one source of delight, but that source is infinite. His works, His gifts, His love to us, and His glory will make a theme which will be ever new. The patriarch looked forward to this sight of God as a *personal* enjoyment when he said, "Whom mine eyes shall behold, and not another" (Job 19:27). Take a deep view of heaven's bliss. Think what it will be *to you.* "Thine eyes shall see the king in his beauty" (Isaiah 33:17). All earthly brightness fades and darkens as we gaze upon it. But here is a brightness which can never dim, a glory which can never fade—*"I shall see God."*

January 11
Morning

"These have no root" (Luke 8:13).

My soul, examine yourself this morning by the light of this text. You have received the Word with joy. Your feelings have been stirred, and a lively impression has been made. Remember that to receive the Word in the ear is one thing, but to receive Jesus into your soul is quite another. In the parable, the seed in one case fell on ground having a rocky bottom covered over with a thin layer of earth. When the seed began to take root, its downward growth was hindered by the hard stone. Therefore, it used its strength in pushing its green shoot up as high as it could. But having no inward moisture derived from root nourishment, it withered away. Is this my case? Have I been making a fair show in the flesh without having a corresponding inner life? Good growth takes place upward and downward at the same time. Am I rooted in sincere allegiance and love to Jesus? If my heart remains unsoftened and unfertilized by grace, the good seed may germinate for a season; but it must ultimately whither, for it cannot flourish on a rocky, unbroken, unsanctified heart. Let me dread a godliness as rapid in growth and as lacking in endurance as Jonah's gourd. Let me count the cost of being a follower of Jesus. Let me feel the energy of His Holy Spirit, and then I will possess an abiding and enduring seed in my soul.

January 11
Evening

"I have prayed for thee" (Luke 22:32).

How encouraging is the thought of the Redeemer's never-ceasing intercession for us. When we pray, He pleads for us. When we are not praying, He is pleading our cause and, by His supplications, shielding us from unseen dangers. Notice the word of comfort addressed to Peter— "Simon, Simon, behold, Satan hath desired to have you, that he may sift you as wheat; But"—what? "But go and pray for yourself?" That would be good advice, but it is not written. Neither does He say, "But I will keep you watchful, and so you shall be preserved." That would have been a great blessing. No, it is, *"But I have prayed for thee, that thy faith fail not"* (Luke 22:31-32). We know little of what we owe to our Savior's prayers. When we reach the hilltops of heaven and look back on the way that the Lord our God has led us, how we will praise Him! As He prayed before the eternal throne, He undid the evil which Satan was doing upon earth. How we thank Him because He never rested, but day and night pointed to the wounds upon His hands and carried our names upon His breastplate! Even before Satan had begun to tempt Him, Jesus stalled him and entered a plea in heaven. Mercy outruns malice. He does not say, "Satan has sifted you, and therefore I will pray," but "Satan hath *desired* to have you." He checks Satan even in his very desire, and nips it in the bud. Jesus does not say, "But I have desired to pray for you." No, but "I *have* prayed for you; I have done it already; I have gone to court and made your defense even before an accusation is made."

January 12
Morning

"Ye are Christ's; and Christ is God's" (1 Corinthians 3:23).

Ye are Christ's. You are His by donation, for the Father gave you to the Son. You were purchased by His blood for He counted the price for your redemption. You are His by dedication, for you have consecrated yourself to Him; His by relation, for you are named by His name, and made one of His brethren and joint-heirs. When tempted to sin, reply, "I cannot do this great wickedness, for I am Christ's." When wealth is before you to be won by sin, say that you are Christ's, and do not touch it. Are you exposed to difficulties and dangers? Stand fast in the evil day, remembering that you are Christ's. Are you placed where others are sitting down idly, doing nothing? Rise to the works with all your powers. When the sweat stands upon your brow, and you are tempted to loiter, cry, "No, I cannot stop, for I am Christ's." When the cause of God invites you, give yourself to it. When the poor need you, give yourself and your goods away, for you are Christ's. Always be one of those whose manners are Christian, whose speech is like the Nazarene, whose conduct and conversation is so suggestive of heaven that all who see you will know that you are the Savior's. Let your argument for holiness be, "I am Christ's."

January 12
Evening

"I have yet to speak on God's behalf" (Job 36:2).

We should not desire to be known by others for our virtue or for our zeal. But at the same time, it is a sin to always try to hide that which God has bestowed upon us for the good of others. A Christian is not to be a village in a valley, but a city set upon a hill. He is not to be a candle under a bushel, but a candle in a candlestick, giving light to all. (See Matthew 5:14-15.) Retirement may be lovely in its season, and to hide one's self is modest, but the hiding of *Christ* in us can never be justified. The keeping back of truth which is precious to us is a sin against others and an offense against God. If you are of a nervous temperament and retiring disposition, take care that you do not indulge in this trembling tendency too much, lest you become useless to the Church. In the name of Him who was not ashamed of you, decide to ignore your feelings. Tell others what Christ has told you. If you cannot speak with the sound of a trumpet, use the still, small voice. If the pulpit is not your platform, if the press does not carry your words, say with Peter and John, "Silver and gold have I none, but such as I have give I unto thee" (Acts 3:6). Talk to the Samaritan woman by the well if you cannot preach a sermon on the mountaintop. Utter the praises of Jesus in the house, if not in the temple; in the field, if not in the city; in your own household, if you cannot speak in the middle of the great family of man. From the hidden springs within let sweetly flowing streams of testimony flow forth, giving drink to every passer-by. Do not hide your talent. To speak for God will be refreshing to ourselves, cheering to saints, useful to sinners, and honoring to the Savior.

January 13
Morning

"Jehoshaphat made ships of Tharshish to go to Ophir for gold but they went not; for the ships were broken at Ezion-geber" (1 Kings 22:48).

Solomon's ships had returned in safety, but Jehoshaphat's vessels never reached the land of gold. Providence prospers one and frustrates the desires of another in the same business and at the same time. Yet, the great ruler is as good and wise at one time as another. May we have grace today, in the remembrance of this text, to bless the Lord for ships broken at Ezion-geber, as well as for vessels loaded with earthly blessings. Let us not envy the more successful or murmur at our losses as though we were singularly and specially tried. The secret cause of Jehoshaphat's loss is worthy of notice, for it is the root of much of the suffering of the Lord's people. It was his alliance with a sinful family, his fellowship with sinners that caused the disaster. In 2 Chronicles 20:37, we are told that the Lord sent a prophet to declare, "Because thou hast joined thyself with Ahaziah, the Lord hath broken thy works." This was a fatherly chastisement, which appears to have been blessed to him. Let Jehoshaphat's experience be a warning to the rest of the Lord's people to avoid being unequally yoked together with unbelievers! Oh, for such love for Jesus that, like Him, we may be holy, harmless, undefiled, and separate from sinners.

January 13
Evening

"The iron did swim" (2 Kings 6:6).

The axe head seemed hopelessly lost. Since it was borrowed, the reputation of the prophetic band was in danger and the name of their God was at risk of being dishonored. Contrary to all expectation, the iron was made to float to the surface of the stream. Things impossible with man are possible with God. (See Luke 18:27.) I knew a Christian who was called to undertake a work far exceeding his strength. It appeared so difficult that the mere idea of attempting it seemed absurd. Yet he was called, and his faith rose to the occasion. God honored his faith, help that was not sought after was sent, and the iron did swim. Another of the Lord's family was in grievous financial straits. He would have been able to meet all claims and much more, if he could have sold a certain portion of his estate. But he was overtaken with a sudden pressure. He sought for friends in vain, but faith led him to the unfailing Helper. The trouble was averted, his footsteps were established, and the iron did swim. A third had a severe case of wickedness to deal with. He had been taught, reproved, warned, and interceded for, but all in vain. Old Adam was too strong for this young Christian. The stubborn spirit would not relent. Then came an agony of prayer, and before long a blessed answer was sent from heaven. The hard heart was broken, and the iron did swim. What is your desperate case? What heavy matter do you have in your hands this evening? Bring it to God. The God of the prophets lives to help His saints. He will not permit you to lack any good thing. Believe in the Lord of Hosts! You too will see the finger of God working marvels for His people. According to your faith, be it done to you and remember that the iron will swim.

January 14
Morning

"Mighty to save" (Isaiah 63:1).

By the words "to save," we understand the whole of the great work of salvation, from the first holy desire onward to complete sanctification. Christ is not only "mighty to save" those who repent, but He is able to make men repent. He will carry those to heaven who believe; but He is, moreover, mighty to give men new hearts and to work faith in them. He is mighty to make the man who hates holiness love it and to constrain the despiser of His name to bend the knee before Him. The life of a believer is a series of miracles formed by the Mighty God. The bush burns, but it is not consumed. He is mighty enough to keep His people holy after He has made them so and to preserve them in His fear and love until He consummates their spiritual existence in heaven. Christ's power does not lie in making a believer and then leaving him to shift for himself. He who begins the good work carries it on. Believer, here is encouragement. Are you praying for some beloved one? Don't stop praying, for Christ is "mighty to save." You are powerless to reclaim the rebel, but your Lord is all powerful. Lay hold on that mighty arm, and rouse it to put forth its strength. Does your own case trouble you? Fear not, for His strength is sufficient for you. Whether to begin with others or to carry on the work in you, Jesus is "mighty to save;" the best proof of which lies in the fact that He saved you.

January 14
Evening

"Beginning to sink, he cried, saying, Lord, save me"(Matthew 14:30).

Sinking times are praying times with the Lord's servants. Peter neglected prayer at the start of his adventurous journey. But when he began to sink, his danger made him a petitioner. His cry, though late, was not too late. In our hours of bodily pain and mental anguish, we find ourselves as naturally driven to prayer as driftwood is driven upon the shore by the waves. The fox dashes to its hole for protection. The bird flies to the woods for shelter. In a similar way, the tried believer hastens to the mercy seat for safety. Heaven's great harbor of refuge is prayer. Thousands of weather-beaten vessels have found a haven there. The moment a storm comes on, it is wise for us to make for it with full sail. *Short prayers are long enough.* There were only three words in the petition that Peter gasped out, but they were sufficient for his purpose. Not length but strength is desirable. A sense of need is a mighty teacher of brevity. If our prayers had less of the tail feathers of pride and more wing, they would be much better. Verbiage is to devotion as chaff to the wheat. All that is a real prayer in many long sermons might have been uttered in a petition as short as that of Peter. *Our extremities are the Lord's opportunities.* Immediately, a keen sense of danger forces an anxious cry that the ear of Jesus hears. His ear and His heart go together, and His hand does not delay to take action. At the last moment we appeal to our Master, but His swift hand makes up for our delays by instant and effective action. Are you nearly drowned by the turbulent waters of affliction? Then lift up your soul to the Savior. Rest assured that He will not allow you to perish. When you can do nothing, Jesus can do all things.

January 15
Morning

"Do as thou hast said" (2 Samuel 7:25).

God's promises were never meant to be thrown aside as waste paper. He intended that they should be used. He loves to see His children bring them up to Him and say, "Lord, do as thou hast said." We glorify God when we plead His promises. Do you think that God will be any poorer for giving you the riches He has promised? He has said, "Come, now, and let us reason together, saith the Lord: though your sins be as scarlet, they shall be as white as snow; though they be red like crimson, they shall be as wool" (Isaiah 1:18). Faith goes straight to the throne and pleads, "Lord, here is the promise. Do as thou hast said." Our Lord replies, "Be it unto thee even as thou wilt." Our heavenly banker delights to cash His own notes. Never let the promise rust. Do not think that God will be troubled by your persistence in reminding Him of His promises. It is His delight to grant favors. He is more ready to hear than you are to ask. The sun is not weary of shining, nor the fountain of flowing. It is God's nature to keep His promises; therefore, go at once to the throne with "Do as thou hast said."

January 15
Evening

"But I give myself unto prayer" (Psalm 109:4).

Lying tongues were busy against the reputation of David, but he did not defend himself. Instead, he moved the case into a higher court and pleaded before the great King. Prayer is the safest method of replying to words of hatred. The psalmist prayed in no cold-hearted manner. He *gave himself* to the exercise. He threw his whole soul and heart into it, straining every sinew and muscle. This is the only way that any of us will find answers at the throne of grace. Supplication in which a man is not thoroughly involved in agonizing earnestness and vehement desire is utterly ineffective. "Fervent prayer," says an old saint, "like a cannon planted at the gates of heaven, makes them fly open." The common fault with most of us is our readiness to yield to distractions. Our thoughts wander, and we make little progress toward our goal. Like quicksilver, our mind will not hold together, but rolls off this way and that. How great an evil this is! It injures us, and, what is worse, it insults our God. What would we think of a petitioner, if, while having an audience with a prince, he was playing with a feather or catching a fly? Continuance and perseverance are expressed in our text. David did not cry once and then lapse into silence. His holy clamor continued until it brought down the blessing. Prayer must not be our occasional work, but our daily business, our habit, and our vocation. As artists give themselves to their models and poets to their classical pursuits, so must we addict ourselves to prayer. We must be immersed in prayer and pray without ceasing.

January 16
Morning

"I will help thee, sayeth the Lord" (Isaiah 41:14).

This morning let us hear the Lord Jesus speak to each one of us. "It is but a small thing for Me, your God, to help you. Consider what I have done already. What! not help you? Why, I bought you with My blood. I have died for you; and if I have done the greater, will I not do the less? It is the least thing I will ever do for you. I have done more and will do more. Before the world began I chose you. I made the covenant for you. I laid aside My glory and became a man for you. I gave My life for you. If I did all this, I will surely help you now. In helping you, I am giving you what I have bought for you already. If you had need of a thousand times as much help, I would give it to you. You require little compared with what I am ready to give. It is much for you to need, but it is nothing for Me to bestow. Help you? Fear not! If there were an ant at the door of your granary asking for help, it would not ruin you to give him a handful of your wheat. You are nothing but a tiny insect at the door of My all-sufficiency. I will help you." Oh, my soul, is this not enough? Do you need more strength than the omnipotence of the united Trinity? Do you want more wisdom than exists in the Father, more love than displays itself in the Son, or more power than is manifest in the influences of the Spirit? Behold, this river of God is full for your supply. What can you desire beside?

January 16
Evening

"The Messiah shall be cut off, but not for himself" (Daniel 9:26).

Blessed be His name, there was no cause of death in Him. No sin defiled Him, and, therefore, death had no claim upon Him. No man could have taken His life from Him justly, for He had done no man wrong. No man could even have slain Him by force unless He deliberately yielded Himself to die. But notice! One sins and another suffers. Justice was offended by us, but found its satisfaction in Him. Rivers of tears, mountains of offerings, seas of the blood of bullocks, and hills of frankincense could not have accomplished the removal of sin. But Jesus was cut off for us, and the cause of wrath was cut off at once. Sin was put away forever. Love led the Redeemer to lay down His life for His enemies! It is not enough, however, to admire the spectacle of the innocent bleeding for the guilty. We must be sure to realize its effect on our lives. The purpose of the Messiah's death was the salvation of His Church. Do we have a part among those for whom He gave His life as a ransom? Did the Lord Jesus stand as our representative? Are we healed by His stripes? It would be a terrible thing if we were to come short of a portion in His sacrifice. It would be better for us if we had never been born. To all who believe on Him, the Lord Jesus is a present Savior. Upon them, all the blood of reconciliation has been sprinkled. Let all who trust in the merit of Messiah's death be joyful at every remembrance of Him. Let their holy gratitude lead them to the fullest consecration to His cause.

January 17
Morning

"And I looked, and, lo, a Lamb stood on the Mount Zion" (Revelation 14:1).

The apostle John was privileged to look within the gates of heaven. In describing what he saw, he begins by saying, "I looked, and lo, a Lamb!" This teaches us that the chief object of contemplation in the heavenly state is "the Lamb of God, which takes away the sins of the world." Nothing else attracted the apostle's attention so much as the person of that divine being, who has redeemed us by His blood. He is the theme of the songs of all glorified spirits and holy angels. In a little while, when tears have been wiped from your eyes, you will see *the same Lamb exalted on His throne.* It is the joy of your heart to hold daily fellowship with Jesus. You will have the same joy to a higher degree in heaven. You will enjoy the constant vision of His presence. You will dwell with Him forever. "I looked, and, lo, a Lamb!" Why, that Lamb is heaven itself. As good Rutherford says, "Heaven and Christ are the same thing." To be with Christ is to be in heaven, and to be in heaven is to be with Christ. That prisoner of the Lord very sweetly writes in one of his glowing letters—"O my Lord Christ, if I could be in heaven without You, it would be a hell; and if I could be in hell, and have You still, it would be a heaven to me, for You are all the heaven I want." It is true, Christian. All you need to make you blessed is "to be with Christ."

January 17
Evening

"And it came to pass in an eveningtide, that David arose from off his bed, and walked upon the roof of the king's house" (Samuel 11:2).

At that hour, David saw Bathsheba. We are never out of the reach of temptation. Both at home and abroad, we are always in danger of meeting with evil allurements. The morning opens with peril, and the shades of evening find us still in jeopardy. Those whom God keeps are well kept. But woe to those who go forth into the world or even dare to walk through their own house unarmed. Those who think that they are secure are more exposed to danger than any others. David should have been engaged in fighting the Lord's battles. Instead, he lingered in Jerusalem and rested in luxury, for he arose from his bed in the evening. Idleness and luxury are the devil's jackals and provide him with abundant prey. Oh, for the constraining love of Jesus to keep us active and useful! When I see the king of Israel sluggishly leaving his couch at the close of the day and falling at once into temptation, let me take warning. I am reminded to set holy watchfulness to guard the door. Is it possible that the king climbed to his housetop for rest and devotion? If so, what a caution is given us to consider no place, however secret, a sanctuary from sin! Our hearts are like kindling, and sparks are plentiful. We need to use diligence at all times to prevent a blaze. Satan can climb housetops and enter closets. Even if we could shut out that foul fiend, our own corruptions are enough to work our ruin unless grace prevents us. Beware of evening temptations. The sun is down, but sin is up. We need a watchman for the night as well as a guardian for the day. Oh blessed Spirit, keep us from all evil this night.

January 18
Morning

"There remaineth therefore a rest to the people of God" (Hebrews 4:9).

How different the state of the believer will be in heaven from what it is here! Here he is born to toil and suffer weariness. In the land of the immortal, fatigue is never known. Anxious to serve his Master, he finds his strength unequal to his zeal. If he is completely active, he will have much labor; not too much for his will, but more than enough for his power, so that he will cry out, "I am not wearied of the labor, but I am wearied in it." Christian, the hot day of weariness will not last forever. The sun is nearing the horizon. It will rise again with a brighter day than you have ever seen, on a land where they serve God day and night, and yet rest from their labors. *Here,* rest is but partial; *there,* it is perfect. Toil-worn laborer, only think when you will rest forever! Can you conceive it? It is a rest *eternal.* There, everything is immortal. The harp abides unrusted, the crown unwithered, the eye undimmed, the voice unfaltering, the heart unwavering, and the immortal being is wholly absorbed in infinite delight. It will be a happy day when mortality will be swallowed up!

January 18
Evening

"He expounded unto them in all the scriptures the things concerning himself" (Luke 24:27).

The two disciples on the road to Emmaus had a most profitable journey. Their companion and teacher was the best of tutors. Their interpreter was one of a thousand, in whom are hid all the treasures of wisdom and knowledge. (See Colossians 2:3.) The Lord Jesus condescended to become a preacher of the gospel, and He was not ashamed to exercise His calling before an audience of two people. Neither does He now refuse to become the teacher of even one. Let us request the company of so excellent an Instructor. This unrivaled tutor used the best of books as His text. Although able to reveal fresh truth, He preferred to expound the old. By turning at once to Moses and the prophets, He showed us that the surest road to wisdom is not speculation, reasoning, or reading man's philosophies, but rather, meditation upon the Word of God. The way to be spiritually rich in heavenly knowledge is to dig in this mine of diamonds and gather pearls from this heavenly sea. When Jesus sought to enrich others, He worked in the quarry of holy Scripture. The favored pair on the road to Emmaus studied the best of subjects. Jesus spoke to them about the things concerning Himself. The one who hid the treasure in the field, guided the searchers to it. Our Lord would naturally discuss the sweetest of topics. He could find none sweeter than His own person and work. We should always search the Word. Oh, for grace to study the Bible with Jesus as both our teacher and our lesson!

January 19
Morning

"I sought him, but I found him not" (Song of Solomon 3:1).

Tell me where you lost the company of Christ, and I will tell you the most likely place to find Him. Have you lost Christ in the closet by restraining prayer? Then it is there you must seek and find Him. Did you lose Christ by sin? You will find Christ in no other way but by the giving up of the sin and seeking by the Holy Spirit to mortify the member in which the lust dwells. Did you lose Christ by neglecting the Scriptures? You must find Christ in the Scriptures. The saying is true, "Look for a thing where you dropped it; it is there." Look for Christ where you lost Him. He has not gone away. It is hard work to go back for Christ. Bunyan tells us that the pilgrim found the piece of the road back to the Arbor of Ease, where he lost his roll, the hardest he had ever traveled. Twenty miles onward is easier than to go one mile back for the lost evidence. Take care, when you find your Master, to cling close to Him. But how is it you have lost Him? One would have thought you would never have parted with such a precious Friend, whose presence is sweet, whose words are comforting. How is it that you did not watch Him every moment for fear of losing sight of Him? Yet, since you have let Him go, what a mercy that you are seeking Him. Go on seeking, for it is dangerous to be without your Lord.

January 19
Evening

"Then opened he their understanding, that they might understand the scriptures" (Luke 24:45).

The One who opened Scripture also opened the understanding. Many can bring the Scriptures to the mind, but the Lord alone can prepare the mind to receive the Scriptures. Our Lord Jesus differs from all other teachers. They reach the ear, but He instructs the heart. They deal with the outward letter, but He imparts an inward taste for the truth, by which we perceive its savor and spirit. The most unlearned of men become scholars in the school of grace when the Lord Jesus, by His Holy Spirit, unfolds the mysteries of the Kingdom to them. He grants the divine anointing by which they are enabled to behold the invisible. How many men of profound learning are ignorant of eternal things! They know the killing letter of revelation, but they cannot discern its living spirit. They have a veil upon their hearts which the eyes of human reason cannot penetrate. We were once as blind as they are. Truth was to us as beauty in the dark, a thing unnoticed and neglected. Had it not been for the love of Jesus, we would have remained in ignorance. Without His gracious opening of our understanding, we could no more have attained to spiritual knowledge than an infant can climb the pyramids. Jesus' College is the only one in which God's truth can be learned. Other schools may teach us what is to be believed, but Christ alone can show us how to believe it. Let us sit at the feet of Jesus. By earnest prayer, let us call upon His blessed aid that our feeble understandings may receive heavenly things.

"Abel was a keeper of sheep" (Genesis 4:2).

As a shepherd, Abel sanctified his work to the glory of God and offered a sacrifice of blood on his altar. The Lord had respect unto Abel and his offering. This early type of our Lord is exceedingly clear and distinct. Like the first streak of light which tinges the east at sunrise, it does not reveal everything, but it clearly manifests the great fact that the sun is coming. As we see Abel, a shepherd and yet a priest, offering a sacrifice of sweet smell unto God, we recognize our Lord, who brings before His Father a sacrifice which Jehovah respects. Abel was hated by his brother—hated without a cause; and the Savior experienced the same hatred. The natural and carnal man hated the accepted man in whom the Spirit of grace was found and rested not until his blood had been shed. Abel fell and sprinkled his altar and sacrifice with his own blood. Likewise, the Lord Jesus was slain by the enmity of man while serving as a priest before the Lord. The good Shepherd layeth down His life for the sheep. Abel's blood spoke. The Lord said unto Cain, "The voice of thy brother's blood crieth unto me from the ground" (Genesis 4:10). The blood of Jesus has a mighty tongue, and its prevailing cry is not vengeance, but mercy. Abel is the first shepherd in order of time, but our hearts will always place Jesus first in order of excellence. Great keeper of the sheep, we the people of Your pasture bless You with our whole hearts when we see You slain for us.

January 20
Evening

"Turn away mine eyes from beholding vanity; and quicken thou me in Thy way" (Psalm 119:37).

There are many kinds of vanity. The laughter of the world, the dance, the music, and the life of the immoral are all known to be vanities. They wear their proper name and title boldly. Far more treacherous are those equally vain things—the cares of this world and the deceitfulness of riches. A man may follow vanity as truly in the accounting office as in the theater. If he spends his life amassing wealth, he passes his days in a vain show. Unless we follow Christ and make our God the great object of life, we differ from the most frivolous only in our appearance. *"Quicken thou me in thy way."* The psalmist confesses that he is dull, heavy, and all but dead. Perhaps you feel the same. We are so sluggish that nothing can revive us apart from the Lord Himself. What! will not hell rouse me? Can I think of sinners perishing and yet not be awakened? Will not heaven rouse me? Can I think of the reward that awaits the righteous and yet be cold? Will not death stir me? Can I think of dying and standing before my God and yet be slothful in my Master's service? Will not Christ's love constrain me? Can I think of His dear wounds, can I sit at the foot of His cross, and not be inflamed with fervency and zeal? No mere consideration can awaken us to zeal, but God Himself must do it; therefore the cry, "Quicken thou me!" The psalmist breathes out his whole soul in vehement pleadings. His body and his soul unite in prayer. "Turn away mine eyes," says the body; "Quicken thou me," cries the soul. This is a suitable prayer for every day.

January 21
Morning

"And so all Israel shall be saved" (Romans 11:26).

When Moses sang at the Red Sea, it was his joy to know that all Israel was safe. Part of that song was, "Thou in thy mercy hast led forth the people which thou hast redeemed" (Exodus 15:13). In the last time, when the elect will sing the song of Moses, the servant of God, and of the Lamb, it will be the boast of Jesus, "Of all whom thou hast given me, I have lost none" (John 18:9). In heaven there will not be a vacant throne. As many as God has chosen, as many as Christ has redeemed, as many as the Spirit has called, as many as believe in Jesus, will safely cross the dividing sea. The front line of the army has already reached the shore. We are marching through the depths; we are at this day following hard after our Leader into the heart of the sea. Let us be of good cheer. The rearguard will soon be where the vanguard already is. The last of the chosen ones will soon have crossed the sea, and then will be heard the song of triumph, when all are secure. But oh, if one were absent. If one of His chosen family should be cast away, it would make an everlasting discord in the song of the redeemed.

January 21
Evening

"He was sore athirst, and called on the Lord, and said, Thou hast given this great deliverance into the hand of thy servant; and now shall I die for thirst?" (Judges 15:18).

Samson was thirsty and ready to die. The difficulty was different from any which the hero had met before. Merely to get thirst quenched is not nearly so great a matter as being delivered from a thousand Philistines! But when the thirst was upon him, Samson felt that a little present difficulty was more weighty than the great past difficulty out of which he had miraculously been delivered. It is very common for God's people, when they have enjoyed a great deliverance, to find a little trouble to be too much for them. Samson slays a thousand Philistines and piles them up in heaps and then faints for a little water! Jacob wrestles with God at Peniel, and overcomes Omnipotence itself, and then "halted upon his thigh!" (Genesis 32:31). It is as if the Lord must teach us our littleness, our nothingness, in order to keep us within bounds. Samson boasted truthfully when he said, "I have slain a thousand men." His boastful throat soon grew hoarse with thirst, and he began to pray. God has many ways of humbling His people. Dear child of God, if after great mercy you are laid very low, your case is not an unusual one. When David mounted the throne of Israel, he said, "I am this day weak, though anointed king" (2 Samuel 3:39). You must expect to feel weakest when you are enjoying your greatest triumph. If God has given you great deliverances in the past, your present difficulty is only like Samson's thirst. The Lord will not let you faint or permit your enemies to triumph over you. Cheer your heart with Samson's words and rest assured that God will deliver you before long.

January 22
Morning

"Son of man, What is the vine tree more than any tree, or than a branch which is among the trees of the forest?" (Ezekiel 15:2).

These words are for the humbling of God's people. They are called God's vine. They, by God's goodness, have become fruitful, having been planted in a good soil. The Lord has trained them on the walls of the sanctuary, and they bring forth fruit to His glory. But what are they without their God? What are they without the continual influence of the Spirit? Oh, believer, learn to reject pride, seeing that you have no ground for it. Whatever you are, you have nothing to make you proud. The more you have, the more you are in debt to God. Consider your origin! Look back to what you were. Consider what you would have been but for divine grace. Look upon yourself as you are now. Does your conscience reproach you? And if He has made you anything, are you not taught that it is grace which has made you to differ? You would have been a great sinner if God had not changed you. Therefore, do not be proud, though you have a large estate—a wide domain of grace; once you did not have a single thing to call your own except your sin and misery.

January 22
Evening

"Doth Job fear God for nought?" (Job 1:9).

This was the wicked question of Satan concerning that upright man of old. But there are many people today about whom this question might be asked. They love God simply because He prospers them. If things went badly with them, however, they would give up all their boasted faith in God. If they clearly see that since the time of their supposed conversion they have enjoyed abundant prosperity, then they will love God in their poor carnal way. But if they have to endure adversity, they rebel against the Lord. Their love is the love of the table, not of the Host. They love the cupboard, not the Master of the house. The promise of the old covenant was prosperity, but the promise of the new covenant is adversity. Remember Christ's words: "Every branch in me that beareth not fruit he taketh away: and every branch that beareth fruit, *he purgeth it, that it may bring forth more fruit*" (John 15:2). If you bring forth fruit, you will have to endure affliction. But this affliction works out precious results because then the Christian learns to rejoice in tribulations. As his tribulations abound, so his consolations abound by Christ Jesus. Sooner or later, every bar of gold must pass through the fire. Do not be afraid but rather rejoice that such fruitful times are in store for you. You will be delivered from clinging to the present and will truly desire those eternal things which will soon be revealed to you. When you feel that you would serve God even for no reward in this life, you will rejoice in the infinite reward of the future.

January 23
Morning

"I have exalted one chosen out of the people" (Psalm 89:19).

Why was Christ chosen out of the people? Was it not that He might be able to be our brother in the blest tie of kindred blood? Oh, what relationship there is between Christ and the believer! The believer can say, "I have a brother in heaven. I may be poor, but I have a brother who is rich and is a King. Will He allow me to be in need while He is on His throne? Oh, no! He loves me; He is my brother." Believer, cherish this blessed thought. He is a brother, born for adversity; treat Him as such. Christ was also chosen out of the people that He might know our wants and sympathize with us. "He was tempted in all points like as we are, yet without sin" (Hebrews 4:15). In all our sorrows, we have His sympathy. Temptation, pain, disappointment, weakness, weariness, poverty—He knows them all, for He has felt all. Remember this, Christian, and let it comfort you. However difficult and painful your road, it is marked by the footsteps of your Savior. Even when you reach the dark valley of the shadow of death and the deep waters of the swelling Jordan, you will find His footprints there. Take courage! Royal feet have left a blood-red track on the road and consecrated the thorny path forever.

January 23
Evening

"We will remember thy love more than wine" (Song of Solomon 1:4).

Jesus will not let His people forget His love. If all the love they have enjoyed is forgotten, He will visit them with fresh love. "Do you forget My cross?" He asks. "I will cause you to remember it; for at My table I will manifest Myself anew to you. Do you forget what I did for you in the council chamber of eternity? I will remind you of it, for you will need a counselor. I will be ready at your call." Mothers do not let their children forget them. If the boy has gone to Australia and does not write home, his mother writes, "Has John forgotten his mother?" Then there comes back a sweet epistle, which proves that the gentle reminder was not in vain. So is it with Jesus. He says to us, "Remember Me;" and our response is, "We will remember Your love. It is as ancient as the glory which You had with the Father before the world began. We remember, O Jesus, Your eternal love when You became our surety and now embrace us as Your betrothed. We remember the love which caused the sacrifice of Yourself. It was the love which, until the fullness of time, mused over that sacrifice and longed for the hour when the Scriptures would be fulfilled. We remember Your love, O Jesus! It was manifest to us in Your holy life, from the manger of Bethlehem to the garden of Gethsemane. Every word and deed of Yours was love. We rejoice in Your love which death did not extinguish. Your love sparkled brilliantly in Your resurrection and shines in our hearts today and for eternity."

January 24
Morning

"Surely he shall deliver thee from the snare of the fowler" (Psalm 91:3).

God delivers His people from the snare of the fowler in two senses: from and out of. First, He delivers them *from* the snare—does not let them enter it. Secondly, if they are caught, He delivers them *out of* it. "He shall deliver thee from the snare" (Psalm 91:3). How? Trouble is often the means whereby God delivers us. God knows that our backsliding will soon end in our destruction, and He, in mercy, sends the rod. At other times, God keeps His people from the snare of the fowler by giving them great spiritual strength, so that when they are tempted to do evil, they say, "How can I do this great wickedness, and sin against God?" But what a blessed thing it is that if the believer does, in an evil hour, come into the net, yet God will bring him out of it! Oh, backslider, be cast down, but do not depair. Hear what your Redeemer says—"Return, backsliding children; I will have mercy upon you" (Jeremiah 3:22). But you say you cannot return, for you are a captive. You will yet be brought out of all the evil into which you have fallen. Repent of your ways. He that has loved you will not cast you away. He will receive you and give you joy and gladness.

January 24
Evening

"Martha was cumbered about much serving" (Luke 10:40).

Her fault was not that she *served*. Every Christian must become a servant. "I serve" should be the motto of all the princes of the royal family of heaven. Nor was it her fault that she had *"much serving."* We cannot do too much. Let our head and heart and hands be engaged in the Master's service. It was no fault of hers that she was busy preparing a feast for the Master. Martha was happy to have an opportunity to entertain her honorable Guest. Her fault was that she grew *"cumbered* with much serving,"* so that she forgot *Him* and only remembered the service. She allowed service to override communion and so presented one duty darkened by the neglect of another. We ought to be Martha and Mary in one. We should do much service and have much communion at the same time. For this we need great grace. It is easier to serve than to commune. Joshua never grew weary in fighting with the Amalekites; but Moses, on the top of the mountain in prayer, needed two helpers to sustain his hands. The more spiritual the exercise, the sooner we tire of it. The choicest fruits are the hardest to grow. The most heavenly graces are the most difficult to cultivate. While we do not neglect external things which are good in themselves, we should also enjoy living, personal fellowship with Jesus. See to it that sitting at the Savior's feet is not neglected, even though it may be under the deceptive pretext of doing service for Him. The first thing for our soul's health, for His glory, and for our own usefulness is to keep ourselves in constant communion with the Lord Jesus. We must see that the vital spirituality of our faith is maintained above everything else in the world.

January 25
Morning

"I will mention the lovingkindnesses of the Lord, and the praises of the Lord, according to all that the Lord hath bestowed on us" (Isaiah 63:7).

Can you do this? Are there mercies which you have experienced? There must surely be some precious milestone along the road of life not quite grown over with moss, on which you can read a happy memorial of His mercy toward you. Have you ever been sick and did He not restore you? Were you ever poor before, and did He not supply your needs? Were you never in trouble before, and did He not deliver you? Do not forget what your God has done for you. Turn over the book of your remembrance and consider the days of old. Have you ever been helped in time of need? I know you have. Go back to the choice mercies of yesterday. Although today's circumstances look dark, light up the lamps of the past. They will glitter through the darkness, and you will trust in the Lord until day breaks and the shadows flee away. "Remember, O Lord, your tender mercies and your lovingkindness, for they have been ever of old."

January 25
Evening

"Do we then make void the law through faith? God forbid: yea, we establish the law" (Romans 3:31).

When the believer is adopted into the Lord's family, his relationship to old Adam and the law ceases at once. He is now under a new rule and a new covenant. Believer, you are God's child; therefore, it is your first duty to obey your heavenly Father. A servile spirit should not be yours because you are not a slave, but a child. Does He ask you to fulfill some spiritual duty? It is at your peril that you neglect it, for you will be disobeying your Father. Jesus tells you, "Be ye therefore perfect, even as your Father which is in heaven is perfect" (Matthew 5:48). Labor to be perfect in holiness, not because the law commands, but because your Savior asks you to. Does He tell His saints to love one another? Do it, not because the law says, "Love thy neighbor," but because Jesus says, "If ye love me, keep my commandments" (John 14:15). This is the commandment that He has given to you, "that ye love one another" (John 13:34). Are you told to give to the poor? Do it, not because charity is a burden which you are required to bear, but because Jesus teaches, "Give to him that asketh thee" (Matthew 5:42). Does the Word say, "Love God with all your heart"? Look at the commandment and reply, "Christ has fulfilled it already; I have no need, therefore, to fulfill it for my salvation, but I rejoice to be obedient because God is my Father." May the Holy Spirit make your heart obedient to the constraining power of Christ's love. Let your prayer be, "Make me to go in the path of thy commandments; for therein do I delight" (Psalm 119:35).

January 26
Morning

"Your heavenly Father" (Matthew 6:26).

God's people are doubly His children. They are His offspring by creation, and they are His sons by adoption in Christ. Hence they are privileged to call Him, "Our Father which art in heaven" (Matthew 6:9). Father! Oh, what a precious word! Here is *authority*. "If I be a Father, where is mine honor?" If you are sons, where is your obedience? Here is *affection* mingled with authority; an authority which does not provoke rebellion; an obedience demanded which is most cheerfully rendered. The obedience which God's children yield to Him must be *loving* obedience. Do not go about the service of God as slaves to their taskmaster's toil, but run in the way of His commands because it is your Father's way. Yield your bodies as instruments of righteousness, because righteousness is your Father's will. His will should be the will of His child. Father! Here is honor and love. How great is a father's love for his children! That which friendship cannot do and mere benevolence will not attempt, a father's heart and hand must do for his sons. They are his offspring, he must bless them. They are his children, he must show himself strong in their defense. If an earthly father watches over his children with unceasing love and care, how much more does our heavenly Father! Abba, Father! He who can say this has uttered better music than cherubim or seraphim can reach. There is heaven in the depth of that word—Father!

January 26
Evening

"All they that heard it wondered at those things" (Luke 2:18).

We must not cease to wonder at the great marvels of our God. It would be very difficult to draw a line between holy wonder and *true worship.* When the soul is overwhelmed with the majesty of God's glory, it may not express itself in song or even utter its voice with bowed head in humble prayer. Yet, it silently adores Him. Our incarnate God is to be worshipped as "Wonderful Counsellor, The mighty God" (Isaiah 9:6). God looks at His fallen creature, man, and instead of sweeping him away to destruction, He becomes the man's Redeemer. This is, indeed, marvelous! But to each believer, redemption is most marvelous as he views it in relation to himself. It is a miracle of grace that Jesus should forsake the thrones and royalties above to suffer and die *for you.* Let your soul lose itself in holy wonder which will lead you to grateful worship and heartfelt thanksgiving. It will cause within you *godly watchfulness* because you will be afraid to sin against such a love as this. You will be moved at the same time to *glorious hope.* If Jesus has done such marvelous things on your behalf, you will feel that heaven itself is not too great for your expectation. What else is wonderful after one has seen the Savior? Perhaps from the quietness and solitude of your life, you are scarcely able to imitate the shepherds of Bethlehem who told what they had seen and heard. But you can at least be a part of the circle of worshippers before the throne as you wonder at what God has done.

January 27
Morning

"And of his fulness have all we received" (John 1:16).

These words tell us that there is a fullness in Christ. There is a fullness of essential Deity, for in Him dwelleth all the fullness of the Godhead. There is a fullness of perfect manhood, for in Him, bodily, that Godhead was revealed. There is a fullness of atoning efficacy in His blood for "the blood of Jesus Christ, his Son, cleanseth us from all sin" (1 John 1:7). There is a fullness of justifying righteousness in His life for "there is therefore now no condemnation to them that are in Christ Jesus" (Romans 8:1). "He is able to save to the uttermost them that come unto God by him; seeing He ever liveth to make intercession for them" (Hebrews 7:25). There is a fullness of victory in His death, for through death He destroyed him that had the power of death, that is, the devil. There is a fullness of efficacy in His resurrection from the dead, for by it, "we are begotten again unto a lively hope" (1 Peter 1:3). There is a fullness of triumph in His ascension for "when he ascended up on high, he led captivity captive, and gave gifts unto men" (Ephesians 4:8). There is a fullness of grace to pardon, of grace to regenerate, of grace to sanctify, of grace to preserve, and of grace to perfect. There is a fullness at all times, a fullness of comfort in affliction, and a fullness of guidance in prosperity. A fullness of every divine attribute, of wisdom, of power, of love; a fullness which is impossible to survey, much less to explore. Come, believer, and get all your need supplied.

January 27
Evening

"But Mary kept all these things, and pondered them in her heart" (Luke 2:19).

This blessed woman exercises three powers of her being: her *memory*—she kept all these things; her *affections*—she kept them in her heart; her *intellect*—she pondered them. Beloved, remember what you have heard of your Lord Jesus and what He has done for you. Make your heart the golden pot of manna to preserve the memorial of the heavenly bread on which you fed in days gone by. Let your memory treasure everything about Christ which you have either felt, known, or believed. Then let your fond affections hold *Him* fast forevermore. Love the *person* of your Lord! Bring forth the alabaster box of your heart, even though it is broken. Let all the precious ointment of your affection come streaming on His pierced feet. Meditate upon what you read. Do not stop at the surface, but dive into the depths. Do not be like the swallow which touches the brook with her wing. Instead, be the fish which penetrates the lowest wave. Abide with your Lord. Do not let Him be like a wanderer who stays for a night before moving on. Constrain Him, saying, "Abide with us: for. . .the day is far spent." (Luke 24:29). Hold Him and do not let Him go. The word "ponder" means to weigh. But where are the scales that can weigh the Lord Christ? "He weighed the mountains in scales" (Isaiah 40:12). In what scales shall we weigh *Him?* If your understanding cannot comprehend Him, let your affection overtake Him. If your spirit cannot enclose the Lord Jesus in the grasp of understanding, let it embrace Him in the arms of love.

January 28
Morning

"Perfect in Christ Jesus" (Colossians 1:28).

Do you feel in your own soul that perfection is not in you? Every tear which trickles from your eye weeps imperfection; every sigh which bursts from your heart cries imperfection; every harsh word which proceeds from your lip mutters imperfection. You have too frequently had a view of your own heart to dream for a moment of any perfection in yourself. But amid this sad consciousness of imperfection, here is comfort for you—you are "perfect *in Christ Jesus."* In God's sight, you are "complete in Him." Even now, you are "accepted in the beloved." But there is a second perfection, yet to be realized, which is promised to all the seed. Is it not delightful to look forward to the time when every stain of sin will be removed from the believer, and he shall be presented faultless before the throne, without spot, or wrinkle, or any such thing? The Church then will be so pure, that not even the eye of omniscience will see a spot or blemish in her. Then we will know and feel the happiness of this vast but short sentence, "Complete in Christ." Not until then will we fully comprehend the heights and depths of the salvation of Jesus. Christ takes a black and deformed thing and makes it clean and matchless in His glory, peerless in His beauty, and fit to be the companion of angels. Oh my soul, stand and admire this blessed truth of perfection in Christ.

January 28
Evening

"And the shepherds returned, glorifying and praising God for all the things that they had heard and seen, as it was told unto them" (Luke 2:20).

What was the subject of their praise? They *praised God for what they had heard*—for the good tidings of great joy that a Savior was born to them. Let us also raise a song of thanksgiving because we have heard of Jesus and His salvation. They also *praised God for what they had seen.* This makes the sweetest music—what we have experienced, what we have felt within, what we have made our own—"the things which I have made touching the king" (Psalm 45:1). It is not enough to *hear* about Jesus. Hearing may tune the harp, but the fingers of living faith must create the music. If you have seen Jesus with the God-given sight of faith, permit no cobwebs to linger among the harpstrings. Use your psaltery and harp for loud praise of His sovereign grace. The shepherds praised God for *the agreement between what they had heard and what they had seen.* Observe the last sentence—"As it was told unto them." Have you found the gospel to be just what the Bible said it would be? Jesus said He would give you rest— have you enjoyed the sweetest peace in Him? He said that you should have joy and comfort and life through believing in Him—have you received all these? Are His ways pleasant and His paths, paths of peace? The King in His beauty outshines all imaginable loveliness. Surely, what we have *seen* exceeds what we have *heard.* Let us glorify and praise God for a Savior who is so precious and so satisfying.

January 29
Morning

"The things which are not seen" (2 Corinthians 4:18).

In our Christian pilgrimage, it is well, for the most part, to be looking forward. Forward lies the crown, and onward is the goal. Whether it is for hope, for joy, for consolation, or for inspiring of our love, the future must, after all, be the grand object of the eye of faith. Looking into the future, we see sin cast out, the body of sin and death destroyed, the soul made perfect and fit to be a partaker of the inheritance of the saints in light. Looking further yet, the believer's enlightened eye can see death's river passed, the gloomy stream forded, and the hills of light attained. He sees himself enter within the pearly gates, hailed as more than conqueror, crowned by the hand of Christ, embraced in the arms of Jesus, glorified with Him. He is made to sit together with Jesus on His throne, even as He has overcome and has sat down with the Father on His throne. The thought of this future may well relieve the darkness of the past and the gloom of the present. The joys of heaven will surely compensate for the sorrows of earth. This world is but a narrow span, and you will soon have passed it. Time, how short—eternity, how long! Death, how brief—immortality, how endless!

January 29
Evening

"The dove came in to him in the evening" (Genesis 8:11).

Praise the Lord for another day of mercy, even though I am now weary with its labor. To my God, who is the preserver of men, I lift my song of gratitude. The dove found no rest away from the ark and, therefore, returned to it. My soul has learned that there is no satisfaction in earthly things. God alone can give rest to my spirit. My business, my possessions, my family, my accomplishments, these are all well enough in their place. But they cannot fulfill the desires of my immortal nature. "Return unto thy rest, O my soul; for the Lord hath dealt bountifully with thee" (Psalm 116:7). It was at the quiet hour, when the gates of the day were closing, that the weary dove came back to her master. O Lord, enable me this evening to return to Jesus in this way. He is the rest of my heart, the home of my spirit. The dove did not merely alight upon the roof of the ark, she "came in to him." My longing spirit looks into the secret of the Lord, piercing to the interior of truth, entering into that which is behind the veil, and reaching to my Beloved. I must come to Jesus. Anything less than the nearest and dearest communion with Him, my panting spirit cannot bear. Blessed Lord Jesus, be with me and reveal Yourself. Abide with me all night, so that when I awake, I may still be with You. My Lord, I give You thanks for Your tender mercies which are new every morning and fresh every evening. Now, put forth Your hand, I pray, and take Your dove into Your bosom.

January 30
Morning

"When thou hearest the sound of a going in the tops of the mulberry trees, then thou shalt bestir thyself" (2 Samuel 5:24).

The members of Christ's Church should be very prayerful, always seeking the anointing of the Holy One to rest upon their hearts, that the Kingdom of Christ may come, and that His "will be done on earth, even as it is in heaven" (Matthew 6:10). There are times when God seems especially to favor Zion. Such seasons ought to be to them like "the sound of a going in the tops of mulberry trees." We should be doubly prayerful, doubly earnest, wrestling more at the throne than has been our habit. Oh, for Pentecostal outpourings and Pentecostal labors! Christian, in yourself there are times "when thou hearest the sound of a going in the tops of the mulberry trees." You have a peculiar power in prayer. The Spirit of God gives you joy and gladness. The Scripture is open to you. The promises are applied. You walk in the light of God's face. You have a peculiar freedom and liberty in devotion and a closer communion with Christ. Now, at such joyous periods, is the time to rouse yourself. Now is the time to get rid of any evil habit, while God the Spirit helps your infirmities.

January 30
Evening

"In whom also we have obtained an inheritance" (Ephesians 1:11).

When Jesus gave Himself for us, He gave us all the rights and privileges that are in Him. As eternal God, He has essential rights which no creature may venture to share. Yet, as Jesus the Mediator who has established the covenant of grace, He has no heritage apart from us. All the glorious consequences of His obedience to the point of death are the possessions of all who are in Him. It is on our behalf that He accomplished the divine will. He enters into glory, but not for Himself alone. It is written, "Whither the forerunner is *for us* entered" (Hebrews 6:20). "He appears in the presence of God *for us*" (Hebrews 9:24). You have no right to heaven in yourself; your right lies in Christ. If you are pardoned, it is through *His* blood. If you are justified, it is through *His* righteousness. If you are sanctified, it is because *He* is your sanctification. If you are kept from falling, it is because you are preserved in Christ Jesus. If you are perfected at last, it will be because you are complete in *Him*. The inheritance is made certain to us, for it is obtained in Him. Each blessing is sweeter and even heaven itself is brighter because it is through Jesus our beloved we have obtained it all. Weigh the riches of Christ in scales and then begin to count the treasures which belong to the saints. "All things are yours. . .and ye are Christ's; and Christ is God's" (1 Corinthians 3:21,23).

January 31
Morning

"The Lord our righteousness" (Jeremiah 23:6).

It will always give a Christian the greatest calm, quiet, ease, and peace, to think of the perfect righteousness of Christ. There are some who are always talking about corruption and the innate evil of the soul. This is quite true, but why not go a little further and remember that we are "perfect in Christ Jesus?" Surely, if we call to mind that Christ is made unto us righteousness, we will be of good cheer. Even though distresses afflict me, Satan assaults me, and there may be many things to be experienced before I get to heaven, those are done for me in the covenant of divine grace. There is nothing wanting in my Lord. Christ has done it all. On the cross, He said, "It is finished" (John 19:30). If it is finished, then I am complete in Him. I can rejoice with unspeakable joy and full of glory, "not having mine own righteousness, which is of the law, but that which is through the faith of Christ, the righteousness which is of God by faith" (Philippians 3:9). When the believer says, "I live on Christ alone; I rest on Him completely for salvation; and I believe that, however unworthy, I am still saved in Jesus," then there rises up as a motive of gratitude this thought—"Will I not live for Christ? Will I not love Him and serve Him, seeing that I am saved by *His* merits?" "The love of Christ constraineth us" (2 Corinthians 5:14).

January 31
Evening

"Then Ahimaaz ran by the way of the plain, and overran Cushi" (2 Samuel 18:23).

Running is not everything. The path which we select is also important. A swift foot over hill and dale will not keep pace with a slower traveler upon level ground. How is it with my spiritual journey? Am I laboring up the hill of my own works and down into the ravines of my own humiliations and resolutions? Or do I run by the plain way of "Believe and live"? The soul runs without weariness and walks without fainting when it moves by faith. Christ Jesus is the way of life. He is a level way, a pleasant way, a way suitable for the tottering feet and feeble knees of trembling sinners. Am I on His path or am I hunting after another track that religion or philosophy may promise me? I read about the way of holiness. The searching man, though a fool, will not go wrong that way. Have I been delivered from proud reason and brought as a little child to rest in Jesus' love and blood? If so, by God's grace, I will outrun the strongest runner who chooses any other path. My wisest course is to go at once to God for help and guidance. He knows my wants and can relieve them. Whom else should I go to but to Him, by the direct appeal of prayer and the plain argument of the promise? If men compete with each other in common matters and one outruns the other, I ought to earnestly run that I may obtain the prize. Lord, help me to renew my mind with Your Word. May I press forward toward the mark for the prize of my high calling of God in Christ Jesus.

February 1
Morning

"They shall sing in the ways of the Lord"
(Psalm 138:5).

The time when Christians begin to sing in the ways of the Lord is when they first lose their burden at the foot of the cross. Not even the songs of the angels seem so sweet as the first song of rapture which gushes from the soul of the forgiven child of God. Believer, do you remember the day when your chains fell off? Do you remember the place where Jesus met you and said, "I have loved thee with an everlasting love; I have blotted out as a cloud thy transgressions, and as a thick cloud thy sins; they shall not be mentioned against thee any more forever" (Jeremiah 31:3). How wonderful it is when Jesus takes away the pain of sin! It is not only at the beginning of the Christian life that believers have reason for song. As long as they live, they discover cause to sing in the ways of the Lord. Their experience of His constant lovingkindness leads them to say, "I will bless the Lord at all times: His praise shall continually be in my mouth" (Psalm 34:1).

February 1
Evening

"Thy love to me was wonderful" (2 Samuel 1:26).

Come and let each one of us speak of the wonderful love of Jesus. We will not relate what we have been told, but the things which we have seen for ourselves. Your love to me, O Jesus, was wonderful when I was a stranger wandering far from You, fulfilling the desires of the flesh and of the mind. Your love restrained me from committing the sin which would have resulted in my death. You withheld me from self-destruction. Your love held back the axe when Justice said, "Cut it down; why cumbereth it the ground?" (Luke 13:7). Your love drew me into the wilderness and made me feel the guilt of my sin and the burden of my iniquity. Your love spoke gently to me when I was dismayed: "Come unto me. . .and I will give you rest" (Matthew 11:28). Oh, how matchless is Your love. You washed my sins away and cleansed my polluted soul. I was black with the grime of my transgressions, but You made me white as the driven snow and pure as the finest wool. You showed me Your love when You whispered in my ear, "I am Yours, and you are Mine." Your voice was so kind when You said, "The Father Himself loveth you" (John 16:27). My soul will never forget those chambers of fellowship where You revealed Yourself to me. Moses was within a cleft in the rock when he saw the back of God. We, too, have clefts in the rock where we may see the full splendor of the Godhead in the person of Christ. Precious Lord Jesus, give us a fresh blessing of Your wondrous love!

February 2
Morning

"Without shedding of blood is no remission"
(Hebrews 9:22).

In none of the Jewish ceremonies were sins, even typically, removed without blood-shedding. By no means can sin be pardoned without atonement. It is clear that there is no hope for me out of Christ. There is no other blood-shedding which is worth a thought as an atonement for sin. Is the blood of His atonement truly applied to my soul? All men are on a level as to their need of Him. What a blessing that there is the one way of pardon! Persons of merely formal religion cannot understand how we can rejoice that all our sins are forgiven us for Christ's sake. Their works, prayers, and ceremonies give them very poor comfort. They are neglecting the one great salvation and endeavoring to get remission without blood. It is in vain, when conscience is aroused, to fly to feelings and evidences for comfort. This is a habit we learned in the past. The only remedy for a guilty conscience is a sight of Jesus suffering on the cross. "The blood is the life thereof," says the Levitical law. Let us rest assured that it is the life of faith and joy and every other holy grace.

February 2
Evening

"And these are ancient things" (1 Chronicles 4:22).

These things are not as ancient as those precious things which are the delight of our souls. Let us recall them, telling them over as misers count their gold. There is *the sovereign choice* of the Father, by which He elected us for eternal life. We were chosen by Him from before the foundation of the world. *Everlasting love* went with the choice. It was not an act of divine will alone which set us apart, but divine affection was also involved. The Father loved us in and from the beginning. *The eternal plan* to redeem us from our certain destruction, to cleanse and sanctify us, and at last to glorify us was conceived from the beginning. It runs side by side with immutable love and absolute sovereignty. *The covenant* is always described as being everlasting. Jesus made His commitment to the sacred promise long before the first star began to shine. It was in Him that the elect were ordained for eternal life. Thus in the divine purpose, a most blessed covenant union was established between the Son of God and His people. It will remain as the foundation of their safety when time is no more. It is shameful that these ancient things are so often neglected and even rejected by most believers. If they knew more of their own sin, they would be more ready to adore His grace. Let us both admire and adore Him tonight.

February 3
Morning

"Therefore, brethren, we are debtors" (Romans 8:12).

As God's creatures, we are all debtors to Him. Having broken His commandments, as we all have, we are debtors to His justice. We owe Him a vast amount which we are not able to pay. It can be said of the Christian that he does not owe God's justice anything, for Christ has paid the debt His people owed. For this reason the believer owes the more to love. I am a debtor to God's grace and forgiving mercy; but I am no debtor to His justice, for He will never accuse me of a debt already paid. Christ said, "It is finished!" By that He meant that whatever His people owed was wiped away forever from the book of remembrance. Christ, to the uttermost, has satisfied divine justice. The account is settled. The handwriting is nailed to the cross, the receipt is given, and we are debtors to God's justice no longer. Christian, pause for a moment. What a debtor you are to divine sovereignty! How much you owe to His love! He gave His own Son that He might die for you. Consider how much you owe to His forgiving grace. After ten thousand affronts, He loves you as infinitely as ever. Consider what you owe to His power. He has raised you from your death in sin and preserved your spiritual life. Though you have changed a thousand times, He has not changed once. To God you owe yourself and all you have.

February 3
Evening

"Tell me. . .where thou feedest, where thou makest thy flock to rest at noon" (Song of Solomon 1:7).

These words express the desire of the believer for communion with Christ. Where do You feed Your flock? In Your *house?* I will go, if I will find You there. In private *prayer?* Then I will pray without ceasing. In the *Word?* Then I will read it diligently. In Your *commandments?* Then I will walk in them with all my heart. Tell me where You feed, for wherever You stand as the Shepherd, there I will lie down as a sheep. I cannot be satisfied apart from You. My soul hungers and thirsts for the refreshment of Your presence. Where does Your flock rest at noon? My only rest must be where You are with Your beloved flock. "Why should I be as one that turneth aside by the flocks of thy companions?" (Song of Solomon 1:7). You have companions—why should I not be one? Satan tells me I am unworthy; but I always was unworthy, and yet You have always loved me. Therefore my unworthiness cannot be a barrier to my fellowship with You now. It is true that I am weak in faith and prone to fall, but my feebleness is the reason why I should always be where You feed Your flock. Then I may be strengthened and preserved in safety beside the still waters. Why should I turn aside? There is no reason why I should, but there are a thousand reasons why I should not. Jesus Himself beckons me to come. If He moves away a little, it is only to make me prize His presence more. Now that I am grieved and distressed at being away from Him, He will lead me again to that sheltered nook. There, the lambs of His fold are sheltered from the burning sun.

February 4
Morning

"The love of the Lord" (Hosea 3:1).

Believer, look back through all your experiences and think of the way the Lord your God led you in the wilderness, and how He has fed and clothed you every day. He has put up with all your murmurings and all your longings after the flesh-pots of Egypt. He has opened the rock to supply you and fed you with manna that came down from heaven. Think of how His grace has been sufficient for you in all your troubles—how His blood has been a pardon to you in all your sins—how His rod and His staff have comforted you. When you have looked back on the love of the Lord, then let faith survey His love *in the future.* Remember that Christ's covenant and blood have something more in them than the *past.* He who has loved you and pardoned you, will never cease to love and pardon. He is the Alpha, and He will be the Omega also. Therefore, when you pass through the valley of the shadow of death, you need fear no evil, for He is with you. When you stand in the cold floods of Jordan, you need not fear, for death cannot separate you from His love. When you come into the mysteries of eternity, you need not tremble, "for I am persuaded, that neither death, nor life, nor angels, nor principalities, nor powers, nor things present, nor things to come, nor height, nor depth, nor any other creature, shall be able to separate us from the love of God, which is in Christ Jesus our Lord" (Romans 8:38-39). Surely as we meditate on "the love of the Lord," our hearts burn within us, and we long to love Him more.

February 4
Evening

"Your refuge from the avenger of blood"
(Joshua 20:3).

The cities of refuge were so arranged that any man might reach one of them in half a day's journey. Likewise, the word of our salvation is near to us. Jesus is a present Savior, and the distance to Him is short. It only requires giving up our own merit and laying hold of Jesus to be our all in all. The roads to the city of refuge were strictly preserved. Every river was bridged and every obstruction removed, so that the man who fled might find an easy passage to the city. Once every year, the elders went along the roads and checked their condition. They made certain that nothing would impede the flight of anyone and cause him to be overtaken and slain. How graciously the promises of the gospel remove stumblingblocks from the way! Wherever there were intersections and turns there were signs with this inscription upon them: "To the city of refuge!" This is a picture of the road to Christ Jesus. It is no roundabout road of the law. It does not involve obeying endless rules. It is a straight road: "Believe and live." It is a road so hard that no self-righteous man can ever tread it. Yet, it is so easy that every sinner may, by following it, find his way to heaven. As soon as the manslayer reached the outskirts of the city, he was safe. It was not necessary for him to pass far within the walls. The suburbs themselves were sufficient protection. If you only touch the hem of Christ's garment, you will be made whole. (See Matthew 9:20-22.) If you lay hold of Him with "faith as a grain of mustard seed" (Matthew 17:20), you are safe.

February 5
Morning

"The Father sent the Son to be the Saviour of the world" (1 John 4:14).

There is peace in knowing that Jesus Christ did not come without His Father's permission, authority, consent, and assistance. He was sent by the Father to be the Savior of men. While there are distinctions as to the *persons* in the Trinity, there are no distinctions of honor. We too frequently ascribe the honor of our salvation more to Jesus Christ than we do to the Father. This is a mistake. Did not His Father send Him? If He spoke wondrously, did not His Father pour grace into His lips that He might be an able minister of the new covenant? He who knows the Father, and the Son, and the Holy Spirit as he should know them, never sets one before another in his love. Since to the Man Christ Jesus you are brother and hold close fellowship, you are also linked with God the Eternal. Did you ever consider the depth of love in the heart of Jehovah, when God the Father equipped His Son for the great enterprise of mercy? The Father sent Him! Contemplate that subject. Think how Jesus works what the Father wills. In the wounds of the dying Savior, see the love of the great I AM. Let every thought of Jesus be also connected with the Eternal, ever-blessed God, for "it pleased the Lord to bruise him; he hath put him to grief" (Isaiah 53:10).

February 5
Evening

"At that time Jesus answered" (Matthew 11:25).

This is a remarkable way in which to begin a verse. If you look at the context, you will notice that no one asked Him a question, and He was not in conversation with any human being. Yet, it is written, "Jesus answered and said, I thank thee, O Father." When a man answers, he answers a person who has been speaking to him. Who, then, had spoken to Christ? It is His Father, of course. Yet, there is no record of it. This should teach us that Jesus had constant fellowship with His Father. God spoke to His heart continually. It was the habit and life of Jesus to talk with God. May *we* likewise have silent fellowship with the Father so that we may often answer Him. Though the world will not know to whom we speak, we may respond to that secret voice unheard by any other ear. Our own ear, opened by the Spirit of God, recognizes it with joy. God has spoken to us. Let us speak to God—either to confirm that God is true and faithful to His promise or to confess the sin of which the Spirit of God has convicted us or to acknowledge the mercy which God's grace has given. What a privilege is intimate communion with the Father of our spirits! It is a secret hidden from the world, a joy which even the closest friend cannot share. If we desire to hear the whispers of God's love, our ear must be ready to listen to His voice. This evening may our hearts be in such a state that when God speaks to us, we, like Jesus, may be prepared to answer Him at once.

February 6
Morning

"Praying always" (Ephesians 6:18).

We have all spoken a large number of prayers since the moment we learned to pray! Our first prayer was a prayer for ourselves. We asked God to have mercy upon us and blot out our sin. He heard us. But when He had blotted out our sins, we had more prayers for ourselves. We have had to pray for sanctifying grace, for constraining and restraining grace; we have been led to crave for a fresh assurance of faith, for deliverance in the hour of temptation, for help in the time of duty, and for relief in the day of trial. We have been compelled to go to God for our souls. Bear witness, children of God, you have never been able to get anything for your souls elsewhere. All the bread your soul has eaten has come down from heaven. All the water of which it drank flowed from the living Rock—Christ Jesus the Lord. Your wants were innumerable, and, therefore, the supplies have been infinitely great. Your prayers have been as varied as the mercies have been countless. You can say, "I love the Lord, because He heard the voice of my supplication." He has heard you in the day of trouble, has strengthened you, and helped you, even when you dishonored Him by trembling and doubting at the mercy seat. Remember this, and let it fill your heart with gratitude to God. "Bless the Lord, O my soul, and forget not all his benefits" (Psalm 103:2).

February 6
Evening

"Pray one for another" (James 5:16).

As an encouragement to cheerfully offer inter-cessory prayer, remember that *such prayer is the sweetest that God hears.* This is because the prayer of Christ is of this same character. In all the incense which our great High Priest puts into the golden censer, there is not a single grain for Him-self. His intercession must be the most acceptable of all supplications—and the more similar our prayer is to Christ's, the sweeter it will be. Peti-tions for our needs will be accepted, but our pleadings for others display more of the fruits of the Spirit—more love, more faith, and more brotherly kindness. These prayers will be, through the precious merits of Jesus, the sweetest offering that we can make to God. *Intercessory prayer is very effective.* The Word of God is filled with its marvelous deeds. Believer, you have a mighty tool in your hand. Use it well, use it constantly, use it with faith, and you will surely be a blessing to your brethren. When you have the King's ear, speak to Him concerning the suffering members of His body. When you are favored to draw near to His throne and the King says to you, "Ask, and I will give you what you desire," let your petitions be, not for yourself alone, but for the many who need His aid. If you have grace at all and are not an intercessor, that grace must be as small as a mus-tard seed. You have just enough grace to pull your soul clear from the quicksand. Deep floods of grace help to carry the weighty cargo of the needs of others. You would bring back from the Lord rich blessings for them, which otherwise might not have been obtained.

February 7
Morning

"Arise ye, and depart" (Micah 2:10).

The hour is approaching when the message will come to us, as it comes to all—"Arise, and go forth from the home in which you have dwelt, from the city in which you have done your business, from your family, from your friends. Arise, and take your last journey." We have read a little and some has been revealed to us by the Spirit, but how little we know of the realms of the future! We know that there is a black and stormy river called "Death." God bids us cross it, promising to be with us. And, after death, what comes? What scene of glory will be unfolded to our view? We know enough of the heavenly land to make us welcome our summons there with joy and gladness. The journey of death may be dark, but we may go forth on it fearlessly, knowing that God is with us as we walk through the gloomy valley, and therefore we need fear no evil. We will be departing from all we have known and loved here, but we will be going to our Father's house—where Jesus is—to that royal "city which hath foundations, whose builder and maker is God" (Hebrews 11:10). This will be our last removal, to dwell forever with Him we love, in the midst of His people, in the presence of God. Christian, meditate much on heaven. It will help you to press on and to forget the toil of the way. This vale of tears is but the pathway to the better country. This world of woe is but the stepping-stone to a world of bliss.

February 7
Evening

"And they heard a great voice from heaven saying unto them, Come up hither" (Revelation 11:12).

Without considering these words in their prophetical connection, let us regard them as the invitation of our great Forerunner to His sanctified people. In time there shall be heard "a great voice from heaven" saying to every believer, "Come up hither." This should be the subject of joyful anticipation for the saints. Instead of dreading the time when we leave this world to go home to the Father, we should be longing for the hour of our freedom. We are not called *down* to the grave, but *up* to the skies. Our heaven-born spirits should long to breathe their native air. Yet, the celestial summons should be *the object of patient waiting.* Our God knows best when to call us saying, "Come up hither." We must not wish to hasten the time of our departure, but patience must have her perfect work. If there could be regrets in heaven, the saints might mourn that they did not live here longer to do more good. Oh, for more wheat for my Lord's granary and more jewels for His crown! When we are fully serving God, and He is giving us precious seed to scatter and reap a hundred fold, we know that it is good for us to stay where we are. Whether our Master says, "Go" or, "Stay," let us be equally well pleased as long as He continues to bless us with His presence.

February 8
Morning

"Thou shalt call his name Jesus" (Matthew 1:21).

When a person is dear, everything connected with him becomes dear. Likewise is the person of the Lord Jesus in the estimation of all true believers. They consider everything about Him to be beyond all price. "All thy garments smell of myrrh, and aloes, and cassia," said David, as if the very vestments of the Savior were so sweetened by His person that he could not but love them. There is not a spot where that hallowed foot walked, a word those blessed lips uttered, or a thought which His loving Word revealed that is not priceless to us. This is true of the names of Christ— they are all sweet in the believer's ear. But if there is one name sweeter than another in the believer's ear, it is the name of *Jesus*. Jesus! it is the name which moves the harps of heaven to melody. Jesus! the life of all our joys. If there is one name more charming, more precious than another, it is this name. Many of our hymns begin with it, and scarcely any, that are good for anything, end without it. It is the sum total of all delights. It is the music with which the bells of heaven ring; a song in a word; an ocean for comprehension, although a drop for brevity; a matchless oratorio in two syllables; a gathering up of the hallelujahs of eternity in five letters.

February 8
Evening

"He shall save his people from their sins" (Matthew 1:21).

Many persons, when asked what they mean by salvation, will reply, "Being saved from hell and taken to heaven." It is true that our Lord Jesus Christ redeems all His people from the wrath to come. He saves them from the fearful condemnation which their sins brought upon them. But His triumph is far more complete than this. He saves His people "from their sins." Where Christ does a saving work, He casts Satan from his throne and will not let him be master any longer. No man is a true Christian if sin reigns in his mortal body. Sin will be *in* us—it will never be utterly expelled until our spirit enters glory. But it will never have *dominion*. There will be a striving for dominion—a lusting against the new law and the new spirit which God has implanted—but sin will never get the upper hand and become the absolute ruler of our nature. Christ will be Master of the heart, and sin must be overcome. The Lion of the tribe of Judah will prevail, and the dragon will be cast out. Is sin subdued in you? If your *life* is unholy, then your *heart* is unchanged. And, if your heart is unchanged, you are an unsaved person. If the Savior has not sanctified you, renewed you, and given you a hatred of sin and a love of holiness, He has done nothing in you of a saving character. The grace which does not make a man better than others is a worthless counterfeit. Christ saves His people not *in* their sins, but *from* them. Without holiness, no man will see the Lord. (See Hebrews 12:14.) "Let every one that nameth the name of Christ depart from iniquity" (2 Timothy 3:19).

February 9
Morning

"And David inquired of the Lord" (2 Samuel 5:23).

The Philistines came in great number, but, with the help of God, David easily put them to flight. Notice that when they came a second time, David did not go up to fight them without inquiring of the Lord. Once he had been victorious, he might have said, as many have in other cases, "I shall be victorious again; I may rest quite sure that if I have conquered once, I shall triumph yet again. Why should I tarry to seek at the Lord's hands?" Not so David. He had gained one battle by the strength of the Lord. He would not venture on another until he insured the same. He inquired, "Shall I go up against them?" He waited until God's sign was given. Learn from David to take no step without God. A Puritan said, "If a Christian carves for himself, he'll cut his own fingers." This is a great truth. A believer once said, "He that goes before the cloud of God's providence goes on a fool's errand;" and so he does. We must have God's providence leading us. If providence tarries, tarry until providence comes. He who goes before providence will be very glad to run back again. "I will instruct thee and teach thee in the way which thou shalt go" (Psalm 32:8). This is God's promise to His people. Let us, then, take all our perplexities to Him and say, "Lord, what will you have me to do?" Do not leave your home this morning without inquiring of the Lord.

February 9
Evening

"Lead us not into temptation; but deliver us from evil" [or the evil one] (Luke 11:4).

Those things which we are taught to seek or shun in prayer, we should also pursue or avoid in our daily lives. Very earnestly, therefore, we should avoid temptation. We must walk so guardedly in the path of obedience that we never encourage the devil to tempt us. We are not to enter the thicket in search of the lion. Such presumption may cost us dearly. This lion may cross our path or leap upon us from the thicket, but we have nothing to do with hunting him. He that meets with the lion, even though he is victorious, will face a difficult struggle. Let the Christian pray that he may be spared the encounter. Our Savior, who experienced temptation, earnestly admonished His disciples—"Pray that ye enter not into temptation" (Luke 22:40). But no matter what we do, we will be tempted; hence the prayer "deliver us from evil." God had one Son without sin, but He has no sons without temptation. We must always be on our guard against Satan, because, like a thief, he gives no warning of his approach. Believers who have experienced the ways of Satan know that there are certain seasons when he will most probably make an attack, just as at certain seasons severe storms may be expected. Thus, the Christian is put on a double guard by fear of danger, and the danger is averted by preparing to meet it. It is better to be so well armed that the devil will not attack you, than to endure the perils of the fight, even though you are the conqueror. Pray this evening that you may not be tempted. Then, pray that if temptation is permitted, you may be delivered from the evil one.

February 10
Morning

"I know how to abound" (Philippians 4:12).

There are many who know "how to be abased," who have not learned "how to abound." When they are set on the top of a pinnacle, their heads grow dizzy, and they are ready to fall. The Christian far more often disgraces his profession in prosperity than in adversity. It is a dangerous thing to be prosperous. The crucible of adversity is a less severe trial to the Christian than the refining-pot of prosperity. Oh, what leanness of soul and neglect of spiritual things have been brought on through the very mercies and bounties of God! Yet, this is not a matter of necessity, for the apostle tells us that he knew how to abound. When he had much, he knew how to use it. Abundant grace enabled him to bear abundant prosperity. It takes more than human skill to carry the brimming cup of mortal joy with a steady hand. Yet, Paul had learned that skill, for he declares, "In all things I am instructed both to be full and to be hungry." It is a divine lesson to know how to be full, for the Israelites were full once. But while the flesh was yet in their mouth, the wrath of God came upon them. Many have asked for mercies that they might satisfy their own hearts' lust. Fullness of bread has often made fullness of blood, and that has brought on wantonness of spirit. We are full, and we forget God. Satisfied with earth, we are content to do without heaven. Take care that you ask in your prayers that God would teach you "how to be full."

February 10
Evening

"I have blotted out, as a thick cloud, thy trans-gressions, and, as a cloud, thy sins: return unto me; for I have redeemed thee" (Isaiah 44:22).

Carefully observe the comparison made here: our sins are like *a cloud.* As clouds are of many shapes and shades, so are our transgressions. Clouds obscure the light of the sun and darken the landscape below. Similarly, our sins hide from us the light of Jehovah's face and cause us to sit in the shadow of death. Our sins, like clouds, are earth-born things and rise from the miry places of our nature. When collected so that their measure is full, they threaten us with storm and tempest. Unlike clouds, our sin yields us no refreshing showers, but rather threatens to deluge us with a fiery flood of destruction. Black clouds of sin, how can there be fair weather in our soul while you remain? Let us now consider the act of divine mercy—*blotting out.* God Himself appears on the scene, and instead of manifesting His anger, He reveals His grace. He forever removes the mis-chief, not by blowing away the cloud but by blow-ing it out of existence. The great transaction of the cross has eternally removed man's transgressions from him. Let us obey the gracious command— *"Return unto me."* Why should pardoned sinners live at a distance from God? If we have been for-given of all our sins, let no fear keep us from the boldest access to our Lord. Let backslidings be lamented, but let us not continue in them. To the greatest possible nearness of communion with the Lord, let us, in the power of the Holy Spirit, strive mightily to return.

February 11
Morning

"And they took knowledge of them, that they had been with Jesus" (Acts 4:13).

A Christian should be a striking likeness of Jesus Christ. If we were what we profess to be and what we should be, we would be pictures of Christ. We are to imitate Him so closely that the world will have no doubt we have been with Jesus. A Christian should be like Christ in his *boldness*. Be like Jesus—very valiant for your God. Imitate Him in your *loving* spirit. Think kindly, speak kindly, and do kindly, that men may say of you, "He has been with Jesus." Imitate Jesus in His *holiness*. Was He zealous for His Master? So should you be always going about doing good. Do not waste time. It is too precious. Was He self-denying, never looking to His own interest? Be the same. Was He devout? Then you should be. Did He defer to His Father's will? So submit yourselves to Him. Was He patient? Then learn to endure. And best of all, as the highest portraiture of Jesus, try to forgive your enemies, as He did. Let those sublime words of your Master, "Father, forgive them; for they know not what they do" (Luke 23:34) always ring in your ears. Forgive, as you have been forgiven. Heap coals of fire on the head of your foe by your kindness to him. Good for evil, remember, is godlike.

February 11
Evening

"Thou hast left thy first love" (Revelation 2:4).

We will always remember the best and brightest of hours when we first saw the Lord. He took our burden, and we received the promise, rejoiced in full salvation, and went on our way in peace. It was springtime in the soul; the winter was past. God and man were reconciled. The law threatened no vengeance, and justice demanded no punishment. Then the flowers appeared in the garden of our heart. Hope, love, peace, and patience sprung from the soil. The hyacinth of repentance, the snowdrop of pure holiness, the crocus of golden faith, and the daffodil of early love all blossomed in the soul. The time of the singing of birds arrived, and we rejoiced with thanksgiving. We magnified the holy name of our forgiving God. Our resolve was, "Lord, I am wholly Yours; all I am, and all I have, I devote to You. You bought me with Your blood—let me spend myself and be spent in Your service. In life and in death, let me be consecrated to You." *How have we kept this resolve?* Our newfound love once burned with a holy flame of devotedness to Jesus—is it the same *now?* Might Jesus say frankly to us, "I have somewhat against thee, because thou hast left thy first love"? We have done little for our Master's glory. Our winter has lasted too long. We are as cold as ice when we should feel a summer's warmth and bloom with sacred flowers. O Lord, after You have so richly blessed us, will we be ungrateful and become indifferent to Your good cause and work? Revive us that we may return to our first love. Send us a refreshing spring, Sun of Righteousness.

February 12
Morning

"For as the sufferings of Christ abound in us, so our consolation also aboundeth by Christ" (2 Corinthians 1:5).

Here is a blessed proportion. The Ruler of providence bears a pair of scales—in this side He puts His people's trials, and in that He puts their consolations. When the scale of trial is nearly empty, you will always find the scale of consolation in nearly the same condition. When the scale of trial is full, you will find the scale of consolation just as heavy. When the black clouds gather most, the light is more brightly revealed to us. It is a blessed thing, that when we are most cast down, then it is that we are most lifted up by the consolations of the Spirit. One reason is, because trials make more room for consolation. Great hearts can only be made by great troubles. The humbler a man lies, the more comfort he will always have. Another reason why we are often most happy in our troubles, is this—then we have the closest dealings with God. When the barn is full, man can live without God. When the purse is bursting with gold, we try to do without so much prayer. But take our food away, and we want our God. Cleanse the idols out of our house, and we are compelled to honor Jehovah. "Out of the depths have I cried unto thee, O Lord" (Psalm 130:1). There is no cry as good as that which comes from the bottom of the mountains; no prayer half as hearty as that which comes up from the depths of the soul, through deep trials and afflictions. They bring us to God, and we are happier; for nearness to God is happiness. Troubled believer, do not fret over your heavy troubles, for they are the heralds of weighty mercies.

February 12
Evening

"He shall abide with you forever" (Psalm 61:7).

The great Father revealed Himself to believers of old before the coming of His Son. He was known to Abraham, Isaac, and Jacob as the Almighty God. Then Jesus came, and the ever-blessed Son was the delight of His people's eyes. At the time of the Redeemer's ascension, the Holy Spirit's power was gloriously manifested on and after Pentecost. He remains today as our Immanuel—God with us. He is dwelling in and with His people, quickening, guiding, and ruling in their midst. Is His presence recognized as it ought to be? We cannot control His working; He is sovereign in all His operations. But are we sufficiently anxious to obtain His help or sufficiently watchful that we do not provoke Him to withdraw His aid? Without Him we can do nothing, but by His almighty energy, the most extraordinary results can be produced. Everything depends upon His manifesting or concealing His power. Do we always look up to Him both for our inner life and our outward service with the respectful dependence which is proper? Do we often run before His call and act independently of His aid? Let us humble ourselves this evening for past failures and entreat the heavenly dew to rest upon us, the sacred oil to anoint us, and the celestial flame to burn within us. The Holy Spirit is not a temporary gift—He abides with the saints. We only have to seek Him, and He will be found by us. He is jealous, but He is compassionate. If He leaves in anger, He returns in mercy. Condescending and tender, He does not grow weary of us, but waits to be gracious.

February 13
Morning

"Behold, what manner of love the Father hath bestowed upon us, that we should be called the sons of God: therefore the world knoweth us not, because it knew him not. Beloved, now are we the sons of God" (1 John 3:1-2).

Consider who we were and what we feel ourselves to be even now when corruption is powerful in us, and you will wonder at our adoption. Yet, we are called "the sons of God." What a high relationship is that of a son, and what privileges it brings! What care and tenderness the son expects from his father, and what love the father feels toward the son! But all that, and more than that, we now have through Christ. As for the temporary drawback of suffering with the elder brother, this we accept as an honor: "Therefore the world knoweth us not, because it knew him not" (1 John 3:1). We are content to be unknown with Him in His humiliation, for we are to be exalted with Him. "Beloved, now are we the sons of God." That is easy to read, but it is not so easy to feel. How is it with your heart this morning? Are you in the lowest depths of sorrow? Does corruption rise within your spirit, and grace seem like a poor spark trampled underfoot? Does your faith almost fail you? Fear not, it is neither your graces nor feelings on which you are to live. You must live simply by faith in Christ. "Ah, but," you say, "see how I am arrayed! my graces are not bright; my righteousness does not shine with apparent glory." But read verse two: *"It doth not yet appear what we shall be: but we know that, when he shall appear, we shall be like him."* The Holy Spirit will purify our minds, and divine power will refine our bodies; then will we see Him as He is.

February 13
Evening

"There is therefore now no condemnation" (Romans 8:1).

Through your faith in Jesus, you are effectively cleared from guilt. You are led out of prison. No longer in chains as a slave, you are delivered *now* from the bondage of the law. You are free from sin and can walk as a freeman. Your Savior's blood has obtained your full release. Now, you have a right to approach the Father's throne. No flames of vengeance are there to frighten you. There is no fiery sword. Justice cannot condemn the innocent. Your disabilities are taken away. Once you were unable to see your Father's face, but you can see it now. You could not speak with Him, but now you have access with boldness. Once there was a fear of hell upon you, but you have no fear of it now, for how can there be punishment for the guiltless? He who believes is not condemned and cannot be punished. All the privileges that you might have enjoyed if you had never sinned are yours now that you are justified. All the blessings which you would have had if you had kept the law, and more, are yours because Christ has kept it for you. All the love and the acceptance which perfect obedience could have obtained from God belong to you because Christ was perfectly obedient on your behalf. All His merits have accrued to your account, that you could be rich through Him, who for your sake became poor. Oh! how great the debt of love and gratitude you owe to your Savior!

February 14
Morning

"And his allowance was a continual allowance given him of the king, a daily rate for every day, all the days of his life" (2 Kings 25:30).

Jehoiachim was not sent away from the king's palace with a store to last him for months, but his provision was given him as a daily pension. He well pictures the happy position of all the Lord's people. A daily portion is all that a man really needs. Sufficient for the day is all that we can enjoy. We cannot eat or drink or wear more than the day's supply of food and raiment. The surplus gives us the care of storing it and the anxiety of watching against a thief. Enough is not only as good as a feast, but is all that even a glutton can truly enjoy. This is all that we should expect. A craving for more than this in ungrateful. When our Father does not give us more, we should be content with his daily allowance. Jehoiachim's case is ours. We have a sure portion, a portion given us by the King, a gracious portion, and a perpetual portion. Here is surely ground for thankfulness. Beloved Christian reader, in matters of grace, you need a daily supply. You have no store of strength. Day by day you must seek help from above. It is a sweet assurance that a daily portion is provided for you. In the Word, through the ministry, by meditation, in prayer, and waiting on God you will receive renewed strength. In Jesus all needful things are laid up for you. Then enjoy your continual allowance.

February 14
Evening

"She was healed immediately" (Luke 8:47).

One of the most touching and instructive of the Savior's miracles is before us tonight. The woman was very ignorant. She imagined that healing came out of Christ without His knowledge or direct will. She was a stranger to the generosity of Jesus' character. Otherwise, she would not have gone behind Him to steal the cure which He was so ready to bestow. Misery should always place itself right in the face of mercy. Had she known the love of Jesus' heart, she would have said, "I need only put myself where He can see me—His omniscience will teach Him my case, and His love at once will work my cure." We admire her faith, but we marvel at her ignorance. After she had obtained the cure, she rejoiced with trembling. She was glad that the divine power had worked a miracle in her. But she feared that Christ might retract the blessing. How little she knew of the fullness of His love! We do not have as clear a view of Him as we could wish. We do not know the heights and depths of His love. But we are certain that He is too good to withdraw the gift from a trembling soul. As little as her knowledge was, her faith, because it was real faith, saved her. There was no tedious delay—faith's miracle was instantaneous. If we have faith as a grain of mustard seed, salvation is our present and eternal possession. In the list of the Lord's children, we may be considered to be the weakest of the family. Yet, being heirs through faith, no power, human or devilish, can eject us from salvation. If we venture in the crowd behind Him and touch the hem of His garment, we are made whole. Take courage, timid one! Your faith has saved you; go in peace. *"Being* justified by faith, *we have* peace with God" (Romans 5:1).

February 15
Morning

"To him be glory both now and forever" (2 Peter 3:18).

Heaven will be full of the ceaseless praises of Jesus. To Him be glory. Is He not a "Priest forever, after the order of Melchizedek?" To Him be glory. Is He not King forever? King of kings and Lord of lords, the everlasting Father? To Him be glory forever. His praises will never cease. That which was bought with blood deserves to last while immortality endures. The glory of the Cross must never be eclipsed. The luster of the grave and of the resurrection must never be dimmed. O Jesus, You will be praised forever! Believer, you are anticipating the time when you will join the saints above in ascribing all glory to Jesus; but are you glorifying Him *now?* The apostle's words are, "To Him be glory both *now* and forever." Will you make it your prayer today? "Lord, help me to glorify You. I have talents; help me to extol You by using them for You. I have time; Lord, help me to redeem it, that I may serve You. I have a head to think; Lord, help me to think of You. You have put me in this world for something. Lord, show me what that is and help me to work out my life-purpose. I cannot do much; but as the widow put in her two mites, which were all her living, I cast my time and eternity, too, into Your treasury. I am all Yours. Take me and enable me to glorify You now, in all that I say, in all that I do, and with all that I have."

February 15
Evening

"Whereby they have made thee glad" (Psalm 45:8).

Who are the ones who have the privilege of making the Savior glad? They are His Church—His people. But is it possible? He makes *us* glad, but how can *we* make Him glad? By *our love*. We think our love is so cold and so faint. Indeed, we must sorrowfully confess it to be; but it is very sweet to Christ. Hear His own description of that love: "How fair is thy love, my sister, my spouse! how much better is thy love than wine!" (Song of Solomon 4:10). See how He delights in you! When you lean your head on His bosom, you not only receive, but you give Him joy. When you gaze with love upon His all-glorious face, you not only obtain comfort, but impart delight. Our *praise*, too, gives Him joy—not the song of the lips alone, but the melody of the heart's deep gratitude. Our *gifts* are very pleasant to Him. He loves to see us lay our time, our talents, and our substance upon His altar, not for the value of what we give, but because of the motive from which the gift springs. *Holiness* is like frankincense and myrrh to Him. Forgive your enemy, and you make Christ glad. Distribute of your substance to the poor, and He rejoices. Take part in saving souls, and you give Him the opportunity to see the fruit of His labor. Proclaim His gospel, and you are a sweet savor to Him. Go among the ignorant and lift up the cross, and you give Him honor. You may break the alabaster box and pour the precious oil of joy upon His head, as did the woman of old. She is remembered to this day wherever the gospel is preached. Will you perfume your beloved Lord with the myrrh and aloes and cinnamon of your heart's praise?

February 16
Morning

"I have learned, in whatsoever state I am, therewith to be content" (Philippians 4:11).

Philippians 4:11 shows us that contentment is not a natural inclination of man. Covetousness, discontent, and murmuring are as natural to man as thorns are to the soil. The precious things of the earth must be cultivated. If we would have wheat, we must plow and sow. If we want flowers, there must be the garden and all the gardener's care. Contentment is one of the flowers of heaven. If we want it, it must be cultivated. It will not grow in us by nature. It is the new nature alone that can produce it, and even then we must be especially careful and watchful that we maintain and cultivate the grace which God has sown in us. Paul says, "I have learned. . .to be content;" as much as to say, he did not know how at one time. It cost him some pains to attain to the mystery of that great truth. No doubt he sometimes thought he had learned, and then broke down. And when at last he had attained it and could say, "I have learned, in whatsoever state I am, therewith to be content," he was an old, gray-headed man, upon the borders of the grave—a poor prisoner shut up in Nero's dungeon at Rome. Do not indulge the notion that you can be contented without learning, or learn without discipline. It is not a power that may be exercised naturally, but a science to be acquired gradually. We know this from experience. Hush that murmur, natural though it be, and continue as a diligent pupil in the Word.

February 16
Evening

"Thy good spirit" (Nehemiah 9:20).

The sin of forgetting the Holy Spirit is much too common. This is folly and ingratitude. He deserves honor for He is supremely good. He is perfect in purity, truth, and grace. He is *benevolently good,* tenderly bearing with our waywardness and striving with our rebellious wills. Making us alive from our death in sin, He trains us for heaven as a loving nurse fosters her child. How generous, forgiving, and tender is this patient Spirit of God. He suggests good thoughts, prompts good actions, reveals good truths, applies good promises, assists in good accomplishments, and leads to good results. There is no spiritual good in all the world of which He is not the author and sustainer. Whether as Comforter, Instructor, Guide, Sanctifier, Life-Giver, or Intercessor, He fulfills His work well. Those who yield to His influences become good. Those who obey His impulses do good. Those who live under His power receive good. Let us revere and adore Him as God over all, blessed forever. Let us acknowledge His power and our need of Him by waiting upon Him in all of our daily tasks. Let us seek His assistance every hour and never grieve Him. Finally, let us praise Him whenever we can. The Church will never prosper until it believes in the Holy Spirit more deeply. He is so good and kind. It is sad indeed that He should be grieved by our sins and neglect.

February 17
Morning

"Isaac dwelt by the well Lahai-roi" (Genesis 25:11).

Hagar had once found deliverance there, and Ishmael drank from the water so graciously revealed by the God who lives and sees the sons of men. But this was merely a casual visit, such as worldlings pay to the Lord in times of need, when it serves their turn. They cry to Him in trouble, but forsake Him in prosperity. Isaac *dwelt* there, and made the well of the living and all-seeing God his constant source of supply. The usual tenor of a man's life, the dwelling of his soul, is the true test of his state. Perhaps the providential visitation experienced by Hagar struck Isaac's mind and led him to revere the place. Its mystical name endeared it to him. His frequent musings by its brim made him familiar with the well. His meeting Rebecca there had made his spirit feel at home near the spot. Best of all, the fact that he enjoyed fellowship with the living God there made him select that hallowed ground for his dwelling. Let us learn to live in the presence of the living God. The well of the Creator never fails. Happy is he who dwells at the well. The Lord has been a sure helper to others: His name is Shaddai, God All-Sufficient. Through Him our soul has found her glorious Husband, the Lord Jesus. In Him we live, move, and have our being. Let us dwell in close fellowship with Him. Glorious Lord, constrain us that we may never leave You but dwell by the well of the living God.

February 17
Evening

"Whereas the Lord was there" (Ezekiel 35:10).

Edom's princes saw the whole country of Israel left desolate, and they felt sure of an easy conquest. But there was one great difficulty in their way that was quite unknown to them—*the Lord was there.* His presence gave special security to the chosen land. Whatever the schemes and devices of the enemies of God's people may be, there is the same barrier to thwart their plan. *The saints* are God's heritage. He is in the midst of them and will protect His own. What comfort this assurance gives us in our troubles and spiritual conflicts! We are constantly opposed and yet perpetually preserved! Satan often shoots his arrows against our *faith,* but our faith defies the power of hell's fiery darts. They are not only turned aside, but they are quenched upon its shield, for *the Lord is there.* Our *good works* are the subjects of Satan's attacks. A saint has never yet had a virtue or a grace which was not the target of hellish bullets. Whether it was hope bright and sparkling or love warm and fervent or patience all enduring or zeal flaming like coals of fire, the enemy of everything that is good has tried to destroy it. The only reason why anything virtuous or lovely survives in us is this—the Lord is there. If the Lord is with us through life, we have no reason to fear death. Our feet will stand on the Rock of Ages when time is passing away. From the first hour of a Christian's life to the last, the only reason he does not perish is because *the Lord is there.* When the God of everlasting love decides to change and leave His elect to perish, only then would the Church be destroyed.

February 18
Morning

"Show me wherefore thou contendest with me" (Job 10:2).

There are some of your graces which would never be discovered if it were not for your trials. Love is too often like a glow-worm showing little light except in the midst of surrounding darkness. Hope itself is like a star—not to be seen in the sunshine of prosperity and only to be discovered in the night of adversity. Afflictions are often the black foils in which God sets the jewels of His children's graces to make them shine the better. How can you know that you have faith until your faith is exercised? God often allows our trials that our graces may be discovered. Besides, it is not merely discovery; real growth in grace is the result of sanctified trials. God often removes our comforts and our privileges in order to make us better Christians. He trains His soldiers, not in tents of ease and luxury, but by turning them out and using them to forced marches and hard service. He has them ford through streams, swim through rivers, climb mountains, and walk many a long mile with heavy knapsacks on their backs. Could this account for the troubles which you are experiencing? Is the Lord bringing out your graces and making them grow? Is this the reason He is contending with you?

February 18
Evening

"Father, I have sinned" (Luke 15:18).

Those whom Christ has washed in His precious blood do not need to make a confession of sin as criminals before God the Judge. Christ has forever taken away all their sins in a legal sense, so that they no longer stand where they can be condemned. Instead, they are forever accepted in the Beloved. But since they have become like children and sin like children do, they must go before their heavenly Father every day and confess their sin. It is the duty of guilty children to make a confession to their earthly father. The grace of God in the heart teaches us that we, as Christians, owe the same duty to our heavenly Father. We daily offend, and we should not rest without daily pardon. If I have not sought forgiveness and been washed from these offenses against my Father, I feel like I am at a distance from Him. I doubt His love for me. I tremble before Him and am afraid to pray to Him. I grow like the prodigal who, although still a child, was far off from his father. If I go to Him with a child's sorrow at offending so gracious and loving a Parent, tell Him all, and rest not until I realize that I am forgiven, I will feel a holy love for my Father. I will go through my Christian life not only as saved, but as one enjoying present peace with God through Jesus Christ my Lord. There is a wide distinction between confessing sin as a *culprit* and confessing sin as a *child*. The Father's bosom is the place for penitent confessions. We have been cleansed once for all, but our feet still need to be washed from the defilement of our daily walk upon this earth.

February 19
Morning

"Thus saith the Lord God: I will yet for this be inquired of by the house of Israel, to do it for them" (Ezekiel 36:37).

Prayer precedes mercy. Turn to sacred history, and you will find that scarcely ever did a great mercy come to this world unheralded by supplication. You have found this true in your own personal experience. God has given you many an unsolicited favor, but still great prayer has always been the prelude of great mercy with you. When you have had rapturous joys, you have been obliged to look on them as answers to your prayers. When you had great deliverances out of trouble and mighty help in danger, you have been able to say, "I sought the Lord, and he heard me, and delivered me from all my fears" (Psalm 34:4). Prayer is always the preface to blessing. When the sunlight of God's mercies rises on our necessities, it cast the shadow of prayer far down on the plain. Prayer is connected with the blessing to show us the value of it. If we had the blessings without asking for them, we would think them common things. Prayer makes our mercies more precious than diamonds. The things we ask for are precious, but we do not realize their preciousness until we have sought for them earnestly.

February 19
Evening

"He first findeth his own brother Simon" (John 1:41).

As soon as a man has found Christ, he begins to find others. One who has tasted of the honey of the gospel cannot eat it all himself. True grace puts an end to all spiritual monopoly. Andrew *first* found his own brother Simon and then others. Andrew did well to begin with Simon. There are Christians who are giving away tracts at other people's houses who should give away a tract at their own. Some are engaged in works of usefulness overseas, but neglect their special sphere of usefulness at home. You may or may not be called to evangelize the people in any particular locality. But certainly you are called to look after your own relatives and acquaintances. Let your religion begin at home. Many merchants export their best commodities, but the Christian should not. He should be a bold witness for Christ everywhere. But let him be sure to put forth the sweetest fruit of spiritual life and testimony in his own family. When Andrew went to find his brother, he could not have imagined how prominent Simon would become. *Simon Peter was worth ten Andrews* from what we can gather from sacred history. Yet, Andrew was instrumental in bringing him to Jesus. You may be very deficient in talent yourself. But you may be the means of drawing one to Christ who will become strong in grace and service. You do not realize the possibilities which are in you. You may merely speak a word to a child who has a noble heart which will stir the Church in years to come. Andrew had only limited talents, but he found Peter. You go and do likewise.

"God, that comforteth those that are cast down" (2 Corinthians 7:6).

Who comforts like Him? Go to some poor, melancholy, distressed child of God. Tell him sweet promises, and whisper in his ear choice words of comfort; he is like the deaf adder; he does not listen. He is in despair, and comfort him as you may, it will be only a sigh of resignation that you get from him. You will bring forth no psalms of praise, no hallelujahs, no joyful sonnets. But let *God* come to His child, let Him lift up His countenance, and the mourner's eyes glisten with hope. You could not have cheered him, but the Lord has done it. "He is the God of all comfort" (2 Corinthians 1:3). There is no balm in Gilead, but there is balm in God. There is no physician among the creatures, but the Creator is Jehovah-rophi. It is marvelous how one sweet word of God will make whole songs for Christians. One word of God is like a piece of gold. The Christian is the goldbeater, and he can hammer that promise out for weeks. Christian, you need not sit down in despair. Go to the Comforter and ask Him to give you consolation. You have heard it said that when a pump is dry, you must pour water down it first of all, and then you will get water. Christian, when you are dry, go to God, ask Him to shed abroad His joy in your heart, and then your joy will be full. Do not go to acquaintances, for you will find them Job's comforters after all. Go first and foremost to your "God, that comforteth those that are cast down" (2 Corinthians 7:6). You will soon say, "In the multitude of my thoughts within me thy comforts delight my soul" (Psalm 94:19).

February 20
Evening

"Then was Jesus led up of the Spirit into the wilderness to be tempted of the devil" (Matthew 4:1).

When Satan tempts us, his sparks fall upon kindling. In Christ's case, however, it was like striking sparks on water. Yet, the enemy continued his evil work. If the devil goes on striking when there is no result, how much more will he tempt when he knows what flammable stuff fills our hearts. Though you become greatly sanctified by the Holy Spirit, you must expect that the great dog of hell will bark at you still. In the company of other men, we expect to be tempted. But even seclusion will not guard us from the same trial. Jesus Christ was led away from human society into the wilderness and was tempted by the devil. Solitude has its benefits, but the devil will follow us into the most lovely retreats. Do not suppose that it is only the worldly-minded who have dreadful thoughts and blasphemous temptations, for even spiritual persons endure the same. The utmost consecration of spirit will not insure you against satanic temptation. It was Christ's food and drink to do the will of Him that sent Him. And yet, He was tempted! Your heart may glow with a flame of love for Jesus, and yet the devil will try to bring you down to lukewarmness. If you tell me when God permits a Christian to lay aside his armor, I will tell you when Satan gives up temptation. Like the old knights in wartime, we must sleep with helmet and breastplate buckled on, for the arch-deceiver will seize our first unguarded hour to make us his prey. May the Lord keep us watchful in all seasons and give us a final escape.

February 21
Morning

"He hath said" (Hebrews 13:5).

If we can only grasp these words by faith, we have an all-conquering weapon in our hand. What fear is there which will not fall smitten with a deadly wound before this arrow from the bow of God's covenant? Yes, whether for delight in our quietude or for strength in our conflict, "He hath said" must be our daily resort. This may teach us the extreme value of searching the Scriptures. There may be a promise in the Word which would exactly fit your case, but you may not know of it, and therefore you miss its comfort. There may be a potent medicine in the Scripture, and you may continue being sick unless you will examine and search the Scriptures to discover what "He hath said." Should you not, besides reading the Bible, store your memories richly with the promises of God? You memorize the sayings of great men; you treasure the verses of renowned poets; should you not be profound in your knowledge of the words of God so that you may be able to quote them readily when you would solve a difficulty or overthrow a doubt? Since "He hath said" is the source of all wisdom and the fountain of all comfort, let it dwell in you richly as "a well of water, springing up into everlasting life" (John 2:14). So you will grow healthy, strong, and happy in the divine life.

February 21
Evening

"Understandest thou what thou readest?"
(Acts 8:30).

We would be better teachers of others and less likely to be carried about by every wind of doctrine if we had a more intelligent understanding of the Word of God. The Holy Spirit is the Author of the Scriptures. He alone can enlighten us to understand them properly. Therefore, we should constantly pray for His teaching and guidance into all the truth. When the prophet Daniel promised to interpret Nebuchadnezzar's dream, he prayed earnestly that God would open up the vision. (See Daniel 2:16-23.) The apostle John, in his vision at Patmos, saw a book sealed with seven seals which no one was worthy to open. The book was later opened by the Lion of the tribe of Judah. But it is written first, "I wept much" (Revelation 5:4). The tears of John were his liquid prayers. They were the sacred keys which opened the sealed book. If for your own and others' benefit you desire to be "filled with the knowledge of his will in all wisdom and spiritual understanding" (Colossians 1:9), remember that prayer is your best means of study. Like Daniel, you will understand the dream and its interpretation when you have sought God. Like John, you will see the seven seals of precious truth loosed after you have wept much. Stones are not broken except by the relentless use of the hammer. The one who shatters them must go down on his knees. Use the hammer of diligence and let the knee of prayer be exercised. Thoughts and reasonings are like the steel wedges which give a hold upon truth. But prayer is the lever which forces open the iron chest of sacred mystery. Then, we may get the treasure hidden within.

February 22
Morning

"His bow abode in strength, and the arms of his hands were made strong by the hands of the mighty God of Jacob" (Genesis 49:24).

The strength God gives to His Josephs is *divine strength.* How did Joseph stand against temptation? God gave him aid. There is nothing we can do without the power of God. All true strength comes from "the mighty God of Jacob." Notice in what a blessedly familiar way God gave this strength to Joseph—"The arms of his hands were made strong by the hands of the mighty God of Jacob." Thus God is represented as putting His hands on Joseph's hands, placing His arms on Joseph's arms. Like a father teaches his children, so the Lord teaches them that fear Him. He puts His arms upon them. God Almighty, Eternal, Omnipotent, stoops from His throne and lays His hand upon the child's hand, stretching His arm upon the arm of Joseph, that he may be made strong! This strength was also covenant strength for it is ascribed to "the mighty God of Jacob." Now, whenever you read of the God of Jacob in the Bible, you should remember the covenant with Jacob. All the power, all the grace, all the blessings, all the mercies, all the comforts, all the things we have, flow to us from the well-head, through the covenant. If there were no covenant, then we would fail indeed, for all grace proceeds from it, as light and heat from the sun.

February 22
Evening

"The Lord is slow to anger, and great in power" (Nahum 1:3).

Jehovah is *slow to anger*. When mercy comes into the world, it rides on the wings of the wind. But when wrath goes forth, it comes with sluggish footsteps, for God takes no pleasure in the sinner's death. God's rod of mercy is always in His outstretched hands. His sword of justice is in its sheath, held down by that pierced hand of love which bled for the sins of men. "The Lord is slow to anger," because He is *great in power*. He is truly great in power who has power over himself. The power that binds omnipotence actually surpasses omnipotence. The weak mind is irritated at a little thing. The strong mind bears it like a rock which does not move though a thousand breakers dash upon it. God sees His enemies, and yet He holds in His anger. If He were less than divine, He would have sent forth His wrath long ago. He would have blasted the earth with the fire, and man would have been destroyed. But the greatness of His power brings us mercy. Can you, by humble faith, look to Jesus and say, "My substitute, You are my rock, my trust"? Then, do not be afraid of God's power. Now that you are forgiven and accepted, now that by faith you have fled to Christ for refuge, the power of God should no more terrify you than the shield and sword of the warrior frightens those whom he loves. Rejoice that He who is "great in power" is your Father and Friend.

February 23
Morning

"I will never leave thee" (Hebrews 13:5).

No promise is of private interpretation. Whatever God has said to any one saint, He has said to all. When He opens a well for one, it is that all may drink. When He opens a granary-door to give out food, there may be one starving man who is the reason its being opened, but all hungry saints may come and feed, too. Whether He gave the Word to Abraham or to Moses, matters not. He has given it to you as one of the covenanted seed. There is not a brook of living water of which you may not drink. If the land flows with milk and honey, eat the honey and drink the milk, for both are yours. Be bold to believe, for He said, "I will never leave thee, nor forsake thee." In this promise, God gives everything to His people. Then no attribute of God can cease to be engaged for us. He will show Himself strong on the behalf of them that trust Him. With loving kindness He will have mercy on us. To summarize, there is nothing you can want, ask for, or need in time or in eternity, which is not contained in this text—"I will never leave thee, nor forsake thee."

February 23
Evening

"Take up the cross, and follow me" (Mark 10:21).

You are not commanded to make your own cross, although unbelief is a master carpenter at cross-making. Neither are you permitted to choose your own cross, although self-will would gladly be lord and master. But your cross is prepared and appointed for you by divine love, and you are to accept it cheerfully. You are to *take up* the cross as your chosen badge and burden, not stand and complain about it. Jesus asks you to submit your shoulder to His easy yoke. Do not kick at it in irritation, trample on it in pride, fall under it in despair, or run away from it in fear. Take it up like a true follower of Jesus. Jesus was a cross-bearer; He leads the way in the path of sorrow. Surely you could not desire a better guide! The way of the cross is the way of safety. Do not be afraid to tread its thorny paths. The cross is not made of feathers or lined with velvet. It is heavy and exasperating to disobedient shoulders. But it is not an iron cross, though fears have painted it with iron colors. It is a wooden cross, and a man can carry it. The Man of Sorrows first carried the load. By the power of the Spirit of God, you will soon be so in love with your cross that, like Moses, you would not exchange the reproach of Christ for all the treasures of Egypt. Remember that it will soon be followed by the crown. The thought of the coming weight of glory will greatly lighten the present heaviness of trouble. The Lord will help you to bow your spirit in submission to the divine will. Then, you may go forth with the holy and submissive spirit which belongs to a follower of the Crucified One.

February 24
Morning

"I will cause the shower to come down in his season: there shall be showers of blessing" (Ezekiel 34:26).

Here is sovereign mercy. There is only one voice which can speak to the clouds and bid them beget the rain. Who sends down the rain upon the earth? Who scatters the showers on the green herb? Do not I, the Lord? So grace is the gift of God and is not to be created by man. It is also needed grace. What would the ground do without showers? As absolutely needful is the divine blessing. In vain you labor, until God the plenteous shower bestows, and sends salvation down. Then, it is plenteous grace. "I will send them showers." It does not say, "I will send them drops," but "showers." So it is with grace. If God gives a blessing, He usually give it in such a measure that there is not room enough to receive it. Plenteous grace! We cannot do without saturating showers of grace. Again, it is *seasonable grace.* "I will cause the shower to come down *in his season.*" What is your season this morning? Is it the season of drought? Then that is the season for showers. Is it a season of great heaviness and depression? Then that is the season for showers. "As thy day, so shall they strength be." And here is a varied blessing. "I will give thee showers of blessing." The word is in the plural. God will send all kinds of blessings. All God's blessings go together, like links in a golden chain. If He gives converting grace, He will also give comforting grace. He will send "showers of blessing." Look up today, parched plant, and open your leaves and flowers for a heavenly watering.

February 24
Evening

"O Lord of hosts, how long wilt thou not have mercy upon Jerusalem?...And the Lord answered the angel...with good words and comfortable words" (Zechariah 1:12–13).

God loves the Church with a love too deep for human understanding. He loves her with all His infinite heart. Therefore, let her sons be of good courage. She cannot be far from prosperity because God has spoken "good words and comfortable words to her. The prophet goes on to tell us what these comfortable words are: "I am jealous for Jerusalem and for Zion with a great jealousy" (Zechariah 1:14). The Lord loves His Church so much that He cannot bear that she would go astray to others. When she has gone astray, He cannot bear that she suffer too much or too heavily. He will not have His enemies afflict her. He is displeased with them because they increase her misery. When God seems to have left His Church, His heart is still warm toward her. History shows us that whenever God uses a rod to chasten His servants, He always breaks it later. It is as if He loathed the rod which gave His children pain. He feels the sting far more than His people. "Like as a father pitieth his children, so the Lord pitieth them that fear him" (Psalm 103:13). His chastening is no evidence of a lack of love. If this is true of His Church *collectively,* it is also true of *each individual member.* You may fear that the Lord has passed you by, but it is not true. He who counts the stars and calls them by their names is in no danger of forgetting His own children. He knows you situation as thoroughly as if you were the only creature He ever made or the only saint He ever loved. Approach Him, and be at peace.

February 25
Morning

"The wrath to come" (Matthew 3:7).

It is pleasant to pass over a country after a rain and to smell the freshness of the herbs. That is the position of a Christian. He is going through a land where the storm has spent itself upon his Savior's head. If there are a few drops of sorrow falling, they distill from clouds of mercy. Jesus cheers him by the assurance that they are not for his destruction. But how terrible to witness the approach of a tempest, to see the forewarnings of the storm. How terrible to await the dread advance of a hurricane—such as occurs, sometimes, in the tropics—to wait in terrible apprehension. And yet, sinner, this is your present position. No hot drops have as yet fallen, but a shower of fire is coming. No terrible winds howl around you, but God's tempest is gathering its dread artillery. As yet the water-floods are dammed up by mercy, but the flood-gates will soon be opened. The thunderbolts of God are yet in His storehouse, but the tempest hastens and how awful will that moment be when God, robed in vengeance, will march forth in fury! Where, Oh sinner, will you hide your head, or where will you flee? Oh, that the hand of mercy may now lead you to Christ! He is freely set before you in the gospel. You know your need of Him. Believe in Him, and then the fury will pass over forever.

February 25
Evening

"But Jonah rose up to fell unto Tarshish from the presence of the Lord and went down to Joppa" (Jonah 1:3).

Instead of going to Nineveh to preach the Word as God commanded him, Jonah went to Joppa to escape from the Lord. There are occasions when God's servants shrink from duty. But what is the result? What did Jonah lose by his conduct? *He lost the presence and comfortable enjoyment of God's love.* When we serve our Lord Jesus as believers should, our God is with us. Though we have the whole world against us, it does not matter as long as we have God with us. But the moment we seek our own desires, we are at sea without a pilot. Then we bitterly groan, "O my God, where have You gone? How could I have been so foolish as to shun Your service? This price is too high. Let me return to You that I may rejoice in Your presence." Jonah also *lost all peace of mind.* Sin soon destroys a believer's comfort. Jonah *lost everything upon which he might have drawn for comfort.* He could not plead the promise of divine protection, for he was not in God's will. He could not say, "Lord, I met with these difficulties in the course of my duty. Help me through them." He was reaping his own deeds; he was filled with his own ways. Christian, do not behave like Jonah unless you wish to have all the waves and the billows rolling over your head. You will find that it is far harder to shun the work and will of God than to immediately yield yourself to it. Finally, *Jonah lost his time,* for he had to go to Tarshish after all. It is hard to contend with God. Let us yield ourselves to Him at once.

February 26
Morning

"Salvation is of the Lord" (Jonah 2:9).

Salvation is the work of God. It is He alone who quickens the soul "dead in trespasses and sins," and it is He also who maintains the soul in its spiritual life. He is both "Alpha and Omega." If I am prayerful, God makes me prayerful. If I have graces, they are God's gift to me. If I hold on in a consistent life, it is because He upholds me with His hand. I do nothing toward my own preservation, except what God Himself first does in me. If I sin, that is my own doing; but if I act rightly, that is of God, wholly and completely. Do I live before men a consecrated life? It is not I, but Christ who lives in me. Am I sanctified? I did not cleanse myself—God's Holy Spirit sanctifies me. Am I weaned from the world? I am weaned by God's chastisement sanctified to my good. Do I grow in knowledge? The great Instructor teaches me. He only is my rock and my salvation. Do I feed on the Word? That Word would be no food for me unless the Lord made it food for my soul and helped me to feed on it. Am I continually receiving fresh increase of strength? Where do I gather my might? My help comes from heaven's hills. Without Jesus I can do nothing. As a branch cannot bring forth fruit except it abide in the vine, no more can I, except I abide in Him. What Jonah learned in the great deep, let me learn this morning in my prayer closet. Salvation is of the Lord.

February 26
Evening

"Behold, if the leprosy have covered all his flesh, he shall pronounce him clean that hath the plague" (Leviticus 13:13).

Although this regulation appears strange, there was wisdom in it. The outward manifestation of the disease proved that the physical make-up of the leper was sound. This evening, let us understand the lesson of so extraordinary a rule. We, too, are lepers and may apply the law of the leper to ourselves. When a man sees himself as completely lost, ruined, and covered with the defilement of sin, he can disclaim all righteousness of his own and plead guilty before the Lord. Then he is clean through the blood of Jesus and the grace of God. Hidden, unfelt, unconfessed iniquity is the true leprosy. But when sin is seen and felt, it has received its death blow, and the Lord looks with eyes of mercy upon the afflicted soul. Nothing is more deadly than self-righteousness or more filled with hope than repentance. We must confess that we are sinful for no other confession will be the whole truth. If the Holy Spirit is at work in us, convicting us of sin, there will be no difficulty in making such an acknowledgment—it will spring spontaneously from our lips. What comfort the text gives to truly awakened sinners! The very circumstance which grievously discouraged them is turned into a sign of a hopeful condition. Digging out the foundation is the first thing necessary in building. Likewise, a thorough consciousness of sin is one of the earliest works of grace in the heart. Oh, poor leprous sinner, come as you are to Jesus.

February 27
Morning

"Thou hast made the Lord, which is my refuge, even the Most High, thy habitation" (Psalm 91:9).

In the wilderness the Israelites were continually exposed to change. When the pillar stopped, the tents were pitched; but tomorrow, before the morning sun had risen, the trumpet sounded, the ark was in motion, and the fiery, cloudy pillar was leading the way through the narrow trails of the mountain, up the hillside, or along the arid waste of the wilderness. They had scarcely time to rest a little before they heard the sound of "Away! this is not your rest; you must still be onward journeying toward Canaan!" Even wells and palm trees could not detain them. Yet they had an abiding home in their God. His cloudy pillar was their roof, and its flame by night their household fire. They must go onward from place to place, continually changing. "Yet," says Moses, "though we are always changing, Lord, thou hast been our dwelling place throughout all generations." The Christian knows no change with regard to God. He may be rich today and poor tomorrow; he may be sickly today and well tomorrow; he may be in happiness today, tomorrow he may be distressed—but there is no change with regard to his relationship to God. If He loved me yesterday, He loves me today. He is my strong habitation whereunto I can continually resort (See Psalm 71:3). I am a pilgrim in the world, but I am at home in my God.

February 27
Evening

"Whose goings forth have been from of old, from everlasting" (Micah 5:2).

The Lord Jesus represented His people before the throne *long before they appeared upon the stage of time.* It was "from everlasting" that He signed the agreement with His Father that He would pay blood for blood, suffering for suffering, agony for agony, and death for death on behalf of His people. It was "from everlasting" that He gave Himself up without a murmuring word, that from the crown of His head to the sole of His foot He might sweat great drops of blood. He was spat upon, pierced, mocked, and crushed beneath the pains of death. Christ loved you before you were born. He has been going forth from everlasting to save you. Will He lose you now? He has carried you in His hand as His precious jewel. Will He let you slip from between His fingers? He chose you before the mountains were brought forth or the channels of the deep were dug. Will He reject you now? Impossible! He would not have loved me so long if He had not been a changeless Lover. If He could grow weary of me, He would have been tired of me long before now. If He had not loved me with a love as deep as hell and as strong as death, He would have turned from me long ago. Oh, joy above all joys, to know that we are His everlasting and inalienable inheritance, given to Him by His Father before the earth ever was! Everlasting love will be the pillow for my head this night.

February 28
Morning

"My expectation is from him" (Psalm 63:5).

If the believer is looking for anything from the world, it is a poor expectation indeed. But if he looks to God for the supply of his wants, whether in temporal or spiritual blessings, his expectation will not be a vain one. Constantly he may draw from the bank of faith and get his need supplied out of the riches of God's lovingkindness. My Lord never fails to honor His promises. When we bring them to His throne, He never sends them back unanswered. Therefore, I will wait only at His door, for He ever opens it with the hand of grace. But we have expectations beyond this life. We will die soon, and then our expectation is from Him. Do we not expect that when death approaches, He will send angels to carry us to His bosom? We believe that when the pulse is faint, and the heart heaves heavily, some angelic messenger will stand and look with loving eyes on us and whisper, "Sister spirit, come away!" We are longing for the time when we will be like our glorious Lord—for "we shall see him as he is" (1 John 3:2). Oh, my soul, live for God; live with the desire to glorify Him from whom comes all your supplies.

February 28
Evening

"The barrel of meal wasted not, neither did the cruse of oil fail, according to the word of the Lord, which he spake by Elijah" (1 Kings 17:16).

See the faithfulness of divine love. Observe that this woman had *daily necessities.* She had to feed herself and her son in a time of famine. Now, the prophet Elijah needed to be fed, too. But though the need was three times as great, she had *a constant supply* of meal. Each day she used what was in the barrel, but each day the amount left over remained the same. You, too, have daily necessities. Because they come so frequently, you may fear that your barrel of meal will one day be empty, and the jar of oil will fail you. Rest assured that, according to the Word of God, this will not happen. Even if you live longer than Methuselah and though your needs are many as the sands of the seashore, God's grace and mercy will last through all your necessities. You will never know a real lack. For three long years in this widow's day, the heavens never saw a cloud and the stars never wept a holy tear of dew upon the wicked earth. Famine and desolation and death made the land a howling wilderness. But this woman was always joyful in abundance. It will be the same with you. You will see the sinner's hope perish, for he trusts his own strength. You will see the proud Pharisee's confidence crumble, for he builds his hope upon the sand. You will even see your own schemes blasted and withered, but you will find your place of defense in the Rock of your Salvation.

February 29
Morning

"With lovingkindness have I drawn thee" (Jeremiah 31:3).

The law and judgment are used to bring us to Christ, but the final victory is affected by lovingkindness. The prodigal set out for his father's house from a sense of need. His father saw him a great way off and ran to meet him. The last steps that he took toward his father's house were with the kiss still warm upon his cheek and the welcome still musical in his ears. The Master came to the door and knocked with the iron hand of the law; the door shook and trembled on its hinges; but the man piled every piece of furniture which he could find against the door, for he said, "I will not admit the Man." The Master turned away, but He came back, and with His own soft hand, he knocked again softly and tenderly. This time the door did not shake, but strange to say, it opened, and there on his knees the once unwilling host was found rejoicing to receive his guest. "Come in, come in; You have so knocked that my heart is drawn to You. I could not think of Your pierced hand leaving its blood-mark on my door, and of You going away homeless. I yield, I yield. Your love has won my heart." So in every case; lovingkindness wins the day. What Moses with the tablets of stone could never do, Christ does with His pierced hand.

February 29
Evening

"Now we have received. . .the spirit which is of God; that we might know the things that are freely given to us of God" (1 Corinthians 2:12).

Have you received the Spirit which is of God? It is necessary for the Holy Spirit to work in the heart of the believer. All that has been done by the Father and the Son will be of no value to us *unless the Spirit reveals these things* to our souls. What effect does salvation have upon any man until the Spirit of God enters into him? Salvation is a dead letter in my consciousness until the Spirit of God calls me out of darkness into marvelous light. Then, through my calling, I see my purpose. I know that I have been chosen in the eternal plan. A covenant was made with the Lord Jesus Christ by His Father. But what good is that covenant to us until the Holy Spirit brings us His blessings and opens our heart to receive them? The blessings are out of our reach. The Spirit of God takes them down and hands them to us. Thus, they truly become ours. Covenant blessings in themselves are like the manna in the skies—far out of mortal reach. But the Spirit of God opens the windows of heaven and scatters the living bread around the camp of the spiritual Israel. Christ's finished work is like wine stored in the wine vat. Because of unbelief, we can neither draw nor drink. The Holy Spirit dips our vessel into this precious wine, and then we drink. Without the Spirit, we are as dead in sin as though the Father had never chosen us, and the Son had never bought us with His blood. The Holy Spirit is absolutely necessary to our well-being. Let us walk lovingly toward Him and tremble at the thought of grieving Him.

March 1
Morning

"Awake, O north wind; and come, thou south; blow upon my garden, that the spices thereof may flow out" (Song of Solomon 4:16).

Anything is better than the dead calm of indifference. Did not the spouse in this verse humbly submit herself to the reproofs of her Beloved? She entreated Him to send forth His grace in some form, making no stipulation as to the peculiar manner in which it should come. Did not she, like ourselves, become so utterly weary of deadness that she sighed for any visitation which would brace her to action? Yet, she desires comfort, too, the smiles of divine love, the joy of the Redeemer's presence; these are often mightily effectual to arouse our sluggish life. She desires either one or the other, or both, so that she may be able to delight her Beloved with the spices of her garden. She cannot endure to be unprofitable, nor can we. How cheering a thought that Jesus can find comfort in our poor feeble graces! It seems far too good to be true. The wisdom of the great Husbandman overrules diverse and opposite causes to produce the one desired result. It makes both affliction and consolation draw forth faith, love, patience, hope, resignation, joy, and the other fair flowers of the garden. May we know by sweet experience what this means!

March 1
Evening

"He is precious" (1 Peter 2:7).

As all the rivers run into the sea, so all delights center on our Beloved. The glance of His eyes outshines the sun. The beauty of His face is fairer than the choicest flowers. Gems of the earth and pearls from the sea are worthless things compared to His preciousness. None of us can compute the value of God's unspeakable gift. Words cannot express the preciousness of the Lord Jesus to His people or fully tell how essential He is to their satisfaction and happiness. Believer, would you find a famine in the midst of plenty if your Lord was not there? Or if the bright, morning star was gone, would you feel that no other star could give you so much as a ray of light? What a howling wilderness is this world without our Lord! If He hides Himself from us for a moment, the flowers of our garden wither, our pleasant fruits decay, the birds suspend their songs, and a tempest overturns our hopes. All earth's candles cannot make daylight if the Sun of Righteousness is eclipsed. What would you do in the world without Him in the midst of its temptations and its cares? What would you do in the morning without Him when you wake up and face another day's battle? What would you do at night when you come home tired and weary, if there was no door of fellowship between you and Christ? He will not permit us to face one day without Him, for Jesus never forsakes His own.

March 2
Morning

"But all the Israelites went down to the Philistines, to sharpen every man his share, and his colter, and his axe, and his mattock" (1 Samuel 13:20).

We are engaged in a great war with the Philistines of evil. Every weapon within our reach must be used. Preaching, teaching, praying, giving, all must be brought into action, and talents which have been thought too useless for service must now be employed. Each moment of time, each fragment of ability, educated or untutored, each opportunity, favorable or unfavorable, must be used, for our foes are many, and our force is slender. Most of our tools need sharpening. We need quickness of perception, tact, energy, promptness—complete adaptation for the Lord's work. Practical common sense is a very scarce thing among the conductors of Christian enterprises. We might learn from our enemies and make the Philistines sharpen our weapons. This morning let us note enough to sharpen our zeal during this day by the aid of the Holy Spirit. Mark the heathen devotees, what tortures they endure in the service of their idols! Are they alone to exhibit patience and self-sacrifice? Observe the prince of darkness, how persevering in his endeavors, how unabashed in his attempts, how daring in his plans, how energetic in all! The devils are united as one man in their infamous rebellion, while we believers in Jesus are divided in our service of God and scarcely ever work with unanimity. Oh, that from Satan's infernal industry we may learn to go about like good Samaritans, seeking whom we may bless!

"Unto me, who am less than the least of all saints, is the grace given, that I should preach among the Gentiles the unsearchable riches of Christ" (Ephesians 3:8).

Paul felt it was a great privilege to be allowed to preach the gospel. He did not look upon his calling as a burden, but he fulfilled it with intense delight. Yet, while Paul was thankful for his ministry, his success in it greatly humbled him. The fuller a vessel becomes, the deeper it sinks in the water. Idlers may enjoy a false pride in their abilities, because they have not been tested. But the earnest worker soon learns his own weakness. If you seek humility, *try hard work*. If you want to know your nothingness, attempt some great thing for Jesus. If you desire to learn how powerless you are apart from the living God, attempt the great work of proclaiming the unsearchable riches of Christ. You will know, as you never knew before, what a weak, unworthy thing you are. Although the apostle knew and confessed his weakness, he was never perplexed about the *subject* of his ministry. From his first sermon to his last, Paul preached nothing but Christ. He lifted up the cross and extolled the Son of God. Follow his example and spread the glad tidings of salvation. The believer must be the flower which yields itself to the Sun of Righteousness. Christ alone is the subject which is both seed for the sower and bread for food. (See 2 Corinthians 9:10.)

March 3
Morning

"I have chosen thee in the furnace of affliction" (Isaiah 48:10).

Comfort yourself, tried believer, with this thought: God saith, "I have chosen thee in the furnace of affliction." Does not the word come like a soft shower, assuaging the fury of the flame? Is it not an asbestos armor, against which the heat has no power? Whatever happens to me in this vale of tears, I know that He has chosen me. If, believer, you require still greater comfort, remember *that you have the Son of Man with you in the furnace.* In that silent room of yours, there sits by your side One whom you have not seen, but whom you love; and when you know it not, He makes all your bed in your affliction and smooths your pillow for you. Your friend sticks closely to you. You cannot see Him, but you may feel the pressure of His hands. Do you not hear His voice? Even in the valley of the shadow of death, He says, "Fear not, I am with thee." He will never leave one whom He has chosen for His own. "Fear not, for I am with thee" (Isaiah 43:5). This is His sure word of promise to His chosen ones in the furnace of affliction.

March 3
Evening

"He saw the Spirit of God descending like a dove" (Matthew 3:16).

As the Spirit of God descended upon the Lord Jesus, so He also descends upon the members of His body. Before we are completely aware of what is happening, we are impelled onward and heavenward beyond all expectations. Yet, it is not done with earthly haste, for the wings of the dove are as soft as they are swift. *Quietness* seems to be essential to many spiritual operations. The Lord is present in the still, small voice, and, like the dew, His grace is distilled in silence. God chose the dove as an expression of *purity,* and the Holy Spirit is holiness itself. When He comes, everything that is pure and lovely and of good report abounds, and sin and uncleanness depart. Peace also reigns where the Holy Spirit comes with power. He bears the olive branch which shows that the waters of divine wrath are calmed. *Gentleness* is another result of His transforming power. Hearts touched by Him are meek and lowly. *Harmlessness* follows as a matter of course. The turtledove can endure wrong, but cannot inflict it. We must be harmless as doves. The dove is a picture of *love,* and its voice is full of affection. The soul visited by the blessed Spirit abounds in love to God, in love to the brethren, and in love to sinners. Above all, it abounds in love to Jesus. The moving of the Spirit of God upon the face of the deep first produced *order and life.* (See Genesis 1:2.) Today, He brings new life and light to our hearts.

March 4
Morning

"My grace is sufficient for thee" (2 Corinthians 12:9).

If none of God's saints were poor and tried, we would not know half so well the consolation of divine grace. We may find a wanderer who has no place to lay his head, but who can say, "Still will I trust in the Lord." We may see a pauper starving on bread and water, but he still glories in Jesus. We may see a bereaved widow overwhelmed in affliction yet still believing in Christ. What honor they reflect on the gospel! God's grace is illustrated and magnified in the poverty and trials of believers. Saints bear up under every discouragement, believing that all things work together for their good. They believe that out of apparent evils a real blessing will ultimately spring—that their God will either work a deliverance for them speedily or most assuredly support them in the trouble. This patience of the saints proves the power of divine grace. The master-works of God are those men who stand, in the midst of difficulties, steadfast and unmovable. He who would glorify his God must set his account on meeting with many trials. No man can be illustrious before the Lord unless his conflicts are many. If, then, yours is a much-tried path, rejoice in it, because you will better show forth the all-sufficient grace of God. Never dream of His failing you. The God who has been sufficient until now can be trusted to the end.

March 4
Evening

"They shall be abundantly satisfied with the fatness of thy house"(Psalm 36:8).

The queen of Sheba was amazed at the richness of Solomon's life style. She marveled at the gathering of servants who feasted at the royal table. (See 1 Kings 10:4-5.) But what is this compared to the hospitalities of the God of grace? Hundreds of thousands of God's people are fed daily. The hungry and thirsty come, bringing large appetites to the banquet. But not one of them leaves unsatisfied. Though the multitude that feed at Jehovah's table is as countless as the stars of heaven, each one receives his portion of meat. Think how much grace even one saint requires—nothing but the Infinite could supply him for one day. Yet, the Lord spreads His table for many saints, generation after generation. The guests at mercy's banquet are "abundantly satisfied" with the abundance of God's house. Such feasting is guaranteed by a faithful promise to all those who put their trust under the shadow of Jehovah's wings. I once thought, "if I could only get some scraps of meat at God's back door of grace, I would be satisfied." I was like the woman who said, "The dogs eat of the crumbs which fall from the master's table" (Matthew 15:27). But no child of God is ever served scraps. They all eat from the King's table. In matters of grace, we all have Benjamin's portion—we have five times more than we could have expected. (See Genesis 43:34.) Though our needs are great, we are continually amazed at the marvelous abundance of grace which God gives us to enjoy.

March 5
Morning

"Let us not sleep, as do others" (1 Thessalonians 5:6).

There are many ways of promoting Christian wakefulness. Let me strongly advise Christians to converse together concerning the ways of the Lord. Christians who isolate themselves and walk alone are very liable to grow drowsy. Keep Christian company, and you will be kept wakeful by it and refreshed and encouraged to make quicker progress in the road to heaven. But as you thus take "sweet counsel" with others in the ways of God, take care that the theme of your conversation is your Lord Jesus. Let the eye of faith be constantly looking unto Him. Let your heart be full of Him. Let your lips speak of His worth. Friend live near to the cross, and you will not sleep. Labor to impress yourself with a deep sense of the value of the place to which you are going. If you think that hell is behind you, and the devil is pursuing you, you will not loiter. Christian, will you sleep while the pearly gates are open—the songs of angels waiting for you to join them—a crown of gold ready for your brow? Ah, no, in holy fellowship continue to watch and pray that you enter not into temptation!

March 5
Evening

"Say unto my soul, I am thy salvation" (Psalm 35:3).

This sweet prayer will be my evening's petition, but first let it give me instruction. *David had his doubts.* Why would he pray, "Say unto my soul, I am thy salvation," if he did not sometimes experience doubts and fears? Let me be encouraged, for I am not the only saint who complains of weakness of faith. If David doubted, I do not need to conclude that *I* am not a Christian because I have doubts. *David was not content while he had doubts and fears.* Instead, he went at once to the mercy seat to pray for the assurance which he valued as much as fine gold. I, too, must seek an abiding sense of my acceptance in the Beloved. I have no joy when His love is not filling my soul. *David knew where to obtain full assurance.* He went to his God in prayer, crying, "Say unto my soul, I am thy salvation." I must be alone with God if I expect to have a clear sense of Jesus' love. If my prayers cease, my eye of faith will grow dim. David would not be satisfied unless *his assurance had a divine source.* "Say unto my soul." Nothing short of a divine testimony in the soul will ever satisfy the true Christian. Moreover, David could not rest unless his assurance had a *vivid personality* about it. "Say unto *my* soul, I am *thy* salvation." Lord, even if You said this to all the saints, it would mean nothing unless You say it to me. Lord, I have sinned. I hardly dare to ask, but say to *my* soul, "I am *thy* salvation." Let me have a present, personal, unfailing, indisputable sense that I am Yours and that You are mine.

March 6
Morning

"Ye must be born again" (John 3:7).

Regeneration is a subject which lies at the very basis of salvation. We should be very diligent to take heed that we really are "born again," for there are many who fancy they are, who are not. Being born in a Christian land and being recognized as professing the Christian religion is of no avail whatever, unless there is something more added to it—the being "born again" by the power of the Holy Spirit. To be "born again" is a matter so mysterious, the human words cannot describe it. "The wind bloweth where it listeth, and thou hearest the sound thereof, but canst not tell whence it cometh, and whither it goeth; so is every one that is born of the Spirit" (John 3:8). Nevertheless, it is a change which is known and felt. This great work is *supernatural.* It is not an operation which a man performs for himself. It is not a change of my name, but a renewal of my nature so that I am not the man I used to be, but a new man in Christ Jesus. If you have been "born again," your acknowledgment will be, "O Lord Jesus, the everlasting Father, You are my spiritual Parent; unless Your Spirit had breathed into me the breath of a new, holy, and spiritual life, I would have been to this day 'dead in trespasses and sins.' My heavenly life is wholly derived from You, to You I ascribe it. My life is hid with Christ in God. It is no longer I who live, but Christ who liveth in me." May the Lord enable us to be well assured on this vital point, for to be unregenerate is to be unsaved, unpardoned, without God, and without hope.

March 6
Evening

"Before destruction the heart of man is haughty" (Proverbs 18:12).

There is an old saying, "Coming events cast their shadows before them." The writer of the Proverbs teaches us that a haughty heart is the prelude to evil. Pride is a sure sign of destruction. David's aching heart shows that man's glory ends when he looks upon his own greatness. (See 2 Samuel 24:10.) Nebuchadnezzar, the mighty builder of Babylon, was reduced to creeping on the earth devouring grass like an ox. (See Daniel 4:33.) Pride made the boaster into a beast, just as it made an angel into a devil. God hates haughty looks and never fails to bring them down. All the arrows of God are aimed at proud hearts. Is your heart haughty this evening? Pride can get into the Christian's heart as well as into the sinner's. It can delude him into dreaming that he is "rich and increased in goods, and in need of nothing" (Revelation 3:17). Are you glorying in your grace or talents? Are you proud of yourself because you have a holy appearance and sweet experiences? Destruction could be coming to you also. Your poppies of conceit will be pulled up by the roots, your grace will wither in the burning heat, and your self-sufficiency will become as straw for the dunghill. If we forget to live at the foot of the cross in deepest humility of spirit, God will not forget to make us suffer under His rod. Destruction will come to you, O self-exalted believer. The destruction of your joys and comforts will come though there can be no destruction of your soul. Therefore, "He that glorieth, let him glory *in the Lord*" (1 Corinthians 1:31).

March 7
Morning

"Have faith in God" (Mark 11:22).

Love can make the feet move more swiftly, but faith is the foot which carries the soul. Faith is the oil enabling the wheels of holy devotion and of earnest piety to move well. Without faith the wheels are taken from the chariot, and we drag heavily. With faith I can do all things. Without faith I will neither have the inclination nor the power to do anything in the service of God. If you would find the men who serve God the best, you must look for the men of the most faith. Little faith will save a man, but little faith cannot do great things for God. Little faith stands desponding, mingling her tears with the flood; but great faith sings, "When you pass through the waters, I will be with you; and through the rivers, they will not overflow you," and she fords the streams at once. Would you be comfortable and happy? Would you have the religion of cheerfulness and not that of gloom? Then have faith in God. If you love darkness and are satisfied to dwell in gloom and misery, then be content with little faith; but if you love the sunshine and would sing songs of rejoicing, covet earnestly this best gift—"great faith."

March 7
Evening

"It is better to trust in the Lord, than to put confidence in man" (Psalm 118:8).

Christians often look to man for help and counsel and mar the noble simplicity of their reliance upon God. Are you anxious about temporal things this evening? You trust in Jesus for your salvation. Then why are you troubled? "Because of my great care," you answer. It is written, "Cast thy burden upon the Lord" (Psalm 55:22). "Be careful for nothing; but in every thing by prayer and supplication with thanksgiving let your requests be made known unto God" (Philippians 4:6). If you cannot trust God for temporal things, how dare you trust Him for spiritual things? Can you trust Him for your soul's redemption and not rely upon Him for a few lesser needs? Is God enough for your need, or is His all-sufficiency too narrow for you? Is His heart faint? Is His arm weary? If so, seek another God; but if He is infinite, omnipotent, faithful, true, and all-wise, then give up your frantic search for another confidence. Why do you think you need another foundation when this is strong enough to bear all the weight you can ever build upon it? Do not alloy the gold of your faith with the dross of human confidence. Wait only upon God and let your expectation be from Him. Let the sandy foundations of earthly trust be the choice of fools. But like one who foresees the storm, build your house upon the Rock of Ages.

March 8
Morning

"We must through much tribulation enter into the kingdom of God" (Acts 14:22).

God's people have their trials. It was never designed by God, when He chose His people, that they should be an untried people. Trials are a part of our lot. They were predestined for us in God's solemn decree and bequeathed us in Christ's last legacy. So surely as the stars are fashioned by His hands, and their orbits fixed by Him, so surely are our trials allotted to us. He has ordained their season and their place, their intensity, and the effect they will have on us. Good men must never expect to escape troubles; if they do, they will be disappointed, for none of their predecessors have been without them. Mark the patience of Job; remember Abraham, for he had his trials, and by his faith under them, he became the "Father of the faithful." Note well the biographies of all the patriarchs, prophets, apostles, and martyrs, and you will discover none of those whom God made vessels of mercy, who were not made to pass through the fire of affliction. It is ordained of old, that the cross of trouble should be engraved on every vessel of mercy, as the royal mark whereby the King's vessels of honor are distinguished. But although tribulation is thus the path of God's children, they have the comfort of knowing that their Master has traversed it before them. They have His presence and sympathy to cheer them, His grace to support them, and His example to teach them how to endure. When they reach the Kingdom, it will more than make amends for the much tribulation through which they passed to enter it.

March 8
Evening

"She called his name Ben-oni (son of sorrow): but his father called him Benjamin (son of my right hand)" (Genesis 35:18).

To every matter there is a bright side as well as a dark side. Rachel was overwhelmed with the pain of a difficult childbirth. Jacob, though weeping at the loss of his wife, could see the beauty of the infant's birth. It is well for us if, while the flesh mourns over trials, our faith triumphs in divine steadfastness. The stormy sea feeds multitudes with its fish; the wild forest blooms with delicate flowers; the stormy wind sweeps away the pestilence; and the biting frost loosens the soil. Dark clouds distill bright drops, and black earth grows brilliant flowers. A vein of good can be found in every mine of evil. Sad hearts have peculiar skill in discovering the worst point of view from which to gaze upon a trial. If there was only one swamp in the world, they would soon be up to their necks in it. If there was only one lion in the jungle, they would hear it roar. We all have this tendency at times. We may cry like Jacob, "All these things are against me" (Genesis 42:36). Faith casts all care upon the Lord and then anticipates good results from the worst calamities. Out of the rough oyster shell of difficulty, faith extracts the rare pearl of honor. From the deep ocean caves of distress, it uplifts the priceless coral of experience. When the flood of prosperity ebbs, faith finds treasures hidden in the sand. When the sun of delight goes down, it turns the telescope of hope to the starry promises of heaven. When death itself appears, faith points to the light of resurrection beyond the grave.

March 9
Morning

"Yea, he is altogether lovely" (Song of Solomon 5:16).

The superlative beauty of Jesus is all-attracting. It is not so much to be admired, as it is to be loved. He is more than pleasant and fair, He is *lovely*. Surely the people of God can fully justify the use of this golden word, for He is the object of their warmest love. Look, disciples of Jesus, to your Master's lips and say, are they not most sweet? Do not His words cause your heart to burn within you as He talks with you by the way? Look up to His head of much fine gold and tell me, are not His thoughts precious to you? Is not your adoration sweetened with affection as you humbly bow before that countenance which is as Lebanon, excellent as the cedars? Is there not a charm in His every feature, and is not His whole person fragrant with such a savor of His good ointments? Our love is not a seal set on His heart of love alone. It is fastened on His arm of power also. There is not a single part of Him on which it does not fix itself. We anoint His whole person with the sweet spikenard of our fervent love. His whole life we would imitate. His whole character we would transcribe. In all other beings we see some lack, but in Him there is all perfection. The best even of His favored saints have had blots upon their garments and wrinkles upon their brows. He is nothing but loveliness. Christ Jesus is gold without alloy—light without darkness—glory without cloud—"Yea, He is altogether lovely."

March 9
Evening

"Abide in me" (John 15:4).

Communion with Christ is a certain cure for every ill. Whether it is a grievous affliction or the overabundance of earthly delight, close fellowship with the Lord Jesus will take bitterness from the one and heaviness from the other. If you live near to Jesus, it is of secondary importance whether you live on the mountain of honor or in the valley of humiliation. You will be covered with the wings of God, and underneath are the everlasting arms. (See Deuteronomy 33:27.) Let nothing keep you from the fellowship which is the privilege of a soul wedded to the Lord. Always seek to be in His company, for only in His presence is there comfort and safety. Jesus should not be a friend who only calls upon us now and then, but rather, one with whom we walk daily. There is a difficult road before you, O traveler to heaven. Do not go without your Guide. You may have to pass through the fiery furnace. Do not enter unless you have the Son of God as your companion. You have to battle the Jericho of your own faults. Do not attempt the warfare until, like Joshua, you have seen the Captain of the Lord's host with His sword drawn in His hand. In every case, in every condition, you will need Jesus. When the iron gates of death open you will need Him most of all. Keep close to your soul's Husband, and lean your head upon His bosom. Since you have lived with Him and lived in Him here on earth, you will abide with Him forever.

March 10
Morning

"In my prosperity I said, I shall never be moved" (Psalm 30:6).

Give a man wealth and let his ships bring home continually rich freights. Let his lands yield abundantly and the weather be favorable to his crops. Let uninterrupted success attend him. Let him enjoy continued health, and give him a happy heart. Let his eyes be ever sparkling with joy, and the natural consequence of such an easy state, even if he is the best Christian who ever breathed, will be *presumption*. Even David said, "I shall never be moved," and we are not better than David or half as good. Beware of the smooth places of the way, if you are treading them. If the way is rough, thank God for it. If God would always rock us in the cradle of prosperity; if there were always few clouds in the sky; if we always had sweet drops in the wine of this life, we would become intoxicated with pleasure. Like the man asleep upon the mast, each moment we would be in jeopardy. We bless God in our afflictions; we thank Him for our changes; we extol His name during loss of property; for we feel that had He not chastened us thus, we might have become too secure. Continual worldly prosperity is a fiery trial.

March 10
Evening

"Man. . .is of few days, and full of trouble" (Job 14:1).

There is nothing very pleasant in the realization that we are not immune to adversity. But it may humble us and prevent our boasting like the psalmist, "I shall never be moved" (Psalm 30:6). It may keep us from sinking our roots too deep in this soil since we are soon to be transplanted into the heavenly garden. Let us recall the frail claim we hold on our *temporal blessings.* If we remember that all the trees of earth are marked for the woodsman's axe, we would not be so ready to build our nests in them. We should love with the love which expects death and separations. Our dear relatives and friends are only loaned to us. The hour when we must return them to the Lender's hand may be near. This is certainly true of our *worldly goods.* Riches grow their own wings and fly away. Our *health* is equally precarious. We are like the frail flowers of the field; we cannot expect to bloom forever. There is no single point where we can hope to escape from the sharp arrows of affliction. Out of our few days, there is not one that is secure from sorrow. Man's life is a cask full of bitter wine; he who looks for joy in it would be better off seeking for honey in an ocean of brine. Do not set your affections upon things of earth, but seek those things which are above. Here the moth devours and the thief breaks in to steal, but in heaven all joys are perpetual and eternal.

March 11
Morning

"Sin. . .exceeding sinful" (Romans 7:13).

Beware of light thoughts of sin. At the time of conversion, the conscience is so tender that we are afraid of the slightest sin. Young converts have a holy timidity, a godly fear, lest they should offend God. But very soon the fine bloom on these first ripe fruits is removed by the rough handling of the surrounding world. It is sadly true that even a Christian may grow so callous that the sin which once startled him does not alarm him in the least. Men get familiar with sin by degrees. The ear in which the cannon has been booming will not notice slight sounds. At first a little sin startles us, but soon we say, "Is it not a little one?" Then there comes another, larger, and then another, until by degrees we begin to regard sin as simply a little slip up. Then follows an unholy presumption: "We have not fallen into open sin. True, we tripped a little, but we stood upright in the main. We may have uttered one unholy word, but as for the most of our conversation, it has been consistent." So we excuse sin; we throw a cloak over it; we call it by dainty names. Take heed lest you fall little by little. Sin, a *little* thing? Is it not a poison? Do not little strokes fell lofty oaks? Will not continual droppings wear away stones? Sin, a *little* thing? It girded the Redeemer's head with thorns and pierced His heart! If you could weigh the least sin in the scales of eternity, you would fly from it as from a serpent and abhor the least appearance of evil. Look on all sin as that which crucified the Savior, and you will see it to be "exceeding sinful."

March 11
Evening

"Thou shalt be called, Sought out" (Isaiah 62:12).

The surpassing grace of God is seen very clearly in that we were not only sought, but sought *out.* We were mingled with the mire. When a precious piece of gold falls into the sewer, men gather around and carefully inspect the mass of filth. They continue to stir and rake and search among the heap until the treasure is found. Or, as another example, it is like we were lost in a maze. We wandered around hopelessly until mercy came after us with the gospel. It did not find us easily; it had to search for us and seek us out. As lost sheep, we were so desperately lost that it did not seem possible that even the Good Shepherd could track us down. Glory be to unconquerable grace, we were sought *out!* No gloom could hide us; no filthiness could conceal us. We were found and brought home. Glory be to infinite love, the Holy Spirit restores us! Strange and marvelous are the ways which God often uses to bring back His own. Blessed be His name, He never gives up the search until the chosen are sought out and found. They are not a people sought today and cast away tomorrow. Almighty power and wisdom combined will make no failures. God's people will be called, "Sought out!" That *any* should be sought out is matchless grace, but that *we* should be sought out is grace beyond degree! We can find no reason for it but God's own sovereign love. Let us lift up our hearts in wonder and praise the Lord that this night *we* wear the name of "Sought out."

March 12
Morning

"Thou shalt love thy neighbor" (Matthew 5:43).

Love your neighbor. Perhaps he rolls in riches, and you are poor and living in your little cottage beside his stately mansion. You see his estates, his fine linen, and his sumptuous banquets every day. God has given him these gifts; do not covet his wealth and think no hard thoughts concerning him. Be content with your own lot, if you cannot better it. But do not look on your neighbor and wish that he were as yourself. Love him, and then you will not envy him. On the other hand, perhaps you are rich, and you reside near the poor. Do not be too proud to call them neighbors. The world calls them your inferiors. In what way are they inferior? They are far more your equals than your inferiors, for God has made of one blood all people that dwell on the face of the earth. It is your coat which is better than theirs, but you are by no means better than they. They are men, and what are you more than that? Take heed that you love your neighbor even though he is in rags. But, perhaps, you say, "I cannot love my neighbors, because for all I do they return ingratitude and contempt." So much the more room for the heroism of love. Would you be a feather-bed warrior, instead of bearing the rough fight of love? He who dares the most will win the most. If rough is your path of love, tread it boldly. Heap coals of fire on their heads. If they are hard to please, seek not to please *them* but to please *your Master.* Love your neighbor, for in so doing you are following in the footsteps of Christ.

March 12
Evening

"To whom belongest thou?" (1 Samuel 30:13).

No neutralities can exist in Christianity. We are either under the banner of King Jesus, to serve and fight His battles, or we are vessels of the wicked prince, Satan. "To whom belongest thou?" Let me assist in your response. *Have you been born again?* If you have, you belong to Christ; but without the new birth you cannot be His. *In whom do you trust?* Those who believe in Jesus are the sons of God. *Whose work are you doing?* You are sure to serve your master, for he whom you serve is obviously your lord. *What company do you keep?* If you belong to Jesus, you will associate with those who wear the distinction of the cross. *What is your conversation?* Is it heavenly, or is it earthly? *What have you learned of your Master?* If you have spent your time with Jesus, it will be said of you, as it was of Peter and John—"They took knowledge of them that they had been with Jesus" (Acts 4:13). The question remains: "To whom belongest thou?" If you are not Christ's, you are in a hard service. *Run away from your cruel master!* Enter into the service of the Lord of love, and you will enjoy a life of blessedness. If you *are* Christ's, there are four things you should do. You belong to Jesus—*obey Him.* Let His Word be your law; let His wish be your will. You belong to the Beloved—*love Him.* Let your heart embrace Him; let your soul be filled with Him. You belong to the Son of God—*trust Him.* Rest nowhere else but on Him. You belong to the King of kings—*be decided for Him.* Thus, your life will show all the world to whom you belong.

March 13
Morning

"Why sit we here until we die" (2 Kings 7:3).

Dear reader, this little book was mainly intended for the edification of believers; but if you are yet unsaved, our heart yearns over you. Open your Bible and read the story of the lepers. Mark their position, which was much the same as yours. If you remain where you are, you will perish. If you go to Jesus, you can only die. If you sit still in despair, no one can pity you when your ruin comes. None will escape who refuse to look to Jesus. To perish is so awful, that if there were but a straw to catch at, the instinct of self-preservation should lead you to stretch out your hand. We have been talking to you on your own unbelieving ground. We assure you, as from the Lord, that if you seek Him, He will be found. Jesus casts out none who come unto Him. You will not perish if you trust Him. On the contrary, you will find treasure far richer than the poor lepers gathered in Syria's deserted camp. May the Holy Spirit encourage you to go at once, and you will not believe in vain. When you are saved yourself, tell the good news to others. Don't keep it to yourself. Tell the Church first and unite with them in fellowship. Let the minister be informed of your discovery, and then proclaim the good news in every place. May the Lord save you before the sun goes down today.

March 13
Evening

"Then he put forth his hand, and took her, and pulled her in unto him into the ark" (Genesis 8:9).

Weary from her wanderings, the dove finally returns to the ark as her only resting place. How heavily she flies—she feels she will drop—she will never reach the ark! But she struggles on. Noah has been looking for his dove all day long and is ready to receive her. She has just enough strength to reach the edge of the ark. She is ready to drop, when Noah puts forth his hand and pulls her in unto him. Notice the phrase *"her in unto him."* She did not fly right in herself, but was too fearful and weary. She flew as far as she could, and then Noah put forth his hand and pulled her in to him. She was not scolded for her wanderings. Just as she was, she was pulled into the ark. So you, sinner, with all your sin, will be received. "Only return"—these are God's two gracious words. The dove had no olive branch in her mouth this time; she brought only herself. But the message is "only return," and she does return. Noah reaches out and pulls her in. Though your soul is black as the raven with the mire of sin, fly back to the Savior. Every moment that you wait only increases your misery. Your attempts to cleanse yourself and make yourself fit for Jesus are all vanity. Come to Him just as you are. "Return, thou backsliding Israel" (Jeremiah 3:12). He does not say, "Return, thou *repenting* Israel" (though there is doubtless such an invitation) but "thou *backsliding* one." Jesus is waiting for you! He will stretch forth His hand and pull you in—in to Himself, to your heart's true home.

March 14
Morning

"Let him that thinketh he standeth take heed lest he fall" (1 Corinthians 10:12).

It is a curious fact that there is such a thing as being proud of grace. A man says, "I have great faith; I shall not fall." "I have fervent love," says another, "I can stand; there is no danger of my going astray." He who boasts of grace has little grace to boast of. Some who do this imagine that their graces can keep them. If a continuous stream of oil does not come to the lamp, though it burn brightly today, it will smoke tomorrow, and its scent will be harmful. Take heed that you do not boast of your graces. Let all your confidence be in Christ and His strength. That is the only way you can be kept from falling. Spend more time in prayer. Spend more time in worship. Read the Scriptures more earnestly and constantly. Watch your life more carefully. Live nearer to God. Take the best example for your pattern. Let your conversation be holy. Show genuine compassion for men's souls. When that happy day comes, when Jesus says, "Come up higher," may it be your happiness to hear Him say, "You have fought a good fight, you have finished your course, and there is laid up for you a crown of righteousness which will not fade away." He alone is able "to keep you from falling and to present you faultless before the presence of his glory with exceeding joy" (Jude 24).

March 14
Evening

"I will take heed to my ways" (Psalm 39:1).

You are never so far from danger of sinning that you can boast of security. The road is very muddy; it will be hard to choose a path that will not soil your garments. This is a world of corruption; you need to be on your guard if you expect to keep your hands clean. There is a thief at every turn of the road to rob you of your jewels. When you reach heaven, it will be by a miracle of divine grace ascribed entirely to your Father's power. Be on your guard. When a man carries a can of gasoline, he makes sure that he does not go near an open flame. You, too, must take care that you do not enter into temptation. Even your daily activities are sharp tools. You must handle them cautiously. There is nothing in this world to foster a Christian's faith, but everything tries to destroy it. You must look up to God, for *He* will keep you! Your prayer should be, "Hold me up, and I will be safe." Guard every thought, word, and action with holy jealousy. Do not expose yourself unnecessarily. If you must go where the darts are flying, never venture forth without your shield. The moment that the devil finds you unprotected, he will rejoice that his hour of triumph has come. Though you cannot be slain, you may be wounded. Therefore, take heed to your ways and pray diligently. No one ever fell into error by being too watchful. May the Holy Spirit guide us in all our ways so that we may always please the Lord.

March 15
Morning

"Be strong in the grace that is in Christ Jesus" (2 Timothy 2:1).

Christ has grace without measure in Himself, but He has not retained it for Himself. As the reservoir empties itself into the pipes, so has Christ emptied out His grace for His people. "Of his fullness have all we received, and grace for grace" (John 1:16). He seems only to have in order to dispense to us. Like a tree, He bears sweet fruit to be gathered by those who need. Grace is always available from Him without price. As the blood of the body, though flowing from the heart, belongs equally to every member, so the influences of grace are the inheritance of every saint united to the Lamb. In this there is a sweet communion between Christ and His Church, inasmuch as they both receive the same grace. This is true communion: when the sap of grace flows from the stem to the branch and when it is perceived that the stem itself is sustained by the very nourishment which feeds the branch. As we receive grace from Jesus and more constantly recognize it as coming from Him, we will behold Him in communion with us and enjoy the happiness of communion with Him. Let us make daily use of our riches, taking from Him the supply of all we need with as much boldness as men take money from their own purse.

March 15
Evening

"He did it with all his heart, and prospered" (2 Chronicles 31:21).

Men who do their work with all their hearts prosper. But those who go to their labor wishing they were someplace else are almost certain to fail. God does not give good harvest to idle men; nor is He pleased to send wealth to those who will not dig in the field to find hidden treasure. If a man desires to prosper, he must be diligent in business. It is the same in your Christian walk. If you long to prosper in your work for Jesus, let it be *heart* work, and let it be done with *all* your heart. Put as much force, energy, and earnestness into your relationship with God as you do into business. The Holy Spirit helps our infirmities, but He does not encourage our idleness. He loves active believers. The most useful men and women in the Church are those who do their work for God *with all their hearts.* The most successful Bible teachers are not necessarily the most scholarly, but rather, the most zealous. Whole-heartedness shows itself in *perseverance.* There may be a failure at first, but the earnest worker will say, "It is the Lord's work, and it must be done. My Lord has called me to do it, and in His strength I will accomplish it." Christian, are you serving your Master with all of your heart? Remember the earnestness of Jesus! He could say, "The zeal of thine house hath eaten me up" (John 2:17). When He sweat great drops of blood, it was no light burden that He had to carry upon those blessed shoulders. When He poured out His heart, it was no weak effort He was making for the salvation of His people. Are we lukewarm?

March 16
Morning

"I am a stranger with thee" (Psalm 39:12).

All my natural alienation from You Lord, your grace has effectually removed. Now, in fellowship with You, I walk through this sinful world as a pilgrim in a foreign country. You are a stranger in Your own world. Man forgets You, dishonors You, sets up new laws and alien customs, and knows You not. When Your dear Son came to His own, His own received Him not. He was in the world, and the world was made by Him, and the world knew Him not. It is no wonder, then, if I, who live the life of Jesus, should be unknown and a stranger here below. Lord, I would not be a citizen where Jesus was an alien. His pierced hand has loosened the cords which once bound my soul to earth, and now I find myself a stranger in the land. My speech seems to these Babylonians, among whom I dwell, an outlandish tongue, and my actions are strange. But here is the sweetness of my lot; I am a stranger with You. You are my fellow-sufferer, my fellow-pilgrim. Oh, what joy to wander in such blessed society! My heart burns within me when You speak to me.

March 16
Evening

"Keep back thy servant also from presumptuous sins" (Psalm 19:13).

This was the prayer of David, the man after God's own heart. (See Acts 13:22.) If David needed to pray like this, we babes in grace must pray even more! It is as if he said, "Keep me back, or I shall rush headlong over the precipice of sin." Our evil nature, like an ill-tempered horse, is tempted to run away. May the grace of God put the bridle upon us that we do not rush into mischief. It is not pleasant to imagine what the best of us might do if it were not for the boundaries the Lord gives us in providence and in grace! Even the holiest persons need to be "kept back" from the vilest transgressions. The apostle Paul solemnly warned the saints against the most loathsome sins. "Mortify therefore your members which are upon the earth; fornication, uncleanness, inordinate affection, evil concupiscence, and covetousness, which is idolatry" (Colossians 3:5). You will surely stumble if you look away from Him who is able to keep you from falling. If your love is fervent, your faith constant, and your hope bright, do not say, "I will never sin," but rather cry, "Lead us not into temptation." There is enough kindling in the heart of the best of men to light a fire that burns to the lowest hell, unless God quenches the sparks as they fall. Hazael said, "Is thy servant a dog, that he should do this great thing?" (2 Kings 8:13). We are inclined to ask the same self-righteous question. May infinite wisdom cure us of the foolishness of self-confidence.

March 17
Morning

"Remember the poor" (Galatians 2:10).

Why does God allow so many of His children to be poor? He could make them all rich if He pleased. He could lay bags of gold at their doors. He could send them a large annual income. He could scatter around their house an abundance of provisions, as He made the quails lie in heaps around the camp of Israel and rained bread out of heaven to feed them. "The cattle upon a thousand hills are his" (Psalm 50:10). He could make the richest and the mightiest bring all their power and riches to the feet of His children, for the hearts of all men are in His control. But He does not choose to do so. Why is this? There are many reasons: one is to give us, who are favored with enough, an opportunity to show our love for Jesus. We show our love for Christ when we sing of Him and pray to Him. But if there were no needy people in the world, we would lose the sweet privilege of evidencing our love by ministering in sacrificial giving to His poorer brethren. He has ordained that thus we should prove that our love stands not in word only, but in deed and in truth. If we truly love Christ, we will care for those who are loved by Him. Those who are dear to Him will be dear to us. Let us then look on it not as a duty, but as a privilege, to relieve the poor of the Lord's flock—remembering the words of the Lord Jesus, "Inasmuch as ye have done it unto one of the least of these my brethren, ye have done it unto me" (Matthew 25:40).

March 17
Evening

"Blessed are the peacemakers: for they shall be called the children of God" (Matthew 5:9).

This is the seventh of the beatitudes. Seven represented the number of perfection among the Hebrews. It may be that the Savior placed the peacemaker seventh upon the list because he most nearly approaches the perfect man in Christ Jesus. The verse which precedes our text speaks of the blessedness of "the pure in heart: for they shall see God" (Matthew 5:8). It is important to understand that we are to be "first pure, then peaceable" (James 3:17). Our peaceable nature is never to be a tolerance of sin or evil. We must be set against everything that opposes God and His holiness. Then, with our purity being a settled matter in our souls, we can go on to peaceableness. But no matter how peaceable we may be in this world, we will be misrepresented and misunderstood. This should not surprise us, for even the Prince of Peace brought fire upon the earth. Though He loved mankind and did no wrong, He was "despised and rejected of men; a man of sorrows, and acquainted with grief" (Isaiah 53:3). Therefore, the peaceable in heart should not be surprised when they meet with enemies. It is added in the following verse, "Blessed are they which are persecuted for righteousness' sake: for theirs is the kingdom of heaven" (Matthew 5:10). The peacemakers are not only pronounced to be blessed, but they are surrounded by blessings. Lord, give us grace to climb to this seventh beatitude! Purify our minds that we may be first pure, then peaceable. Strengthen our souls that our peaceableness may not lead us into cowardice and despair when, for Your sake, we are persecuted.

March 18
Morning

"Ye are all the children of God by faith in Christ Jesus" (Galatians 3:26).

The fatherhood of God is common to all His children. Ah, Little-faith, you have often said, "O that I had the courage of Great-heart, that I could wield His sword and be as valiant as He! But, alas, I stumble at every straw, and a shadow makes me afraid." Listen, Little-faith, Great-heart is God's child, and you are God's child, too. Great-heart is not one bit more God's child than you are. Peter and Paul, the highly favored aspostles, were of the family of the Most High. So are you also. The weak Christian is as much a child of God as the strong one. All the names are in the same family register. One may have more grace than another, but God, our heavenly Father, has the same tender heart toward all. One may do more mighty works and may bring more glory to his Father, but he whose name is the least in the Kingdom of heaven is as much the child of God as he who stands among the King's mighty men. Let this cheer and comfort us when we draw near to God and say, "Our Father." Yet, while we are comforted by knowing this, let us not rest contented with weak faith, but ask, like the apostles, to have it increased. However feeble our faith may be, if it is real faith in Christ, we will reach heaven at last. If, then, you would live to Christ's glory and be happy in His service, seek to be filled with the spirit of adoption more completely, until perfect love casts out fear.

March 18
Evening

"As the Father hath loved me, so have I loved you" (John 15:9).

What is divine love like? The Father loved Jesus *without beginning,* and Jesus loves His people in the same way. "I have loved thee with an everlasting love" (Jeremiah 31:3). You can easily find the beginning of your love for Christ. But His love for us is a stream whose source is hidden in eternity. The Father loves Jesus *without any change.* There is no change in Jesus Christ's love to those who rest in Him. Yesterday, you may have been on the mountaintop, and you said, "He loves me." Today, you may be in the valley of humiliation, but He loves you still the same. On the high elevations, you heard His voice speak so sweetly and clearly with the music of love. Now, on the sea or even *in* the sea, when the waves and billows roll over you, His heart is faithful to His ancient choice. The Father loves the Son *without any end,* and this is how the Son loves His people. You need not fear, for His love for you will never cease. Rest confident that Christ will go with you even down to the grave. He will then be your guide up to the celestial hills. The Father loves the Son *without any measure,* and the Son bestows the same immeasurable love upon His chosen ones. The whole heart of Christ is dedicated to His people. He loved us and gave Himself for us. (See Galatians 2:20.) His love surpasses knowledge. We have an unchanging Savior, a precious Savior, one who loves without measure, without change, without beginning, and without end, even as the Father loves Him!

March 19
Morning

"Strong in faith" (Romans 4:20).

Remember, *faith is the only way you can obtain blessings.* Prayer cannot draw down answers from God's throne except it be the earnest prayer of the man who believes. Faith is the angelic messenger between the soul and the Lord Jesus in glory. If faith is withdrawn, we can neither send up prayer nor receive the answers. Faith is the telegraphic wire which links earth and heaven—on which God's messages of love fly so fast that before we call, He hears us. But if that telegraphic wire of faith is snapped, how can we receive the promise? Am I in trouble? I can obtain help for trouble by faith. Am I beaten about by the enemy? My soul leans by faith on her dear refuge in God. But take faith away—in vain I call to God. There is no road between by soul and heaven. Faith links me with divinity. Faith clothes me with the power of God. Faith engages on my side the omnipotence of Jehovah. Faith insures every attribute of God in my defense. It helps me defy the hosts of hell. It makes me march triumphant over the necks of my enemies. But without faith how can I receive anything of the Lord? Let not him that wavereth expect that he will receive anything of God!" "If thou canst believe, all things are possible to him that believeth" (Mark 9:23).

March 19
Evening

"And she did eat, and was sufficed, and left" (Ruth 2:14).

Whenever we are privileged to eat of the bread which Jesus gives, we are, like Ruth, satisfied with a full and sweet meal. When Jesus is the Host, no guest leaves the table hungry. Our *head* is satisfied with the precious truth which Christ reveals. Our *heart* is content with Jesus, the lovely object of affection. Our *hope* is satisfied, for who do we have in heaven but Jesus? And, our *desire* is fulfilled, for what can we wish for more than to know Christ and to "be found in him" (Philippians 3:9)? Jesus fills our *conscience* so that it is at perfect peace. Our *judgment* is secure with the certainty of His teaching. Our *memory* glows with recollections of what He has done, and our *imagination* rejoices at the prospects of what He will do. As Ruth was "sufficed, *and left,*" so it is with us. We thought that we could take in all of Christ. We sat at the table of the Lord's love and said, "Nothing but the infinite can ever satisfy me; I am such a great sinner that I must have infinite grace to wash my sin away." But there are certain sweet things in the Word of God which we have not enjoyed yet. We are like the disciples to whom Jesus said, "I have yet many things to say unto you, but ye cannot bear them now" (John 16:12). There are graces to which we have not attained, places of fellowship nearer to Christ which we have not reached, and heights of communion which our feet have not climbed. At every banquet of love there are many baskets of fragments left. Let us praise the generosity of our glorious Lord.

March 20
Morning

"My beloved" (Song of Solomon 2:8).

This was a golden name which the ancient Church gave to the Anointed of the Lord. She sang, "My beloved is mine, and I am his: he feedeth among the lilies" (Song of Solomon 2:16). Ever in her song of songs does she call Him by that delightful name, "My beloved!" Even in the long winter, when idolatry had withered the garden of the Lord, her prophets found space to lay aside the burden of the Lord for a little season and to say, as Isaiah did, "Now will I sing to my well-beloved a song of my beloved touching His vineyard" (Isaiah 5:1). Though the saints never saw His face, though as yet He was not made flesh or had dwelt among us or had man beheld His glory, yet He was the consolation of Israel, the hope and joy of all the chosen, the "beloved" of all those who were upright before the Most High. We, in the summer days of the Church, desire to speak of Christ as the Beloved of our soul and to feel that He is very precious, the chiefest among ten thousand, and the altogether lovely. So true is it that the Church loves Jesus and claims Him as her Beloved, that the apostle dares to defy the whole universe to separate her fom the love of Christ and declares that neither persecution, distress, affliction, perils, or the sword have been able to do it. He joyously boasts, "In all these things we are more than conquerors through him that loved us" (Romans 8:37). Oh, that we knew more of the ever precious One!

March 20
Evening

"Husbands, love your wives. even as Christ also loved the church"(Ephesians 5:25).

Few masters could venture to say, "If you want to practice my teaching, imitate my life." But the life of Jesus is the exact likeness of perfect virtue. Therefore, He can point to Himself as the paragon of holiness as well as the teacher of it. The Christian should take nothing less than Christ for his model. Under no circumstances should we be content unless we reflect the grace which was in Him. As a husband, the Christian is to look upon the portrait of Christ Jesus, and he is to live according to that copy. The love of a husband is *special.* The Lord Jesus has a special affection for the Church. He said in John 17:9, "I pray for them: I pray not for the world." The Church is the favorite of heaven and the treasure of Christ. It is the crown of His head, the bracelet of His arm, the breastplate of His heart, and the very center of His love. A husband should love his wife with a *constant* love, for this is how Jesus loves His Church. He may change in His display of affection, but the affection itself is still the same. A husband should love his wife with an *enduring* love, for nothing "shall be able to separate us from the love of God, which is in Christ Jesus our Lord" (Romans 8:39). A true husband loves his wife with a *hearty* love, fervent and intense. It is not mere lip service. What more could Christ have done in proof of His love than He has done? Jesus has a *delighted* love for His spouse. He prizes her affection and delights in her. In your domestic relationships, is this the rule and measure of your love— *"even as Christ loved the church"?*

March 21
Morning

Ye shall be scattered, every man to his own, and shall leave me alone" (John 16:32).

Few were involved with the sorrows of Gethsemane. The majority of the disciples were not sufficiently advanced in grace to be admitted to behold the mysteries of "the agony." Occupied with the passover feast at their own houses, they represent the many who live according to the letter, but are mere babes as to the spirit of the gospel. To eleven men only was the privilege given to enter Gethsemane and see "this great sight." Out of the eleven, eight were left at a distance. Only three highly favored ones could approach the veil of our Lord's mysterious sorrow. Within that veil even these must not intrude. A stone's-cast distance must be left between. He must tread the wine-press alone. To some selected spirits it is given, for the good of others and to strengthen them for future conflict, to enter the inner circle and hear the pleadings of the suffering High Priest. They have fellowship with Him in His sufferings and are made conformable unto His death. Yet, even these cannot penetrate the secret places of our Saviour's woe. There was an inner chamber in our Master's grief, shut out from human knowledge and fellowship. There Jesus is "left alone." Here Jesus was more than ever an "unspeakable gift."

March 21
Evening

"Canst thou blind the sweet influences of Pleiades, or loose the bands of Orion?" (Job 38:31).

If we are inclined to boast of our abilities, the splendor of nature soon shows us how insignificant we are. We cannot move the least of all the twinkling stars or quench even one of the beams of the morning sun. We speak of power, but the heavens laugh us to scorn. When the Pleiades, a magnificient cluster of stars, shines forth in the spring, we cannot restrain its brilliance. And, when Orion reigns aloft and the year is bound in winter's grip, we cannot relax the icy bands. The seasons revolve according to divine appointment. The whole race of men cannot change their schedule. Lord, "what is man that thou art mindful of him?" (Psalm 8:4). In the spiritual as in the natural world, man's power is limited. All the cunning and malice of men cannot halt the life-giving power of the Comforter. When He comes down to visit a church and revive it, the most antagonistic enemies cannot resist the good work. They may ridicule it, but they can no more restrain it than they can push back the springtime when the Pleiades is in the sky. God wills it, and so it must be. God alone can remove the winter of spiritual death from an individual or a church. What a blessing it is that He can do it! Lord, end my winter and let my spring begin. I cannot raise my soul out of her death and dullness, but all things are possible with You. I need heavenly influences, the clear shining of Your love, the beams of Your grace, and the light of Your countenance. These are the Pleiades to me. I suffer much from sin and temptation. These are my wintry signs, my terrible Orion. Lord, work wonders in me and for me.

March 22
Morning

"And he went a little farther, and fell on his face, and prayed." (Matthew 26:39).

There are several instructive features in our Savior's prayer in His hour of trial. It was *lonely prayer.* He withdrew even from His three favored disciples. Believer, be much in solitary prayer, especially in times of trial. Family prayer, social prayer, or prayer in the church will not suffice. These are very precious, but the best devotions are held where no ear hears but God's. It was *humble prayer.* Luke says He knelt, but another evangelist says, "He. . .fell on His face." Humility gives us good foot-hold in prayer. There is no hope of prevalence with God unless we humble ourselves so that He may exalt us in due time. It was the prayer of a Son. "Abba, Father." You will find it a stronghold in the day of trial to plead your adoption. Do not be afraid to say, "My Father, hear my cry." Observe that it was *persevering prayer.* He prayed three times. Cease not until you prevail. Be as the persistent widow whose continual coming earned what her first supplication could not win. Continue in prayer and watch with thanksgiving. Lastly, *it was the prayer of resignation.* "Nevertheless, not as I will, but as thou wilt" (Luke 22:42). Yield, and God yields. Let it be as God wills, and God will determine the best. Be content to leave your prayer in His hands, who knows when to give, how to give, what to give, and what to withhold. So pleading, earnestly, yet with humility and resignation, you will surely prevail.

March 22
Evening

"Father, I will that they also, whom thou hast given me, be with me where I am" (John 17:24).

Death! Why do you snatch away the excellent ones of the earth, in whom is all our delight? Oh, stop your work and spare the righteousness! Death takes the dearest of our friends. The most generous, the most prayerful, the most holy, the most devoted must die. And why? Jesus prayed, "Father, I will that they also, whom thou hast given me, be with me where I am." This prayer bears them on eagles' wings to heaven. Every time a believer mounts from this earth to Paradise, it is an answer to Christ's prayer. An old saint remarked, "Many times Jesus and His people pull against one another in prayer. You bend your knee in prayer and say, 'Father, I will that Thy saints be with me where *I* am;' Christ says, 'Father, I will that they also whom Thou hast given Me, be with Me where *I* am.' " Thus the disciple is opposing the purpose of his Lord. The soul cannot be in both places— the beloved one cannot be with Christ and with you, too. Now, which prayer will be answered? I am sure, though it causes great agony, you would say, "Jesus, not my will, but Thine be done." You would give up your prayer for your loved one's life, if you could realize that Christ is praying in the opposite direction. Lord, You shall have our loved ones. By faith, we let them go.

March 23
Morning

"His sweat was as it were great drops of blood falling down to the ground" (Luke 22:44).

The mental pressure on our Lord forced His frame to an unnatural excitement. His pores sent forth great drops of blood which fell down to the ground. This demonstrates the mighty power of His love. If men suffer great pain of mind, apparently, the blood rushes to the heart. The cheeks are pale; fainting may occur; the blood has gone inward, as if to nourish the inner man while passing through its trial. But see our Savior in His agony. He is so utterly oblivious of self that instead of His agony driving His blood to the heart to nourish Himself, it drives it outward. The agony of Christ, inasmuch as it pours Him out on the ground, pictures the fullness of the offering which He made for men. Do we not perceive how intense the wrestling must have been through which He passed, and will we not hear its voice to us? "Ye have not yet resisted unto blood, striving against sin" (Hebrews 12:4) Behold the great High Priest of our profession sweat blood rather than yield to the great tempter of your souls.

March 23
Evening

"I tell you that, if these should hold their peace, the stones would immediately cry out" (Luke 19:40).

But could the stones cry out? They could if He who opens the mouth of the dumb commanded them to lift up their voice. If they were able to speak, they would have much to testify in praise of Him who created them by the word of His power. Will *we* speak well of Him who made us new creatures and out of stones raised up children of Abraham? The old rocks could tell of chaos and order. They could describe the handiwork of God in successive stages of creation's drama. *We* can talk of God's decrees, of God's great work in ancient times, and all that He did for His Church in the days of old. If the stones were to speak, they could tell of their *breaker* who took them from the quarry and made them fit for the temple. Our glorious Breaker broke our hearts with the hammer of His Word, that He might build us into His temple. If the stones cried out, they would magnify their *builder* who polished them and fashioned them into a palace. Our Architect and Builder has put us in our place in the temple of the living God. If the stones could cry out, they might have a long story to tell by way of *memorial*. A great stone has often been set up as a memorial before the Lord. We, too, can testify of the great things God has done for us. The broken stones of the law cry out against us, but Christ Himself, who has rolled away the stone from the door of the tomb, speaks for us. We will not let the stones cry out. We will break forth into sacred song and forever glorify Him who is the Shepherd and Stone of Israel.

March 24
Morning

"He was heard in that he feared" (Hebrews 5:7).

Did this fear arise from the infernal suggestion that Jesus was utterly forsaken? There may be sterner trials than this, but surely it is one of the worst to be utterly forsaken. "See," said Satan, "You have a friend nowhere! Your Father has shut up the bowels of His compassion against You. Not an angel in His courts will stretch out his hand to help You. All heaven is alienated from You. Son of Mary, see Your brother James, see Your loved disciple John, and Your bold apostle Peter: how the cowards sleep when You are in your sufferings! You have no friend left in heaven or in earth. All hell is against You. I have stirred up my infernal den. I have sent my letters throughout all regions, summoning every prince of darkness to come against You this night. We will spare no arrows. We will use all our infernal might to overwhelm You. What will You do?" He was heard in that He feared. He was no more alone, but heaven was with Him. Jesus was heard in His deepest woe. My soul, you will be heard also.

March 24
Evening

"In that hour Jesus rejoiced in spirit" (Luke 10:21).

The Savior was "a man of sorrows" (Isaiah 53:3). But deep in His innermost soul He carried an inexhaustible treasury of heavenly joy. There was never a man who had a deeper, purer, or more abiding peace than our Lord Jesus Christ. He was anointed with the oil of gladness above His fellows. (See Psalm 45:7.) His vast benevolence must have given Him the greatest delight, for benevolence is joy. There were a few recorded times when this joy manifested itself in Jesus' life on earth. "In that hour Jesus rejoiced in spirit, and said, I thank thee, O Father, Lord of heaven and earth" (Luke 10:21). Christ had His songs though darkness surrounded Him. His face was marred, and His countenance lost the glow of earthly happiness. Yet He radiated unparalleled satisfaction as He thought about the final reward for His work. In the midst of the congregation, He sang His praise to God. In this way, the Lord Jesus is a blessed picture of His Church on earth. At this hour, the Church expects to walk closely with her Lord along a thorny road. To bear the cross is her calling, and to be scorned by her brothers is her lot. Yet, the Church has a deep well of joy which will sustain the saints of God. Like our Savior, we have times of intense delight for "there is a river, the streams whereof shall make glad the city of our God" (Psalm 46:4). Though we are exiles, we rejoice in our King.

March 25
Morning

"Betrayest thou the Son of man with a kiss" (Luke 22:48).

Be on guard when the world puts on a loving face, for it will betray you, as it did your Master, with a kiss. Whenever a man is about to stab religion, he usually professes very great reverence for it. Beware of the sleek-faced hypocrisy which is armor-bearer to heresy and infidelity. Knowing the deceivableness of unrighteousness, be wise as a serpent to detect and avoid the designs of the enemy. The young man, void of understanding, was led astray by the kiss of the strange woman. May your soul be so graciously instructed all this day that "the much fair speech" of the world may have no effect upon you! But what if you should be guilty of the same accursed sin as Judas, that son of perdition? You have been baptized into the name of the Lord Jesus. You are a member of His visible Church; you sit at His communion table. All these are so many kisses of my lips. Are you sincere in them? Do you live in the world as carelessly as others do, and yet make a profession of being a follower of Jesus? Surely you act inconsistently. You are a Judas. It would be better for you if you had never been born. O Lord, make us sincere and true. Preserve us from every false way. Never let us betray our Savior. We do love you, Jesus; and although we often grieve You, yet we desire to abide faithful even to death.

March 25
Evening

"The Son of man" (John 3:13).

How constantly our Master used the title, "the Son of man!" If He had chosen, He could always have spoken of Himself as the Son of God, the Everlasting Father, the Wonderful, the Counselor, the Prince of Peace. But behold the lowliness of Jesus! He prefers to call Himself the Son of man. Let us learn a lesson of humility from our Savior. Let us never become devoted to seeking great titles or proud degrees. There is, however, a far sweeter meaning to His name. Jesus loved manhood so much that He delighted to honor it. It is a high honor, and indeed, the greatest dignity of manhood, that Jesus is the Son of man. He displays this name that He may hang royal stars upon the breast of manhood and show forth the love of God to Abraham's seed. *Son of man*—whenever He said that word, He shed a halo around the head of Adam's children. Yet, there is an even more precious thought. Jesus Christ called Himself the Son of man to express His oneness and sympathy with His people. He reminds us that we may approach Him without fear. We may take all our griefs and troubles to Him, for He knows them by experience. Since He Himself suffered as the "Son of man," He is able to comfort us. All hail, blessed Jesus! You gave Yourself the sweet name which acknowledges that You are a brother and a friend. Your name is to us a dear token of Your grace, Your humility, and Your love.

March 26
Morning

"Jesus said unto them, If ye seek me, let these go their way" (John 18:8).

Mark, my soul, the care Jesus manifested, even in His hour of trial, toward the sheep of His hand! The ruling passion is strong in death. He resigns Himself to the enemy, but He interposes a word of power to set His disciples free. As to Himself, like a sheep before her shearers, He is dumb and opens not His mouth. Yet, for His disciples' sake, He speaks with Almighty energy. This is love—constant, unselfish, faithful love. But is there more here than is to be found on the surface? Have we not the very soul and spirit of the atonement in these words? The Good Shepherd lays down His life for the sheep and pleads that they must therefore go free. The Surety is bound, and justice demands that those for whom He stands a substitute should go their way. In the midst of Egypt's bondage, that voice rings as a word of power, "Let these go their way." The redeemed must come out of the slavery of sin and Satan. In every cell of the dungeons of despair the sound is echoed, "Let these go their way." Satan hears the well-known voice and lifts his foot from the neck of the fallen. Death hears it, and the grave opens her gates to let the dead arise. Their way is one of progress, holiness, triumph, and glory, and none will dare to stop them in it. "The hind of the morning" has drawn the cruel hunters on himself, and now the most timid roes and hinds of the field may graze at perfect peace among the lilies of his loves. The thundercloud has burst over the Cross of Calvary, and the pilgrims of Zion will never be smitten by the bolts of vengeance. Come, rejoice in the immunity your Redeemer has secured for you, and bless His name all the day and every day.

March 26
Evening

"When he cometh in the glory of his Father with the holy angels"(Mark 8:38).

If we have been partakers with Jesus in His shame, we will share in His glory when He comes again. Are you with Christ Jesus today? Does a vital union knit you together with Him? Then you must be with Him in His shame. You must take up His cross and go with Him outside the camp, bearing His reproach. (See Hebrews 13:13.) Then you will surely be with Him when the cross is exchanged for the crown. But if you are not with Him in the new-birth experience, you will not be with Him when He comes in His glory. If you back away from suffering with Him, you will not understand the fullness of joy when the King comes and *all His holy angels with Him.* Notice that the angels are with Him! And yet, He took up the seed of Abraham. If you are His own beloved, you cannot be far from Him. If you are married to Him, will you be distant? Though it is a day of judgment, you cannot be far from that heart which admitted angels into intimacy and brought you into union. He said to you, "I will betroth thee unto me in righteousness, and in judgment, and in loving kindness, and in mercies" (Hosea 2:19). His own lips have said, "I am married unto you" (Jeremiah 3:14). If the angels will be with Him, it is certain that His own beloved in whom is all His delight will be near to Him and sit at His right hand. Here is a morning star of hope of such exceeding brilliance that it will light up the darkest and most desolate experience.

175

March 27
Morning

"Then all the disciples forsook him and fled" (Matthew 26:56).

He never deserted them, but they, in cowardly fear of their lives, fled from Him in the very beginning of His sufferings. This is but one instance of the frailty of all believers if left to themselves. They are but sheep at best, and they flee when the wolf comes. They had all been warned of the danger and had promised to die rather than leave their Master. Yet, they were seized with sudden panic and took to their heels. It may be that I, at the opening of this day, have braced my mind to bear a trial for the Lord's sake, and I imagine myself to be certain to exhibit perfect fidelity. But let me be very jealous of myself, lest, having the same evil heart of unbelief, I should depart from my Lord as the apostles did. It is one thing to promise, and quite another to perform. It would have been to their eternal honor to have stood at Jesus' side. They fled from honor. May I be kept from imitating them! Where else could they have been so safe as near their Master who could easily call for twelve legions of angels? They fled from their true safety. O God, do not let me play the fool also. Divine grace can make the coward brave. These very apostles, who were timid as hares, grew to be bold as lions after the Spirit had descended on them. Even so, the Holy Spirit can make my spirit brave to confess my Lord and witness for His truth. What anguish must have filled the Savior as He saw His friends so faithless! This was one bitter ingredient in His cup, but that cup is drained dry. Let me not put another drop in it. If I forsake my Lord, I will crucify Him afresh and put Him to an open shame. Keep me, O blessed Spirit, from an end so shameful!

March 27
Evening

"And she said, Truth, Lord: yet the dogs eat of the crumbs which fall from their master's table" (Matthew 15:27).

This woman gained comfort in her misery by thinking *great thoughts of Christ*. The Master spoke of the children's bread. She reasoned, "Since You are the Master of the table of grace, I know that You are a generous Host. There is sure to be abundance of bread on Your table. There will be such an abundance for the children that there will be crumbs to throw on the floor for the dogs. The children will be no worse off because the dogs are fed." She thought of Jesus as one who had such an abundance to give that all that she needed would only be a crumb in comparison. Remember that she wanted to have the devil cast out of her daughter. It was a very great thing to her, but she had such high esteem of Christ that she said, "It is nothing to Him, it is but a crumb for Christ to give." Great thoughts of your sin alone will drive you to despair; but great thoughts of Christ will pilot you into the haven of peace. My sins are many, but it is nothing to Jesus to take them all away. The weight of my guilt presses me down as a giant's foot would crush a worm. But it is no more than a grain of dust to Him, because He has already borne its curse in His own body on the tree. (See 1 Peter 2:24.) It will be a small thing *for Him* to give me full remission, although it will be an infinite blessing *for me* to receive it. The woman opened her soul's mouth very wide, expecting great things from Jesus, and He filled it with His love. Her case is an example of prevailing faith. If we wish to conquer like her, we must imitate her tactics.

March 28
Morning

"The love of Christ, which passeth knowledge" (Ephesians 3:19).

The love of Christ passes all human comprehension. Words cannot describe His matchless love toward men. It is so vast and boundless that, as the swallow skims the water and dives not into its depths, so all descriptive words only touch the surface, while depths immeasurable lie beneath. Before we can have any right idea of the love of Jesus, we must understand His previous glory. But who can tell us the majesty of Christ? When He was enthroned in the highest heavens, He was very God of very God. By Him were the heavens made and all the hosts thereof. His own almighty arm upheld the spheres. The praises of cherubim and seraphim perpetually surrounded Him. The full chorus of the hallelujahs of the universe unceasingly flowed to the foot of His throne. He reigned supreme above all His creatures. God over all, blessed forever. And who, on the other hand, can tell how low He descended? To be a man was something, but to be a man of sorrows was far more. To bleed, to die, and to suffer were much for Him who was the Son of God. But to suffer such unparalleled agony and to endure a death of shame and desertion by His Father, this is a depth of condescending love which the most inspired mind must utterly fail to fathom.

March 28
Evening

"I will accept you with your sweet savour" (Ezekiel 20:41).

The merits of our great Redeemer are a sweet savor to the Most High. The active and passive righteousness of Christ have an equal fragrance. There was a sweet savor in His active life. By it, He honored the law of God and made every precept glitter like a precious jewel in the pure setting of His own person. In his passive obedience, He endured with unmurmuring submission, hunger, thirst, cold, and nakedness. He sweat great drops of blood in Gethsemane, gave His back to the smiters, and His cheeks to them that plucked out His beard. (See Isaiah 50:6.) Finally, He was fastened to the cross that He might suffer the wrath of God in our behalf. Because of His substitutionary suffering and His obedience, the Lord our God accepts us. What a sweet savor is needed to put away our ill savor! What cleansing power there must be in His blood to take away sin such as ours! And what glory in His righteousness makes such unacceptable creatures to be accepted in the Beloved! How sure and unchanging our acceptance must be since it is *in Him!* Never doubt your acceptance in Jesus. You cannot be accepted without Christ; but when you have received His grace, you cannot be unaccepted. Despite all your doubts, fears, and sins, Jehovah's gracious eye never looks on you in anger. When He looks at you through Christ, He sees no sin. You are always accepted in Christ and are always blessed and dear to the Father's heart. Therefore, lift up a song to heaven. As you see the smoking incense of the merit of the Savior rising before the sapphire throne, let the incense of your praise go up also.

March 29
Morning

"Though be were a Son, yet learned be obedience by the things which be suffered" (Hebrews 5:8).

The Captain of our salvation was made perfect through suffering. Therefore, we who are sinful and far from being perfect must not wonder if we are called to pass through suffering too. Will the head be crowned with thorns, and will the other members of the body be rocked on the dainty lap of ease? Must Christ pass through seas of His own blood to win the crown, and are we to walk to heaven in silver slippers? No, our Master's experience teaches us that suffering is necessary. But there is one very comforting thought in the fact of Christ's "being made perfect through suffering." It is that He can have complete sympathy with us. He is not a high priest who cannot be touched with the feelings of our infirmities. In this sympathy of Christ, we find a sustaining power. Believer, lay hold of this thought in all times of agony. Let the thought of Jesus strengthen you as you follow in His steps. Find a sweet support in His sympathy. Remember that to suffer is an honorable thing. To suffer for Christ is glory. The apostles rejoiced that they were counted worthy to do this. The Lord will give us grace to suffer *for* and *with* Christ. The jewels of a Christian are his afflictions. The regalia of the kings whom God has anointed are their troubles, their sorrows, and their griefs. "If we suffer, we shall also reign with him" (2 Timothy 2:12).

March 29
Evening

"I called him, but he gave me no answer"
(Song of Solomon 5:6).

Prayer sometimes waits like a petitioner at the gate until the King comes forth to grant her request. The Lord has been known to try great faith by long delays. He has permitted His servant's voices to echo in their ears as from a brazen sky. They have knocked at the golden gate, but it has remained immovable, as though it was rusted upon its hinges. Like Jeremiah, they have cried, "Thou hast covered thyself with a cloud, that our prayer should not pass through" (Lamentations 3:44). True saints have continued long in patient waiting without reply. This was not because their prayers were not intense or because they were unaccepted. But the delay pleased Him who is Sovereign and who gives according to His own pleasure. If it pleases Him for our patience to be exercised He will do as He desires with His own! Beggars must not be choosers concerning the time, place, or form of their answer. But we must be careful not to take delays in prayer for denials. We must not allow Satan to shake our confidence in the God of truth by pointing to our unanswered prayers. Unanswered petitions are not unheard. There is a registry in the court of heaven where every prayer is recorded. The Lord has a bottle in which the costly tears of sacred grief are stored and a book in which your holy groanings are numbered. (See Psalm 56:8.) You will prevail. Only be content to wait a little while. Your Lord's time will be better than your own. He will answer you and make you put away the sackcloth and ashes of long waiting. He will clothe you with the scarlet and fine linen of your heart's desire.

"He was numbered with the transgressors" (Isaiah 53:12).

This wonderful condescension was justified by many powerful reasons. In such a character He could better become their advocate. In some trials there is an identification of the counselor with the client. Now, when the sinner is brought to the court, Jesus appears there Himself. He stands to answer the accusation. He points to His side, His hands, His feet and challenges Justice to bring anything against the sinners whom He represents. He pleads His blood so triumphantly that the Judge proclaims, "Let them go their way; deliver them from going down into the pit, for He hath found a ransom." Our Lord Jesus was numbered with the transgressors in order that they might feel their hearts drawn toward Him. Who can be afraid of one who is written in the same list with us? Surely we may come boldly to Him and confess our guilt. He who is numbered with us cannot condemn us. He was holy, while we were guilty. He transfers His name from the list of the holy to this black indictment, and our names are taken from the indictment and written in the roll of acceptance. There is a complete transfer made between Jesus and His people. All our estate of misery and sin Jesus has taken, and all that Jesus has comes to us. Rejoice, believer, in your union to Him who was numbered among the transgressors. Prove that you are truly saved by being manifestly numbered with those who are new creatures in Him.

March 30
Evening

"Let us search and try our ways, and turn again to the Lord"(Lamentations 3:40).

The spouse who loves her absent husband longs for his return. A long separation from the man whom she loves leaves a painful emptiness in her spirit. It is the same with souls who love the Savior so much that they *must* see His face. They cannot bear that He should be away upon the mountaintop and not hold communion with them. A reproaching glance or an uplifted finger will be grievous to loving children who fear to offend their tender father. Beloved, it was once the same way with you. A text of Scripture, a threatening, a touch of the rod of affliction, and you went to your Father's feet, crying, "Show me why You are angry with me." Is it so now? Are you content to follow Jesus from far off? Can you contemplate ending your communion with Christ without alarm? Have your sins separated you and God, and is your heart at rest? It is a grievous thing when we can live contentedly without the enjoyment of the Savior's face. *Let us consider what an evil thing this is—* little love for our dying Savior, little joy in our precious Jesus, little fellowship with the Beloved! Truly repent in your soul, while you sorrow over your hardness of heart. Do not stop at sorrow! Remember where you first received salvation. *Go at once to the cross.* There only can your spirit be made alive. No matter how hard, how insensible, how dead you may have become, go again in all the rags, poverty, and defilement of your natural condition. Clasp that cross. Jesus will bring back to us our first love. This will restore the simplicity of your faith and the tenderness of your heart!

"With his stripes we are healed" (Isaiah 53:5).

Pilate delivered our Lord to the Roman officers to be scourged. The Roman scourge was a most dreadful instrument of torture. It was made of the sinews of oxen, and sharp bones were intertwined among the sinews so that every time the lash came down these pieces of bone inflicted terrible lacerations and tore off the flesh from the bone. The Savior was, no doubt, bound to the column and thus beaten. He had been beaten before, but this beating by the Roman officers was probably the most severe of His flagellations. My soul, stand here and weep over His poor stricken body. Believer in Jesus, can you gaze on Him without tears as He stands before you in the mirror of agonizing love? He is at once fair as the lily for innocence and red as the rose with the crimson of His own blood. As we feel the sure and blessed healing which His stripes have wrought in us, does not our heart melt at once with love and grief? If ever we have loved our Lord Jesus, surely we must feel that affection glowing now within our bosoms. Beloved, print the image of Your bleeding self on the tablets of our hearts all day, and at nightfall we will return to commune with You and feel sorrow that our sins have cost You so much.

March 31
Evening

"And Rizpah the daughter of Aiah took sackcloth, and spread it for her upon the rock, from the beginning of harvest until water dropped upon them out of heaven, and suffered neither the birds of the air to rest on them by day, nor the beasts of the field by night" (2 Samuel 21:10).

If the love of a woman for her slain sons could make her continue her mournful vigil for so long a period, will we grow weary of considering the sufferings of our blessed Lord? She drove away the birds of prey. Will we not chase from our meditations those worldly and sinful thoughts which defile our minds? Away, birds of evil wing! Rizpah bore the heat of summer, the night dews and the rains, unsheltered and alone. Sleep was chased from her weeping eyes. Behold how she loved her children! We complain at the first little inconvenience or trial. Are we such cowards that we cannot bear to suffer with our Lord? She chased away even the wild beasts with mighty courage. Are we ready to encounter every foe for Jesus' sake? Her children were slain, and yet, she wept and watched. What should we do who have crucified our Lord by our sins? Our obligations are boundless, our love should be fervent, and our repentance thorough. To watch with Jesus should be our business, to protect His honor should be our occupation, to abide by His cross should be our peace. Those ghastly corpses might have frightened Rizpah, especially at night. But in our crucified Lord, there is nothing terrifying, but everything attractive. Jesus, we will watch with You. Graciously reveal Yourself to us. Then we will not sit beneath sackcloth, but in a royal pavilion.

April 1
Morning

"Let him kiss me with the kisses of his mouth" (Song of Solomon 1:2).

In beginning a new month, let us seek the same desires after our Lord as those which glowed in the heart of the elect spouse. See how she leaps at once to Him. She does not even mention His name. How bold is her love! It was much condescension which permitted the weeping woman to anoint His feet with spikenard. It was rich love which allowed the gentle Mary to sit at His feet and learn of Him. Esther trembled in the presence of Ahashuerus, but the spouse in joyful liberty of perfect love knows no fear. If we have received the same free spirit, we may ask the same question. By kisses, we mean those varied manifestations of affection by which the believer is made to enjoy the love of Jesus. The kiss of *reconciliation* we enjoyed at our conversion. The kiss of *acceptance* is still warm on our brow, as we know that He has accepted us and our works through rich grace. The kiss of daily *communion* is desired day after day, until it is changed into the kiss of *reception,* which removes the soul from earth, and the kiss of *consummation,* which fills it with the joy of heaven. Faith is our walk, but fellowship sensibly felt is our rest. Faith is the road, but communion with Jesus is the well from which the pilgrim drinks.

April 1
Evening

"It is time to seek the Lord" (Hosea 10:12).

This month of April derives its name from the Latin verb *aperio,* which means *to open.* All the buds and blossoms are now opening, and we have arrived at the gates of the flowery season. May your heart, in accord with the universal awakening of nature, be opened to receive the Lord. Every blossoming flower warns you that *it is time to seek the Lord.* Do not be out of tune with nature, but let your heart bloom with holy desires. Are you filled with the vitality of youth? Then, give your vigor to the Lord. Salvation is priceless at whatever age it is received. But an early salvation has a double value in it. Young men and women, since you may perish before you grow old, *it is time to seek the Lord.* You who feel the first signs of decay, quicken your pace. That hollow cough, that shortened breath are warnings you must not take lightly. *It is indeed time to seek the Lord.* Is there a little gray mingled with your once dark and luxuriant tresses? Years swiftly move along, and death is drawing near. Let each return of spring inspire you to set your house in order. If you are now advanced in life, delay no longer. There is a day of grace for you now—be thankful for that. But it is a limited season which grows shorter every time the clock ticks. Here in this silent room on this first night of another month, I lay before you this warning, *it is time to seek the Lord.* Do not ignore that word. It may be your last call from destruction, the final syllable from the lip of grace.

April 2
Morning

"He answered him to never a word" (Matthew 27:14).

He had never been slow of speech when He could bless the sons of men, but He would not say a single word for Himself. Never did a man speak like this man, and never was a man silent like Him. Was this singular silence the index of His perfect self-sacrifice? Did it show that He would not utter a word to stay the slaughter of His sacred person which He had dedicated as an offering for us? Had He so entirely surrendered Himself that He would not interfere in His own behalf, even in the minutest degree, but be bound and slain an unstruggling, uncomplaining victim? Nothing can be said to excuse human guilt; and, therefore, He who bore its whole weight stood speechless before His judge. Is not patient silence the best reply to a gainsaying world? Calm endurance answers some questions infinitely more conclusively than the loftiest eloquence. Did not the silent Lamb of God furnish us with a grand example of wisdom? Evidently our Lord, by His silence, furnished a remarkable fulfillment of prophecy. A long defense of Himself would have been contrary to Isaiah's prediction: "He is brought as a lamb to the slaughter, and as a sheep before her shearers is dumb, so he openeth not his mouth" (Isaiah 53:7). By His silence, He conclusively proved Himself to be the true Lamb of God. As such we salute Him this morning. Be with us, Jesus, and in the silence of our heart let us hear the voice of Your love.

April 2
Evening

"He shall see his seed, he shall prolong his days, and the pleasure of the Lord shall prosper in his hand" (Isaiah 53:10).

Plead for the speedy fulfillment of this promise, all you who love the Lord. It is easy to pray when our desires are based on God's own promise. How can He that gave the word refuse to keep it? Unchangeable truth cannot demean itself by a lie, and eternal faithfulness cannot degrade itself by neglect. Whenever you are praying for the Kingdom of Christ, let your eyes behold the dawning of the blessed day which is drawing near. The Crucified One will receive His crown in the place where men rejected Him. Be encouraged, you that prayerfully work for Christ with little apparent success. Borrow the telescope of faith, wipe the misty breath of your doubts from the glass, and look through it and behold the coming glory. Do you make this your constant prayer? Remember that the same Christ who tells us to say, "Give us this day our daily bread," had first given us this petition, "Hallowed be thy name. Thy kingdom come. Thy will be done in earth, as it is in heaven" (Matthew 6:11,9-10). Do not let your prayers only concern your own sins, your own wants, your own imperfections, and your own trials. Climb the starry ladder and come to Christ Himself. Then, as you draw near to the blood-sprinkled mercy seat, offer this prayer continually, "Lord, extend the Kingdom of Your dear Son." Such a petition, fervently presented, will elevate the spirit of all your devotions. Prove the sincerity of your prayer by working to promote the Lord's glory.

April 3
Morning

"They took Jesus, and led him away" (John 19:16).

He had been in agony all night. He spent the early morning at the hall of Caiaphas. He had been hurried from Caiaphas to Pilate, from Pilate to Herod, and from Herod back again to Pilate. He had, therefore, little strength left, and neither refreshment nor rest was permitted Him. They were eager for His blood and led Him out to die, loaded with the cross. Do you recall how the high priest brought the scapegoat and put both his hands on its head, confessing the sins of the people that those sins might be laid on the goat and cease from the people? Then the goat was led away into the wilderness. It carried away the sins of the people. Now we see Jesus brought before the priests and rulers, who pronounce Him guilty. God Himself imputes our sins to Him: "The Lord hath laid on Him the iniquity of us all" (Isaiah 53:6). "He was made sin for us" (2 Corinthians 5:21). As the substitute for our guilt, bearing our sin on His shoulders, represented by the cross, we see the great Scapegoat led away by the appointed officers of justice. As you look at the cross on His shoulders, does it represent your sin? There is one way you can tell whether He carried your sin or not. Have you laid your hand on His head, confessed your sin, and trusted in Him? Then your sin does not lie on you. It has all been transferred to Christ, and He bears it on His shoulder as a load heavier than the cross.

April 3
Evening

"All we like sheep have gone astray; we have turned every one to his own way; and the Lord hath laid on him the iniquity of us all" (Isaiah 53:6).

There is a confession of sin that belongs to all of the people of God. They have all fallen. Therefore, they all say, from the first who entered heaven to the last who shall enter there, "All we like sheep have gone astray." The confession, while unanimous, is also *personal* and particular: "We have turned every one to his own way." There is a peculiar sinfulness about every individual. All are sinful, but each one has some special transgression not found in his brother. "We have turned every one to his own way" is a confession that each man sinned in a way that was peculiar to himself or sinned with an offense he could not perceive in others. This confession is *unreserved.* There is not a word to detract from its force or a syllable that offers an excuse. The confession *gives up all pleas of self-righteousness.* It is the declaration of men who are consciously guilty—guilty without excuse. They stand with their weapons of rebellion broken in pieces and cry, "All we like sheep have gone astray; we have turned every one to his own way." Yet, the next sentence makes it almost a song. "The Lord hath laid on him the iniquity of us all." It is the most grievous sentence of the three, but it overflows with comfort. Where misery was concentrated, mercy reigned. Where sorrow reached her climax, weary souls find rest. The bruised Savior heals broken hearts. Humble repentance gives place to assured confidence by simply gazing at Christ on the cross!

April 4
Morning

"For he hath made him to be sin for us, who knew no sin; that we might be made the righteousness of God in him" (2 Corinthians 5:21).

Mourning Christian, why do you weep? Are you mourning over your own corruptions? Look to your perfect Lord, and remember you are complete in Him. You are in God's sight as perfect as if you had never sinned. More than that, the Lord our righteousness has put a divine garment on you so that you have more than the righteousness of man—you have the righteousness of God. You who are mourning by reason of inbred sin and depravity, remember, none of your sins can condemn you. You have learned to hate sin, but you have also learned that sin is not yours—it was laid on Christ's head. Your standing is not in yourself—it is in Christ. Your acceptance is not in yourself but in your Lord. You are as much accepted of God today, with all your sinfulness, as you will be when you stand before His throne, free from all corruption. Lay hold on this precious thought, *perfection in Christ!* For you are complete in Him. With your Savior's garment on, you are as holy as the Holy One. It is Christ who died and was risen again, who is at the right hand of God making intercession for us. When your time comes, you will rise up where Jesus sits and reign at His right hand, even as He has overcome and has sat down at His Father's right hand. All this because the divine Lord "was made to be sin for us, who knew no sin; that we might be made the righteousness of God in him" (2 Corinthians 5:21).

April 4
Evening

"Come ye, and let us go up to the mountain of the Lord" (Isaiah 2:3).

It is beneficial to our souls to rise above this present evil world to something nobler and better. The cares of this world and the deceitfulness of riches attempt to choke everything that is good within us. We grow fretful and discouraged or perhaps proud and carnal. It is good for us to cut down these thorns and briers because heavenly seed sown among them is not likely to yield a harvest. There is no better sickle to cut them down than communion with God and the things of the Kingdom. In the valleys of Switzerland, many of the inhabitants are sickly. This is because the atmosphere is polluted, and the air is stagnant. But up on the mountain, the people are healthy because they breathe the clear, fresh air as it blows from the virgin snows of the Alpine summits. The dwellers in the valley would be strengthened if they frequently left their homes among the marshes and the fever mists and inhaled the bracing mountain air. May the Spirit of God help us leave the mist of fear, the fevers of anxiety, and all the illness which gathers in this valley of earth. Let us ascend the mountains of joy and blessedness. May the Holy Spirit cut the cords that keep us here below and help us to climb! We sit like chained eagles fastened to the rock. Unlike the eagle, however, we begin to love our chain, and would, perhaps, loathe to have it snapped. May God grant us grace, if we cannot escape from the chain of our flesh to enable our spirits to be set free. Leaving the flesh at the foot of the hill, may our soul reach the top of the mountain and enjoy communion with the Most High.

April 5
Morning

"On him they laid the cross, that he might bear it after Jesus" (Luke 23:26).

We see in Simon's carrying the cross a picture of the work of the Church throughout all generations. The Church is the cross-bearer after Jesus, and He did not suffer so as to exclude your suffering. He bears a cross, not that you may escape it, but that you may endure it. Christ exempts you from sin but not from sorrow. Remember that and expect to suffer. But let us comfort ourselves with this thought, that in our case, as in Simon's, it is not our cross but Christ's cross which we carry. When you are attacked for your piety, when your religion brings the trial of cruel mocking on you, then remember it is not your cross but Christ's cross which you carry. How delightful it is to carry the cross of our Lord Jesus! You carry the cross after Him. You have blessed company. Your path is marked with the footprints of your Lord. The mark of His blood-red shoulder is upon that heavy burden. It is His cross, and He goes before you as a shepherd goes before his sheep. Take up your cross daily and follow Him. Do not forget, also, that you bear this cross in partnership. You only carry the light end of the cross. Christ bore the heavier end. And remember, though Simon had to bear the cross for only a little while, it gave him lasting honor. Even so the cross we carry is only for a little while, and then we will receive the crown, the glory.

April 5
Evening

"Before honour is humility" (Proverbs 15:33).

Humility of soul always *brings a blessing with it*. If we empty our hearts of self, God will fill us with His love. He who desires close communion with Christ should remember the Word of the Lord: "To this man will I look, even to him that is poor and of a contrite spirit, and trembleth at my word" (Isaiah 66:2). The sweetest fellowship with heaven is only enjoyed by humble souls. God will deny no blessing to a thoroughly humbled spirit. "Blessed are the poor in spirit: for theirs is the kingdom of heaven" (Matthew 5:3). The whole treasury of God will be given to the soul which is humble enough to receive it without growing proud because of it. God blesses us all up to the full measure that it is safe for Him to do so. If you do not get a blessing, it is because it is not safe for you to have one. If our heavenly Father allowed your unhumbled spirit to win a victory in His holy war, you would seize the crown for yourself. Then, meeting with a fresh enemy, you would be defeated. Therefore, you are kept low for your own safety. When a man is sincerely humble and never ventures to touch even a grain of the praise, there is no limit to what God will do in his life. Humility makes us ready to be blessed by the God of all grace. It also enables us to deal efficiently with our fellowmen. True humility is a flower which will adorn any garden. It is an herb with which you may season every dish of life. Whether in prayer or praise, in work or suffering, the genuine salt of humility cannot be used in excess.

April 6
Morning

"Let us go forth therefore unto him without the camp" (Hebrews 13:13).

Jesus, bearing His cross, went forth to suffer. The Christian's reason for leaving the camp of the world's sin and religion is not because he loves to be different but because Jesus did so. The disciple must follow his Master. Christ was "not of the world." His life and His testimony were a constant protest against conformity with the world. Jesus would have His people go forth without the camp for their own sanctification. You cannot grow in grace to any high degree while you are conformed to the world. The life of separation may be a path of sorrow, but it is the highway of safety. The separated life may cost you many pangs, and make every day a battle, yet it is a happy life after all. No joy can excel that of the soldier of Christ. Jesus reveals Himself so graciously and gives such sweet refreshment that the warrior feels more calm and peace in his daily strife than others in their hours of rest. The highway of holiness is the highway of communion. It is thus we will hope to win the crown if we are enabled by divine grace faithfully to follow Christ without the camp. The crown of glory will follow the cross of separation. A moment's shame will be well recompensed by eternal honor. A little while of witness-bearing will seem nothing when we are forever with the Lord.

April 6
Evening

"In the name of the Lord I will destroy them" (Psalm 118:12).

Our Lord Jesus, by His death, purchased a right to reign in our *entire* being. His death and resurrection accomplished the sanctification of our spirit, soul, and body. The newborn nature which God has given to the believer must assert the rights of the Lord Jesus Christ. Since you are a child of God, you must conquer each part of self that is not submitted to Christ. Never be satisfied until He who is King by purchase becomes Lord over all and reigns supreme in your heart. Sin has no right to any part of us. Therefore, we fight a good and lawful battle when we seek, in the name of Jesus, to drive it out. My body is a member of Christ. I must not tolerate any subjection to the prince of darkness. Christ suffered for my sins and redeemed me with His precious blood. Should I permit my memory to become a storehouse of evil or my passions to be full of iniquity? Shall I surrender my judgment to be perverted by error or my will to be bound in the chains of sin? No, I belong to Christ and sin has no right to me. O Christian, do not be discouraged into thinking that your spiritual enemies could never be destroyed. You are not able to overcome them in your own strength; but you can and will overcome them through the blood of the Lamb. Go to the Mighty One for strength, and wait humbly upon God. He will surely come to your rescue, and you will sing of victory through His grace.

April 7
Morning

"O ye sons of men, how long will ye turn my glory into shame" (Psalm 4:2).

What honors did the blinded people of Israel award their long-expected King? (1.) They gave him a procession of honor in which Roman legionaries, Jewish priests, men and women, took a part, He Himself bearing His cross. This is the triumph which the world awards to Him who comes to overthrow man's direct foes. Shouts of ridicule are His only acclamations, and cruel taunts are His only praise. (2.) They presented Him with the wine of honor. Instead of a golden cup of generous wine, they offered Him the criminal's stupefying death-draught, which He refused. Afterwards when He cried, "I thirst" (John 19:28), they gave Him vinegar mixed with gall, thrust to His mouth on a sponge. Oh, what wretched, detestable inhospitality to the King's Son. (3.) He was provided with a guard of honor, who showed their esteem of Him by gambling over His garments, which they had seized as their booty. (4.) A throne of honor was found for Him on the bloody tree. The cross was, in fact, the full expression of the world's feeling toward Him. (5.) The title of honor was nominally "King of the Jews." But the blinded nation distinctly repudiated that title and really called Him "King of thieves" by placing Jesus in the place of highest shame between two thieves. His glory was thus in all things turned into shame by the sons of men, but it will yet gladden the eyes of saints and angels, world without end.

April 7
Evening

"Deliver me from bloodguiltiness, O God, thou God of my salvation: and my tongue shall sing aloud of thy righteousness" (Psalm 51:14).

In this solemn confession David plainly names his sin. He does not call it manslaughter or speak of it as a mistake by which an unfortunate accident killed a good man. Rather, he calls it by its true name—bloodguiltiness. He did not actually kill the husband of Bathsheba, but he planned in his heart that Uriah would be slain. Therefore, David stood before the Lord as a murderer. Learn to be honest with God. Do not give fair names to foul sins. No matter what you call them, they will smell no sweeter. See your sins as God does, and, with all openness of heart, acknowledge their real character. David was evidently oppressed with the seriousness of his sin. It is easy to use words, but it is difficult to feel their deep meaning. The Fifty-first Psalm is the portrait of a contrite spirit. Let us seek to have the same brokenness of heart. Although our words may be remorseful, if our heart is not conscious that our sins are deserving of hell, we cannot expect to find forgiveness. Our text expresses an earnest prayer to the God of salvation. It is His prerogative to forgive. His very name promises to save those who seek His face. He is the God of *my* salvation. The psalmist ends with a *commendable vow:* if God will deliver him, he will *sing aloud.* Who can sing in any other style in the face of such great mercy! Notice the subject of the song—*God's righteousness.* We must sing of the finished work of a precious Savior. He who knows the most of forgiving love will sing the loudest.

April 8
Morning

"If they do these things in a green tree, what shall be done in the dry" (Luke 23:31).

When God saw Jesus in the sinner's place, He did not spare Him. When He finds the unregenerate without Christ, He will not spare them. Oh, sinner, Jesus was led away by His enemies; so will you be dragged away to the place appointed for you. Jesus was deserted by God; and if He, who was only imputedly a sinner, was deserted, how much more will you be! "Eloi, Eloi, lama, sabachthani?" (See Mark 15:34.) What an awful shriek! But what will be your cry when you say, "O God! O God! Why have you forsaken me?" The answer will come back, "Because ye have set at nought all my counsel, and would none of my reproof: I also will laugh at your calamity; I will mock when your fear cometh" (Proverbs 1:25-26). If God spared not His own Son, how much less will He spare you! Self-righteous sinners, who would stand in your place when God says, Awake, O sword, against the man that rejected Me; smite him, and let him feel the pain forever? Jesus was spit on. Sinner, what shame will be yours? We cannot sum up in one word all the mass of sorrows which met on the head of Jesus, who died for us. Therefore, it is impossible for us to tell you what oceans of grief must roll over your spirit if you die as you are now. By the agonies of Christ, by His wounds and by His blood, do not bring on yourselves the wrath to come! Trust in the Son of God, and you will never die.

April 8
Evening

"I will fear no evil: for thou art with me"
(Psalm 23:4).

Behold, how independent of outward circumstances the Holy Spirit can make the Christian! A bright light may shine within us when it is all dark around us. How firm, how happy, how calm, how peaceful we may be, when the world shakes and the pillars of the earth are removed! Even death itself has no power to suspend the music of a Christian's heart. Instead, it makes that music become more sweet, more clear, and more heavenly. The last kind act which death can do is to let the earthly melody melt into the heavenly chorus, the temporal joy into the eternal bliss! Let us have confidence, then, in the blessed Spirit's power to comfort us. Are you facing poverty? Fear not. The divine Spirit can give you a greater abundance than the rich. Do not be sad! Every pang may be a refining fire to consume your dross and a beam of glory to light up the secret parts of your soul. Are your eyes growing dim? Jesus will be your light. Do your ears fail you? Jesus' name will be your soul's best music. Socrates used to say, "Philosophers can be happy without music." Christians can be happier than philosophers when all outward causes of rejoicing are withdrawn. In God, my heart will triumph, come what may. By your power, O blessed Spirit, my heart will be glad though all things fail me here below.

April 9
Morning

"And there followed him a great company of people, and of women, which also bewailed and lamented him" (Luke 23:27).

Among the riotous mob which hounded the Redeemer to His doom, there were some gracious souls whose bitter anguish was released in wailing and lamentations—fit music to accompany that march of woe. When my soul can, in imagination, see the Savior bearing His cross to Calvary, it joins the godly women and weeps with them; for, indeed, there is true cause for grief. My sins were the scourges which lacerated those blessed shoulders and crowned those thorn-bleeding brow. My sins cried, "Crucify Him! Crucify Him!" and laid the cross on His gracious shoulders. His being led forth to die is sorrow enough for one eternity, but my having been His murderer is more grief than one poor fountain of tears can express. Why those women loved and wept is not hard to guess. They could not have had greater reasons for love and grief than my heart has. Nain's widow saw her son restored—but I myself have been raised to newness of life. Peter's wife's mother was cured of the fever—but I was healed of the greater plague of sin. Seven devils were cast out of Magdalene—but a whole legion were cast out of me. Mary and Martha were favored with visits—but He dwells with me. His mother bore His body—but He is formed in me the hope of glory. Let me not be behind the holy women in gratitude or sorrow.

April 9
Evening

"Thy gentleness hath made me great" (Psalm 18:35).

These words may be translated, "Thy *goodness* hath made me great." David gratefully ascribed all his greatness to the goodness of God. "Thy *providence"* is another reading. Providence is goodness in action. Goodness is the bud, and providence is the flower. Goodness is the seed while providence is the harvest. Some render it, "Thy *help"* which is another word for providence. Providence is the firm ally of the saints, aiding them in the service of their Lord. "Thy *condescension"* combines the ideas mentioned, including that of *humility.* Regardless of the translation, God's humbling Himself is the cause of our being made great. There are other interpretations, as for instance the Septuagint, which reads, "Thy discipline (fatherly correction) hath made me great." The Chaldee paraphrase reads, "Thy word hath increased me." The idea remains the same. David ascribes all his greatness to the goodness of his Father in heaven. May this sentiment be echoed in our hearts this evening while we cast our crowns at Jesus' feet and cry, "Thy gentleness hath made me great." How marvelous has been our experience of God's gentleness! How gentle are His corrections, forbearance, and teachings! Let gratitude be awakened in your heart and let humility be deepened. Let your love be rekindled before you fall asleep tonight.

April 10
Morning

"The place which is called Calvary" (Luke 23:33).

The hill of comfort is the hill of Calvary; the house of consolation is built with the wood of the cross; the temple of heavenly blessing is founded on the riven rock—riven by the spear which pierced His side. No scene in sacred history ever gladdens the soul like Calvary's tragedy. Light springs from the midday-midnight of Golgotha, and every herb of the field blooms sweetly beneath the shadow of the once accursed tree. In that place of thirst, grace has dug a fountain which ever gushes with waters pure as crystal, each drop capable of alleviating the woes of mankind. You who have had your seasons of conflict will confess that it was not at Olivet that you found comfort, not on the hill of Sinai, nor on Tabor; but Gethsemane, Gabbatha, and Golgotha have been a means of comfort to you. The bitter herbs of Gethsemane have often taken away the bitterness of your life; the scourge of Gabbatha has often scourged away your cares, and the groans of Calvary put all other groans to flight. Thus Calvary yields us comfort rare and rich. We never would have known Christ's love in all its heights and depths if He had not died. We could not guess the Father's deep affection if He had not given His Son to die.

April 10
Evening

"For there stood by me this night the angel of God" (Acts 27:23).

The storm and darkness, along with imminent risk of shipwreck, brought the crew of the vessel into a dangerous situation. One man alone remained perfectly calm, and by his word, the rest were reassured. Paul was the only man who had the courage to say, "Sirs. . .be of good cheer" (Acts 27:21-22). There were veteran Roman soldiers and brave old mariners on board. Yet, their poor Jewish prisoner had more courage than they all. The Lord Jesus dispatched a heavenly messenger to whisper words of consolation in the ear of His faithful servant. Therefore, Paul wore a shining countenance and spoke like a man filled with confidence. If we fear the Lord, we may expect timely intervention when our circumstances are at their worst. Angels are not kept from us by storms or hindered by darkness. If angels' visits are rare at ordinary times, they will be frequent in our nights of tempest and tossing. Friends may avoid us when we are under pressure, but our dealings with the inhabitants of the angelic world will increase. We will be strengthened by words of love brought to us from the throne by way of Jacob's ladder. Then, we will be strong to do great things for God. Are you in an hour of distress? Jesus is the Angel of the covenant. If His presence is earnestly sought, His assistance will not be denied. Like Paul, believers can know the comfort of having the Angel of God stand by them in a night of storm when anchors no longer hold and rocks are near.

April 11
Morning

"I am poured out like water, and all my bones are out of joint" (Psalm 22:14).

Did earth or heaven ever behold a sadder spectacle of woe? In soul and body, our Lord felt Himself to be weak as water poured on the ground. The placing of the cross in its socket had shaken Him with great violence, had strained all the ligaments, had pained every nerve, and more or less dislocated all His bones. Burdened with His own weight, the Sufferer felt the strain increasing every moment of those six long hours. His sense of faintness and general weakness was overpowering, while to His own consciousness He became nothing but a mass of misery and swooning sickness. How faint He must have been when He saw the dread vision of the wrath of God and felt it in His own soul! To us, sensations such as our Lord endured would have been insupportable, and kind unconsciousness would have come to our rescue. But in His case, He was wounded and felt the sword. He drained the cup and tasted every drop. As we kneel before our now ascended Savior's throne, let us remember well the way by which He prepared it as a throne of grace for us. Let us, in spirit, drink of His cup that we may be strengthened for our hour of heaviness whenever it may come.

April 11
Evening

"Look upon mine affliction and my pain; and forgive all my sins" (Psalm 25:18).

It is good to have our prayers about our sorrows linked with pleas concerning our sins. We should not be so overwhelmed with our pain that we forget our offenses against God. It was to God that David carried his sorrow and confessed his sin. *We must take our sorrows to God.* Your little sorrows may be rolled upon God, for He counts the hairs of your head. Your great sorrows may be committed to Him, for He holds the ocean in the hollow of His hand. Go to Him, whatever your present trouble may be, and you will find Him able and willing to relieve you. *But we must take our sins to God, too.* We must carry them to the cross. The blood of Christ will purge their guilt and destroy their defiling power. Finally, we are to go to the Lord with sorrows and with sins *in the right spirit.* All that David asks concerning his sorrow is, *"Look* upon mine affliction and my pain." But the next petition is more definite— *"Forgive all my sins."* Many sufferers would have put it, "Remove my affliction and my pain, and look at my sins." But David cries, "Lord, as for my affliction and my pain, I will not dictate to Your wisdom. Lord, look at them; I will leave them to You. As for my sins, Lord, I know that I must have them forgiven; I cannot endure to lie under their curse for a moment." A Christian knows that sorrow is easier to tolerate than sin. He can bear the continuation of his troubles, but he cannot support the burden of his transgressions.

April 12
Morning

"My heart is like wax; it is melted in the midst of my bowels" (Psalm 22:14).

Our blessed Lord experienced a terrible sinking and melting of soul. "The spirit of a man will sustain his infirmity, but a wounded spirit who can bear?" (Proverbs 18:14). Deep depression of spirit is the most grievous of all trials. Believer, humbly adore the King of glory as having more mental distress and inward anguish than anyone among us. As our faithful High Priest, He can be touched with a feeling of our infirmities. Especially let those of us whose sadness springs directly from the withdrawal of a present sense of our Father's love enter into near and intimate communion with Jesus. Do not give way to despair, since through this dark room the Master has passed before us. Our souls may sometimes long and faint and thirst to behold the light of the Lord's countenance. Come in, strong and deep love of Jesus, like the sea at the flood in spring tides, drown all my sins, wash out all my cares, lift up my earth-bound soul, and float it right up to my Lord's feet. There let me lie, a poor broken shell, washed up by His love, having no virtue or value. Only venturing to whisper to Him that if He will put His ear to me, He will hear within my heart faint echoes of the vast waves of His own love which have brought me where it is my delight to lie, even at His feet forever.

April 12
Evening

"The king's garden" (Nehemiah 3:15).

The mention of the king's garden by Nehemiah brings to mind the *paradise* which the King of kings prepared for Adam. Sin ruined that fair abode of all delights. The children of men were driven out to till the ground which yielded only thorns and briers. Remember the fall of Adam, for it was your fall, too. Weep because the Lord of love was so shamefully treated by the head of the human race. Behold how dragons and demons dwell on this fair earth which once was a garden of delights. There is another garden which the King waters with His bloody sweat—*Gethsemane*. The bitter herbs of this garden are far sweeter to renewed souls than even Eden's luscious fruits. At Gethsemane, the mischief of the serpent in the first garden was undone. The curse was lifted from earth and borne by the woman's promised seed. Meditate upon the agony and the passion of our Lord. Return to the garden of the olive press, and see the great Redeemer rescuing the world from its lost state. This is the garden of gardens where the soul may see the guilt of sin and the power of love. *My heart* should also be His garden. How do the flowers flourish? Do any choice fruits appear? Does the King walk within and rest in the shelter of my spirit? Let me make certain that the plants are trimmed and watered and the mischievous foxes hunted out. Come Lord, and let the heavenly wind blow at Your coming. Let the spices of Your garden flow abroad. I must not forget the King's garden of *the Church*. O Lord, send prosperity to it. Rebuild her walls, nourish her plants, and ripen her fruits. Reclaim the barren waste from the wilderness and make it into "a King's garden."

April 13
Morning

"A bundle of myrrh is my well-beloved unto me" (Song of Solomon 1:13).

Myrrh may well be chosen as the type of Jesus on account of its preciousness, its perfume, its pleasantness, its healing, preserving, disinfecting qualities, and its connection with sacrifice. But why is He compared to "a *bundle* of myrrh?" First, for *plenty*. He is not a drop of it; He is a treasure chest full. He is not a sprig or a flower of it, but a whole bundle. There is enough in Christ for all my necessities. "In him dwelleth all the fulness of the Godhead bodily" (Colossians 2:9). Everything needful is in Him. Take Jesus in His different characters, and you will see a marvelous variety— Prophet, Priest, King, Husband, Friend, Shepherd. View Him in His virtue, gentleness, courage, self-denial, love, faithfulness, truth, righteousness— everywhere He is a bundle of preciousness. He is a "bundle of myrhh" for *preservation*—not loose myrrh, to be dropped on the floor or trodden on, but myrrh tied up, myrrh to be stored in a treasure chest. We must value Him as our best treasure. We must prize His words and His ordinances. Moreover, Jesus is a "bundle of myrrh" for *speciality*. The emblem suggests the idea of distinguishing, discriminating grace. From before the foundation of the world, He was set apart for His people. He gives forth His perfume only to those who understand how to enter into communion with Him, and how to have close dealings with Him. Happy are you who can say, "A bundle of myrrh is my well-beloved unto me."

April 13
Evening

"And he shall put his hand upon the head of the burnt offering; and it shall be accepted for him to make atonement for him" (Leviticus 1:4).

An example of our Lord's being made "sin for us" is shown here by the significant transfer of sin to the bullock. The laying of the hand was more than a touch of contact. In some other places of Scripture, the original word has the meaning of *leaning heavily*, as in the expression, "Thy wrath lieth hard upon me" (Psalm 88:7). Surely this is the very essence and nature of faith. It not only brings us into contact with the great Substitute, but it teaches us to lean upon Him with all the burden of our guilt. Jehovah placed all the offenses of His covenant people upon the head of the Substitute. But each one of the chosen must personally ratify this solemn covenant act. By grace, he may lay his hand upon the head of the "Lamb slain from the foundation of the world" (Revelation 13:8). Believer, do you remember that rapturous day when you first obtained pardon through Jesus the Sin-bearer? My soul recalls its day of deliverance with delight. Laden with guilt and full of fear, I saw my Savior as my Substitute. I laid my hand upon Him so timidly at first. But my courage grew, and my confidence was confirmed. Finally, I leaned my soul entirely upon Him. Now it is my unceasing joy to know that my sins are no longer counted against me, but laid on Him. In addition to all of this, Jesus has said of all my future sinfulness, "Charge that to My account."

April 14
Morning

"All they that see me laugh me to scorn: they shoot out the lip, they shake the head" (Psalm 22:7).

Mockery was a great ingredient in our Lord's woe. Judas mocked Him in the garden; the chief priests and scribes laughed Him to scorn; Herod set Him at nought; the servants and the soldiers jeered at Him and brutally insulted Him; Pilate and his guards ridiculed His royalty; and on the tree, all sorts of horrid jests and hideous taunts were hurled at Him. Ridicule is always hard to bear, but when we are in intense pain, it is so heartless and cruel that it cuts us to the quick. Imagine the Savior crucified, racked with the anguish far beyond all mortal guess, and then picture that motley multitude, all wagging their heads or thrusting out their lips in bitterest contempt of one poor suffering victim! Surely there must have been something more in the crucified One than they could see, or else such a great and mingled crowd would not unanimously have honored Him with such contempt. Was it not evil confessing, in the very moment of its greatest apparent triumph, that after all it could do no more than mock at that victorious goodness which was then reigning on the cross? O Jesus, despised and rejected of men, how could You die for men who treated You so cruelly? We, too, have despised You in the days of our obstinance, and even since our new birth we have set the world on high in our hearts. Yet You bleed to heal our wounds and die to give us life.

April 14
Evening

"Say ye to the righteous, that it shall be well with him" (Isaiah 3:10).

It is well with the righteous *always*. If the prophet had said, "Say ye to the righteous that it is well with him in his prosperity," we would be thankful for so great a blessing. If the verse had been written, "It is well with him when under persecution," we would be thankful for the sustaining assurance because persecution is hard to bear. Since no time is mentioned, however, all time is included. From the beginning of the year to the end of the year, from the first gathering of evening shadows until the morning star shines, in all conditions, and under all circumstances, it will be well with the righteous. He is *well fed* because he feeds upon the flesh and blood of Jesus. He is *well clothed* because he wears the righteousness of Christ. He is *well housed* for he dwells in God. He is *well married* for his soul is knit in bonds of marriage union to Christ. He is *well provided for* because the Lord is his Shepherd. He is *well endowed* for heaven is his inheritance. It is well with the righteous—*well upon divine authority.* The mouth of God speaks the comforting assurance. Even if ten thousand devils declare our circumstances to be hopeless, we will laugh them all to scorn. Praise God for a faith which enables us to believe God when the circumstances contradict Him. It is at all times well with you, the righteous one. If you cannot see it, believe God's Word instead of your sight. The one whom God blesses is blessed indeed.

April 15
Morning

"My God, my God, why hast thou forsaken me" (Psalm 22:1).

No other place so well shows the griefs of Christ as Calvary, and no other moment at Calvary is so full of agony as that in which His cry rends the air—"My God, my God, why hast thou forsaken me?" At this moment, physical weakness was united with acute mental torture from the shame and disgrace through which He had to pass. To make His grief culminate with emphasis, He suffered spiritual agony surpassing all expression, resulting from the departure of His Father's presence. This was the black midnight of His horror. It was then that He descended the abyss of suffering. No man can enter into the full meaning of these words. Some of us think at times that we could cry, "My God, my God, why hast thou forsaken me?" There are seasons when the brightness of our Father's smile is eclipsed by clouds and darkness, but let us remember that God never does really forsake us. It is only a *seeming* forsaking of us, but in Christ's case it was a *real* forsaking. In our case, our cry is often dictated by unbelief. In His case, it was the utterance of a dreadful fact, for God had really turned away from Him for a season. Since even the thought that He has forsaken us gives us agony, what must the woe of the Savior have been when He exclaimed, "My God, my God, why hast thou forsaken me?"

April 15
Evening

"Lift them up for ever" (Psalm 28:9).

God's people need lifting up. They need divine grace to make them mount on wings covered with silver and with feathers of gold. By nature, sparks fly upward, but the sinful souls of men fall downward. O Lord, lift them up forever! David himself said, "Unto thee, O Lord, do I lift up my soul" (Psalm 25:1). When you ask this blessing for yourself, do not forget to seek it for others also. There are three ways in which God's people require to be lifted up. They must be *elevated in character.* Lift them up, O Lord; do not let Your people be like the world's people! The world lies in the power of the wicked one. Lift Your children out of it! The world's people are looking for silver and gold, seeking their own pleasures and the gratification of their lusts. Lord, lift Your people up above all this. Keep them from being "muck-rakers," as John Bunyan calls the man who was always scraping after gold. Set their hearts upon their risen Lord and the heavenly heritage. Moreover, believers need to be *prospered in conflict.* In the battle, if they seem to fall, O Lord, give them the victory. If the foot of the foe is upon their necks for a moment, help them to grasp the sword of the Spirit and win the battle. Lord, lift up Your children's spirit in the day of conflict. Keep the adversary from tormenting them. But if they have been persecuted, let them sing of the mercy of a delivering God. We may also ask our Lord to *lift them up on the last day!* Lift their bodies from the tomb, and raise their souls to Your eternal Kingdom in glory.

April 16
Morning

"The precious blood of Christ" (1 Peter 1:19).

Standing at the foot of the cross, we see hands, feet, and side, all distilling crimson streams of precious blood. It is "precious" because of its redeeming and atoning power. By it the sins of Christ's people are atoned for; they are redeemed from under the law; they are reconciled to God; they are made one with Him. Christ's blood is also "precious" in its cleansing power. It "cleanseth from all sin" (1 John 1:7). "Though your sins be as scarlet, they shall be as white as snow" (Isaiah 1:18). Through Jesus' blood there is not a spot left on any believer. The precious blood, which makes us clean, removes the stains of abundant iniquity and permits us to stand accepted in the Beloved, notwithstanding the many ways in which we have rebelled against our God! The blood of Christ is likewise "precious" in its preserving power. We are safe from the destroying angel under the sprinkled blood. Remember, it is God's *seeing* the blood that is the true reason for our being spared. The blood of Christ is "precious" also in its sanctifying influence. There is no motive for holiness so great as that which streams from the veins of Jesus. And "precious," unspeakably precious, is this blood, because it has an overcoming power. It is written, "They overcame through the blood of the Lamb" (Revelation 12:11). The blood of Jesus! Sin dies at its presence, death ceases to be death, and heaven's gates are opened.

April 16
Evening

"And his hands were steady until the going down of the sun" (Exodus 17:12).

The prayer of Moses was so mighty that everyone depended upon it. The petitions of Moses defeated the enemy more than the fighting of Joshua. Yet, both were needed. In spiritual conflict, force and fervor, decision and devotion, and valor and vehemence must join together. You must wrestle with your sin, but the major part of the wrestling must be done alone with God. Prayer, like Moses, holds up the covenant before the Lord. The Lord cannot deny His own declarations. Hold up the rod of promises, and you will receive your answer. When Moses grew weary, his friends assisted him. When your prayer loses its vitality, let faith support one hand and let holy hope uplift the other. Then prayer, seating itself upon the rock of our salvation, will persevere and prevail. Beware of faintness in devotion. If Moses felt it, who can escape? It is far easier to fight with sin in public than to pray against it in private. Joshua never grew weary in fighting, but Moses did grow weary in praying. The more spiritual an exercise, the more difficult it is for flesh and blood to maintain it. May the Spirit of God who helps our infirmities enable us, like Moses, to continue with our hands steady "until the going down of the sun." Intermittent supplication avails little. We must wrestle all night and hold up our hands "until the going down of the sun." We must remain steadfast until the evening of life is over and we come to the rising of a better sun, in the land where prayer is swallowed up in praise.

April 17
Morning

"We are come to the blood of sprinkling, that speaketh better things than that of Abel" (Hebrews 12:24).

Reader, have *you* come to the blood of sprinkling? The question is not whether you have come to a knowledge of doctrine or an observance of ceremonies or to a certain form of experience, but have you come to the blood of Jesus? The blood of Jesus is the life of all vital godliness. If you have truly come to Jesus, we know how you came—the Holy Spirit sweetly brought you there. You came to the blood of sprinkling with no merits of your own. Guilty, lost, and helpless, you came to take that blood, and that blood alone, as your everlasting hope. You came to the cross of Christ with a trembling and an aching heart. Oh, what a precious sound it was for you to hear the voice of the blood of Jesus! The dropping of His blood is as the music of heaven to the penitent sons of earth. We are full of sin, but the Savior bids us lift our eyes to Him, and, as we gaze on His streaming wounds, each drop of blood, as it falls, cries, "It is finished; I have made an end of sin; I have brought in everlasting righteousness." Oh, sweet language of the precious blood of Jesus! If you have come to that blood once, you will come to it constantly. It is only by daily coming to Christ alone that you will find joy and comfort.

April 17
Evening

"We would see Jesus" (John 12:21).

The growing cry of humanity is, "Who will show us any good?" People seek satisfaction in earthly comforts, enjoyments, and riches. But the convicted sinner knows of only one good. "O that I knew where I might find *Him!"* When he is truly awakened to feel his guilt, you could pour gold at his feet, and he would say, "Take it away. I want to find *Him."* It is a blessed thing for a man to bring his desires into focus so that they all center on one object. When he has fifty different desires, his heart resembles a stagnant pool breeding disease. But when all his desires are brought into one channel, his heart becomes like a river of pure water, running swiftly to irrigate the fields. Happy is he whose one desire is set on Christ. If Jesus is a soul's desire, it is a blessed sign of divine work within. Such a man will never be content with mere religion. He will say, "I want Christ; I *must* have Him—mere religious ordinances are of no use to me. I want *Him.* You offer me the empty pitcher while I am dying of thirst. Give me water, or I die. Jesus is my soul's desire. I would see Jesus!" Is this your plea? Is your only desire for Christ? Then you are not far from the Kingdom of heaven. Can you say, "I would give all that I have to be a Christian. I would give up everything I hope for, if I might know that I have a part of Christ"? Then, despite all your fears, be of good cheer. The Lord loves you, and you will come out into daylight soon. Rejoice in the liberty, because Christ has set you free.

April 18
Morning

"She bound the scarlet line in the window"
(Joshua 2:21).

Rahab depended on the promise of the spies for her preservation. She looked on them as the representatives of the God of Israel. Her faith was simple and firm, but it was very obedient. To tie the scarlet line in the window was a trivial act in itself, but she dared not run the risk of omitting it. Come, my soul, is there not here a lesson for you? Have you been attentive to all your Lord's will, even though some of His commands should seem nonessential? Have you observed in His own way the two ordinances of believers' baptism and the Lord's Supper? Have I implicitly trusted in the precious blood of Jesus? Can I look out toward the Dead Sea of my sins, or the Jerusalem of my hopes, without seeing the blood? The passer-by can see a cord of a conspicuous color if it hangs from the window. It will be well for me if my life makes the atonement conspicuous to all onlookers. What is there to be ashamed of? Let men or devils gaze if they will. The blood is my boast and my song. My soul, there is One who will see that scarlet line, even when from weakness of faith you cannot see it yourself. Jehovah, the Avenger, will see it and pass over you. Jericho's walls fell flat. Rahab's house was on the wall, and yet it stood unmoved. My nature is built into the wall of humanity; and yet, when destruction smites the race, I will be secure. My soul, tie the scarlet thread in the window afresh and rest in peace.

April 18
Evening

"And thou saidst, I will surely do thee good" (Genesis 32:12).

When Jacob was on the other side of the brook Jabbok, and Esau was coming toward him with armed men, he earnestly sought God's protection. He pleaded, "And thou saidst, I will surely do thee good." Oh, the force of that plea! He was holding God to His word—"Thou saidst." We can always depend upon the faithfulness of God. Will He not do as He has said? "Let God be true, and every man a liar" (Romans 3:4). Every word that comes from His lips will stand fast and be fulfilled. Solomon, at the opening of the temple, used this same mighty plea. He pleaded with God to remember the word He had spoken to David and to bless that place. When a man gives a promissory note, his honor is pledged. He signs his name, and he must pay the note when the time comes, or else he loses credit. It will never be said that God dishonors His bills. He is punctual to the moment—He is never before His time, but He never is behind it either. Search God's Word and compare it with the experience of God's people. You will find that the two agree from the beginning to the end. Many patriarchs have said with Joshua, "Not one thing hath failed of all the good things which the Lord your God spake concerning you; all are come to pass"(Joshua 23:14). If you have a divine promise, you may claim it with certainty. The Lord meant to fulfill the promise, or He would not have given it. When He speaks, it is because He means to do as He has said.

April 19
Morning

"Behold, the veil of the temple was rent in twain from the top to the bottom" (Matthew 27:51).

The rending of so strong and thick a veil was not intended merely as a display of power—many lessons were taught us. The old law of ordinances was put away. When Jesus died, the sacrifices were all finished. That tear also revealed all the hidden things of the old dispensation: the mercy-seat could now be seen, and the glory of God gleamed forth above it. By the death of our Lord Jesus, we have a clear revelation of God. He was not like Moses who put a veil over his face. Life and immortality are now brought to light, and things which have been hidden since the foundation of the world are manifest in Him. The annual ceremony of atonement was thus abolished. The atoning blood, which was once every year sprinkled within the veil, was now offered once for all by the great High Priest. No blood of bullocks or of lambs is needed now, for Jesus has entered within the veil with His own blood. Access to God is now permitted and is the privilege of every believer in Christ Jesus. There is no small space laid open through which we may peer at the mercy-seat, but the tear reaches from the top to the bottom. We may come with boldness to the throne of the heavenly grace. Our Lord is the key to heaven. Let us enter in with Him into the heavenly places and sit with Him there until our common enemies are made His footstool.

April 19
Evening

"The Amen" (Revelation 3:14).

The word *Amen* solemnly confirms that which was spoken before. Jesus is the great Confirmer. The *Amen* in all His promises is forever the same. Jesus Christ said, "Come unto me, all ye that labour and are heavy laden, and I will give you rest" (Matthew 11:28). If you come to Him, He will say "Amen" in your soul. His promise will be true *to you*. Jesus fulfilled the words of the prophet, "The bruised reed shall he not break" (Isaiah 42:3). Bring your poor, broken, and bruised heart to Him. He will say "Amen" to you, and it will be as true in *your soul* as in hundreds of cases in years past. There is not a word which has gone out of the Savior's lips which He has ever retracted. The words of Jesus will stand when heaven and earth pass away. Jesus is *Amen* in all His offices. He was a Priest to pardon and cleanse once, and He is Amen as Priest still. He was a King to rule and reign for His people and to defend them with His mighty arm. He is an Amen King, the same still. He was a Prophet of old to foretell good things to come. His lips are sweet and drop with honey still—He is an Amen Prophet. He is *Amen* concerning the merit of His blood. He is the *Amen* of His righteousness. That sacred robe will remain fair and glorious when all of nature decays. He is *Amen* in every single title He bears. He is your Husband who will never seek a divorce; your Friend who sticks cioser than a brother; your Shepherd who is with you in death's dark valley. He is your help and your deliverer, your castle and your high tower. He is the horn of your strength, your confidence, your joy, your all in all. Jesus is your *Amen*.

April 20
Morning

"That through death he might destroy him that had the power of death" (Hebrews 2:14).

Child of God, cease to fear dying. Living near the cross of Calvary you may think of death with pleasure. Welcome it when it comes with intense delight. It is sweet to die in the Lord. It is a covenant-blessing to sleep in Jesus. Death is no longer banishment. It is a return from exile, a going home to the many mansions where the loved ones already dwell. The distance between glorified spirits in heaven and militant saints on earth seems great, but it is not so. We are not far from home— a moment will bring us there. How long will that soul be tossed on the waves before it comes to that sea which knows no storm? Listen to the answer: "Absent from the body, present with the Lord" (2 Corinthians 5:8). Like that ship of old, on the lake of Galilee, a storm had tossed it; but Jesus said, "Peace, be still," and immediately it came to the land. Do not think that a long period intervenes between the instant of death and the eternity of glory. When the eyes close on earth, they open in heaven. Child of God, what is there for you to fear in death, seeing that through the death of your Lord its curse and sting are destroyed? It is a Jacob's ladder whose foot is in the dark grave, but its top reaches to glory everlasting!

April 20
Evening

"Fight the Lord's battles" (1 Samuel 18:17).

God's elect are still battling on earth, and Jesus Christ is the Captain of their salvation. He said, "Lo, I am with you alway, even unto the end of the world" (Matthew 28:20). Harken to the shouts of war! Let the people of God stand fast in their ranks, and let no man's heart be afraid. It is true that the battle is turned against us. Unless the Lord Jesus lifts His sword, we do not know the outcome of the Church. But let us be of good courage. There never was a day when Christianity seemed to tremble more than now. A fierce effort is being made to place the antichrist in his seat of power. We need a bold voice and a strong hand to preach and publish the old gospel for which martyrs bled and confessors died. The Savior is, by His Holy Spirit, still on earth. He is in the midst of the fight. Therefore, the outcome of the battle is certain. As the conflict rages, the Lord Jesus is in His office as our great Intercessor, pleading for His people! Do not look so much at the battle below, for there you will be surrounded by smoke and overwhelmed by the garments rolled in blood. But lift your eyes to where your Savior lives and pleads. As long as He intercedes, the cause of God is safe. Let us fight as if it all depended upon us, but let us look up and know that all depends upon Him. By the lilies of Christian purity and by the roses of the Savior's atonement, you who love of Jesus will contend valiantly in the Holy War. Fight for the sake of the Kingdom and the crown of your Master. "For the battle is not yours, but God's" (2 Chronicles 20:15).

April 21
Morning

"I know that my Redeemer liveth" (Job 19:25).

The marrow of Job's comfort lies in that little word "my"—"my Redeemer," and in the fact that the Redeemer lives. Oh, to get hold of a living Christ. Do not be content until by faith you can say, "Yes, I cast myself on my living Lord, and He is mine." You may think it is presumption to say, "He lives as *my* Redeemer;" yet, remember, if you have but faith as a grain of mustard seed, that little faith entitles you to say it. But there is also another word here, expressive of Job's strong confidence—"I *know.*" To say, "I hope so, I trust so," is comfortable; and there are thousands in the fold of Jesus who hardly ever get much further. But to reach the essence of consolation you must say, "I know." Ifs and buts are sure murderers of peace and comfort. Doubts are dreary things in time of sorrow. If I have any suspicion that Christ is not mine, then there is vinegar mingled with the gall of death. But if I know that Jesus lives for me, then darkness is not dark. Even the night is light about me. Surely if Job, in those ages before the coming and advent of Christ, could say, "I know," we should not speak less positively. A living Redeemer, truly mine, is joy unspeakable.

April 21
Evening

"Who is even at the right hand of God" (Romans 8:34).

He who was once despised and rejected of men now occupies the position of a beloved and honored Son. The right hand of God is the *place of majesty and favor.* Our Lord Jesus is His people's Representative. When He died for them, they had forgiveness. When He rose again for them, they had liberty. When He sat down at His Father's right hand, they had favor, honor, and dignity. The raising and elevation of Christ is the elevation, the acceptance, and the glorifying of all His people. His seat at the right hand of God displays the acceptance of Christ as the Surety of our salvation. The reception of the Representative means the acceptance of *our* souls. This provides freedom from condemnation. "Who is he that condemneth?" (Romans 8:34). Who will condemn the ones who are, in Jesus, at the right hand of God? The right hand is the *place of power.* Christ at the right hand of God has all power in heaven and in earth. Who can fight against the people who have such power vested in their Captain? What can destroy you if Omnipotence is your helper? If the wings of the Almighty cover you, what sword can harm you? Rest secure. Jesus is your all-prevailing King and has crushed your enemies beneath His feet. Sin, death, and hell are all vanquished by Him, and you are represented in Him. There is no possibility that you can be destroyed.

April 22
Morning

"Him hath God exalted" (Acts 5:31).

Jesus, our Lord, once crucified, dead and buried, now sits on the throne of glory. The highest place that heaven affords is His by undisputed right. He is exalted at the Father's right hand. As Jehovah, He has eminent glories in which finite creatures cannot share. As the Mediator, He wears in heaven the honors which are the heritage of all the saints. It is delightful to reflect how close Christ's union is with His people. We are actually one with Him. We are members of His body, and His exaltation is our exaltation. He has a crown, and He gives us crowns too. He has a throne, but He is not content with having a throne to Himself. On His right hand there must be His bride arrayed in gold. He cannot be glorified without His bride. Look up to Jesus now. Let the eye of your faith behold Him with many crowns on His head. You will one day be like Him, when you will see Him as He is. You will not be as great as He is, or as divine, but you will still, in a measure, share the same honors and enjoy the same happiness and the same dignity which He possesses. Be content to live unknown for a little while. You will reign with Christ, for He has made us kings and priests unto God, and we will reign forever and ever. What a wonderful thought for the children of God! We have Christ for our glorious representative in heaven's courts now. Soon He will come and receive us to Himself, to be with Him there, to behold His glory, and to share in His joy.

April 22
Evening

"Thou shalt not be afraid for the terror by night" (Psalm 91:5).

What is this terror? It may be the shout of fire, the noise of thieves, or the cry of sudden death. We live in the world of death and sorrow. Therefore, we may expect difficulties in the night watches as well as beneath the glare of the afternoon sun. Nothing should alarm us because of the promise that the believer shall not be afraid. God our Father is here and will be here all through the lonely hours. He is an almighty Watcher, a sleepless Guardian, a faithful Friend. Darkness is not dark to Him. He has promised to be a wall of fire around His people—who can break through such a barrier? Those who do not know God should be afraid, for they have an angry God above them, a guilty conscience within them, and a yawning hell beneath them. But we who rest in Jesus are saved from all these through rich mercy. If we give way to foolish fear, we will dishonor our profession of faith and lead others to doubt the reality of godliness. We should be afraid of being afraid, lest we grieve the Holy Spirit by our foolish distrust. Put down dismal forebodings and groundless apprehensions. God has not forgotten to be gracious or shut up His tender mercies. It may be night in the soul, but there should be no terror, for the God of love does not change. Children of light may walk in darkness, but they are not cast away. They prove their adoption by trusting in their heavenly Father.

April 23
Morning

"Nay, in all these things we are more than conquerors through him that loved us" (Romans 8:37).

We go to Christ for forgiveness, and then too often look to ourselves for power to fight our sins. Paul thus rebukes us: "O foolish Galatians, who hath bewitched you, that ye should not obey the truth? This only would I learn of you: Received ye the Spirit by the works of the law, or by the hearing of faith? Are ye so foolish? Having begun in the Spirit, are ye now made perfect by the flesh" (Galatians 3:1-3). Take your sins to Christ's cross, for the old man can only be crucified there. We are crucified with Him. For instance, how would you go about overcoming a bad temper? It is very possible you have never tried the right way of going to Jesus with it. How did I get salvation? I came to Jesus just as I was, and I trusted Him to save me. I must kill my angry temper in the same way. It is the only way I can ever kill it. I must go to the cross with it and say to Jesus, "Lord, I trust you to deliver me from it." This is the only way to give it a death-blow. Are you covetous? Do you feel the world entangling you? You may struggle against this evil as long as you please, but only the blood of Jesus will deliver you from your sinful ways. Give it to Christ. Your prayers, repentances, and tears—all of them put together—are worth nothing apart from Jesus. None but Jesus can do helpless sinners good—or helpless saints either. If you are to be a conqueror, it *must* be through Him.

April 23
Evening

"Lo, in the midst of the throne. . .stood a Lamb as it had been slain" (Revelation 5:6).

Why should our exalted Lord appear in His wounds in glory? The wounds of Jesus are His glories, His jewels, and His sacred ornaments. To the eye of the believer, Jesus is more than beautiful because He is "white and ruddy." (See Song of Solomon 5:10.) Jesus is white with innocence and ruddy with His own blood. We see Him as the lily of matchless purity and as the rose crimsoned with His own gore. Christ is lovely as He teaches upon Olivet and by the sea, but there never was such a matchless Christ as He that hung upon the cross. There we behold all His beauties in perfection, all His attributes developed, all His love drawn out, and all His character expressed. The wounds of Jesus are far more fair than all the splendor and pomp of kings. The thorny crown is more than an imperial diadem. His scepter is no longer a reed, but there was a glory in it that never flashed from a scepter of gold. Jesus appears as the slain Lamb who sought our souls and redeemed them by His complete atonement. His wounds are the trophies of His love and His victory. He has divided the spoil with the strong. He redeemed for Himself a great multitude which no man can number. His scars are the memorials of the fight. If Christ loves to remember His sufferings for His people, *how precious should His wounds be to us!*

April 24
Morning

"And because of all this we make a sure covenant" (Nehemiah 9:38).

There are many occasions when we may have a desire to renew our covenant with God. After recovery from sickness, when, like Hezekiah, we have had a new term of years added to our life, we may fitly do it. After any deliverance from trouble, when our joys bud forth anew, let us again visit the foot of the cross and renew our consecration. Especially, let us do this after any sin which has grieved the Holy Spirit or brought dishonor on the cause of God. Let us then look to that blood which can make us whiter than snow and again offer ourselves to the Lord. We should not only let our troubles confirm our dedication to God, but our prosperity should do the same. If we ever meet with occasions which deserve to be called "crowning mercies," then surely, if He has crowned us, we should also crown our God. If we would learn to profit by our prosperity, we would not need so much adversity. Have we received some blessing which we little expected? Has the Lord put our feet in a large room? Can we sing of His mercies? Then let us put our hand on the horns of the altar now and say, "Bind me here, my God; bind me here with cords forever." Let us make with Him a sure covenant because of our gratitude to Jesus.

April 24
Evening

"The flowers appear on the earth; the time of the singing of birds is come, and the voice of the turtle is heard in our land" (Song of Solomon 2:12).

Sweet is the season of spring. The long and dreary winter helps us to appreciate spring's gentle warmth, and the promise of summer enhances its present delights. After periods of depression of spirit, it is delightful to behold again the light of the Sun of Righteousness. Our slumbering hearts rise from their lethargy like the crocus and the daffodil from their beds of earth. We rejoice with delicious notes of gratitude, far more melodious than the warbling of birds. The comforting assurance of peace, infinitely more delightful than the dove's song, is heard within the soul. Now is the time for the soul to seek communion with her Beloved. She must rise from her sordidness and come away from her old associations. If we do not hoist the sail when the breeze is favorable, it is our own fault when the times of refreshing pass us by. When Jesus visits us in tenderness and entreats us to arise, can we be so foolish as to refuse His request? He has risen that He may draw us to Himself. He revived us that we may ascend in newness of life to the heavenlies and share communion with Him. Our wintry state may fill us with coldness and indifference. But when the Lord creates the season of spring within, our sap will flow with vigor, and our branch will blossom with high resolve. O Lord, if it is not springtime in my chilly heart, please make it so. Come, Holy Spirit, and renew my soul! Restore me, and have mercy upon me. Take pity upon Your servant and send me a happy revival of spiritual life!

April 25
Morning

"Rise up, my love, my fair one, and come away" (Song of Solomon 2:10).

I hear the voice of my Beloved! He speaks to me! He bids me, "Rise up," and well He may, for I have long enough been lying among the pots of worldliness. He is risen, and I am risen in Him. Why then should I cleave to the dust? From lower loves, desires, pursuits, and aspirations, I would rise toward Him. He calls me by the sweet title of "My love," and He counts me fair. If He has exalted me and thinks I am beautiful, how can I linger and find congenial associates among the sons of men? He bids me, "Come away." Farther and farther from everything selfish He calls me. "Come away" has no harsh sound to my ear, for what is there to hold me in this wilderness of vanity and sin? Oh, my Lord, I would, if it were possible, have neither eyes nor ears nor heart for sin. To come to You is to come home from exile, to come to land out of the raging storm, to come to rest after long labor, to come to the goal of my desires and the summit of my wishes. But Lord, how can a stone rise? How can a lump of clay come away from the horrible pit? Your grace can do it. Send Your Holy Spirit to kindle sacred flames of love in my heart, and I will continue to rise until I leave earthly life behind me and indeed come away.

April 25
Evening

"If any man hear my voice, and open the door, I will come in to him" (Revelation 3:20).

What is your desire this evening? Is it set upon heavenly things? Do you long to enjoy the eternal love of your heavenly Father? Do you desire liberty in very close communion with God? Do you aspire to know the heights and depths and lengths and breadths of God? Then, you must draw near to Jesus. You must get a clear sight of Him in His preciousness and completeness. You must view Him in His work, in His offices, and in His person. He who understands Christ receives an anointing from the Holy One, by which he knows all things. (See 1 John 2:27.) Christ is the great Master-key to all the chambers of God. There is no room in the house of God which will not open and yield all its wealth to the soul that lives near to Jesus. Are you saying, "If only He would make my heart His dwelling place forever"? Open the door, and He will come in. He has been knocking for a long time so that He may fellowship with you and you with Him. He dines with you because you have invited Him into your heart. You dine with Him because He brings the provision. Open the portals of your soul. He will come with that love which you long to feel and the joy that you cannot find on your own. He will bring peace with the wine and sweet apples of His love and cheer you until you have no sickness but that of "love o'erpowering, love divine." Only open the door to Him, drive out His enemies, give Him the keys of your heart, and He will dwell there forever. Oh, wondrous love, that brings such a Guest to dwell in such a heart!

April 26
Morning

"This do in remembrance of me" (1 Corinthians 11:24).

It appears almost impossible that those who have been redeemed by the blood of the dying Lamb and have been loved with an everlasting love by the eternal Son of God, would forget their gracious Savior. Forget Him who never forgot us? Forget Him who poured His blood forth for our sins? Forget Him who loved us even to the death? Can it be possible? Yes, it is not only possible, but conscience confesses that it is too sadly a fault with all of us, that we allow Him to be as wayfaring man tarrying but for a night. He whom we should make the abiding tenant of our memories is but a visitor. The cross where one would think that memory would linger, and unmindfulness would be an unknown intruder, is desecrated by the feet of forgetfulness. Do you find yourselves forgetful of Jesus? Some creature steals away your heart, and you are unmindful of Him. Some earthly business engrosses your attention when you should fix your eye steadily on the cross. It is the incessant turmoil of the world, the constant attraction of earthly things, which takes away the soul from Christ. We must be determined that whatever else we let slip through our fingers and from our minds, we will hold fast to Jesus.

April 26
Evening

"Blessed is he that watcheth" (Revelation 16:15).

"I die daily," said the apostle in 1 Corinthians 15:31. The early Christians risked their lives everywhere they went. We are not called to pass through these same fearful persecutions today. If we were, the Lord would give us grace to bear the test. But the tests of Christian life that we face today are more likely to overcome us than even those of the fiery age. If we have to bear the ridicule of the world, that is an easy test. Its flattery, its soft words, and its hypocrisy are far worse. Our danger is that we may grow rich and become proud or take on the values of this present evil world and lose our faith. If wealth does not bring a trial, worldly care is just as dangerous. If we cannot be torn in pieces by the roaring lion, we may be hugged to death by the bear. The devil does not care which it is as long as he destroys our love for Christ and our confidence in Him. The Church is far more likely to lose her integrity in these soft and silken days than in those rougher times. We must be awake now for we travel upon a hazardous road. We are likely to fall asleep to our own destruction unless our faith in Jesus is a reality and our love for Him is a burning flame. Many who claim to be Christians in these days of easy believism will one day prove to be tares and not wheat. Christian, do not think that these are times in which you can dispense with watchfulness or holy zeal. You need these things now more than ever. May the eternal Spirit display His omnipotence in you. He will enable you to say, in these softer times as well as in the rougher, "We are more than conquerors through him that loved us" (Romans 8:37).

April 27
Morning

"God, even our own God" (Psalm 46:6).

It is strange how little use we make of the spiritual blessings which God gives us, but it is stranger still how little use we make of God Himself. How seldom do we ask counsel of the Lord! How often do we go about our business without seeking His guidance! In our troubles how constantly we strive to bear our burdens ourselves, instead of casting them on the Lord that He may sustain us! This is not because we may not, for the Lord seems to say, "I am yours, soul; come and make use of Me as you will. You may freely come to My store; you are welcome." It is our own fault if we do not avail ourselves of our God. Since you have such a friend, and He invites you, draw from Him daily. There is no reason for lack while you have God to go to. Never fear or faint while you have God to help you. He can supply you with all. Let me urge you to make use of your God. Make use of Him in prayer. Go to Him often, because He is your God. Tell Him all your needs. Use Him by faith at all times. If some circumstance has clouded your way, use God as your direction. If some strong enemy has troubled you, find in Jehovah a shield; for He is guidance and protection to His people. If you have lost your way in the maze of life, use Him as a guide, for He will direct you. "God, even our own God, shall bless us."

April 27
Evening

"The Lord is King for ever and ever" (Psalm 10:16).

Jesus Christ makes no despotic claim of *divine right,* but He is truly the Lord's anointed. "It pleased the Father that in him should all fulness dwell" (Colossians 1:19). God has given all power and authority to Him. As the Son of man, He is now head over all things to His Church. He reigns over heaven, earth, and hell with the keys of life and death. Certain princes have delighted to call themselves kings by *the popular will.* Surely this is true concerning our Lord Jesus Christ in His Church. If it could be decided by vote whether He should be King in the Church, every believing heart would crown Him. We would count no expense wasted that glorified Christ. Suffering would be pleasure, and loss would be gain if we could surround His brow with brighter crowns and make Him more glorious in the eyes of men and angels. Yes, He shall reign! Go forth, you who love your Lord. Bow at His feet, cover His path with the lilies of your love and the roses of your gratitude. "Bring forth the royal diadem and crown Him Lord of all." Our Lord Jesus is King in Zion by *right of conquest.* He has reclaimed the hearts of His people and has destroyed their enemies who held them in cruel bondage. In the Red Sea of His own blood, our Redeemer drowned the Pharaoh of our sins. He delivered us from the iron yoke and heavy curse of the law. He has taken us out of the powers of darkness with His sword. Who will snatch His conquest from His hand? All hail, King Jesus! Rule in our hearts forever, lovely Prince of Peace.

April 28
Morning

"Remember the word unto thy servant, upon which thou hast caused me to hope" (Psalm 119:49).

Whatever your need may be, you may readily find a promise in the Bible regarding it. Are you weary? Here is the promise—"He giveth power to the faint" (Isaiah 40:29). When you read such a promise, take it back to the great Promiser, and ask Him to fulfill His own Word. Are you seeking Christ and thirsting for closer communion with Him? This promise shines like a star on you— "Blessed are they that hunger and thirst after righteousness, for they shall be filled" (Matthew 5:6). Take that promise to the throne continually. Go to God over and over again with this—"Lord, You said it; do as You said." Are you distressed because of sin and burdened with the heavy load of your iniquities? Listen to these words—"I, even I, am he that blotteth out thy transgressions, and will no more remember thy sins" (Isaiah 43:25). Are you afraid you may not be able to hold on until the end? If that is your state, take this word of grace to the throne and plead it: "The mountains shall depart, and the hills be removed; but my kindness shall not depart from thee" (Isaiah 54:10). If you have lost the sweet sense of the Savior's presence and are seeking Him with a sorrowful heart, remember the promises: "Return unto me, and I will return unto you" (Malachi 3:7). Base your faith on God's own Word. Whatever your fears or wants, go to your heavenly Father saying, "Remember the word unto thy servant, upon which thou hast caused me to hope."

April 28
Evening

"All the house of Israel are impudent and hardhearted" (Ezekiel 3:7).

Are there no exceptions? No, not one. Even the favored race is described as impudent and hardhearted. Consider your share in this universal accusation, and be ready to acknowledge your guilt. The first charge is *impudence.* This refers to a hardness of forehead, a lack of holy shame, or boldness in evil. Before my conversion, I could sin and feel no remorse, hear of my guilt and yet remain unhumbled, even confess my iniquity and experience no inward sorrow because of it. For a sinner to go to God's house and pretend to pray to Him and praise Him displays a brazen-faced hypocrisy of the worst kind! But since the day of my new birth, I have doubted my Lord to His face, murmured insolently in His presence, worshipped before Him in a slovenly manner, and sinned without honest repentance. If my forehead was not so adamant, I would have a far more holy fear and a far deeper contrition of spirit. The second charge is *hardheartedness.* I cannot plead innocent here either. Once I had nothing but a heart of stone. Although through grace I now have a new and fleshy heart, much of my former stubbornness remains. I am not affected by the death of Jesus as I ought to be. Neither am I moved by the ruin of my fellowmen, the wickedness of the times, the chastisement of my heavenly Father, and my own failures, as I should be. O that my heart would melt at the mention of my Savior's sufferings and death. The Savior's precious blood is the universal solvent. It will soften even me, until my heart melts as wax before the fire.

April 29
Morning

"Thou art my hope in the day of evil" (Jeremiah 42:17).

The path of the Christian is not always bright with sunshine. He has his seasons of darkness and of storm. True, it is written in God's Word, "Her ways are ways of pleasantness, and all her paths are peace" (Proverbs 3:17). It is a great truth that trust in God brings a man happiness below as well as bliss above. Experience tells us that the course of the just is "as the shining light, that shineth more and more unto the perfect day" (Proverbs 4:18). Sometimes, however, that light is eclipsed. At certain periods, clouds cover the believer's sun, and he walks in darkness and sees no light. There are many who have rejoiced in the presence of God for a season. They have walked along the "green pastures" by the side of the "still waters," but suddenly they find the glorious sky is clouded. They say, "Surely, if I were a child of God, this would not happen." Oh, do not say this. The best of God's saints must experience trials. The dearest of His children must bear the cross. No Christian has enjoyed perpetual prosperity. Perhaps the Lord allotted you a smooth and unclouded path at first because you were weak and timid. Now that you are stronger in the spiritual life you must enter on the rougher experience of God's full-grown children. We need winds and tempest to exercise our faith, to tear off the rotten bough of self-dependence, and to root us more firmly in Christ. The day of evil reveals to us the value of our glorious hope.

April 29
Evening

"The Lord taketh pleasure in his people"
(Psalm 149:4).

The love of Jesus is sufficient for all the needs of His people. There is nothing which concerns their welfare that is not important to Him. He thinks of you as an eternal being, but He knows that you are mortal, too. "The very hairs of your head are all numbered" (Matthew 10:30). "The steps of a good man are ordered by the Lord: and he delighteth in his way" (Psalm 37:23). His mantle of love covers all our concerns. Believer, rest assured that the heart of Jesus cares about your daily affairs. His tender love is abundant enough that you may run to Him in all matters. "Like as a father pitieth his children, so the Lord pitieth them that fear him" (Psalm 103:13). The interests of all His saints are borne upon the broad bosom of the Son of God. His heart comprehends the diverse and innumerable concerns of all His people. Do you think that you can measure the love of Christ? Think of what His love has brought you— justification, adoption, sanctification, eternal life. The riches of His goodness are unsearchable. Oh, how matchless is the love of Christ! Shall such a love as this receive only half our hearts? Shall it have a cold love in return? Shall Jesus' marvelous lovingkindness and tender care meet with faint response and delayed acknowledgement? Tune your heart to a glad song of thanksgiving! Go to sleep rejoicing for you are not a desolate wanderer, but a beloved child. You are watched over, cared for, supplied, and defended by the Lord.

April 30
Morning

"And all the children of Israel murmured" (Numbers 14:2).

There are murmurers among Christians now, as there were in the camp of Israel. There are those who, when the rod falls, cry out against the afflictive dispensation. They ask, "Why am I afflicted? What have I done to be chastened like this?" Allow me a word with you who murmur. Why should you murmur against the dispensations of your heavenly Father? Can He treat you more harshly than you deserve? Consider what a rebel you once were, but He pardoned you! Surely, if He in His wisdom sees fit to chasten you, you should not complain. Does not that proud, rebellious spirit of yours prove that your heart is not thoroughly sanctified? Those murmuring words are contrary to the holy, submissive nature of God's children. Is not the correction needed? But if you murmur against the chastening, take heed, for it will go hard with murmurers. But know one thing—"He doth not afflict willingly, nor grieve the children of men" (Lamentations 3:33). All His corrections are sent in love, to purify you, and to draw you nearer to Himself. Surely it must help you bear the chastening if you are able to recognize your Father's hand. For "whom the Lord loveth He chasteneth, and scourgeth every son whom He receiveth. If ye endure chastening, God dealeth with you as with sons" (Hebrews 12:6-7). "Neither murmur ye as some of them also murmured and were destroyed of the destroyer" (1 Corinthians 10:10).

April 30
Evening

*"How precious also are thy thoughts unto me,
O God"* (Psalm 139:17).

The thought of divine omniscience offers no
comfort to the ungodly mind, but to the child of
God it overflows with consolation. God is always
thinking about us. It would be dreadful to exist for
a moment beyond the observation of our heavenly
Father. His thoughts are always tender, loving,
wise, prudent, far-reaching, and they bring us
countless benefits. The Lord always thought about
His people. He provided the covenant of grace
which secured their salvation. Now, He gives them
strength in their perseverance which will bring
them safely to their final rest. In all our wanderings, the eyes of the Eternal Watcher are constantly fixed upon us—we never roam beyond the
Shepherd's care. In our sorrows He observes us
incessantly, and not a pang escapes Him. In our
toils He sees all our weariness and writes all the
struggles of His faithful one in His book. These
thoughts of the Lord encompass us in all our paths
and penetrate our innermost being. Not a nerve or
tissue, valve or vessel, of our body is uncared for.
All the problems of our little world are thought
upon by the great God. Never be led astray by
philosophic fools who preach an impersonal God
and talk of self-existent, self-governing matters.
The Lord lives and thinks about us. Let no one rob
you of this assurance. The favor of a king is valued
so highly that he who has it considers his fortune
made. But how much greater is it to be thought
about by the King of kings! If the Lord thinks of us,
all is well, and we may rejoice evermore.

May 1
Morning

"His cheeks are as a bed of spices, as sweet flowers" (Song of Solomon 5:13).

The flowery month is here! March winds and April showers have done their work, and the earth is clothed with beauty. To you the "beds of spices" are well known. You have often smelled the perfume of the "sweet flowers." Go at once to your Beloved and find in Him all loveliness and all joy. That cheek once so rudely smitten with a rod, often wet with tears of sympathy, and then defiled with spittle—that cheek, as it smiles with mercy, is a fragrant aroma to my heart. You did not hide Your face from shame and spitting, O Lord Jesus, and therefore I will find my dearest delight in praising You. Those cheeks were furrowed by the plow of grief and crimsoned with red lines of blood from Your thorn-crowned temples; such marks of love unbounded cannot but charm my soul far more than "pillars of perfume." In Jesus I find not only fragrance, but a bed of spices; not one flower, but all manner of sweet flowers. He is to me my rose and my lily, my hearts-ease and my cluster of camphor. When He is with me, it is May all year round. My soul goes forth to wash its happy face in the morning-dew of His grace and to solace itself with the singing of the birds of His promises. Precious Lord Jesus, let me know the blessedness which dwells in abiding, unbroken fellowship with You.

May 1
Evening

*"How precious also are thy thoughts unto me,
O God"* (Psalm 139:17).

The thought of divine omniscience offers no comfort to the ungodly mind, but to the child of God it overflows with consolation. God is always thinking about us. It would be dreadful to exist for a moment beyond the observation of our heavenly Father. His thoughts are always tender, loving, wise, prudent, far-reaching, and they bring us countless benefits. The Lord always thought about His people. He provided the covenant of grace which secured their salvation. Now, He gives them strength in their perseverance which will bring them safely to their final rest. In all our wanderings, the eyes of the Eternal Watcher are constantly fixed upon us—we never roam beyond the Shepherd's care. In our sorrows He observes us incessantly, and not a pang escapes Him. In our toils He sees all our weariness and writes all the struggles of His faithful one in His book. These thoughts of the Lord encompass us in all our paths and penetrate our innermost being. Not a nerve or tissue, valve or vessel, of our body is uncared for. All the problems of our little world are thought upon by the great God. Never be led astray by philosophic fools who preach an impersonal God and talk of self-existent, self-governing matters. The Lord lives and thinks about us. Let no one rob you of this assurance. The favor of a king is valued so highly that he who has it considers his fortune made. But how much greater is it to be thought about by the King of kings! If the Lord thinks of us, all is well, and we may rejoice evermore.

May 2
Morning

"I pray not that thou shouldest take them out of the world" (John 17:15).

It is a sweet and blessed event which will occur to all believers in God's own time—the going home to be with Jesus. In a few more years, the Lord's soldiers who are now fighting the good fight of faith will be through with conflict and enter into the joy of their Lord. But although Christ prays that His people may eventually be with Him where He is, He does not ask that they be taken at once from this world to heaven. He wishes them to stay here. He leaves us in His Father's hands, until, like shocks of corn fully ripe, we will each be gathered into our Master's garner. To abide in the flesh is needful for others, if not profitable for ourselves. Jesus asks that we be kept from evil, but He never asks for us to be admitted to the inheritance in glory until we are of full age. Christians often want to die when they have any trouble. Ask them why, and they will tell you, "Because we would be with the Lord." We fear it is not so much because they are longing to be with the Lord, as it is their desire to get rid of their troubles. Otherwise, they would feel the same wish to die at other times, when not under the pressure of trial. Now it is quite right to desire to depart, if we can do it in the same spirit that Paul did. To be with Christ is far better. But the wish to escape from trouble is a selfish one. Let your wish be to glorify God by your life here as long as He pleases. Even though it is in the midst of toil, conflict, and suffering, and allow Him to say when "it is enough."

May 2
Evening

"These all died in faith" (Hebrews 11:13).

Behold the epitaph of all those blessed saints who passed away before the coming of our Lord! It does not matter how they died, whether of old age or by violent means. This one point in which they all agree is the one most worthy of record: "These all died in faith." In faith they lived. It was their comfort, their guide, their motive, and their support. In the same spiritual grace they died, ending their life with the sweet melody they had sung for so long. They did not die resting in the flesh or upon their own achievements. They never wavered from their first commitment to God, but held to the way of faith to the end. Faith is as precious to die by as it is to live by. Dying in faith has distinct reference to *the past*. They believed the promises which had been made before. They were assured that their sins were blotted out through the mercy of God. Dying in faith also concerns *the present*. These saints were confident of their acceptance by God. They enjoyed the beams of His love and rested in His faithfulness. Dying in faith looks into *the future.*They fell asleep trusting that the Messiah would surely come. When He appears upon the earth in the last day, they will rise from their graves to behold Him. To them, the pains of death were only the birth pangs of a better state. Take courage as you read this epitaph. Your journey through this life is one of faith, and the circumstances seldom bring joy. The brightest and the best have followed the same path. Look to Jesus, the Author and Finisher of your faith. Thank Him for giving you the same precious faith that belonged to the souls now in glory.

May 3
Morning

"In the world ye shall have tribulation" (John 16:33).

Are you asking the reason for this, believer? Look upward to your heavenly Father and behold Him pure and holy. You are to be like Him one day. Will you be conformed to His image easily? Will you require much refining? Will it be an easy thing to get rid of your corruptions and make you perfect, even as your Father which is in heaven is perfect? Next, Christian, turn your eye downward. Do you know what foes you have beneath your feet? You were once a servant of Satan, and no king will willingly lose his subjects. Do you think that Satan will let you alone? No, he will always be at you, for he "goeth about like a roaring lion, seeking whom he may devour" (1 Peter 5:8). Expect trouble, Christian. Look around you. You are in an enemy's country, a stranger and a sojourner. The world is not your friend. If it is, then you are not God's friend, for he who is the friend of the world is the enemy of God. Be assured that you will find enemies everywhere. When you sleep, think that you are resting on the battlefield. When you walk, suspect an ambush in every hedge. As mosquitos are said to bite strangers more than natives, so will the trials of earth be sharpest to you. Lastly, look within your own heart and observe what is there. Sin and self are still within. Expect trouble. But do not despair because God said, "I will be with thee in trouble; I will deliver thee and honor thee" (Psalm 91:15).

May 3
Evening

"A very present help" (Psalm 46:1).

Covenant blessings are meant to be appropriated. Believer, you do not depend upon Christ as you should. When you are in trouble, do you tell Him all of your grief? His sympathizing heart can comfort and relieve you. Or do you go to all of your friends except your very best Friend? Do you spread your tale of woe everywhere, except upon the bosom of your Lord? Are you burdened with today's sins? Here is a fountain filled with blood—use it. Has a sense of guilt returned to you? The pardoning grace of Jesus may be proved again and again. Come to Him at once for cleansing. Do you despise your weakness? He will be your strength if you lean upon Him. Do you feel naked? Here is the robe of Jesus' righteousness. Do not stand looking at it, but wear it. Strip off your own righteousness and fears and put on the fair white linen. Do you feel sick? Pull the night-bell of prayer, and call the Beloved Physician! He will give the medicine that will revive you. You are poor, but you have "a kinsman. . .a mighty man of wealth" (Ruth 2:1). Go to Him and ask Him to give out of His abundance. He has made you a joint-heir with Him. All that He is and all that He has is available to you. There is nothing Christ dislikes more than for His people to make a display of Him and not use Him. He loves to be employed by us. The more burdens we put on His shoulders, the more precious He will be to us.

May 4
Morning

"Shall a man make gods unto himself, and they are no gods?" (Jeremiah 41:20).

One great troublesome sin of ancient Israel was idolatry. Spiritual Israel, however, has a tendency to lean in the same direction. Self, in various forms, struggles to place the chosen ones under its dominion. Favorite children are often the cause of much sin in believers. The Lord is grieved when He sees us doting on them in the above measure. Spoiled children may live to be as great a curse to us as Absalom was to David. If Christians desire to grow thorns to stuff their sleepless pillows, let them dote on their dear ones. Why are we so vain? We pity the poor heathen who adores a god of stone, and yet we worship a god of flesh. Where is the vast superiority between a god of flesh and one of stone? The principle is the same in either case; only in ours, the crime is more aggravated because we have more light and sin in the face of it. The heathen bows to a false deity, but he has never known the true God. We commit two evils. We forsake the living God and turn to idols. May the Lord purge us all from this grievous iniquity.

May 4
Evening

"Being born again, not of corruptible seed, but of incorruptible"(1 Peter 1:23).

Peter earnestly exhorted the scattered saints to love each other "with a pure heart fervently" (1 Peter 1:22). He wisely based his argument upon the high and divine nature which God implanted in His people rather than laws of human nature or philosophy. God's people are heirs of glory, princes of the royal blood, and descendants of the King of kings, earth's truest and oldest aristocracy. Peter admonished them, "Love one another because of your noble birth, being born of incorruptible seed. You have descended from God, the Creator of all things. Because of your immortal destiny, you shall never pass away, although the glory of flesh shall fade, and even its existence shall cease." (See 1 Peter 1:22-25). In the spirit of humility, we should recognize the true dignity of our reborn nature and then live up to it. What is a Christian? If you compare him with a king, he adds priestly sanctity to royal dignity. The king's royalty is often seen only in his crown. But with a Christian, it is infused into his inmost nature. He is as much above other men through his new birth as the man is above the beast. Surely he ought to conduct himself in all his dealings as one who is not of this world, but chosen and distinguished by sovereign grace. Therefore, he cannot live in the same way as the world's citizens. Let the dignity of your nature and the brightness of your future constrain you to cling to holiness and to avoid every appearance of evil.

May 5
Morning

"I will be their God, and they shall be my people" (2 Corinthians 6:16).

What a sweet title—"My people"! What a cheering revelation—"their God"! The whole world is God's. But of those He has chosen, whom He has purchased for Himself, He says what He does not say of others—"My people." In this word there is the idea of ownership. All the nations upon earth are His. The whole world is in His power. Yet, His people, His chosen, are His special possession. He has done more for them than others. He bought them with His blood. He brought them close to Himself. He has loved them with an everlasting love. Dear friends, can you, by faith, see yourselves in that number? Can you look up to heaven and say, "My Lord and my God?" Can you read your name written in precious blood? Can you, by humble faith, lay hold of Jesus' garments and say, "My Christ"? If you can, then God says of you and of others like you, "My people." If God is your God, and Christ is your Christ, the Lord pays special attention to you. You are the object of His choice, accepted in His beloved Son.

May 5
Evening

"He that handleth a matter wisely shall find good: and whoso trusteth in the Lord, happy is he" (Proverbs 16:20).

Wisdom is man's true strength. Under its guidance, he best accomplishes his life's goals. Walking in wisdom gives man the richest enjoyment and presents the noblest occupation for his talents. Hence, by it he finds good in the fullest sense. Without wisdom, man is like a wild pony running in circles, wasting strength which might be profitably employed. Wisdom is the compass by which man is to steer across the trackless waste of life. Without it, he is like an abandoned ship, tossed about by the wind and waves. A man must be prudent in this world or he will have unnumbered difficulties. If we follow where our great Teacher leads, we will find good even in this dark abode. There are celestial fruits to be gathered this side of Eden's garden and songs of praise to be sung amid the groves of earth. But where may this wisdom be found? Many have dreamed of it, but have not possessed it. Where may we learn it? Let us listen to the voice of the Lord, for He declared the secret. We have it in the text, "Whoso trusteth in the Lord, happy is he." *The true way to handle a matter wisely is to trust in the Lord.* This is the sure solution to the most intricate labyrinths of life. Follow it, and you will find eternal bliss. He who trusts in the Lord has a diploma for wisdom granted by inspiration. Lord, walk with me in the garden this evening and teach me the wisdom of faith.

May 6
Morning

"We dwell in him" (1 John 4:13).

Do you want a house for your soul? Do you ask, "What is the price?" It is something less than proud human nature would like to give. It is without money and without price. Would you like to pay a respectable rent? Would you love to do something to win Christ? Then you cannot have the house, for it is without price. Will you take my Master's house on a lease for all eternity, with nothing to pay for it but the rent of loving and serving Him forever? Will you take Jesus and dwell in Him? See, this house is furnished with all you want. It is filled with more riches than you will spend as long as you live. Here you can have intimate communion with Christ and feast on His love. In it, when weary, you can find rest with Jesus. From it, you can look out and see heaven itself. Will you have the house? If you are houseless, you will say, "I would like to have the house. May I have it?" Yes, the key is, "Come to Jesus." "But," you say, "I am too shabby for such a house." Never mind, for there are garments inside. If you feel guilty and condemned, Christ will make you good enough for the house in time. He will wash you and cleanse you, and you will be able to sing, "We dwell in Him." Dwelling in Him, you have not only a perfect and secure house, but an everlasting one. When this world melts like a dream, our house will live and stand more imperishable than marble, more solid than granite, self-existent as God, for it is God Himself. "We dwell in him."

May 6
Evening

"All the days of my appointed time will I wait" (Job 14:14).

Our time here on earth will make heaven seem even more heavenly. Nothing makes rest as sweet as toil. Nothing renders security as pleasant as exposure to danger. The bitter fruit of earth will give more enjoyment to the new wine which sparkles in the golden bowls of glory. Our battered armor and scarred countenances will make our victory seem even more illustrious when we are welcomed to the seats of those who have overcome the world. We would not have full *fellowship with Christ* if we did not sojourn for a while upon this earth. He was baptized with a baptism of suffering, and we must be baptized with the same if we desire to share His Kingdom. Fellowship with Christ is honorable, and the most severe sorrow is an inexpensive price for it. Another reason for our lingering here is *for the good of others.* We should not wish to enter heaven until our work is done. We are called to minister light to souls trapped in the dark wilderness of sin. Our stay here is *for God's glory.* A tried saint, like a well-cut diamond, glitters brilliantly in the King's crown. Nothing reflects the skill of a workman as accurately as a severe trial of his work. Its triumphant endurance of the ordeal honors its builder. We are God's workmanship, and He will be glorified by our steadfastness. It is for the honor of Jesus that we endure the trial of our faith with sacred joy. Let each man surrender his own longings to the glory of Jesus. Our time is fixed and settled by eternal decree. Let us not be anxious about it, but wait with patience until the gates of pearl open at last.

May 7
Morning

"Multitudes followed him, and he healed them all" (Matthew 12:15).

What a multitude of hideous sickness must have thrust itself under the eye of Jesus! Yet, we do not read that He was disgusted. What a variety of evils must have met at His feet! Yet, He was ready for every new shape of evil and was victor over it in every form. It did not matter if it was fever, palsy, madness, leprosy, or blindness—all knew the power of His word and fled at His command. It is even so this morning. Whatever my own case may be, the beloved Physician can heal me. Whatever may be the state of others whom I may remember in prayer, I have hope in Jesus that He will heal them of their diseases. My friend, I have hope for all when I remember the healing power of my Lord. He still dispenses His grace and works wonders among the sons of men. Let me go to Him at once in earnest. Let me praise Him this morning as I remember how He performed His spiritual cures by taking on Himself our sicknesses. "By his stripes we are healed" (Isaiah 53:5). The Church on earth is full of souls healed by our beloved Physician. The inhabitants of heaven itself confess that He healed them all. Come, then, publish abroad the virtue of His grace, and let it be "to the Lord for a name; for an everlasting sign which shall not be cut off" (Isaiah 55:13).

May 7
Evening

"Jesus saith unto him, Rise, take up thy bed, and walk" (John 5:8).

Like many others, the crippled man had been waiting for a wonder to take place and a sign to be given. Wearily, he watched the pool, but no angel came for him. Yet, thinking it was his only chance, he continued to wait. He did not know that there was One near him whose word could heal him in a moment. Many are having the same problem— they are waiting for some extraordinary emotion, remarkable impression, or celestial vision. They wait in vain. Remarkable signs are seen in a few cases, yet these are rare, and no man has a right to look for them. It is very sad that tens of thousands are now waiting, using their religion, vows, and resolutions in vain. Meanwhile, these poor souls forget the present Savior who bids them to look to Him to be saved. *He* could heal them at once, but they prefer to wait for an angel and a wonder. To trust Him is a sure way to every blessing. He is worthy of absolute confidence. But unbelief makes them prefer the cold porches of Bethesda to the warm bosom of His love. May the Lord turn His eye upon the multitudes who are in this situation tonight. May He forgive their doubts of His divine power and call them by that sweet voice to rise from the bed of despair. In the energy of faith, let them take up their bed and walk. O Lord, hear our prayer at this calm hour of sunset. Before the new day dawns, may we all look to You and live.

May 8
Morning

"He that was healed wist not who it was" (John 5:13).

Years are short to the happy and healthy, but thirty-eight years of disease must have dragged into a long time for the poor, impotent man. When Jesus healed him by a word while he lay at the pool of Bethesda, he was delightfully aware of a change. Likewise, the sinner who has been paralyzed with despair is very conscious of the change when the Lord Jesus speaks the word of power and gives joy and peace in believing. The evil removed is too great to be removed without our discerning it. The change brought about is too marvelous not to be noticed. Yet, the poor man was ignorant of the Author of his cure. He did not know the sacredness of His person on the errand which brought Him among men. We must not hastily condemn men for lack of knowledge. Where we can see the faith which saves the soul, we must believe that salvation has been bestowed. The Holy Spirit makes men penitent long before He makes them divine. Ignorance is, however, an evil. This poor man was tantalized by the Pharisees and was unable to cope with them. It is good to be able to answer opposition, but we cannot do so if we do not know the Lord Jesus clearly and with understanding. His ignorance, however, was soon cured when he was visited by the Lord in the temple. After that gracious manifestation, he was found testifying that it was Jesus who had made him whole.

May 8
Evening

"Acquaint now thyself with him" (Job 22:21).

If we desire to acquaint ourselves with God and be at peace, we must know Him as He has revealed Himself. God said, "Let *us* make man in our image" (Genesis 1:26). Man should not be content until he knows something about the "us" from whom his being was derived. Make a conscious effort to know *the Father.* Bury your head in His bosom in deep repentance and confess that you are not worthy to be called His son. Receive the kiss of His love and let the ring which is the token of His eternal faithfulness be on your finger. Sit at His table and let your heart rejoice in His grace. Then, press forward and seek to know *the Son* of God who is the brightness of His Father's glory. Know Him in the remarkable complexity of His nature. He is eternal God, and yet He suffered as a finite man. Follow Him as He walks upon the waters with the step of Deity and as He sits at the well in the weariness of humanity. Do not be satisfied until you know Jesus Christ as your Friend, your Brother, your Husband, your all. Do not forget *the Holy Spirit.* Seek to obtain a clear view of His character, His attributes, and His works. The Spirit of the Lord first moved upon chaos and brought forth order. (See Genesis 1:2.) He now visits the chaos of your soul and creates the order of holiness. Behold Him as the Lord and Giver of spiritual life, the Illuminator, the Instructor, the Comforter, and the Sanctifier. Such an intelligent and scriptural belief in the Trinity is yours if you truly know God. Such knowledge brings *deep and abiding peace.*

May 9
Morning

"Who hath blessed us with all spiritual blessings" (Ephesians 1:3).

All the goodness of the past, the present, and the future, Christ bestows on His people. In the mysterious ages of the past, the Lord Jesus was His Father's first elect. He had from all eternity the prerogatives of Sonship. By adoption and regeneration, He has elevated us to Sonship also. The eternal covenant, based on suretyship and confirmed by oath, is ours. In the everlasting settlements of predestinating wisdom and omnipotent decree, the eye of the Lord Jesus was ever fixed on us. The marvelous incarnation of the God of heaven, with all the amazing condescension and humiliation which attended it, is ours. The bloody sweat, the scourge, and the cross are ours forever. Whatever blissful consequences flow from perfect obedience, finished atonement, resurrection, ascension, or intercession, are all ours by His own gift. Upon His breastplate He is now bearing our names. He employs His dominion over principalities and powers for those who trust in Him. His high estate is as much at our service as was His condition of abasement. He who gave Himself for us in the depths of woe and death, does not withdraw the grant now that He is enthroned in the highest heavens.

May 9
Evening

"Come, my beloved, let us go forth into the field. . .let us see if the vine flourish" (Song of Solomon 7:11,12).

The Church was prepared to engage in earnest labor and desired her Lord's company in it. She did not say, "I will go," but "let us go." It is a joy to work when Jesus is at your side! Like our first parents, we are put into the garden of the Lord for a purpose. Let us go forth into the field. The Church desires to enjoy communion with Christ while she works for Him. Some imagine that they cannot serve Christ actively and still have fellowship with Him. They are mistaken. True, it is easy to fritter away our inward spiritual life through outward activity. We may reach the point where we complain, "They made me the keeper of the vineyards; but mine own vineyard have I not kept" (Song of Solomon 1:6). There is no reason why, however, this should be the case except due to our own folly and neglect. A believer may do nothing and grow as lifeless in spiritual things as those who are the busiest. Mary was not praised for sitting still, but for sitting at Jesus' feet. (See Luke 10:39-42.) Even so, Christians are not to be praised for neglecting duties under the pretense of having secret fellowship with Jesus. It is not sitting, but *sitting at Jesus' feet* which is commendable. Do not think that activity is in itself an evil. It is a great blessing and a means of grace to us. Those who have most fellowship with Christ are not the hermits who have much time to spare. Rather, they are the untiring laborers who are toiling for Jesus. He is by their side making them workers together with God. Let us remember that in anything we have to do for Jesus, we can and should do it in close communion with Him.

May 10
Morning

"But now is Christ risen from the dead" (1 Corinthians 15:20).

Christianity rests on the fact that Christ is risen from the dead. "If Christ be not risen, then is our preaching vain, and your faith is also vain. . . .ye are yet in your sins" (1 Corinthians 15:14-17). The divinity of Christ finds its surest proof in His resurrection, since He was "declared to be the Son of God with power, according to the spirit of holiness, by the resurrection from the dead" (Romans 1:4). Christ's sovereignty and deity depends on His resurrection, "for to this end Christ both died, and rose, and revived, that he might be Lord both of the dead and living" (Romans 14:9). Our justification, that choice blessing of the covenant, is linked with Christ's triumphant victory over death and the grave. "He was delivered for our offenses, and was raised again for our justification" (Romans 4:25). Our very regeneration is connected with His resurrection. We are "begotten again unto a lively hope by the resurrection of Jesus Christ from the dead" (1 Peter 1:3). And most certainly our ultimate resurrection rests here. "If the Spirit of him that raised up Jesus from the dead dwell in you, he that raised up Christ from the dead shall also quicken your mortal bodies by his Spirit that dwelleth in you" (Romans 8:11). If Christ is not risen, then we will not rise. But if He is risen, then they who are asleep in Christ have not perished, but in their flesh will surely behold their God. The silver thread of resurrection runs through all the believer's blessings, from his regeneration onward to his eternal glory, and binds them together.

May 10
Evening

"The only begotten of the Father, full of grace and truth" (John 1:14).

Believer, you can give your testimony that Christ is the only begotten of the Father as well as the first begotten from the dead. You can say, "He is divine to me, even if He is human to all the world. He has done for me what only God could do. He subdued my stubborn will and melted my heart of stone. He turned my mourning into laughter and my desolation into joy. He made my heart rejoice with joy unspeakable and full of glory. He is *full of grace.* If this were not true, I would never have been saved. He drew me when I struggled to escape from His grace. At last when I came trembling like a condemned culprit to His mercy seat, He said, "Your sins, which are many, are all forgiven. Be of good cheer." He is *full of truth.* His promises are all true; not one has failed. A servant never had such a master as I have. No spouse had such a husband as Christ has been to my soul. A sinner never had a better Savior or a mourner a better comforter than Christ. I want no one else other than Him. In life He is my life, and in death He will be the end of death. In poverty, Christ is my riches. In darkness He is my star, and in brightness He is my sun. He is the manna of the camp in the wilderness, and He will be the new corn of the multitude when they come to Canaan. Jesus is to me all grace and no wrath, all truth and no falsehood. He is infinitely full of truth and grace.

May 11
Morning

"I am with you alway" (Matthew 28:20).

It is good to know there is One who is always the same and who is always with us. It is good there is one stable rock in the midst of the billows of the sea of life. Oh, my soul, set not your affections on rusting, moth-eaten, decaying treasures, but set your heart on Him who abides forever faithful to you. Do not build your house on the moving quicksands of a deceitful world, but found your hopes on this Rock which stands immovably secure. Put everything in Christ. Set all your affections on His person, all your hope in His merit, all your trust in His efficacious blood, and all your joy in His presence so you may laugh at loss and defy destruction. Remember that the day is coming when nothing will be left but the black, cold earth. Death's extinguisher must soon put out your candle. Oh, how sweet to have sunlight when the candle is gone! The dark flood must soon roll between you and all you have. Wed your heart then to Him who will never leave you. Trust yourself to Him who will go with you through the black and surging current of death's stream, will land you safely on the celestial shore, and will make you sit with Him in heavenly places forever. Tell your secrets to the Friend who sticks closer than a brother. Trust all your concerns to Him who never can be taken from you, who will never leave you, and who will never let you leave Him, even "Jesus Christ, the same yesterday, and today, and forever" (Hebrews 13:8). "Lo, I am with you alway" (Matthew 28:20) is enough for my soul to live on.

May 11
Evening

"Only be thou strong and very courageous" (Joshua 1:7).

God's tender love for His servants makes Him concerned about the state of their emotions. He wants them to be of good courage. Some consider it a small thing for a believer to be troubled with doubts and fears, but God does not agree. He wants us to be free from care, doubt, and cowardice. Our Master takes our unbelief more seriously than we do. When we are discouraged, we are subject to a grievous disorder that should not be trifled with, but carried at once to the beloved Physician. It grieves our Lord to see our sad countenance. It was a law of King Ahasuerus that no one should come into his court dressed in mourning. (See Nehemiah 2:1-2.) This is not the law of the King of kings, for we may come and tell Him how we feel. But He wants us to be free from the spirit of heaviness and to wear the garment of praise. Then, we may glorify the Lord by enduring trials in an heroic manner. If we are fearful and fainthearted, *it will dishonor God. Besides, what a bad example it is!* This disease of doubt and discouragement is an epidemic which soon spreads among the Lord's flock. One downcast believer makes twenty souls sad. Unless your courage is kept up, *Satan will be too much for you.* The joy of the Lord is your strength, and no fiend of hell can make headway against you. *Labor is light* to a man of cheerful spirit. *Success waits upon cheerfulness.* The man who toils while rejoicing in God and believing with all his heart has success guaranteed. Therefore, "be thou strong and very courageous."

May 12
Morning

"And will manifest myself to him" (John 14:21).

The Lord Jesus gives special revelations of Himself to His people. Even if Scripture did not declare this, there are many of the children of God who could testify to the truth of it from their own experience. In the biographies of eminent saints, you will find many instances recorded in which Jesus has been pleased, in a very special manner, to speak to their souls and to unfold the wonders of His person. Their souls have been so steeped in happiness that they thought themselves to be in heaven. Even though they were not there, they were on the threshold of it. When Jesus manifests Himself to His people, it has a holy influence on the believer's heart. One effect will be *humility*. If a man says, "I have had such and such spiritual communications, I am a great man," he has never had any communion with Jesus at all. "God hath respect unto the lowly; but the proud he knoweth afar off" (Psalm 138:6). Another effect will be *happiness*; for in God's presence there are pleasures forevermore. *Holiness* will be sure to follow. A man who has no holiness has never had this manifestation. Some men profess a great deal, but we must not believe anyone unless we see that his deeds answer to what he says. "Be not deceived, God is not mocked" (Galatians 6:7). He will not bestow His favors upon the wicked. While He will not cast away a perfect man, neither will He respect an evildoer.

May 12
Evening

"Fear not to go down into Egypt; for I will there make of thee a great nation: I will go down with thee into Egypt; and I will also surely bring thee up again" (Genesis 46:3-4).

Jacob must have shuddered at the thought of leaving the land of his father and dwelling among heathen strangers. It was *a new scene and likely to be a trying one.* Yet, the way was evidently appointed for him, and, therefore, he resolved to go. Believers today are sometimes called to perils and temptations. At such times *they should imitate Jacob's example* by offering sacrifices of prayer to God and seeking His direction. They should not take a step until they have waited upon the Lord for His blessing. Then, Jacob's Companion will be their friend and helper. The Lord condescends to go down into our humiliations with us. We cannot hesitate to go where Jehovah promises His presence. Even the valley of death grows bright with the radiance of this assurance. Marching onward with faith in God, believers will be brought up again from the troubles of life and the chambers of death. Jacob's seed came out of Egypt in due time. All the faithful will pass unscathed through the tribulation of life and the terror of death. Let us *exercise Jacob's confidence.* "Fear not" is the Lord's command and divine encouragement to those who are launching upon new seas in obedience to His will. His divine presence and preservation forbid the slightest fear or unbelief. Without God, we should be afraid to move; but when He commands us to go, it would be dangerous to remain. Therefore, go forward and fear not.

May 13
Morning

"Weeping may endure for a night, but joy cometh in the morning" (Psalm 30:5).

Christian, if you are in a time of trial, think of the future. Lift up your heart with the thought of the coming of your Lord. Be patient because He comes with clouds descending. Be patient! The Husbandman waits until He reaps His harvest. Jesus has said, "Behold, I come quickly; and my reward is with me, to give to every man according as his work shall be" (Revelation 22:12). Your life may be full of troubles now, but it will soon be free from care. Your garments may be soiled with dust now, but they will be white soon. Wait a little longer. How trivial our trials will seem when we look back on them! Looking at them here in the present, they seem immense. Let us go on boldly. If the night is dark, the morning is coming, which is more than they can say who are shut up in the darkness of hell. Do you know what it is to live on expectation—to anticipate heaven? Happy believer, it may be all dark now, but it will soon be light. It may be all trial now, but it will soon be all happiness! What does it matter though "weeping may endure for a night," when "joy cometh in the morning"?

May 13
Evening

"Thou art my portion, O Lord" (Psalm 119:57).

Look at your possessions and compare them with those of your fellowmen. Some make their living in the field. They are rich, and their harvests yield them a golden increase. But what are harvests worth compared with God who is the God of harvests? What are bursting granaries compared with the One who feeds you with the bread of heaven? Some have their business in the city. Their wealth is abundant and flows to them in constant streams until they possess a reservoir of gold. But what is gold compared with God? You cannot eat it. Your spiritual life could not be sustained by it. Apply it to a discouraged heart, and see if it could stop a single groan or make one grief seem less painful. But in God, you have more than gold or riches ever could buy. Some receive applause and fame. But does not God mean more to you than that? If you are applauded by thousands, would this prepare you to cross the Jordan or help you to face judgment? There are griefs in life which wealth cannot alleviate. There is the deep need at the hour of death for which no riches can provide. But in God every need is met, whether in life or in death. With God as your portion, you are truly rich. He will supply your need, comfort your heart, assuage your grief, guide your steps, be with you in the dark valley, and then take you home to enjoy Him forever. "I have enough," said Esau in Genesis 33:9. This is the best thing a worldly man can say. But Jacob replies, "I have all things," which is too high for carnal minds to understand.

May 14
Morning

"Joint heirs with Christ" (Romans 8:17).

As heir of all things, Jesus is the sole proprietor of the vast creation of God. He has permitted us to claim the whole world as ours by virtue of that deed of joint-heirship which the Lord has ratified with His chosen people. The golden streets of paradise, the pearly gates, the river of life, the transcendent bliss, and the unutterable glory are, by our blessed Lord, given to us for our everlasting possession. All that He has He shares with His people. Crown the head, and the whole body shares the honor. Behold here is the reward of every Christian conqueror! Christ's throne, crown, scepter, palace, treasure, robes, and heritage are yours. Christ deems His happiness completed by His people sharing it. "The glory which thou gavest me have I given them" (John 17:22). "These things have I spoken unto you, that my joy might remain in you, and that your joy might be full" (John 15:11). The honors of His Kingdom are more pleasing, because His people appear with Him in glory. More valuable to Him are His conquests, since they have taught His people to overcome. He delights in His throne because on it there is a place for them. He rejoices in His royal robes, since over them His skirts are spread. He delights all the more in His joy because He calls them to enter into it.

May 14
Evening

"He shall gather the lambs with his arm, and carry them in his bosom" (Isaiah 40:11).

The Good Shepherd carries the lambs in His bosom because He has a tender heart. The sighs, ignorance, and feebleness of the little ones of His flock bring out His compassion. It is *His responsibility* as a faithful High Priest to consider the weak. He purchased them with His blood, and they are *His property*. He is responsible for each lamb, bound by a covenant not to lose one. They are all a part of His glory and reward. But how may we understand the expression, "He will carry them"? Sometimes He carries them by *not permitting them to endure much trial.* Or, they are carried by being filled with an *unusual degree of love* so that they have the ability to stand firm. Though their knowledge may not be deep, they have great sweetness in what they do know. Frequently, He carries them by giving them a *very simple faith* which takes the promise just as it stands. They run straight to Jesus with every problem. The simplicity of their faith gives them an unusual degree of confidence which carries them above the world. *He carries the lambs in His bosom.* Here is boundless affection. Would He put them in His bosom if He did not love them deeply? Here is tender nearness. They could not possibly be closer. Here is perfect safety. Who can hurt them when they are carried in His bosom? An enemy would have to hurt the Shepherd first. Here is perfect rest and sweetest comfort. May we become more fully aware of the infinite tenderness of Jesus!

May 15
Morning

"All that believe are justified" (Acts 13:39).

The believer in Christ receives a present justification. Faith does not produce this fruit by and by, but now. Since justification is the result of faith, it is given to the soul in the moment when it accepts Him. Are they who stand before the throne of God justified now? So are we, as truly and as clearly justified as they who walk in white and sing melodious praises to celestial harps. The thief on the cross was justified the moment he turned the eye of faith to Jesus. Paul the aged, after years of service, was not more justified than was the thief with no service at all. We are *today* accepted in the Beloved, *today* absolved from .sin, *today* acquitted. God supplies us in our journeying to and fro. We are pardoned *now*; *now* our sins are put away; *now* we stand in the sight of God accepted as though we had never been guilty. "There is therefore now no condemnation to them which are in Christ Jesus" (Romans 8:1). There is not a sin in the Book of God, even now, against one of His people. Who can lay anything to their charge? There is neither speck nor spot nor wrinkle nor any such thing remaining on any believer. Let present privilege awaken us to present duty; and now, while life lasts, let us spend and be spent for our sweet Lord Jesus.

May 15
Evening

"Made perfect" (Hebrews 12:13).

There are two kinds of perfection that the Christian needs to walk in—justification in the person of Jesus and sanctification by the Holy Spirit. Corruption still remains in the heart of the reborn Christian—experience soon teaches us this. But the day is coming when God will finish the work which He has begun. He will present my soul, not only perfect in Christ, but perfect through the Spirit, without spot or blemish. Can this poor, sinful heart of mine become holy, even as God is holy? My spirit often cries, "Oh, wretched man that I am! who shall deliver me from the body of this death?" (Romans 7:24). One day, I will be completely free from sin and death with no evil things to harass my ears or unholy thoughts to disturb my peace. When I cross the Jordan, the work of sanctification will be finished. My spirit will then have its last baptism in the Holy Spirit's fire. I long to die and receive that last and final purification which will usher me into heaven. I will be able to say, "I am clean," through Jesus' blood and through the Spirit's work. We should extol the power of the Holy Spirit for making us fit to stand before our Father in heaven! But the hope of perfection hereafter should not make us content with imperfection now. If it does this, our hope cannot be genuine. The work of grace must be abiding in us now or it cannot be perfected then. Let us pray to "be filled with the Spirit" (Ephesians 5:18), that we may bring forth the fruits of righteousness.

May 16
Morning

"Who giveth us richly all things to enjoy" (1 Timothy 6:17).

Our Lord Jesus is ever giving and does not for a solitary instant withdraw His hand. As long as there is a vessel of grace not yet full to the brim, the oil will not stop. The rain of His grace is always dropping. The river of His bounty is ever-flowing, and the well-spring of His love is constantly overflowing. As the King can never die, so His grace can never fail. Daily we pluck His fruit, and daily His branches bend down to our hand with a fresh store of mercy. There are seven feast days in His weeks. Who has ever returned from His door unblessed? Who has ever risen from His table unsatisfied? His mercies are new every morning and fresh every evening. Who can know the number of His benefits or recount the list of His bounties? The countless stars are like the standard bearers of a more innumerable host of blessings. Who can count the dust of the benefits which He bestowed on Jacob or tell the number of the fourth part of His mercies toward Israel? How will my soul extol Him who daily loads us with benefits and who crowns us with lovingkindness? Oh, that my praise could be as ceaseless as His bounty!

May 16
Evening

"And he said, Thus saith the Lord, Make this valley full of ditches. For thus saith the Lord, Ye shall not see wind, neither shall ye see rain; yet that valley shall be filled with water, that ye may drink, both ye, and your cattle, and your beasts" (2 Kings 3:16-17).

The armies of the three kings were dying for lack of water. God was ready to send it, and the prophet announced the coming blessing. Here was a case of *human helplessness.* All the valiant men could not obtain a drop of water from the wells of the earth. The people of the Lord saw their own inadequacy and knew that their help must be found in God alone. They were instructed to make *a believing preparation* for the divine blessing. They dug the trenches in which the precious liquid would be held. Likewise, the Church must prepare herself to be blessed. She must make the pools, and the Lord will fill them. This must be done in the full assurance that the blessing is about to descend. Finally, there was a *miraculous supply* of the water. In Elijah's case, the shower poured from the clouds, but here, the pools were filled in a silent and mysterious manner. The Lord has His own sovereign methods of action. Our job is to gratefully receive from Him and not to dictate to Him. We must also notice the *remarkable abundance* of the supply—there was enough for the need of all. It is the same with the gospel. All the needs of the entire Church will be met by the divine power in answer to prayer. What am I doing for Jesus? What trenches am I digging? O Lord, make me ready to receive the blessing which You are so willing to bestow.

May 17
Morning

"So to walk even as he walked" (1 John 2:6).

Why should Christians imitate Christ? They should do it for *their own sakes*. If they desire to be in a healthy state of soul—if they would escape the sickness of sin and enjoy the vigor of growing grace, let Jesus be their model. There is nothing which can so assist you to walk toward heaven with good speed, as wearing the image of Jesus on your heart to rule all its actions. It is when, by the power of the Holy Spirit, you are enabled to walk with Jesus in His very footsteps, that you are most happy and most known to be the sons of God. Next, for *faith's sake,* strive to be like Jesus. Faith has been sorely shot at by cruel enemies but has not been wounded half as dangerously by its enemies as by its friends. Who made those wounds in the fair hand of godliness? The professor who used the dagger of hypocrisy. The man who enters the fold, being nothing but a wolf in sheep's clothing, and worries the flock more than the lion outside. There is no weapon half as deadly as a Judas-kiss. Inconsistent professors injure the gospel more than the sneering critic or the infidel. But especially for *Christ's own sake*, imitate His example. Christian, do you love your Savior? Is His name precious to you? Would you see the kingdom of the world become His? Is it your desire that He should be glorified? Are you longing for souls to be won to Him? If so, imitate Jesus. Be an epistle of Christ, known and read of all men.

May 17
Evening

"Thou art My servant; I have chosen thee"
(Isaiah 41:9).

The grace of God in our hearts has made us God's servants. We may be unfaithful servants, and we certainly are unworthy ones. Yet, we *are* His servants, feeding at His table and obeying His commands. We were once the servants of sin. But He who made us free has taken us into His family and taught us obedience to His will. We do not serve our Master perfectly, but we would if we could. As we hear God's voice saying unto us, "Thou art My servant," we can answer with David, "I am thy servant. . .thou hast loosed my bonds" (Psalm 116:16). The Lord calls us not only His *servants,* but His *chosen ones.* We did not choose Him first, but He chose us. The eye of sovereignty singled us out, and the voice of unchanging grace declared, "I have loved thee with an everlasting love" (Jeremiah 31:3). Long before time began or space was created, God had written upon His heart the names of His elect people. He chose them to be conformed to the image of His Son and ordained them as heirs of all the fullness of His love, grace, and glory. He understood that our hearts were evil, and yet He made the choice. Our Savior is no fickle lover. He does not feel enchanted for a while with some gleam of beauty from His Church's eye, and then cast her off because of her unfaithfulness. No, He married her from eternity. It is written of Jehovah, "He hateth putting away" (Malachi 2:16). The eternal choice is a bond upon our gratitude and upon His faithfulness, which neither of us can disown.

May 18
Morning

"In him dwelleth all the fulness of the God-head bodily. And ye are complete in him" (Colossians 2:9-10).

All the attributes of Christ, as God and man, are at our disposal. He cannot endow us with the attributes of deity, but He has done all that can be done. How vast His grace, how firm His faithfulness, how unchangeable, how infinite His power, how limitless is His knowledge! All these are made the pillars of the temple of salvation by the Lord Jesus, and all are covenanted to us as our inheritance. The whole of Christ, in His adorable character as the Son of God, is given to us to enjoy. His wisdom is our direction, His knowledge our instruction, His power our protection, His justice our surety, His love our comfort, and His mercy our solace. He holds back nothing from us. Instead, He opens the recesses of the Mountain of God and bids us dig in the mines for the hidden treasures. "Everything is yours," He says, "Be filled and satisfied with the goodness of the Lord." Oh, how sweet to behold Jesus and to call on Him with the certain confidence that in seeking His love or power, we are only asking for what He already faithfully promised!

May 18
Evening

"Afterward" (Hebrews 12:11).

How happy are tried Christians, *afterward!* No calm is deeper than that which follows a storm. Who has not rejoiced in the sparkling sunshine after the rain? After climbing the Hill of Difficulty, we sit down in the shade to rest. After journeying through the Valley of Humiliation, after fighting with the prince of darkness, the Shining One appears with the healing branch from the tree of life. Our sorrow, like the passing wake of a vessel upon the sea, leaves a silver line of holy light behind it, "afterward." Sweet, deep peace follows the horrible turmoil which once reigned in our guilty souls. The Christian receives the best things last. But even his worst things are "afterward" good things, just as difficult plowing yields a joyful harvest. Even now he grows rich by his losses, he rises by his falls, he lives by dying, and becomes full by being emptied. Since his grievous afflictions yield him so much peaceable fruit in this life what will be the full measure of joy "afterward" in heaven? If he can sing in a dungeon, how sweetly will he sing in heaven! If difficulties seem good to him *now,* what will be the overflowing goodness of God to him *then?* Who would not bear the present cross for the crown which will come afterward? But patience is required for the rest is not for today, and the triumph is not for the present, but "afterward." Wait, and let patience have her perfect work.

May 19
Morning

"I have seen servants upon horses, and princes walking as servants upon the earth" (Ecclesiastes 10:7).

Upstarts frequently usurp the highest places, while the truly great pine away in obscurity. This is a riddle in providence whose solution will one day gladden the hearts of the upright, but it is a common fact that none of us should murmur if it should fall to our own lot. When our Lord was on earth, He walked the footpath of weariness and service as the Servant of servants. The world is upside down. Therefore, the first are last, and the last first. When the wheel turns, those who are lowest rise, and the highest sink. Have patience believer! Eternity will right the wrongs of time. Grace must reign as a prince and make the members of the body instruments of righteousness. The Holy Spirit loves order, and He therefore sets our powers and faculties in due rank and place, giving the highest room to those spiritual faculties which link us with the great King. Let us not disturb the divine arrangement but ask for grace that we may keep our bodies under subjection. We were not recreated to allow our passions to rule over us, but that we, as kings, may reign in Christ Jesus over the triple kingdom of our spirit, soul, and body, to the glory of God the Father.

May 19
Evening

"And he requested for himself that he might die" (1 Kings 19:4).

This was a remarkable prayer from the man who was never to die. Elijah was to be carried to heaven in a chariot of fire. Yet, he had come to a point of severe discouragement, and he prayed, "Let me die; I am no better than my fathers." God does not always give us exactly what we pray for, though He always does answer our prayers. He gave Elijah something better than what he requested. Thus, God truly heard and answered him. It seems strange that the lionhearted Elijah would be depressed by Jezebel's threat and ask to die. Our heavenly Father was blessedly kind in that He did not take His discouraged servant at his word. There is a limit to the doctrine of the prayer of faith. We are not to expect that God will grant our every request. We know that we sometimes ask and do not receive because we ask wrongly. (See James 4:3.) We may ask for something that is not promised, or we may be opposing the spirit which the Lord wants us to cultivate. We sometimes ask contrary to His will or to the decrees of His providence. Or we ask merely for the gratification of our own ease and without consideration of His glory; then, we must not expect to receive. When we ask in unwavering faith and do not receive the precise thing asked for, we will receive more than an equivalent for it. As one remarks, "If the Lord does not pay in silver, He will in gold; and if He does not pay in gold, He will in diamonds." If He does not give you precisely what you ask for, He will give you something that is equal or better.

May 20
Morning

"Marvellous lovingkindness" (Psalm 17:7).

When we give our hearts with our alms, we give well; but we often fail in this respect. Not so our Master and our Lord. His favors are always performed with the love of His heart. He does not send us the cold meat and the broken pieces from the table of His luxury. Instead, He dips our morsel in His own dish, seasoned with the spices of His fragrant affections. He will come into our homes on His errands of kindness and will not act as some visitors do in the poor man's cottage. He will sit by our side and not despise our poverty. What comforting words come from His gracious lips! What embraces of affection He bestows upon us! It is impossible to doubt the sincerity of His love, for there is a bleeding heart stamped on the face of all His charitable donations. He gives liberally and upbraideth not with not one hint that we are burdensome to Him. He instead rejoices in His mercy and presses us to His bosom while He is pouring out His life for us. There is a sweetness in His honeycomb which could not be in it unless the very essence of His soul's affection had been mingled with it. May we continually taste and know the blessedness of it!

May 20
Evening

"I drew them with cords of a man, with bands of love" (Hosea 11:4).

Our heavenly Father often draws us with the cords of love. But how hesitant we are to run toward Him! How slowly we respond to His gentle impulses! He draws us to *exercise a more simple faith in Him.* We do not leave our worldly cares with God, but like Martha, we burden ourselves with much serving. Our meager faith brings leanness into our souls. We do not open our mouths wide, though God has promised to fill them. (See Psalm 81:10.) He draws us to Himself this evening. We can hear Him say, "Come My child and trust Me. The veil has been torn. Enter into My presence and boldly approach the throne of My grace. I am worthy of your fullest confidence. Shake off the dust of your cares, and put on the beautiful garments of joy." The Father also *draws us to closer communion* with Himself. We have been sitting on the doorstep of God's house. He invites us to come into the banquet hall and dine with Him. But we decline the honor. There are secret rooms which are not yet opened to us. Jesus calls us to enter them, but we hold back. We are poor lovers of our sweet Lord Jesus, not fit to be His servants, much less to be His brides. Yet, He exalted us to be bone of His bone and flesh of His flesh. We are married to Him by a glorious marriage covenant. This is true love! But it is love which *takes no denial.* What foolish children we are to refuse those bands of love.

May 21
Morning

"If so be ye have tasted that the Lord is gracious" (1 Peter 2:3).

"If"—then there is a possibility that some may not have tasted that the Lord is gracious. There is no spiritual favor which is not a matter for heart searching. But while this should be a matter of earnest and prayerful inquiry, no one should be content while there is any such thing as an "if" about his having tasted that the Lord is gracious. A jealous and holy distrust of self may give rise to the question even in the believer's heart, but the continuance of such a doubt would be an evil. We must not rest without a desperate struggle to clasp the Savior in the arms of faith and say, "I know whom I have believed, and I am persuaded that he is able to keep that which I have committed unto him" (2 Timothy 1:12). Let nothing satisfy you until, by the infallible witness of the Holy Spirit bearing witness with your spirit, you are certified that you are a child of God. Do not trifle here. Let no "perhaps" or "if" or "maybe" satisfy your soul. Get the sure mercies of David. Advance beyond these dreary "ifs." Abide no more in the wilderness of doubts and fears. Cross the Jordan of distrust and enter the Canaan of peace, where the Canaanite still lingers, but where the land does not cease to flow with milk and honey.

May 21
Evening

"There is corn in Egypt" (Genesis 42:2).

Famine had a strangle hold on all the nations. It seemed inevitable that Jacob and his family would suffer greatly because of it. But the God of providence who never forgets the object of His love stored a granary for His people. He gave the Egyptians warning of the scarcity and led them to treasure up grain during the years of plenty. Jacob did not expect assistance from Egypt, but there was corn in store for him there. Believer, though all things appear to be against you, rest assured that God has made a provision on your behalf. In the midst of your grief, there is a saving grace. Somehow He will deliver you, and somewhere He will provide for you. The place from which your rescue arises may be a very unexpected one. But help will surely come. If men do not feed you, ravens will. If earth does not yield wheat, heaven will drop with manna. Therefore, be of good courage and rest quietly in the Lord. God can make the sun rise in the west if He pleases. He will make the source of distress become the channel of delight. The corn in Egypt was all in the control of Joseph. Likewise, the richest blessings are all in the absolute power of our Lord Jesus. He will dispense them liberally to His people. Jesus is unceasing in His faithful care for His brethren. Prayer will bring us into the presence of our royal Brother. Once before His throne, we must only ask and receive. Lord, forgive our unbelief. This evening, cause us to draw upon Your fullness and receive grace for grace.

May 22
Morning

"He led them forth by the right way" (Psalm 107:7).

Changes often lead the anxious believer to inquire, "Why is it like this with me? I looked for light, but darkness came. I looked for peace but experienced trouble. I said in my heart, 'My mountain stands firm; I will never be moved.' It was only yesterday that I could read my title clear. Today, my hopes are clouded. Is this part of God's plan for me? Can this be the way in which God would bring me to heaven?" Yes, it could be. The eclipse of your faith, the darkness of your mind, the fainting of your hope—all these things are part of God's method of making you ready for the great inheritance which you will soon receive. These trials are for the testing and strengthening of your faith—they are waves that wash you farther upon the rock—they are winds which waft your ship more swiftly toward the desired haven. According to David's words, so it might be said of you, "So he bringeth them to their desired haven" (Psalm 107:30). By honor and dishonor, by evil report and by good report, by plenty and by poverty, by joy and by distress, by persecution and by peace, by all these things is the life of your soul maintained. Do not think, believer, that your sorrows are out of God's plan; they are necessary parts of it. "We must, through much tribulation, enter the kingdom" (Acts 14:22). Learn then to "count it all joy when ye fall into divers temptations" (James 1:2).

May 22
Evening

"Behold, thou art fair, my beloved" (Song of Solomon 1:16).

From every point of view, our Beloved is most beautiful. We have seen Him from the mountaintop, and He has shone upon us as the sun in its strength. But we have seen Him also "from the lions' dens, from the mountains of the leopards" (Song of Solomon 4:8). Even there, He has lost none of His loveliness. From the sick bed to the borders of the grave, we turned our eyes to our soul's Spouse. He has never been otherwise than "all fair." Many of His saints looked upon Him from the gloom of dungeons and from the red flames of the stake. They never uttered an ill word of Him, but died extolling His surpassing greatness. How noble and pleasant it is to be forever gazing at our sweet Lord Jesus! It is unspeakably delightful to view the Savior in all His offices and find that He is matchless in each. It is as if we shift the kaleidoscope of His character and find fresh combinations of peerless grace. In the manger and in eternity, on the cross and on His throne, in the garden and in His Kingdom, among thieves or in the midst of cherubim, He is everywhere "altogether lovely." Carefully examine every act of His life and every trait of His character. He will not be found lacking in any good thing. As ages revolve, His hidden glories will shine forth with even more splendor, and His loveliness will fill all celestial hearts with rapturous joy.

May 23
Morning

"The Lord will perfect that which concerneth me" (Psalm 138:8).

The confidence which the psalmist expressed here was a divine confidence. He did not say, "I have grace enough to perfect that which concerneth me—my faith is so steady that it will not stagger—my love is so warm that it will never grow cold—my resolution is so firm that nothing can move it." No, his dependence was on the Lord alone. If we indulge in any confidence which is not grounded on the Rock of Ages, our confidence is worse than a dream. It will fall on us and cover us with its ruins, to our sorrow and confusion. All that nature spins, time will unravel, to the eternal confusion of all who are clothed therein. The psalmist was wise. He rested on nothing short of the Lord's work. It is the Lord who has begun the good work within us. It is He who has carried it on. If He does not finish it, it never will be complete. This is our confidence, the Lord who began will perfect. Our confidence must not be in what *we* have done, but entirely in what *the Lord* will do. Unbelief insinuates that You will never be able to stand. Yes, we would indeed perish if left to our own strength. But thanks be to God, He will perfect that which concerns us and bring us to the desired haven. We can never be too confident when we confide in Him alone.

May 23
Evening

"Thou hast bought me no sweet cane with money" (Isaiah 43:24).

Worshippers at the temple usually brought presents of sweet perfume to be burned upon the altar of God. But backsliding Israel became selfish and made few votive offerings to her Lord. This was evidence of the coldness of her heart toward God and His house. Could the complaint of the text be occasionally, if not frequently, brought against you? Those who are poor in pocket but rich in faith will be no less accepted because their gifts are small. Do you give in fair proportion to the Lord or is the widow's mite kept back from the sacred treasury? The rich believer should be thankful for the wealth entrusted to him, but he should not forget his large responsibility. Where much is given, much will be required. (See Luke 12:48.) Do you realize your obligation to give to the Lord according to the benefit received? Jesus gave His blood for us. What shall we give to Him? We and all that we have are His, for He has purchased us for Himself. How can we continue to act as if we were our own? Oh, for more consecration and more love! Blessed Jesus, nothing is too costly to give as a tribute to Your unrivaled love. Yet, You receive with favor the smallest sincere token of affection! You receive our poor forget-me-nots as though they were infinitely precious, though they are like the bunch of wild flowers which the child brings to its mother. May we never grow stingy toward You. From this hour on, may we never hear You complain of us withholding the gifts of our love.

May 24
Morning

"Blessed be God, which hath not turned away my prayer" (Psalm 66:20).

In looking back on the character of our prayers, if we do it honestly, we will be filled with wonder that God ever answered them. There may be some who think their prayers are worthy of acceptance—as the Pharisee did. The true Christian, in a more enlightened retrospect, weeps over his prayers. If he could retrace his steps, he would desire to pray more earnestly. Remember, Christian, how cold your prayers have been. In your prayer closet you should have wrestled as Jacob did. Instead, your petitions have been faint and few—far removed from that humble, believing, persevering faith which cries, "I will not let thee go except thou bless me" (Genesis 32:26). Yet, wonderful to say, God has heard these cold prayers of yours. Not only has He heard, but He has answered them. Reflect, also, how infrequently you have prayed. God has not ceased to bless. It is marvelous that the Lord should regard those intermittent prayers which come and go with our necessities. What a God He is to hear the prayers of those who come to Him when they have pressing needs but neglect Him when they have received a mercy. They approach Him when they are forced to come but forget to address Him when mercies are plentiful and sorrows are few! Let His gracious kindness in hearing such prayers touch our hearts, so that we may henceforth be found "praying always with all prayer and supplication in the spirit" (Ephesians 6:18).

May 24
Evening

"Only let your conversation be as it becometh the gospel of Christ" (Philippians 1:27).

The word *conversation* includes the whole course of our life and behavior in the world. The Greek word signifies the actions and the privileges of citizenship. Thus, we are commanded to let our actions, as citizens of the New Jerusalem, give glory to the gospel of Christ. *The gospel is very simple.* There should be a simplicity about our manner, our speech, our dress, and our whole behavior. This is the very soul of beauty. The gospel is *perfectly true.* The Christian's life will be lusterless and valueless without the jewel of truth. The gospel is a very *fearless gospel.* It boldly proclaims the truth, whether men like it or not. We must be equally faithful and unflinching. But the gospel is also *very gentle.* Notice the spirit of its Founder: "A bruised reed shall he not break" (Matthew 12:20). Let us seek to win others by the gentleness of our words and acts. The gospel is *very loving.* It is the message of the God of love to a lost and fallen race. Christ's last command to His disciples was, "Love one another" (John 13:34). Let there be more unity and love among the saints. Let there be more tender compassion toward the souls of the worst and vilest of men! We must not forget that the gospel of Christ is *holy.* It never excuses sin. It pardons it, but only through an atonement. If our life is to resemble the gospel, we must shun everything that would hinder our perfect conformity to Christ. For His sake, for our own sakes, and for the sake of others, we must strive day by day to let our conversation be more in accordance with His gospel.

May 25
Morning

"Forsake me not, O Lord" (Psalm 38:21).

We frequently pray that God will not forsake us in times of trial and temptation, but we forget that we need to use this prayer at all times. There is no moment of our life, however holy, in which we can do without His constant upholding. Whether in light or in darkness, in communion or in temptation, we need the prayer, "Forsake me not, O Lord. Hold me up, and I shall be safe." A little child, while learning to walk, always needs aid. The ship left by the pilot drifts at once from her course. We cannot do without continued aid from above. Father, do not forsake Your child, lest he fall by the hand of the enemy. Shepherd, do not forsake Your lamb, lest he wander from the safety of the fold. Do not forsake me in my joys, lest they absorb my heart. Do not forsake me in my sorrows, lest I murmur against You. Do not forsake me, for without You I am weak, but with You I am strong. Do not forsake me, for my path is dangerous and full of snares. I cannot do without Your guidance. "Be not far from me, O Lord, for trouble is near, for there is none to help" (Psalm 22:11). "Leave me not, neither forsake me, O God of my salvation" (Psalm 27:9).

May 25
Evening

"And they rose up the same hour, and returned to Jerusalem...And they told what things were done in the way, and how he was known of them" (Luke 24:33,35).

When the two disciples reached Emmaus, they refreshed themselves at the evening meal. The mysterious stranger who had fascinated them on the road took bread and broke it, thus making Himself known to them. He then vanished out of their sight. They had convinced Him to stay with them because it was already early evening. But now, although it was much later, their love was a lamp to their eyes and wings on their feet. They journeyed back seven and a half miles to tell the glorious news of a risen Lord. When they reached the disciples in Jerusalem, they were greeted by another burst of joyful news. They were on fire to speak of Christ's resurrection and to proclaim what they knew of the Lord. We too must bear our witness concerning Jesus. John's account of the empty tomb needed to be supplemented by Peter, and Mary added more details. Combined, we have a full testimony from which nothing can be spared. Each of us has peculiar gifts and special abilities. But God's ultimate purpose is the perfecting of the whole body of Christ. We must bring our spiritual possessions and share what God has given to us with everyone. Speak what you know and testify what you have seen. Do not let the toil, darkness, or possible unbelief of your friends weigh one moment in the scale. Rise up, and march to the place of duty. There, tell what great things God has done for you.

May 26
Morning

"Cast thy burden upon the Lord, and he shall sustain thee" (Psalm 55:22).

Worry, if carried to excess, has the nature of sin in it. The precept to avoid worry is repeated frequently by our Savior. It is reiterated by the apostles. It is a principle which cannot be neglected without involving transgression. We labor to take on ourselves our weary burden, as if He were unable or unwilling to take it for us. This disobedience to His principle, this unbelief in His Word, is all sinful. More than this, worry often leads to acts of sin. He who cannot calmly leave his affairs in God's hand is very likely to be tempted to use wrong means to help himself. This sin leads to forsaking God as our Counselor and resorting instead to human wisdom. This is going to the "broken cistern" instead of to the "fountain;" a sin which was laid against Israel of old. Anxiety makes us doubt God's lovingkindness, and our love for Him grows cold. We feel mistrust and grieve the Spirit of God, so that our prayers become hindered, our consistent example marred, and our life one of self-seeking. Thus, lack of confidence in God leads us to wander far from Him. If we cast each burden as it comes on Him and we are "careful for nothing" because He undertakes to care for us, it will keep us close to Him and strengthen us against such temptation. "Thou wilt keep him in perfect peace whose mind is stayed on thee because he trusteth in thee" (Isaiah 26:3).

May 26
Evening

"Continue in the faith" (Acts 14:22).

Perseverance is the badge of true saints. The Christian life is more than a beginning in the ways of God. It is also a continuance in the faith as long as life lasts. It is the same with a Christian as it was with the great Napoleon who said, "Conquest has made me what I am, and conquest must maintain me." The only true conqueror who will be crowned is the one that continues until war's trumpet is blown no more. Perseverance is, therefore, the target of all our spiritual enemies. The *world* does not object to you being a Christian for a time if she can tempt you to give up your journey and settle down in her Vanity Fair. The *flesh* will seek to entangle you and prevent you from pressing on to glory. "It is weary work being a Christian. Come, give it up. Must I always be humble? Am I never to be indulged? Give me at least a vacation from this constant warfare." *Satan* will make many fierce attacks on your perseverance. It will be the target for all his arrows. He will strive to hinder you *in service.* He will insinuate that you are doing no good. He will endeavor to make you weary of *suffering.* He will whisper, "Curse God, and die" (Job 2:9). He will attack your *steadfastness:* "What is the good of being so zealous? Be quiet like the rest." He will assail your *doctrinal beliefs:* "Why do you hold to these denominational creeds? Sensible men are getting more liberal. They are removing the old landmarks. Blend in with the times." Wear your shield, Christian, close to your armor. Pray to God that, by His Spirit, you may endure to the end.

May 27
Morning

"So Mephibosheth dwelt in Jerusalem: for he did eat continually at the king's table; and was lame on both his feet" (2 Samuel 9:13).

Mephibosheth was no great ornament to a royal table, yet he had a continual place at David's table because the king could see in his face the features of the beloved Jonathan. Like Mephibosheth, we may cry to the King of Glory, "What is thy servant, that thou shouldst look upon such a dead dog as I am?" (2 Samuel 9:8). But still the Lord indulges us in communion with Himself, because He sees in our countenances the remembrance of His dearly-beloved Jesus. Such is the love which the Father bears to His only begotten. For His sake He raises His lowly brethren from poverty to courtly companionship, noble rank, and royal provision. Their deformity shall not rob them of their privileges. Lameness is no bar to sonship. The cripple is as much the heir as if he could run like Asahel. Yet, grievous disability may mar the persons of the best-loved saints. Saints whose faith is weak and whose knowledge is slender are great losers. They are exposed to many enemies and cannot follow the king everywhere he goes. Bad nursing in their spiritual infancy often causes converts to fall into a despondency from which they never recover. Lord, help the lame to leap like a hart and satisfy all Your people with the bread of your table!

May 27
Evening

"What is thy servant, that thou shouldest look upon such a dead dog as I am?" (2 Samuel 9:8).

The more grace we have, the less we think of ourselves with pride. Grace, like light, reveals our impurity. Distinguished saints have scarcely known what to compare themselves to because of their keen sense of unworthiness. "I am," says holy Rutherford, "a dry and withered branch, a piece of dead carcass, dry bones, and not able to step over a straw." The most vile objects in nature have an advantage because they have never contracted sin. A dog may be greedy, fierce, or filthy, but it has no conscience to violate, no Holy Spirit to resist. A dog may be a worthless animal, and yet, by a little kindness, it will love its master and be faithful until death. We forget the goodness of the Lord, however, and do not follow Him when He calls. The term *dead dog* is the most expressive of all terms of contempt. But it is not too strong to express the self-abhorrence of instructed believers. They do not only pretend to be modest. They have weighed themselves in the balance of the sanctuary and discovered the vanity of their nature. At best, we are mere clay and animated dust. But viewed as sinners, we are monsters indeed. It is a wonder that the Lord Jesus loves us. Though we are dust and ashes, we must and will "magnify the exceeding greatness of his power" (Ephesians 1:19). Could His heart find rest in heaven? Must He look elsewhere for His pure and unblemished bride?

May 28
Morning

"Whom he justified, them he also glorified" (Romans 8:30).

Believer, here is a precious truth for you. You may be poor or suffering, but for encouragement take a review of your "calling" and the consequences that flow from it. Especially that blessed result spoken of here. As surely as you are God's child today, so surely will all your trials be at an end. Your weary head will wear the crown of glory, and hand of labor will grasp the palm branch of victory. Do not lament your troubles, but rather rejoice that before long you will be where "there shall be neither sorrow nor crying, neither shall there be any more pain" (Revelation 21:4). The chariots of fire are at your door, and a moment will suffice to bear you to the glorified. The everlasting song is almost on your lips. The portals of heaven stand open for you. If He has called you, nothing can divide you from His love. Distress cannot sever the bond. The fire of persecution cannot burn the link. The hammer of hell cannot break the chain. You are secure. That voice which called you at first will call you again from earth to heaven, from death's dark gloom to immortality's unuttered splendors. Rest assured; the heart of Him who has justified you beats with infinite love toward you. You will soon be with the glorified, where your portion is. You are only waiting here to be made meet for the inheritance. Once that is done, the wings of angels will lift you far away to the mount of peace, joy, and blessedness where you will rest forever and ever.

May 28
Evening

"This I recall to my mind, therefore have I hope" (Lamentations 3:21).

Memory is frequently the slave of depression. Despairing minds call to remembrance every dark experience in the past and expand upon every gloomy prospect in the present. Memory, clothed in sackcloth, presents a cup of mingled gall and bitterness to the mind. There is, however, no necessity for this. Wisdom can readily transform memory into an angel of comfort. That same recollection which brings so many gloomy omens may also bear a wealth of hopeful signs. This was Jeremiah's experience. Memory brought him to deep humiliation of soul: "My soul hath them still in remembrance, and is humbled in me" (Lamentations 3:20). Now, this same memory restored him to life and comfort. "This I recall to my mind, therefore have I hope." If we exercise our memories more wisely, we might, in our very darkest distress, strike a match which would immediately kindle the lamp of comfort. There is no need for God to create a new way to restore believers to joy. If they would prayerfully rake the ashes of the past, they would find light for the present. If they would turn to the Book of truth and the throne of grace, their candle would soon shine again. It is our duty to remember the lovingkindness of the Lord and to recall His deeds of grace. Let us open the volume of recollection which is richly illuminated with memorials of mercy. Memory may be, as Coleridge calls it, "the bosom-spring of joy." When the divine Comforter bends it to His service, memory may be chief among earthly comforters.

May 29
Morning

"Thou hatest wickedness" (Psalm 45:7).

Be ye angry and sin not. There can hardly be goodness in a man if he is not angry at sin. He that loves truth must hate every false way. How our Lord Jesus hated it when the temptation came. Three times it assailed Him in different forms, but He met it with "Get thee behind me, Satan" (Mark 8:33). He hated it when temptation came to others. He showed His hate more often in tears of pity than in words of rebuke. Yet, what language could be more stern, more Elijah-like, than the words, "Woe unto you, Scribes and Pharisees, hypocrites! for ye devour widows' houses, and for a pretense make long prayers" (Matthew 23:14). He hated wickedness so much that He bled on the cross to destroy it. He rose that He might forever trample it beneath His feet. Christ is in the gospel, and that gospel is opposed to wickedness in every shape. Wickedness arrays itself in fair garments and imitates the language of holiness. But the precepts of Jesus, like His famous scourge of small cords, chase it out of the temple and will not tolerate it in the Church. When our Redeemer comes to be our Judge, His words will manifest His abhorrence of iniquity. As perfect as is His righteousness, so complete will be the destruction of every form of wickedness. Oh, glorious champion of right and destroyer of wrong, for this cause has God, even your God, anointed you with the oil of gladness.

May 29
Evening

"Cursed be the man before the Lord, that riseth up and buildeth this city Jericho" (Joshua 6:26).

Since he was cursed who rebuilt Jericho, much more cursed are those who labor to spread the kingdom of Satan among us. Gigantic strongholds of sin will fall by the power of our faith, the perseverance of our efforts, and the blast of our gospel trumpets. We should be serious about removing every error which may foster the spirit of bondage to ungodly principles and a lukewarm love for Christ. When we have made a clean sweep at home, we should seek in every way to oppose sin's all too rapid spread abroad in the Church and in the world. This can be done in secret by fervent prayer and in public by bold testimony. We must warn those who are inclined to believe the errors of false religions. We must instruct the young in gospel truth. We must aid in spreading the light more thoroughly through the land, for messengers of Satan, like owls, hate daylight. Are we doing all we can for Jesus and the gospel? If not, our negligence plays into the hands of the enemy. What are we doing to spread the Bible which is the devil's bane and poison? Are we sending out good, sound gospel writings? Luther once said, "The devil hates goose quills." Doubtless, he has good reason, for ready writers, by the Holy Spirit's blessing, have done Satan's kingdom much damage. If the thousands who will read this short word this night will do all they can to hinder the rebuilding of this accursed Jericho, the Lord's glory will make a rapid advance among the sons of men. What can you do? What will you do?

May 30
Morning

"Take us the foxes, the little foxes that spoil the vines" (Song of Solomon 2:15).

A little thorn may cause much suffering. A little cloud may hide the sun. Little foxes spoil the vines, and little sins do mischief to the tender heart. These little sins burrow in the soul and make it full of that which is hateful to Christ, so that He will hold no comfortable fellowship and communion with us. A great sin cannot destroy a Christian, but a little sin can make him miserable. Jesus will not walk with His people unless they drive out every known sin. He says, "If ye keep my commandments, ye shall abide in my love, even as I have kept my Father's commandments and abide in his love" (John 15:10). Some Christians very seldom enjoy their Savior's presence. Why is this? Surely it must be an affliction for a tender child to be separated from his father. How can you be the spouse of Christ and be content without His company? Ask the question—What has driven Christ from me? If you want to live with Christ, walk with Christ, and have fellowship with Christ, take heed of the little foxes that spoil the vines. Our vines have tender grapes. Jesus invites you to go with Him. He will surely, like Samson, easily take the foxes at once. Go with Him to the hunting.

May 30
Evening

"That henceforth we should not serve sin"
(Romans 6:6).

Christian, what have you to do with sin? Has it not cost you enough already? Burnt child, will you continue to play with fire? When you have already been between the jaws of the lion, will you step into his den a second time? Have you not had enough of the old serpent? He poisoned you once. Will you play near the hole of the viper and put your hand upon the cobra's den a second time? Oh, do not be so foolish! Did sin ever give you any real pleasure? Did you find solid satisfaction in it? If so, go back to your old drudgery and wear the chain again. But sin never did give you what it promised to bestow. Rather, it deluded you with lies. Do not be snared again. Be free and let the remembrance of your ancient bondage forbid you to enter the net again. Sin is contrary to the designs of eternal love. God desires your purity and holiness. Do not oppose the purposes of your Lord. *Christians can never sin cheaply.* Transgression destroys peace of mind, obscures fellowship with Jesus, hinders prayer, and brings darkness over the soul. Therefore, do not be the slave of sin. Each time you serve sin, you "crucify. . .the Son of God afresh, and put Him to an open shame" (Hebrews 6:6). Can you bear *that* thought? If you have fallen into any sin during this day, the Master has sent this admonition this evening to bring you back before you have backslidden very far. Turn to Jesus anew. He has not forgotten His love for you. His grace is still the same. With weeping and repentance, come to His footstool. You will be received once more into His heart.

May 31
Morning

"The king also himself passed over the brook Kidron" (2 Samuel 15:23).

David passed that gloomy brook when fleeing from his traitor son. The man after God's own heart was not exempt from trouble. In fact, his life was full of it. He was both the Lord's anointed and the Lord's afflicted. Why then should we expect to escape? Why should we complain as though some strange thing had happened to us? The King of kings Himself was not favored with a more cheerful or royal road. He passed over the filthy ditch of Kidron through which the filth of Jerusalem flowed. God had one Son without sin, but not a single child without the rod. It is a great joy to believe that Jesus has been tempted in all points like we are. What is our Kidron this morning? Is it a faithless friend, a sad bereavement, or a slanderous reproach? The King has passed over all these. Is it bodily pain, poverty, persecution, or contempt? Over each of these Kidrons, the King has gone before us. "In all our afflictions he was afflicted" (Isaiah 63:9). The idea of strangeness in our trials must be banished at once and forever. He, who is the Head of all saints, knows by experience the grief which we think so peculiar. David's Lord arose victorious from the grave. Let us then be of good courage, for we will be victorious also. We will draw water out of the wells of salvation with joy, though for a season we have to pass by the noxious streams of sin and sorrow. Have courage, soldiers of the Cross. The King Himself triumphed after going over Kidron, and so will you.

May 31
Evening

"Who healeth all thy diseases" (Psalm 103:3).

We are all to some degree suffering under the disease of sin. What a comfort to know that we have a great Physician who is both able and willing to heal us! His cures are *speedy*. There is life in a look at Him. His cures are *radical*. He strikes at the center of the disease. He never fails, and *the disease never returns*. There is no relapse where Christ heals. His patients are not merely patched up temporarily. He makes new men of them. He gives a new heart and places a right spirit within them. He is well skilled in all diseases. Physicians generally have some area of specialty. Although they may know a little about almost all our pains and ills, there is usually one disease which they have studied above all others. But Jesus Christ is thoroughly acquainted with all of human nature. He is as much at home with one sinner as with another. Never yet did He meet an unusual case that was difficult for Him to cure. He has had extraordinary complications of strange diseases to deal with, but He always knows exactly how to treat the patient. The medicine He gives is the only true remedy in every instance. Whatever our spiritual malady may be, we should call the divine Physician at once. There is no brokenness of heart which Jesus cannot bind up. "The blood of Jesus Christ his Son cleanseth from all sin" (1 John 1:7). Countless thousands have been delivered from all sorts of diseases through the power of His touch. Let us joyfully put ourselves in His hands.

June 1
Morning

"The evening and the morning were the first day" (Genesis 1:5).

Did light and darkness divide the realm of time in the first day? Then little wonder is it if I also have changes in my circumstances from the sunshine of prosperity to the midnight of adversity. I must expect at seasons to mourn the absence of my former joys and to seek my Beloved in the night. I'm not alone in this, for all the Lord's beloved ones have had to sing the mingled song of judgment and of mercy, of trial and deliverance, of mourning and of delight. It is one of the arrangements of divine providence that day and night will not cease, either in the spiritual or natural creation, until we reach the land of which it is written, "There is no night there" (Revelation 22:5). What our heavenly Father ordains is wise and good. What then, my soul, is best for you to do? Learn first to be content with this divine order. Praise the Lord for the sun of joy when it rises and for the gloom of evening as it falls. There is beauty both in sunrise and sunset. Like the nightingale, pour forth your notes at all hours. Believe that the night is as useful as the day. The stars of promise shine forth gloriously amid the darkness of grief. Continue your service under all changes. Continue in your calling as the Lord's servant until He suddenly appears in His glory.

June 1
Evening

"He will make her wilderness like Eden"
(Isaiah 51:3).

I see a vision of a howling wilderness, a great and terrible desert like the Sahara. I am surrounded by hot and arid sand which is covered with ten thousand bleached skeletons of wretched men. They have expired in anguish, having lost their way in the pitiless waste. What an appalling sight!—a sea of sand without end and without an oasis, a cheerless graveyard for a forlorn race! But behold and wonder! Suddenly, springing from the scorched sand, I see a green plant. As it grows, it buds, and the bud expands. It is a rose, and at its side a lily bows its modest head. As the fragrance of the flowers is diffused, the wilderness is transformed into a fruitful field. The desert begins to blossom as the glory of Lebanon is given to it. Where the skeletons lay bleaching in the sun, behold, a resurrection is proclaimed. The dead spring up as a mighty army, full of eternal life. Jesus is that plant in the desert. His presence makes all things new. The wonder of life springing from death is no less in each individual's salvation. The Father describes you as an infant, naked, unwashed, and defiled with blood, left to be food for beasts of prey. (See Ezekiel 16:3-6.) But you have been pitied and rescued by divine providence. You are washed and cleansed from your defilement. You are adopted into heaven's family, the fair seal of love is upon your forehead, and the ring of faithfulness is on your hand. Oh, how precious is the matchless power and grace which changes deserts into gardens and makes the barren heart sing for joy.

June 2
Morning

"For the flesh lusteth against the Spirit, and the Spirit against the flesh" (Galatians 5:17).

There is a constant struggle between the old nature and the new in every believer's heart. The old nature is very active and loses no opportunity of plying all the weapons of its deadly armory against new-born grace. On the other hand, the new nature is ever on the watch to resist and destroy its enemy. Grace within us will employ prayer, faith, hope, and love to cast out evil. It puts on the "whole armor of God" and wrestles earnestly. These two opposing natures will never cease to struggle so long as we are in this world. With Jesus, who is always with us, the new-born nature is more than a match for its foes. Are you fighting with the adversary today? Are Satan, the world, and the flesh all against you? Do not be discouraged. Fight on! For God Himself is with you. *Jehovah Nissi* is your banner, and *Jehovah Rophi* is the healer of your wounds. You will overcome, for who can defeat omnipotence? Fight on, looking to Jesus. Although the conflict may be long and hard, the victory will be sweet. Jesus, the Captain of our salvation, assures us that we will eventually become more than conquerors through Him who loves us.

June 2
Evening

"Good Master" (Matthew 19:16).

If the young man in the gospel used this title in speaking to our Lord, how much more proper it is for me to address Him this way! He is indeed my Master—a ruling Master and a teaching Master. I delight to run His errands and to sit at His feet. I am both His servant and His disciple. If He asks me why I call Him *good,* I have a ready answer. "There is none good but one, that is, God" (Matthew 19:17). But He is God, and all the goodness of Deity shines forth in Him. All the good I have has come to me through Him. He was good to me when I was dead in sin, for He raised me by His Spirit's power. He has been good to me in all my needs, trials, struggles, and sorrows. Never could there be a better Master, for His service is freedom, and His rule is love. When He teaches me as my Rabbi, He is unspeakably good. His doctrine is divine, His manner is patient, and His Spirit is gentleness itself. No error mingles with His instruction—the golden truth He brings forth is pure, and all His teachings sanctify as well as edify the disciple. The ancient saints proved Him to be a good Master. Each of them rejoiced to sing, "I am Thy servant, O Lord!" My humble testimony must be the same. I will speak of His greatness to my friends and neighbors, for they may be led by my testimony to seek my Lord Jesus as their Master. They would never regret so wise a deed. If they would take His easy yoke, they would find themselves in so royal a service that they would enlist in it forever.

June 3
Morning

"These were potters, and those that dwelt among plants and hedges: there they dwelt with the king for his work" (1 Chronicles 4:23).

Potters were not the very highest grade of workers, but the king needed potters. Therefore, they were in royal service even though the material they worked on was nothing but clay. We, too, may be engaged in the most menial part of the Lord's work, but it is a great privilege to do anything for the King. Those who dwelt among plants and hedges had rough, rustic, hedging and ditching work to do. They may have desired to live in the city amid its refinement, but they kept their appointed places because they also were doing the king's work. The place of our habitation is fixed. We are not to leave it out of whim, but we are to seek to serve the Lord in it by being a blessing to those among whom we reside. These potters and gardeners had royal company, for they dwelt with the king. No menial occupation can keep us from communion with our divine Lord. In visiting crowded dwellings, workplaces, or jails, we may go *with the King.* In all works of faith, we may count on Jesus' fellowship. When we are in His work, we are confident of His approval. You unknown workers who are occupied for your Lord amid the dirt and wretchedness of the lowest of the low, be of good cheer for jewels have been found on dunghills, earthen pots have been filled with heavenly treasure, and ill weeds have been transformed into precious flowers. Dwell with the King for His work, and when He writes His chronicles your name will be recorded.

June 3
Evening

"He humbled himself" (Philippians 2:8).

Jesus is the great teacher of true humility. See the Master taking a towel and washing His disciples' feet! Follower of Christ, will you humble yourself? See Him as the Servant of servants, and surely you cannot be proud! The sentence, "He humbled Himself" offers a summary of His life on this earth. He stripped off first one robe of honor and then another until, naked, He was fastened to the cross. There He emptied His inmost self, pouring out His lifeblood, giving Himself for all of us. Finally, they laid Him in a borrowed grave. How low was our dear Redeemer brought! How then, can we be proud? Stand at the foot of the cross and count the scarlet drops by which you have been cleansed. See the thorny crown and His scourged shoulders still gushing with the crimson flow of blood. See His hands and feet given up to the rough iron, and His whole self mocked and scorned. See the bitterness, the pangs, and the throes of inward grief show themselves in His outward frame. Hear the chilling shriek, "My God, my God, why hast thou forsaken me?" (Matthew 27:46). If you are not humbled in the presence of Jesus, you do not know Him. You were so lost that nothing could save you but the sacrifice of God's only begotten Son. As Jesus stooped for you, bow in humility at His feet. A realization of Christ's amazing love has a greater tendency to humble us than even a consciousness of our own guilt. Pride cannot live beneath the cross. Let us sit there and learn our lesson. Then let us rise and carry it into practice.

June 4
Morning

"The kindness and love of God our Saviour"
(Titus 3:4).

How sweet it is to behold the Savior communing with His own beloved people! Let your mind consider for an instant the history of the Redeemer's love, and a thousand acts of affection will suggest themselves. When we meditate on this amazing love, our soul may well faint for joy. Who can endure such a weight of love? That partial sense of it which the Holy Spirit is sometimes pleased to afford is more than the soul can contain. How glorious must be a complete view of it! When our soul is able to discern all the Savior's gifts, have wisdom to estimate them, and time to meditate upon them, we will then be able to commune with Jesus more closely. But who can imagine the sweetness of such fellowship? It may be one of the things which has not entered into the heart of man, but which God has prepared for them that love Him. Oh, to burst open the door of our Joseph's granaries and see the plenty which He has stored up for us! This will overwhelm us with love. By faith we see, as in a glass darkly, the reflected image of His unbounded treasures. But when we actually see the heavenly things themselves, with our own eyes, how deep will be the stream of fellowship in which our soul will bathe itself!

June 4
Evening

"Received up into glory" (1 Timothy 3:16).

We have seen our beloved Lord become humiliated and cruelly forsaken. He was "despised and rejected of men; a man of sorrows, and acquainted with grief" (Isaiah 53:3). Yet now, He has triumphed over all the powers of darkness. Our faith beholds our King, robed in the splendor of victory. How glorious He must have been in the eyes of the angels when a cloud received Him, and He ascended up to heaven! Now He wears the glory which He had with God before the earth existed. Yet, there is another glory beyond this. He has earned it in the fight against sin, death, and hell. As victor, He wears the illustrious crown. Hark how the song swells high! "Worthy is the Lamb that was slain, for He redeemed us to God by His blood!" (See Revelation 5:9-14.) He wears the glory of an Intercessor who can never fail, of a Prince who can never be defeated, and of a Conqueror who has vanquished every foe. He is the Lord who has the heart's allegiance of every Christian. Jesus wears all the glory which the pomp of heaven can bestow upon Him and which ten thousand times ten thousand angels can minister to Him. You cannot begin to comprehend His exceeding greatness. Yet, there will be a further revelation of it when He descends from heaven in great power, with all the holy angels. "Then shall he sit upon the throne of his glory" (Matthew 25:31). This is only the beginning, for eternity will sound His praise, "Thy throne, O God, is for ever and ever" (Psalm 45:6). If you desire to rejoice in Christ's glory hereafter, He must be glorious in your sight now.

June 5
Morning

"The Lord shut him in" (Genesis 7:16).

Noah was shut in *away from all the world* by the hand of divine love. We are not of the world, even as our Lord Jesus was not of the world. We cannot enter into the sin and pursuits of the multitude. We cannot play with the children of darkness, for our heavenly Father has shut us in. Noah was shut in with his God. "Come thou into the ark" was the Lord's invitation by which He clearly showed that He Himself intended to dwell in the ark with His servant and his family. The chosen are enclosed in the same circle which contains God in the Person of the Father, Son, and Spirit. Let us never be inattentive to that gracious call. Come, my people, enter into your chambers. Shut your doors behind you and hide yourself for a little moment. Noah was so shut in that no evil could reach him. Floods only lifted him heavenward, and winds only wafted him on his way. Outside of the ark all was ruin, but inside all was rest and peace. Without Christ we perish, but in Christ Jesus there is perfect safety. Noah was so shut in that he did not even desire to come out. Those who are in Christ Jesus are in Him forever. Eternal faithfulness has shut them in. In the last days, the Master of the house will rise up and shut the door. It will be in vain for mere philosophers to knock and cry, "Lord, Lord, open unto us." That same door which shuts in the wise virgins will shut out the foolish forever. Lord, shut me in by your grace.

June 5
Evening

"He that loveth not knoweth not God" (1 John 4:8).

The distinguishing mark of a Christian is his confidence in the love of Christ and the depth of his affection for Christ. First, faith enables the soul to say with the apostle, "the Son of God, who loved me, and gave himself for me" (Galatians 2:20). Then, love offers gratitude and love to Jesus in return. "We love him, because he first loved us" (1 John 4:19). In the days of the early Church, which is the heroic period of the Christian faith, this double mark was clearly seen in all believers in Jesus. The love they felt for the Lord was not a quiet emotion which they hid in the secret chamber of their souls. It was not something that they spoke of in their private Sunday services where they sang hymns in honor of Christ Jesus. Rather, it was a passion with them of vehement and all-consuming energy. It was visible in their actions, spoken in their conversation, and flashed out of their eyes even in a casual glance. Their love for Jesus was a flame which fed upon the core and heart of their being. The fire burned its way to the outer man and shone there. Because of their dependence upon Christ's love, they *dared* much, and because of their love for Christ, they *did* much. It is the same now. The children of God are ruled in their innermost being by love. "The love of Christ constraineth us" (2 Corinthians 5:14). They rejoice that divine love is shed abroad in their hearts by the Holy Spirit, who has been given to them. Filled with gratitude, they love the Savior with a pure heart, fervently. Do *you* love Him? Before you sleep, give an honest answer to that weighty question.

June 6
Morning

"Behold, I am vile" (Job 40:4).

Lost sinner, I have a word of encouragement for you! You think you cannot come to God because you are vile. There is not a saint living on earth who has not been made to feel that he is vile. If Job, Isaiah, and Paul were all obliged to say, I am vile, will you be ashamed to join in the same confession? If divine grace does not eradicate all sin from the believer, how do you hope to do it yourself? If God loves His people while they are yet vile, do you think your vileness will prevent His loving you? Believe on Jesus. Jesus calls you just as you are! Even now say, "You have died for sinners. I am a sinner. Lord Jesus, sprinkle your blood on me." If you confess your sin, you will find pardon. If, now, with all your heart, you will say, "I am vile; wash me," you will be washed *now*. You can rise from reading this morning's portion with all your sins pardoned. Although you woke this morning with every sin that man has ever committed on your head, you will rest tonight accepted in the Beloved. Once degraded with the rags of sin, you will be adorned with a robe of righteousness and appear white as the angels are. For *now* is the accepted time. If you believe on Him who justifies the ungodly, you are saved. May the Holy Spirit give you saving faith in Him who receives the vilest.

June 6
Evening

"Are they Israelites? so am I" (2 Corinthians 11:22).

We have here *a personal claim* that needs proof. There are many with no right to the title who claim to belong to the Israel of God. If we confidently declare, "So am I also an Israelite," let us only say it after having searched our heart in the presence of God. We can prove that we are following Jesus if we can say from the heart, "I trust Him wholly, trust Him only, trust Him simply, trust Him now, and trust Him forever." The position which the saints of God hold belongs to us, and all their enjoyments are our possessions. We may be the very least in Israel, "less than the least of all saints" (Ephesians 3:8). Yet, since the mercies of God belong to the *saints*, we may put in our plea and say, "Are they Israelites? so am I. Therefore, the promises are mine, grace is mine, glory will be mine." When God's people are rejoicing that they are His, what a blessing if I can say, "So am I!" When they speak of being pardoned, justified, and accepted in the Beloved, I may respond joyfully, "Through the grace of God so am I!" But this claim also has its conditions and duties. We must share with God's people in darkness as well as in sunshine. When we hear them spoken of with contempt and ridicule for being Christians, we must come boldly forward and say, "So am I." When we see them working for Christ, giving their time, their talent, and their whole heart to Jesus, we must be able to say, "So do I." Let us live as those who, having claimed a privilege, are willing to take the responsibility connected with it.

June 7
Morning

"Ye that love the Lord, hate evil" (Psalm 97:10).

You have good reason to hate evil. Consider what harm it has already brought you. Sin blinds you so that you cannot see the beauty of the Savior. It made you deaf so that you could not hear the Redeemer's tender invitations. Sin turned your feet into the way of death and poured poison into the very fountain of your being. It tainted your heart and made it "deceitful above all things, and desperately wicked" (Jeremiah 17:9). You were an heir of wrath even as others. You ran with the multitude to do evil. Such were all of us. But Paul reminds us, "but ye are washed, but ye are sanctified, but ye are justified in the name of the Lord Jesus, and by the Spirit of our God" (1 Corinthians 6:11). We have good reason for hating evil when we look back and trace its deadly workings. Our soul would have been lost had not omnipotent love interfered to redeem us. Even now it is an active enemy, ever watching to do us harm. Therefore, hate evil, Christian, unless you desire trouble. Live a happy life and die a peaceful death. Walk in all the ways of holiness, hating evil, even to the end. If you truly love your Savior and would honor Him, then hate evil. When you spend ample time with Jesus, it is impossible for you to be at peace with sin.

June 7
Evening

"Be zealous" (Revelation 3:19).

If you desire to see souls converted; if you long to hear the cry that "The kingdoms of this world are become the kingdoms of our Lord" (Revelation 11:15); if you wish to place crowns upon the head of the Savior and see His throne lifted high, then be filled with zeal. The world will be converted by the zeal of the Church. Prudence, knowledge, patience, and courage will follow in their places, but zeal must lead the march. It is not the depth of your knowledge or the extent of your talent that will triumph. It is your zeal that will do great exploits. Zeal draws its power from the continued operations of the Holy Spirit in the soul. If our spiritual life dwindles, we will not know zeal. But if we are strong and vigorous within, we will feel a loving eagerness to see the Kingdom of Christ come and His will done on earth, even as it is in heaven. A deep sense of gratitude will nourish Christian zeal. When we look at what we were redeemed from, we find many reasons why we should live and give for God. Zeal is also stimulated by the thought of the eternal future. It looks with tearful eyes down to the flames of hell, and it cannot slumber. It looks up with a longing gaze to the glories of heaven, and it cannot help but rouse itself. Time is short compared with the work to be done. Therefore, it devotes all that it has to the cause of its Lord. Finally, it is strengthened by the remembrance of Christ's example. He was clothed with zeal as with a cloak. Let us prove that we are His disciples by manifesting the same spirit of zeal.

June 8
Morning

"There fell down many slain, because the war was of God" (1 Chronicles 5:22).

Warrior, fighting under the banner of the Lord Jesus, observe this verse with holy joy; for as it was in the days of old, so it is now. If the war is of God, the victory is sure. The sons of Reuben, the Gadites, and half the tribe of Manasseh could barely muster forty-five thousand fighting men. Yet, in their war with the Hagarites, they slew "men a hundred thousand." They cried to God in the battle, and He interceded for them because they put their trust in Him. If we go forth in Jehovah's name, the Lord of Hosts is with us as our Captain. They did not neglect buckler, sword, and bow, neither did they place their trust in these weapons. We must use all fitting means, but our confidence must rest in the Lord alone. He is the sword and the shield of His people. The great reason for their extraordinary success lay in the fact that "the war was of God." Beloved, in fighting with sin without and within, with error doctrinal or practical, with spiritual wickedness in high places or low places, with devils and the devil's allies, you are waging Jehovah's war. The battle is the Lord's, and He will deliver His enemies into our hands.

June 8
Evening

"Thou shalt see now whether my word shall come to pass unto thee or not" (Numbers 11:23).

God promised Moses that He would feed the multitude in the wilderness with meat for a whole month. Moses, overtaken by unbelief, looked to the outward circumstances and was at a loss to know how the promise could be fulfilled. He looked to the creature instead of the Creator. But did the Creator expect the creature to fulfill His promise for Him? No, He who made the promise fulfilled it by His own omnipotence. If He speaks, it is done. His promises do not depend upon the puny strength of man for their fulfillment. We can easily see the mistake which Moses made. And yet, how often we do the same! God has promised to supply our needs, but we look to the creature to do what God has promised to do. Then, because we realize that the creature is weak and feeble, we indulge in unbelief. Why do we bother to look to man at all? Do you go to the top of the Alps to feel the summer heat? Will you journey to the North Pole to gather fruits ripened in the sun? This is no more foolish than looking to the weak for strength and expecting the creature to do the Creator's work. Faith is not based upon the visible means for the performance of the promise. Rather, it depends upon the all-sufficiency of the invisible God who will surely do as He said. After clearly seeing that the responsibility lies with the Lord, will we dare to indulge in mistrust? The question of God comes mightily to us: "Is the Lord's hand waxed short?" (Numbers 11:23). "Thou shalt see now whether my word shall come to pass unto thee or not."

June 9
Morning

"The Lord hath done great things for us, whereof we are glad" (Psalm 126:3).

Some Christians are sadly prone to look on the dark side of everything and to dwell more on what they have gone through than on what God has done for them. Ask for their impression of the Christian life, and they will describe their continual conflicts, their deep afflictions, their sad adversities, and the sinfulness of their hearts with scarcely any allusion to the mercy and help which God has given them. But a Christian whose soul is in a healthy state will come forward joyously and say, "I will speak, not about myself, but to the honor of my God. He brought me up out of a horrible pit and out of the miry clay. He set my feet on a rock and established my goings. He put a new song in my mouth, even praise to our God. The Lord has done great things for me, whereof I am glad." Such an abstract of experience as this is the very best that any child of God can present. It is true that we endure trials, but it is just as true that we are delivered out of them. In looking back, it would be wrong to deny that we have had trials, but it would be equally wicked to forget that we have been through them safely and profitably. The deeper our troubles, the louder our thanks to God who has led us through all and preserved us until now.

June 9
Evening

"Search the scriptures" (John 5:39).

The Greek word for *search* signifies a strict, close, diligent, and curious investigation. We must not be content with a superficial reading of a chapter or two of the Bible. With the candle of the Spirit, we must deliberately seek out the hidden meaning of the Word. Holy Scripture *requires searching*—much of it can only be learned by careful study. There is milk for babes, but also meat for strong men. The great theologian Tertullian exclaims, "I adore the fulness of the Scriptures." No man who merely skims the Book of God can profit by it. We must dig until we obtain the hidden treasure. The door of the Word is only opened by the key of diligence. The Scriptures *are worthy of searching*. They are the writings of God, bearing the divine stamp of approval. Who shall dare to treat them lightly? He who despises them despises the God who wrote them. The Word of God *will repay searching*. God does not tell us to sift through a mountain of chaff with a grain of wheat in it here and there. The Bible is winnowed corn—we have only to open the granary door and find it. Under the teaching of the Holy Spirit, Scripture glows with splendor of revelation. It is like a vast temple paved with gold and roofed with rubies and emeralds. The *Scriptures reveal Jesus.* "They are they which testify of me" (John 5:39). No more powerful motive can be given to Bible readers than this: he who finds Jesus finds life, heaven, and all things. Great joy is in store for the one who searches his Bible and discovers his Savior.

June 10
Morning

"We live unto the Lord" (Romans 14:8).

If God had willed it, each of us might have entered heaven at the moment of conversion. It was not absolutely necessary for our preparation for immortality that we should tarry here. He could have changed us from imperfection to perfection and taken us to heaven at once. Why then are we here? Would God keep His children out of paradise a single moment longer than was necessary? Why is the army of the living God still on the battlefield, when one charge might give them the victory? The answer is—They are here that they may *"live unto the Lord"* and bring others to know His love. We remain on earth as sowers to scatter good seed; as plowmen to break up the fallow ground; as heralds publishing salvation. We are here as the "salt of the earth," to be a blessing to the world. We are here to glorify Christ in our daily life. We are here as workers for Him and as workers together with Him. Let us see that our life answers its end. Let us live earnest, useful, holy lives to the praise of the glory of His grace.

June 10
Evening

"They are they which testify of me" (John 5:39).

Jesus Christ is the Alpha and Omega of the Bible. He is the constant theme of its sacred pages. From first to last, they testify of Him. At the creation, we discern Him as one of the sacred Trinity. We catch a glimpse of Him in the promise of the woman's seed. We see Him typified in the ark of Noah. We walk with Abraham as he sees the Messiah's day. We dwell in the tents of Isaac and Jacob, feeding upon the gracious promise. We hear the venerable Israel talking of Shiloh. In the numerous types of the law, we find the Redeemer foreshadowed. Prophets, kings, priests, and preachers all look to Jesus. They stand as the cherubs did over the ark of the covenant, desiring to look within and read the mystery of God's great redemption of man. In the New Testament, we find our Lord to be the one pervading subject. The whole substance of the New Testament is Jesus crucified. Even its closing sentence is bejewelled with the Redeemer's name. We should always read Scripture in this light. We should consider the Word to be as a mirror into which Christ looks down from heaven. The reflection is dark, but it is still a blessed preparation for when we will see Him face to face. The Bible contains Jesus Christ's letters to us, perfumed by His love. The pages are the garments of our King, and they all smell of myrrh, aloes, and cinnamon. The Scriptures are the swaddling bands of the holy child Jesus. Unroll them and you find your Savior. The essence of the Word of God is Christ.

June 11
Morning

"We love him because he first loved us" (1 John 4:19).

There is no light in the planet but that which proceeds from the sun, and there is no true love for Jesus in the heart but that which comes from the Lord Jesus Himself. From this overflowing fountain of the infinite love of God, all our love for God springs. This is a certain truth, that we love Him for no other reason than because He first loved us. Our love for Him is the fair offspring of His love for us. Anyone may have cold admiration when studying the works of God. The warmth of love can only be kindled in the heart by God's Spirit. How marvelous that when we had rebelled against Him, He would by a display of such amazing love, seek to draw us back. We would never have had a grain of love toward God unless it had been sown in us by the sweet seed of His love for us. Love, then, has for its parent the love of God shed abroad in the heart; but after it is divinely born, it must be divinely nourished. Love is not a plant which will flourish naturally in human soil. It must be watered from above. Love for Jesus is a flower of delicate nature. If it received no nourishment but that which could be drawn from the rock of our hearts, it would soon wither. As love comes from heaven, so it must feed on heavenly bread. It cannot exist in the wilderness unless it is fed by manna from on high. Love must feed on love. The very soul and life of our love for God is His love for us.

June 11
Evening

"There brake he the arrows of the bow, the shield, and the sword, and the battle" (Psalm 76:3).

Our Redeemer's glorious cry of "It is finished" was the death knell of all the adversaries of His people. It signified the breaking of "the arrows of the bow, the shield, and the sword, and the battle." The hero of Golgotha used His cross as an anvil and His woes as a hammer. He destroyed bundle after bundle of our sins, those poisoned "arrows of the bow." He trampled upon every indictment against us and destroyed every accusation. The diabolical darts were reduced to fragments, and the infernal bucklers were broken like potters' vessels! Jesus drew the dread sword of Satanic power from its sheath of hellish workmanship and snapped it across His knee, as a man breaks dry wood. The punishment of our sin was borne by Christ. A full atonement was made for all our iniquities by our blessed Substitute. Who can accuse us? Who can condemn us? "It is Christ that died, yea rather, that is risen again" (Romans 8:34). Jesus emptied the quivers of hell, quenched every fiery dart, and broke off the head of every arrow of wrath. The ground is strewn with the splinters of the weapons of hell's warfare, which are only visible to us to remind us of our former danger and of our great deliverance. "Sin shall not have dominion over you" (Romans 6:14). Jesus has made an end of it and put it away forever. The destructions of the enemy have come to an end.

June 12
Morning

"Thou art weighed in the balances and found wanting" (Daniel 5:27).

It is well to frequently weigh ourselves in the scale of God's Word. You will find it a holy exercise to read daily some psalm of David. As you meditate on each verse, ask yourself, "Can I say this? Have I felt as David felt? Has my heart ever been broken on account of sin, as his was when he penned his penitential psalms? Has my soul been full of true confidence in the hour of difficulty? Do I take the cup of salvation and call on the name of the Lord?" As you read ask yourself how far you are conformed to His likeness. Endeavor to discover whether you have the meekness, the humility, the lovely spirit which He constantly displayed. Then, read the epistles to see whether you can go with the apostle in what he said of his experience. Have you ever cried out as he did— "O wretched man that I am! who shall deliver me from the body of this death" (Romans 7:24). Have you seemed to yourself the chief of sinners and less than the least of all saints? Could you join with him and say, "For me to live is Christ, and to die is gain" (Philippians 1:21). If we thus read God's Word as a test of our spiritual condition, we will have good reason to stop many times and say, "Lord, give me true penitence. Give me real faith, warmer zeal, and more fervent love. Make me more like Jesus. Let me no longer be found wanting when weighed in the balances of the sanctuary, lest I be found wanting in the scales of judgment."

June 12
Evening

"Who hath saved us, and called us with an holy calling" (2 Timothy 1:9).

The apostle says, "Who *hath* saved us." Believers in Christ Jesus are not persons who are hopeful that they may ultimately be saved. They *are* already saved. Salvation is not a blessing to be enjoyed upon the deathbed and to be sung of as a future promise. Rather, it should be obtained, received, and enjoyed now. God ordained the believer for salvation, and that purpose is complete. He is saved because of the *price which has been paid for him.* "It is finished" (John 19:30) was the cry of the Savior before He died. As the believer sinned in Adam, so he lives in Christ. This complete salvation is accompanied by a *holy calling.* Those whom the Savior redeemed are called by the power of the Holy Spirit to holiness. They leave their sins and endeavor to be like Christ. They choose holiness, not out of any compulsion, but from the drawing of a new nature. Believers are able to rejoice in holiness just as naturally as they once delighted in sin. God neither chose them nor called them because they were holy. He called them that they might *be holy.* Holiness is the beauty produced by His workmanship in them. The Christlike qualities we see in a believer are as much the work of God as the atonement itself. Salvation must be by grace because the Lord is the author of it. The Lord works in such a manner that our righteousness is forever excluded. A present salvation is the believer's privilege. The evidence that he is called to it is his holy life.

June 13
Morning

"Whosoever will, let him take the water of life freely" (Revelation 22:17).

Jesus says, "Take freely." He wants no payment or preparation. He seeks no recommendation from our virtuous emotions. You have no belief and no repentance. Come to Him, and He will give them to you. Come just as you are. He gives Himself to needy ones. We can hardly imagine anyone so foolish as to stand before a drinking fountain and to cry, "I cannot drink because I do not have enough money." However poor the man is, the fountain is there for him to freely drink of it. Thirsty people whether they are dressed in silk or in broadcloth, do not look for any warrant for drinking. The fountain itself is their warrant for taking its water freely. Perhaps the only persons who need go thirsty are those who think it would demean them to drink at a common fountain. Instead, they pass by with parched lips. Oh, how many there are who are rich in their own good works and cannot therefore come to Christ! "I will not be saved," they say, "in the same way as the harlot or the profane. What? Go to heaven in the same way as a chimneysweep? Is there no pathway to glory but the path which led the thief there? I will not be saved that way." Such proud boasters must remain without the living water, but, "Whosoever will, let him take the water of life freely."

June 13
Evening

"Remove far from me vanity and lies" (Proverbs 30:8).

"My God, be not far from me" (Psalm 38:21).

Here we have two great lessons—what to pray for deliverance from and what to request. The happiest state of a Christian is the holiest state. No Christian enjoys comfort when his eyes are fixed on worldly pleasures. He finds no satisfaction unless his soul is made alive in the ways of God. The world may find happiness elsewhere, but he cannot. I do not blame ungodly men for rushing to their pleasures. That is all they have to enjoy. A converted wife who despaired of her husband's salvation was always very kind to him. She said, "I fear that this is the only world in which he will be happy, and, therefore, I have made up my mind to make him as happy as I can in it." Christians must seek their delights at a higher level than the sinful enjoyments of the world. Vain pursuits are dangerous to renewed souls. No Christian is safe when he is spiritually sluggish. Although every Christian is secure concerning his salvation, he is vulnerable in his experience in holiness and communion with Jesus in this life. Satan does not often attack a Christian who is living near God. It is when the Christian departs from God, becomes spiritually starved, and tries to feed on vanities that the devil discovers his opportunity. He may sometimes stand against the child of God who is active in his Master's service, but the battle is generally short. He who slips into the Valley of Humiliation every time he takes a false step invites Satan to attack him. Pray for grace to walk humbly with God!

June 14
Morning

"Delight thyself also in the Lord" (Psalm 37:4).

The teaching of these words must seem very surprising to those who are strangers to vital godliness. But to the sincere believer it is only the repetition of a recognized truth. The life of the believer is described as a delight in God, and we are certified of the great fact that true religion overflows with happiness and joy. Ungodly persons and nominal Christians never look on religion as a joyful thing. To them it is service, duty, or necessity but never pleasure or delight. If they attend to religion at all, it is either that they may gain thereby or because they dare not do otherwise. The thought of delight in religion is so strange to most men that no two words in their language stand farther apart than "holiness" and "delight." But believers who know Christ understand that delight and faith are so blessedly united that the gates of hell cannot prevail to separate them. They who love God with all their hearts find that His ways are ways of pleasantness and all His paths are peace. Our faith is no fetter, and our profession is no bondage. We are not dragged to holiness or driven to duty. No, our piety is our pleasure, our hope is our happiness, and our duty is our delight.

June 14
Evening

"O Lord, to us belongeth confusion of face...because we have sinned against thee" (Daniel 9:8).

A deep sense and clear sight of sin, its bitterness, and the punishment it deserves, should make us bow low before the throne. We have sinned as Christians. Although we have been abundantly blessed, we have been ungrateful. Privileged beyond most, we have not brought forth fruit in proportion to our benefits. What Christian will not blush when he looks back upon the past? Our days before we were saved are to be forgiven and forgotten. Since that time, however, we have sinned against light and against love—light which has penetrated our minds and love in which we have rejoiced. An unpardoned sinner transgresses cheaply compared with the sin of one of God's own elect who has had communion with Christ. Look at David! Many will talk of his sin, but look at his repentance. Hear his broken bones as each one of them moans out its sorrowful confession! See his tears as they fall upon the ground, and hear the deep sighs which accompany the softened music of his harp! We have sinned. Let us, therefore, seek the spirit of penitence. Look again at Peter! We speak much of Peter's denying his Master. Remember that he wept bitterly. (See Luke 22:62.) Have *we* no denials of our Lord to be lamented with tears? These sins of ours, before and after conversion, would send us to the place of inextinguishable fire if it were not for God's sovereign mercy. Bow down under a sense of sinfulness and worship God. Admire the grace which saves you, the mercy which spares you, and the love which pardons you!

June 15
Morning

"And Sarah said, God hath made me to laugh, so that all that hear will laugh with me" (Genesis 21:6).

It was far above the power of nature and even contrary to its laws that the aged Sarah should be honored with a son. It is also beyond all ordinary rules that I, a sinner, should find grace to bear the indwelling Spirit of the Lord Jesus in my soul. I, whose nature was as dry, withered, barren, and accursed as a howling wilderness, have been made to bring forth fruit unto holiness. My mouth is filled with joyous laughter because of the grace which I have received from the Lord. I have found Jesus, the promised seed, and He is mine forever. This day I will lift up psalms of triumph to the Lord, who has remembered my low estate. "My heart rejoiceth in the Lord, mine horn is exalted in the Lord: my mouth is enlarged over mine enemies; because I rejoice in thy salvation" (1 Samuel 2:1). I surprise my family with my abundant peace. I delight my friends with my ever-increasing happiness. I edify the Church with my grateful confessions. I even impress the world with the cheerfulness of my daily conversation. The Lord Jesus is a deep sea of joy. My soul will dive therein and will be swallowed up in the delights of His companionship. Sarah looked on her Isaac and laughed with excess of rapture, and all her friends laughed with her. You, my soul, look on Jesus and bid heaven and earth unite in your unspeakable joy.

June 15
Evening

"He that openeth, and no man shutteth" (Revelation 3:7).

Jesus is the Keeper of the gates of Paradise. He sets an open door in front of every believer which no man or devil is able to close. Faith in Him is the golden key to the everlasting doors. Do you carry this key close to your heart, or are you trusting some deceitful means of entrance which will fail you in the end? Hear this parable of the preacher, and remember it. The great King made a banquet, and He proclaimed that only those who bring the fairest flower that blooms will enter. Men advance to the gate by thousands, each bringing the flower which he esteems to be the queen of the garden. But they are all driven from the royal presence and cannot enter into the festive halls. They clutch the deadly nightshade of superstition or the flaunting poppies of religion or the hemlock of self-righteousness. But these are not dear to the King, and the bearers are shut out of the pearly gates. Have you gathered the rose of Sharon? Do you wear the lily of the valley in your bosom? If so, when you come to the gates of heaven, you will discover its value. When you show those choicest of flowers, the heavenly door will open. You will find your way, with the rose of Sharon in your hand, to the throne of God Himself. Heaven possesses nothing that excels its radiant beauty. All the flowers that bloom in Paradise can never rival the lily of the valley. Get Calvary's blood-red rose into your hand by faith. By love wear it, by communion preserve it, by daily watchfulness make it your all in all. Then you will be blessed beyond all bliss and happy beyond a dream.

June 16
Morning

"And I give unto them eternal life, and they shall never perish" (John 10:28).

The Christian should never think or speak lightly of unbelief. For a child of God to mistrust His love, His truth, His faithfulness must be greatly displeasing to Him. How can we ever grieve Him by doubting His upholding grace? Christian, it is contrary to every promise of God's precious Word that you would ever be forgotten or left to perish. If it could be so, how could He be true who has said, "Can a woman forget her sucking child, that she should not have compassion on the son of her womb? Yea, they may forget, yet will I never forget thee" (Isaiah 49:15). What would be the value of the promise: "The mountains shall depart, and the hills be removed; but my kindness shall not depart from thee, neither shall the covenant of my peace be removed, saith the Lord that hath mercy on thee?" (Isaiah 54:10). Where would be the truth of Christ's words: "I give unto my sheep eternal life; and they shall never perish, neither shall any man pluck them out of my hand. My father which gave them me is greater than all, and no man is able to pluck them out of my Father's hand?" (John 10:29). Where is the veracity of God, His honor, His power, His grace, His covenant, His oath, if any of those who have put their trust in Christ should nevertheless be cast away? Banish those unbelieving fears which so dishonor God. Remember it is sinful to doubt His Word wherein He has promised you that you will never perish.

June 16
Evening

"The Lord is my light and my salvation; whom shall I fear? the Lord is the strength of my life; of whom shall I be afraid?" (Psalm 27:1).

"The Lord is my light and my salvation." Here is personal interest: *my light* and *my salvation*. The soul is assured of it, and therefore declares it boldly. Divine light is poured into the soul before salvation can be obtained. Where there is not enough light to reveal our darkness and to make us long for the Lord Jesus, there is no evidence of salvation. After conversion, God is our joy, comfort, guide, teacher, and in every sense our light. He is light within, light around, light reflected from us, and light to be revealed to us. The Lord does not merely give light, but He *is* light. He not only gives salvation, but He *is* salvation. When you, by faith, lay hold upon God, all of the covenant blessings are yours. "Whom shall I fear?" The powers of darkness are not to be feared, for the Lord, our light, destroys them. The damnation of hell is not to be dreaded by us, for the Lord is our salvation. This is a very different challenge from that of boastful Goliath. It does not depend upon the conceited strength of a man, but upon the real power of the omnipotent I AM. "The Lord is the strength of my life." It is easy to give praise where the Lord lavishes deeds of grace. Our life derives all its strength from God. If He makes us strong, we cannot be weakened by all the schemes of the adversary. "Of whom shall I be afraid?" The bold question looks into the future as well as the present. "If God be for us, who can be against us" (Romans 8:31), either now or in time to come?

June 17
Morning

"Help, Lord" (Psalm 12:1).

David mourned the fewness of faithful men and therefore lifted up his heart in supplication. When the creature failed, he flew to the Creator. He evidently felt his own weakness, or he would not have cried for help. But at the same time, he intended honestly to exert himself for the cause of truth, for the word "help" is inapplicable where we ourselves do nothing. The psalmist runs straight to his God with a well-considered prayer. He knows what he is seeking and where to seek it. Lord, teach us to pray in the same blessed manner. The occasions for the use of this prayer are frequent. How suitable it is in providential afflictions for tried believers who find all helpers failing them. Students in doctrinal difficulties may often obtain aid by lifting up this cry of "Help, Lord," to the Holy Spirit, the great Teacher. Spiritual warriors in inward conflicts may send to the throne for reinforcements, and this will be a model for their request. Workers in heavenly labor may thus obtain grace in time of need. Seeking sinners in doubts and alarms may offer up the same weighty supplications. In fact, in all cases, times, and places, this will serve the turn of needy souls. "Help, Lord," will suit us living and dying, suffering or laboring, rejoicing or sorrowing. In Him our help is found. Let us not be slack to cry to Him. The answer to the prayer is certain, if it is sincerely offered through Jesus. The Lord's character assures us that He will not leave His people. His gift of Jesus is a pledge of every good thing.

June 17
Evening

"Then Israel sang this song, Spring up, O well; sing ye unto it"(Numbers 21:17).

The well in the wilderness was famous because it was *the subject of a promise*. "That is the well whereof the Lord spake unto Moses, Gather the people together, and I will give them water" (Numbers 21:16). The people needed water, and it was promised by their gracious God. We need fresh supplies of heavenly grace. The Lord pledged Himself to give all we require. The well became *the cause of a song*. Before the water gushed forth, cheerful faith prompted the people to sing. As they saw the crystal fount bubbling up, the music grew even more joyous. We who believe the promise of God should rejoice in the prospect of divine revivals in our souls. As we experience them, our holy joy should overflow. Are we thirsting? Let us not murmur, but sing. Spiritual thirst is bitter to bear, but the promise indicates a well. Let us be encouraged to look for it. The well was *the center of prayer.*"Spring up, O well." We must seek after what God promised to give, or we show that we have neither desire nor faith. This evening, let us ask that the scripture we have read and our devotional readings may not be an empty formality. Rather, let them be a channel of grace to our souls. The well was *the object of effort*. "The nobles of the people digged it" (Numbers 21:18). The Lord wants us to be active in obtaining grace. Prayer must not be neglected; the fellowship with other believers must not be forsaken; worship must not be slighted. The Lord will generously give us His grace, but not as a reward for our idleness. Let us seek Him to whom are all our fresh springs of joy.

June 18
Morning

"Thy Redeemer" (Isaiah 54:5).

Jesus the Redeemer is ours forever. He is king for us, priest for us, and prophet for us. Whenever we read a new title for our Redeemer, let us appropriate Him as ours in that name also. He is the Shepherd, the Captain, the Prince, and the Prophet. Jesus has no dignity which He will not employ for our exaltation and no prerogative which He will not exercise for our defense. His fullness in the Godhead is our unfailing, inexhaustible treasure house. His manhood also, which He took on Him for us, is ours in all its perfection. To us our gracious Lord communicates the spotless virtue of a stainless character. On us He bestows the reward procured by obedient submission and incessant service. He bequeaths us His manger that we may learn how God came down to man. His cross teaches us how man may go up to God. All His thoughts, emotions, actions, utterances, miracles, and intercessions were for us. He trod the road of sorrow on our behalf and has given us as His heavenly legacy the full results of all the labors of His life. Oh, my soul, by the power of the Holy Spirit, call Him your Redeemer this morning.

June 18
Evening

"I am come into my garden, my sister, my spouse" (Song of Solomon 5:1).

The heart of the believer is Christ's garden. He bought it with His precious blood, and He enters it and claims it as His own. A garden implies *separation*. It is not public property, and it is not a wilderness. It is walled around and hedged in. The wall of separation between the Church and the world must be made broader and stronger. Christians say, "Well, there is no harm in this; there is no harm in that," thus getting as near to the world as possible. Grace is at a low level in that soul which can even ask how far it may go in worldly conformity. A garden is *a place of beauty.* It far surpasses the wild, uncultivated lands. The genuine Christian must seek to be more excellent in his life than the best moralist, because Christ's garden ought to produce the best flowers in the world. The rarest, richest, choicest lilies and roses should bloom in the place which Jesus calls His own. The garden is *a place of growth.* The saints are not to remain undeveloped, always mere buds and blossoms. We should "grow in grace, and in the knowledge of our Lord and Savior Jesus Christ" (2 Peter 3:18). Growth should be rapid where Jesus is the Gardener and the Holy Spirit is the dew from above. A garden is *a place of retirement.* The Lord Jesus Christ calls us to reserve our souls as a place where He can manifest Himself to us. We often worry and trouble ourselves with much serving, like Martha. We do not have the room for Christ that Mary had, and we do not sit at His feet as we should. May the Lord grant the sweet showers of His grace to water His garden this day.

June 19
Morning

"And they were all filled with the Holy Ghost" (Acts 2:4).

It is a rich blessing to be filled with the Holy Spirit. It would be impossible to over-estimate the consequences of this sacred filling of the soul. Life, comfort, light, purity, power, peace, and many other precious blessings are inseparable from the Spirit's presence. As sacred oil, He anoints the head of the believer, sets him apart to the priesthood of saints, and gives him grace to execute his office right. As the only truly purifying water, He cleanses us from the power of sin and sanctifies us, working in us to do the Lord's good pleasure. As the light, He manifested to us at first our lost estate. Now He reveals the Lord Jesus to us and in us and guides us in the way of righteousness. Enlightened by His pure celestial ray, we are no more darkness, but light in the Lord. He is the sacrificial flame by which we are enabled to offer our whole souls as a living sacrifice to God. As heavenly dew, He removes our barrenness and fertilizes our lives. As the dove, with wings of peaceful love, He broods over His Church and over the souls of believers. As the Comforter, He dispels the cares and doubts which mar the peace of His beloved. He descends on the chosen and bears witness to their sonship by working in them a filial spirit by which they cry, Abba, Father. As the wind, He brings the breath of life to men. Blowing where He wills, He performs the quickening operations by which the spiritual creation is animated and sustained. Pray to God that we might feel His presence this day and every day.

344

June 19
Evening

"My beloved is mine, and I am his: he feedeth among the lilies. Until the day break, and the shadows flee away, turn, my beloved, and be thou like a roe or a young hart upon the mountains of Bether" (Song of Solomon 2:16-17).

Surely if there is a joyous verse in the Bible, it is this—"My beloved is mine, and I am his." It is peaceful, full of assurance, and overflowing with happiness and contentment. The verse reminds us of Him who, before He went to Gethsemane, said, "Peace I leave with you, my peace I give unto you: not as the world giveth, give I unto you" (John 14:27). "In the world ye shall have tribulation: but be of good cheer; I have overcome the world" (John 16:33). Let us ring the silver bell again: "My beloved is mine, and I am his: he feedeth among the lilies." And yet, there is a shadow. Though the surroundings are fair and lovely, it is not entirely a sunlit landscape. There is a cloud in the sky which casts a shadow over the scene, "until the day break, and the shadows flee away." There is a word, too, about the "mountains of Bether" or "the mountains of division." To our love, any division is bitterness. Although you do not doubt your salvation, and you know that He is yours, you are not feasting with Him. Do not permit a shadow of a doubt to cloud the assurance that you are His and He is yours.

June 20
Morning

"For, lo, I will command, and I will sift the house of Israel among all nations, like as corn is sifted in a sieve, yet shall not the least grain fall upon the earth" (Amos 9:9).

Every sifting comes by divine command and permission. Satan had to ask for permission before he could lay a finger on Job. Satan may hold the sieve, hoping to destroy the corn; but the overruling hand of the Master is accomplishing the purity of the grain by the very process which the enemy intended to be destructive. Be comforted by the blessed fact that the Lord directs the sieve to His own glory and to your eternal profit. The Lord Jesus will surely use the fan which is in His hand and will divide the precious from the vile. In the sieve true weight alone has power. Husks and chaff, being devoid of substance, must fly before the wind, and only solid corn will remain. Observe the complete safety of the Lord's wheat. Even the smallest grain has a promise of preservation. God Himself sifts in all places, in all nations, and in the most effectual manner. Yet through all of this, not the smallest, lightest, or most shriveled grain is permitted to fall to the ground. Every individual believer is precious in the sight of the Lord, and He will not lose one of His redeemed people. No matter how little we may be, if we are the Lord's, we may rejoice that we are preserved in Christ Jesus.

June 20
Evening

"Straightway they forsook their nets, and followed him" (Mark 1:18).

When they heard the call of Jesus, Simon and Andrew obeyed at once without question. If we would always, immediately and with resolute zeal, put into practice what we hear, our reading of the Bible could not fail to enrich us spiritually. A man will not lose his bread if he eats it at once. Neither can he be deprived of the benefit of doctrine if he has already acted upon it. Most readers and hearers become moved by a message and intend to change. But the proposal is a blossom which falls from the tree too soon, and no fruit is ever harvested from it. They wait, they waver, and then they forget. Like puddles during nights of frost and days of sunshine, they are only thawed in time to be frozen again. That fatal tomorrow is blood red with the murder of fair resolutions; it is the slaughterhouse of good intentions. Be a doer of the Word. Truth that is both read and practiced is the most profitable. If you are impressed with any duty while meditating upon these pages, hasten to fulfill it before the holy glow departs from your soul. Leave your nets and all that you have, rather than be found rebellious to the Master's call. Do not give place to the devil by delay! Make haste while opportunity and desire are in happy conjunction. Do not be caught in your own nets, but break the mesh of worldliness, and come away to where glory calls you.

June 21
Morning

"Thou art fairer than the children of men"
(Psalm 45:2).

Jesus is altogether complete. He is a picture of beauty and a breastplate of glory. In Him all the things of good repute are in their proper places and assist in adorning each other. Not one feature in His glorious person attracts attention at the expense of others. But He is perfectly and altogether lovely. Oh, Jesus, Your power, Your grace, Your justice, Your tenderness, Your truth, Your majesty, and Your immutability, make up such a God-man, as neither heaven nor earth has seen elsewhere. Your infancy, Your eternity, Your sufferings, Your triumphs, Your death, and Your immortality are all woven in one gorgeous tapestry without seam or rent. You are music without discord. You are many and yet not divided. You are all things and yet not diverse. As all the colors blend into one resplendent rainbow, so all the glories of heaven and earth meet in You and unite so wondrously, that there is none like You in all things. If all the virtues of the most excellent were bound in one bundle, they could not rival You. You have been anointed with the holy oil of myrrh and cassia, which Your God has reserved for you alone. As for Your fragrance, it is as the holy perfume, the like of which none other can ever mingle. Even with the art of the apothecary, each spice is fragrant, but the compound is divine.

June 21
Evening

"The foundation of God standeth sure" (2 Timothy 2:19).

The foundation upon which our faith rests is this: "God was in Christ, reconciling the world unto himself, not imputing their trespasses unto them" (2 Corinthians 5:19). Genuine faith relies upon the fact that, "the Word was made flesh, and dwelt among us" (John 1:14). "Christ also hath once suffered for sins, the just for the unjust, that he might bring us to God" (1 Peter 3:18). "Who his own self bare our sins in his own body on the tree" (1 Peter 2:24). "The chastisement of our peace was upon him; and with his stripes we are healed" (Isaiah 53:5). In one word, the great pillar of the Christian's hope is *substitution*. Christ Himself was the sacrifice for the guilty. He was made sin for us that we might be made the righteousness of God in Him. (See 2 Corinthians 5:21.) This foundation stands as firm as the throne of God. Our delight is to hold it, to meditate upon it, and to proclaim it. Gratitude for our salvation should permeate every part of our life and conversation. A direct attack is being made upon the doctrine of the atonement. Some men cannot accept substitution. They gnash their teeth at the thought of the Lamb of God bearing the sin of man. But we who have experienced the preciousness of this truth will proclaim it confidently and unceasingly. We will neither dilute it nor change it in any way. We cannot, we dare not, give it up, for it is our life. Despite every controversy, we know that "nevertheless the foundation of God standeth sure."

June 22
Morning

"He shall build the temple of the Lord; and he shall bear the glory" (Zechariah 6:13).

Christ Himself is the builder of His spiritual temple. He has built it on the mountains of His unchangeable affection, His omnipotent grace, and His infallible truthfulness. But as it was in Solomon's temple, so in this. The materials need to be made ready. The cedars of Lebanon are not framed for the building. They are not cut down, shaped, and made into those planks of cedar, whose odoriferous beauty will make glad the courts of the Lord's house in Paradise. The rough stones are still in the quarry. They must be hewn and squared. All this is Christ's own work. Each individual believer is being prepared, polished, and made ready for his place in the temple. But Christ's own hand performs the preparation work. Afflictions cannot sanctify, except as they are used by Him to this end. Our prayers and efforts cannot make us ready for heaven apart from the hand of Jesus, who fashions our hearts. In the building of Solomon's temple, there was neither hammer nor axe nor any tool of iron heard in the house, because all was brought perfectly ready for the exact spot it was to occupy. So it is with the temple which Jesus builds—the making ready is all done on earth. When we reach heaven, there will be no sanctifying us there, no squaring us with afflictions, no planing us with suffering.

June 22
Evening

"That those things which cannot be shaken may remain" (Hebrews 12:27).

We have many things in our possession which *can* be shaken. It is foolish for a Christian to depend upon them, for there is nothing stable on this earth. Yet, we have certain "things which *cannot* be shaken." If the things which can be shaken should all be taken away, you may derive comfort from the things that cannot be shaken which will remain. Whatever your losses have been, you enjoy *present salvation.* You are standing at the foot of His cross, trusting in the merit of Jesus' precious blood. No rise or fall of the markets can interfere with your salvation in Him. No failures and bankruptcies can touch that. You are a *child of God.* No change of circumstances can ever rob you of that. If you are brought to poverty and stripped bare, you can say, "He is my Father still. In my Father's house are many mansions; therefore, I will not be troubled." Another permanent blessing is *the love of Jesus Christ.*He who is God and Man loves you with all the strength of His affectionate nature—nothing can affect that. Nothing on this earth matters to the man who can sing, "My beloved is mine, and I am his" (Song of Solomon 2:16). We cannot lose our richest heritage. Whenever trouble comes, let us stand firm. Let us show that we are not little children to be cast down by what may happen in this fleeting time. Our country is Immanuel's land, and our hope is above the sky. Therefore, calm as the summer's ocean, we will see the wreck of everything earthborn and still rejoice in the God of our salvation.

June 23
Morning

"Ephraim is a cake not turned" (Hosea 7:8).

A pancake not turned is unbaked on one side. Ephraim was like this in many respects. He had areas in his life that were untouched by divine grace. Although there was some partial obedience, there was much rebellion left. Are you thorough in the things of God? Has grace gone through the very center of your being? To be sanctified in your spirit, soul, and body should be your aim and prayer. There must not be the appearance of holiness in one place and reigning sin in another, or you, too, will be a cake not turned. The assumed appearance of superior sanctity frequently accompanies a total absence of all vital godliness. The saint in public is sometimes a devil in private. He deals in flour by day and in soot by night. The cake which is burned on one side is dough on the other. If it is so with me, O Lord, turn me! Turn my unsanctified nature to the fire of Your love and let it feel the sacred glow. Let my burned side cool a little while I learn of my own weakness and desire heat when I am removed from Your heavenly flame. Let me not be found a double-minded man, but one entirely under the powerful influence of reigning grace. I know if I am left like a cake unturned and am not on both sides the subject of Your grace, I must be consumed forever amid everlasting burnings.

June 23
Evening

"Waiting for the adoption" (Romans 8:23).

Saints are God's children, but men cannot see this except by certain moral characteristics. The adoption is not manifested. The children are not yet openly declared. A Roman was permitted to adopt a child and keep it private a long time. But there was a second adoption in public when the child was brought before the authorities. His old garments were taken off, and the father who took him as his child gave him clothing suitable to his new station in life. "Beloved, now are we the sons of God, and it doth not yet appear what we shall be" (1 John 3:2). We are not yet arrayed in the apparel which befits the royal family of heaven. We are still wearing this flesh and blood of the sons of Adam. But we know that when *He* appears who is the "firstborn among many brethren" (Romans 8:29), we will be like Him, for we will see Him as He is. (See 1 John 3:2.) A child taken from the lowest ranks of society and adopted by a Roman senator would say to himself, "I long for the day when I will be publicly adopted. Then I will remove these beggar's garments and be robed as becomes my senatorial rank." So it is with us today. We are waiting to put on our proper garments and be manifested as the children of God. We are young nobles and have not yet worn our crowns. We are young brides, and the marriage day is not yet come. Our joy, like a swollen spring, longs to well up like a geyser, leaping to the skies. It heaves and groans within our spirit for room to manifest itself to men.

June 24
Morning

"A certain woman of the company lifted up her voice, and said unto him, Blessed is the womb that bare thee, and the paps which thou hast sucked. But he said, Yea rather, blessed are they that hear the word of God, and keep it." (Luke 11:27-28).

It is fondly imagined by some that it must have involved very special privileges to have been the mother of our Lord. They suppose that she had the benefit of looking into His very heart in a way in which we cannot hope to do. We do not know that Mary knew more than others. She does not appear from anything we read in the gospels to have been a better-instructed believer than any other of Christ's disciples. All that she knew, we also may discover. Do you wonder that we should say so? Here is a text to prove it: "The secret of the Lord is with them that fear him, and he will show them his covenant" (Psalm 25:14). Remember the Master's words: "Henceforth I call you not servants; for the servant knoweth not what his Lord doeth: but I have called you friends; for all things that I have heard of my Father I have made known unto you" (John 15:15). This divine Revealer of secrets tells us His heart and keeps nothing back which is profitable to us. Therefore, we will not ignorantly cry out, "Blessed is the womb that bare thee." We will instead intelligently bless God that, having heard the Word and kept it, we have as true an acquaintance with the secrets of His heart as Mary was supposed to have obtained. How happy we are to have this privilege!

June 24
Evening

"Shadrach, Meshach, and Abed-nego, answered and said,. . .Be it known unto thee, O king, that we will not serve thy gods" (Daniel 3:16,18).

The bold courage and marvelous deliverance of the three Hebrew children illustrates firmness and steadfastness in upholding truth in the teeth of tyranny and in the jaws of death. Both in matters of faith in God and matters of uprightness in business, never sacrifice your conscience. It is better to lose all rather than to lose your integrity. When all else is gone, still hold fast to a clear conscience as the rarest jewel which can adorn the human heart. Do not be guided by the shifting sands of policy, but follow the unwavering star of divine authority. When you see no present advantage, walk by faith and not by sight. Honor God by trusting Him when it comes to matters of loss for the sake of principle. He will prove His word that "godliness with contentment is great gain" (1 Timothy 6:6). "Seek ye first the kingdom of God, and his righteousness; and all these things shall be added unto you" (Matthew 6:33). It may happen that, in the providence of God, you suffer a loss by following your conscience. You will find that if the Lord does not pay you back in the silver of earthly prosperity, He will fulfill His promise in the gold of spiritual joy. Remember that "a man's life consisteth not in the abundance of the things which he possesseth" (Luke 12:15). An honest spirit, a heart void of offense, and the favor of God are greater riches than mines of diamonds. "Better is a dinner of herbs where love is, than a stalled ox and hatred therewith" (Proverbs 15:17). An ounce of deep and abiding peace is worth a ton of gold.

June 25
Morning

"Get thee up into the high mountain" (Isaiah 40:9).

Our knowledge of Christ is somewhat like climbing a mountain. When you are at the base you see very little. The mountain itself appears to be half as high as it really is. Confined in a little valley, you discover scarcely anything but the rippling brooks as they descend into the stream at the foot of the mountain. Climb the first rising knoll, and the valley lengthens and widens beneath your feet. Go higher, and you see the country for four or five miles round and are delighted with the widening prospect. Mount still, and the scene enlarges; until at last, you are on the summit. The Christian life is of the same order. When we first believe in Christ, we see little of Him. The higher we climb, the more we discover of His beauties. But who has ever gained the summit? Who has known all the heights and depths of the love of Christ which passes knowledge? Paul, when grown old, sitting gray-haired, shivering in a dungeon in Rome, could say with greater emphasis than we can, "I know whom I have believed." Each experience had been like the climbing of a hill, each trial had been like ascending another summit, and his death seemed like gaining the top of the mountain. From there he could see the faithfulness and the love of Him to whom he had committed his soul. Get up, dear friend, to the high mountain.

June 25
Evening

"The dove found no rest for the sole of her foot" (Genesis 8:9).

Can you find rest apart from Christ Jesus? Then be assured that your religion is vain. Are you satisfied with anything less than the knowledge of your union and interest in Christ? Then your faith is worthless. If you profess to be a Christian, yet find full satisfaction in worldly pleasures and pursuits, your profession is false. If your soul can feel comfortable in the chambers of sin, then you are a hypocrite. But if you feel that indulging in sin without punishment would be a severe punishment in itself; if you could have the whole world and abide here forever, yet you would be miserable without God for He is what your soul craves after; then be of good courage, for you are a child of God. Despite all of your sins and imperfections, be comforted in this: If your soul has no rest in sin, you are not as the sinner is! If you are still crying and craving after something better, Christ has not forgotten you, for you have not forgotten Him. The believer cannot live without his Lord. We cannot live on the sand of the wilderness; we want the manna which drops from on high. Our bottles of self-confidence cannot yield us a drop of moisture. We drink from the Rock which follows us, and that Rock is Christ. (See 1 Corinthians 10:4.) When you feed on Him, your soul can sing, "He satisfied my mouth with good things, so that my youth is renewed like the eagle's." (See Psalm 103:5.) But if you are not His own, your riches and success can give you no satisfaction. You will one day lament over them in the words of wisdom, "Vanity of vanities, all is vanity" (Ecclesiastes 1:2).

June 26
Morning

"Art thou become like unto us" (Isaiah 14:10).

What must be the apostate's doom when his naked soul appears before God? How will he bear that voice, "Depart, ye cursed; you have rejected Me, and I reject you; you have played the harlot and departed from Me. I also have banished you forever from My presence and will not have mercy on you"? What will be this wretch's shame at the last great day when, before assembled multitudes, the apostate will be unmasked? No greater eagerness will ever be seen among Satanic tormentors than in that day when devils drag the hypocrite's soul down to perdition. Bunyan pictures this with massive but awful grandeur of poetry when he speaks of the back way to hell. Seven devils bound the wretch with nine cords and dragged him from the road to heaven, in which he had professed to walk, and thrust him through the back door into hell. Mind that back way to hell! Examine yourselves whether you are in the faith. Look well to your state and see whether you be in Christ or not. It is the easiest thing in the world to give a lenient verdict when one's self is to be tried. Be just to all, but be rigorous to yourself. Remember, if it is not a rock on which you build, when the house falls, great will be the fall of it. May the Lord give you sincerity, constancy, and firmness; and in no day, however evil, may you be led to turn aside.

June 26
Evening

"Having escaped the corruption that is in the world through lust" (2 Peter 1:4).

Banish forever all thoughts of indulging the flesh if you want to live in the power of your risen Lord. It is tragic when a man who is alive in Christ dwells in the corruption of sin. "Why seek ye the living among the dead?" (Luke 24:5). Should the living dwell in a tomb? Should divine life be buried in the grave of fleshly lust? How can we partake of the cup of the Lord and yet drink the cup of Satan? Surely you are delivered from open lusts and sins. Have you also escaped from the secret and delusive traps of the Satanic hunter? Have you escaped from slothfulness? Are you free from carnal security? Are you seeking day by day to live above worldiness, the pride of life, and greed? Remember, it is for this reason that you have been enriched with the treasures of God. Do not permit all the lavish treasure of grace to be wasted upon you. Follow after holiness; it is the Christian's crown and glory. An unholy church is useless to the world and has no esteem among men. It is an abomination, hell's laughter, and heaven's abhorrence. The worst evils which have ever come upon the world have been brought upon it by an unholy church. You are God's priest—act as such. You are God's king—reign over your lusts. You are God's chosen—do not associate with sin. Heaven is your inheritance. Live like a heavenly spirit, and you will prove that you have true faith in Jesus. There cannot be faith in the heart unless there is holiness in the life.

June 27
Morning

"Only ye shall not go very far away" (Exodus 8:28).

This is a crafty word from the Pharaoh. If the poor bondaged Israelites must go out of Egypt, then he bargains with them that it will not be very far away—at least not far enough to escape the terror of his arms and the observation of his spies. After the same fashion, the world would have us be more charitable and not carry matters with too severe a hand. Death to the world and burial with Christ are experiences which carnal minds treat with ridicule. Worldly wisdom recommends the path of compromise and talks of moderation. According to this carnal policy, purity is admitted to be very desirable, but we are warned against being too precise. Truth is of course to be followed, but error is not to be severely denounced. "Yes," says the world, "be spiritually minded by all means, but do not deny yourself a little frivolity. What's the good of criticizing something when it is so fashionable and everybody does it?" Multitudes of professing Christians yield to this cunning advice to their own eternal ruin. If we would follow the Lord wholly, we must go right away into the wilderness and leave the carnal world behind us. We must leave its maxims, pleasures, and religion and go far away to the place where the Lord calls His sanctified ones. When the town is on fire, our house cannot be too far from the flames. To all true believers, let the trumpet-call be sounded, "Come ye out from among them; be ye separate" (2 Corinthians 6:17).

June 27
Evening

"Let every man abide in the same calling wherein he was called" (1 Corinthians 7:20).

Some persons have the foolish notion that the only way they can live for God is by becoming ministers or missionaries. Many would be shut out from any opportunity of magnifying the Most High if this was true! Beloved, it is not the work, it is the earnestness with which it is performed. It is not position, it is the grace which will enable us to glorify God. God is most glorified in that factory where the godly worker, as he operates his machine, sings of the Savior's love. He is glorified far more there than in many pulpits where official *religiousness* performs its scanty duties. The name of Jesus is glorified by the clerk at the drugstore who praises God or speaks to her co-workers about Jesus as much as by the popular preacher who is thundering the gospel throughout the country. God is glorified by our serving Him in our proper vocations. Do not forsake the path of duty by leaving your occupation, and take care you do not dishonor your profession while in it. Do not think too little of your calling. Every lawful trade may be sanctified by the gospel. Turn to the Bible, and you will find the most menial forms of labor connected with daring deeds of faith. Therefore, be not discontented with your calling. Whatever God has made your position, abide in that, unless you are *quite sure* that He calls you to something else. Let your first concern be to glorify God to the utmost of your power where you are. If He needs you somewhere else, He will show you. This evening, lay aside troublesome ambition, and embrace peaceful content.

June 28
Morning

"Looking unto Jesus" (Hebrews 12:2).

It is the Holy Spirit's work to turn our eyes away from self to Jesus. Satan's work is just the opposite of this. He is constantly trying to make us regard ourselves instead of Christ. Satan implants thoughts about self, and we will never find comfort of assurance by looking within. But the Holy Spirit turns our eyes entirely away from self. He tells us that we are nothing, but that "Christ is all in all" (Colossians 3:11). Remember, therefore, it is not your hold on Christ that saves you—it is Christ. It is not even faith in Christ, though that be the instrument—it is Christ's blood and merits. Therefore, look not so much to your hand with which you are grasping Christ, as to look at Christ Himself. Look to Jesus, the source of your hope, the author and finisher of your faith. We will never find happiness by looking at our prayers, our doings, or our feelings. It is what *Jesus* is, not what *we* are, that gives rest to the soul. If we would at once overcome Satan and have peace with God, it must be by "looking unto Jesus." Simply keep your eye on Him. Let His death, His sufferings, His merits, His glories, and His intercession be fresh on your mind. When you wake in the morning, look to Him. When you lie down at night, look to Him. He will never fail you!

June 28
Evening

"But Aaron's rod swallowed up their rods" (Exodus 7:12).

This incident shows the sure victory of the divine handiwork over all opposition. Whenever a divine principle is cast into the heart, the devil may fashion a counterfeit and produce swarms of opponents. But God's work will swallow up all its foes. If God's grace takes possession of a man, the world's magicians may throw down all their rods. But even if every rod is as cunning and poisonous as a serpent, Aaron's rod will swallow up their rods. The sweet attractions of the cross will win the man's heart. He who lived only for this deceitful earth will now have an eye for the upper spheres and a wing to mount into celestial heights. Our faith has to meet a multitude of foes! The devil throws our old sins down before us, and they turn to serpents. But the cross of Jesus destroys them all. Then the devil launched forth another host of serpents in the form of worldly trials, temptations, and unbelief. But faith in Jesus is more than a match for them and overcomes them all. The same principle shines in the faithful service of God. With an enthusiastic love for Jesus, difficulties are surmounted, sacrifices become pleasures, and sufferings are honors. But there are many persons who profess religion, but do not possess it. The religion that they have will not pass this test. Examine yourself on this point. Aaron's rod *proved* its heaven-given power. Is your life doing so? If Christ is anything to you, He must be everything. Oh, do not rest until love and faith in Jesus are the master passions of your soul!

June 29
Morning

"Them also which sleep in Jesus will God bring with him" (1 Thessalonians 4:14).

Do not think that the soul sleeps in insensibility. "Today shalt thou be with me in Paradise" is the whisper of Christ to every dying saint. They "sleep in Jesus," but their souls are before the throne of God, praising Him day and night in His temple, singing hallelujahs to Him who washed them from their sins in His blood. The body sleeps in its lonely bed of dirt beneath the coverlet of grass. But what is this sleep? The idea connected with sleep is *rest,* and that is the thought which the Spirit of God would convey to us. Sleep shuts the door of the soul and bids all intruders to wait for a while. The toil-worn believer quietly sleeps like a weary child who slumbers on his mother's breast. Happy are they who die in the Lord. They rest from their labors, and their works follow them. Guarded by angel watchers, curtained by eternal mysteries, their earthly bodies sleep on, until the fullness of time brings the fullness of redemption. They went to their rest with the furrowed brow and the wasted features, but they will wake up in beauty and glory. The shriveled seed, so destitute of form and comeliness, rises from the dust a beautiful flower. The winter of the grave gives way to the spring of redemption and the summer of glory. Blessed are those who "sleep in Jesus."

June 29
Evening

"Howbeit in the business of the ambassadors of the princes of Babylon, who sent unto him to inquire of the wonder that was done in the land, God left him, to try him, that he might know all that was in his heart" (2 Chronicles 32:31).

Hezekiah was growing spiritually great and priding himself upon the favor of God to such an extent that self-righteousness crept into his heart. Because of his carnal security, the grace of God was withdrawn for a time. This explains his difficulties with the Babylonians. If the grace of God left the best Christian, there is enough sin in his heart to make him the worst of transgressors. If left to yourselves, you who are on fire for Christ would cool down like Laodicea into sickening lukewarmness. You who are strong in the faith would be white with the leprosy of false doctrine. You who now walk before the Lord in excellence and integrity would stagger with the drunkenness of evil passion. Like the moon, we borrow our light. Although we are bright when grace shines on us, we are darkness itself when the Sun of Righteousness withdraws Himself. Lord, do not withdraw Your indwelling grace! You said in Isaiah 27:3, "I the Lord do keep it; I will water it every moment: lest any hurt it, I will keep it night and day." Lord, keep us everywhere. Keep us in the valley, that we do not murmur against Your humbling hand. Keep us on the mountain, that we do not become full of pride. Keep us in youth, when our passions are strong. Keep us in old age, when, becoming conceited by our wisdom, we prove to be greater fools than the young and naive. Keep us living, keep us dying, keep us laboring, keep us suffering, keep us fighting, keep us resting, keep us everywhere, for everwhere we need You, O God!

June 30
Morning

"And the glory which thou gavest me I have given them" (John 17:22).

Behold the unsurpassed openhandedness of the Lord Jesus for He has given us His all. Although a tithe of His possessions would have made a universe of angels rich beyond all thought, He was not content until He had given us all that He had. We would have been satisfied if He had allowed us to eat the crumbs of His bounty beneath the table of His mercy; but He will do nothing by halves. He makes us sit with Him and share the feast. Had Jesus given us some small pension from His royal chambers, we would have had cause to love Him eternally. But no, He wants His bride to be as rich as Himself. He will not have a glory or a grace in which she will not share. He has not been content with less than making us joint-heirs with Himself, so that we might have equal possessions. He gives His people the keys to every room in His house. He gives them full liberty to take all that He has to be their own. Christ has put the flask of His love and grace to the believer's lip and bidden him drink forever. If the believer could drain it, he is welcome to do so; but since he cannot exhaust it, he is bidden to drink abundantly, for it is all his own. What truer proof of fellowship can heaven or earth afford?

June 30
Evening

"Ah Lord God! behold, thou hast made the heaven and the earth by thy great power and stretched out arm, and there is nothing too hard for thee"(Jeremiah 32:17).

When the Chaldeans surrounded Jerusalem, and the sword, famine, and pestilence had desolated the land, Jeremiah was commanded by God to purchase a field and have the deed of transfer legally sealed and witnessed. This was a strange purchase for a rational man to make. Prudence could not justify it, for there was scarcely a chance that Jeremiah could ever enjoy the possession. But it was enough for Jeremiah that God had asked him to do it. He reasoned thus: "Ah, Lord God! You can make this plot of ground useful to me. You can rid this land of these oppressors. You can yet make me sit under my vine and my fig tree in the heritage which I have bought; for You made the heavens and the earth, and there is nothing too hard for You." This gave a majesty to the early saints. They dared to do at God's command things which human reason would condemn. Noah built a ship on dry land, Abraham offered up his only son, Moses despised the treasures of Egypt, and Joshua beseiged Jericho for seven days using no weapons but the blasts of rams' horns. They all acted upon God's command, contrary to the dictates of human reason. The Lord gave them a rich reward for their obedient faith. May we have a more potent infusion of this heroic faith in God. Let Jeremiah's place of confidence be ours—nothing is too hard for the God that created the heavens and the earth.

July 1
Morning

"In summer and in winter shall it be"
(Zechariah 14:8).

The streams of living water which flow from Jerusalem are not dried up by the parching heat of sultry midsummer anymore than they were frozen by the cold winds of blustering winter. Rejoice, Oh my soul, that you are spared to testify of the faithfulness of the Lord. The seasons change and you change, but your Lord remains the same. The streams of His love are as deep, as broad, and as full as ever. The heat of business cares and scorching trials make me need the cooling influences of the river of His grace. Job said his brothers were like deceitful brooks, but he found his God to be an overflowing river of consolation. The Nile is the great confidence of Egypt, but its floods are variable. Our Lord is always the same. By turning the course of the Euphrates, Cyrus took the city of Babylon; but no power, human or infernal, can divert the current of divine grace. The tracks of ancient rivers have been found all dry and desolate; but the streams which take their rise on the mountains of divine sovereignty and infinite love will always be full to the brim. Generations melt away, but the course of grace is unaltered. My soul, how blessed you are to be led beside such still waters! Never wander to other streams or you might hear the Lord's rebuke.

July 1
Evening

"The voice of the Lord God walking in the garden in the cool of the day" (Genesis 3:8).

Now that the cool of the day has come, rest awhile and listen to the voice of God. He is always ready to speak when you are prepared to hear. If there are any hindrances to communication, it is not on His part for He stands at the door and knocks. If His people will open their hearts, He rejoices to enter. But what is the state of my heart, my Lord's garden? Is it well trimmed and watered, and does it bring forth good fruit for Him? If not, He will have much to reprove, but I still ask Him to come to me. Nothing can bring my heart into a right condition like the presence of the Sun of Righteousness who brings healing in His wings. Come, therefore, O Lord my God. My soul invites You earnestly and waits for You eagerly. Plant fresh flowers in my garden, like those I see blooming in such perfection in Your matchless character! Deal with me in Your tenderness and wisdom, and rain upon my whole nature, as the herbs are now moistened with the evening dews. Speak, Lord, for Your servant is listening. Oh, that He would walk with me. I am ready to give up my whole heart and mind to Him. I am sure that He will want to have fellowship with me, for He has given me His Holy Spirit to abide with me forever. The cool twilight is sweet when every star shines like the eye of heaven and the cool wind as the breath of celestial love. My Father, my elder Brother, my sweet Comforter, speak now in lovingkindness, for You have opened my ear.

July 2
Morning

"Our heart shall rejoice in him" (Psalm 33:21).

The fact that Christians can rejoice, even in the deepest distress, is a blessing. The waves may roll over them, but their souls soon rise to the surface and see the light of God's countenance. They have a bouyancy about them which keeps their head always above the water and helps them to sing amid the tempest. Trouble does not necessarily bring consolation with it to the believer, but the presence of the Son of God in the trial with him fills his heart with joy. He is sick and suffering, but Jesus visits him. The cold, chilly waters of Jordan are gathering about him up to his neck. Jesus puts His arms around him and cries, "Fear not, beloved; to die is to be blessed; the waters of death have their fountain-head in heaven; they are not bitter; they are sweet as nectar, for they flow from the throne of God." As the departing saint wades through the stream, the billows gather around him, and heart and flesh fail him, the same voice sounds in his ear, "Fear not; I am with thee; be not dismayed; I am thy God" (Isaiah 41:10). As he nears the borders of the infinite unknown, Jesus says, "Fear not, little flock; for it is your Father's good pleasure to give you the kingdom" (Luke 12:32). Thus strengthened and consoled, the believer is not afraid to die. He is even willing to depart, for he has seen Jesus as the morning star and longs to gaze on Him as the sun in His strength. Truly, the presence of Jesus is all the heaven we desire.

July 2
Evening

"Unto thee will I cry, O Lord my rock; be not silent to me: lest, if thou be silent to me, I become like them that go down into the pit" (Psalm 28:1).

A cry is the natural expression of sorrow and a suitable utterance when all other expressions fail us. But the cry must be directed to the Lord, for to cry to man is a waste of time. When we consider the readiness of the Lord to hear and His ability to aid, we see the reason for directing all our appeals at once to the God of our salvation. It will be useless to call the rocks in the day of judgment, but our Rock hears our cries. "Be not silent to me." Those who merely go through the motions of prayer may be content without answers to their prayers, but genuine suppliants cannot. They must obtain actual replies from heaven, or they cannot rest. They long to receive their reply at once and dread even a little of God's silence. God's voice is often so terrible that it shakes the wilderness, but His silence is equally awe-inspiring. When God seems to close His ear, we must cry with more earnestness. When our voice grows shrill with eagerness and grief, He will not deny us a hearing for long. What a dreadful position we would be in if the Lord became forever silent to our prayers! "Lest if thou be silent to me, I become like them that go down into the pit." If deprived of the God who answers prayer, we would be in a worse plight than the dead in the grave. We would soon sink to the same level as the lost in hell. We *must* have answers to prayer because ours is an urgent case of dire necessity. Surely the Lord will speak peace to our agitated minds, for He will never permit His beloved children to perish.

July 3
Morning

"The ill-favoured and lean-fleshed kine did eat up the seven well-favoured and fat kine" (Genesis 41:4).

Pharaoh's dream has too often been my waking experience. My days of sloth have ruinously destroyed all that I had achieved in times of zealous industry. My seasons of coldness have frozen all the genial glow of my periods of fervency and enthusiasm. My fits of wordliness have thrown me back from my advances in the divine life. I need to beware of lean prayers, lean praises, lean duties, and lean experiences, for these will eat up the fat of my comfort and peace. If I neglect prayer for a short time, I lose all the spirituality to which I had attained. If I draw no fresh supplies from heaven, the old corn in my granary is soon consumed by the famine which rages in my soul. How anxious I am to have no lean-fleshed days, no ill-favored hours! If every day I journeyed toward the goal of my desires I would soon reach it, but backsliding leaves me still far off from the prize of my high calling and robs me of the advances which I had so laboriously made. The only way in which all my days can be like the healthy cattle is to feed in the right meadow and to spend time with the Lord in His service, in His company, in His fear, and in His way. Why wouldn't every year be richer than the past, in love, usefulness, and joy? I have had more experience of my Lord and should be more like Him. O Lord, keep the curse of leanness of soul far from me.

July 3
Evening

"If we suffer, we shall also reign with him" (2 Timothy 2:12).

We must not imagine that we are suffering for and with Christ if we are not *in* Christ. Are you trusting Jesus only? If not, whatever you may mourn over on earth is not "suffering with Christ." Such suffering gives no hope of reigning with Him in heaven. We must not conclude that all of a Christian's sufferings are sufferings with Christ. It is *essential* that he be *called by God* to suffer. If we are rash and imprudent and run into positions for which neither providence nor grace has prepared us, we should question whether we are sinning rather than communing with Jesus. If we let our emotions take the place of judgment and permit self-will to reign instead of scriptural authority, we will fight the Lord's battles with the devil's weapons. If we are injured in the fight, we should not be surprised. When troubles come upon us *as the result of sin,* we must not dream that we are suffering with Christ. Suffering which God accepts must have *God's glory as its end.* If I suffer that I may earn a name or win applause, I will get no other reward than that of the Pharisee. Love for Jesus and our brothers and sisters must be the reason for all our patience. We should manifest the character of Christ in meekness, gentleness, and forgiveness. Let us search our hearts and see if we truly suffer with Jesus. If we do, what is our light affliction compared with *reigning with Him?* It is a blessing to be in the furnace with Christ and an honor to stand in the face of ridicule and abuse with Him. If there was no future reward, we might count ourselves fortunate in our present honor. But when the recompense is infinitely more than we had any right to expect, shall we not take up the cross willingly and go on our way rejoicing?

July 4
Morning

"Sanctify them through thy truth" (John 17:17).

Sanctification begins in regeneration. The Spirit of God infuses into man that new living principle by which he becomes a new creature in Christ Jesus. This work, which begins in the new birth, is carried on in two ways: mortification, where the lusts of the flesh are subdued and kept under; and vivification, by which the life which God has put within us is made a well of water springing up to everlasting life. This is carried on every day in what is called perseverance, by which the Christian is preserved and continued in a gracious state and is made to abound in good works to the praise and glory of God. While the Spirit of God is the author of sanctification, there is a visible agency employed which must not be forgotten. "Sanctify them," said Jesus, "through thy truth. Thy word is truth" (John 17:17). Many passages of Scripture prove that the instrument of our sanctification is the Word of God. The Spirit of God brings to our minds the precepts and doctrines of truth and applies them with power. These are heard in the ear but received in the heart. They work in us to will and to do of God's good pleasure. The Word is the sanctifier. If we do not hear or read the truth, we will not grow in sanctification. "Thy word is a lamp unto my feet and a light unto my path" (Psalm 119:105).

July 4
Evening

"He that hath clean hands, and a pure heart; who hath not lifted up his soul unto vanity, nor sworn deceitfully" (Psalm 24:4).

Outward holiness is a precious mark of grace. Many have perverted the doctrine of justification by faith in such a way as to treat good works with scorn. They will receive everlasting contempt on Judgment Day. If our hands are not clean, let us wash them in Jesus' precious blood and lift up pure hands to God. But *clean hands* will not suffice unless they are connected with *a pure heart*. True religion is heart work. We may wash the outside of the cup and the platter, but if the inward parts remain filthy, we are filthy in the sight of God. The very life of our being lies in the inner nature, which is the reason for the need of purity within. The pure in heart will see God. (See Matthew 5:8.) All others are blind. The man who is born for heaven "hath not lifted up his soul unto vanity." All men have their joys which lift up their souls. The unbeliever lifts up his soul in carnal delights which are mere empty vanities, but the saint rejoices in the ways of the Lord. The one who is content with husks will be placed with the swine. Does the world satisfy you? Then you have your reward in this life. Make the most of it, for you will know no other joy. The saints are still men of honor. The Christian's word is his only oath, but it is as good as twenty oaths of other men. False speaking will shut any man out of heaven, for a liar will not enter into God's house. Does the Scripture condemn you this evening, or do you hope to ascend to the hill of the Lord?

July 5
Morning

"Called to be saints" (Romans 1:7)

We tend to regard the apostolic saints as if they were saints in a more special manner than the other children of God. All are saints whom God has called by His grace and sanctified by His Spirit. The nearer a man lives to God, the more intensely he mourns over his own evil heart. The more his Master honors him in His service, the more also does his evil flesh tease him daily. The fact is, if we had seen the apostle Paul, we would have thought him remarkably like the rest of the chosen family. If we had talked with him, we would have said, "We find that his experience and ours are much the same. He is more faithful, more holy, and more deeply taught than we are, but he has the same trials to endure." Do not look on the ancient saints as being exempt from infirmities or sins. Do not regard them with that mystic reverence which will almost make us idolaters. Their holiness is attainable even by us. We are called to be saints by that same voice which constrained them to their high vocation. It is a Christian's duty to force his way into the inner circle of saintship. We have the same light that they had, and the same grace is accessible to us. Why should we rest satisfied until we have equaled them in heavenly character? They lived *with* Jesus and *for* Jesus. Therefore, they grew *like* Jesus. Let us live by the same Spirit as they did, "looking unto Jesus," and our saintship will soon be apparent.

July 5
Evening

"Trust ye in the Lord for ever: for in the Lord Jehovah is everlasting strength" (Isaiah 26:4).

Seeing that we have such a God to trust, let us rest upon Him. Let us resolutely drive out all unbelief and get rid of the doubts and fears which mar our comfort. There is no excuse for fear when God is the foundation of our trust. A loving parent would be deeply grieved if his child could not trust him. How ungenerous, how unkind is our conduct when we put so little confidence in our heavenly Father who has never failed us and who never will! Doubting should be banished from the household of God. But old Unbelief is as nimble today as when the psalmist asked, "Is his mercy clean gone for ever? doth his promise fail for evermore?" (Psalm 77:8). Despite temptations to doubt, we should speak well of our God. There is none like Him in the heaven above or the earth beneath. "To whom then will ye liken me, or shall I be equal? saith the Holy One" (Isaiah 40:25). There is no rock like the rock of Jacob. Our enemies themselves realize this. Rather than permit doubts to live in our hearts, we will take the whole detestable crew, as Elijah did the prophets of Baal, and slay them over the brook. We will kill them at the sacred stream which wells forth from our Savior's wounded side. We have been in many trials, but we have never yet been in a place where we could not find all that we needed in God. Let us be encouraged to trust in the Lord forever, assured that His everlasting strength will be, as it has been, our help and fortress.

July 6
Morning

"Whoso hearkeneth unto me shall dwell safely, and shall be quiet from fear of evil" (Proverbs 1:33).

The Israelites provoked the Most High by their continued idolatry. He punished them by withholding both dew and rain, so that their land was visited by a sore famine. But while He did this, He took care that His own chosen ones would be secure. If all other brooks are dry, yet there will be one reserved for Elijah. When that fails, God will still preserve for him a place of sustenance. The Lord had not simply one Elijah, but He had a remnant who were hidden by fifties in a cave. Though the whole land was subject to famine, yet these fifties in the cave were fed from Ahab's table by the faithful, God-fearing steward, Obadiah. Let us draw from this the inference that, come what may, God's people are safe. Let convulsions shake the solid earth, and let the skies themselves be rent in two. Yet, amid the wreck of worlds the believer will be as secure as in the calmest hour of rest. If God cannot save His people under heaven, He will save them in heaven. If the world becomes too hot to hold them, then heaven will be the place of their reception and their safety. Be confident when you hear of wars and rumors of wars. Let no agitation distress you, but be quiet from fear of evil. Whatever comes on the earth, you, beneath the broad wings of Jehovah, will be secure.

July 6
Evening

"How many are mine iniquities and sins" (Job 13:23).

Have you ever considered how great the sin of God's people is? Think of the seriousness of your own transgressions. What a collection of sin there is in the life of even the most sanctified of God's children! Multiply the sin of one by the multitude of the redeemed, "a great multitude which no man can number" (Revelation 4:9), and you will have some conception of the great mass of the guilt of the people for whom Jesus shed His blood. We get a better idea of the magnitude of sin by the greatness of the remedy provided. It is the blood of Jesus Christ, God's only and well-beloved Son. God's Son! Angels cast their crowns before Him! All the choral symphonies of heaven surrounded His glorious throne. He is "over all, God blessed forever. Amen." (Romans 9:5). Yet, He takes upon Himself the form of a servant and is scourged and pierced, bruised and torn, and at last crucified. Nothing but the blood of the incarnate Son of God could make atonement for our offenses. No human mind can estimate the infinite value of the divine sacrifice. Great as the sin of God's people is, the atonement which takes it away is immeasurably greater. Therefore, even when sin rolls like a flood and the remembrance of the past is bitter, the believer can stand before the blazing throne of the great and holy God and cry, "Who is he that condemneth? It is Christ that died, yea rather, that is risen again" (Romans 8:34). While the recollection of his sin fills him with shame and sorrow, he uses it to show the brightness of mercy. Guilt is the dark night in which the fair star of divine love shines with serene splendor.

July 7
Morning

"Brethren, pray for us" (1 Thessalonians 5:25).

We implore every Christian household to grant this fervent request first uttered by an apostle. A very heavy responsibility rests on all ministers of the gospel. As officers in Christ's army, they are the special targets of the enmity of men and devils. Their sacred calling involves temptations from which you are exempt. Above all, it too often draws them away from personal enjoyment of truth into a ministerial and official consideration of it. They observe very sad backslidings, and their hearts are wounded. They see millions perishing, and their spirits sink. They want to profit from their preaching. They desire to be a blessing to your children. They long to be useful both to saints and sinners. Therefore, dear friends, intercede for those in the ministry. You do not look to them but to the Master for spiritual blessings. Yet, how many times has He given those blessings through His ministers! Ask, then, again and again, that they may be the earthen vessels into which the Lord may put the treasures of the gospel. The whole company of missionaries, ministers, teachers, and students, in the name of Jesus, beseech you—"Brethren, pray for us."

July 7
Evening

"When I passed by thee. . .I said unto thee. . .Live" (Ezekiel 16:6).

Saved one, gratefully consider this statement of mercy. Note that this command of God is *majestic.* In our text, we perceive a sinner with nothing in him but sin and expecting nothing but wrath. But the eternal Lord passes by in His glory. He looks, He pauses, and He pronounces the solitary but royal word—*Live.* This command is *manifold.* When He says, "Live," it includes many things. The sinner is ready to be condemned, but the mighty One says, Live, and he rises pardoned and absolved. The command is spiritual life. We did not know Jesus. Our eyes could not see Christ, and our ears could not hear His voice. Jehovah said, "Live," and we who were dead in trespasses and sins were made alive. The command includes glory-life which is the perfection of spiritual life. "I said unto thee. . .Live," and that word rolls on through all the years of time until death comes. In the midst of the shadows of death, the Lord's voice is still heard, "Live!" In the morning of the resurrection it is that same voice which is echoed by the archangel, "Live." As redeemed spirits rise to heaven to be blessed forever in the glory of God, it is by the power of this same word, "Live." It is an *irresistible* command. Saul of Tarsus was on the road to Damascus to arrest the saints of God. A voice was heard from heaven, and a light was seen that was brighter than the sun. Saul cried out, "Lord, what wilt thou have me to do?" (Acts 9:6). This mandate is one of *free grace.* When sinners are saved, it is only because God does it to magnify His free, unpurchased, unsought grace. Christian, see your position as a debtor to grace. Show your gratitude by an earnest, Christlike life.

July 8
Morning

"Tell me, I pray thee, wherein thy great strength lieth" (Judges 16:6).

Where lies the secret strength of faith? It lies in the food it feeds on. Faith studies *what the promise is*—an emanation of divine grace, an overflowing of the great heart of God. Faith says, "My God gave this promise out of love and grace; therefore, I am certain His Word will be fulfilled." Then faith thinks, "Who is the author of this promise?" It remembers that it is God, who cannot lie—God omnipotent and God immutable. Faith, therefore concludes that the promise must be fulfilled. It remembers why the promise was *given*—namely, for God's glory. He will never stain His own character or mar the luster of His own crown. Therefore, the promise must and will stand. Then faith also considers the amazing *work of Christ* as being a clear proof of the Father's intention to fulfill His Word. "He that spared not his own Son, but freely delivered him up for us all, how shall he not with him also freely give us all things?" (Romans 8:32). Faith looks back on *the past* and remembers that God never failed it. Faith recollects times of great peril when deliverance came and hours of awful need when its strength was found. It cries, "Hitherto the Lord has helped me, and He will help me still." Thus faith can say with assurance, "Surely goodness and mercy shall follow me all the days of my life!" (Psalm 23:6).

July 8
Evening

"Lead me in thy truth, and teach me: for thou art the God of my salvation; on thee do I wait all the day" (Psalm 25:5).

The believer begins with trembling feet to walk in the way of the Lord. He asks to be led onward like a little child upheld by his parent's helping hand. He craves to be further instructed in the alphabet of truth. The burden of the prayer in tonight's text is the instruction of the saints in the things of God. David knew much, but he realized his ignorance. He still desired to be in the Lord's school. Four times in two verses, he applies for a scholarship in the college of grace. Many believers, instead of following their own devices and cutting out new paths of thought for themselves, should inquire for the good ways of God's truth. They need to beseech the Holy Spirit to give them sanctified understandings and teachable spirits. *"For thou art the God of my salvation."* Jehovah is the Author and Perfecter of salvation to His people. Is He the God of *your* salvation? Do you find in the Father's mercy, in the Son's atonement, and in the Spirit's quickening, all the grounds of your eternal hopes? If the Lord has chosen to save you, surely He will not refuse to instruct you in His ways. We can address the Lord with the confidence which David manifests here. It gives us great power in prayer and comfort in trial. *"On thee do I wait all the day."* Patience is the fair daughter of faith. We cheerfully wait when we are certain that we shall not wait in vain. It is our duty and our privilege to wait upon the Lord in service, in worship, in expectancy, and in trust, all the days of our life. If our faith is true, it will bear continued trial without yielding. We will not grow weary of waiting upon God if we remember how long and how graciously He once waited for us.

July 9
Morning

"Forget not all his benefits" (Psalm 103:2).

It is delightful to observe the hand of God in the lives of ancient saints, His goodness in delivering them, His mercy in pardoning them, and His faithfulness in keeping His covenant with them. But it is even more interesting for us to mark the hand of God in our own lives. We do our Lord an injustice when we suppose that He performed all His mighty acts for those in the early time but does not perform wonders for the saints who are now on the earth. Let us review our own lives. Surely in these we may discover some happy incidents, refreshing to ourselves and glorifying to our God. Have you had no deliverances? Have you passed through rivers supported by the divine presence? Have you walked through fires unharmed? Have you had no manifestations? Have you had choice favors? Has God never listened to you and answered your requests? Surely the goodness of God has been the same to us as to the saints of old. Let us weave His mercies into a song. Let our souls give forth music as sweet and as exhilarating as came from David's harp while we praise the Lord whose mercy endureth forever.

July 9
Evening

"And God divided the light from the darkness" (Genesis 1:4).

A believer has two principles at work within him. In his natural state, he was subject to one principle only—darkness. Now light has entered, and the two principles are engaged in conflict. This is described by the apostle Paul in Romans 7:21-23. "I find then a law, that, when I would do good, evil is present with me. For I delight in the law of God after the inward man: But I see another law in my members, warring against the law of my mind, and bringing me into captivity to the law of sin which is in my members." How does this state of things come about? "God divided the light from the darkness." Darkness by itself is quiet and undisturbed. When the Lord sends in light, there is a conflict, for the one is in opposition to the other. This conflict will never cease until the believer has become completely light in the Lord. If there is a *division within* the individual Christian, there is certain to be a *division without.* As soon as the Lord gives light to any man, he begins to separate himself from the darkness around him. He secedes from mere worldly religion of outward ceremonies, for nothing short of the gospel of Christ will satisfy him now. He withdraws himself from worldly society and frivolous amusements and seeks the company of the saints. What God has divided, let us never try to unite. As Christ went outside the camp, bearing His reproach, so let us come out from the ungodly and be a peculiar people. He was holy, harmless, undefiled, and separate from sinners. So we are to be distinguished from the rest of mankind by our likeness to our Master.

July 10
Morning

"Fellow-citizens with the saints" (Ephesians 2:19).

What is meant by our being citizens in heaven? It means that we are under heaven's government. Christ, the King of heaven, reigns in our hearts. Our daily prayer is, "Thy will be done on earth as it is in heaven" (Matthew 6:10). The proclamations issued from the throne of glory are freely received by us. We cheerfully obey the decrees of the Great King. Then, as citizens of the New Jerusalem, we share heaven's honors. The glory which belongs to beautified saints belongs to us, for we are already sons of God. We have Christ for our Brother, God for our Father, and a crown of immortality for our reward. We share the honors of citizenship. We have common rights to all the property of heaven. Also, as citizens of heaven, we enjoy its delights. Do they there rejoice over sinners that repent—prodigals that have returned? So do we. Do they chant glories of triumphant grace? We do the same. Do they cast their crowns at Jesus' feet? We cast our honors there too. Are they charmed with His smile? It is not less sweet to us who dwell below. Do they look forward, waiting for His second advent? We also look and long for His appearing. Since we are *citizens of heaven,* let our walk and actions be consistent with our high dignity.

July 10
Evening

*"And the evening and the morning were the
first day"* (Genesis 1:5).

The evening was "darkness" and the morning
was "light." Yet, the two together are called by
the name that is given to the light alone—
day! This has an exact analogy in spiritual experience. In every believer there is darkness and light.
Yet, he is not to be called a sinner because there is
sin in him. He is to be named a saint because he
possesses some degree of holiness. This will be a
most comforting thought to those who ask, "Can I
be a child of God while there is so much darkness
in me?" Yes! you, like the day, do not take your
name from the evening, but from the morning.
You are spoken of in the Word of God as if you
were now perfectly holy, as you will be soon. You
are called the child of light, though there is darkness in you still. You are named after the predomi-
nating quality in the sight of God, which will one
day be the only principle remaining. Observe that
the evening comes first. Naturally, we are in darkness first. Gloom is often first in our mournful
apprehension, driving us to cry out in deep humiliation, "God be merciful to me a sinner." The
place of the morning is second. It dawns when
grace overcomes sin. John Bunyan said, "That
which is last, lasts forever." The first yields in due
season to the last; but nothing comes after the last.
Though you are darkness by nature, once you
become light in the Lord, there is no evening to
follow. "Thy sun shall no more go down" (Isaiah
60:20). The first day in this life is an evening and a
morning. But the second day, when we will be
with God forever, will be a day with no evening,
but one sacred, high, eternal noon.

July 11
Morning

"After that ye have suffered awhile, make you perfect, stablish, strengthen, settle you" (1 Peter 5:10).

You have seen the rainbow as it spans the plain. It is beautiful, but it passes away. The fair colors give way to the fleecy clouds, and the sky is no longer brilliant with the tints of heaven. It is not *established*. How can it be? How can a glorious show made up of transitory sunbeams and passing raindrops remain? The graces of the Christian character must not resemble the rainbow in its transitory beauty. Seek, believer, that every good thing you have may be an established, settled thing. May your character not be a writing on the sand but an inscription on the rock. Be rooted and grounded in love. May your whole life be so settled and established that all the blasts of hell and all the storms of earth will never be able to remove you. Notice how this blessing of being established in the faith is gained. The apostle's words point us to *suffering* as the means employed— *"After that ye have suffered awhile."* It is of no use to hope that we will be well rooted if no rough winds pass over us. Do not shrink from the tempestuous winds of trial, but take comfort, believing that by their rough discipline God is fulfilling this benediction to you.

July 11
Evening

"Tell ye you, children of it, and let your children tell their children, and their children another generation" (Joel 1:3).

In this simple way, by God's grace, a living testimony for truth is always to be kept alive in the land. The people of the Lord are to hand down their witness for the gospel to their heirs. These, in turn, share the truth with their next descendants. This is our *first* duty. He is a bad preacher who does not begin his ministry at home. The heathen are to be witnessed to by all means. But home has a prior claim, and woe to those who reverse the order of the Lord's arrangements. To teach our children is a *personal* duty. We cannot delegate it to Sunday school teachers or pastors. These can assist us, but they cannot deliver us from the sacred obligation. Mothers and fathers must, like Abraham, instruct their households in the fear of God and talk with their offspring concerning the wondrous works of the Most High. Parental teaching is a *natural* duty. Who is more qualified to look to the child's spiritual well-being as those who are the authors of his physical being? To neglect the instruction of our offspring is worse than cruel. Family prayer and Bible study are *necessary* for the nation, for the family, and for the Church. The kingdom of Satan is constantly trying to advance in our land. One of the most effectual means for resisting its inroads is left almost neglected—the instruction of children in the faith. Parents must realize the importance of this matter. It is a *pleasant* duty to talk of Jesus to our sons and daughters, and it has often proved to be an *accepted* work. God has saved the children through the parents' prayers and admonitions.

July 12
Morning

"Sanctified by God the Father" (Jude 1); *"Sanctified in Christ Jesus"* (1 Corinthians 1:2); *"Through sanctification of the Spirit"* (1 Peter 1:2).

How unwisely do those believers talk who make preferences in the Persons of the Trinity. They think of Jesus as if He were the embodiment of everything lovely and gracious, while the Father they regard as severely just and destitute of kindness. Equally wrong are those who magnify the decree of the Father and the atonement of the Son so as to depreciate the work of the Spirit. In deeds of grace, none of the Persons of the Trinity act apart from the rest. They are as united in their deeds as in their essence. In their love toward the chosen, they are one. In the actions which flow from that great central source, they are still undivided. Especially notice this in the matter of sanctification. While we may without mistake speak of sanctification as the work of the Spirit, we must take heed that we do not view it as if the Father and the Son had no part therein. It is correct to speak of sanctification as the work of the Father, of the Son, and of the Spirit. Jehovah said, "Let *us* make man in our own image after our likeness" (Genesis 1:26) and thus we are "His workmanship, created in Christ Jesus unto good works, which God hath before ordained that we should walk in them" (Ephesians 2:10). See the value which God sets on real holiness. You, as the follower of Christ, must also set a high value on holiness—on purity of life and godliness of conversation. Let us begin today to live in a manner that will manifest the work of the Triune God in us.

July 12
Evening

"His heavenly kingdom" (2 Timothy 4:18).

The city of the great King is a place of *active service*. Redeemed spirits serve Him day and night in His temple. They never cease to fulfill the good pleasure of their King. They always rest, as far as ease and freedom from care is concerned. Yet, they never rest in the sense of inactivity. Jerusalem is the place of *communion* with all the people of God. We will sit with Abraham, Isaac, and Jacob in eternal fellowship. We will converse with the noble host of the saints, all reigning with Him who, by His love and His mighty power, has brought them safely home. We will not sing solos, but in chorus we will praise our King. Heaven is a place of *realized victory*. Whenever you achieve a victory over your lusts, whenever, after hard struggling, you lay a temptation dead at your feet, you experience a foretaste of the joy that awaits you when the Lord will soon tread Satan under your feet. Then you will find yourself to be more than conqueror through Him who loved you. Paradise is a place of *security*. When you enjoy the full assurance of faith, you have the pledge of that glorious security which will be yours when you are a citizen of the heavenly Jerusalem. O my sweet home, Jerusalem, the happy harbor of my soul! I give thanks to Him whose love taught me to long for you. But I will shout louder thanks in eternity when I will live within your heavenly gates.

July 13
Morning

"God said to Jonah, Doest thou well to be angry" (Jonah 4:9).

Anger is not always sinful, but it has a tendency to run wild. Whenever it displays itself, we should be quick to question its character with this inquiry, "Doest thou well to be angry?" It may be that we can answer, "Yes." Very frequently anger is the madman's firebrand, but sometimes it is Elijah's fire from heaven. We do well when we are angry with sin because of the wrong which it commits against our good and gracious God. We are rightfully angry with ourselves if we remain so foolish after so much divine instruction. He who is not angry at transgression becomes a partaker in it. Sin is a loathsome and hateful thing, and no renewed heart can patiently endure it. God Himself is angry with the wicked every day. It is written in His Word, "Ye that love the Lord, hate evil" (Psalm 97:10). Far more frequently it is to be feared that our anger is not commendable or even justifiable. Then we must answer, "No." Why should we be fretful with children, irritable with workers, or irate with friends? Is such anger honorable to our Christian profession or glorifying to God? It is the old evil heart seeking to gain dominion. We should resist it with all the might of our new-born nature. Many believers give way to temper as though it were useless to attempt resistance. But let the believer remember that he must be a conqueror in every point, or else he cannot be crowned. If we cannot control our tempers, what has grace done for us? We must not make natural infirmity an excuse for sin. We must ask the Lord to crucify our tempers and renew us in gentleness and meekness after His own image.

July 13
Evening

*"When I cry unto thee, then shall mine ene-
mies turn back: this I know; for God is for me"*
(Psalm 56:9).

It is impossible for any words to express the full
meaning of this delightful phrase, *"God is for
me."* He was *for us* before the worlds were made.
He was *for us,* or He would not have given His
beloved Son. He was for us when He wounded the
Only-begotten and laid the full weight of His
wrath upon Him. He was *for us,* though He was
against *Him.* He was *for us* when we were ruined
in the fall—He loved us anyway. He was *for us*
when we were defiant rebels against Him. He was
for us, or He would not have brought us humbly
to seek His face. He has been *for us* in many struggles. We have encountered hosts of dangers. We
have been assailed by temptation from without
and within. How could we have remained
unharmed to this hour if He had not been *for us?*
He is *for us* with all the infinity of His being; with
all the omnipotence of His love; with all the infal-
libility of His wisdom. Arrayed in all His divine
attributes, He is eternally and immutably *for us.*
Because He is *for us,* the voice of prayer will
always insure His help. *"When I cry unto thee,
then shall mine enemies be turned back."* This is
no uncertain hope, but a well-grounded assurance— *"this I know."* I will direct my prayer to
God and look up for the answer, assured that it
will come. My enemies will be defeated because
God is for me. O believer, how happy you are with
the King of kings at your side! How safe with such
a Protector! How sure is your cause, pleaded by
such an Advocate! If God is for you, who can stand
against you?

July 14
Morning

"If thou lift up thy tool upon it, thou hast polluted it" (Exodus 20:25).

God's altar was to be built of unhewn stones, so that no trace of human skill or labor might be seen on it. Human wisdom delights to trim and arrange the doctrines of the cross into a system more artificial and more congenial with the depraved tastes of fallen nature. Instead of improving the gospel, carnal wisdom pollutes it until it becomes another gospel and not the truth of God at all. All alterations and amendments of the Lord's own Word are defilements. The proud heart of man is very anxious to have a hand in the justification of the soul before God. Preparations for Christ are dreamed of, humblings and repentings are trusted in, good works are cried up, and natural ability is much boasted. The Lord alone must be exalted in the work of atonement, and not a single mark of man's chisel or hammer will be endured. There is an inherent blasphemy in seeking to add to what Christ Jesus in His dying moments declared to be finished. Trembling sinner, put away your tools and fall on your knees in humble supplication. Accept the Lord Jesus to be the altar of your atonement, and rest in Him alone. Many believers may take warning from this morning's text as to the doctrines which they believe. There is far too much inclination among Christians to reconcile the truths of revelation. This is a form of irreverence and unbelief. Strive against it, and receive truth as you find it. Rejoice that the doctrines of the Word are unhewn stones and are all the more fit to build an altar for the Lord.

July 14
Evening

"As it began to dawn. . .came Mary Magdalene. . .to see the sepulchre" (Matthew 28:1).

Let us learn from Mary Magdalene how to obtain fellowship with the Lord Jesus. Notice how she looked for Him. She sought the Savior *very early* in the morning. If you can wait for Christ and be patient in the hope of having fellowship with Him at some distant hour, you will never have fellowship at all. The heart that is prepared for communion is a hungering and a thirsting heart. She sought Him with *great boldness.* Other disciples ran and hid, but Mary stood at the sepulcher. (See John 20:11.) If you desire to have Christ with you, let nothing hold you back. Defy the world. Press on where others flee. She sought Christ *faithfully*—she stood at the sepulcher. Some find it hard to stand by a living Savior, but she stood by a dead one. Let us seek Christ in this way, remaining faithful though all others forsake Him. She sought Jesus *earnestly.* She stood *weeping.* Those tears led the Savior to come forth and show Himself to her. If you desire Jesus' presence, weep after it! If you cannot be happy unless He comes and says to you, "You are My beloved," you will soon hear His voice. She sought the Savior *only.* She did not care for the angels. Her search was only for her Lord. If Christ is your one and only love, if your heart has cast out all rivals, you will not lack the comfort of His presence. Mary Magdalene sought Jesus *because she loved much.* Let us experience the same intensity of affection. Let our heart, like Mary's, be full of Christ. Then our love, like hers, will be satisfied with nothing but Him.

July 15
Morning

"The fire shall ever be burning upon the altar; it shall never go out" (Leviticus 6:13).

Keep the altar of private prayer burning. This is the very life of all piety. Burn here the fat of your sacrifices. Let your private devotions be, if possible, regular, frequent, and undisturbed. Effectual prayer availeth much. Have you nothing to pray for? Let us suggest the Church, the ministry, your own soul, your children, your relations, your neighbors, your country, and the cause of God and truth throughout the world. Let us examine ourselves on this important matter. Do we engage in private devotion with lukewarmness? Is the fire of devotion burning dimly in our hearts? If so, be alarmed at this sign of decay. Let us ask for the spirit of grace and of supplication. Let us set apart special periods for extraordinary prayer. For if this fire should be smothered beneath the ashes of a worldly conformity, it will dim the fire on the family altar and lessen our influence both in the Church and in the world. The text will also apply to the altar of the heart. This is a golden altar indeed. God loves to see the hearts of His people glowing toward Himself. Let us give God our hearts, blazing with love and seeking His grace, that the fire may never be quenched. It will not burn if the Lord does not keep it burning. Many adversaries will attempt to extinguish it. Let us use Scriptures as fuel for our heart's fire; they are live coals. Let us attend sermons, but above all let us be much alone with Jesus.

July 15
Evening

"He appeared first to Mary Magdalene" (Mark 16:9).

Jesus "appeared first to Mary Magdalene," probably not only on account of her great love and perseverance, but because she had a special experience with Christ's delivering power. The greatness of our sin before conversion does not determine the grade of fellowship that we may enjoy. She left all to become a *constant follower of the Savior.* He was her first and her chief object. Many who were on Christ's side did not take up Christ's cross, but *she* did. *She spent her substance in serving Him.* If we long to see much of Christ, let us also *serve* Him. Those who sit under the banner of His love and drink deeply from the cup of communion are those who give most, serve best, and abide closest to the bleeding heart of their dear Lord. Notice *how* Christ revealed Himself to this sorrowing one—by a *word,* "Mary." One word *in His voice,* and at once she knew Him. She replied with another word, and her heart was too full to say more. She said, "Master." When your spirit glows most with the heavenly fire you will say, "I am thy servant. . .thou hast loosed my bonds" (Psalm 116:16). If you can say, "Master," if you feel that His will is your will, then you stand in a happy, holy place. Christ honors those who honor Him, and love draws our Beloved. It needs but one word of His to turn our weeping to rejoicing, and His presence makes the heart's sunshine.

July 16
Morning

"They gathered manna every morning" (Exodus 16:21).

Labor to maintain a sense of your entire dependence on the Lord's good will and pleasure for the continuance of your richest enjoyments. Never try to live on the old manna or seek to find help in the world. All must come from Jesus. Old anointings will not suffice to impart unction to your spirit. Your head must have fresh oil poured on it from the golden horn of the sanctuary, or it will cease from its glory. Today you may be on the summit of the mount of God, but He who has put you there must keep you there, or you will sink. Your mountain only stands firm when He settles it in its place. If He hides His face, you will soon be troubled. Only Jesus can supply the joy of your heart, the light of your eyes, and the strength of your life. Comfort lies in His hand. Our Lord is determined that we will feel and recognize this hourly dependence, for He only permits us to pray for daily bread. He only promises that "as thy days, so shall thy strength be" (Deuteronomy 33:25). Is it not best for us that it should be so, that we may often approach His throne and constantly be reminded of His love? Oh, how rich the grace which supplies us so continually and does not refrain itself because of our ingratitude! The golden shower never ceases, the cloud of blessing hovers continually above our habitation. O Lord Jesus, we would bow at Your feet, conscious of our utter inability to do anything without You.

July 16
Evening

"Thou shalt arise, and have mercy upon Zion: for the time to favour her, yea, the set time is come. For thy servants take pleasure in her stones, and favour the dust thereof" (Psalm 102:13-14).

A selfish man in trouble is very hard to comfort because the springs of his comfort lie entirely within himself. But a Christian has other springs which supply comfort besides those which lie within. He can go to God and find abundant help. He can receive consolation in things relating to the world at large, to his country, and above all, to the Church. David was exceedingly sorrowful when he wrote, "I am like an owl of the desert. I watch, and am as a sparrow alone upon the house top" (Psalm 102:6-7). The only way he could comfort himself was in the reflection that God would have mercy upon Zion. Though *he* was sad, yet Zion would prosper; however desperate his own circumstances, Zion would arise. Learn to comfort yourself in God's gracious dealing toward the Church. Although your way is dark, you can still rejoice with the triumphs of His cross and the spread of His truth. Our personal troubles are forgotten while we look, not only upon what God *has* done and *is* doing for Zion, but on the glorious things He *will yet do* for His Church. Whenever you are sad of heart and heavy in spirit, forget yourself and your little concerns and seek the welfare and prosperity of God's people. When you bend your knee in prayer to God, do not limit your petition to the narrow circle of your own life. Send out prayers for the Church's prosperity. "Pray for the peace of Jerusalem" (Psalm 122:6), and your own soul will be refreshed.

July 17
Morning

"Knowing, brethren beloved, your election of God" (1 Thessalonians 1:4).

Many people want to know their election before they look to Christ. But they cannot because it is only discovered by looking to Jesus. Do you think you are a lost, guilty sinner? Go straight to the cross of Christ and tell Jesus so. Tell Him that you have read in the Bible, "Him that cometh unto me I will in no wise cast out" (John 6:37). Look to Jesus and believe on Him, and you will prove your election directly. For as surely as you believe, you are elect. If you have given yourself wholly to Christ and trust Him, then you are one of God's chosen ones. But if you stop and say, "I want to know first whether I am elect," you do not know what you have asked. Go to Jesus just as you are. Leave all curious inquiry about election alone. Go straight to Christ and you will know your election. The assurance of the Holy Spirit will be given to you so that you will be able to say, "I know whom I have believed, and am persuaded that he is able to keep that which I have committed unto him" (2 Timothy 1:12). Christ was at the everlasting council. He can tell you whether you were chosen or not. But you cannot find it out in any other way. Go and put your trust in Him, and His answer will be, "I have loved thee with an everlasting love; therefore with lovingkindness have I drawn thee" (Jeremiah 31:3). There will be no doubt about His having chosen *you*, when you have chosen *Him*.

July 17
Evening

"Let not one of them escape" (1 Kings 18:40).

The prophet Elijah received the answer to his prayer. Fire from heaven consumed the sacrifice in the presence of all the people. He called upon the assembled Israelites to take the priests of Baal, and he sternly cried, "Let not one of them escape." He took them all down to the brook Kishon and killed them. We must do the same with our sins. They are all doomed; not one must be preserved. Do not spare it though it cries and begs. Strike, though it is something dear to you. Strike, for God struck at sin when it was laid upon His own Son. With stern, unflinching purpose you must condemn to death that sin which was once the idol of your heart. Jesus will be your power. You have strength to win the victory in the crusade against sin because Christ Jesus has promised to be with you to the end. If you want to triumph over darkness, stand in the presence of the Sun of Righteousness. There is no better place for the discovery of sin and recovery from its power and guilt than the immediate presence of God. Job never knew how to get rid of sin as well as he did when his eye of faith rested upon God. Then he repented in dust and ashes. The fine gold of the Christian often grows dim. We need the sacred fire to consume the dross. Let us run to God. He is a consuming fire. He will not consume our spirit, but He will destroy our sins. Let the goodness of God stir in us a sacred jealousy and a holy revenge against iniquities which are hateful in His sight. Go forth to battle in the strength of the Lord and utterly destroy the accursed crew. Let not one of them escape.

July 18
Morning

"They shall go hindmost with their standards" (Numbers 2:31).

The camp of Dan brought up the rear when the armies of Israel were on the march. The Danites occupied the hindmost place. But what did the position matter since they were as truly part of the host as were the foremost tribes? They followed the same fiery cloudy pillar. They ate the same manna, drank of the same spiritual rock, and journeyed to the same inheritance. Come, my heart, cheer up, though last and least, it is your privilege to be in the army and to fare as those who lead. Someone must be hindmost in honor and esteem. Someone must do menial work for Jesus, and why not I? The Danites occupied a very useful place. Stragglers have to be picked up on the march, and lost property has to be gathered from the field. Fiery spirits may dash forward over untrodden paths to learn fresh truth and win more souls to Jesus. But some of a more conservative spirit may be engaged in reminding the Church of her ancient faith and restoring her fainting sons. Every position has its duties, and the slowly moving children of God will find their peculiar state an eminent blessing to the whole host. The rear guard is a place of danger. There are foes behind us as well as before us. Attacks may come from any quarter. The experienced Christian will find much work for his weapons in aiding those poor, doubting, and wavering souls who are hindmost in faith, knowledge, and joy. These must not be left unaided. My soul, tenderly watch to help the hindmost this day.

402

July 18
Evening

"Neither shall one trust another: they shall walk every one in his path" (Joel 2:8).

Locusts always keep their rank. Although they are numbered in the thousands, they do not crowd each other and throw their race into confusion. This remarkable fact in nature shows how thoroughly the Lord has placed the spirit of order into His universe. The smallest creatures are as much controlled by it as are the orbiting planets. It would be wise for believers to be ruled by the same influence in their spiritual life. In *Christian graces* no one virtue should unsurp the sphere of another or eat the food of the rest for its own support. Affection must not smother honesty, courage must not elbow meekness out of the way, modesty must not jostle energy, and patience must not trample resolution. It is the same with *our duties*. One must not interfere with another. Public usefulness must not injure private prayer; church work must not push family worship into a corner. It is worthless to offer God one duty stained with the blood of another. Jesus told the Pharisee, "These ought ye to have done, and not to have left the other undone" (Matthew 23:23). The same rule applies to our *personal position*. We must minister as the Spirit has given us ability and not intrude upon our fellow servant's domain. Our Lord Jesus taught us not to covet the high places, but to be willing to be the least among the brethren. Keep an envious, ambitious spirit far from us. Let us feel the force of the Master's command and do as He tells us, keeping in rank with the rest of the believers. Tonight, let us see whether we are keeping the unity of the Spirit in the bond of peace. (See Ephesians 4:3.)

July 19
Morning

"The Lord our God hath showed us his glory"
(Deuteronomy 5:24).

How will the glory of God be manifested to such fallen creatures as we are? Man's eye is not single. He always has a side glance toward his own honor and too high an estimate of his own powers. He is not qualified to behold the glory of the Lord. It is clear, then, that self must get out of the way that there may be room for God to be exalted. This is the reason He allows His people to experience straits and difficulties. Being made conscious of their own folly and weakness, they will be fit to behold the majesty of God when He comes forth to work their deliverance. He whose life is one even and smooth path will see little of the glory of the Lord. He has few occasions of self-emptying and, therefore, little fitness for being filled with the revelation of God. Among the huge waves of bereavement, poverty, temptation, and reproach, we learn the power of Jehovah because we feel the littleness of man. Thank God, then, if you have been led by a rough road. This has given you your experience of God's greatness and lovingkindness. Your troubles have enriched you with a wealth of knowledge to be gained by no other means. Praise God that you have not been left to the darkness and ignorance which continued prosperity might have involved. In the fight of affliction you have been capacitated to excel in His glory because of His wonderful dealings with you.

July 19
Evening

"A bruised reed shall he not break, and smoking flax shall he not quench" (Matthew 12:20).

What is weaker than the bruised reed or the smoking flax? A reed that grows in the marsh snaps as soon as the wild duck touches it. If the foot of a man brushes against it, it is bruised and broken. Every wind that flits across the river moves it to and fro. Nothing is more frail or brittle, with an existence that is more in jeopardy, than a bruised reed. Look at the smoking flax. It has a spark within it, but it is almost smothered. An infant's breath might blow it out; nothing has a more precarious existence than its flame. *Weak things* are described here, yet Jesus says of them, "The smoking flax I will not quench; the bruised reed I will not break." Some of God's children are made strong to do mighty works for Him. But the majority of His people are a timid, trembling race. They are like starlings, frightened at every passer-by—a fearful little flock. If temptation comes, they are caught like birds in a snare. If trial threatens, they are ready to faint. Tossed by every turbulent breeze, they drift along like a sea bird on the crest of the billows—weak things, without strength, without wisdom, without foresight. Yet, because they are so weak, they have this promise made especially to them. How this shows us the compassion of Jesus—so gentle, tender, and considerate! We need never shrink back from *His* touch. We need never fear a harsh word from *Him.* Though He will chide us for our weakness, He does not rebuke. Bruised reeds will have no blows from Him, and the smoking flax will receive no dampening frowns.

July 20
Morning

"The earnest of our inheritance" (Ephesians 1:14).

Oh, what enlightenment, what joys, what consolation, what delight of heart is experienced by that man who has learned to feed on Jesus alone. Yet, the realization which we have of Christ's preciousness is, in this life, imperfect at best. As an old writer has said, " 'Tis but a taste!' " We have tasted that the Lord is gracious, but we do not yet know *how* good and gracious He is. What we know of His sweetness makes us long for more. We have enjoyed the first-fruits of the Spirit, and they have set us hungering and thirsting for the fullness of the heavenly vintage. We groan within ourselves, waiting for the adoption. Here we see the manna falling small like coriander seed, but there we will eat the bread of heaven. We are beginners in spiritual education. Although we have learned the first letters of the alphabet, we cannot read words yet, much less put sentences together. We have many ungratified desires at present, but soon every wish will be satisfied. Within time you will be rid of all your trials and troubles. Your eyes, now filled with tears, will weep no longer. You will gaze in ineffable rapture on the splendor of Him who sits on the throne. You will share in His triumph. You will be co-heir with Him who is the Heir of all things.

July 20
Evening

"And now what hast thou to do in the way of Egypt, to drink the waters of Sihor?" (Jeremiah 2:18).

By a variety of miracles, mercies, and deliverances, Jehovah proved Himself to be worthy of Israel's trust. Yet, they forsook their true and living God and followed false gods. The Lord constantly reproved them for their unfaithfulness. Our text contains one instance of God's reasoning with them: "What hast thou to do in the way of Egypt, to drink the waters of the muddy river?"— for so it may be translated. "Why do you wander afar and leave your own cool stream from Lebanon? Why are you so strangely set on mischief that you cannot be content with the good and healthful, but instead follow after that which is evil and deceitful?" Is this a word of warning to the Christian? O true believer, called by grace and washed in the precious blood of Jesus, you have tasted a better drink than the muddy river of this world's pleasure can give. You have had fellowship with Christ, and the joy of seeing Jesus and leaning your head upon His bosom. Do the songs, honors, and merriment of this earth give you satisfaction after that? You have eaten the bread of angels; can you now live on husks? Good Rutherford once said, "I have tasted of Christ's own manna, and it hath put my mouth out of taste for the brown bread of this world's joys." It should be the same with you. If you are seeking the waters of Egypt, return quickly to the one living fountain. The waters of Sihor may be sweet to the Egyptians, but they will offer only bitterness to you. What do you have to do with them?

July 21
Morning

"The daughter of Jerusalem hath shaken her head at thee" (Isaiah 37:22).

Reassured by the Word of the Lord, the poor, trembling citizens of Zion grew bold and shook their heads at Sennacherib's boastful threats. Strong faith enables the servants of God to look with calm contempt on their most haughty foes. We know that our enemies are attempting impossibilities. They seek to destroy the eternal life which cannot die while Jesus lives. They seek to overthrow the citadel against which the gates of hell will not prevail. We know their weakness. What are they but men? And what is man but a worm? When the Lord arises, they will fly as chaff before the wind and be consumed as crackling thorns. Their utter powerlessness to do damage to the cause of God and His truth may make the weakest soldiers in Zion's ranks laugh them to scorn. Above all, we know that the Most High is with us. When He dresses Himself for battle, where are His enemies? His rod of iron will dash them in pieces like a potter's vessel, and their very remembrance will perish from the earth. The Kingdom is safe in the King's hands. Let us shout for joy for the Lord reigns, and His foes will be as straw for the dunghill.

July 21
Evening

"Why go I mourning?" (Psalm 42:9).

Can you find any reason why you mourn instead of rejoice? Why yield to gloomy anticipations? Who said that the night would never end in day? Who told you the sea of circumstances would drain until nothing is left but the mud of horrible poverty? Who said that the winter of your discontent would proceed from frost to frost, from snow and ice and hail to deeper snow and more heavy tempest of despair? Day follows night, flood comes after ebb, and spring and summer give way to winter. Be filled with hope! God will never fail you! He loves you in the midst of all this. Mountains, though hidden by darkness, are as real as in day, and God's love is as true now as it was in your brightest moments. No father punishes His children always. The Lord hates the rod as much as you do. He only uses it for the same reason that should make you willing to receive it—it works your lasting good. You will yet climb Jacob's ladder with the angels and behold Him who sits at the top of it—your covenant God. Amid the splendors of eternity, you will forget the trials of time. Or you will only remember them to bless God who led you through them and brought about lasting good by them. Come, sing in the midst of tribulation. Rejoice even while passing through the furnace. Make the wilderness blossom like the rose! Cause the desert to ring with exultant joys, for these light afflictions will soon be over, and then, forever with the Lord, your bliss will never fade.

July 22
Morning

"I am married unto you" (Jeremiah 3:14).

Christ Jesus is joined to His people in marriage. In love He espoused His Church as a chaste virgin long before she fell under the yoke of bondage. Full of burning affection, He toiled like Jacob for Rachel, until the whole of her purchase-money had been paid. Now, having sought her by His Spirit and brought her to know and love Him, He awaits the glorious hour when their mutual bliss will be consummated at the marriage-supper of the Lamb. The glorious Bridegroom has not yet presented His betrothed, perfect and complete, before the Majesty of heaven. She is still a wanderer in a world of woe, a dweller in the tents of Kedar. But she is even now the bride, the spouse of Jesus, dear to His heart, precious in His sight, written on His hands, and united with His person. On earth He exercises toward her all the affectionate offices of Husband. He makes rich provision for her needs, pays all her debts, allows her to assume His name and to share in all His wealth. He will never act otherwise to her. He will never mention the word divorce, for "He hateth putting away" (Malachi 2:16). Death must sever the conjugal tie between the most loving mortals, but it cannot divide the links of this immortal marriage. In heaven they marry not but are as the angels of God. Yet, there is this one marvelous exception to the rule, for in heaven Christ and His Church will celebrate their joyous nuptials.

July 22
Evening

"Behold the man!" (John 19:5).

Our Lord Jesus fully became the joy and comfort of His people when He plunged deepest into the depths of sorrow. Come and behold the Man in the garden of Gethsemane. Behold His heart, so brimming with love that He cannot hold it in and so full of sorrow that it must find a vent. Behold the bloody sweat as it falls upon the ground. Behold the Man as they drive the nails into His hands and feet. Look up, repenting sinners and see the sorrowful image of your suffering Lord. The ruby drops stand on the thorn-crown and adorn the diadem of the King with priceless gems. Behold the Man when all His bones are out of joint, and He is poured out like water and brought into the dust of death. God forsook Him, and hell surrounded Him. Behold and see: was there ever sorrow like His sorrow? Draw near and look upon this spectacle of grief—unique, unparalleled, a wonder to men and angels. Gaze upon Him, for if there is not consolation in a crucified Christ, there is no joy in earth or heaven. If the ransom price of His blood offers no hope, there can be no joy in your heart. As we sit at the foot of the cross, we become less troubled with our doubts and fears. When we see His sorrows, we will be ashamed to mention our own. We need only gaze into His wounds to heal our own. If we live uprightly, it will be by the contemplation of His death. If we rise to dignity, it must be by considering His humiliation and His sorrow.

July 23
Morning

"Even thou wast as one of them" (Obadiah 1:11).

Special stress in the sentence before us is laid on the word *thou*. A bad action may be all the worse because of the person who has committed it. When God's chosen people sin, we sin with an emphasis. If an angel should lay his hand on us when we are doing evil, he need not use any other rebuke than the question, "What dost thou here?" Much forgiven, much delivered, much instructed, and much blessed, will we dare to put our hand to evil? God forbid! A few minutes of confession may be beneficial to you this morning. Have you ever behaved as the wicked? At an evening party, certain men laughed at an unclean joke. *You were as one of them, and it was not altogether offensive to your ears.* When hard things were spoken concerning the ways of God, you were bashfully silent and seemed to be *as one of them*. Is there any difference? Here we come to close quarters. Be honest with yourself and make sure that you are a new creature in Christ Jesus. When this is sure, walk jealously lest any would again be able to say, "Even you were as one of them." You would not desire to share their eternal doom, why be like them here? Side with the afflicted people of God and not with the world.

July 23
Evening

"The blood of Jesus Christ his Son cleanseth us from all sin" (1 John 1:7).

"Cleanseth," says the text—not *"shall* cleanse." There are multitudes who think that as a dying hope they may look forward to pardon. Oh, how infinitely better to have cleansing now than to depend on the mere possibility of forgiveness when death is near. Some imagine that a sense of pardon is only obtainable after many years of Christian experience. But forgiveness of sin is a *present* thing—a privilege for this day, a joy for this very hour. The moment a sinner trusts Jesus, he is fully forgiven. The text also indicates *continuance.* It was "cleanseth" yesterday, it is "cleanseth" today, it will be "cleanseth" tomorrow. It will always be so with you, Christian, until you cross the river. You may come to this fountain every hour for it still cleanses you. Notice the *completeness* of the cleansing. "The blood of Jesus Christ his Son cleanseth us from *all* sin"— not only from sin, but "from *all* sin." The Holy Spirit will give you a taste of the sweetness of this word. Our sins against God are many. Whether the bill is little or great, the same check paid them all. The blood of Jesus Christ is as blessed and divine a payment for the transgressions of blaspheming Peter as for the shortcomings of loving John. Our iniquity is gone forever. Blessed completeness! What a sweet theme to dwell upon as one drifts off to sleep.

July 24
Morning

"Stand still, and see the salvation of the Lord" (Exodus 14:13).

These words contain God's command to the believer when he is brought into extraordinary difficulties. He cannot retreat or go forward. He is shut up on the right hand and on the left. What is he to do now? The Master's Word to him is, "Stand still." It will be well for him if at such times he listens only to his Master's word, for other and evil advisers come with their suggestions. Despair whispers, "Lie down and die; give it all up." But God would have us walk in cheerful courage and rejoice in His love and faithfulness. Cowardice says, "Retreat and go back to the world's way of acting. You cannot play the Christian's part. It is too difficult. Relinquish your principles." However much Satan may urge this course on you, you cannot follow it if you are a child of God. If you are called to stand still for a while, it is to renew your strength for some greater advance in due time. Hastiness cries, "Do something. Stir yourself because to stand still and wait is sheer idleness." Presumption boasts, "If the sea is before you, march into it and expect a miracle." But faith does not listen to presumption, despair, cowardice, or hastiness. It hears God say, "Stand still," and it stands immovable as a rock. "Stand still"—keep the posture of a man ready for action, expecting further orders, while cheerfully and patiently awaiting the directing voice. It will not be long before God will say to you, as distinctly as Moses said it to the people of Israel, "Go forward."

July 24
Evening

"His camp is very great" (Joel 2:11).

Consider the mightiness of the Lord who is your glory and defense. He is a Man of war; Jehovah is His name. All *the forces of heaven* listen for His call. Cherubim and seraphim, watchers and holy ones, principalities and powers, are all attentive to His will. If our eyes were not blinded by the nearsightedness of our flesh, we would see horses and chariots of fire surrounding the Lord's beloved. The powers of nature are all subject to the absolute control of the Creator. Stormy wind and tempest, lightning and rain, snow and hail, and the soft dews and cheering sunshine come and go at His decree. Earth, sea, air, and the places under the earth are the barracks for Jehovah's great armies. Space is His campground, light is His banner, and flame is His sword. When He goes forth to war, famine ravages the land, pestilence smites the nations, hurricane sweeps the sea, tornado shakes the mountains, and earthquake makes the solid world tremble. See to it that you are at peace with this mighty King. Be sure to enlist under His banner, for to fight against Him is madness, and to serve Him is glory. Jesus is ready to receive recruits for the army of the Lord. If you are not already enlisted, go to Him before you sleep and beg to be accepted through His merits. If you are already a soldier of the cross, be of good courage. The enemy is powerless compared with your Lord, whose camp is very great.

"He left his garment in her hand, and fled and got him out" (Genesis 39:12).

In contending with certain sins there remains no mode of victory but by flight. He who would be safe from acts of evil must run away from occasions of it. A covenant must be made with our eyes not even to look on the cause of temptation for such sins only need a spark to begin with and a blaze follows in an instant. Who would enter the leper's prison and sleep amid its horrible corruption? Only he who desires to be leprous himself would thus court contagion. If the mariner knew how to avoid a storm, he would do anything rather than run the risk of weathering it. Today I may be exposed to great peril; let me have the wisdom to keep out of it and avoid it. The wings of a dove may be of more use to me today than the jaws of a lion. It is true I may be an apparent loser by declining evil company, but I had better leave my cloak than lose my character. It is not needful that I be rich, but it is imperative for me to be pure. No ties of friendship, no chains of beauty, no flashings of talent, or no unfair ridicule must turn me from the wise resolve to flee from sin. I am to resist the devil, and he will flee from me; but the lusts of the flesh I must flee, or they will surely overcome me.

July 25
Evening

"In their affliction they will seek me early"
(Hosea 5:15).

Losses and adversities are frequently used by the great Shepherd to fetch home His wandering sheep. Like fierce dogs, they draw the wanderers back to the fold. Lions cannot be tamed if they are too well fed. They must be brought down from their great strength, and then they will submit to the tamer's hand. The Christian often becomes obedient to his Lord's will by receiving dry bread and hard labor. When rich and increased in goods, many believers carry their heads much too loftily and speak boastfully. Like David, they flatter themselves saying, "I shall never be moved" (Psalm 30:6). When the Christian grows wealthy, is surrounded by friends, has good health and a happy family, he too often permits Mr. Carnal Security to feast at his table. Then, if he is a true child of God, there is a rod being prepared for him. His substance will melt away as a dream. There goes a portion of his estate—how soon the acres change hands! How fast his losses roll in! Where will they end? It is a blessed sign of divine life if, when these embarrassments occur, he begins to be distressed about his backsliding and returns to God. Blessed are the waves that wash the mariner upon the rock of salvation! Losses in business are often sanctified to enrich our souls. If the chosen soul will not come to the Lord with full hands, it will come empty. If we fail to honor Him on the pinnacle of riches, He will allow us to be brought into the valley of poverty. Yet, faint not, heir of sorrow, when you are rebuked. Rather, recognize the loving hand which chastens, and say like the prodigal son, "I will arise and go to my father" (Luke 15:18).

July 26
Morning

"Giving all diligence, add to your faith virtue, and to virtue knowledge" (2 Peter 1:5-6).

Take care that your faith is of the right kind—that it is not a mere belief of doctrine but a simple faith depending on Christ alone. Give diligent heed to your courage that you may, with a consciousness of right, go on boldly. Study well the Scriptures and get knowledge, for a knowledge of doctrine will tend to confirm faith. Try to understand God's Word; let it dwell in your heart richly. When you have done this, add to your knowledge temperance. Take heed to your body; be temperate without. Take heed to your soul; be temperate within. Get temperance of lip, life, heart, and thought. Add to this, by God's Holy Spirit, patience. Ask Him to give you that patience which endures affliction; which, when it is tried, will come forth as gold. Array yourself with patience that you may not murmur or be depressed in your afflictions. When that grace is won, look to godliness. Godliness is something more than religion. Make God's glory your object in life. To that add brotherly love. Have a love for all the saints. To that add charity which opens its arms to all men and loves their souls. When you are adorned with these jewels, you will come to know by clearest evidence your calling and election. Remember, lukewarmness and doubting very naturally go hand in hand.

July 26
Evening

"That he may set him with princes" (Psalm 113:8).

Our spiritual privileges are of the highest order. "Among princes" is the *place of select society.* "Truly our fellowship is with the Father, and with his Son Jesus Christ" (1 John 1:3). There is no select society like this! We are "a chosen generation, a royal priesthood, an holy nation, a peculiar people" (1 Peter 2:9). We have come "to the general assembly and church of the firstborn, which are written in heaven" (Hebrews 12:23). The saints have the right to a *royal audience.* The child of God has free access to the inner courts of heaven. "For through him we both have access by one Spirit unto the Father" (Ephesians 2:18). "Let us therefore come boldly," says the apostle in Hebrews 4:16, "to the throne of grace." Among princes there is *abundant wealth;* but what is the abundance of princes compared with the riches of believers? For "all are yours; and ye are Christ's; and Christ is God's" (1 Corinthians 3:22-23). "He that spared not his own Son, but delivered him up for us all, how shall he not with him also freely give us all things?" (Romans 8:32). Princes have *power.* A prince of heaven's empire has great influence, for Jesus "hath made us kings and priests unto God" (Revelation 1:6). We reign over the kingdom of time and eternity. Princes have *special honor.* We may look down upon all earthborn dignity from the high position upon which grace has seated us. He "hath raised us up together, and made us sit together in heavenly places in Christ Jesus" (Ephesians 2:6). We share the honor of Christ—compared with this, earthly splendors are not worth a thought. Communion with Jesus is a richer gem than ever glittered in an imperial diadem.

July 27
Morning

"Exceeding great and precious promises" (2 Peter 1:4).

If you know the preciousness of the promises and enjoy them in your own heart, take time to meditate on them. Thinking over the hallowed words will often be the prelude to their fulfillment. Many a Christian who has thirsted for the promise has found the sought after blessing gently distilling into his soul while he is meditating on the promise. He rejoiced that he was led to lay the promise near his heart. But besides meditating on the promises, receive them as being the very words of God. Speak to your soul thus: "If I were dealing with a man's promise, I would carefully consider the ability and the character of the man who had covenanted with me. So with the promise of God. My eye must not be so much fixed on the greatness of the mercy as on the greatness of the Promiser. My soul, it is God, even your God, who cannot lie, and who speaks to you. This Word of His which you are now considering is as true as His own existence. He is an unchangeable God. He has not altered the thing which has gone out of His mouth or called back one single consolatory sentence. It is the God who made the heavens and the earth who has spoken. He cannot fail in wisdom as to the time when He will bestow the favors because He knows when it is best to give and when better to withhold. Therefore, I will and must believe the promise." If we meditate on the promises and consider the Promiser, we will experience their sweetness and obtain their fulfillment.

July 27
Evening

"Who shall lay any thing to the charge of God's elect?" (Romans 8:33).

Most blessed challenge! How unanswerable it is! Every sin of the elect was laid upon the great Champion of our salvation, and by the atonement, carried away. There is no sin recorded in God's book against His people; they are justified in Christ forever. When the guilt of sin was taken away, the punishment of sin was removed. For the Christian, there is no stroke from God's angry hand—not even a single frown of judgment. The believer may be chastised by his Father, but God the Judge has nothing to say to the Christian except, "I have absolved you. You are acquitted." The Christian is completely freed from all the punishment and guilt of sin. The power of sin is removed, too. It may stand in our way and agitate us with perpetual warfare. But sin is a conquered foe to every soul in union with Jesus. There is no sin which a Christian cannot overcome if he will only rely upon God for the victory. Those who wear the white robes in heaven overcame through the blood of the Lamb and the word of their testimony. (See Revelation 12:11.) We may do the same. No lust is too mighty, no sin too strongly entrenched. We can overcome through the power of Christ. Christian, your sin is a condemned thing. It may kick and struggle, but it is doomed to die. God has written condemnation across its brow. Christ has crucified it, nailing it to His cross. Go now and destroy it, and the Lord will help you to live to His praise. At last, sin, with all its guilt, shame, and fear, is gone.

July 28
Morning

"So foolish was I, and ignorant: I was as a beast before thee" (Psalm 73:22).

Remember, this is the confession of the man after God's own heart. In telling us his inner life, he writes, "So foolish was I, and ignorant." The word *foolish,* here, means more than it signifies in ordinary language. David, in a former verse of the Psalm, writes, "I was envious of the foolish when I saw the prosperity of the wicked." This shows that the folly he intended had sin in it. He puts himself down as being *foolish.* It was sinful folly, a folly which was to be condemned because of its perverseness, for he had been envious of the present prosperity of the ungodly—forgetful of the dreadful end awaiting them. Are we better than David that we should call ourselves wise? Do we profess that we have attained perfection or have been so chastened that the rod has taken all our stubbornness out of us? This would be pride indeed! Look back believer. Think of your doubting God when He has been so faithful to you. Think how often you have chosen sin because of its pleasure when that pleasure was a root of bitterness to you! Surely if we know our own heart, we must plead guilty to the indictment of a sinful folly and resolve that God will be our counsel and guide.

July 28
Evening

"Who went about doing good" (Acts 10:38).

These few words give us an exquisite picture of the Lord Jesus Christ. Only of the Savior is the statement true in the fullest and most unqualified sense—He went about doing good. From this description, it is evident that He did good *personally*. The gospels tell us that He touched the leper with His own finger, and He anointed the eyes of the blind. When He was asked to speak the word only at a distance, He usually went Himself to the sick bed and there personally healed the afflicted one. A lesson to us, if we want to do good, is to do it ourselves. Give alms with your own hand—a kind look or word will enhance the value of the gift. Speak to a friend about his soul—your loving appeal will have more influence than a whole library of tracts. Our Lord's method of doing good shows us His *incessant activity!* He not only did the good which came close to Him, but He "went about" on His errands of mercy. Throughout the whole land of Judea, there was scarcely a village which was not gladdened by the sight of Him. How this reproves the sluggish manner in which many believers serve the Lord! Let us be energetic in doing good. The text implies that Jesus Christ *went out of His way* to do good. "He went *about* doing good." He was never deterred by danger or difficulty. He sought out the objects of His gracious intentions. Christ's *perseverance* and the *unity* of His purpose are also implied. The practical application of the subject may be summed up in the words: "He left us an example that we should follow in His steps." (See 1 Peter 2:21.)

July 29
Morning

"Nevertheless, I am continually with thee" (Psalm 73:23).

Nevertheless—As if, notwithstanding all the foolishness and ignorance which David had just been confessing to God, not one atom the less was it true and certain that David was saved, accepted, and blessed by God's constant presence. Believer, endeavor in like spirit to say, "Nevertheless, since I belong to Christ I am continually with God!" He is always thinking of me for my good and I am continually on His mind. The Lord never sleeps, but He is perpetually watching over my welfare. I am continually in His hand so that none will be able to pluck me out. I am continually on His heart, worn there as a memorial, even as the high priest bore the names of the twelve tribes on his heart forever. God is always making providence work for our good. Suprising grace! You see me in Christ, and, though in myself abhorred, You behold me as wearing Christ's garments and washed in His blood. I stand accepted in His presence. I am continually in His favor. Here is comfort for the tried and afflicted soul who is troubled within. Look at the calm in Jesus. *"Nevertheless"*—say it in your heart and take the peace it gives. "Nevertheless, I am continually with thee."

July 29
Evening

"All that the Father giveth me shall come to me" (John 6:37).

This declaration involves *the doctrine of election*—there are some souls whom the Father gave to Christ. It involves *the doctrine of effectual calling*—these who are given must and will come to Him. Although they set themselves against it, they will be brought out of darkness into God's marvelous light. It teaches us *the necessity of faith*—even those who are given to Christ are not saved unless they come to Him. There is no other way to heaven but by the door, Christ Jesus. All that the Father gives to our Redeemer *must come to Him;* therefore, none can come to heaven unless they come to Christ. Oh, the power and majesty in the words *"shall come!"* The Lord Jesus uses His messengers, His Word, and His Spirit to sweetly and graciously compel men to come that they may eat of His marriage supper. He does not violate the free choice of man, but draws him by the power of His grace. I may exercise power over another man's will. Yet, that other man's will may be perfectly free, because the constraint is exercised in a manner which is agreeable with the laws of the human mind. Jesus uses irresistible arguments addressed to the understanding, mighty reasons appealing to the heart, and the mysterious influence of His Holy Spirit to operate upon all the powers and passions of the soul. Where the man was once rebellious, he now yields cheerfully to Jesus' rule, subdued by sovereign love. Those whom God has chosen willingly and joyfully accept Christ and come to Him with simple and pure faith. They rest upon Him as all their salvation and all their desire. Have you come to Jesus in this way?

July 30
Morning

"And when he thought thereon, he wept" (Mark 14:72).

Some feel that as long as Peter lived his tears flowed when he remembered how he denied his Lord. This may be so, for his sin was very great and grace in him had afterward done a perfect work. This same experience is common to all the redeemed family according to the degree in which the Spirit of God has removed the natural heart of stone. We, like Peter, remember our boastful promise: "Though all men forsake You, yet I will not." When we think of what we vowed to be and of what we have been, we may weep whole showers of grief. Can we, when we are reminded of our sins and their exceeding sinfulness, remain stolid and stubborn? Do we cry to the Lord for renewed assurances of pardoning love? May we never take a dry-eyed look at sin unless, before long, we have a tongue parched in the flames of hell. Peter thought of his Master's look of love. The Lord followed up the cock's warning voice with an admonitory look of sorrow, pity, and love. That glance was never out of Peter's mind so long as he lived. It was far more effectual than ten thousand sermons would have been without the Spirit. The penitent apostle would be sure to weep when he recollected the Savior's full forgiveness which restored him to his former place. To think that we have offended so kind and good a Lord is more than sufficient reason for constant weeping. Lord, smite our rocky hearts and make the waters flow.

July 30
Evening

"Him that cometh to me I will in no wise cast out" (John 6:37).

No limit is set to the *duration* of this promise. It does not merely say, "I will not cast out a sinner when he comes to Me for the first time," but, "I will in no wise cast out." The original reads, "I will *not, not* cast out," or "I will *never, never* cast out." The text means that Christ will not reject a believer the first time he comes, and He will not reject him to the end. But suppose the believer sins after coming? "If any man sin, we have an advocate with the Father, Jesus Christ the righteous" (1 John 2:1). But suppose the believers backslide? "I will heal their backsliding, I will love them freely: for mine anger is turned away from him" (Hosea 14:4). But believers may fall under temptation! "God is faithful, who will not suffer you to be tempted above that ye are able; but will with the temptation also make a way to escape, that ye may be able to bear it" (1 Corinthians 10:13). The believer may fall into sin as David did, but God also answered David's prayer of repentance: "Purge me with hyssop, and I shall be clean: wash me, and I shall be whiter than snow" (Psalm 51:7). "And I will cleanse them from all their iniquity" (Jeremiah 33:8). "I give unto them, eternal life," Jesus promises. "And they shall never perish, neither shall any man pluck them out of my hand" (John 10:28). When you come to Christ, He will receive you and make you His bride. You will be His forever.

July 31
Morning

"I in them" (John 17:23).

If such is the union which subsists between our souls and the person of our Lord, how deep and broad is the channel of our communion! This is no narrow pipe through which a thread-like stream may wind its way. It is a channel of amazing depth and breadth along whose glorious length a ponderous volume of living water may roll. This city of communion has many pearly gates. Each gate is thrown wide open, that we may enter assured of welcome. How much we are blessed in having so large an entrance! Had the Lord Jesus been far away from us, with many a stormy sea between, we would have longed to send a messenger to tell Him of our love and bring us tidings from His Father's house. See His kindness. He takes lodging with us and tabernacles in poor humble hearts. How foolish we are if we do not live in habitual communion with Him! When the road is long, dangerous, and difficult, we need not wonder that friends seldom meet each other. But when they live together, will Jonathan forget his David? A wife may, when her husband is on a journey, live many days without holding a conversation with him, but she could never be separated from him if she knew he was in one of the rooms of her own house. Seek your Lord for He is near. Embrace Him for He is your Brother. Hold Him fast for He is your Husband. Press Him to your heart for He is of your own flesh.

July 31
Evening

"And these are the singers. . .they were employed in that work day and night" (1 Chronicles 9:33).

It was ordered in the temple that the sacred chant would never cease. The singers constantly praised the Lord whose mercy endures forever. As mercy did not cease to rule either by day or night, so neither did music hush its holy ministry. There is a lesson for believers in the ceaseless song of Zion's temple. You, too, are a debtor. See to it that your gratitude, like love, never fails. God's praise is constant in heaven, your final dwelling place. Learn to practice the eternal hallelujah. As the sun scatters its light over the earth, its beams awaken grateful believers to tune their morning hymn. By the priesthood of the saints, perpetual praise is kept up at all hours. It wraps our globe in a mantle of thanksgiving and fastens it with a golden belt of song. The Lord always deserves to be praised for who He is, for His works of creation and providence, for His goodness toward His creatures, and especially for the act of redemption. In addition to this, there are all the marvelous blessings flowing in an endless stream. It is always beneficial to praise the Lord. It cheers the day and brightens the night. It lightens the toil and softens sorrow. It sheds a sanctifying radiance over earthly gladness which makes the world less able to blind us with its glare. Do we have something to sing about at this moment? Can we weave a song out of our present joys, our past deliverances, or our future hopes? By the love of Jesus, let us be stirred to close the day with a psalm of sanctified gladness.

August 1
Morning

"Let me now go to the field, and glean ears of corn" (Ruth 2:2).

Downcast and troubled Christian, come and glean today in the broad field of promise. Here are abundant promises which exactly meet your wants. Take this one: "He will not break the bruised reed, nor quench the smoking flax" (Matthew 12:20). Does that suit your case? A reed, helpless and weak, yet, He will not break you but will restore and strengthen you. You are like the smoking flax. No light or warmth can come from you, but He will not quench you. Would you glean another ear? "Come unto me, all ye that labor and are heavy laden, and I will give you rest" (Matthew 11:28). What soft words! Your heart is tender, and the Master knows it. Therefore, He speaks so gently to you. Will you obey Him and come to Him now? Take another ear of corn: "Fear not, thou worm Jacob; I will help thee, saith the Lord and thy Redeemer, the Holy One of Israel" (Isaiah 41:14). How can you be afraid when He offers this wonderful assurance? You may gather ten thousand such golden ears as these: "I have blotted out thy sins like a cloud, and like a thick cloud thy transgressions" (Isaiah 44:22). Or this: "Though your sins be as scarlet, they shall be as wool; though they be red like crimson, they shall be whiter than snow" (Isaiah 1:18). Our Master's field is very rich. They lie before you believer! Gather them up, make them your own, for Jesus bids you take them. Do not be afraid—only believe! Grasp these sweet promises, thresh them out by meditation, and feed on them with joy.

August 1
Evening

"Thou crownest the year with thy goodness"
(Psalm 65:11).

God blesses us richly every hour of every day. When we sleep and when we wake, His mercy waits upon us. The sun may leave us a legacy of darkness, but God never ceases to shine upon His children with beams of love. Like a river, His lovingkindness always flows with a fullness that is as inexhaustible as His own nature. Like the atmosphere which surrounds the earth and supports the life of man, the benevolence of God surrounds all His creatures. Rivers are swollen at certain seasons by the rain, and the atmosphere itself is sometimes filled with more fresh, more bracing, or more balmy influences than usual. It is the same with the mercy of God. It has its golden hours and its days of overflowing joy, when the Lord magnifies His grace before the sons of men. *The joyous days of harvest* are a special season of favor. The glory of autumn is in the ripe gifts of providence that are abundantly bestowed. It is the mellow season of realization where all before was mere hope and expectation. Great is the joy of harvest. Happy are the reapers who fill their arms with the liberality of heaven. The psalmist tells us that the harvest is the crowning of the year. Surely these crowning mercies call for crowning thanksgiving! Let us offer thanks by the *inward emotions of gratitude.* Let our hearts be warmed, and let our spirits remember and meditate upon the goodness of the Lord. Then, let us *praise Him with our lips* and magnify His name, from whose bounty all this goodness flows. Let us glorify God by yielding our gifts to Him.

August 2
Morning

"Who worketh all things after the counsel of his own will" (Ephesians 1:12).

Our belief in God's wisdom supposes that He has a settled purpose and plan in the work of salvation. What would creation have been without His design? In every bone, joint, muscle, sinew, gland, and blood vessel, you see the presence of a God working everything according to the design of infinite wisdom. And will God be present in creation, ruling over all, and not in grace? Will the new creation have the fickle genius of free will to preside over it when divine counsel rules the old creation? Look at Providence! Even the hairs of your head are all numbered. God weighs the mountains of our grief in scales and the hills of our tribulation in balances. And will there be a God in providence and not in grace? No! He knows the end from the beginning. He sees, in its appointed place, not merely the cornerstone which He has laid in fair colors in the blood of His dear Son, but He beholds in their ordained position each of the chosen stones taken out of the quarry of nature and polished by His grace. He has in His mind a clear knowledge of every stone which will be laid in its prepared space, how vast the divide will be, and when the topstone will be brought forth with shoutings of, "Grace! Grace! unto it." At the last it will be clearly seen that, in every chosen vessel of mercy, Jehovah did as He willed with His own. In every part of the work of grace, He accomplished His purpose and glorified His own name.

August 2
Evening

"So she gleaned in the field until even" (Ruth 2:17).

As Ruth went out to gather the ears of corn, so I must go forth into the fields of prayer, meditation, and hearing the Word to gather spiritual food. *The gleaner gathers her portion ear by ear*—her gains are little by little. Every ear helps to make a bundle, and every gospel lesson assists in making us wise concerning salvation. *The gleaner keeps her eyes open.* If she stumbled along in a dream, she would have no load to carry home rejoicing. I must be watchful in religious exercises lest they become unprofitable to me. May I rightly value my opportunities and glean with greater diligence! *The gleaner stoops for all she finds,* and so must I. Proud spirits criticize and object, but lowly minds glean and receive benefit. A humble heart is a great help toward profitably hearing the gospel. The word of salvation is only received with meekness. Pride is a vile robber, not to be endured for a moment. *What the gleaner gathers, she holds.* If she dropped one ear to find another, her day's work would be of little value. She is as careful to retain as to obtain; therefore, her gains are great. I often forget all that I hear! The second truth pushes the first out of my head, and so my reading and hearing become much learning with little application. Do I realize the importance of storing up the truth? *A hungry belly makes the gleaner wise*—if there is no corn in her hand, there will be no bread on her table. I have an even greater need. Lord, help me to feel it, that it may urge me onward to glean in fields which yield so great a reward to diligence.

August 3
Morning

"The Lamb is the light thereof" (Revelation 21:23).

Quietly contemplate the Lamb as the light of heaven. Light in Scripture is the emblem of joy. The joy of the saints in heaven is comprised in this: Jesus chose us, loved us, bought us, cleansed us, robed us, kept us, and glorified us. We are here entirely through the Lord Jesus. Light is also the cause of beauty. Without light, no radiance flashes from the sapphire, and no peaceful ray proceeds from the pearl. Thus, all the beauty of the saints above comes from Jesus. As planets, they reflect the light of the Sun of Righteousness. They live as beams proceeding from the central orb. If He withdrew, they must die. If His glory were veiled, their glory must expire. Light is also the emblem of knowledge. In heaven our knowledge will be perfect, but the Lord Jesus Himself will be the fountain of it. Dark providences which were never understood before will then be clearly seen. All that puzzles us now will become plain to us in the light of the Lamb. Oh, what glorifying of the God of love! Light also means manifestation. Light manifests. In this world it does not yet appear what we will be. What a transformation! We were stained with sin; but with one touch of His finger, we are bright as the sun and clear as crystal. Oh, what a manifestation! All this proceeds from the exalted Lamb. Oh, to be present and to see Him in His own light, the King of kings and Lord of lords!

August 3
Evening

"But as he went" (Luke 8:42).

Jesus is passing through the throng to the house of Jairus to raise the ruler's dead daughter. But He is so overflowing with goodness that He works another miracle while on the road. If we have one purpose, it is good to go immediately and accomplish it. It would be unwise to expend our energies on the way. When hastening to rescue a drowning friend, we cannot afford to exhaust our strength upon a person in similar danger. It is enough for a man to fulfill his own peculiar calling. But our Master knows no limit of power or boundary of mission. His grace is so abundant that even His path radiates lovingkindness. He is a swift arrow of love which not only reaches its ordained target, but it perfumes the air through which it flies. Virtue constantly flows from Jesus as sweet odors waft from flowers. It will always emanate from Him as water bubbles from a sparkling fountain. What delightful encouragement this truth offers us! If our Lord is ready to heal the sick and bless the needy, then put yourself in His path. Do not neglect asking because He is so generous in giving. Give earnest heed to His Word at all times that Jesus may speak through it to your heart. Dwell with Him that you may obtain His blessing. When He is present to heal, He will surely heal you. He is present even now, for He always comes to hearts which need Him. Do you need Him? He knows how much! Lord, look upon the distress which is now before You and make Your servant whole.

August 4
Morning

"The people that do know their God shall be strong" (Daniel 11:32).

Every believer understands that to know God is the highest and best form of knowledge. This spiritual knowledge is a source of strength to the Christian. It strengthens his faith. Believers are constantly spoken of in the Scriptures as being persons who are enlightened and taught of the Lord. They are said to have an unction from the Holy One, and it is the Spirit's peculiar office to lead them into all truth. Knowledge strengthens love as well as faith. Knowledge opens the door; and then through that door, we see our Savior. Or, to use another similitude, knowledge paints the portrait of Jesus; and when we see that portrait, then we love Him. We cannot love a Christ whom we do not know, at least in some degree. If we know little of the excellencies of Jesus, what He has done for us and what He is doing now, we cannot love Him much. But the more we know Him, the more we will love Him. Knowledge also strengthens hope. How can we hope for a thing if we do not know of its existence? Knowledge supplies us reasons for patience. There is not a single grace of the Christian which, under God, will not be fostered and brought to perfection by holy knowledge. How important it is that we grow not only in grace but in the knowledge of our Lord and Savior Jesus Christ!

August 4
Evening

"I smote you with blasting and with mildew and with hail in all the labours of your hands" (Haggai 2:17).

How destructive hail is to the standing crops as it relentlessly beats out the precious grain upon the ground! But even more to be dreaded are those mysterious destroyers—disease and mildew. These turn an ear of corn into a mass of soot and dry up the grain. Innumerable minute fungi attack the crops, and if not for the goodness of God, famine would soon spread over the land. When we consider the active agents which are ready to destroy the harvest, we must pray, "Give us this day our daily bread" (Matthew 6:11). The curse is rampant; we have constant need of the blessing. When blight and mildew come, they are often chastisements from heaven. Men must learn to bear the rod made from their own wrongdoing. Spiritually, mildew is a common evil. When our work is most promising, this blight appears. We hoped for many conversions, and instead, a general apathy, an abounding worldliness, or a cruel hardness of heart launches out against us. There may be no open sin in those for whom we are laboring, but there is a lack of sincerity and decision which sadly disappoints our desires. We learn from this experience our dependence upon the Lord and the need of prayer. Spiritual pride or laziness will soon bring the dreadful evil upon us, and only the Lord of the harvest can remove it. Mildew may even attack our own hearts and shrivel our prayers and devotion. May God keep us from so serious a calamity. Shine, blessed Sun of Righteousness, and drive the blights away.

August 5
Morning

"We know that all things work together for good to them that love God" (Romans 8:28).

On some points a believer is absolutely sure. He knows, for instance, that God sits in the stern-sheets of the vessel when it rocks most. He believes that an invisible hand is always on the world's tiller and that wherever providence may drift, Jehovah steers it. That reassuring knowledge prepares him for everything. He looks over the raging waters, sees the Spirit of Jesus treading the billows, and hears a voice saying, "It is I; be not afraid" (Mark 6:50). He knows, too, that God is always wise. Knowing this, he is confident that there can be no accidents and no mistakes. He can say, "If I would lose all I have, it is better to lose than to have, if God so wills." "We know that all things work together for good to them that love God." The Christian does not merely hold this as a theory, but *he knows it* as a matter of fact. Everything has worked for good as yet. Every event as yet has worked out the most divinely blessed results; and so, believing that God rules all, that He governs wisely, that He brings good out of evil, the believer's heart is assured. He is able to calmly meet each trial as it comes. The believer can, in the spirit of true resignation, pray, "Send me what You will, my God, so long as it comes from You. There never came an ill portion from Your table to any of Your children."

August 5
Evening

"Shall your brethren go to war, and shall ye sit here?" (Numbers 32:6).

Family relationships have their obligations. The Reubenites and Gadites would have been most unbrotherly if they had claimed the land which had been conquered and left the rest of the people to fight for their portions alone. We have received much by the efforts and sufferings of the saints in the past. If we do not make some return to the Church by giving her our best energies, we are unworthy to be enrolled in her ranks. Others are bravely combating the errors of the age or excavating perishing ones from amid the ruins of the fall. If we fold our hands in idleness, we must be warned lest the curse of Meroz who "came not to the help of the Lord" fall upon us. (See Judges 5:23.) The Master of the vineyard asks, "Why stand ye here all the day idle?" (Matthew 20:6). The toils of devoted missionaries and fervent ministers shame us if we sit in laziness. Shrinking from trial is the temptation of those who are at ease in Zion. They would gladly escape the cross and still wear the crown. If the most precious are tried in the fire, are we to escape the crucible? If the diamond must be buffed upon the wheel, are we to be made perfect without suffering? Why should we be treated better than our Lord? The First-born felt the rod, why not the younger brethren? Cowardly pride chooses a downy pillow and a silken couch for a soldier of the cross. He who is resigned to the divine will learns by grace to be pleased with it.

August 6
Morning

"Watchman, what of the night?" (Isaiah 21:11)

What enemies are abroad? What heresy must I guard against? Sins creep from their lurking-places when the darkness reigns. I must mount the watch-tower and watch in prayer. Our heavenly Protector foresees all the attacks which are about to be made on us. When Satan desires evil for us, He prays for us that our faith will not fail when we are sifted as wheat. What weather is coming for the Church? We must care for the Church with anxious love. Let us observe the signs of the times and prepare for conflict. "Watchman, what of the night?" What stars are visible? What precious promises suit our present case? You sound the alarm and give us the consolation, also. Christ, the polestar, is ever fixed in His place, and all the stars are secure in the right hand of their Lord. But, watchman, when comes the morning? The Bridegroom tarries. Are there no signs of His coming forth as the Sun of Righteousness? Has not the morning star arisen as the pledge of day? When will the day dawn and the shadows flee away? O Jesus, come in Spirit to my sighing heart and make it sing for joy.

August 6
Evening

"Let the whole earth be filled with his glory; Amen, and Amen."(Psalm 72:19).

This is a great request. There are times when a prayer for one man is enough to stagger us. But how far-reaching was the psalmist's intercession! "Let the whole earth be filled with his glory." It does not leave out a single country, however crushed by the foot of superstition; it includes every nation, however barbarous. For the cannibal as well as for the civilized, for all climates and races, this prayer is uttered. The whole circle of the earth that it encompasses omits no son of Adam. We must be up and working for our Master, or we cannot honestly offer such a prayer. The petition is not asked with a sincere heart unless we endeavor, as God helps us, to extend the Kingdom of our Master. Is this *your* prayer? Turn your eyes to Calvary. Behold the Lord of Life nailed to a cross, with the crown of thorns upon His brow, with bleeding head and hands and feet. Can you look upon this miracle of miracles, the death of the Son of God, without feeling a marvelous adoration that language never can express? When you feel the blood applied to your conscience and know that He has blotted out your sins, *you are not a man* unless you fall to your knees and cry, "Let the whole earth be filled with his glory; Amen, and Amen." Can you pretend to love your Prince and not desire to see Him as the universal Ruler? Your faith is worthless unless it leads you to pray that the same mercy which has been extended to you may bless the whole world.

August 7
Morning

"The upright love thee" (Song of Solomon 1:4).

Believers love Jesus with a deeper affection than they dare to give to any other being. They would sooner lose father and mother than part with Christ. They hold all earthly comforts with a loose hand, but they carry Him locked in their bosoms. They voluntarily deny themselves for His sake, but they are not to be driven to deny *Him.* It is scant love which the fire of persecution can dry up. The true believer's love is a deeper stream than this. Men have labored to divide the faithful from their Master, but their attempts have been fruitless in every age. Neither crowns of honor nor frowns of anger have untied this knot. This is no everyday attachment which the world's power may at length dissolve. Neither man nor devil has found a key which opens this lock. Never has the craft of Satan been more at fault than when he has exercised it in seeking to tear apart this union of two divinely welded hearts. It is written, and nothing can blot out the sentence, "The upright love thee." The intensity of the love of the upright, however, is not so much to be judged by what it appears as by what the upright long for. It is our daily lament that we cannot love enough. If only our hearts were capable of holding more and reaching farther. Measure our love by our intentions, and it is high indeed. If only we could give all the love in all hearts, in one great mass, to Him who is altogether lovely!

August 7
Evening

"Satan hindered us" (1 Thessalonians 2:18).

Since the first hour that goodness came into conflict with evil, Satan continually works to hinder us in our spiritual experience. From all directions, all along the line of battle, in the vanguard and in the rear, at the dawn of day and in the midnight hour, Satan hinders us. If we toil in the field, he seeks to break the plow; if we build the wall, he tries to cast down the stones; if we serve God in suffering or in conflict, everywhere Satan hinders us. He hinders us when we are first coming to Jesus Christ. We had fierce conflicts with Satan when we first looked to the cross and lived. Now that we are saved, he attempts to hinder the completeness of our personal character. You may be congratulating yourself, "I have walked consistently; no man can challenge my integrity." Beware of boasting, for your virtue will yet be tried. If you have been a firm believer, your faith will be attacked; if you have been as meek as Moses, expect to be tempted to speak foolishly with your lips. Satan is sure to hinder us when we are earnest in prayer. He discourages our intercession and weakens our faith in order that, if possible, we may miss the blessing. Satan is no less vigilant in obstructing Christian effort. There was never a spiritual revival without a revival of his opposition. As soon as Ezra and Nehemiah begin to labor, Sanballat and Tobiah were stirred up to hinder them. (See Nehemiah 2:19.) We should not be alarmed when Satan hinders us, for that proves that we are on the Lord's side and are doing the Lord's work. In His strength, we will win the victory and triumph over our adversary.

August 8
Morning

"They weave the spider's web" (Isaiah 59:5).

See the spider's web and behold in it a most suggestive picture of the hypocrite's religion. It is meant to catch his prey. Foolish persons are easily entrapped by the loud professions of pretenders, and even the more judicious cannot always escape. Custom, reputation, praise, advancement, and other flies are the small game which hypocrites take in their nets. A spider's web is a marvel of skill. Look at it and admire the cunning hunter's wiles. Is not a deceiver's religion equally amazing? How does he make so barefaced a lie appear to be truth? A spider's web comes from the creature's own bowels. The bee gathers her wax from flowers. The spider sucks no flowers, yet she spins out her material to any length. Even so hypocrites find their trust and hope within themselves. They lay their own foundation and hew out the pillars of their own house, refusing to be debtors to the sovereign grace of God. But a spider's web is very frail. It is not enduringly manufactured. It is no match for the servant's broom or the traveler's staff. Hypocritical cobwebs will soon come down when the broom of destruction begins its purifying work. This reminds us of one more thought—that such cobwebs are not to be endured in the Lord's house. He will see to it that they and those who spin them will be destroyed forever. Oh, my soul, be resting on something better than a spider's web. Let the Lord Jesus be your eternal hiding place.

August 8
Evening

"All things are possible to him that believeth"
(Mark 9:23).

Many Christians are always filled with doubt and fear, and they forlornly think that this is the normal state of believers. This is a mistake. It is possible for us to cause doubt and fear to become like a bird flitting across the soul, but never lingering there. When you read of the high and sweet communion enjoyed by believers, you sigh and murmur in your heart, "Alas! these are not for me." If you only have faith, you will yet stand upon the sunny pinnacle of the temple. You hear of the exploits which holy men have done for Jesus; what they have enjoyed of Him; how much they have been like Him; how they have been able to endure great persecutions for His sake. You say, "Ah! as for me, I am only a worm; I can never attain to this." But there is nothing which one saint was, that you may not be. There is no elevation of grace, no attainment of spirituality, no clearness of assurance, no post of duty, which is not open to you if you have the power to believe. Lay aside your sackcloth and ashes and rise to the dignity of your true position. You are little in the Kingdom because you want to be so, not because there is any necessity for it. Ascend! The golden throne of assurance is waiting for you. The crown of communion with Jesus is ready to be placed upon your brow. Wrap yourself in scarlet and fine linen, and feast sumptuously every day. If you believe, you may eat the fat of the land. Your land will flow with milk and honey, and your soul will be satisfied as with marrow and fatness. Gather golden sheaves of grace, for they await you in the fields of faith. "All things are possible to him that believeth."

August 9
Morning

"The city hath no need of the sun, neither of the moon, to shine in it" (Revelation 21:23).

In the better world, the inhabitants are independent of all creature comforts. They have no need of raiment. Their white robes never wear out, and they will never be defiled. They need no medicine to heal diseases. They need no sleep to refresh themselves. They rest not day or night but untiringly praise Him In His temple. They need no social relationship to minister comfort. Whatever happiness they may derive from association with their fellows is not essential to their bliss, for their Lord's society is enough for their largest desires. They need no teachers there. They doubtless commune with one another concerning the things of God, but they will all be taught of the Lord. Ours are the alms at the king's gate, but they feast at the table itself. Here we lean on the friendly arm, but there they lean on their Beloved. Here we must have the help of our companions, but there they find all they want in Christ Jesus. Here the angels bring us blessings, but we will not need messengers from heaven then. We will not need Gabriels there to bring love-notes from God, for there we will see Him face to face. What a glorious hour when God and not His creatures—when the Lord and not His works—will be our daily joy! Our souls will then have attained the perfection of bliss.

August 9
Evening

"He appeared first to Mary Magdalene, out of whom he had cast seven devils" (Mark 16:9).

Mary of Magdala was the victim of a fearful evil. She was possessed by not one devil only, but seven. These dreadful inmates caused much pain and pollution to the poor frame in which they had found a lodging. Hers was a hopeless, horrible case. She could not help herself, neither could any human lessen her pain. But Jesus passed that way. Although He was unsought and probably even resisted by the poor demoniac, He uttered the word of power. Mary of Magdala became a testimony of the healing power of Jesus. All the seven demons left her, never to return, forcibly ejected by the Lord of all. What a blessed deliverance! From delirium to delight, from despair to peace, from hell to heaven! She immediately became a constant follower of Jesus, catching His every word, following His steps, sharing His life. She became His generous helper, first among that group of healed and grateful women who ministered to Him. When Jesus was lifted up in crucifixion, Mary remained the sharer of His shame. She could not die on the cross with Jesus, but she stood as near to it as she could. When His body was taken down, she watched to see where it was laid. She was the faithful and watchful believer—last at the sepulcher where Jesus slept, first at the grave when He arose. Her beloved Rabbi called her by her name and made her His messenger of good news to the trembling disciples and Peter. Thus, grace found her as a maniac and made her a minister, cast out devils and let her behold angels, delivered her from Satan and united her forever to the Lord Jesus. May I also be such a miracle of grace!

August 10
Morning

"Christ, who is our life" (Colossians 3:4).

Paul's marvelously rich expression indicates that Christ is the *source* of our life. "You hath he quickened, who were dead in trespasses and sins" (Ephesians 2:1). That same voice which brought Lazarus out of the tomb raised us to newness of life. He is now the *substance* of our spiritual life. It is by His life that we live. He is in us. *Christ is the sustenance of our life.* "This is the bread which cometh down from heaven, that a man may eat thereof, and not die" (John 6:50). *Christ is the solace of our life.* All our true joys come from Him. In times of trouble, His presence is our consolation. There is nothing worth living for but Him, and His lovingkindness is better than life! *Christ is the object of our life.* As the soldier fights for his captain and is crowned in his captain's victory, so the believer contends for Christ and gets his triumph out of the triumphs of his Master. "For him to live is Christ" (Philippians 1:21). *Christ is the example of our life.* Where there is the same life within, there will be, to a great extent, the same developments without. If we live in near fellowship with the Lord Jesus, we will grow like Him. We will set Him before us as our divine copy, and we will seek to tread in His footsteps, until He becomes *the crown of our life* in glory.

August 10
Evening

"The Son of man hath power on earth to forgive sins" (Matthew 9:6).

Behold one of the great Physician's mightiest arts—He has power to forgive sin! While He lived on this earth, before the ransom had been paid, before the blood had been sprinkled on the mercy seat, He had power to forgive sin. Does He not have the power to do it now that He has died and risen again? What power must dwell in Christ who faithfully paid the debts of His people! He has boundless power now that He has finished transgression and made an end of sin. If you doubt this, see Him rising from the dead! Behold Him ascending in splendor to the right hand of God! Hear Him pleading before the eternal Father, pointing to His wounds, claiming the merit of His sacred passion! What power to forgive is here! "He ascended up on high. . .and gave gifts unto men" (Ephesians 4:8). He is exalted on high to give repentance and remission of sins. (See Acts 5:31.) The most crimson sins are removed by the crimson of His blood. At this moment, whatever your sin, Christ has power to pardon you. A prayer will accomplish it. Jesus has nothing more to do to buy your pardon—all the atoning work is done. He can, in answer to your tears, forgive your sins today. He can breathe into your soul this very moment a peace with God which passes all understanding. It will spring from the perfect remission of your iniquities. May you now experience the power of Jesus to forgive sin! Waste no time in calling upon the Physician of souls.

August 11
Morning

"O that I were as in months past" (Job 29:2).

Some Christians look back on the past with pleasure but regard the present with dissatisfaction. Once they lived near to Jesus, but now they feel they have wandered from Him. They say, "O that I were as in months past!" They complain that they do not have peace of mind or that they have no enjoyment in the means of grace or that conscience is not so tender or that they have not so much zeal for God's glory. The causes of this mournful state of things are manifold. It may arise through a *neglect of prayer,* for a neglected prayer closet is the beginning of all spiritual decline. Or it may be the result of *idolatry.* The heart has been occupied with something else more than with God. The affections have been set on the things of earth instead of the things of heaven. A jealous God will not be content with a divided heart. He must be loved first and best. He will withdraw the sunshine of His presence from a cold, wandering heart. Or the cause may be found in *self-confidence* and *self-righteousness.* Pride is busy in the heart, and self is exalted instead of lying low at the foot of the cross. Christian, if you are not now as you "were in months past," do not rest satisfied with wishing for a return of former happiness, but go at once to seek your Maker and tell Him your sad state. Ask His grace and strength to help you walk more closely with Him. Humble yourself before Him, and He will lift you up. Do not sit down to sigh and lament. While the beloved Physician lives there is hope and certainty of recovery for the worst cases.

August 11
Evening

"Everlasting consolation" (2 Thessalonians 2:16).

Consolation—there is music in the word. Like David's harp, it charms away the evil spirit of melancholy. It was a distinguished honor for Barnabas to be called "the son of consolation." (See Acts 4:36.) It is also one of the illustrious names of One greater than Barnabas, for the Lord Jesus is "the consolation of Israel" (Luke 2:25). *Everlasting consolation*—this is the cream of all, the precious perfume, for the eternity of comfort is its crown and glory. All earthborn consolations are fleeting in essence and short-lived in their existence. They are as brilliant and as fragile as the rainbow hues of a soap bubble. But the consolations which God gives to His people do not fade or lose their freshness. They can stand all tests—the shock of trial, the flame of persecution, and the passing of years. They can even endure death itself. What is this everlasting consolation? It includes a sense of pardoned sin. A Christian has received the witness of the Spirit in his heart. His iniquities are put away like a thick cloud. The Lord also gives His people an abiding sense of acceptance in Christ. The Christian knows that God looks upon him as standing in union with Jesus. It is sweet to know that God accepts us. Union to the risen Lord is a consolation of the highest order; it is everlasting. Are you pining and refusing to be comforted? Is this honorable to God? Will it make others want to know Jesus? Cheer up, then! When Jesus gives eternal consolation, it is a sin to murmur.

August 12
Morning

"The Lord reigneth, let the earth rejoice" (Psalm 97:1).

There is no cause for fear once we believe in this blessed scripture. On earth the Lord's power as readily controls the rage of the wicked as the rage of the sea. His love as easily refreshes the poor with mercy as the earth with showers. Majesty gleams in flashes of fire amid the tempest's horrors, and the glory of the Lord is seen in its grandeur in the fall of empires and the crash of thrones. In all our conflicts and tribulations, we may behold the hand of the divine King. In hell, evil spirits recognize with misery His undoubted supremacy. When permitted to roam abroad, it is with a chain at their heel. Death's darts are under the Lord's lock, and the grave's prisons have divine power as their warden. The terrible vengeance of the Judge of all the earth makes fiends cower and tremble, even as dogs in the kennel fear the hunter's whip. In heaven, none doubt the sovereignty of the eternal King, but all fall on their faces to do Him homage. Angels are His courtiers, the redeemed are His favorites, and all delight to serve Him day and night. May we soon reach the city of the great King.

August 12
Evening

"The bow shall be seen in the cloud" (Genesis 9:14).

The rainbow, the symbol of the covenant with Noah, is a type of our Lord Jesus who is the Father's witness to the people. When may we expect to see the token of the covenant? The rainbow is only seen when it is painted upon a *cloud.* When the sinner remembers his past sin and mourns before God, Jesus Christ is revealed to him as the covenant Rainbow. He displays all the glorious hues of His divine character, and He bestows His deep and abiding peace. When trials and temptations surround the believer, it is sweet to behold our Lord Jesus Christ—to see Him bleeding, dying, rising, and pleading for us. God's rainbow is hung over the cloud of our sins, our sorrows, and our woes, to prophesy deliverance. A cloud alone does not give a rainbow; there must be the *crystal drops* to reflect the light of the sun. So our sorrows must not only threaten, they must fall heavily upon us. There would have been no redemption for us if the vengeance of God had been merely a threatening cloud. Until there is true anguish in the sinner's conscience, there is no Christ for him. Until the chastisement which he feels becomes grievous, he cannot see Jesus. But there must also be a *sun.* Clouds and drops of rain will not make a rainbow unless the sun shines. Our God, who is as the sun to us, always shines, but we do not always see Him. Clouds may hide His face. But no matter what drops fall or what clouds threaten, if He shines, there will be a rainbow. It is said that when we see the rainbow, the shower is over. When we behold Jesus, our sins vanish and our doubts and fears subside. When Jesus walks the waters of the sea, how profound is the calm!

August 13
Morning

"The cedars of Lebanon which he hath planted" (Psalm 104:16).

Lebanon's cedars are symbolic of the Christian in that they owe their planting entirely to the Lord. This is quite true of every child of God. He is not man-planted or self-planted but God-planted. The mysterious hand of the divine Spirit dropped the living seed into a heart which He had Himself prepared for its reception. Every true heir of heaven owns the great Husbandman as his planter. Moreover, the cedars of Lebanon are not dependent on man for their watering. They stand on the lofty rock, unmoistened by human irrigation, yet our heavenly Father supplies them. This is the way it is with the Christian who has learned to live by faith. He is independent of man, even in temporal things. He looks to the Lord his God for his continued maintenance and to Him alone. He is not a hot-house plant sheltered from temptation. He stands in the most exposed position. He has no shelter or protection, except the broad wings of the eternal God who always covers the cedars which He Himself has planted. Like cedars, believers are full of sap, having vitality enough to be ever green, even amid winter's snows. Lastly, the flourishing and majestic condition of the cedar is to the praise of God only. The Lord alone has been everything to the cedars. Therefore, David very sweetly puts it in one of the psalms, "Praise ye the Lord, fruitful trees and all cedars" (Psalm 148:9). In the believer there is nothing that can magnify man. He is planted, nourished, and protected by the Lord's own hand. To Him let all the glory be given.

August 13
Evening

"And I will remember my covenant" (Genesis 9:15).

God does not say, "And when *you* shall look upon the bow, and *you* shall remember My covenant, then I will not destroy the earth." It does not depend upon *our* memory which is fickle and frail, but upon *God's* memory which is infinite and immutable. "The bow shall be in the cloud; and *I* will look upon it, that *I* may remember the everlasting covenant" (Genesis 9:16). It is not *my* remembering God, it is God's remembering *me* which is the reason for my safety. It is not *my* laying hold of His covenant, but His covenant's laying hold on *me.* The whole foundation of salvation is secured by divine power. Even the *remembrance* of the covenant is not left to our memories, for we might forget. But our Lord cannot forget the saints whom He has engraved on the palms of His hands. (See Isaiah 49:16.) When Israel was in Egypt, and the blood was upon the lintel and the two side posts, the Lord did not say, "When *you* see the blood I will pass over you," but, "When *I* see the blood I will pass over you." (See Exodus 12:23.) Looking to Jesus brings me joy and peace, but God looking to Jesus secures my salvation. It is impossible for God to look at Christ, our bleeding Surety, and then be angry with us. Our sins are already punished in Him. No, it is not up to us to be saved by remembering the covenant. We *should* remember the covenant, and we *will* do it through divine grace. But our safety hinges upon God's remembering *us,* not our remembering *Him;* therefore, the covenant is *an everlasting covenant.*

August 14
Morning

"Thou, Lord, hast made me glad through thy work" (Psalm 92:4).

Do you believe that your sins are forgiven and that Christ has made a full atonement for them? Then what a joyful Christian you ought to be! You should live above the common trials and troubles of the world! Since sin is forgiven, can it matter what happens to you now? Luther said, "Smite, Lord, smite, for my sin is forgiven; if Thou hast but forgiven me, smite as hard as Thou wilt." Christian, if you are saved, be grateful and loving. Cling to that cross which took your sin away. Paul wrote, "I beseech you, therefore, by the mercies of God, that ye present your bodies a living sacrifice, holy, acceptable unto God, which is your reasonable service" (Romans 12:1). Do not let your zeal evaporate. Show your love. Love the brethren of Him who loved you. If there is a Mephibosheth anywhere who is lame, help him for Jonathan's sake. If there is a poor, tried believer, weep with him and bear his cross for the sake of Him who wept for you and carried your sins. Since you are forgiven, for Christ's sake, go and tell the joyful news of pardoning mercy to others. Do not be content with this blessing for yourself alone. Holy gladness and holy boldness will make you a good preacher, and all the world will be a pulpit for you to preach in. Cheerful holiness is the most forcible of sermons, but the Lord must give it to you. Seek it this morning before you go into the world. When it is the Lord's work in which we rejoice, we need not be afraid of being too glad.

August 14
Evening

"I know their sorrows" (Exodus 3:7).

The child is cheered as he sings, "This my father knows." We will be comforted when we realize that our dear Friend and tender Husband of our soul knows all about us. *He is the Physician.* If He knows all, there is no need that the patient should know. Hush, fluttering heart, which is always prying, peeping, and suspecting! The things that you do not know now, you will understand hereafter. Jesus, the beloved Physician, knows your soul in adversities. Why should the patient analyze all the medicine or ponder all the symptoms? This is the physician's work, not mine. It is my business to trust, and his to prescribe. If he writes his prescription in characters which I cannot read, I will not be uneasy on that account. Rather, I will rely upon his unfailing skill to make all clear in the result, however mysterious in the working. *He is the Master.* We are to obey, not to judge. "The servant knoweth not what his lord doeth" (John 15:15). Shall the architect explain his plans to every construction worker on the site? If he knows his own intent, is it not enough? The vessel on the potter's wheel cannot guess to what pattern it shall be conformed. But if the potter understands his art, what does the ignorance of the clay matter? My Lord must not be questioned any longer by one so ignorant as I am. *He is the Head.* All understanding centers there. What judgment has the arm? What comprehension has the foot? Why should the member have a brain of its own when the head fulfills for it every intellectual duty? Sweet Lord, be the eye, soul, and head for us. Let us be content to know only what You choose to reveal.

August 15
Morning

"Isaac went out to meditate in the field at the eventide" (Genesis 24:63).

If those who spend so many hours in idle company, light reading, and useless pastimes could learn wisdom, they would find more interesting engagements in meditation than in the vanities which now have such charms for them. We would all know more, live nearer to God, and grow deeper in grace. Meditation chews the cud and extracts the real nutrition from the mental food gathered elsewhere. When Jesus is the theme, meditation is sweet indeed. Isaac found Rebecca while engaged in private thoughts. Very admirable was the choice of place. In the field we have innumerable texts for thought. From the cedar to the hyssop, from the soaring eagle to the chirping grasshopper, from the blue expanse of heaven to a drop of dew, all things are full of teaching. When the eye is divinely opened, that teaching flashes on the mind far more vividly than from written books. Our little rooms are neither so healthy, so suggestive, so agreeable, nor so inspiring as the fields. Let us count nothing common or unclean but feel that all created things point to their Maker, and the field will at once be hallowed. The glory of the setting sun excites our wonder, and the solemnity of approaching night awakens our awe. If the business of this day will permit it, it will be well, dear reader, if you can spare an hour to walk in the field in the evening. But if not, the Lord is in the town, too, and will meet with you in your room or in the crowded street. Let your heart go forth to meet Him.

August 15
Evening

"And I will give you an heart of flesh" (Ezekiel 36:26).

A heart of flesh is known by its *tenderness concerning sin.* To have indulged a foul imagination or to have allowed a vile desire to remain for a moment is enough to make a heart of flesh grieve before the Lord. Only a heart of stone calls a great iniquity nothing. The heart of flesh is *tender toward God's will.* When the heart of flesh is given to God, the will quivers like an aspen leaf in every breath of heaven and bows like a willow in every breeze of God's Spirit. The natural will is cold, hard iron which cannot be hammered into form; but the renewed will, like molten metal, is soon molded by the hand of grace. In the fleshy heart there is a *tenderness of the affections.* The hard heart does not love the Redeemer, but the renewed heart burns with affection toward Him. The hard heart is selfish and coldly demands, "Why should I weep for sin? Why should I love the Lord?" But the heart of flesh says, "Lord, You know that I love You. Help me to love You more!" This renewed heart is prepared to receive every spiritual blessing, and every blessing comes to it. It will yield every heavenly fruit to the honor and praise of God, and, therefore, the Lord delights in it. A tender heart is the best defense against sin and the best preparation for heaven. A renewed heart stands on its watchtower looking for the coming of the Lord Jesus. Do you have this heart of flesh?

August 16
Morning

"Give unto the Lord the glory due unto his name" (Psalm 29:2).

God's glory is the result of His nature and acts. He is glorious in His character for there is such a store of everything that is holy, good, and lovely in God that He must be glorious. The actions which flow from His character are also glorious. He intends that they should manifest to His creatures His goodness, mercy, and justice. He is equally concerned that the glory associated with them should be given only to Himself. There is nothing in ourselves in which we may glory. What do we have that we did not receive from God? Then how careful ought we to be to walk humbly before the Lord! The moment we glorify ourselves, since there is room for one glory only in the universe, we set ourselves up as rivals to the Most High. Will the dust of the desert strive with the whirlwind or the drops of the ocean struggle with the tempest? Give the Lord all the honor and glory that is due His name. Yet it is, perhaps, one of the hardest struggles of the Christian life to learn this sentence—"Not unto us, O Lord, not unto us, but unto thy name give glory" (Psalm 115:1). It is a lesson which God is teaching us. Let a Christian begin to boast, "I can do all things," without adding, "through Christ which strengtheneth me" (Philippians 4:13), and before long he will have to groan, "I can do nothing." When we do anything for the Lord, and He is pleased to accept our doings, let us lay our crown at His feet and exclaim, "Not I, but the grace of God which was with me!"

August 16
Evening

"Ourselves also, which have the firstfruits of the Spirit" (Romans 8:23).

At this moment, we have the first fruits of the Spirit. We have the gem of repentance; faith, that priceless pearl; hope, the heavenly emerald; and love, the glorious ruby. We are already made new creatures in Christ Jesus by the work of the Holy Spirit. (See 2 Corinthians 5:17.) This is called the first fruit because *it comes first.* As the Israelites used the first of the harvest for the wave offering, so the spiritual life and all the grace which adorns that life are the first operations of the Spirit of God in our souls. The first fruits were the *pledge of the harvest.* As soon as the Israelite plucked the first handful of ripe ears, he looked forward with glad anticipation to the time when the wagon would creak beneath the sheaves. When God gives us things which are pure, lovely, and of good report, these forecast the coming glory. The first fruits were always *holy to the Lord.* Our new nature, with all its powers, is a consecrated thing. The new life is not ours, that we should ascribe its excellence to our own merit—it is Christ's image and creation and is ordained for His glory. But *the first fruits were not the harvest,* and the works of the Spirit in us at this moment are not the consummation. The perfect is yet to come. We must not boast that we have "arrived" and consider the wave offering to be all the produce of the year. We must hunger and thirst after righteousness and pant for the day of full redemption. This evening, open your mouth wide, and God will fill it. Seek higher degrees of consecration, and your Lord will grant them to you. He is "able to do exceeding abundantly above all that we ask or think" (Ephesians 3:20).

August 17
Morning

"The mercy of God" (Psalm 52:8).

Meditate a little on this tender mercy of the Lord. With a gentle, loving touch, He heals the broken in heart and binds up their wounds. It is a great mercy. There is nothing little in God. His mercy is like Himself—it is infinite. You cannot measure it. It is undeserved mercy, as indeed all true mercy must be, for deserved mercy is only a misnomer for justice. There was no right on the sinner's part to the kind consideration of the Most High. Had the rebel been doomed at once to eternal fire he would have merited the doom; and if delivered from wrath, sovereign love alone has found a cause, for there was none in the sinner himself. It is rich mercy. Some things are great but have little efficacy in them. This mercy is a cordial to your drooping spirits. It is manifold mercy. As Bunyan says, "All the flowers in God's garden are double." There is no single mercy. You may think you have only one mercy, but you will find it to be a whole cluster of mercies. It is abounding mercy. Millions have received it. Yet, far from its being exhausted, it is as fresh, as full, and as free as ever. It is unfailing mercy. It will never leave you. If mercy is your friend, mercy will be with you in temptation to keep you from yielding, and it will be with you in trouble to prevent you from sinking. Mercy is with you while you are living, to be the light and life of your countenance. And when you are dying, mercy will be the joy of your soul when earthly comfort is ebbing fast.

August 17
Evening

"He doth not afflict willingly nor grieve the children of men"(Lamentations 3:33).

From our Lord's words we learn that there is a limit to affliction. Its ultimate end is restrained, and it cannot go beyond a specific point. Lazarus passed through death, but death was not to be the final result of his affliction. The Lord says to the waves of pain, "You may go no farther." God does not send destruction, but He does send instruction to His people. Wisdom hangs the thermometer at the furnace mouth and regulates the heat. The God of providence limits the time, manner, intensity, repetition, and effects of all our trials. Each sanctifying result is eternally purposed. Nothing great or small escapes the watchful eye of Him who numbers the hair of our heads. This limit is wisely adjusted to our strength. Affliction is not haphazard—the weight of every stroke of the rod is accurately measured. He who made no mistakes in balancing the clouds and the heavens commits no errors in measuring the ingredients which compose the medicine of souls. We cannot suffer too much or be relieved too late. The limit is tenderly appointed. The knife of the heavenly Surgeon never cuts deeper than is absolutely necessary. When we consider how stubborn we are, it is a wonder that we are not afflicted with worse trials. He who has fixed the bounds of our habitation has also fixed the bounds of our tribulation. No mother is more compassionate than our gracious God; no father is more loving than our merciful God.

August 18
Morning

"Strangers are come into the sanctuaries of the Lord's house" (Jeremiah 51:51).

On this account the faces of the Lord's people were covered with shame, for it was a terrible thing that men should intrude into the Holy Place reserved for the priests alone. Everywhere about us we see cause for sorrow. How many ungodly men are now being educated to enter into the ministry! How fearful it is that ordination would be placed on the unconverted and that among the more enlightened churches of our land there would be such laxity of discipline. If the thousands who will read this portion will all take this matter before the Lord Jesus this day, He will interfere and avert the evil which will come on His Church. To adulterate the Church is to pollute a well, to pour water on fire, to sow a fertile field with stones. May we all have grace to maintain in our own proper way the purity of the Church as being an assembly of believers and not an unsaved community of unconverted men. Our zeal must, however, begin at home. Let us examine ourselves as to our right to eat at the Lord's table. Let us see to it that we have our wedding garment on, lest we ourselves be intruders in the Lord's sanctuaries. Many are called, but few are chosen; the way is narrow, and the gate is straight. Oh, for grace to come to Jesus with the faith of God's elect! Heart searching is the duty of all who are baptized or come to the Lord's table. "Search me, O God, and know my heart: try me, and know my thoughts" (Psalm 139:23).

August 18
Evening

"And they gave him to drink wine mingled with myrrh: but he received it not" (Mark 15:23).

A golden truth is revealed in the fact that the Savior refused to drink from the myrrhed wine-cup. The Son of God had previously looked down upon our world and measured the long descent to the depths of human misery. He added up the agonies which the atonement would require and did not refuse a single one. He solemnly determined that to offer a sufficient atoning sacrifice, He must go the whole way, from the throne of highest glory to the cross of deepest woe. This myrrhed cup, with its anesthetic influence, would have relieved a little of the misery; therefore, He refused it. He would not stop short of all He had undertaken to suffer for His people. How many of us have pined after reliefs from our grief which would have been injurious to us! Did you ever pray for freedom from hard service or suffering with a petulant and willful eagerness? Suppose it had been said to you, "If you desire, you may keep what you love, but God will be dishonored by it." Could you put away the temptation and say, "Thy will be done?" It is sweet to be able to say, "My Lord, I would rather not suffer, yet if I can honor You more by suffering and if the loss of my earthly all will bring You glory, then so let it be. I refuse the comfort, if it comes in the way of Your honor." Oh, that we would promptly and willing put away the thought of self and comfort when it interferes with finishing the work which He has given us to do.

August 19
Morning

"He shall stand and feed in the strength of the Lord" (Micah 5:4).

Christ's reign in His Church is that of a Shepherd-King. He has supremacy, but it is the superiority of a wise and tender Shepherd over His needy and loving flock. He commands and receives obedience, but it is the willing obedience of the well-cared-for sheep rendered joyfully to their beloved Shepherd. He rules by the force of love and the energy of goodness. The great Head of the Church is actively engaged in providing for His people. He does not sit down on the throne in an empty state or hold a scepter without wielding it in government. No! He stands and feeds. The expression "feed," in the original, means to shepherdize, to do everything expected of a shepherd: to guide, watch, preserve, restore, and tend, as well as to feed. It is said, "He shall stand and feed;" not, "He shall feed now and then and leave His position;" not, "He shall one day grant a revival and then the next day leave His Church to barrenness." His eyes never slumber, and His hands never rest. His heart never ceases to beat with love, and His shoulders are never weary of carrying His people's burdens. Wherever Christ is, there is God; and whatever Christ does is the act of the Most High. It is a joyful truth to consider that He who stands today representing the interests of His people is God to whom every knee will bow. We are happy to belong to such a Shepherd. Let us worship and bow down before Him as the people of His pasture.

August 19
Evening

"Pull me out of the net that they have laid privily for me: for thou art my strength" (Psalm 31:4).

Our spiritual foes are part of the serpent's brood. They seek to ensnare us by subtle lies and illusions. The psalmist's prayer expresses the possibility of the believer being caught like a bird. The fowler does his work skillfully, and careless ones are soon surrounded by the net. The text asks that the captive one may be delivered out of Satan's meshes. Eternal love can rescue the saint from between the jaws of the lion and out of the belly of hell. It may require a sharp pull to save a soul from the net of temptation and mighty power to free a man from the snares of malicious cunning. But the Lord is equal to every emergency, and the most skillfully placed nets of the hunter will never be able to hold His chosen ones. Those who tempt others will be destroyed themselves. *"For thou art my strength."* What inexpressible sweetness is found in these words! How joyfully we encounter toils and how cheerfully we endure sufferings when we lay hold of heavenly strength. Divine power will tear apart all the schemes of our enemies, confound their politics, and frustrate their deceitful tricks. He is a happy man who has the matchless might of God the Father on his side. Our own strength would be of little use when entangled in the nets of shrewd cunning, but the Lord's strength is always available. We only have to request it, and we will find it near at hand.

August 20
Morning

"The sweet psalmist of Israel" (2 Samuel 23:1).

Among all the saints whose lives are recorded, David possesses the most striking, varied, and instructive character. In his history, we meet with trials and temptations not to be discovered, as a whole, in other saints of ancient times, and he is all the more suggestive a type of our Lord. David knew the trials of all ranks and conditions of men. Kings have their troubles, and David wore a crown. The peasant has his cares, and David handled a shepherd's crook. The wanderer has many hardships, and David abode in the caves of Engedi. The psalmist was also tried in his friends. His counselor Ahithophel forsook him. "He which did eat of my bread, hath lifted up his heel against me" (Psalm 41:9). His worst foes were of his own household, and his children were his greatest affliction. The temptations of poverty and wealth, of honor and reproach, and of health and weakness all tried their power on him. David no sooner escaped from one trial than he fell into another. It is probably from this cause that David's psalms are so universally the delight of experienced Christians. Whatever our frame of mind, whether ecstasy or depression, David has exactly described our emotions. He was an able master of the human heart because he had been tutored in the best of all schools—the school of heartfelt, personal experience. As we are instructed in the same school, we increasingly appreciate David's psalms and find them to be green pastures. My soul, let David's experience cheer and counsel you this day.

August 20
Evening

"And they fortified Jerusalem unto the broad wall" (Nehemiah 3:8).

Well-fortified cities have broad walls, just as Jerusalem had in her glory. The New Jerusalem must also be surrounded and preserved by a broad wall of non-conformity to the world and separation from its customs and spirit. The tendency these days is to break down the holy barrier and make the distinction between the Church and the world appear nominal. Believers are no longer strict and Puritanical. Questionable literature is eagerly read, and frivolous pastimes are indulged. A general relaxation of standards threatens to deprive the Lord's people of those sacred differences which separate them from sinners. It will be a sad day for the Church and the world when there is no distinction between the children of God and the children of this world. Let it be your aim in heart, word, dress, and action to maintain the broad wall, remembering that the friendship of this world is enmity against God. (See James 4:4.) The broad wall provided a pleasant place from which the inhabitants of Jerusalem could rule the surrounding country. We may overlook the scenes of earth and behold the glories of heaven. Although we are separated from the world and deny ourselves all ungodliness and fleshly lusts, we are not in prison or restricted with narrow bounds. Rather, we walk at liberty, because we keep His precepts. Come and walk with God in His statutes. As friends meet each other on the city wall, so meet God in the way of prayer and meditation.

August 21
Morning

"He that watereth shall be watered also himself" (Proverbs 11:25).

In this morning's scripture we are taught the great lesson that to get, we must give; to accumulate, we must scatter; to make ourselves happy, we must make others happy; and in order to become spiritually vigorous, we must seek the spiritual good of others. In watering others, we are watered ourselves. How? Our efforts to be useful bring out our powers for usefulness. We have latent talents and dormant faculties, which are brought to light by exercise. We do not know what tender sympathies we possess, until we try to dry the widow's tears and soothe the orphan's grief. We often find in attempting to teach others that we gain instruction for ourselves. What gracious lessons some of us have learned as we have attempted to help others. We went to teach the Scriptures and came away blushing that we knew so little of them. Watering others makes us humble. Our own comfort is also increased by our working for others. We endeavor to cheer them, and the consolation gladdens our own heart. Like the two men in the snow—one rubbed the other's limbs to keep him from dying, and in so doing kept his own blood in circulation and saved his own life. The poor widow of Sarepta gave from her scanty store for the prophet's wants, and from that day she never again knew what want was. Give, and it will be given to you, good measure, pressed down, and running over.

August 21
Evening

"I said not unto the seed of Jacob, Seek ye me in vain" (Isaiah 45:19).

We may gain much solace by considering what God has *not* said. What He *has* said is full of comfort and delight; what He has *not* said is no less rich in consolation. It was one of these "said nots" which preserved the kingdom of Israel in the days of Jeroboam, for "the Lord said not that he would blot out the name of Israel from under heaven" (2 Kings 14:27). In our text, we have the assurance that God will answer prayer because He has "said *not* unto the seed of Israel, Seek ye me in vain." Let your doubts and fears say what they will, if God has not cut you off from mercy, there is no room for despair. Even the voice of conscience is worth little if it is not in agreement with the voice of God. Tremble at what God *has* said! But do not permit your imagination to overwhelm you with despondency and sinful despair. Many timid persons have suspected that there may be something in God's decree which shuts *them* out from hope. But God refutes that troublesome fear, for no true seeker can be given over to wrath. "I have not spoken in secret, in a dark place of the earth; I have not said, even in the secret of my unsearchable decree, Seek ye me in vain." God has clearly revealed that He *will* hear the prayer of those who call upon Him. His declaration cannot be disputed. He does not reveal His mind in unintelligible words, but He speaks plainly and positively. "Ask, and it shall be given to you" (Matthew 6:7). Prayer must and will be heard. Never, even in the secrets of eternity, has the Lord said to any soul, "Seek ye me in vain."

August 22
Morning

"I charge you, O daughters of Jerusalem, if ye find my beloved, that ye tell him that I am sick of love" (Song of Solomon 5:8).

Gracious souls are never perfectly at ease unless they are in a state of nearness to Christ. When they are away from Him, they lose their peace. The nearer to Him, the nearer they are to the perfect calm of heaven. The nearer to Him, the fuller the heart is, not only of peace, but of life, vigor, and joy, for these all depend on constant communion with Jesus. What the sun is to the day, what the moon is to the night, what the dew is to the flower, such is Jesus Christ to us. What bread is to the hungry, clothing to the naked, the shadow of a great rock to the traveler in a weary land, such is Jesus Christ to us. Supremely blessed are they who thirst after the Righteous One. Blessed is that hunger, since it comes from God. There is a hallowness about that hunger, since it sparkles among the beatitudes of our Lord. But the blessing involves a promise. Such hungry ones will be filled with what they are desiring. If Christ causes us to long after Himself, He will certainly satisfy those longings. When He does come to us, how sweet it will be!

August 22
Evening

"The unsearchable riches of Christ" (Ephesians 3:8).

The Master has riches beyond the count of mathematics, the measurement of reason, the dream of imagination, or the eloquence of words. They are *unsearchable!* You may look, study, and weigh, but Jesus is a greater Savior than you can comprehend. He is more ready to pardon than you are to sin and more able to forgive than you are to transgress. The Master is more willing to supply your wants than you are to confess them. *The Master has riches of happiness to bestow upon you now.* He can make you lie down in green pastures and lead you beside still waters. (See Psalm 23:2.) There is no music like the music of His pipe. He is the Shepherd, and you are the sheep. You may lie down peacefully at His feet. There is no love like His; neither earth nor heaven can match it. To know Christ and to be found in Him is life and joy. The Master treats His servants generously; He gives them two heavens—a heaven below for serving Him here and a heaven above to delight in Him forever. *His unsearchable riches will be best known in eternity.* During your time on earth, He will give you all you need. Your place of defense will be the munitions of rocks, your bread shall be given you, and your waters shall be sure. (See Isaiah 33:16.) Then one day you will have a face-to-face view of the glorious and beloved King. The unsearchable riches of Christ is the tune for the minstrels of earth and the song for the harpists of heaven. Lord, teach us more and more of Jesus, and we will tell the good news to others.

"The voice of weeping shall be no more heard"
(Isaiah 65:19).

The glorified weep no more, for all outward causes of grief are gone. There are no broken friendships or blighted prospects in heaven. Poverty, famine, peril, persecution, and slander are unknown there. They weep no more, for they are perfectly sanctified. No evil heart of unbelief prompts them to depart from the living God. They are without fault before His throne and are fully conformed to His image. Well may they cease to mourn who have ceased to sin. They weep no more, because all fear of change is past. They know that they are eternally secure. Sin is shut out, and they are shut in. They dwell within a city which will never be stormed. They bask in a sun which will never set. They drink of a river which will never dry, and they pluck fruit from a tree which will never wither. Countless cycles may revolve, but eternity will not be exhausted. While eternity endures, their immortality and blessedness will co-exist with it. They are forever with the Lord. They weep no more, because every desire is fulfilled. Imperfect as our present ideas are of the things which God has prepared for them that love Him, yet we know enough by the revelation of the Spirit to know the saints above are supremely blessed. The joy of Christ, which is an infinite fullness of delight, is in them. That same joyful rest remains for us. Before long the weeping willow will be exchanged for the palm branch of victory, and sorrow's dewdrops will be transformed into the pearls of everlasting bliss. "Wherefore comfort one another with these words" (1 Thessalonians 4:18).

August 23
Evening

"That Christ may dwell in your hearts by faith" (Ephesians 3:17).

We believers should have Jesus constantly before us to inflame our love toward Him and to increase our knowledge of Him. All Christians should enter as diligent scholars into Jesus' college as students of the body of Christ, resolved to attain a degree in the teachings of the cross. In order to have Jesus ever near, the heart must be full of Him, welling up with His love to overflowing. The apostle prays, "That Christ may dwell in your hearts." See how near he wants Jesus to be! You cannot get anything closer to you than to have it in the heart itself. "That He may dwell"—not that He may call on you sometimes as a casual visitor enters into a house and stays for a night. That He may dwell *in your heart*—the best room of the house; not in your thoughts alone, but in your affections; not merely in the mind's meditations, but in the heart's emotions. Our love for Christ should not be a love that flames up and then dies out into the darkness of a few embers, but a constant flame, fed by sacred fuel. This cannot be accomplished except by faith. Faith must be strong, or love will not be fervent. The root of the flower must be healthy, or we cannot expect the bloom to be sweet. Faith is the lily's root, and love is the lily's bloom. Jesus cannot be in your heart's love unless you have a firm hold of Him by your heart's faith. If your love grows cold, be sure that your faith is drooping.

August 24
Morning

"The breaker is come up before them" (Micah 2:13).

Because Jesus has gone before us, things are much different than they would have been had He never passed that way. He has conquered every foe that obstructed the way. Cheer up now. Not only has Christ traveled the road, but He has slain your enemies. Do you dread sin? He has nailed it to His cross. Do you fear death? He has been the death of death. Are you afraid of hell? He has barred it against the advent of any of His children. They will never see the gulf of perdition. Whatever foes may be before the Christian, they are all overcome. There are lions, but their teeth are broken; there are serpents, but their fangs are extracted; there are rivers, but they are bridged or fordable. The sword that has been forged against us is already blunted. The instruments of war which the enemy is preparing have already lost their point. God has taken away in the person of Christ all the power that anything can have to hurt us. Well then, you may go joyously along your journey, for all your enemies are conquered beforehand. You will, it is true, often engage in combat; but your fight will be with a vanquished foe. His head is under your foot. He may attempt to injure you, but his strength will not be sufficient for his malicious design. Your victory is certain.

August 24
Evening

"If fire break out, and catch in thorns, so that the stacks of corn, or the standing corn, or the field, be consumed therewith; he that kindled the fire shall surely make restitution" (Exodus 22:6).

What restitution can be made for one who shoots flaming arrows of error or lust and sets men's soul on a blaze with the fire of hell? If such an offender repents and is forgiven, his past will cause him sorrow since he cannot undo the mischief he has done. A bad example may kindle a flame which years of amended character cannot quench. To burn the food of a man is bad enough, but how much worse to destroy the soul! Let us consider how we may have been guilty in the past and inquire whether there is still sin in us which may damage the souls of our relatives, friends, or neighbors. The fire of strife is a terrible evil when it breaks out in a church. Where converts were multiplied and God was glorified, jealousy and envy effectively do the devil's work. The fire of enmity comes in and leaves little else but smoke and a heap of ashes. Those who cause the offenses commit a serious sin. May they never come through us. Although we cannot make restitution, we certainly will be the chief sufferers if we are the chief offenders. Those who feed the fire deserve reproach, but he who first kindles it is most to blame. Discord usually takes first hold upon the thorns. It is nurtured among the hypocrites and away it goes among the righteous, blown by the winds of hell. No one knows where it may end. O Lord, Giver of peace, make us peacemakers. Never let us aid the men of strife or even unintentionally cause the least division among Your people.

"His fruit was sweet to my taste" (Song of Solomon 2:3).

Faith, in the Scripture, is spoken of as pertaining to all the senses. It is hearing. "Hear, and your soul shall live" (Isaiah 55:3). One of the first performances of faith is hearing. We hear the voice of God, not with the outward ear alone, but with the inward ear. We hear it as God's Word, and we believe it to be so; that is the *"hearing"* of faith. Then our mind looks on the truth as it is presented to us; that is to say, we understand it; we perceive its meaning. This is *sight.* "Unto them that look for him shall he appear the second time without sin unto salvation" (Hebrews 9:28). We begin to admire it and find how fragrant it is; that is faith in its *"smell."* Faith is smelling. "All thy garments smell of myrrh, aloes, and cassia" (Psalm 45:8). Then we appropriate the mercies which are prepared for us in Christ; that is faith in its *"touch."* By faith the woman came behind and touched the hem of Christ's garment, and by this we handle the things of the good word of life. Faith is equally the spirit's *taste.* "How sweet are thy words to my taste! yea, sweeter than honey to my lips" (Psalm 119:103). "Except ye eat the flesh of the Son of man, and drink his blood, ye have no life in you" (John 6:53). That which gives true enjoyment is the aspect of faith wherein Christ is received into us and made to be the food of our souls. It is then we sit under His shadow with great delight and find His fruit sweet to our taste.

August 25
Evening

"If thou believest with all thine heart, thou mayest" (Acts 8:37).

These words may answer your question about your relationship to Christian doctrines. Perhaps you say, "I am afraid to be baptized. It is such a serious thing to acknowledge that I am dead with Christ and buried with Him. I do not feel free to come to the Master's table; I am afraid of eating and drinking damnation unto myself for not discerning the Lord's body." (See 1 Corinthians 11:29.) Jesus has given you liberty. Do not be afraid. If a stranger came to your house, he would stand at the door or wait in the hall. But your child feels very comfortable in the house. So it is with the child of God. A stranger may not intrude where a child may venture. When the Holy Spirit has given you the spirit of adoption, you may come to Christian ordinances without fear. The same rule holds true of the Christian's *inward privileges.* You think that you are not allowed to rejoice with joy unspeakable and full of glory. If you are permitted to get inside Christ's door or sit at the bottom of His table, you will be content. But you will not have less privileges than the very greatest of the saints. God shows no partiality in His love to His children. When Jesus comes into the heart, He issues a general license to be glad in the Lord. No chains are worn in the court of King Jesus. Our admission into the full privileges may be gradual, but it is sure. You may say, "I wish I could enjoy the promises and walk in my Lord's commands." "If thou believest with all thine heart, thou mayest."

August 26
Morning

"He hath commanded his covenant forever"
(Psalm 111:9).

The Lord's people delight in the covenant. It is an unfailing source of consolation to them as the Holy Spirit leads them into His banqueting house and waves His banner of love. They delight to contemplate *the antiquity* of that covenant, remembering that before planets ran their round, the interests of the saints were made secure in Christ Jesus. It is peculiarly pleasing to them to remember *the sureness* of the covenant. They delight to celebrate it as signed, sealed, and ratified in all things. It often makes their hearts dilate with joy to think of its *immutability,* as a covenant which neither time nor eternity, life nor death, will ever be able to violate—a covenant as old as eternity and as everlasting as the Rock of ages. They rejoice to feast on *the fullness* of this covenant, for they see all things provided for them in it. God is their portion, Christ their companion, the Spirit their Comforter, earth their lodge, and heaven their home. They see in it an inheritance reserved for every soul possessing salvation. How their souls were gladdened when they saw in the last will and testament of their divine Kinsman that it was bequeathed to them! More especially it is the pleasure of God's people to contemplate *the graciousness* of this covenant. They see that the law was made void because it was a covenant of works and depended on merit. But this they perceive to be enduring because grace is the basis. The covenant is a treasury of wealth, a fountain of life, a storehouse of salvation, a charter of peace, and a haven of joy.

August 26
Evening

"The people, when they beheld him, were greatly amazed, and running to him saluted him" (Mark 9:15).

How great is the difference between Moses and Jesus! When the prophet of Horeb had been on the mountain for forty days, he underwent a kind of transfiguration that made his countenance shine with great brightness. He put a veil over his face, for the people could not look upon his glory. (See Exodus 34:29-33.) Our Savior had been transfigured with a greater glory than that of Moses. Yet, it is not written that the people were blinded by the blaze of His countenance. Rather, they were amazed, ran to Him, and saluted Him. The glory of the law repels, but the greater glory of Jesus attracts. Jesus is holy and just, yet blended with His purity there is so much truth and grace that sinners run to Him, amazed at His goodness and fascinated by His love. They salute Him, become His disciples, and take Him to be their Lord and Master. It may be that you feel blinded by the dazzling brightness of the law of God. You sense its claims on your conscience, but you cannot keep it in your life. Not that you find fault with the law; on the contrary, it commands your highest esteem. Still, it does not draw you to God. Instead, you are hardened in heart and are verging toward desperation. Turn your eye from Moses and look to Jesus. He is the Son of God, and He is greater than Moses. But He is the Lord of love and, therefore, more tender than the lawgiver. He bore the wrath of God and in His death revealed more of God's justice than Sinai on a blaze. But justice is now satisfied, and it is now the guardian of believers in Jesus. Look, sinner, to the bleeding Savior. As you feel drawn by His love, run to His arms, and you will be saved.

August 27
Morning

"How long will it be ere they believe me?" (Numbers 14:11).

Strive, with all diligence, to keep out unbelief. Among hateful things it is the most to be abhorred. Its injurious nature is so venemous that he who exercises it, and he on whom it is exercised, are both hurt by it. In your case, believer, it is most wicked, for the mercies of your Lord in the past increase your guilt in doubting Him now. It is very cruel for a well-beloved wife to mistrust a kind and faithful husband. The sin is needless, foolish, and unwarranted. Jesus has never given the slightest ground for suspicion, and it is hard to be doubted by those to whom our conduct is uniformly affectionate and true. This is crowning His head with thorns of the sharpest kind. Jesus is the Son of the Highest and has unbounded wealth. It is shameful to doubt Omnipotence and distrust All-Sufficiency. The cattle on a thousand hills will suffice for our most hungry feeding, and the granaries of heaven are not likely to be emptied by our eating. If Christ were only a cistern, we might soon exhaust His fullness; but who can drain a fountain? Myriad spirits have drawn their supplies from Him, and not one of them has murmured at the scantiness of His resources. Put away this lying traitor unbelief, for his only errand is to cut the bonds of communion and make us mourn an absent Savior.

August 27
Evening

"Into thine hand I commit my spirit: thou hast redeemed me, O Lord God of truth" (Psalm 31:5).

These words have been frequently spoken by holy men in their hour of death. The object of the faithful man's concern in life and death is not his body or his estate, but his spirit. This is his treasure—if his spirit is safe, all is well. What is this mortal state compared with the soul? The believer commits his soul to the hand of God. It came from Him, it is His own, He has sustained it, He is able to keep it, and it is only right that He should receive it. All things are safe in Jehovah's hands. What we entrust to the Lord will be secure, both now and in the days to come. It is peaceful living and glorious dying to rest in the care of God. At all times we should commit everything to Jesus' faithful hand. Then, though life may hang by a thread and adversities multiply as the sands of the sea, our soul will dwell at ease and delight itself in quiet resting places. *"Thou hast redeemed me, O Lord God of truth."* Redemption is a solid basis for confidence. David had not known Calvary as we have, but temporal redemption cheered him. Shall not eternal redemption yet more deeply console us? Past deliverances encourage our strong pleas for present assistance. What the Lord has done in the past, He will do again, for He does not change. He is faithful to His promises and gracious to His saints. He will not turn away from His people.

August 28
Morning

"Oil for the light" (Exodus 25:6).

My soul, how much you need this! Your lamp will not continue to burn long without it. You have no oil well springing up in your human nature. Even the consecrated lamps could not give light without oil. Under the most happy circumstances you cannot give light for another hour unless fresh oil of grace is given you. Not every oil could be used in the Lord's service. Neither the petroleum which exudes so plentifully from the earth nor the produce of fishes nor that extracted from nuts would be accepted. Only the best olive oil was selected. Pretended grace from natural goodness or imaginary grace from outward ceremonies will never serve the true saint of God. He knows that the Lord would not be pleased with these. He goes to the olive-press of Gethsemane and draws his supplies from Him who was crushed therein. The oil of gospel grace is pure, and hence the light which is fed thereon is clear and bright. Our churches are the Savior's golden candelabra. If they are to be lights in this dark world, they must have much holy oil. Let us pray for ourselves, our ministers, and our churches, that they may never lack oil for the light. Truth, holiness, joy, knowledge, and love are all beams of the sacred light. But we cannot exemplify them unless we receive oil from God the Holy Spirit in private.

August 28
Evening

"Sing, O barren" (Isaiah 54:1).

We have brought forth some fruit for Christ and have a joyful hope that we are "the planting of the Lord, that he might be glorified" (Isaiah 61:3). Yet, there are times when we feel very barren. Prayer is lifeless, love is cold, faith is weak, each grace in the garden of our heart languishes and droops. We are like flowers in the hot sun, thirsting for a refreshing shower. The text is addressed to us in just such a state. *"Sing, O barren, break forth and cry aloud."* But what can I sing about? I cannot talk about the present, and even the past looks empty. I *can* sing of *Jesus Christ.* I can magnify His great love for His people when He came from the heights of heaven for their redemption. I will go to the cross again. Perhaps that very cross which gave me life may give me fruitfulness. My barrenness is the platform for His fruit-creating power. My desolation is the black setting for the sapphire of His everlasting love. I will go in poverty; I will go in helplessness; I will go in all my shame and backsliding. I am still His child. In confidence in His faithful heart, even I, the barren one, will sing and cry aloud. Sing, believer, for it will cheer your own heart and the hearts of other desolate ones. Sing on, for you will be fruitful soon. The experience of barrenness is painful, but the Lord's visitations are delightful. A sense of our own poverty drives us to Christ, and in Him we find our fruit.

"Have mercy upon me, O God" (Psalm 51:1).

When Dr. Carey was suffering from a serious illness, he was asked, "If this sickness would prove fatal, what passage would you select as the text for your funeral sermon?" He replied, "I feel that such a poor, sinful creature is unworthy to have anything said about him. But if a funeral sermon must be preached, let it be from the words, 'Have mercy upon me, O God, according to Thy lovingkindness; according unto the multitude of Thy tender mercies blot out my transgressions' " (Psalm 51:1). In the same spirit of humility, he directed in his will that the following inscription, and nothing more, should be cut on his gravestone:

WILLIAM CAREY, BORN AUGUST 17th, 1761;
DIED—.
"A wretched, poor, and helpless worm,
On Thy kind arms I fall."

The best of men are conscious, above all others, that they are men at the best. We need the Lord's mercy on our good works, our prayers, our preachings, our alms-givings, and our holiest things. The blood was not only sprinkled on the door-posts of Israel's houses, but on the sanctuary, the mercy seat, and the altar; as sin intrudes into our holiest things, the blood of Jesus is needed to purify them from defilement.

August 29
Evening

"All the days of his separation shall he eat nothing that is made of the vine tree, from the kernels even to the husk" (Numbers 6:4).

Nazarites had taken, among other vows, one which barred them from the use of wine. To make the rule clearer, they were not to touch the unfermented juice of grapes or even eat the fruit, either fresh or dried. In order to secure the integrity of the vow, they were not allowed anything that had to do with the vine. They were to avoid the appearance of evil. Surely this is a lesson to the Lord's separated ones, teaching them to come away from sin in every form. We are called to avoid not merely the grosser shapes of disobedience, but even its spirit and likeness. Strict walking is not popular in these days, but it is both the safest and the happiest way to live. He who yields a point or two to the world is in fearful peril. He who eats the grapes of Sodom will soon drink the wine of Gomorrah. Worldly conformity in any degree is a snare to the soul and makes it more inclined to commit presumptuous sins. The Nazarite who drank grape juice could not be sure whether it had undergone a degree of fermentation. Consequently, he could not be certain that his vow was intact. We must not flirt with temptation, but flee from it with speed. It is better to be sneered at as a Puritan than despised as a hypocrite. Careful walking may involve much self-denial, but it has pleasures of its own which are more than a sufficient reward.

August 30
Morning

"Wait on the Lord" (Psalm 27:14).

Sometimes it takes years of teaching before we learn to *wait*. It is much easier to forge ahead than to stand still. There are hours of perplexity when the most willing spirit, anxiously desirous to serve the Lord, does not know what part to take. Then what will it do? Fly back in cowardice, turn to the right hand in fear, or rush forward in presumption? No, it must simply wait. *Wait in prayer,* however. Call on God and spread the case before Him. Tell Him your difficulty and plead His promise of aid. In dilemmas between one duty and another, it is sweet to be humble as a child and wait with simplicity of soul on the Lord. It is sure to be well with us when we are heartily willing to be guided by the will of God. But *wait in faith.* Express your unstaggering confidence in Him. Unfaithful, untrusting waiting is an insult to the Lord. Believe that He will come at the right time. The vision will come and will not tarry. *Wait in quiet patience,* not rebelling because you are under the affliction, but blessing your God for it. Never murmur as the children of Israel did against Moses. Never wish you could go back to the world again, but accept the case as it is and put it, without any self-will, into the hand of your covenant God, saying, "Now, Lord, not my will, but Yours be done. I do not know what to do. But I will wait until You drive back my foes. I will wait, for my heart is fixed on You alone, O God, and my spirit waits for You in the full conviction that You will be my joy and my salvation, my refuge and my strong tower."

August 30
Evening

"Heal me, O Lord, and I shall be healed" (Jeremiah 17:14).

"I have seen his ways, and will heal him" (Isaiah 57:18).

It is the prerogative of God to remove spiritual disease. Physical disease may be healed by men, but even then, the glory is to be given to God. He provides doctors with wisdom to use medicine, and He grants power to the human body to cast off disease. As for spiritual sicknesses, the power to heal remains with the great Physician alone. He claims it as His right: "I kill, and I make alive; I wound, and I heal" (Deuteronomy 32:39). One of the Lord's titles is Jehovah-Rophi, the Lord that healeth thee. (See Exodus 15:26.) "I will heal thee of thy wounds" (Jeremiah 30:17) is a promise which could not come from man, but only from the mouth of the eternal God. For this reason, the psalmist cried to the Lord, "Heal my soul; for I have sinned against thee" (Psalm 41:4). The godly praise the name of the Lord, saying, "He heals all our diseases." (See Psalm 103:3.) He who made man can restore man. The Creator of our nature can create it anew. Whatever your disease may be, this great Physician can heal you. He is God—there is no limit to His power. Come, then, with the blind eye of darkened understanding, and come with the limping foot of wasted energy. Come with the maimed hand of weak faith, the fever of an angry temper, or the sickness of shivering despondency. Come just as you are, for God will restore you to health. Nothing can restrain the healing power which flows from Jesus our Lord. Legions of devils have attacked the power of the beloved Physican, and never once has He been defeated. All His patients have been cured in the past and will be in the future.

August 31
Morning

"On mine arm shall they trust" (Isaiah 51:5).

In times of severe trial, the Christian has nothing on earth that he can trust and is therefore compelled to cast himself on his God alone. He must simply and entirely trust himself to the providence and care of God. When a man is so poor, so friendless, so helpless that he has nowhere else to turn, he flies into his Father's arms and is blessedly clasped therein! He will learn more of his Lord then than at any other time. Tempest-tossed believer, it is a happy trouble that drives you to your Father! Now that you have only your God to trust, see that you put your full confidence in Him. Do not dishonor your Lord and Master by unworthy doubts and fears; but be strong in faith, giving glory to God. Show rich men how rich you are in your poverty when the Lord God is your helper. Show the strong man how strong you are in your weakness when underneath you are the everlasting arms. Now is the time for feats of faith. Be strong and very courageous; God will certainly, as surely as He built the heavens and the earth, glorify Himself in your weakness and magnify His might in the midst of your distress. The grandeur of the arch of heaven would be spoiled if the sky were supported by a single visible column, and your faith would lose its glory if it rested on anything discernible by the carnal eye. May the Holy Spirit give you rest in Jesus this closing day of the month.

August 31
Evening

"If we walk in the light, as he is in the light" (1 John 1:7).

Will we ever be able to walk as clearly in the light as He is whom we call "Our Father?" It is written, "God is light, and in him is no darkness at all" (1 John 1:5). This is the model which is set before us, for the Savior Himself said, "Be ye therefore perfect, even as your Father which is in heaven is perfect" (Matthew 5:48). Although we may feel that we can never rival the perfection of God, we are to seek after it and never be satisfied until we reach it. The youthful artist can hardly hope to equal Raphael or Michelangelo. But if he did not have a model of excellence in his mind, he would only create something crude and ordinary. The expression that the Christian is to walk in light as God is in the light refers to *likeness,* but not *degree.* We are truly, heartily, sincerely, honestly in the light, but we cannot be there in the same measure that Jesus is. I cannot dwell in the sun because it is too bright for my residence. But I can *walk* in the light of the sun. Though I cannot achieve that perfection of purity and truth which belongs to the Lord of Hosts, I can keep my eyes on Jesus. Therefore, I can strive, by the help of the indwelling Spirit, to conform to His image. John Trapp, who wrote a commentary on the New Testament, says, "We may be in the light as God is in the light for *quality*, but not for *equality."* We are to have the same light and walk in it as God does. Equality with God in His holiness and purity, however, must be left until we cross the Jordan and enter into the perfection of the Most High. The blessings of sacred fellowship and perfect cleansing are bound up with walking in the light.

September 1
Morning

"Thou shalt guide me with thy counsel, and afterward receive me to glory" (Psalm 73:24).

The psalmist felt his need for divine guidance. He had just been discovering the foolishness of his own heart, and he resolved that God's counsel would henceforth guide him. A sense of our own folly is a great step toward being wise when it leads us to rely on the wisdom of the Lord. The blind man leans on his friend's arm and reaches home in safety. Likewise, we should give ourselves up implicitly to divine guidance, nothing doubting, assured that though we cannot see, it is always safe to trust the All-seeing God. *"Thou shalt"* is a blessed expression of confidence. He was sure that the Lord would not decline the condescending task. Be assured that your God will be your counselor and friend. He will guide you. He will direct all your ways. In His written Word you have this assurance in part fulfilled, for holy Scripture is His counsel to you. We have God's Word always to guide us! This is the unerring chart from the quicksands of destruction to the haven of salvation, mapped and marked by One who knows all the way. Bless You, O God, that we may trust You to guide us to the end! After this guidance through life, the psalmist anticipates a divine reception at last—*"And afterward receives me to glory"* (Psalm 73:24). What a thought for you, believer! *God* Himself will receive *you* to glory—*you!* Wandering, erring, straying, yet He will bring you safe at last to glory! This is your portion; live on it this day.

September 1
Evening

"Trust in him at all times" (Psalm 62:8).

Faith is as much the rule of physical as of spiritual life. We should have faith in God for our earthly affairs as well as for our heavenly business. It is only as we learn to trust in God for the supply of all our daily need that we will live above the world. We are not to be idle. Our inactivity would show we did *not* trust in God, but in the devil—the father of idleness. We are not to be impulsive or rash—that would be trusting chance and not the God of economy and order. By trusting in God for temporal things, you will not have to mourn because you used sinful means to grow rich. Serve God with integrity. If you achieve no success, at least no sin will weigh upon your conscience. By trusting God, you will not be guilty of self-contradiction. He who trusts in deceit sails one way today and another way tomorrow, like a vessel tossed about by the wind. But he that trusts in the Lord is like a vessel propelled by steam. It cuts through the waves, defies the wind, and makes one straightforward track to her destined haven. Be a person with living principles within. Never bow to the varying customs of the worldy wisdom. Walk in your path of integrity with steadfast steps and show that you are invincibly strong in the strength which confidence in God alone can confer. You will be delivered from worry. You will not be troubled with evil tidings, for your heart will be fixed, trusting in the Lord. (See Psalm 112:7.) There is no more blessed way of living than a life of dependence upon a covenant-keeping God. We have no care, for He cares for us. We have no troubles, because we cast our burdens upon the Lord.

September 2
Morning

"But Simon's wife's mother lay sick of a fever, and anon they tell him of her" (Mark 1:30).

This little peep into the house of the apostolic fisherman is very interesting. We see at once that household joys and cares are no hindrance to the full exercise of the ministry. A few may decry marriage, but true Christianity and household life agree well together. Peter's house was probably a poor fisherman's hut, but the Lord of Glory entered it, lodged in it, and wrought a miracle in it. If this little book is read this morning in some humble cottage, let this fact encourage those who reside there to seek the company of King Jesus. God is in little huts more often than in rich palaces. Jesus is looking around your room now and is waiting to be gracious to you. Sickness had entered Simon's house, and fever in a deadly form had prostrated his mother-in-law. As soon as Jesus came they told Him of the sad affliction, and He hastened to the patient's bed. Do you have any sickness in the house this morning? You will find Jesus the best Physician by far. Go to Him at once and tell Him all about the matter. It concerns one of His people, and therefore it will not be trivial to Him. Observe that *at once* the Savior restored the sick woman. None can heal as He does. We know that believing prayer for the sick is far more likely to be followed by restoration than anything else in the world. Where this does not avail, we must meekly bow to His will by whom life and death are determined. The tender heart of Jesus waits to hear our griefs. Pour them into His patient ear.

September 2
Evening

"Except ye see signs and wonders, ye will not believe" (John 4:48).

Craving after miracles was a symptom of the sickly state of men's minds in our Lord's day. They refused the gospel which they so greatly needed. Instead, they eagerly demanded the miracles which Jesus did not always choose to give. Many people today must see signs and wonders, or they will not believe. Some have said in their heart, "I must feel deep trouble in my soul, or I never will believe in Jesus." But what if you never feel it? Will you go to hell out of spite against God because He will not treat you like another? Another has said to himself, "If I had a dream or if I could feel a sudden shock that I could not explain, then I would believe." You undeserving mortals dream that the Lord is to be dictated to by you! You are beggars at His gate, asking for mercy, and yet, you draw up regulations as to how He shall give that mercy. The Master is generous, but He spurns all dictation and maintains His sovereignty of action. Why do you crave for signs and wonders? Is not the gospel its own sign and wonder? This is a miracle of miracles—"God so loved the world, that he gave his only begotten Son, that whosoever believeth in him should not perish" (John 3:16). Surely that precious word, "Whosoever will, let him take the water of life freely" (Revelation 22:17) and that solemn promise, "Him that cometh to me I will in no wise cast out" (John 6:37) are better than signs and wonders? Why will you ask proof from One who cannot lie? The devils themselves declared Him to be the Son of God. (See Matthew 8:29.) Will you mistrust Him?

September 3
Morning

"Thou whom my soul loveth" (Song of Solomon 1:7).

It is wonderful to be able to say of the Lord Jesus—*"Thou whom my soul loveth."* Many can only say they *hope* they love Him; they *trust* they love Him; but only a poor and shallow experience will be content to stay here. No one should give any rest to his spirit until he feels quite sure about this vitally important matter. We should not be satisfied with a superficial *hope* that Jesus loves us and with a bare trust that we love Him. The old saints spoke positively and plainly. Paul said, "I know whom I have believed" (2 Timothy 1:12). "I know that my Redeemer liveth," said Job. Get positive knowledge of your love for Jesus. True love for Christ is the Holy Spirit's work in every case. He is the cause of it. *Why* do we love Jesus? *Because He first loved us and gave Himself for us.* We have life through His death. We have peace through His blood. Though He was rich, for our sakes He became poor. *Why* do we love Jesus? Because of the *excellency of His person.* We are filled with a sense of His beauty! His greatness, goodness, and loveliness combine to enthrall the soul until it is so overcome with love that it exclaims, "Yea, He is altogether lovely." This is a blessed love—a love which binds the heart with chains softer than silk and firmer than stone!

September 3
Evening

"The Lord trieth the righteous" (Psalm 6:5).

All events take place under the watchful eye of Almighty God. Consequently, no trials come to us without His knowledge. All blessings are potential doors to trial. Men may be drowned in seas of prosperity as well as in rivers of affliction. Temptations and trials lurk on all roads. Because this world is under the dominion of Satan, we are surrounded with dangers. Yet, no shower falls unpermitted from the threatening cloud; every drop has its order before it descends to the earth. The trials which come allow us to prove and strengthen our faith. By them, we may illustrate the power of divine grace, test the genuineness of our virtues, and increase our spiritual energy. Our Lord, in His infinite wisdom and superabundant love, sets such a high value upon His people's faith that He permits them to experience trials which strengthen their faith. You would never have possessed the precious faith which now supports you if the trial of your faith had not been like a fire. You are a tree that never would have rooted so well if the wind had not shaken you and made you take firm hold upon the precious truths of the covenant of grace. Worldly ease is a great enemy to faith. It loosens the joints of holy valor and snaps the sinews of sacred courage. The balloon never rises until the cords are cut. Testing accomplishes this sharp service for believing souls. While the wheat sleeps comfortably in the husks, it is useless to man. It must be threshed out of its resting place before its value can be known. It is good that the righteous are tried for it causes them to grow rich toward God.

September 4
Morning

"I will; be thou clean" (Mark 1:41).

Primeval darkness heard the Almighty command, "Let there be light," and immediately there was light. The Word of the Lord Jesus is equal in majesty to that ancient word of power. Redemption, like creation, has its word of might. Jesus speaks, and it is done. Leprosy yielded to no human remedies, but it fled at once at the Lord's "I will." The disease exhibited no hopeful signs or tokens of recovery. The sinner is in a plight more miserable than the leper. Let him go to Jesus, beseeching Him, and kneeling down to Him. Let him exercise what little faith he has, even if it can go no farther than, "Lord, if You will, You can make me clean." There need be no doubt as to the result. Jesus heals all who come and casts out none. In reading this morning's Scripture, notice that Jesus touched the leper. This unclean person had broken through the regulations of the ceremonial law and pressed into the house, but Jesus broke through the law Himself in order to meet him. Jesus Christ was made sin for us, although in Himself He knew no sin, that we might be made the righteousness of God in Him. If only poor sinners would go to Jesus, believing in the power of His blessed substitutionary work, they would soon learn the power of His gracious touch. That hand which multiplied the loaves, which saved sinking Peter, which upholds afflicted saints, which crowns believers—that same hand will touch every seeking sinner and in a moment make him clean. The love of Jesus is the source of salvation.

September 4
Evening

"Just balances, just weights, a just ephah, and a just hin, shall ye have" (Leviticus 19:36).

Weights, scales, and measures were to be used according to the standard of justice. Surely no Christian needs to be reminded of this in his business. If honesty was banished from all the world, it would find a shelter in believing hearts. There are, however, other balances which weigh moral and spiritual things, and these often need examining. Are the balances in which we weigh our own and other men's characters accurate? Do we turn our own ounces of goodness into pounds, and other persons' bushels of excellence into pecks? Are the scales in which we measure our trials and troubles set according to standard? Paul, who had more to suffer than we have, called his afflictions light. (See 2 Corinthians 4:17.) Yet, we often consider ours to be heavy—surely something must be wrong with the weights! Those scales which weigh our doctrinal belief—are they fair? The doctrines of grace should have the same weight with us as the commandments of the Word. Unfortunately for many Christians, one scale or the other is unfairly weighted. It is important to give correct measure in truth. Those measures in which we estimate our obligations and responsibilities look rather small. When a rich man gives no more to the cause of God than the poor contribute is that "a just ephah and just hin?" When ministers are half starved, is that honest dealing? When the poor are despised and ungodly rich men are held in admiration, is that a just balance? Find out and destroy all unrighteous balances, weights, and measures.

September 5
Morning

"Woe is me, that I sojourn in Mesech, that I dwell in the tents of Kedar!" (Psalm 120:5).

Even though you are a Christian, you have to live in the midst of an ungodly world, and it is of little use for you to cry, "Woe is me." Jesus did not pray that you would be taken out of the world. It is better to meet the difficulty in the Lord's strength and glorify Him in it. The enemy is always on the watch to detect inconsistency in your conduct; therefore, be very holy. Remember that the eyes of all are on you, and more is expected from you than from other men. Strive to give no occasion for blame. Let your goodness be the only fault they can discover in you. Seek to be useful as well as consistent. Perhaps you think, "If I were in a more favorable position, I might serve the Lord's cause; but I cannot do any good where I am." But the worse the people are among you, the more they need your example. If they are crooked, you should set them straight. If they are perverse, they need you to turn their proud heart to the truth. Where would the physicians be but where there are many sick? When you become weary of the strife and sin that meet you on every hand, remember that all the saints have endured the same trial. Some of them had to endanger their lives to the death, and you will not be crowned until you also have endured hardness as a good soldier of Jesus Christ. Therefore, "stand fast in the faith; quit you like men; be strong" (1 Corinthians 16:13).

September 5
Evening

"Hast thou entered into the springs of the sea?" (Job 38:16).

Some things in nature must remain a mystery to the most intelligent and enterprising investigators. Universal knowledge is for God alone. If this is true concerning the things which are seen and temporal, it is even more so in matters that are spiritual and eternal. Why, then, have I been torturing my brain with speculations as to destiny, will, fixed fate, and human responsibility? I am no more able to comprehend these deep and dark truths than I can find out the depth from which the ocean draws her watery stores. Why am I so curious to know the reason of my Lord's providences and the motives of His actions? Will I ever be able to clasp the sun in my fist and hold the universe in my palm? Yet, these are as a drop in a bucket compared with the Lord my God. Let me not strive to understand the infinite, but rather spend my strength in love. What I cannot gain by intellect, I can possess by affection. Let that satisfy me. I cannot penetrate the heart of the sea, but I can enjoy the healthful breezes which sweep over its bosom, and I can sail over its blue waves. If I could enter the springs of the sea, the feat would serve no useful purpose either to myself or others. It would not save the sinking ship or give back the drowned mariner to his weeping wife and children. Neither would my solving deep mysteries prove anything. The least love to God and the simplest act of obedience to Him are better than the most profound knowledge. My Lord, I leave the infinite to You and pray that You would keep me from a love for the tree of knowledge that would deprive me of the tree of life.

September 6
Morning

"In the midst of a crooked and perverse nation, among whom ye shine as lights in the world" (Philippians 2:15).

A Christian man should so shine in his life that a person could not live with him a week without knowing the gospel. His conversation should be such that all who are around him would clearly perceive whose he is and whom he serves. People should see the image of Jesus reflected in his daily actions. Lights are intended for *guidance*. We are to help those around us who are in the dark. We are to hold forth the Word of life to them. We are to point sinners to the Savior and the weary to a divine resting place. Men sometimes read their Bibles and fail to understand them. We should be ready, like Philip, to instruct the inquirer in the meaning of God's Word, the way of salvation, and the life of godliness. Lights are also used for *warning*. Christian men should know that there are many false lights shining everywhere in the world, and therefore the right light is needed. The wreckers of Satan are always abroad, tempting the ungodly to sin under the name of pleasure. They hoist the wrong light. It is our responsibility to put up the true light on every dangerous rock, to point out every sin, and tell what it leads to so we may be clear of the blood of all men. Lights also have a very *cheering* influence and so have Christians. A Christian ought to be a comforter with kind words on his lips and sympathy in his heart. He should carry sunshine wherever he goes and diffuse happiness around him.

September 6
Evening

"If ye be led of the Spirit, ye are not under the law" (Galatians 5:18).

He who looks at his own character and position from a legal point of view will despair when he comes to the end of his self-examination. If we are to be judged based on the law, no one will be justified. How blessed to know that we dwell in the domains of grace and not of law! The question is not, "Am I perfect in myself before the law?" but, "Am I perfect in Christ Jesus?" That is a very different matter. We need not inquire, "Am I without sin naturally?" but, "Have I been washed in the fountain opened for sin and for uncleanness?" It is not, "Am I in myself well-pleasing to God?" but it is, "Am I accepted in the Beloved?" The Christian views his failures from the top of Sinai and grows alarmed concerning his salvation. It would be far better if he read his title by the light of Calvary. He says, "My faith has unbelief in it. It is not able to save me." If he had considered *the object* of his faith instead of his faith, then he would have said, "There is no failure in *Him*, and therefore I am safe." He sighs over his hope, "Ah! my hope is marred and dimmed by anxiety about present things. How can I be accepted?" Had he regarded *the basis* of his hope, he would have seen that the promise of God is certain. Whatever our doubts may be, the oath and promise never fail. It is always safer to be led of the Spirit into gospel liberty than to wear legal chains. Judge yourself by what *Christ* is rather than what *you* are. Satan will try to destroy your peace by reminding you of your sinfulness and imperfections. You can only meet his accusations by faithfully holding to the gospel and refusing to wear the yoke of bondage.

September 7
Morning

"And when they could not come nigh unto him for the press, they uncovered the roof where he was: and when they had broken it up, they let down the bed wherein the sick of the palsy lay" (Mark 2:4).

Faith is full of inventions. The house was full, a crowd blocked the door, but faith found a way of getting at the Lord and placing the palsied man before Him. If we cannot get sinners where Jesus is by ordinary methods, we must use extraordinary ones. It seems, according to Luke 5:19, that the roofing had to be removed, which would make dust and cause a measure of danger to those below. But where the case is very urgent, we must not mind running some risks and shocking some proprieties. Jesus was there to heal, and come what may, faith ventured all so that her poor paralyzed charge might have his sins forgiven. Oh, that we had more daring faith among us! Try today to perform some gallant act for the love of souls and the glory of the Lord. Cannot faith invent also and reach by some new means the outcasts who lie perishing around us? It was the presence of Jesus which excited victorious courage in the four bearers of the palsied man. Is the Lord not among us now? Have we seen His face this morning? Have we felt His healing power in our own souls? If so, let us, breaking through all impediments, labor to bring souls to Jesus. O Lord, make us quick to suggest methods of reaching Your sin-sick ones and bold to carry them out at all hazards.

September 7
Evening

"There is sorrow on the sea; it cannot be quiet" (Jeremiah 49:23).

Little do we know what sorrow may be upon the sea at this moment. We are safe in our quiet home, but far away on the sea, a hurricane may be cruelly seeking to destroy the lives of men. Hear how death howls upon the deck. The hull quivers as the waves beat like battering rams upon the vessel! God help you, poor, drenched, and wearied ones! My prayer goes up to the great Lord of sea and land, that He will calm the storm and bring you to your desired haven! I should do more than pray. I should try to benefit those hardy men who risk their lives constantly. How often the boisterous sea swallows up the mariner! The sorrow of death on the sea is echoed in the long wail of widows and orphans. The salt of the sea is in many eyes of mothers and wives. Remorseless billows, you have devoured the love of women and the support of households. What a resurrection there will be from the caverns of the deep when the sea gives up her dead! Until then, there will be sorrow on the sea. As if in sympathy with the woes of earth, the sea is forever fretting along a thousand shores, wailing with a sorrowful cry like her own birds. She booms with a hollow crash of unrest, raving with uproarious discontent, chafing with hoarse wrath, or jangling with the voices of ten thousand murmuring pebbles. This is not our place of rest, and the surging billows tell us so. There is a land where there is no sea—our faces are steadfastly set toward it. We are going to the place which the Lord has told us about. Until then, we cast our sorrows on the Lord who walked upon the sea of old. He makes a way for His people through the ocean's depths.

September 8
Morning

"From me is thy fruit found" (Hosea 14:8).

The fruit of the branch is directly traceable to the root. Sever the connection, the branch dies, and no fruit is produced. By virtue of our union with Christ, we bring forth fruit. Every bunch of grapes has been first in the root. It has passed through the stem, flowed through the sap vessels, and fashioned itself externally into fruit. But it was first in the stem. Also, every good work was first in Christ, and then it is brought forth in us. Christian, prize this precious union in Christ, for it must be the source of all the fruitfulness which you can hope to know. If you were not joined to Jesus Christ, you would be a barren bough indeed. Our fruit comes from God. The fruit owes much to the root, but it also owes much to external influences. How much we owe to God's grace and providence! He provides us contantly with quickening, teaching, consolation, strength, or whatever else we need. To this we owe all of our usefulness or virtue. The gardener's sharp-edged knife promotes the fruitfulness of the tree by thinning the clusters and by cutting off superfluous shoots. So it is, Christian, with that pruning which the Lord gives to you. "My Father is the husbandman. Every branch in me that beareth not fruit he taketh away; and every branch that beareth fruit, he purgeth it, that it may bring forth more fruit" (John 15:2). Since our God is the author of our spiritual graces, let us give to Him all the glory of our salvation.

September 8
Evening

"The exceeding greatness of his power to usward who believe, according to the working of his mighty power, Which he wrought in Christ, when he raised him from the dead" (Ephesians 1:19-20).

What shall we say of those who think that conversion is accomplished by the free will of man and is due to the improvement of his disposition? When we see the dead rise from the grave by their own power, then we may expect to see ungodly sinners turning to Christ of their own free will. It is not the Word preached or the Word read in itself. All life-giving power proceeds from the Holy Spirit. All the soldiers and the high priests could not keep the body of Christ in the tomb. Death itself could not hold Jesus in its bonds. This same irresistible power is put forth in the believer when he is raised to newness of life. No sin, corruption, devils in hell, or sinners upon earth can stop the hand of God's grace when it intends to convert a man. The power which raised Christ from the dead was *glorious.* It reflected honor upon God and brought dismay to the hosts of evil. Therefore, great glory is given to God in the conversion of every sinner. It was *everlasting power.* "Christ being raised from the dead dieth no more; death hath no more dominion over him" (Romans 6:9). So we, being raised from the dead, do not go back to our dead works or to our old corruptions, but we live unto God. "For ye are dead, and your life is hid with Christ in God" (Colossians 3:3). "Like as Christ was raised up from the dead by the glory of the Father, even so we also should walk in newness of life" (Romans 6:4). The same power which raised the Head works life in the members. What a blessing to be made alive together with Christ!

September 9
Morning

"I will answer thee, and show thee great and mighty things which thou knowest not" (Jeremiah 33:3).

There are different translations of these words. One version renders it, "I will show thee great and fortified things;" another, "great and reserved things." Now, there are reserved and special things in Christian experience. There are the common frames and feelings of repentance, faith, joy, and hope, which are enjoyed by the entire family. But there is an upper realm of rapture, of communion, and conscious union with Christ which is far from being the common dwelling-place of believers. Not all of us have John's high privilege to lean on Jesus' bosom or Paul's to be caught up into the third heaven. There are heights in knowledge of the things of God which the eagle's eye and philosophic thought has never seen. God alone can bear us there. But the chariot in which He takes us up, and the fiery steeds with which that chariot is dragged, are prevailing prayers. Prevailing prayer takes the Christian to Carmel and enables him to cover heaven with clouds of blessing and earth with floods of mercy. Prevailing prayer bears the Christian aloft and shows him the inheritance reserved. It elevates and transfigures us. If you desire to reach to something higher than ordinary, look to the Rock that is higher than you and gaze with the eye of faith through the window of persistent prayer. When you open the window on your side, it will not be bolted on the other!

September 9
Evening

"And round about the throne were four and twenty seats: and upon the seats I saw four and twenty elders sitting, clothed in white raiment" (Revelation 4:4).

These representatives of the saints in heaven are said to be *around the throne*. In Song of Solomon 1:12, Solomon sings of the king sitting at his table. Some expositors supposed it to be a round table and have concluded that there is an equality among the saints. That idea is conveyed by the equal nearness of the four and twenty elders. The glorified spirits in heaven are blessed with nearness to Christ, clear vision of His glory, constant access to His court, and intimate fellowship with Him. There is no difference in this respect between one saint and another. All the people of God—apostles, martyrs, ministers, or obscure believers—will all be seated *near the throne*. They will all be near to Christ, all delighting in His love, all eating and drinking at the same table with Him, all equally beloved as His favorites and friends, even if they are not all equally rewarded as servants. Let believers on earth imitate the saints in heaven in their nearness to Christ. May Christ be the object of our thoughts and the center of our lives. How can we bear to live at such a distance from our Beloved? Lord Jesus, draw us nearer to You! Permit us to sing, "His left hand is under my head, and his right hand doth embrace me" (Song of Solomon 2:6).

September 10
Morning

"And he goeth up into a mountain, and calleth unto him whom he would: and they came unto him" (Mark 3:13).

Here was sovereignty. Impatient spirits may fret and fume because they are not called to the highest places in the ministry. But reader, rejoice that Jesus calls whom He will. If He calls me to be a doorkeeper in His house, I will cheerfully bless Him for His grace in permitting me to do anything in His service. The call of Christ's servants comes from above. Those whom He calls must go up the mountain to Him. They must seek to rise to His level by living in constant communion with Him. They may not be able to mount to classic honors or attain scholastic eminence, but they must, like Moses, go up into the mount and have constant communion with the unseen God. Jesus went apart to hold fellowship with the Father. We must enter into the same divine companionship if we would bless our fellow men. No wonder the apostles were clothed with power when they came down from the mountain where Jesus was. This morning we must endeavor to ascend the mount of communion that we may be ordained to the lifework for which we are set apart. Let us not see the face of man today until we have seen Jesus. We, too, will cast out devils and work wonders if we go down into the world girded with that divine energy which Christ alone can give. We *must* see Jesus. We must linger at the mercy-seat until we can truthfully say, "We were with Him in the Holy Mount."

September 10
Evening

"Evening wolves" (Habakkuk 1:8).

The evening wolf, infuriated by a day of hunger, was more fierce and ravenous than he was in the morning. This furious creature may represent our doubts and fears after a day of distraction of mind, losses in business, and perhaps unkind taunting from our fellowmen. Our thoughts howl in our ears, "Where is God now?" How voracious and greedy they are, swallowing up all suggestions of comfort and remaining as hungry as before. Great Shepherd, slay these evening wolves. Let Your sheep lie down in green pastures, undisturbed by insatiable unbelief. The fiends of hell are very similar to evening wolves. When the flock of Christ is in a cloudy and dark day, and their sun seems to be going down, the wolves hasten to tear and devour. O Lord, You have laid down Your life for the sheep. Preserve them from the fangs of the wolf. False teachers who craftily and industriously hunt for the precious life, devouring men by their falsehoods, are as dangerous and detestable as evening wolves. They are most dangerous when they wear the sheep's skin. Blessed is he who is kept from them, for thousands are made the prey of grievous wolves that enter into the fold of the Church. What a wonder of grace it is when fierce persecutors are converted! Then the wolf dwells with the lamb, and men of cruel, ungovernable dispositions become gentle and teachable. O Lord, convert many of these wolves. We pray for their salvation tonight.

September 11
Morning

"Be ye separate" (2 Corinthians 6:17).

The Christian, while *in* the world, is not to be *of* the world. To him, to live, should be Christ. Whether he eats or drinks or whatever he does, he should do all to God's glory. You may lay up treasure, but lay it up in heaven where neither moth nor rust corrupts or where thieves cannot break through or steal. You may strive to be rich, but let it be your ambition to be rich in faith and good works. You may have pleasure; but when you are merry, sing psalms and make melody in your heart to the Lord. In your spirit, as well as in your aim, you should differ from the world. Waiting humbly before God, always conscious of His presence, delighting in communion with Him, and seeking to know His will, you will prove that you are of the heavenly race. And you should be separate from the world in your actions. If a thing is right, though you lose by it, it must be done. If it is wrong, though you would gain by it, you must scorn the sin for your Master's sake. You must have no fellowship with the unfruitful works of darkness, but rather reprove them. Walk worthy of your high calling and dignity. Do not let those eyes, which are soon to see the King in His beauty, become the windows of lust. Do not let those hearts, which are before long to be filled with heaven and to overflow with ecstatic joy, be filled with pride and bitterness.

September 11
Evening

"Lead me, O Lord, in thy righteousness because of mine enemies"(Psalm 5:8).

The enmity of the world against the people of Christ is very bitter. Men will forgive a thousand faults in others, but they will magnify the most trivial offense in the followers of Jesus. Instead of uselessly regretting this, let us turn it to our good. Since so many are watching for us to stumble, let this be a special motive for walking very carefully before God. If we live carelessly, the world will soon see it. They will shout triumphantly, "Aha! See how these Christians act! They are hyocrites, every one!" Thus much damage will be done to the cause of Christ, and His holy name will be insulted. The cross of Christ is in itself an offense to the world. Let us take heed that we add no offense of our own. It is "unto the Jews a stumbling block, and unto the Greeks foolishness" (1 Corinthians 1:23). Let us be certain that we put no stumbling blocks where there are enough already. Let us not add our folly to increase the scorn with which the worldy-wise deride the gospel. In the presence of adversaries who will misrepresent our best deeds and question our motives where they cannot disapprove of our actions, how circumspect we should be! Christians travel as suspected persons through this world. Not only are we under surveillance, but there are more spies than we imagine. If we fall into the enemies' hands, we may sooner expect kindness from a wolf or mercy from a fiend than anything like patience with our infirmities from men who spice their infidelity toward God with scandals against His people. O Lord, lead us always, lest our enemies succeed in making us stumble.

September 12
Morning

"God is jealous" (Nahum 1:2).

Your Lord is very jealous of your love, believer. Did He choose you? He cannot bear that you should choose another. Did He buy you with His own blood? He cannot endure that you should think that you are your own or that you belong to this world. He loved you with such love that He would sooner die than see you perish. He cannot endure anything standing between your heart's love and Himself. When we lean on Him, He is glad; but when we transfer our dependence to another, He is displeased and will chasten us so that He may bring us to Himself. He is also very jealous of our company. There should be no one with whom we converse so much as with Jesus. To abide in Him only, this is true love; but to commune with the world, to find sufficient solace in our carnal comforts, to prefer even the society of our fellow-Christians to fellowship with Him, this is grievous to our jealous Lord. He is happy when we abide in Him and enjoy constant fellowship with Himself. Many of the trials we experience wean our hearts from the creature and fix them more closely on Himself. Let this jealousy, which should keep us near to Christ, be a comfort to us. If He loves us so much as to care thus about our love, we may be sure that He will not allow anything to harm us and will protect us from all our enemies. Oh, that we may have grace this day to keep our hearts in sacred chastity for our Beloved alone, with sacred jealousy shutting our eyes to all the fascinations of the world!

September 12
Evening

"I will sing of mercy and judgment" (Psalm 101:1).

Faith triumphs in trial. When Reason is thrust into the inner prison, Faith makes the dungeon walls ring with her merry notes. She cries, "I will sing of mercy and of judgment: unto thee, O Lord, will I sing." Faith pulls the black mask from the face of trouble and discovers the angel beneath. There is a reason for a song even in the judgments of God toward us. This is because the trial is not as heavy as it might have been. The trouble is not so severe as we deserved to experience. Our affliction is not as crushing as the burden which others have to carry. Faith sees that her worst sorrow is not given to her as punishment. There is not a drop of God's wrath in it—it is all sent in love. Faith discerns love gleaming like a jewel on the breast of an angry God. Faith says of her grief, "This is a badge of honor, for the child must feel the rod of discipline." Then she sings of the sweet result of her sorrows, because they bring about her spiritual good. "For our light affliction, which is but for a moment, worketh for us a far more exceeding and eternal weight of glory" (2 Corinthians 4:17). Faith rides forth on the black horse, trampling down carnal reason and fleshly sense and chanting notes of victory in the midst of the battle.

September 13
Morning

"Who passing through the valley of Baca make it a well, the rain also filleth the pools" (Psalm 84:6).

This teaches us that the comfort obtained by one may often prove serviceable to another, just as wells would be used by the company who came after. We read a book full of consolation, which is like Jonathan's rod, dropping with honey. We think our brother has been here before us and dug this well for us as well as for himself. We notice this in the Psalms, such as that beginning, "Why art thou cast down, O my soul" (Psalm 42:5). Travelers have been delighted to see the footprint of man on a barren shore while passing through the valley of tears. We dig a well, but heaven fills it with rain. The means are connected with the end, but they do not of themselves produce it. See here the rain fills the pools so that the wells become useful as reservoirs for the water. Labor is not lost, but yet it does not supersede divine help. Grace may well be compared to rain for its purity, for its refreshing influence, for its coming from above, and for the sovereignty with which it is given or withheld. May our readers have showers of blessing, and may the wells they have dug be filled with water. They are as clouds without rain and pools without water. O God of love, open the windows of heaven and pour us out a blessing!

September 13
Evening

"This man receiveth sinners" (Luke 15:2).

Observe the *condescension* revealed by this statement. This Man who towers above all other men, holy, harmless, undefiled, and separate from sinners—*this* Man receives sinners. That any of *us* are willing to seek after the lost is nothing wonderful—they are part of our own race. But the holy God against whom the transgression has been committed took upon Himself the form of a servant. He bore the sin of many and then became willing to receive the vilest of the wicked. This is marvelous! He does not receive sinners that they may remain sinners. He receives them that He may pardon their sins, justify and cleanse their hearts by His purifying Word, and preserve their souls by the indwelling of the Holy Spirit. He enables them to serve Him, to show forth His praise, and to have communion with Him. Into His heart's love He receives sinners, takes them from the pit of misery, and wears them as jewels in His crown. He rescues them from the burning fire and preserves them as costly monuments of His mercy. None are as precious in Jesus' sight as the sinners for whom He died. When Jesus receives sinners, it is not at some outdoor reception place where He charitably entertains them as passing beggars. Rather, He opens the golden gates of His royal heart and receives the sinner right into Himself. He admits the humble penitent into personal union and makes him a member of His body, of His flesh, and of His bones. He is still receiving sinners this evening. Pray that sinners would receive Him.

September 14
Morning

"There were also with him other little ships"
(Mark 4:36).

Jesus was the Lord High Admiral of the sea that night, and His presence preserved the whole convoy. If we go with Jesus, we must be content to fare as He fares. When the waves are rough to Him, they will be rough to us. It is by the tempest and tossing that we will come to land, as He did before us. When the storm swept over Galilee's dark lake, all faces gathered blackness, and all hearts dreaded shipwreck. When all creature-help was useless, the slumbering Savior arose and, with a word, transformed the riot of the tempest into the deep quiet of a calm. Jesus is the star of the sea; and although there is sorrow on the sea, when Jesus is on it there is joy also. May our hearts make Jesus their anchor, their rudder, their lighthouse, their lifeboat, and their harbor. His Church is the Admiral's flagship. He Himself is the great attraction. Let us follow in His wake, mark His signals, steer by His chart, and never fear while He is within hail. Not one ship in the convoy will suffer wreck; the great Commodore will steer each one safely to the desired haven. Winds and waves will not spare us, but they all obey Him; and, therefore, whatever squalls may occur without, faith will feel a blessed calm within. His vessel has reached the haven, and so will ours.

September 14
Evening

"I acknowledged my sin unto thee, and mine iniquity have I not hid. I said, I will confess my transgressions unto the Lord; and thou forgavest the iniquity of my sin" (Psalm 32:5).

David's grief for sin was bitter. He could find no remedy until he made a full confession before the throne of heavenly grace. He tells us that for a time he kept silent and his heart became more filled with grief. Like a mountain stream whose outlet is blocked up, his soul was swollen with torrents of sorrow. He made excuses, he tried to divert his thoughts, but it was all in vain. His anguish gathered, and since he would not use the release of confession, his spirit was full of torment and knew no rest. At last David realized that he must return to God in humble penitence or die outright. He hastened to the mercy seat and confessed his iniquities before the all-seeing One. Having done this, a work so simple and yet so difficult to pride, he immediately received divine forgiveness. The bones which had been broken began to rejoice. He came forth to sing of the blessedness of the man whose transgression is forgiven. See the value of a heartfelt confession of sin! It should be highly prized. In every case where there is a genuine, gracious confession, mercy is freely given, not because the repentance and confession *deserve* mercy, but for *Christ's sake*. There is always healing for the broken heart. The fountain is ever flowing to cleanse us from our sins. Truly, O Lord, You are a God "ready to forgive" (Psalm 86:5). Therefore, we will acknowledge our iniquities.

September 15
Morning

"He shall not be afraid of evil tidings" (Psalm 112:7).

Christian, you should not dread the arrival of evil tidings. If you are distressed by them, how are you different from other men? Other men do not have your God to go to. They have never proved His faithfulness as you have done. It is no wonder if they are bowed down with fear. But you profess to be of another spirit. You have been begotten again unto a lively hope, and your heart lives in heaven and not on earthly things. Now, if you are seen to be distracted as other men, what is the value of that grace which you profess to have received? Where is the dignity of that new nature which you claim to possess? If you should be filled with alarm as others are, you would, doubtless, be led into the sins common to others under trying circumstances. The ungodly, when they are overtaken by evil tidings, rebel against God. They murmur and think that God deals harshly with them. Will you fall into that same sin? Unconverted men often run to wrong means in order to escape from difficulties, and you will be sure to do the same if your mind yields to the present pressure. Trust in the Lord, and wait patiently for Him. Your wisest course is to do as Moses did at the Red Sea—"stand still, and see the salvation of God" (Exodus 14:13). If you give way to fear when you hear of evil tidings, you will be unable to meet the trouble with that calm composure which sustains under adversity. Saints have often sung God's high praises in the fires. But if you doubt, will it magnify the Most High? Then take courage, and "let not your heart be troubled, neither let it be afraid" (John 14:27).

September 15
Evening

"A people near unto him" (Psalm 148:14).

The old covenant required that a distance be kept between God and man. When God appeared to His servant Moses, He said, "Draw not nigh hither: put off thy shoes from off they feet" (Exodus 3:5). When He manifested Himself upon Mount Sinai to His own chosen and separated people, one of the first commands was, "Set bounds about the mount" (Exodus 19:23). Both in the sacred worship of the tabernacle and in the temple, the thought of distance was always prominent. Only the priests dared to venture into the inner court. The innermost place, the holy of holies, was entered once in the year and only by the high priest. It was as if the Lord, in those early ages, wanted to teach man that sin was utterly loathsome to Him. When He came nearest to them, He still made them feel the separation between a holy God and an impure sinner. When the gospel came, we received a new invitation. The word "Go" was exchanged for "Come." Distance gave way to nearness. We who were far off were brought near by the blood of Jesus Christ. (See Ephesians 2:13.) Incarnate Deity has no wall of fire surrounding it. "Come unto me, all ye that labour and are heavy laden, and I will give you rest" (Matthew 11:28) is the joyful proclamation of God as He appears in human flesh. What safety and privilege is available in this nearness to God through Jesus! Do you know it by experience? If you know it, are you living in the power of it? This nearness is marvelous, yet it is to be followed by an even greater nearness. It will be said, "The tabernacle of God is with men, and he will dwell with them" (Revelation 21:3).

September 16
Morning

"Partakers of the divine nature" (2 Peter 1:4).

To be a partaker of the divine nature is not, of course, to become God. That cannot be. The essence of Deity is not to be participated in by the creature. Between the creature and the Creator there must be a gulf fixed in respect of essence. But as the first man Adam was made in the image of God, so we, by the renewal of the Holy Spirit, are in a diviner sense made in the image of the Most High and are partakers of the divine nature. We are, by grace, made like God. "God is love" (1 John 4:16). "He that loveth is born of God" (1 John 4:7). God is good, and He makes us good by His grace, so that we become the pure in heart who will see God. Do we not become members of the Body of Christ? Yes, the same blood which flows in the head flows in the hand; and the same life which quickens Christ quickens His people, for, "Ye are dead, and your life is hid with Christ in God" (Colossians 3:3). As if this were not enough, we are married to Christ. He has betrothed us unto Himself in righteousness and in faithfulness, and he who is joined to the Lord is one spirit. Oh, marvelous mystery! We look into it, but who can understand it? One with Jesus—so one with Him that the branch is not more one with the vine than we are a part of the Lord, our Savior and our Redeemer! While we rejoice in this, let us remember that those who are made partakers of the divine nature will manifest their high and holy relationship in their fellowship with others. It will be evident, by their daily walk and conversation, that they have escaped the corruption that is in the world through lust.

September 16
Evening

"Am I a sea, or a whale, that thou settest a watch over me?" (Job 7:12).

This was a strange question for Job to ask the Lord. He thought he was too insignificant to be so strictly watched and chastened. He did not feel that he was so unruly that he needed to be restrained. The inquiry was natural from one surrounded with such unexplainable miseries. But Job's question received a very humbling answer. It is true that man is not the sea—he is even more troublesome and unruly. The sea obediently respects its boundary, though it is a mere belt of sand. But self-willed man defies heaven and oppresses earth. There is no end to his rebellious rage. The sea, obedient to the moon, ebbs and flows with ceaseless regularity. It renders an active as well as a passive obedience. Man, however, is restless beyond his sphere. He sleeps within the lines of duty, and he is lazy where he should be active. He will neither come nor go at the divine command, but sullenly prefers to do what he should not and to leave undone that which is required of him. Every drop in the ocean, every beaded bubble, every foamy wave, and every shell and pebble feel the power of law and move at once. Oh, that our nature was even one thousandth part as much conformed to the will of God! We call the sea fickle and false, but how constant it is! Centuries before our fathers' days, the sea is where it was, beating on the same cliffs to the same tune. But where is vain, fickle man? Can the wise man guess by what foolish sin he will next be seduced from his obedience? We require more watching than the billowy sea, for we are far more rebellious. Lord, rule us for Your own glory.

September 17
Morning

"Bring him unto me" (Mark 9:19).

The disappointed father turned away from the disciples to their Master in despair. His son was in the worst possible condition, and all means had failed. The child was soon delivered from the evil one when the parent, in faith, obeyed the Lord Jesus' word, "Bring thy son hither" (Luke 9:41). Children are a precious gift from God, but much anxiety comes with them. They may be a great joy or a great bitterness to their parents. They may be filled with the Spirit of God or possessed with the spirit of evil. We must spend time in more prayer on their behalf, while they are still babes. Sin is there, so let our prayers begin to attack it. Our cries for our offspring should precede those cries which accompany their actual advent into a world of sin. When they are grown up, they may wallow in sin and display enmity against God. Then, when our hearts are breaking, we should remember the great Physician's words, "Bring them unto me." We must not cease to pray until they cease to breathe. No case is hopeless while Jesus lives. Ungodly children, when they show us our own powerlessness against the depravity of their hearts, drive us to flee to the Strong One for strength. This is a great blessing to us. Whatever our morning's need may be, let it, like a strong current, bear us to the ocean of divine love. Jesus can soon remove our sorrow. He delights to comfort us. Let us hasten to Him while He waits to meet us.

September 17
Evening

"Encourage him" (Deuteronomy 1:38).

God calls His *people* to encourage one another. He did not say to an angel, "Gabriel, My servant Joshua is about to lead My people into Canaan— go, encourage him." God never works needless miracles. If His purposes can be accomplished by ordinary means, He will not use miraculous power. Gabriel would not have been half as well suited for the work as Moses was. A brother's sympathy is more precious than an angel's ministry. An angel had never experienced the hardness of the road or seen the fiery serpents or led the stiffnecked multitude in the wilderness as Moses had done. We should be glad that God usually works for man through other men. It forms a bond of brotherhood, and being mutually dependent on one another, we are fused more completely into one family. Take this evening's text as God's message to you. Labor to help others and especially strive to *encourage* them. Talk cheerfully to the young and anxious inquirer. Lovingly try to remove stumbling blocks out of his way. When you find a spark of grace in the heart, kneel down and blow it into a flame. Allow the young believer to discover the roughness of the road by degrees, but tell him of the strength which dwells in God, of the sureness of the promise, and of the beauty of communion with Christ. Aim to comfort the sorrowful and to refresh the weary in spirit. Encourage those who are fearful to go on their way with gladness. God encourages you by His promises. Christ encourages you as He points to the heaven He has won for you. The Spirit encourages you as He works in you to do His will. Imitate divine wisdom and encourage others.

September 18
Morning

"If we live in the Spirit, let us also walk in the Spirit" (Galatians 5:25).

The two most important things in our holy religion are the *life of faith* and the *walk of faith*. You will never find true faith unattended by true godliness. On the other hand, you will never discover a truly holy life which is not rooted in living faith on the righteousness of Christ. There are some who cultivate faith and forget holiness. There are others who have strained after holiness of life but have denied the faith. We must have faith, for this is the foundation; we must have holiness of life, for this is the superstructure. Of what service is the mere foundation of a building to a man in the day of tempest? Can he hide himself there? He wants a house to cover him, as well as a foundation for that house. Even so we need the superstructure of spiritual life if we would have comfort in the day of doubt. But seek not a holy life without faith, for that would be to erect a house which can afford no permanent shelter, because it has no foundation on a rock. Let faith and life be put together; and, like the two abutments of an arch, they will make our piety enduring. Like light and heat streaming from the same sun, they are alike full of blessing. O Lord, give us this day life within, and it will reveal itself without to Your glory.

September 18
Evening

"And they follow me" (John 10:27).

We should follow our Lord as unhesitatingly as sheep follow their shepherd, for *He has a right to lead us wherever He pleases.* We are not our own, but we are bought with a price. (See 1 Corinthians 6:20.) Let us recognize the rights of the redeeming blood. The soldier follows his captain, and the servant obeys his master. We must follow our Redeemer, who purchased us as His own possession. We are not true to our profession of being Christians if we question the commands of our Lord. Submission is our duty; complaints are our shame. Our Lord might say to us as to Peter, "What is that to thee? follow thou me" (John 21:22). Wherever Jesus leads us, He goes before us. With such a companion, who will dread the perils of the road? The journey may be long, but His everlasting arms will carry us to the end. The presence of Jesus is the assurance of eternal salvation. Because He lives, we will live also. We should follow Christ in simplicity and faith, because the paths in which He leads us all end in glory and immortality. They may not be smooth paths, but they lead to the "city which hath foundations, whose builder and maker is God" (Hebrews 11:10). "All the paths of the Lord are mercy and truth unto such as keep his covenant" (Psalm 25:10). Let us put full trust in our Leader. We know that, come prosperity or adversity, sickness or health, popularity or contempt, His pure and perfect purpose will be fulfilled. His love will make us far more blessed than those who sit at home and warm their hands at the world's fire. To the top of the mountains or to the dens of lions we will follow our Beloved.

"The liberty wherewith Christ hath made us free" (Galatians 5:1).

This liberty makes us *free* to heaven's charter—*the Bible*. Here is a choice passage, believer: "When thou passest through the rivers I will be with thee" (Isaiah 43:2). You are free to that. Here is another: "The mountains shall depart, and the hills be removed, but my kindness shall not depart from thee" (Isaiah 54:10). You are a welcome guest at the table of the promises. Scripture is a never-failing treasury filled with boundless stores of grace. It is the bank of heaven. You may draw from it as much as you please. Come in faith, and you are welcome to all covenant blessings. There is not a promise in the Word which will be withheld. In the depths of tribulations, let this freedom comfort you. Amid waves of distress, let it cheer you. When sorrow surrounds you, let it be your solace. This is your Father's love-token. You are free to it at all times. It is the believer's privilege to have access at all times to his heavenly Father. Whatever our desires, our difficulties, our needs, we are at liberty to spread all before Him. No matter how much we may have sinned, we may ask and expect pardon. And remember, we may plead His promise that He will provide for all our needs. This does not depend on *our* wealth. You are free to all that is treasured up *in Christ*—wisdom, righteousness, sanctification, and redemption. Your inheritance includes freedom from condemnation, freedom to the promises, freedom to the throne of grace, and freedom to enter heaven!

September 19
Evening

"For this child I prayed" (1 Samuel 1:27).

Devout souls delight to look upon the blessings they obtained by prayer, for they can see God's special love in His answer to them. When we can name our blessings Samuel, which means "asked of God," they will be as dear to us as the child was to Hannah. Peninnah had many children, but they came as common blessings unsought in prayer. Hannah's one, heaven-given child was far dearer because he was the fruit of earnest pleadings. The cup of prayer puts a sweetness into the refreshments it brings. Did we pray for the conversion of our children? How doubly sweet, when they are saved, to see our petitions fulfilled in them! It is better to rejoice over them as the fruit of our pleadings than as the fruit of our bodies. Have we sought some spiritual gift from the Lord? When it comes to us, it will be wrapped up in the gold cloth of God's faithfulness and truth, and therefore be doubly precious. Have we prayed for success in the Lord's work? How joyful is the prosperity which comes flying upon the wings of prayer! It is always best to get blessings into our house by the door of prayer. Then, they are blessings indeed and not temptations. Even when the answer does not arrive immediately, the blessings grow richer for the delay. The child Jesus was all the more lovely in the eyes of Mary when she found Him in the temple, after searching for Him in Jerusalem for three days. (See Luke 2:43-49.) That which we win by prayer should be dedicated to God, as Hannah dedicated Samuel. Since the gift came from heaven, let it go to heaven. Let devotion consecrate it.

September 20
Morning

"The sword of the Lord and of Gideon" (Judges 7:20).

Gideon ordered his men to do two things. Covering up a torch in an earthen pitcher, he told them, at an appointed signal, to break the pitcher and let the light shine. Then, they were to the trumpet, crying, "The sword of the Lord and of Gideon! the sword of the Lord and of Gideon!" This is precisely what all Christians must do. First, *you must shine;* break the pitcher which conceals your light. Throw aside the bushel that has been hiding your candle and shine. Let your light shine before men. Let your good works be such, that, when men look at you, they will know that you have been with Jesus. Then, *there must be the sound,* the blowing of the trumpet. Take the gospel to sinners. Carry it to their door. Put it in their way. Do not allow them to escape it. Remember, that the true war-cry of the Church is Gideon's watchword, "The sword of the Lord and of Gideon!" God must do it. It is His own work. But we are not to be idle. We can do nothing of ourselves, but we can do everything by the help of our God. Let us, therefore, in His name determine to go out personally, and God will be with us. They will be put to confusion, and the Lord of hosts will reign forever and ever.

September 20
Evening

"In the evening withhold not thine hand"
(Ecclesiastes 6:6).

In the evening of the day, opportunities are plentiful to witness for Christ. Men return from their labor, and the zealous soul-winner finds time to tell them of the love of Jesus. Do I have any evening work for Jesus? If not, let me no longer withhold my hand from a service which requires abundant labor. Sinners are perishing for lack of knowledge. He who loiters may find his hands crimson with the blood of souls. Jesus gave both His hands to the nails. How can I keep back one of mine from His blessed work? Night and day, He toiled and prayed for me. How can I give a single hour to the pampering of my flesh with luxurious ease? Get up, idle heart. Stretch out your hand to work or uplift it to pray. Heaven and hell are in earnest. Let me be the same and sow good seed for the Lord this evening. Life is so brief that no man can afford to lose a day. If a king brought us a great heap of gold and told us to take as much as we could count in a day, we would make a long day of it. We would begin early in the morning and in the evening we would not withhold our hand. Winning souls is far nobler work. Why do we withdraw from it so quickly? Some are given a long evening of old age. If this is my case, let me use the talents that I retain and serve my blessed and faithful Lord to the last hour. By His grace, I will die in His service and lay down my task only when I lay down my body. In the evening I will not withhold my hand.

September 21
Morning

"I will rejoice over them to do them good"
(Jeremiah 32:41).

The delight which God has in His saints is cause for jubilation in the believer. We cannot see any reason in ourselves why the Lord should take pleasure in us. We cannot take delight in ourselves, for we often have to groan, being burdened and conscious of our sinfulness. We feel that God's people cannot take much delight in us, for they must perceive so much of our imperfections and lament our infirmities rather than admire our graces. But we love to dwell on this transcendent truth, this glorious mystery. As the bridegroom rejoices over the bride, so does the Lord rejoice over us. We do not read anywhere that God delights in the cloud-capped mountains or the sparkling stars. But we do read that He delights in the sons of men. We do not find it written that even angels give His soul delight, yet He expresses His delight in His people in strong language. Who could have conceived of the eternal One as bursting forth into a song? Yet it is written, "He will rejoice over thee with joy; he will rest in his love; he will joy over thee with singing" (Zephaniah 3:17). As He looked on the world He had made, He said, "It is very good." But when He beheld those who are the purchase of Jesus' blood, His own chosen ones, it seemed as if the great heart of the Infinite could restrain itself no longer, and overflowed in divine exclamation of joy. Our grateful response should be, "I will rejoice in the Lord, I will joy in the God of my salvation."

September 21
Evening

"Gather not my soul with sinners" (Psalm 26:9).

Fear made David pray this way. Something inside of him whispered, "Perhaps after all, I may be gathered with the wicked." That fear, although marred by unbelief, springs from holy anxiety concerning past sin. Even the pardoned man will inquire, "What if my sins should be remembered, and I should be left out of the Book of Life?" He recollects his present unfruitfulness—so little grace, so little love, so little holiness. Looking to the future, he considers his weakness and the many temptations which beset him. He fears that he may fall and become a prey to the enemy. A sense of sin, present evil, and his prevailing corruptions compel him to pray in fear and trembling, "Gather not my soul with sinners." If you have prayed this prayer, you need not be afraid that you will be gathered with sinners. Do you have the two virtues which David had—the outward walking in integrity and the inward trusting in the Lord? Are you resting upon Christ's sacrifice? Can you approach the altar of God with humble hope? If so, rest assured that it is impossible for you to be gathered with the wicked. The gathering at the judgment is like to like. "Gather ye together first the tares, and bind them in bundles to burn them: but gather the wheat into my barn" (Matthew 13:30). If you are *like* God's people, then you will be *with* God's people. You are loved too much to be cast away with reprobates. Shall one dear to Christ perish? Impossible! Hell cannot hold you! Heaven claims you! Trust in your Savior, and fear not!

September 22
Morning

"Let Israel rejoice in him" (Psalm 149:2).

Be glad of heart, believer, but take care that your gladness springs from the Lord. You have much cause for gladness in your God. Be glad that the Lord reigns, that Jehovah is King! Rejoice that He sits on the throne and rules all things! Every attribute of God should become a fresh ray in the sunlight of our gladness. Knowing that He is *wise* should make us glad, as we look at our own foolishness. Knowing that He is *mighty* should cause us to rejoice, as we tremble at our own weakness. Knowing that He is *everlasting* should always be a theme of joy when we know that we wither as the grass. Knowing that He is *unchanging* should perpetually yield us a song, since we change every hour. This gladness in God is as a deep river. We have only as yet touched its brink. We know a little of its clear, sweet, heavenly streams. But onward, the depth is greater, and the current more impetuous in its joy. The Christian feels that he may delight himself not only in what God is, but also in all that God has done in the past. Let God's people tell of His mighty acts and "sing unto the Lord, for He hath triumphed gloriously" (Exodus 15:1). They should never cease to sing, for as new mercies flow to them day by day, so should their gladness in the Lord's loving acts in providence and in grace show itself in continued thanksgiving. Be glad children of Zion and rejoice in the Lord your God.

"When my heart is overwhelmed; lead me to the rock that is higher than I" (Psalm 61:2).

Most of us know what it is to be overwhelmed in heart. Discoveries of inward corruption will do this if the Lord permits the deep waters of our sinful nature to become troubled and cast up mire and dirt. Disappointments and heartbreaks will do this when billow after billow rolls over us, and we are like a broken shell hurled about by the surf. Blessed be God, at such times we are not without an all-sufficient solace. Our God is the harbor of weather-beaten ships, the hospice of forlorn pilgrims. He is higher than we are. His mercy is higher than our sins, and His love is higher than our thoughts. It is pitiful to see men put their trust in something lower than themselves. Our confidence is fixed upon our high and glorious Lord. He is a Rock since He never changes, and He is a high Rock because the tempests which overwhelm us roll far below at His feet. If we get under the shelter of this lofty rock, we may defy the hurricane, for all is calm under the protection of the towering cliff. The confusion of the troubled mind is often so severe that we need a heavenly Guide to this divine shelter. O Lord, by Your Holy Spirit, teach us the way of faith and lead us into Your rest. The wind blows us out to sea, and the helm does not respond to our weak hand. You alone can steer us between the sunken rocks and bring us safely into the fair haven. How dependent we are upon You to direct us wisely and steer us into safety and peace.

"Accepted in the beloved" (Ephesians 1:6).

What a privilege! It includes our justification before God; but the term "acceptance," in the Greek, means more than that. It signifies that we are the objects of *divine delight.* How marvelous that we should be the objects of divine love! But it is only *"in the beloved."* Some Christians seem to be accepted in their own experience; at least, that is their apprehension. When their spirit is lively and their hopes bright, they think God accepts them, for they feel so high, so heavenly-minded, so drawn above the earth! But when their souls cleave to the dust, they are the victims of the fear that they are no longer accepted. They must see that all their high joys do not exalt them and all their low despondencies do not really depress them in their Father's sight. They stand accepted in One who never alters, in One who is always the beloved of God, always perfect, and always without spot or wrinkle. How much more they would honor the Savior if they realized this truth! Believer, rejoice! You look within and say, "There is nothing acceptable *here!"* But look at Christ and see there is everything acceptable *there.* If your sins trouble you, God will cast your sins behind His back and accept you in the Righteous One. If the devil tempts you, be of good cheer. You are accepted in Him who has broken Satan's head, and he cannot destroy you. Even glorified souls are not more accepted than you are. They are only accepted in heaven "in the beloved," and you are even now accepted in Christ after the same manner.

September 23
Evening

"Jesus said unto him, If thou canst believe" (Mark 9:23).

A certain man had a son who was afflicted with a dumb spirit. The father saw the futility of the disciple's efforts to heal his child, and he had little or no faith in Christ. Therefore, when he was asked to bring his son to Jesus, he said to Him, "If thou canst do any thing, have compassion on us, and help us" (Mark 9:22). There should have been an *if* in the father's question, but the poor, trembling man put the *if* in the wrong place. Jesus seemed to say, "There should be no *if* about My power or concerning My willingness. *If you can believe,* all things will be possible to you. The man's trust was strengthened, and he offered a humble prayer for an increase of faith. Jesus spoke the word, and the devil was cast out with an order never to return. We, like this man, often see that there is a condition to the promise, but we are always blundering by putting it in the wrong place. *If* Jesus can help me; *if* He can give me grace to overcome temptation; *if* He can give me pardon; *if* He can make me successful. The truth is, *if* you can believe, He both can and will. If you confidently trust in the Lord, all things that are possible to Christ will be possible to you. Faith stands in God's power and is robed in God's majesty. Girding itself with the glorious might of the Spirit, it becomes, in the omnipotence of God, mighty to do, to dare, and to suffer. All things, without limit, are possible to him who believes.

September 24
Morning

"For I was ashamed to require of the king a band of soldiers and horsemen to help us against the enemy in the way; because we had spoken unto the king, saying, The hand of our God is upon all them for good that seek him; but his power and his wrath is against all them that forsake him" (Ezra 8:22).

An armed regiment would have been desirable, but Ezra feared that the heathen king would think his professions of faith in God to be mere hypocrisy or imagine that the God of Israel was not able to preserve His own worshippers. He could not bring his mind to lean on an arm of flesh in a matter so evidently of the Lord. Therefore, the caravan set out with no visible protection, guarded by Him who is the sword and shield of His people. Few believers feel this holy jealousy for God. Even those who walk by faith occasionally mar the luster of their life by craving aid from man. It is a most blessed thing to stand upright on the Rock of Ages, upheld by the Lord alone. Would any believer seek state endowments for their Church if they remembered that the Lord is dishonored by their asking government aid? Cannot the Lord supply the needs of His own cause? Would we run hastily to friends and relations for assistance if we remembered that the Lord is magnified by our implicit reliance on His solitary arm? My soul, wait only on God. "But," says one, "are we not to make use of any other sources?" Assuredly, but our fault seldom lies in their neglect. Far more frequently it springs out of foolishly believing in them instead of believing in God.

September 24
Evening

"I sleep, but my heart waketh" (Song of Solomon 5:2).

Paradoxes abound in Christian experience. In our text this evening, the spouse was asleep, and yet she was awake. Only those who have experienced Christianity can understand the paradox of a believer's life. The two points this evening are a mournful sleepiness and a hopeful wakefulness. *I sleep.* Through sin that dwells in us, we may become lax in spending time with God, slothful in prayer, dull in spiritual joy, and altogether lazy and careless. This is a shameful state for one in whom the Holy Spirit dwells. It is also extremely dangerous. It is time for all to shake off the bands of sloth. Many believers lose their strength, as Samson lost his locks of hair, while sleeping on the lap of carnal security. With a perishing world around us, it is cruel to sleep. Since eternity is so near at hand, it is madness. Yet, none of us are as awake as we should be. A few thunderclaps would do us all good. Unless we soon rouse ourselves, we may have them in the form of war, pestilence, or personal losses. May we leave the couch of fleshly ease forever and go forth with flaming torches to meet the coming Bridegroom! *My heart waketh.* This is a happy sign. Life is not extinct, though sadly smothered. When our renewed heart struggles against our natural heaviness, we should be grateful to sovereign grace for keeping vitality within the body of this death. Jesus will hear, help, and visit our hearts. The voice of the vigilant heart is the voice of our Beloved, saying, "Open to me." Holy zeal will surely unbar the door.

September 25
Morning

"Just, and the justifier of him which believeth"
(Romans 3:26).

We have peace with God because we are justified by faith. Conscience no longer accuses. Judgment now decides *for* the sinner instead of *against* him. Memory looks back on past sins with deep sorrow for the sin, but yet with no dread of any penalty to come. Christ paid the debt of His people to the last jot and tittle and received the divine receipt. Unless God can be so unjust as to demand double payment for one debt, no soul for whom Jesus died as a substitute can ever be sent into hell. It seems to be one of the very principles of our enlightened nature to believe that God is just. This very same belief that God is just becomes the pillar of our confidence and peace! If God is just, I, a sinner must be punished. But Jesus stands in my stead and is punished for me. Now, if God is just, I, a sinner, standing in Christ, can never be punished. God must change His nature before one soul for whom Jesus was a substitute can ever by any possibility suffer the lash of the law. My hope lives, not because I am not a sinner, but because I am a sinner for whom Christ died. My trust is not that I am holy, but that He is my righteousness. My faith does not rest on what *I* am or will be or feel or know, but in what *Christ* is, in what He has done, and in what He is now doing for me.

September 25
Evening

"Who of God is made unto us wisdom" (1 Corinthians 1:30).

Man's intellect seeks after rest, and by nature he seeks it apart from the Lord Jesus Christ. Educated men, even when converted, often look upon the simplicities of the cross of Christ with too little reverence and love. The temptation of a man with refined thought and high education is to depart from the simple truth of Christ crucified and to invent a more *intellectual* doctrine. This led the early Christian churches into Gnosticism and confused them with all sorts of heresies. This is the root of many new philosophies which spring up and become fashionable while they ensnare entire groups of believers. Whoever you are and whatever your education may be, if you belong to the Lord, you will find no rest in philosophizing divinity. You may receive a dogma of one great thinker or a dream of another profound reasoner. But they will be like chaff compared to the wheat of the pure Word of God. In Christ Jesus there is treasured up all the fullness of wisdom and knowledge. (See Colossians 2:3.) All attempts on the part of Christians to be content with religious systems that embrace false doctrines while they deny the deity of Jesus Christ, must fail. True heirs of heaven must come back to the grandly simple reality that "Jesus Christ came into the world to save sinners" (1 Timothy 1:15). Jesus satisfies the most elevated intellect when He is believingly received, but apart from Him the mind of the philosopher discovers no rest. "The fear of the Lord is the beginning of knowledge" (Proverbs 1:7). "A good understanding have all they that do his commandments" (Psalm 111:10).

September 26
Morning

"The myrtle trees that were in the bottom"
(Zechariah 1:8).

The vision in this chapter describes the condition of Israel in Zechariah's day. Being interpreted in its aspect toward *us,* it describes the Church of God as we find it now in the world. The Church is compared to a myrtle grove flourishing in a valley. It is hidden, unobserved, secreted. It courts no honor and attracts no observation from the careless gazer. The Church, like her Head, has a glory, but it is concealed from carnal eyes. The time of her breaking forth in all her splendor is not here yet. The idea of *tranquil security* is also suggested to us. The myrtle grove in the valley is still and calm, while the storm sweeps over the mountain summits. How great is the inward tranquility of God's Church! Even when opposed and persecuted, she has a peace which the world cannot give, and which, therefore, it cannot take away. The peace of God which passes all understanding keeps the hearts and minds of God's people. The metaphor forcibly pictures the peaceful, perpetual growth of the saints. The myrtle does not shed its leaves; it is always green. The Church, in her worst time, still has a blessed strength about her. She has sometimes exhibited this strength most when her winter has been sharpest. She has prospered most when her adversities have been most severe. The myrtle is the emblem of peace and a significant token of triumph. The brows of conquerors were bound with myrtle and with laurel. Yet the Church is always victorious, and every Christian is more than a conqueror through Him that loved him. Living in peace, the saints fall asleep in the arms of victory.

September 26
Evening

"Howl, fir tree; for the cedar is fallen" (Zechariah 11:2).

When the crash of a falling oak is heard in the forest, it is a sign that the woodman is at work. Every tree in the area trembles because tomorrow the sharp edge of the axe may find it. We are all like trees marked for the axe. The fall of one should remind us that for everyone, whether great as the cedar or humble as the fir, the appointed hour is rapidly approaching. We should not become callous to death simply because it happens all the time. May we regard death as the most weighty of all events and be sobered by its approach. It is foolish to frolic while our eternal destiny hangs on a thread. The sword is out of its scabbard, and the edge is sharp—let us not play with it. He who does not prepare for death is worse than an ordinary fool—he is a madman. Be ready, servant of Christ, for your Master comes suddenly, when an ungodly world least expects Him. See to it that you are faithful in His work, for the grave will soon be dug for you. Be ready, parents. See that your children are brought up in the fear of God, for they will someday be orphans. Be ready, businessmen. Take care that your affairs are in order and that you serve God with all your heart. The days of your earthly service will soon be ended, and you will be called to give account for your deeds whether they were good or evil. May we all carefully prepare for the tribunal of the great King that we may be rewarded with the gracious commendation, "Well done, good and faithful servant" (Matthew 25:21).

"Happy art thou, O Israel; who is like unto thee, O people saved by the Lord?" (Deuteronomy 33:29).

The person who feels Christianity makes men miserable is himself an utter stranger to it. It would be strange, indeed, if it made us wretched, for see *to what a position it exalts us!* It makes us sons of God. Do you suppose that God will give all the happiness to His enemies and reserve all the mourning for His own family? Will His foes have joy and His children inherit sorrow and wretchedness? No, we will rejoice in the Lord always and glory in our inheritance, for we "have not received the Spirit of bondage again to fear; but we have received the Spirit of adoption, whereby we cry, Abba, Father" (Romans 8:15.) The rod of chastisement must rest on us in measure, but it works fruits of righteousness; and therefore, by the aid of the divine Comforter, we, the people saved of the Lord will joy in the God of our salvation. We are married to Christ. Would our great Bridegroom permit His spouse to linger in constant grief? For a while we may suffer as our Head once suffered, yet we are even now blessed with heavenly blessings in Him. We have the earnest of our inheritance in the comforts of the Spirit, which are neither few nor small. Inheritors of joy forever, we have foretastes of our portion. It is true, "Happy art thou, O Israel; who is like unto thee, O people saved by the Lord!"

September 27
Evening

"My Beloved put in his hand by the hole of the door, and my bowels were moved for him" (Song of Solomon 5:4).

Knocking was not enough, for my heart was too full of sleep, too cold and ungrateful to arise and open the door. But the touch of His grace has awakened my soul. Oh, the long-suffering of my Beloved! He waited for me when He found Himself shut out and me asleep because of my own laziness. Oh, the greatness of His patience, to knock and knock again and to call out, asking me to open to Him! How could I have refused Him! My heart bows in shame. But He displays His great kindness when He reaches and unbars the door Himself. Now I see that nothing but my Lord's own power can save me from my own wickedness. Religion fails, even the gospel has no effect upon me until His hand is stretched out. He can open my heart when nothing else will. My soul should be stirred for Him when I think of all that He has suffered for me and of my ungenerous response. I have allowed my affections to wander. I have set up rivals. I have grieved Him. Sweetest and dearest of all beloveds, I treated You as an unfaithful wife treats her husband. Oh, my cruel sins, my cruel self! What can I do? Tears are a poor show of my repentance. My whole heart boils with indignation at myself. Wretch that I am, to treat my Lord, the Joy of my life, as though He were a stranger. Jesus, You forgive freely, but this is not enough. Prevent my unfaithfulness in the future. Kiss away these tears, and then purge my heart and bind it to You that I may never wander again.

September 28
Morning

"The Lord looketh from heaven; he beholdeth all the sons of men" (Psalm 33:13).

Perhaps no figure of speech represents God in a more gracious light than when He is spoken of as stooping from His throne and coming down from heaven to attend to the wants and to behold the problems of mankind. We love Him, who, when Sodom and Gomorrah were full of iniquity, would not destroy those cities until He had made a personal visitation of them. We cannot help pouring out our heart in affection for our Lord, who inclines His ear from the highest glory and puts it to the lip of the dying sinner. His heart longs after reconciliation. How can we but love Him, when we know that He numbers the very hairs of our heads, marks our path, and orders our ways? This great truth is brought near to our heart when we recollect how attentive He is, not merely to the temporal interests of His creatures but to their spiritual concerns. Though a long distance separates the finite creatures and the infinite Creator, there are links uniting both. When you weep, God is very aware of it. "Like as a father pitieth his children, so the Lord pitieth them that fear him" (Psalm 103:13). Your sigh is able to move the heart of Jehovah. Your whisper can incline His ear to you. Your prayer can stay His hand, and your faith can move His arm. Do not think that God sits on high taking no account of you. For the eyes of the Lord run to and fro throughout the whole earth, to show Himself strong on behalf of them whose heart is perfect toward Him (2 Chronicles 16:9).

September 28
Evening

"Go again seven times" (1 Kings 15:43).

Success is certain when the Lord has promised it. Although you may have pleaded month after month without evidence of an answer, the Lord always hears when His people are serious about a matter which concerns His glory. The prophet on the top of Mount Carmel continued to wrestle with God and never for a moment gave way to a fear that he did not belong in Jehovah's courts. Six times the servant returned, but on each occasion the prophet only said, "Go again." Faith sends expectant Hope to look from Carmel's brow, and if nothing is beheld, she sends again and again. Rather than being crushed by repeated disappointment, Faith is determined to plead more fervently with God. She is humbled, but not ashamed. Her groans are deeper, and her sighings become more vehement, but she never relaxes her hold. A speedy answer would be more agreeable to the flesh, but believing souls have learned to be submissive. They find it good to wait *for* as well as *upon* the Lord. Delayed answers often set the heart searching itself and so lead to repentance and spiritual reformation. Thus, deadly blows are struck at our corruption, and the inner chambers of our hearts are cleansed. The great danger is that men may give up and miss the blessing. Do not fall into that sin, but continue in watchful prayer. When the little cloud was seen, it was the sure forerunner of torrents of rain. It will be the same with you. The token for good will surely be given, and you will rise as a prevailing prince to enjoy the answer you have sought. Elijah was a man like us. His power with God did not lie in his own merits. If his believing prayer accomplished so much, why not yours? Plead with unwavering faith, and it will be given to you according to your desire.

September 29
Morning

"Behold, if the leprosy have covered all his flesh, he shall pronounce him clean that hath the plague" (Leviticus 13:13).

This regulation appears strange. Yet, there was wisdom in it, for the throwing out of the disease proved that the constitution was sound. We, too, are lepers and may read the law of lepers as applicable to ourselves. When a man sees himself to be altogether lost and ruined and pleads guilty before the Lord, then he is made clean through the blood of Jesus and the grace of God. When sin is seen and felt, it has received its death-blow, and the Lord looks with eyes of mercy on the soul afflicted with it. Nothing is more deadly than self-righteousness or more hopeful than contrition. We must confess that we are nothing else but sin, for no confession short of this will be the whole truth. If the Holy Spirit is at work within us, convincing us of sin, there will be no difficulty about making such an acknowledgment. It will spring spontaneously from our lips. What comfort this scripture provides. Sin that is mourned and confessed, however black and foul, will never shut a man out from the Lord Jesus. Whosoever comes to Him, He will in no wise cast out. Though dishonest as the thief, though unchaste as the woman who was a sinner, though fierce as Saul of Tarsus, though rebellious as the prodigal, the great heart of love will look on the man who feels he has no righteousness in himself and will pronounce him clean when he trusts in Jesus crucified. Come to Him, then, poor, heavy-laden sinner.

"I found him whom my soul loveth: I held him, and would not let him go" (Song of Solomon 3:4).

Does Christ receive us when we come to Him, despite all our past sinfulness? Does He chide us for having tried all other refuges before we came to Him? And is there anyone on earth like Him? Is He the best and fairest of all? Oh, then let us praise Him! Daughters of Jerusalem, extol Him with timbrel and harp! Cast down your idols, and lift up the name of the Lord Jesus. Let the worldly standards of pride be trampled underfoot, but let the cross of Jesus, which the world frowns and scoffs at, be lifted on high. Let our King be sent on high forever. Let my soul sit at His footstool and kiss His feet and wash them with my tears. Oh, how precious is Christ! How can I search elsewhere for joy or comfort when He is so full, so rich, so satisfying? Believer, make a covenant with your heart that you will never depart from Him. Implore Him to keep you as a ring upon His finger and as a bracelet upon His arm. Ask Him to bind you about Him as the bride adorns herself with jewels. I want to live in Christ's heart. In the clefts of that rock, my soul would eternally abide. "Yea, the sparrow hath found an house, and the swallow a nest for herself, where she may lay her young, even thine altars, O Lord of hosts, my King and my God" (Psalm 84:3). Lord, I also long to make my home in You. May the soul of Your turtledove never go forth again, but may I nestle close to You, O Jesus, my true and only rest.

September 30
Morning

"Sing forth the honor of his name, make his praise glorious" (Psalm 66:2).

Whether we will praise God or not is not an option for us. Praise is God's due; and every Christian, as the recipient of His grace, is bound to praise God from day to day. It is true we have no commandment prescribing certain hours of song and thanksgiving, but the law written on the heart teaches us that it is right to praise God. The unwritten mandate comes to us with as much force as if it had been recorded on tables of stone or handed to us from the top of thundering Sinai. Yes, it is the Christian's *duty* to praise God. It is not only a pleasurable exercise, but it is the absolute obligation of his life. Do not think that you are guiltless in this respect or imagine that you can discharge your duty to your God without songs of praise. You are bound by the bonds of His love to bless His name so long as you live, and His praise should continually be in your mouth. "This people have I formed for myself; they shall show forth my praise" (Isaiah 43:21). If you do not praise God, you are not bringing forth the fruit which He, as the divine Husbandman, has a right to expect at your hands. Arise and sing His praise. With every morning's dawn, lift up your notes of thanksgiving and let every setting sun be followed with your songs. Cover the earth with your praises. Surround it with an atmosphere of melody, and God Himself will hearken from heaven and accept your music.

September 30
Evening

"A living dog is better than a dead lion" (Ecclesiastes 9:4).

Life is a precious thing, and in its humblest form it is superior to death. This truth is also certain in spiritual things. It is better to be the least in the Kingdom of heaven than the greatest outside of it. The lowest degree of grace is superior to the noblest development of the unredeemed nature. The Holy Spirit implants divine life in a man's soul and makes a precious deposit which none of the refinements of education can equal. The thief on the cross excels Caesar on his throne. Lazarus among the dogs is better than Cicero among the senators. The most unlettered Christian is superior to Plato in the sight of God. Life is the badge of nobility in the realm of spiritual things. Men without it are only coarser or finer specimens of the same lifeless material. They all need to be made alive, for they are dead in trespasses and sins. A living, loving, gospel sermon, however unlearned in matter and awkward in style, is better than the finest discourse that lacks the Holy Spirit's anointing and power. The poorest spiritual preacher is infinitely preferred to the exquisite orator who has no wisdom except words and no energy but that of the sound of his voice. The same holds true of our prayers and other religious exercises. If we are quickened in them by the Holy Spirit, they are acceptable to God through Jesus Christ. Our grand religious formalities in which our hearts are absent, like dead lions, are mere carrion in the sight of the living God. Oh, for living groans and living sighs rather than lifeless songs and dead calms. The snarling of the dog of hell will at least keep us awake, but what greater curse can a man have than dead faith? Make us alive in You, O Lord!

October 1
Morning

"Pleasant fruits, new and old, which I have laid up for thee, O my beloved" (Song of Solomon 7:13).

The spouse desires to give all that she produces to Jesus. Our heart has all manner of pleasant fruits, both new and old, and they are laid up for our Beloved. At this rich autumn season, let us survey our harvest. We have *new* fruits. We desire to feel new life, new joy, and new gratitude. We wish to make new resolves and carry them out by new labors. But we have some *old* fruits, too. There is our first love—a choice fruit! There is our first faith. It is the simple faith by which, having nothing, we became possessors of all things. There is our joy when first we knew the Lord; let us revive it. We have our old remembrances of the promises. How faithful God has been! Old sins we must regret. But we have repented and wept our way to the cross, and we have learned of the merit of His blood. We have fruits this morning, both new and old. But here is the point—*they are all laid up for Jesus.* Let our many fruits be laid up only for our Beloved. Let us display them when He is with us and not hold them up before the gaze of men. Jesus, none will enter to rob You of one good fruit from the soil which You have watered. All we have is Yours!

October 1
Evening

"The Lord will give grace and glory" (Psalm 84:11).

Jehovah is bountiful in His nature. It is His delight to give. His gifts are precious beyond measure and are as freely given as the light of the sun. He gives grace to His elect because He wills it; to His redeemed because of His covenant; to the called because of His promise; to believers because they seek it; to sinners because they need it. He gives grace abundantly, seasonably, constantly, readily, and sovereignly. He freely renders all forms of grace to His people: comforting, preserving, sanctifying, directing, instructing, and assisting grace. He generously pours it all into their souls without ceasing. Sickness may befall us, but the Lord will give grace. We may experience poverty, but grace will surely be provided. Death must come, but grace will light a candle at the darkest hour. How blessed it is, as seasons change and the leaves begin to fall, to enjoy such an unfading promise as this: "The Lord will give grace." The little word *and* in this verse is a diamond rivet binding the present with the future—grace and glory always go together. The Lord will never deny glory to a soul whom He has freely given His grace. Indeed, glory is nothing more than grace in its Sunday dress, grace in full bloom, grace like autumn fruit, mellow and perfected. How soon we may have glory, none can tell! But whether our wait is long or short, we know that we will be glorified one day. Glory—the glory of heaven, the glory of eternity, the glory of Jesus, the glory of the Father—the Lord will surely give to His chosen.

October 2
Morning

"The hope which is laid up for you in heaven"
(Colossians 1:5).

Our hope in Christ for the future is the mainstay of our joy here. This hope will animate our hearts to think often of heaven for all that we can desire is promised there. Here we are weary and toilworn, but heaven is the land of *rest*. Fatigue will be forever banished. Now, we are always in the field of battle. We are so tempted within and so molested by foes without that we have little time to rest. We have suffered bereavement after bereavement, but we are going to the land of the *immortal,* where graves are unknown things. Here sin is a constant grief to us, but there we will be perfectly holy. Nothing that defiles will enter into that Kingdom. What a joy that you are not to dwell eternally in this wilderness but will soon inherit Canaan. Nevertheless, let it never be said of us that we are dreaming about the *future* and forgetting the *present.* Let the future sanctify the present to highest uses. Through the Spirit of God, the hope of heaven is the most potent force for the product of virtue. It is a fountain of joyous effort. It is the cornerstone of cheerful holiness. The man who has this hope in him goes about his work with vigor, for the joy of the Lord is his strength! He fights against temptation with ardor, for the hope of the next world repels the fiery darts of the adversary. He can labor without present reward, for he looks for a reward in the world to come.

October 2
Evening

"A man greatly beloved" (Daniel 10:11).

Child of God, do you hesitate to claim this title? Has your unbelief made you forget that *you* are greatly beloved, too? You must have been greatly beloved to have been bought with the precious blood of Christ, a Lamb without blemish and without spot. God sent His only begotten Son to die for you. You lived in sin and rioted in it. You must have been greatly beloved for God to have borne so patiently with you. You were called by grace, led to a Savior, and made a child of God and an heir of heaven. All this proves a very great and super-abundant love. Since that time, whether your path has been rough with troubles or smooth with blessings, it has been full of proof that you are greatly beloved. If the Lord has chastened you, it was not in anger. The more unworthy you feel, the more evidence you have that nothing but unspeakable love could have led the Lord Jesus to save your soul. The more humble you feel, the clearer is the display of the abounding love of God who chose you and called you and made you an heir of grace. Since there is this love between God and us, let us live in the influence and sweetness of it. Let us not approach our Lord as though we were strangers or as though He were unwilling to hear us. "He that spared not his own Son, but delivered him up for us all, how shall he not with him also freely give us all things?" (Romans 8:32). Come boldly, O believer, despite the whispering of Satan and the doubt of your own heart, you are greatly beloved. Meditate on the greatness and faithfulness of divine love this evening, and go to sleep in peace.

October 3
Morning

"Are they not all ministering spirits, sent forth to minister for them who shall be heirs of salvation?" (Hebrews 1:14).

Angels are the unseen attendants of the saints of God. They bear us up in their hands lest we dash our foot against a stone. Loyalty to their Lord leads them to take a deep interest in the children of His love. They rejoice over the return of the prodigal to his father's house below, and they welcome the advent of the believer to the King's palace above. In olden times, the sons of God were favored with their visible appearance, and at this day, although unseen by us, heaven is still opened. The angels of God ascend and descend from the Son of man that they may visit the heirs of salvation. If our eyes could be opened, we would see horses and chariots of fire about the servants of the Lord. We have come to an innumerable company of angels, who are all watchers and protectors of the royal seed. To what dignity are the chosen elevated when the brilliant courtiers of heaven become their willing servants! We are defended since all twenty thousand chariots of God are armed for our deliverance! To whom do we owe all this? Let the Lord Jesus Christ be forever endeared to us, for through Him we are made to sit in heavenly places far above principalities and powers. He it is whose camp is round about them that fear Him. He is the true Michael whose foot is on the dragon. All hail, Jesus!

October 3
Evening

"He himself hath suffered being tempted"
(Hebrews 2:18).

This simple thought is so encouraging that it tastes like honey to the weary heart: Jesus was tempted. You have heard that truth many times—have you grasped it? You may be going through a dark valley, but Jesus went through it before. It is a difficult battle which you are waging, but Jesus stood against the same enemy. Let us be of good cheer. Christ has borne the load before us. Jesus was tempted, but He never sinned. Then, it is not necessary for me to sin. Jesus was a man, and He endured temptation and did not sin. Then in His power, His members may also cease from sin. Some beginners in the Christian life think that they cannot be tempted without sinning, but they are mistaken. There is no sin in *being tempted,* but there *is* sin in *yielding to temptation.* Here is comfort for the tempted ones. The Lord Jesus, though tempted, gloriously triumphed. As He overcame, so surely shall His followers, for Jesus is the representative of His people. The Head has triumphed, and the members share in the victory. Fears are needless, for Christ is with us, armed for our defense. Our place of safety is the bosom of the Savior. Perhaps our temptations will drive us nearer to Him. Blessed be any wind that blows us into the port of our Savior's love! Happy are the wounds which make us seek the beloved Physician. You who are tempted, come to your tempted Savior. He can be touched with a feeling of your infirmities and will comfort every tried and tempted one.

October 4
Morning

"At evening time it shall be light" (Zechariah 14:7).

We often look forward with forebodings to the time of old age. To many saints, old age is the choicest season in their lives. A balmier air fans the mariner's cheek as he nears the shore of immortality. Fewer waves ruffle his sea, and quiet reigns deep, still, and solemn. The pilgrims have reached the Beulah land, that happy country whose days are as the days of heaven on earth. Angels visit it, celestial gales blow over it, flowers of paradise grow in it, and the air is filled with seraphic music. Some dwell here for years, and others come to it but a few hours before their departure. But it is an Eden on earth. The setting sun seems larger than when high in the sky, and a splendor of glory tinges all the clouds which surround his going down. Ripe fruits of choice experience are gathered as the rare repast of life's evening, and the soul prepares itself for rest. The Lord's people will also enjoy light in the hour of death. Unbelief laments, the shadows fall, the night is coming, and existence is ending. No, cries faith, the night is far spent, and the true day is at hand. Light is come—the light of immortality, the light of a Father's countenance. Gather your feet into the bed, and see the waiting bands of spirits! Angels carry you away. Farewell, beloved one. Now it is light. The pearly gates are open, the golden streets shine in the jasper light. You now behold the unseen. Adieu, brother; you have light at eventide, such as we have not yet known.

October 4
Evening

"If any man sin, we have an advocate with the Father, Jesus Christ the righteous" (1 John 2:1).

Though we sin, we still have our advocate. John does not say, "If any man sin, he has forfeited his advocate." We *have* an advocate, though we are sinners. All the sin that a believer can ever commit cannot destroy his relationship to the Lord Jesus Christ as his advocate. The name here given to the Lord is expressive—*Jesus*. He is the advocate that we need, for Jesus is the name of One whose business and delight it is to save. "Thou shalt call his name JESUS: for he shall save his people from their sins" (Matthew 1:21). Next, it is Jesus *Christ*— Christos, the anointed. This shows His *authority* to plead for us. The Christ has a right to plead, for He is the Father's own appointed advocate and elected priest. God appointed One that is mighty, and we may safely lay our trouble where God has laid His help. He is Christ, and therefore authorized; He is Christ, and therefore *qualified,* for the anointing has fully fitted Him for His work. He can plead so as to move the heart of God and prevail. What words of tenderness, what sentences of persuasion, will the Anointed One use when He stands up to plead for me! One more part of His title remains—Jesus Christ *the righteous.* If the Righteous One is my advocate, then my cause is good, or He would not have embraced it. It is His plea, for He meets the charge of unrighteousness against me by the plea that *He* is righteous. He declares Himself to be my substitute and credits His obedience to my account. Believers have a Friend who is well fitted to be their Advocate. Oh believers, leave yourself entirely in His hands.

October 5
Morning

"He arose, and did eat and drink, and went in the strength of that meat forty days and forty nights" (1 Kings 19:8).

All the strength supplied to us by our gracious God is meant for service, not for wantonness. When the prophet Elijah found the cake baked on the coals and the jug of water placed at his head as he lay under the juniper tree, he was commissioned to go forty days and forty nights in the strength of it. The Master invited the disciples to come and dine with Him, and after the feast was concluded, He said to Peter, "Feed my sheep." He further added, "Follow me." This is true with us also. We eat the bread of heaven that we may expend our strength in the Master's service. Some Christians are for living *on* Christ, but are not so anxious to live *for* Christ. Earth should be a preparation for heaven, and heaven is the place where saints feast and work most. They sit down at the table of our Lord and serve Him day and night in His temple. They eat of heavenly food and render perfect service. Believer, labor for Christ in the strength you gain from Him daily. We are not to retain the precious grains of truth. We must sow it and water it. Why does the Lord send down the rain on the thirsty earth and give the genial sunshine? It is to help the fruits of the earth yield food for man. Even so the Lord feeds and refreshes our souls that we may afterward use our renewed strength in the promotion of His glory.

October 5
Evening

"He that believeth and is baptized shall be saved" (Mark 16:16).

Mr. MacDonald asked the inhabitants of the island of St. Kilda how a man must be saved. An old man replied, "We shall be saved if we repent, forsake our sins, and turn to God." "Yes," said a middle-aged female, "and with a true heart, too." "Aye," added a third, "and with prayer;" and said a fourth, "it must be the prayer of the heart." "And we must be diligent, too," said a fifth, "in keeping the commandments." Thus, each contributed his thoughts. Feeling that a very decent creed had been made up, they all looked and listened for the preacher's approval. But they had aroused his deepest pity. The carnal mind always maps out a way in which self can work and become great. But the Lord's way is quite the opposite. Believing and being baptized are no matters of merit to be gloried in—they are so simple that boasting is excluded, and free grace bears the honor. It may be that you are unsaved—what is the reason? Do you think that the way of salvation explained in the text is dubious? How can that be when God has pledged His own Word for its certainty? Do you think it is too easy? Why then do you not listen to it? To believe is simply to trust, to depend, and to rely upon Christ Jesus. To be baptized is to submit to the ordinance which our Lord fulfilled at Jordan. The converted ones submitted to baptism at Pentecost, and the jailer yielded obedience the very night of this conversion. (See Acts 2:41; Acts 16:30-33.) The outward sign does not save us, but it is a symbol of our death, burial, and resurrection with Jesus. Do you believe in Jesus? Then, dear friend, dismiss your fears; you will be saved. Are you still an unbeliever? Then remember there is only one door, and if you will not enter by it, you will perish in your sins.

October 6
Morning

"Whosoever drinketh of the water that I shall give him shall never thirst" (John 4:14).

He who is a believer in Jesus finds enough in his Lord to satisfy him now and keep him content forevermore. The believer is not the man whose days are weary for comfort and whose nights are long from absence of heart-cheering thought. He finds in Christ such a spring of joy, such a foundation of consolation, that he is content and happy. Put him in a dungeon, and he will find good company. Place him in a barren wilderness, and he will eat the bread of heaven. Drive him away from friendship, and he will meet the friend that sticketh closer than a brother. Sap the foundation of his earthly hopes, and his heart will still be fixed, trusting in the Lord. The heart is as insatiable as the grave until Jesus enters it, and then it is a cup full to overflowing. There is such a fullness in Christ. The true saint is completely satisfied with the all-sufficiency of Jesus. Is this the feeling in your heart? Do you feel that all your desires are satisfied in Jesus, and that you have no want now but to know more of Him and to have closer fellowship with Him? Then come continually to the fountain, and take of the water of life freely. Jesus will never think you take too much, but will always welcome you, saying, "Drink, yea, drink abundantly, O beloved."

October 6
Evening

"He had married an Ethiopian woman" (Numbers 12:1).

Moses made a strange choice for his wife. But more unusual is the choice of Him who is even greater than Moses! Our Lord, who is fair as the lily, has married one who confesses herself to be "black, because the sun hath looked upon me" (Song of Solomon 1:6). Each believer must, when filled with a sense of Jesus' love, be overwhelmed with astonishment that such love is lavished on an object utterly unworthy of it. Knowing as we do our secret guilt and unfaithfulness, we bow in grateful admiration of the freeness and sovereignty of grace. Jesus must have found the reason for His love in His own heart. He could not have found it in us, for it is not there. Even since our conversion, we have been black due to our old nature, though grace has made us beautiful. Rutherford said of himself, "His relation to me is, that I am sick, and He is the Physician of whom I stand in need. Alas! how often play I fast and loose with Christ! He bindeth, I loose; He buildeth, I cast down; I quarrel with Christ, and He agreeth with me twenty times a day!" Tender and faithful Husband of our souls, continue Your gracious work of conforming us to Your image. We know that one day You will present us to Yourself without spot or wrinkle or any such thing. Moses met with opposition because of his marriage. Both he and his spouse were the subjects of suspicion. Can we wonder if this vain world opposes Jesus and His spouse, especially when sinners are converted? This remains the Pharisee's reason for objection, "This man receiveth sinners" (Luke 15:2).

October 7
Morning

"Wherefore hast thou afflicted thy servant?"
(Numbers 11:11).

If our faith is worth anything, it will stand the
test when trials come. The true jewel fears no test.
It is a weak faith which can only trust God when
friends are true, the body full of health, and the
business profitable. True faith holds by the Lord's
faithfulness when friends are gone, when the body
is sick, when spirits are depressed, and the light of
our Father's countenance is hidden. A faith which
can say in the direst trouble, "Though he slay me,
yet will I trust in him" (Job 13:15) is heaven-born
faith. The Lord is greatly glorified in the graces of
His people. When "tribulation worketh patience;
and patience, experience; and experience, hope"
(Romans 5:3-4), the Lord is honored by these
growing virtues. We would never know the music
of the harp if the strings were left untouched or
enjoy the juice of the grape if it were not trodden
in the wine-press. We would never discover the
sweet perfume of cinnamon if it were not pressed
and beaten or feel the warmth of fire if the coals
were not utterly consumed. The wisdom and
power of the great Workman are discovered by the
trials through which His vessels of mercy are permitted to pass. There must be shades in the picture to bring out the beauty of the lights. Could
we be so supremely blessed in heaven if we had
not known the curse of sin and the sorrow of
earth? Peace will be sweeter after conflict and rest
more welcome after toil. The recollection of past
sufferings will enhance the bliss of the glorified.

October 7
Evening

"Now on whom dost thou trust" (Isaiah 36:5).

This is an important question. Listen to the Christian's answer, and see if it is yours. I trust *the Father,* believing that He has chosen me from before the foundations of the world. I trust Him to provide for me, to teach me, to guide me, to correct me, and to bring me home to Him. I trust *the Son.* True God of true God is He—the man Christ Jesus. I trust in Him to take away all my sins by His own sacrifice and to adorn me with His perfect righteousness. I trust Him to be my Intercessor and to present my prayers and desires before His Father's throne. I trust Him to be my Advocate at the last great day, to plead my cause, and to justify me. I trust Him for what He is, for what He has done, and for what He has promised to do. I trust *the Holy Spirit.* He has saved me from my sins. I trust Him to drive them all out of my life. I trust Him to curb my temper, to subdue my will, to enlighten my understanding, to check my passions, to comfort my despondency, to help my weakness, and to illuminate my darkness. I trust Him to dwell in me as my life, to reign in me as my King, to sanctify me wholly, spirit, soul, and body, and then to take me up to dwell with the saints in light forever. I trust Him whose power will never be exhausted, whose love will never diminish, whose kindness will never change, whose faithfulness will never fail, whose wisdom will never be confused, and whose perfect goodness can never know a decrease! By trusting, I may enjoy sweet peace now, and glory hereafter.

October 8
Morning

"Launch out into the deep, and let down your nets for a draught" (Luke 5:4).

We learn from this narrative the necessity of human involvement. The draught of fishes was miraculous, yet neither the fisherman nor his boat nor his fishing tackle were ignored. All were used to take the fishes. In the saving of souls, God uses many different instruments. He has selected this plan as being that by which He is most magnified in the earth. "Master, we have toiled all the night and have taken nothing" (Luke 5:5). What was the reason for this? They understood the work. Had they gone about the toil unskillfully? No. Had they lacked industry? No. They had *toiled*. Had they lacked perseverance? No. They had toiled *all the night*. Was there a deficiency of fish in the sea? Certainly not, for as soon as the Master came, they swam to the net in schools. What, then, is the reason? It is because there is no power in themselves apart from the presence of Jesus! Without Christ we can do nothing, but with Him we can do all things. *Christ's presence confers success.* Jesus sat in Peter's boat, and His will drew the fish to the net. When Jesus is lifted up in His Church, His presence is the Church's power—the shout of a King is in the midst of her. "I, if I be lifted up, will draw all men unto me" (John 12:32). Let us go out this morning on our work of soul-fishing, looking up in faith and around us in solemn anxiety. Let us toil until night comes, and we will not labor in vain. He who bids us let down the net will also fill it with fishes.

October 8
Evening

"Praying in the Holy Ghost" (Jude 20).

Observe the grand characteristic of true prayer—*in the Holy Ghost.* Only the prayer which comes from God can go to God. The desire He writes upon our heart will move His heart and bring down a blessing, but the desires of the flesh have no power with Him. Praying in the Holy Spirit means praying *fervently.* Cold prayers ask the Lord not to hear them. Those who do not plead with fervency, do not plead at all. Think of lukewarm fire like lukewarm prayer—it is essential that it be red-hot. It is praying *perseveringly.* The true supplicant gathers force as he proceeds and grows more fervent when God delays to answer. The longer the gate is closed, the more vehemently he knocks. Beautiful in God's sight is tearful, agonizing, unconquerable prayer. It means praying *humbly,* for the Holy Spirit never puffs us up with pride. It is His job to convict of sin and to bow us down in contrition and brokenness of spirit. It is *loving* prayer. Prayer should be perfumed and saturated with love—love for our fellow saints and love for Christ. Moreover, it must be a prayer full of *faith.* A man prevails only as he believes. The Holy Spirit is the author of faith and strengthens it so that we pray believing God's promise. May this blessed combination of excellent graces be fragrant within us because the Holy Spirit is in our hearts!

October 9
Morning

"Able to keep you from falling" (Jude 24).

In one sense the path to heaven is very safe. In other respects there is no road so dangerous. It is surrounded with difficulties. One false step—and how easy it is to take that, if grace is absent—and down we go. How many times have we exclaimed as the psalmist, "My feet were almost gone; my steps had well nigh slipped" (Psalm 73:2). If we were strong, sure-footed mountaineers, this would not matter so much; but in ourselves, how weak we are! A straw may throw us, and a pebble can wound us. We are mere children tremblingly taking our first steps in the walk of faith. Our heavenly Father holds us by the arms, or we would soon be down. Oh, if we are kept from falling, how must we bless the patient power which watches over us day by day! Think how prone we are to sin, how apt to choose danger, and how strong our tendency to cast ourselves down. These reflections will make us sing more sweetly than we have ever done, "Glory be to him who is able to keep you from falling" (Jude 24). We have many foes who try to push us down. The road is rough, and we are weak. In addition to this, enemies lurk in ambush who rush out when we least expect them. They labor to trip us up or hurl us down the nearest cliff. Only an Almighty arm can preserve us from these unseen foes who are seeking to destroy us. Such an arm is engaged for our defense. He is faithful and able to keep us from falling. With a deep sense of our utter weakness, we cherish a firm belief in our perfect safety.

October 9
Evening

"But he answered her not a word" (Matthew 15:23).

Genuine seekers who have not yet obtained the blessing may take comfort from this evening's Scripture. The Savior did not immediately bestow the blessing, even though the woman had great faith in Him. He intended to give it, but He waited awhile. "He answered her not a word." There were no better prayers than hers in the world. She was intensely earnest. She had such a high degree of faith that even Jesus said, "O woman, great is thy faith" (Matthew 15:28). Therefore, although it is true that faith brings answers to prayer, it does not always bring them instantly. There may be reasons for the trial of faith, rather than the reward of faith. Genuine faith may be in the soul like a hidden seed. But as yet it may not have budded and blossomed into joy and peace. A painful silence from the Savior is the grievous trial of many seeking souls. But heavier still is the affliction of a harsh, cutting reply such as this: "It is not meet to take the children's bread and to cast it to dogs" (Matthew 15:26). Many, in waiting upon the Lord, find immediate answers, but this is not the case with all. Some are turned from darkness to light in a moment, but others are plants of slower growth. A deeper sense of sin may be given to you instead of a sense of pardon, and in such a case you will need patience to bear the heavy blow. Though you may be beaten and bruised, trust God. Though He gives you an angry word, believe in the love of His heart. Do not give up seeking or trusting the Master because you have not yet obtained the blessed joy which you long for. Cast yourself on Him, and perseveringly depend even when you cannot joyfully hope.

October 10
Morning

"Faultless before the presence of his glory" (Jude 24).

In your mind examine that wondrous word *"faultless."* We are far from it now; but as our Lord never stops short of perfection in His work of love, we will reach it one day. The Savior who will keep His people to the end will also present them at last to Himself as a glorious Church, not having spot, wrinkle, or any such thing. They will be holy and without blemish. All the jewels in the Savior's crown are without a single flaw. But how will Jesus make us faultless? He will wash us from our sins in His own blood until we are white and fair as God's purest angel. We will be clothed in His righteousness. We will be innocent and uncondemned even in His eyes. His law will not only have no charge against us, but it will be magnified in us. Moreover, the work of the Holy Spirit within us will be altogether complete. He will make us so perfectly holy that we will have no lingering tendency to sin. We will dwell in His presence forever. The beauty of the saints will be as great as that of the place prepared for them. Oh, the joy of that hour when the everlasting doors will be lifted up, and we, being made meet for the inheritance, will dwell with the saints in light. Sin gone, Satan shut out, temptation past forever, and ourselves *"faultless"* before God—this will be heaven indeed!

October 10
Evening

"And I will deliver thee out of the hand of the wicked and I will redeem thee out of the hand of the terrible" (Jeremiah 15:21).

The Lord Jehovah Himself intervenes to deliver and redeem His people. He pledges Himself to rescue them. His own arm will do it, and He will receive the glory. Nothing is mentioned about our own effort which may be needed to assist the Lord. Neither our strength nor our weakness is taken into the account. Why then do we calculate our forces and consult with flesh and blood to our grievous downfall? Jehovah has enough power without borrowing from our puny strength. Be at peace, unbelieving thoughts, be still and know that the Lord reigns. The Lord says nothing of friends and helpers. He does the work alone and feels no need for human assistance. All our dependence upon companions and relatives is useless. They are broken reeds if we lean upon them—often unwilling to help when able, and unable when they are willing. Since the promise comes from God, it would be wise to wait only upon Him. When we do so, we are never disappointed. Who are the wicked that we should fear them? The Lord will utterly consume them. They are to be pitied rather than feared. As for the terrible ones, they are only terrors to those who have no God to run to. When the Lord is on our side, whom shall we fear? If we run into sin to please the wicked, we have cause to be alarmed; but if we hold fast our integrity, the rage of tyrants will be overruled for our good. In all times of fiery trial, let us patiently endure and trust in the promises of our mighty God.

October 11
Morning

"Let us lift up our heart with our hands unto God in the heavens" (Lamentations 3:41).

The act of prayer teaches us our unworthiness, which is a very beneficial lesson for such proud beings as we are. If God gave us favors without constraining us to pray for them, we would never know how poor we are. A true prayer is an inventory of wants, a catalogue of necessities, and a revelation of hidden poverty. The most healthy state of a Christian is to be constantly depending on the Lord for supplies, rich in Jesus, and mighty through God to do great exploits. Hence, the use of prayer because it lays the creature where he should be—in the very dust. Prayer is in itself, apart from the answer which it brings, a great benefit to the Christian. As the runner gains strength for the race by daily exercise, so for the great race of life we acquire energy by the hallowed labor of prayer. Prayer plumes the wings of God's young eaglets that they may learn to mount above the clouds. Prayer girds the loins of God's warriors and sends them forth to combat with their muscles firm. An earnest pleader comes out of his prayer closet rejoicing like a strong man to run his race. Prayer is that uplifted hand of Moses which routs the Amalekites more than the sword of Joshua. Prayer girds human weakness with divine strength, turns human folly into heavenly wisdom, and gives to troubled mortals the peace of God. We cannot think of anything prayer cannot do! We thank You, God, for the mercy-seat, a choice proof of Your marvelous lovingkindness. Help us to use it aright throughout this day!

October 11
Evening

"Whom he did predestinate, them he also called" (Romans 8:30).

The apostle Paul wrote to Timothy, "Who hath saved us, and called us with an *holy* calling" (2 Timothy 1:9). Here is a standard by which we may test our calling. It is a holy calling, not according to our works, but according to His own purpose and grace. This calling forbids all trust in our own works and leads us to Christ alone for salvation. Afterward, it purges us from dead works to serve the living and true God. As He who called you is holy, so you must also be holy. If you are truly Christ's you can say, "Nothing pains me as much as sin; I desire to be rid of it. Lord, help me to be holy." Is this the desire of your heart? Is this the substance of your life toward God and His divine will? In Philippians 3:13-14, we are told of "the *high* calling of God in Christ Jesus." Has your calling ennobled your heart and set it upon heavenly things? Has it elevated your hopes, your tastes, and your desires? Has it raised the purpose of your life so that you spend it with God and for God? We find another test in Hebrews 3:1—"partakers of the *heavenly* calling." Heavenly calling means a call *from* heaven. If man alone called you, then you are uncalled. Is your calling of God? Is it a call *to* heaven as well as from heaven? Unless you are a stranger here, and heaven is your home, you have not been called with a heavenly calling. Those who have been called declare that they look for a city which has foundations, whose builder and maker is God. (See Hebrews 11:10.) They themselves are strangers and pilgrims upon the earth. Is your calling like theirs—holy, high, and heavenly? Then, beloved, you have been called by God.

October 12
Morning

"I will meditate in thy precepts" (Psalm 119:15).

There are times when solitude is better than society and silence is wiser than speech. We would be better Christians if we spent more time waiting on God and gathering, through meditation on His Word, spiritual strength for labor in His service. We ought to meditate on the things of God, because we thus get the real nutrition out of them. Truth is something like the cluster of the vine. If we would have wine from it, we must bruise it. We must press and squeeze it many times. So we must, by meditation, tread the clusters of truth if we would get the wine of consolation from it. Our bodies are not supported by merely taking food into the mouth. The process which really supplies the muscle, nerve, sinew, and the bone is the process of digestion. It is by digestion that the outward food becomes assimilated with the inner life. Our souls are not nourished merely by listening awhile to this and then to that and then to the other part of divine truth. Hearing, reading, marking, and learning all require inward digesting to complete their usefulness. The inward digesting of the truth lies for the most part in meditating on it. Why is it that some Christians, although they hear many sermons, make slow advances in the divine life? Because they do not thoughtfully meditate on God's Word. They love the wheat, but they do not grind it. They want the corn, but they will not go forth into the fields to gather it. The fruit hangs on the tree, but they will not pluck it. The water flows at their feet, but they will not stoop to drink it. Lord, deliver us from such folly as we resolve to meditate on Your Word this morning.

October 12
Evening

"The Comforter, which is the Holy Ghost" (John 14:26).

We live in an age that has experienced the outpouring of the Holy Spirit. Jesus does not cheer us by His physical presence as He will do one glorious day, but by the indwelling and constant abiding of the Holy Spirit, the Comforter of the Church. It is His job to console the hearts of God's people. He convicts of sin; He illuminates and instructs; but the main parts of His work include making glad the hearts of the renewed, strengthening the weak, and lifting up all that are bowed down. He does this by revealing Jesus to them. The Holy Spirit consoles, but *Christ is the consolation.* As an illustration, the Holy Spirit is the Physician, but Jesus is the medicine. *He* heals the wound, but it is by applying the holy ointment of Christ's name and grace. If we give the Holy Spirit the Greek name of *Paraclete* meaning Comforter or Advocate, then our heart gives our blessed Lord Jesus the title of the *Paraclesis* or Comfort and Consolation. With this rich provision for his need, why should the Christian be sad and discouraged? The Holy Spirit has graciously come to be your Comforter. Do you suppose, O weak and trembling believer, that He will be negligent of His sacred trust? Has He undertaken something that He cannot or will not perform? If it is His work to strengthen and to comfort you, do you suppose He has forgotten His business, or that He will fail to accomplish His loving work? Do not think so little of the tender and blessed Spirit whose name is *the Comforter.* He delights to give the oil of joy for mourning and the garment of praise for the spirit of heaviness. Trust in Him, and He will surely comfort you until the house of mourning is closed forever, and the marriage feast begins.

October 13
Morning

"Godly sorrow worketh repentance" (2 Corinthians 7:10).

Genuine repentance is the work of the Spirit of God. Repentance is too choice a flower to grow in nature's garden. Pearls grow naturally in oysters, but penitence never shows itself in sinners unless divine grace works it in them. If you have one particle of real hatred for sin, God must have given it to you. That which is born of flesh is flesh. True repentance has a distinct reference to the Savior. When we repent of sin, we must have one eye on sin and another on the cross. It will be better still if we fix both our eyes on Christ and see our transgressions only in the light of His love. True sorrow for sin is eminently practical. No man may say he hates sin if he lives in it. Repentance makes us see the evil of sin, not merely as a theory, but experimentally—as a burnt child dreads fire. True mourning for sin will make us very jealous over our tongues lest we say a wrong word. We are very watchful over our daily actions lest in anything we offend, and each night we will close the day with painful confessions of shortcomings. Each morning we will awaken with prayers that this day God would hold us up that we may not sin against Him. Sincere repentance is continual. Believers repent until their dying day. Every other sorrow yields to time, but this dear sorrow grows with our growth. We thank God we are permitted to enjoy and to suffer it until we enter our eternal rest.

October 13
Evening

"Love is strong as death" (Song of Solomon 8:6).

Would it be an exaggeration if this description was applied to my poor, weak, and scarcely living love for Jesus my Lord? I do love Him. Perhaps, by His grace, I could even die for Him. But as for my love in itself, it can scarcely endure a scoffing jest, much less a cruel death. Surely it is my Beloved's love which is spoken of here—the love of Jesus, the matchless lover of souls. His love was indeed stronger than the most terrible death, for it endured the trial of the cross triumphantly. It was a lingering death, but love survived the torment; a shameful death, but love despised the shame; an unrighteous death, but love bore our iniquities; a forsaken, lonely death, from which the eternal Father hid His face, but love endured the curse and triumphed over all. Never has there been such love, never such death. It was a desperate duel, but love remained strong through the fight. Are my emotions stirred at the contemplation of such heavenly affection? Lord, I long to feel Your love flaming like a furnace within me. Why should I despair of loving Jesus with a love as strong as death? He deserves it; I desire it. The martyrs felt this love, and they were flesh and blood; then why not I? They mourned their weakness, and yet out of weakness were made strong. Grace gave them their unflinching constancy. This same grace is available for me. Jesus, shed abroad Your love in my heart this evening.

October 14
Morning

"I count all things but loss for the excellency of the knowledge of Christ Jesus my Lord" (Philippians 3:8).

Spiritual knowledge of Christ will be a *personal* knowledge. I cannot know Jesus through another person's acquaintance with Him. No, I must know Him *myself*. It will be an *intelligent* knowledge. I must know Him as the Word reveals Him. I must know His natures, both the divine and the human. I must know His offices, His attributes, His works, His shame, and His glory. I must meditate on Him until I comprehend with all saints what is the breadth, length, depth, and height of His love. It will be an *affectionate* knowledge of Him. Indeed, if I know Him at all, I must love Him. An ounce of heart-knowledge is worth a ton of head-knowledge. Our knowledge of Him will be a *satisfying* knowledge. When I know my Savior, my mind will be full to the brim. I will feel that I have that which my spirit longed for. At the same time, it will be an *exciting* knowledge. The more I know of my Beloved, the more I want to know. Like the miser's treasure, my gold will make me covet more. In conclusion, this knowledge of Christ Jesus will be a most happy one. In fact, sometimes it will completely bear me up above all trials, doubts, and sorrows. Come, sit at Jesus' feet, and learn of Him all this day.

October 14
Evening

"And be not conformed to this world" (Romans 12:2).

If a Christian can possibly be saved while he conforms to this world, it will be by fire. Such a bare salvation is almost as much to be dreaded as desired. Do you wish to leave this world in the darkness of a bed of affliction and enter heaven as a shipwrecked mariner climbs the rocks of his native country? Then be worldly; be mixed up with the kingdom of darkness and refuse to go outside the camp bearing Christ's reproach. Or would you rather have a heaven below as well as a heaven above? Do you want to receive glorious entrance into the joy of your Lord? Then "come out from among them, and be ye separate, saith the Lord, and touch not the unclean thing; and I will receive you" (2 Corinthians 6:17). Does your soul long to obtain the full assurance of faith? You cannot gain it while you commune with sinners. Does your heart wish to burn with the flame of love? Your love will be dampened by the drenchings of godless society. You may be a babe in grace, but you can never be a perfect man in Christ Jesus while you yield yourself to the values and philosophies of men of the world. It is dangerous for an heir of heaven to be a great friend with the heirs of hell. Even small inconsistencies are dangerous. Little thorns make great blisters, little moths destroy fine garments, and a little frivolity and mischief will rob faith of a thousand joys. O believer, you do not realize what you lose by your conformity to the world. It cuts the tendons of your strength and makes you crawl where you ought to run. For your own comfort's sake and for the sake of your growth in grace, if you are a Christian, then be a marked and distinct Christian.

October 15
Morning

"But who may abide the day of his coming?"
(Malachi 3:2).

His first coming was without external pomp or show of power. Yet, in truth, there were few who could abide its testing might. Herod and all Jerusalem were stirred at the news of the wondrous birth. Those who supposed themselves to be waiting for Him showed the fallacy of their professions by rejecting Him when He came. But what will His second advent be? What sinner can endure to think of it? "He shall smite the earth with the rod of his mouth, and with the breath of his lips shall he slay the wicked" (Isaiah 11:4). When, in His humiliation, His only words to the soldiers were, "I am He," they fell backward. What will be the terror of His enemies when He more fully reveals Himself as the "I Am"? His death shook earth and darkened heaven. What will be the dreadful splendor of that day in which, as the living Savior, He summons the living and dead before Him? Oh, that the terrors of the Lord would persuade men to forsake their sins! Though a Lamb, He is still the Lion of the tribe of Judah, rending the prey in pieces. Although He does not break the bruised reed, yet will He break His enemies with a rod of iron and dash them in pieces like a potter's vessel. But His beloved blood-washed people look for His appearing with joy and hope to witness it without fear. Let us search ourselves this morning and make our calling and election sure, so that the coming of the Lord may cause no dark forebodings in our mind. Oh, for grace to cast away all hypocrisy and to be found sincere without rebuke in the day of His appearing!

October 15
Evening

"But the firstling of an ass thou shalt redeem with a lamb; and if thou redeem him not, then shalt thou break his neck" (Exodus 34:20).

Every firstborn creature must be the Lord's, but since the ass was unclean, it could not be presented in sacrifice. What then? Should it be allowed to go free from the universal law? By no means. God allows no exceptions to His rules. The beast is His due, but He will not accept it. No way of escape remained but redemption—the creature must be saved by the substitution of a lamb in its place. If not redeemed, it must die. My soul, here is a lesson for you. That unclean animal is like you. You are the property of the Lord, who made you and preserves you. But you are so sinful that God will not and cannot accept you. The Lamb of God must stand in your place, or you will have to die eternally. Let all the world know of your gratitude to that spotless Lamb who bled for you and redeemed you from the fatal curse of the law. Must it not sometimes have been a question with the Israelite which should die, the ass or the lamb? Would not the good man pause to estimate and compare? Assuredly there was no comparison between the value of the soul of man and the life of the Lord Jesus, and yet the Lamb dies, and the man is spared. My soul, admire the boundless love of God for you and others of the human race. Worms are bought with the blood of the Son of the Highest! Dust and ashes are redeemed with a price far above silver and gold! What a doom would have been mine if redemption had not been found. Infinitely precious is the glorious Lamb who has redeemed us from death.

October 16
Morning

"Jesus saith unto them, Come and dine" (John 21:12).

In these words, the believer is invited to a holy nearness to Jesus. "Come and dine," implies the same table and the same meat. Sometimes it means to sit side by side and lean our head on the Savior's bosom. "Come and dine" gives us a vision of union with Jesus. Oh, what union this is! It is a depth which reason cannot fathom. "He that eateth my flesh, and drinketh my blood, dwelleth in me, and I in him" (John 6:56). It is also an invitation to enjoy fellowship with the saints. Christians may differ on a variety of points, but they have all one spiritual appetite. If we cannot all feel alike, we can all feed alike on the bread of life sent down from heaven. At the table of fellowship with Jesus, we are one bread and one cup. Get nearer to Jesus, and you will find yourself linked more and more in spirit to all who are, like yourself, supported by the same heavenly manna. If we were closer to Jesus, we would be closer to one another. We likewise see in these words the source of strength for every Christian. To look at Christ is to live, but for strength to serve Him you must "come and dine." We labor under much unnecessary weakness on account of neglecting this precept of the Master. We should feed on the marrow and fatness of the Word that we may accumulate strength therein and urge every power to its full tension in the Master's service. Thus, then, if you desire nearness to Jesus, union with Jesus, love for His people, and strength from Jesus, "come and dine" with Him by faith.

October 16
Evening

"With thee is the fountain of life" (Psalm 36:9).

There are times in our spiritual experience when human counsel, sympathy, or religion fail to comfort or help us. Why does our gracious God permit this? Perhaps it is because we have been living too much without Him. He, therefore, permits everything which we have been depending upon to be taken away that He may draw us to Himself. It is a blessed thing to live at the fountainhead. While our provisions are full, we are content, like Hagar and Ishmael, to go into the wilderness; but when those are dry, nothing will help us but the knowledge that "Thou God seest me" (Genesis 16:13). We are like the prodigal. We long for the food of the swine and forget our Father's house. Remember, we can make husks even out of forms of religion. They are blessed things, but if we put them in God's place, they are of no value. Anything becomes an idol when it keeps us away from God. A famine in the land may make us seek after our Lord all the more. The best position for a Christian is depending wholly and directly on God's grace, "having nothing, and yet possessing all things" (2 Corinthians 6:10). Let us never for a moment think that our standing is due to our sanctification, our humility, or our feelings. We are saved only because Christ offered a full atonement. We are complete in Him. We have nothing of our own to trust in, but when we rest upon the merits of Jesus, we stand upon the only sure ground of confidence. Beloved, when we are brought to a thirsting condition, we are sure to turn to the fountain of life with eagerness.

"And David said in his heart, I shall now perish one day by the hand of Saul" (1 Samuel 27:1).

The thought of David's heart at this time was a false thought. He certainly had no ground for thinking that God's anointing him was intended to be left as an empty, meaningless act. On no occasion had the Lord deserted His servant. He had been placed in perilous positions very often, but not one instance had occurred in which divine intervention had not delivered him. The trials to which he had been exposed had been varied. Yet, in every case, God graciously ordained a way of escape. David should have realized from what God had done for him that God would be his defender still. Do we doubt God's help in this same way? Is it not mistrust without a cause? Have we ever had the shadow of a reason to doubt our Father's goodness? Has He once failed to justify our trust? Our God has not left us at any time. We have gone through many trials. They have never been to our detriment but always to our advantage. The conclusion from our past experience is that He who has been with us in six troubles will not forsake us in the seventh. What we have known of our faithful God proves that He will keep us to the end. Let us not, then, reason contrary to evidence. How can we ever be so ungenerous as to doubt our God? Lord, throw down the Jezebel of our unbelief and let the dogs devour it.

October 17
Evening

"He shall gather the lambs with his arm" (Isaiah 40:11).

Our Good Shepherd has quite a variety of sheep in His flock. Some are strong in the Lord, and others are weak in faith. He is impartial in His care for all His sheep, and the weakest lamb is as dear to Him as the most advanced of the flock. Lambs tend to lag behind, to wander, and to grow weary. But the Shepherd protects them from these dangerous habits with His arm of power. He finds newborn souls, like young lambs, ready to perish, and He nourishes them until their life becomes vigorous. He finds weak minds ready to faint and die, and He consoles them and renews their strength. He gathers all the little ones, for it is not the will of our heavenly Father that one of them should perish. What a quick eye He must have to see them all! What a tender heart to care for them all! What a far-reaching and strong arm to gather them all! In His lifetime on earth He was a great gatherer of the weak. Now that He dwells in heaven, His loving heart yearns toward the meek and contrite, the timid and feeble, and the fearful and fainting here below. He gently gathered me to Himself, to His truth, to His blood, to His love, and to His Church. Since my conversion, He has frequently restored me from my wanderings and once again folded me within the circle of His everlasting arms! The best part is that He does it all personally, not delegating the task of love, but condescending to rescue and preserve His most unworthy servant. How shall I love Him enough or serve Him worthily? Great Shepherd, I pray for a heart to love You more truly.

October 18
Morning

"Thy paths drop fatness" (Psalm 65:11).

Many are "the paths of the Lord" which "drop fatness," but a special one is the path of prayer. No believer who is much in the prayer closet will need to cry, "My leanness, my leanness; woe unto me" (Isaiah 24:16). Starving souls live at a distance from the mercy-seat and become like the parched fields in times of drought. Prevalence with God in wrestling prayer is sure to make the believer strong. The nearest place to the gate of heaven is the throne of heavenly grace. Spend much time alone with Jesus, and you will have much assurance. Spend little time alone with Jesus, and your faith will be shallow, polluted with many doubts and fears, and lacking in the joy of the Lord. The soul-enriching path of prayer is open to the very weakest saint and no high attainments are required. See to it, dear reader, that you are often in private devotion and fellowship with Jesus. Earth has no words which can set forth the holy calm of a soul leaning on Jesus' bosom. Few Christians understand it. They live in the lowlands and seldom climb to the top. They live in the outer court. They do not enter the holy place. At a distance they see the sacrifice, but they do not sit down with the priest to eat and enjoy the fat of the burnt offering. But, reader, sit under the shadow of Jesus. Let your Beloved be as the apple tree among the trees of the woods, and you will be satisfied as with marrow and fatness. O Jesus, visit us with Your salvation.

October 18
Evening

"Behold, to obey is better than sacrifice" (1 Samuel 15:22).

Saul had been commanded to slay all the Amalekites and their cattle. Instead of doing so, he preserved the king and permitted the people to take the best of the oxen and sheep. When called to account for this, he declared that he did it with the intention of offering a sacrifice to God. But Samuel assured him that sacrifices were no excuse for an act of direct rebellion. The sentence before us this evening is worthy to be printed in letters of gold and to be hung before the eyes of the present idolatrous generation. They are very fond of following their own will, but they utterly neglect the laws of God. Always remember that to keep strictly in the path of your Savior's command is better than any outward form of religion. If you are failing to keep the least of Christ's commands to His disciples, be disobedient no longer. All the pretensions you make of devotion to your Master, and all the devout actions which you may perform are no recompense for disobedience. "To obey," even in the slightest and smallest thing, "is better than sacrifice," however pompous. Do not be distracted by ornate cathedrals, sumptuous robes, incense, and banners. The first thing God requires of His child is obedience. Although you give your body to be burned as a martyr and give all your goods to feed the poor, if you do not obey the Lord's precepts, all your formalities profit you nothing. It is a blessed thing to be teachable as a little child, but it is a much more blessed thing to carry out the lesson to the letter. How many adorn their temples but refuse to obey the Word of the Lord! Do not be like one of them.

October 19
Morning

"Babes in Christ" (1 Corinthians 3:1).

Are you mourning because you are so weak in the divine life? Because your faith is so little, and your love so feeble? Cheer up, for you have cause for gratitude. Remember that in some things you are equal to the greatest and most full-grown Christian. You are as much bought with blood as he is. You are as much an adopted child of God as any other believer. An infant is as truly a child of its parents as is the full-grown man. You are completely justified, for your justification is not a thing of degrees. Your little faith has made you completely clean. You have as much right to the precious things of the covenant as the most advanced believers, for your right to covenant mercies lies not in your growth but in the covenant itself. Your faith in Jesus is not the measure but the token of your inheritance in Him. The smallest star that gleams is set in heaven. The faintest ray of light has affinity with the great orb of day. In the family register of glory, the small and the great are written with the same pen. You are as dear to your Father's heart as the greatest in the family. Jesus is very tender over you. You are like a bruised reed. He will never break the bruised reed. Instead of being downcast by reason of what you are, you should triumph in Christ. In Christ I am made to sit in heavenly places. Am I poor in faith? Still in Jesus I am heir of all things. I will rejoice in the Lord and glory in the God of my salvation.

October 19
Evening

"God my maker, who giveth songs in the night" (Job 35:10).

Any man can sing in the daylight. When wealth rolls in abundance around him, any man can praise the God who gives a plentiful harvest or sends home a merchant ship loaded with rich cargo. It is easy enough for chimes to whisper music when the winds blow—the difficulty is for music to swell forth when no wind is stirring. It is easy to sing when we can read the notes by daylight; but the one who is skillful sings from his heart. No man can make a song in the night of his soul. He may attempt it, but he will find that a song in the night must be divinely inspired. When all things go well, I can weave songs wherever I go, rejoicing in the flowers that grow upon my path. But put me in a desert where no green thing grows, and how shall I lift a hymn of praise to God? If my voice is clear, and my body healthy I can sing God's praise. Silence my tongue, lay me upon the bed of sickness and how can I chant God's high praises, unless He gives me the song? No, it is not in man's power to sing when all is against him, unless music from heaven fills his soul. It was a divine song which Habakkuk sang when he said, "Although the fig tree shall not blossom, neither shall fruit be in the vines; the labour of the olive shall fail, and the fields shall yield no meat; the flock shall be cut off from the fold, and there shall be no herd in the stalls: Yet I will rejoice in the Lord, I will joy in the God of my salvation" (Habakkuk 3:17-18). Since our Maker gives songs in the night, let us wait upon Him for the music. O Chief Musician, let us not remain silent because of our circumstances. Tune our lips to the melody of thanksgiving.

October 20
Morning

"Grow up into him in all things" (Ephesians 4:15).

Many Christians remain stunted and dwarfed in spiritual things. They exist but do not "grow up into him in all things." But should we rest content with being in the green blade when we might advance to the ear and eventually ripen into the full corn in the ear? Should we be satisfied to believe in Christ and to say, "I am safe," without wishing to know in our own experience more of the fullness which is to be found in Him? It should not be so. We should, as good traders in heaven's market, covet to be enriched in the knowledge of Jesus. It is all very well to keep other men's vineyards, but we must not neglect our own spiritual growth and ripening. Why should it always be winter time in our hearts? We must have our seedtime, it is true; but, Oh, for a springtime and a summer season which will give promise of an early harvest! If we would ripen in grace, we must live near to Jesus. We must hold sweet communion with Him. We must come near, as John did, and pillow our head on His breast. Then we will find ourselves advancing in holiness, love, faith, and hope—in every precious gift. As the sun rises first on mountaintops and gilds them with its light, it is one of the most delightful contemplations in the world to notice the glow of the Spirit's light on the head of a saint who has risen up in spiritual stature.

October 20
Evening

"Keep not back" (Isaiah 43:6).

Although this message referred to the children of Israel, it is an exhortation to us also. We are naturally opposed to all good things, and we need grace to learn to go forward in the ways of God. Are you unconverted, but do you desire to trust in the Lord Jesus? Then *keep not back.* Love invites you, and the precious blood prepares the way. Do not let sins or fears hinder you, but come to Jesus just as you are. Do you long to pray? Would you pour out your heart before the Lord? *Keep not back.* The mercy seat is prepared for those who need mercy. A sinner's cries will prevail with God. You are invited, you are even commanded to pray. Come with boldness to the throne of grace. Are you already saved? Then *keep not back* from fellowship with the Lord's people. Do not neglect baptism and the Lord's Supper. You may have a timid disposition, but you must strive against it, lest it lead you into disobedience. If you have talents, *keep not back* from using them. Do not hoard your wealth or waste your time. Keep your abilities from rusting and your influence from being unused. Jesus kept not back; imitate Him by self-denials and self-sacrifice. *Keep not back* from close communion with God, from boldly appropriating covenant blessings, from advancing in the Christian life, and from discovering the precious mysteries of the love of Christ. Neither be guilty of keeping others back by your coldness, harshness, or suspicions. For Jesus' sake, go forward yourself and encourage others to do the same. Hell and its armies of superstition and infidelity are ready for the fight. O soldiers of the cross, *keep not back.*

October 21
Morning

"The love of Christ constraineth us" (Matthew 5:47).

How much do you owe my Lord? Has He ever done anything for you? Has He forgiven your sins? Has He covered you with a robe of righteousness? Has He set your feet on a rock? Has He established your goings? Has He prepared heaven for you? Has He prepared you for heaven? Has He written your name in His book of life? Has He given you countless blessings? Has He laid up for you a store of mercies, which eye has not seen or ear heard? Then do something for Jesus worthy of His love. How will you feel when your Master comes if you have to confess that you did nothing for Him but kept your love shut up, like a stagnant pool, neither flowing forth to His poor or to His work. What do men think of a love which never shows itself in action? Why, they say, "Open rebuke is better than secret love" (Proverbs 27:5). Who will accept a love so weak that it does not move you to a single deed of self-denial, generosity, heroism, or zeal? Think how He has loved you and given Himself for you! Do you know the power of that love? Then let it be like a rushing, mighty wind to your soul to sweep out the clouds of your worldliness and clear away the mists of sin. The divine Spirit will make you bold as lions and swift as eagles in your Lord's service. Love should give wings to the feet of service and strength to the arms of labor. Fixed on God with a constancy that is not to be shaken, let us manifest the constraints of our love for Jesus.

October 21
Evening

"Why are ye troubled? and why do thoughts arise in your hearts?"(Luke 24:38).

The Lord cares for all things, but He is particularly concerned about His saints. "The angel of the Lord encampeth round about them that fear him" (Psalm 34:7). "Precious in the sight of the Lord is the death of his saints" (Psalm 116:15). "We know that all things work together for good to them that love God, to them who are the called according to his purpose" (Romans 8:28). While He is the Savior of all men, He is especially the Savior of them that believe. Let that assurance cheer and comfort you. You are His special masterpiece; His treasure which He guards as the apple of His eye; His vineyard over which He watches day and night. "The very hairs of your head are all numbered" (Matthew 10:30). Let the thought of His love for you be a spiritual painkiller, a sweet quieter to your woe: "I will never leave thee, nor forsake thee" (Hebrews 13:5). God says that as much to you as to any saint of old. "Fear not. . .I am thy shield, and thy exceeding great reward" (Genesis 15:1). We lose much consolation by relating His promises to the whole Church, instead of taking them directly home to ourselves. Believer, grasp the divine word with a personal, appropriating faith. Hear Jesus say, "I have prayed for thee, that thy faith fail not" (Luke 22:32). Do you see Him walking on the waters of your trouble? He is there, and He is saying, "Be of good cheer; it is I; be not afraid" (Matthew 14:27). Accept the voice of Jesus as spoken to you and say, "Jesus whispers consolation, and I cannot refuse it. I will sit under His shadow with great delight."

October 22
Morning

"I will love them freely" (Hosea 13:4).

He who understands the meaning of this sentence is a theologian, and he who can dive into its fullness is a true master in Israel. It is a condensation of the glorious message of salvation which was delivered to us in Christ Jesus our Redeemer. The sense hinges on the word "freely." This is the glorious, suitable, divine way by which love streams from heaven to earth. It is a spontaneous love flowing forth to those who neither deserved it, purchased it, or sought after it. It is, indeed, the only way in which God can love us. "I will love them *freely.*" Now, if there were any fitness necessary in us then He would not love us freely. But it stands, "I will love you *freely.*" We complain, "Lord, my heart is so hard, and I do not feel my need of Christ. I do not feel that softening of spirit which I should desire." Remember, there are no conditions. The covenant of grace has no conditionality whatever. We, without any worthiness, may venture on the promise of God which was made to us in Christ Jesus when He said, "He that believeth on him is not condemned" (John 3:18). It is blessed to know that the grace of God is free to us at all times, without preparation, fitness, money, or price! "I will love them freely." These words invite backsliders to return. Indeed, the text was especially written for such—"I will heal their backsliding; I will love them freely" (Hosea 14:4). Backslider, surely the generosity of the promise will at once break your heart, and you will return and seek your Father's face.

October 22
Evening

"He shall take of mine, and shall shew it unto you" (John 16:15).

There are times when all the promises and doctrines of the Bible are of no avail unless a gracious hand applies them to us. We are thirsty, but too faint to crawl to the stream. When a soldier is wounded in battle, it is useless for him to know that there are those at the hospital who can bind up his wounds. He needs to be carried there and have the remedies applied. It is the same with our souls. To meet this need, the Spirit of truth takes of the things of Jesus and applies them to us. Christ draws near and sheds His peace abroad in our hearts. If you are distressed tonight, your Father does not give promises and then leave you to draw them up from the Word like buckets from a well. He will write the promises anew on your heart. He will manifest His love to you and, by His blessed Spirit, dispel your cares and troubles. O mourner, God wipes every tear from the eyes of His people. The good Samaritan did not say, "Here is the wine, and here is the oil for you;" he poured the oil and the wine on the injured man's wounds. Jesus not only gives you the sweet wine of the promise, but He holds the golden chalice to your lips and pours the lifeblood into your mouth. The poor, sick, weary pilgrim is not merely strengthened to walk, but he is borne on eagles' wings. The glorious gospel provides everything for the helpless, draws near to us when we cannot go after it, and brings us grace before we seek for grace! Happy are the people who have the Holy Spirit to bring Jesus to them.

October 23
Morning

"Will ye also go away?" (John 6:67).

Many have forsaken Christ. Yet, has Jesus not proved Himself all-sufficient? He appeals to you this morning. "Have I been a wilderness unto you?" (Jeremiah 2:31). When your soul has simply trusted Jesus, have you ever been confounded? Have you not up until now found your Lord to be a compassionate and generous friend to you? Has not simple faith in Him given you all the peace your spirit could desire? Can you so much as dream of a better friend than He has been to you? What can compel you to leave Christ? When we are troubled by this world or with the severer trials within the Church, we find it a blessed thing to pillow our head on the bosom of our Savior. This is the joy we have today, that we are saved in Him. If this joy is satisfying, why would we think of changing? We will not reject the sun until we find a better light or leave our Lord until a brighter lover appears. Since this can never be, we will hold Him with an immortal grasp and bind His name as a seal on our arm. As for the future, can you suggest anything which can arise that will render it necessary for you to forsake Him? If we are poor, what is better than to have Christ, who can make us rich? When we die, is it not written that "neither death, nor life, nor things present, nor things to come, shall be able to separate us from the love of God, which is in Christ Jesus our Lord" (Romans 8:38-39)? We say with Peter, "Lord, to whom will we go?"

October 23
Evening

"Why sleep ye? rise and pray, lest ye enter into temptation" (Luke 22:46).

When is the Christian most likely to sleep? Is it not when his temporal circumstances are prosperous? When you had daily troubles to take to the throne of grace, were you more spiritually alert than you are now? Easy roads make sleepy travelers. The Christian did not sleep when lions were in the way or when fighting with the enemy of his soul; but when he climbed halfway up the Hill of Difficulty, he came to a delightful arbor and sat down. He promptly fell asleep, to his great sorrow and loss. Remember Bunyan's description: "Then they came to an arbor, warm, and promising much refreshing to the weary pilgrims; for it was finely wrought above head, beautified with greens, and furnished with benches and settles. It had also in it a soft couch, where the weary might lean. . . .The arbor was called the Slothful's Friend, and was made on purpose to allure, if it might be, some of the pilgrims to take up their rest there when weary." In easy places, men shut their eyes and wander into the dreamy land of forgetfulness. Old Erskine wisely remarked, "I like a roaring devil better than a sleeping devil." There is no temptation half as dangerous as not being tempted. The distressed soul does not sleep; it is after we enter into peaceful confidence and full assurance that we are in danger of slumbering. The disciples fell asleep after they had seen Jesus transfigured on the mountaintop. Take heed, joyous Christian—pleasant circumstances are near neighbors to temptations. Be as happy as you will, only be watchful.

October 24
Morning

"The trees of the Lord are full of sap" (Psalm 104:16).

Without sap the tree cannot flourish or even exist. *Vitality* is essential to a Christian. There must be *life*—a vital principle infused into us by God the Holy Spirit—or we cannot be trees of the Lord. The mere name of being a Christian is but a dead thing. We must be filled with the Spirit of divine life. This life is *mysterious.* Regeneration is wrought by the Holy Spirit entering into man and becoming man's life. This divine life in a believer afterward feeds on the flesh and blood of Christ and is thus sustained by divine food. But where it comes from and where it goes, who can explain to us? What a secret thing the sap is! The roots go searching through the soil, but we cannot see them suck out the various gases or transform the mineral into the vegetable. This work is done down in the dark. Our root is Christ Jesus, and our life is hid in Him. This is the secret of the Lord. In the Christian, the divine life is always full of energy. The believer's graces are not all in constant motion, but his life never ceases to palpitate within. He is not always working for God, but his heart is always living on Him. As the sap manifests itself in producing the foliage and fruit of the tree, so it must be with a truly healthy Christian. His grace is externally manifested in his walk and conversation. If you talk with him, he cannot help speaking about Jesus. If you notice his actions, you will see that he has been with Jesus. He has so much sap within that it must fill his conduct and conversation with life.

October 24
Evening

"He. . .began to wash the disciples' feet" (John 13:5).

The Lord Jesus loves His people so much that every day He is still doing many things for them that may be compared to washing their soiled feet. Their poorest actions He accepts; their deepest sorrow He feels; their slightest wish He hears, and their every transgression He forgives. He is still their Servant as well as their Friend and Master. He not only performs majestic deeds when He stands up to plead for them; but humbly, patiently, He goes among His people with the basin and the towel. He does this when He daily puts away from us our constant infirmities and sins. Last night when you prayed, you mournfully confessed that much of your conduct was not worthy of your name, Christian. Even tonight, you mourn that you have fallen into the same sin from which grace delivered you long ago. Yet, Jesus has great patience with you. He will hear your confession of sin, and He will say, "I will, be thou clean" (Luke 5:13). He will again apply the blood of atonement and speak peace to your conscience. It is a great act of eternal love when Christ absolves the sinner and puts him into the family of God. But what patience there is when the Savior bears the recurring follies of His wayward disciple. Day by day and hour by hour, He washes away the multiplied transgressions of His erring, yet beloved child! To dry up a flood of rebellion is something marvelous, but to endure the constant dripping of repeated offenses and to bear with a perpetual trying of patience—this is divine indeed! While we find comfort and peace in our Lord's daily cleansing, His influence on us will increase our watchfulness and strengthen our desire for holiness.

October 25
Morning

"For the truth's sake which dwelleth in us, and shall be with us forever" (2 John 2).

Let the truth of God obtain an entrance into the human heart where no power, human or infernal, can dislodge it. We entertain it not as a guest, but as the master of the house—this is a Christian necessity. Those who feel the vital power of the gospel and know the might of the Holy Spirit would sooner be torn to pieces than be rent away from the gospel of their salvation. What a thousand mercies are wrapped up in the assurance that the truth will be with us forever. Some truths we outgrow and leave behind, for they are but rudiments and lessons for beginners. But we cannot deal this way with divine truth. Although it is sweet food for babes, it is in the highest sense strong meat for men. The truth that we are sinners is painfully with us to humble us and make us watchful. The more blessed truth, that whosoever believes on the Lord Jesus will be saved, abides with us as our hope and joy. Our grounds and motives for believing are now stronger and more numerous than ever, and we have reason to expect that it will be so until in death we clasp the Savior in our arms. Wherever this abiding love of truth can be discovered, we are bound to exercise our love. Much error may be mingled with truth received. Let us war against the error but still love the brother for the measure of truth which we see in him. Above all, let us love and spread the truth ourselves!

October 25
Evening

"She. . .gleaned in the field after the reapers: and her hap was to light on a part of the field belonging unto Boaz, who was of the kindred of Elimelech" (Ruth 2:3).

Her *hap was.* The situation seemed to result from nothing but an accident, but how divinely it was arranged! Ruth had gone forth with her mother's blessing, under the care of her mother's God, to humble but honorable toil, and the providence of God was guiding her every step. Little did she know that amid the sheaves she would find a husband who would make her the joint owner of all those broad acres, and that she, a poor foreigner, would become one of the ancestors of the great Messiah. God is very good to those who trust in Him, and He often surprises them with unexpected blessings. We do not know what may happen to us tomorrow, but no good thing will be withheld. Chance is banished from the faith of Christians, for they see the hand of God in everything. The trivial events of today may involve consequences of the highest importance. How blessed would it be if, in wandering in the field of meditation tonight, we would happen to come upon the place where our Kinsman will reveal Himself to us! O Spirit of God, guide us to Him. Search for the footsteps of His flock, which may lead us to the green pastures where He dwells! This is a weary world when Jesus is away; we could do without sun and moon before we could do without Him. But how divinely fair all things become in the glory of His presence! May we wait in prayer this night until we come upon a part of the field belonging to Jesus, where He will manifest Himself to us.

October 26
Morning

"Ye looked for much, and, lo, it came to little; and when ye brought it home, I did blow upon it. Why? saith the Lord of hosts. Because of mine house that is waste, and ye run every man unto his own house" (Haggai 1:9).

Many people limit their contributions to the ministry and missionary endeavors and call such saving good economy. Little do they dream that they are impoverishing themselves. Their excuse is that they must care for their own families, and they forget that to neglect the house of God is the sure way to bring ruin on their own houses. Our God has a method in providence by which He can bless our endeavors beyond our expectations or defeat our plans to our confusion and dismay. Scripture teaches that the Lord enriches the liberal and leaves the miserly to find out that withholding tends to poverty. In a very wide sphere of observation, I have noticed that the most generous Christians have always been the most happy and almost invariably the most prosperous. I have seen the liberal giver rise to wealth of which he never dreamed. I have as often seen the stingy, ungenerous person descend to poverty by the very thriftiness by which he thought to rise. Men trust good stewards with larger and larger sums and so does the Lord. He gives by cartloads to those who give by bushels. Selfishness looks first at home, but godliness seeks first the Kingdom of God and His righteousness. Yet, in the long run, selfishness is loss, and godliness is great gain. It takes faith to act toward our God with an open hand, but surely He deserves it of us.

October 26
Evening

"All the rivers run into the sea; yet the sea is not full; unto the place from whence the rivers come, thither they return again" (Ecclesiastes 1:7).

Everything is on the move; time knows nothing of rest. The solid earth is a rolling ball, and the great sun itself is a star obediently fulfilling its course around some greater luminary. Tides move the sea, winds stir the ocean, and friction wears the rock—change and death rule everywhere. Men are born to die; everything is hurry, worry, and vexation of spirit. Friend of the unchanging Jesus, what a joy it is to reflect upon your changeless heritage! Your sea of bliss will be forever full, since God Himself pours eternal rivers of pleasure into it. We seek an abiding city beyond the skies, and we will not be disappointed. The Scripture before us this evening may teach us about gratitude. Father Ocean is a great receiver, but he is also a generous distributer. What the rivers bring him, he returns to the earth in the form of clouds and rain. The man who takes all but makes no return is out of harmony with the universe. To give to others means sowing seeds for ourselves. He who is a good steward is willing to use his substance for his Lord, and he will be entrusted with more. Are you rendering to Him according to the benefit received? Much has been given you— what is your fruit? To be selfish is to be wicked. Suppose the ocean gave up none of its watery treasure; it would bring ruin upon our race. God forbid that any of us should follow the ungenerous and destructive policy of living for ourselves alone. Jesus did not please Himself. All fullness dwells in Him, but of His fullness we have all received. (See John 1:16.)

October 27
Morning

"It is a faithful saying" (2 Timothy 2:11).

Paul has four of these *"faithful sayings."* The first occurs in 1 Timothy 1:15: "This is a faithful saying, and worthy of all acceptance, that Christ Jesus came into the world to save sinners." The next is in 1 Timothy 4:8-9: "Godliness is profitable unto all things, having promise of the life that now is, and of that which is to come." The third is in 2 Timothy 2:12: "If we suffer, we shall also reign with him." The fourth is in Titus 3:8: "This is a faithful saying. . . .that they which have believed in God might be careful to maintain good works." We may trace a connection between these faithful sayings. The first one lays the foundation of our eternal salvation in the free grace of God as shown to us in the mission of the great Redeemer. The next affirms the double blessedness which we obtain through this salvation—the blessings of time and eternity. The third shows one of the duties to which the chosen people are called. We are ordained to suffer for Christ with the promise that "if we suffer, we shall also reign with him." The last sets forth the active form of Christian service, bidding us diligently to maintain good works. Treasure these faithful sayings. Let them be the guides of your life, comfort, and instruction. The apostle of the Gentiles proved them to be faithful, and they are faithful still. Not one word will fall to the ground. They are all worthy of acceptance. Let us accept them now and prove their faithfulness. Let these four sayings be written on the four corners of your house.

October 27
Evening

"We are all as an unclean thing" (Isaiah 64:6).

The believer is a new creature; he belongs to a holy generation and a peculiar people. The Spirit of God is in him, and in all respects, he is far removed from the natural man. But despite all that, the Christian is still entangled by the imperfection of his nature and will continue in this way to the end of his earthly life. The black fingers of sin leave stains upon our fairest robes. Selfishness defiles our tears, and unbelief tampers with our faith. The best thing we ever did, apart from receiving Jesus, only swelled the number of our sins. When we have been most pure in our own sight, we are not pure in God's sight. As He charged His angels with folly, He must charge us with it even more. The song which ascends to heaven and seeks to emulate celestial hymns has human discord in it. The prayer which moves the arm of God is still a bruised and battered prayer. It only moves that arm because the sinless One, the great Mediator, has stepped in to take away the sin of our supplication. The most golden faith or the purest degree of sanctification to which a Christian ever attained on earth still has so much dross in it that it is only worthy of the flames. Every night when we look in the mirror, we see a sinner. We must confess, "We are all as an unclean thing, and all our righteousness is filthy rags." How priceless a gift is His perfect righteousness! Even now, though sin dwells in us, *its power is broken.* It has no dominion; it is a snake with a broken back. We are in bitter conflict with it, but it is with a vanquished foe.

October 28
Morning

"I have chosen you out of the world" (John 15:19).

Here is distinguishing grace and discriminating regard, for some are made the special objects of divine affection. Do not be afraid to dwell on this high doctrine of election. When your mind is most heavy and depressed, you will find this scripture to be soothing. Those who doubt the doctrines of grace or cast them into the shade miss one of our richest blessings. There is no balm comparable to it. If the honey Jonathan ate enlightened his eyes, this is honey which will enlighten your heart to love and learn the mysteries of the Kingdom of God. Live on this choice dainty without fear. Meat from the King's table will not hurt His courtiers. Desire to have your mind enlarged so that you may comprehend more and more the eternal, everlasting, discriminating love of God. When you have mounted as high as election, tarry on its sister mount, the covenant of grace. Covenant engagements are the ramparts of stupendous rock which we lie behind. Covenant engagements with the Surety, Christ Jesus, are the quiet resting places of trembling spirits. The Father promised that He would give me to the Son to be a part of the infinite reward of the travail of His soul. Then, until God Himself is unfaithful or until Jesus ceases to be the truth, my soul is safe. When David danced before the ark, he told Michal that election made him do so. Come, my soul, exalt before the God of grace and leap for joy of heart.

October 28
Evening

"His head is as the most fine gold, his locks are bushy and black as a raven" (Song of Solomon 5:11).

Comparisons all fail to describe the Lord Jesus, but the spouse uses the best expression within her reach. By *the head* of Jesus we may understand His deity, "for the head of Christ is God" (1 Corinthians 11:3). The ingot of purest gold is the best conceivable metaphor, but even that is too poor to describe One who is infinitely precious, pure, dear, and glorious. Jesus is not a grain of gold, but a vast globe of it, a priceless mass of treasure such as earth and heaven cannot excel. The creatures are mere iron and clay; they all will perish like wood, hay, and stubble. But the eternal Head of the creation of God will shine on forever. He is infinitely holy and altogether divine. *The bushy locks* depict His manly vigor. Our Beloved is the manliest of men. He is bold as a lion, laborious as an ox, and swift as an eagle. Every conceivable and inconceivable beauty is to be found in Him, though once He was despised and rejected of men. Now He is eternally crowned with peerless majesty. *The black hair* indicates youthful freshness, for Jesus has the dew of His youth upon Him. Others grow weak with age, but He is forever a Priest. Others come and go, but He abides as God upon His throne, world without end. We will behold Him tonight and adore Him. Angels are gazing upon Him, and His redeemed must not turn away their eyes from Him. Where else is there such a Beloved? Jesus draws me, and I must run after Him.

"After this manner therefore pray ye: Our Father, which art in heaven" (Matthew 6:9).

This prayer begins where all true prayer must commence—with the spirit of adoption, "Our Father." There is no acceptable prayer until we can say, "I will arise and go to my Father." This childlike spirit soon perceives the grandeur of the Father in heaven and ascends to devout adoration—"Hallowed be thy name. Thy kingdom come. Thy will be done on earth, as it is in heaven." Next follows the heartfelt expression of dependence on God—"Give us this day our daily bread." Being further illuminated by the Spirit, he discovers that he is not only dependent, but sinful; hence he entreats for mercy—"Forgive us our debts as we forgive our debtors." Being pardoned, having the righteousness of Christ imputed, and knowing his acceptance with God, he humbly supplicates for holy perseverance—"Lead us not into temptation." The man who is really forgiven is anxious not to offend again. The possession of justification leads to an anxious desire for sanctification. "Forgive us our debts"—that is justification. "Lead us not into temptation, but deliver us from evil—that is sanctification in its negative and positive forms. As the result of all this, there follows a triumphant praise—"Thine is the kingdom, the power, and the glory, forever. Amen." We rejoice that our King reigns in providence and will reign in grace, and there will be no end of His dominion. Thus, this short model of prayer conducts the soul from a sense of adoption up to fellowship with our reigning Lord.

October 29
Evening

"But their eyes were holden that they should not know him" (Luke 24:16).

The disciples should have known Jesus. They had heard His voice often and gazed upon that marred face frequently. Yet, is it the same with you also? You have not seen Jesus lately. You have been to His table, and you have not met Him there. You may be in dark trouble this evening, and though He plainly says, "It is I, be not afraid," you cannot discern Him. Our eyes are prevented from seeing Him. We know His voice; we have looked into His face; we have leaned our head upon His bosom. Although Christ is near us, we say, "Oh, if only I knew where I might find Him!" We should know Jesus, for we have the Scriptures to reflect His image. Yet it is possible for us to open that precious Book and have no glimpse of the Well-beloved. Jesus waits among the lilies of the Word; you walk among those lilies, and yet, you do not behold Him. He walks through the glades of Scripture to commune with His people, as the Father did with Adam in the cool of the day. You are in the garden of Scripture, but you cannot see Him, though He is always there. Why do we not see Him? It must be ascribed in our case, as in the disciples', to unbelief. They evidently did not expect to see Jesus, and, therefore, they did not know Him. To a great extent, in spiritual things, we get what we expect of the Lord. Faith alone can bring us to see Jesus. Make this your prayer: "Lord, open my eyes, that I may see my Savior present with me." It is a blessed thing to *want* to see Him, but it is far better to gaze upon Him. To those who seek Him, He is kind. But to those who find Him, He is precious beyond all imagination!

October 30
Morning

"I will praise thee, O Lord" (Psalm 9:1).

Praise should always follow answered prayer as the mist of earth's gratitude rises when the sun of heaven's love warms the ground. Has the Lord been gracious to you and inclined His ear to the voice of your supplication? Then praise Him as long as you live. Do not deny a song to Him who has answered your prayer and given you the desire of your heart. To be silent over God's mercies is to incur the guilt of ingratitude. It is to act as basely as the nine lepers, who, after they had been cured of their leprosy, did not return to give thanks to the healing Lord. To forget to praise God is to refuse to benefit ourselves. Praise, like prayer, is one great means of promoting the growth of the spiritual life. It helps to remove our burdens, to excite our hope, and to increase our faith. It is a healthful and invigorating exercise which quickens the pulse of the believer and prepares him for fresh enterprises in his Master's service. To bless God for mercies received is also the way to benefit our fellowmen; "the humble shall hear thereof and be glad" (Psalm 34:2). Others, who have been in like circumstances, will take comfort if we can say, "Oh! magnify the Lord with me, and let us exalt His name together. . . .this poor man cried, and the Lord heard him" (Psalm 34:3-6). Weak hearts will be strengthened and drooping saints will be revived as they listen to our songs of deliverance.

October 30
Evening

"Thou that dwellest in the gardens, the companions hearken to the voice: cause me to hear it" (Song of Solomon 8:13).

Jesus remembers the garden of Gethsemane well. Although He left that garden, He now dwells in the garden of His Church. There He reveals Himself to those who keep His blessed company. His voice of love is more musical than the harps of heaven. There is a depth of melodious love within it which leaves all human music far behind. Tens of thousands on earth and millions above are indulged with its harmonious accents. Oh, that I could share in their joys! It is true some of these are poor, others bedridden, and some near the gates of death. But I would cheerfully starve with them, hurt with them, or die with them, if I could only hear Your voice, O Lord! Once I heard it often, but I have grieved Your Spirit. Return to me in compassion and say to me, "I am your salvation." No other voice can satisfy me. Let me hear You, I pray. I do not know what You will say, neither do I make any demands. O my Beloved, let me hear You speak, and if it is a rebuke, I will bless You for it. Perhaps cleansing my dull ear requires an operation which will be very grievous to the flesh, but whatever the cost, I will not turn from my one consuming desire—to hear Your voice. Open my ear, pierce my ear with Your precious notes. Only do not permit me to continue to be deaf to Your call. Tonight, Lord, grant Your unworthy one his desire, for I am Yours. You have opened my eyes to see You, and the sight has saved me. Lord, open my ears and let me hear Your voice.

October 31
Morning

"Renew a right spirit within me" (Psalm 51:10).

A backslider, if there is a spark of life left in him, will groan after restoration. The same exercise of grace is required in this renewal as at our conversion. We needed repentance then, and we certainly need it now. At first, we needed faith to come to Christ. Now, only the same grace can bring us to Jesus. We wanted a word from the Most High to end our fears then, and we will soon discover, when under a sense of present sin, that we need it now. No man can be renewed without as real and true a manifestation of the Holy Spirit's power as he felt at first, because the work is as great. Let your personal weakness, Christian, be an argument to make you pray earnestly to your God for help. Remember, David, when he felt himself to be powerless, hastened to the mercy-seat with, "Renew a right spirit within me" (Psalm 51:10). Let this scripture be a goad in your side to drive you with an awful earnestness to Israel's strong Helper. Plead with God as though you pleaded for your very life—"Lord, renew a right spirit within me." He who sincerely prays to God to do this will prove his honesty by using the means through which God works. Be much in prayer. Live on the Word of God. Kill the lusts which have driven your Lord from you. Be careful to watch over the future uprisings of sin. Sit by the wayside and be ready when He passes by. Continue in all those blessed ordinances which will foster and nourish your dying graces. Know that all power must proceed from Him, cease not to cry, "Renew a right spirit within me."

October 31
Evening

"I did know thee in the wilderness, in the land of great drought"(Hosea 8:5).

Lord, You knew me in my *fallen state,* and even then You chose me for Yourself. When I was loathsome and self-abhorred, You received me as Your child and satisfied my craving wants. Blessed forever be Your name for this free, rich, and abounding mercy. Since that time, *my spiritual life* has often been a wilderness. But I remained as Your beloved. You poured streams of love and grace into me to cheer me and make me fruitful. When my *outward circumstances* have been at the worst, and I have wandered in a desert, Your sweet presence comforted me. Men forgot me during the hard times, but You knew my soul in adversities, for no affliction dims the luster of Your love. Most gracious Lord, I magnify You for all Your faithfulness to me in trying circumstances. I lament that I should at any time have forgotten You and been exalted in my heart. I owe all to Your gentleness and love. My soul, if Jesus acknowledged you in your low estate, be sure that you are a part of both Jesus Himself and His cause now that you are in prosperity. Do not be so lifted up by worldly success that you become ashamed of the truth or of the poor Church with which you have been associated. Follow Jesus into the wilderness. Bear the cross with Him when the heat of persecution grows intense. He claimed your soul in its poverty and shame—never be so treacherous as to be ashamed of Him. You should be filled with shame at the thought of being ashamed of your best Beloved!

November 1
Morning

"The church in thy house" (Philemon 2). Is there a church in your house? Are parents, children, friends, and servants all members of it? Or are some still unconverted? How a father's heart would leap for joy and a mother's eyes fill with holy tears if all were saved from the oldest to the youngest! Let us pray for this great mercy until the Lord grants it to us. Probably it had been the dearest of Philemon's desires to have all his household saved, but it was not at first granted him in its fullness. He had a wicked servant, Onesimus, who, having wronged him, ran away from his service. But his master's prayers followed him, and as God would have it, Onesimus was led to hear Paul preach. His heart was touched, and he returned to Philemon, not only to be a faithful servant, but a beloved brother. Is there an unconverted child absent this morning? Make special supplication that such may, on their return to their home, gladden all hearts with good news of what grace has done! Is there one present? Let him partake in the same earnest plea. If there is such a church in your house, order it well. Let all act as in the sight of God. Move in the common affairs of life with holiness, diligence, kindness, and integrity. More is expected of a church than of an ordinary household. Family worship must, in such a case, be more devout and hearty. Internal love must be more warm and unbroken, and external conduct must be more sanctified and Christlike. As a church let us draw near to the great Head of the one Church universal, and let us beseech Him to give us grace to shine before men to the glory of His name.

November 1
Evening

"And knew not until the flood came, and took them all away; so shall also the coming of the Son of man be" (Matthew 24:39).

The doom of the flood was universal. Neither rich nor poor escaped—the learned and the illiterate, the admired and the despised, the religious and the profane, the old and the young all sank in one common ruin. Some had ridiculed the patriarch—where are their merry jests now? Others threatened him for his zeal which they thought was madness—where are their boastings and hard speeches? The critic who judged the old man's work was drowned in the same sea which covered his sneering companions. Those who spoke patronizingly of the good man's strength of convictions but did not share them sunk into the deep to rise no more. The workers who were paid to help build the wondrous ark were all lost also. The flood swept them *all* away and made no single exception. Even so, no rank, possession, or character will save a single soul who has not believed in the Lord Jesus. How amazing was the general apathy of the people! They were all eating and drinking, marrying and giving in marriage, until the awful morning dawned. Sin duped the whole race with the folly of self-preservation—the most foolish of all follies. All men are negligent of their souls until grace gives them reason to be concerned. Then they leave their madness and act like rational beings, but not until then. *All* were safe in the ark. From the huge elephant down to the tiny mouse, all were safe. The timid hare was equally secure with the courageous lion, and the helpless gazelle as safe as the laborious ox. All are safe in Jesus. Are you in Him this evening?

November 2
Morning

"I am the Lord, I change not" (Malachi 3:6).

It is well for us that, amidst all the variableness of life, there is One whom change cannot affect; One whose heart can never alter and on whose brow mutability can make no furrows. Everything else has changed. The sun itself grows dim with age. The world is growing old. The folding up of the wornout vesture has commenced. The heavens and earth must soon pass away. They will perish; but there is One who has immortality, and in whose person there is no change. The mariner feels delight when, after having been tossed about for many days, he steps again on the solid shore. This is like the satisfaction of a Christian, when, amidst all the changes of this troublesome life, he rests his foot on this truth—*"I am the Lord, I change not."* With God "is no variableness, neither shadow of turning" (James 1:17). Whatever His attributes were of old, they are now. His power, wisdom, justice, and truth are all unchanged. He has always been the refuge of His people and their stronghold in the day of trouble. He is their sure helper still. He is unchanged in His love. He has loved His people with an everlasting love, and He loves them now as much as He ever did. Precious is the assurance that He changes not!

November 2
Evening

"Horror hath taken hold upon me because of the wicked that forsake thy law" (Psalm 119:53).

Do you feel this holy shuddering at the sins of others? If not, you lack inward holiness. David's cheeks were wet with rivers of tears because of prevailing unholiness. Jeremiah desired eyes like fountains that he might lament the iniquities of Israel. Lot was troubled by the life style of the men of Sodom. Those upon whom the mark was set in Ezekiel's vision were those who sighed and cried because of the abominations of Jerusalem. It must grieve gracious souls to see what pains men take to go to hell. They have experienced the evil of sin, and they are alarmed to see others flying like moths into its blaze. Sin makes the righteous shudder because it violates a holy law which is in every man's highest interest to keep. Sin in others horrifies a believer, because it reminds him of the impurity of his own heart. When he sees a transgressor, he cries out with the realization, "He fell today, and I may fall tomorrow." Sin to a believer is horrible because it crucified the Savior. He sees the nails and spear in every iniquity. How can a saved soul behold that cursed sin without abhorrence? The good God deserves better treatment, the great God claims it, the just God will have it, or He will repay His adversary to his face. An awakened heart trembles at the audacity of sin and stands alarmed at the contemplation of its punishment. How monstrous is rebellion! How terrible a doom is prepared for the ungodly! Never laugh at sin's foolishness, lest you begin to smile at sin itself. It is your enemy and your Lord's enemy— view it with the utmost hatred, for only then can you possess the holiness, without which no man can see the Lord.

November 3
Morning

"Behold, he prayeth" (Acts 9:11).

Prayers are instantly noticed in heaven. The moment Saul began to pray, the Lord heard him. Here is comfort for the distressed but praying soul. Often a poor, brokenhearted one bends his knee but can only utter his wailing in the language of sighs and tears. Yet, that groan has made all the harps of heaven thrill with music. That tear has been caught by God and treasured in heaven. The supplicant whose fears prevent his words will be well understood by the Most High. He may only look up with misty eyes. Tears are the diamonds of heaven, and sighs are part of the music of Jehovah's court. They are numbered with the sublimest strains that reach the Majesty on high. Do not think that your prayer, however weak or trembling, will be unregarded. Jacob's ladder is lofty, but our prayer will climb its starry rounds. Our God not only hears prayer but also loves to hear it. "He forgetteth not the cry of the humble" (Psalm 9:12). True, He does not regard high looks and lofty words. He does not care for the pomp and pagentry of kings. He does not listen to the swell of martial music. He does not regard the triumph and pride of man; but wherever there is a heart big with sorrow, a lip quivering with agony, a deep groan or a penitential sigh, the heart of Jehovah is open. He marks it down in the registry of His memory. He puts our prayers, like rose leaves, between the pages of His book of remembrance, and when the volume is opened at last, there will be a precious fragrance springing up from it.

November 3
Evening

"Their prayer came up to his holy dwelling place, even unto heaven" (2 Chronicles 30:27).

Prayer is the never-failing resort of the Christian. When you cannot use your sword, you may take up the weapon of all-prayer. Your powder may be damp, your bowstring may be relaxed, but the weapon of all-prayer is never out of order. The enemy laughs at the javelin, but he trembles at prayer. Sword and spear need regular repairs, but prayer never rusts. When we think it is the most blunt, it cuts the best. Prayer is an open door which none can shut. Devils may surround you, but the way upward is always open. We can never be taken by blockade, ambush, mine, or storm, as long as heavenly assistance can come down to us to relieve us in the time of our need. Prayer is never out of season—in summer and in winter its results are precious. Prayer gains audience with heaven in the dead of night, in the midst of business, in the heat of noonday, and in the shades of evening. In every condition, whether of poverty, sickness, obscurity, slander, or doubt, your covenant God will welcome your prayer and answer it from His holy place. Prayer is never futile. True prayer is true power. You may not always get what you ask, but you will always have your true needs supplied. When God does not answer His children according to the letter, He does so according to the Spirit. If you ask for coarse grain, will you be angry because He gives you the finest flour? This evening, do not forget to make your request, for the Lord is ready to grant your desires.

November 4
Morning

"For my strength is made perfect in weakness"
(2 Corinthians 12:9).

A primary qualification for serving God with any amount of success is a sense of our own weakness. When God's warrior marches forth to battle boasting, "I know that I will conquer; my own right arm and my conquering sword will get me the victory," then defeat is not far away. God will not go forth with that man. He who reckons on victory in this way has reckoned wrongly, for "it is not by might, nor by power, but by my Spirit, saith the Lord of hosts" (Zechariah 4:6). They who go forth to fight, boasting of their prowess will return with their banners trailing in the dust and their armor stained with disgrace. Those who serve God must serve Him in His way and in His strength, or He will never accept their service. He casts away the mere fruits of the earth. He will only reap that seed sown from heaven, watered by grace, and ripened by the sun of divine love. God will empty out all that you have before He will put His own into you. The river of God is full of water, but not one drop of it flows from earthly springs. God will have no strength used in His battles but the strength which He Himself imparts. Are you mourning over your own weakness? Take courage, for there must be a consciousness of weakness before the Lord will give you victory. Your emptiness is but the preparation for your being filled, and your casting down is but the making ready for your lifting up.

November 4
Evening

"In thy light shall we see light" (Psalm 36:9).

No words can explain the love of Christ to the heart until Jesus Himself speaks within. Descriptions all fall flat and lifeless unless the Holy Spirit fills them with His power. Until our Emmanuel reveals Himself, the soul does not see Him. If you want to see the sun, would you take out a candle and search for it? No, the wise man knows that the sun must reveal itself, and only by its own blaze can that mighty lamp be seen. The same is true with Christ. "Blessed art thou, Simon Bar-jona," said He to Peter, "for flesh and blood hath not revealed it unto thee" (Matthew 16:17). Purify flesh and blood by any educational process you choose, elevate mental faculties to the highest degree of intellectual power, yet none of these can reveal Christ. The Spirit of God must come with power and overshadow the man with His wings. Then the Lord Jesus will reveal Himself to the sanctified eye. The great mass of this bleary-eyed world can see nothing of the magnificent glories of Emmanuel. He stands before them without form or beauty, a root out of a dry ground, rejected by the vain and despised by the proud. Only where the Spirit has touched the eye with eyesalve, filled the heart with divine life, and educated the soul to a heavenly taste, only there is He understood. "Unto you therefore which believe he is precious" (1 Peter 2:7). To you He is the chief cornerstone, the Rock of your salvation, your all in all; but to others He is "a stone of stumbling and a rock of offence" (1 Peter 2:8). O Jesus, our Lord, our heart is open. Come in, and never leave us.

November 5
Morning

"No weapon that is formed against thee shall prosper" (Isaiah 54:17).

Today is notable in English history for three great deliverances wrought by God for us. The first, in 1588, was the total destruction of the Spanish Armada by the breath of the Almighty. In 1605, on this day, the plot to destroy the House of Parliament was discovered. Today is also the anniversary of the landing of King William III at Torbay. Religious liberty was secured in 1688. This day ought to be celebrated by the songs of saints. Our Puritan forefathers most devoutly made it a special time of thanksgiving. There is a record of the annual sermons preached by Matthew Henry on this day. Our love of liberty should make us regard its anniversary with holy gratitude. Let our hearts and lips exclaim, "We have heard with our ears, and our fathers have told us, the wondrous things which You did in their day and in the old time before them." You have made this nation the home of the gospel. When the foe has risen against her, You have shielded her. Grant us more and more a hatred of evil and hasten the day of its entire extinction. We will stand on Your promise, "No weapon that is formed against thee shall prosper."

November 5
Evening

"Be thankful unto him, and bless his name"
(Psalm 100:4).

Jesus is not pleased that His brethren think of Him in a poor manner. It is His pleasure that His precious ones should be delighted with His beauty. We are not to regard Him as a bare necessity, like bread and water, but as a luxurious delicacy and a rare delight. He revealed Himself as the *pearl of great price* in its peerless beauty, as the *bundle of myrrh* in its refreshing fragrance, as the *rose of Sharon* in its lasting perfume, and as the *lily* in its spotless purity. Think how God esteems the only Begotten, His unspeakable gift to us. Consider what the angels think of Him, as they count it their highest honor to veil their faces at His feet. Consider what the redeemed think of Him, as they sing His well-deserved praises throughout the endless days. High thoughts of Christ will enable us to act consistently in our relationship with Him. The more loftily we see Christ enthroned and the more humble we are when bowing before the foot of the throne, the more truly we will be prepared to act our part toward Him. Our Lord Jesus desires us to think well of Him that we may submit cheerfully to His authority. High thoughts of Him increase our love. Love and esteem go together. Therefore, believer, think much of your Master's excellent greatness. Study Him in His heavenly glory, before He took upon Himself your nature. Think of the mighty love which drew Him from His throne to die upon the cross. Admire Him as He conquers all the powers of hell. See Him risen, crowned, and glorified. Bow before Him as the Wonderful, the Counselor, the mighty God, for only in this way will your love to Him be what it should.

November 6
Morning

"I will pour water upon him that is thirsty"
(Isaiah 44:3).

When a believer has fallen into a low, sad state of feeling, he often tries to lift himself out of it by chastening himself with dark and doleful fears. This is not the way to rise from the dust but to continue in it. It is not the law but the gospel which saves the seeking soul at first, and it is not a legal bondage but gospel liberty which can restore the fainting believer afterward. It is not fear that brings the backslider back to God but the sweet wooings of love allure him to Jesus' bosom. Are you thirsting for the living God this morning and unhappy because you cannot find Him to be the delight of your heart? Have you lost the joy of faith and is this your prayer, "Restore to me the joy of my salvation"? Are you conscious, also, that you are barren like the dry ground and that you are not bringing forth the fruit to God which He has a right to expect of you? Are you aware that you are not as useful in the Church or in the world as your heart desires to be? Then here is exactly the promise which you need: "I will pour water upon him that is thirsty." You will receive the grace you so much require, and you will have it to the utmost reach of your needs. Water refreshes the thirsty and quickens the sleeping plant life. Your life will be quickened and refreshed by fresh grace. Water swells the buds and makes the fruits ripen, and you will be made fruitful in the ways of God. Whatever good quality there is in divine grace, you will enjoy it to the full. All the riches of divine grace will be yours in plenty.

November 6
Evening

"Saying, This is the blood of the testament which God hath enjoined unto you" (Hebrews 9:20).

There is a strange power about the very name of blood, and the sight of it is always affecting. A kind heart cannot bear to see a sparrow bleed, and it turns away with horror at the slaughter of an animal. The blood of men is a consecrated thing. It is murder to shed it in wrath, and it is a dreadful crime to squander it in war. When we contemplate the blood of the Son of God, our awe is increased. We shudder as we think of the guilt of sin and the terrible penalty which the Sin-bearer endured. Blood, always precious, is priceless when it streams from Emmanuel's side. The blood of Jesus seals the *covenant* of grace and makes it forever sure. Covenants of old were made by sacrifice, and the everlasting covenant was ratified in the same manner. Oh, the delight of being saved upon the sure foundation of divine justification which cannot be dishonored! Salvation by the works of the law is a frail and broken vessel whose shipwreck is certain; but the covenant vessel fears no storms, for the blood insures it completely. The blood of Jesus made His *testament* valid. A will has no power unless the person who made it dies. In this way, the soldier's spear is a blessed aid to faith since it proved that our Lord was dead. Happy are those who see their title to heavenly blessings assured to them by a dying Savior. Does this blood call us to sanctify ourselves to Him by whom we have been redeemed? Does it call us to newness of life and incite us to entire consecration to the Lord? Oh that the power of the blood might be known and felt in us this night!

November 7
Morning

Behold, I have graven thee upon the palms of my hand" (Isaiah 49:16).

Zion said, "The Lord hath forsaken me, and my Lord hath forgotten me" (Isaiah 49:14). How amazed the divine mind seems to be at this wicked unbelief! What can be more astounding than the unfounded doubts and fears of God's favored people? The Lord's loving word of rebuke should make us blush. He cries, "How can I have forgotten thee, when I have graven thee upon the palms of My hands?" Unbelief is a strange marvel! God keeps His promise a thousand times, but the trial makes us doubt Him. He never fails. He is never a dry well. Yet, we are as continually vexed with anxieties, molested with suspicions, and disturbed with fears as if our God were the mirage of the desert. "Behold" is a word intended to excite admiration. Heaven and earth may well be astonished that rebels should obtain so great a nearness to the heart of infinite love as to be written on the palms of His hands. "I have graven *thee.*" It does not say, "thy name." The name is there, but that is not all: "I have graven *thee.*" Absorb the fullness of this! Everything about you and all that concerns you have I put there. Will you ever say again that your God has forsaken you, since He has graven *thee* on His own palms?

November 7
Evening

"And ye shall be witnesses unto me" (Acts 1:8).

In order to learn how to fulfill your duty as a witness for Christ, look at His example. He is always witnessing—by the well of Samaria or in the Temple of Jerusalem; by the lake of Gennesaret or on the mountain's brow. He is witnessing night and day. His mighty prayers are as vocal to God as His daily services. He witnesses under all circumstances. Scribes and Pharisees cannot shut His mouth; even before Pilate He witnesses the truth. He witnesses clearly and distinctly, and there is no mistake in Him. Christian, make your life a clear testimony. Let your heart's love for God and man be visible to all. You do not need to *say,* "I am true;" *be* true. Do not boast of integrity, but *be* upright. Your testimony will be such that men cannot help seeing it. Never, for fear of feeble man, restrain your witness. Your lips have been warmed with a coal from the altar. Let them speak as heaven-touched lips should. "In the morning sow thy seed, and in the evening withhold not thine hand" (Ecclesiastes 11:6). Witness for the Savior in season and out of season. If you endure suffering of any kind for Christ's sake and the gospel's, do not be discouraged. Rather, rejoice in the honor conferred upon you, that you are counted worthy to suffer for your Lord. Your sufferings, losses, and persecutions will make you a platform from which you shall witness for Christ Jesus more vigorously and with greater power. Study your great Example and be filled with His Spirit. Remember that you need much teaching, much prayer, much grace, and much humility if your witnessing is to be to your Master's glory.

November 8
Morning

"As ye have received Christ Jesus the Lord"
(Colossians 2:6).

The life of faith is represented as *receiving*. It is simply the acceptance of a gift. As the earth drinks in the rain, as the sea receives the streams, as night accepts light from the stars, so we, giving nothing, partake freely of the grace of God. The saints are not, by nature, wells or streams. They are but cisterns into which the living water flows. They are empty vessels into which God pours His salvation. One cannot very well receive a shadow. We receive that which is substantial. In the life of faith, Christ becomes real to us. While we are without faith, Jesus is a mere name to us—a person who lived a long while ago, so long ago that His life is only history to us now! By an act of faith, Jesus becomes a real person in the consciousness of our heart. But receiving also means getting possession of. The thing which I receive becomes my own. When I receive Jesus, He becomes *my* Savior, so much mine that neither life nor death will be able to rob me of Him. Salvation may be described as the blind receiving sight, the deaf receiving hearing, the dead receiving life; but we have not only received these blessings, we have received Christ Jesus Himself. It is true that He gave us life from the dead. He gave us pardon of sin; He gave us imputed righteousness. These are all precious things, but we are not content with them; we have received Christ Himself. The Son of God has been poured into us, and we have received Him. How full we must be, for heaven itself cannot contain Him!

November 8
Evening

"The Master saith, Where is the guestchamber, where I shall eat the passover with my disciples?" (Mark 14:14).

Jerusalem at the time of the Passover was one great gathering of humanity. Each household had invited guests for the holiday, but no one invited the Savior. It was by His supernatural power that He found an upper room in which to celebrate the feast. It is the same even to this day—Jesus is not received among the sons of men except where His supernatural power and grace prepare the heart. All doors are wide open to the prince of darkness, but Jesus must clear a way for Himself or lodge in the streets. We do not know the identity of the owner of the upper room, but he readily accepted the honor which the Redeemer proposed to confer upon him. It is still easy to see who are the Lord's chosen and who are not. When the gospel comes to some, they fight against it and want nothing to do with it. But where men receive it joyfully, it is a sure indication that there is a secret work going on in the soul and that God has chosen them for eternal life. Are you willing to receive Christ? Then no difficulty can stand in the way. Christ will be your guest. His own power is working with you, making you willing. What an honor to entertain the Son of God! The heavens cannot contain Him, and yet, He condescends to find a home within our hearts! We are not worthy for Him to come under our roof, but what an amazing privilege when He enters anyway! He makes a feast for us to enjoy with Him where the food gives immortality to those who eat it. Blessed is the one who entertains the Lord.

November 9
Morning

"So walk ye in him" (Colossians 2:6).

If we have received Christ Himself in our heart, our new life will manifest its intimate acquaintance with Him by a walk of faith in Him. Walking implies action. Our faith is not to be confined to our prayer closet. We must carry out into daily life that which we believe. If a man walks in Christ, he acts as Christ would act. Men will say of that man, "He is like his Master; he lives like Jesus Christ." Walking signifies progress. "So walk ye in him." Proceed from grace to grace, and run forward until you reach the uttermost degree of knowledge that a man can attain concerning our Beloved. There must be a perpetual abiding in Christ. Many Christians think that in the morning and evening they ought to come into the company of Jesus, but they give their heart to the world all day! This is poor living. We should always be with Him, treading in His steps and doing His will. Walking also implies habit. When we speak of a man's walk and conversation, we mean his habit. If we sometimes enjoy Christ and then later forget Him, sometimes call Him ours and later lose our hold, that is not a habit. We do not *walk* in Him. We must keep close to Him, cling to Him, and never let Him go. "As ye have received Christ Jesus the Lord, so walk ye in him." In the beginning Christ Jesus was the trust of your faith, the source of your life, the principle of your action, and the joy of your spirit. Let Him be the same until life's end.

November 9
Evening

"His place of defence shall be the munition of rocks: bread shall be given him; his waters shall be sure" (Isaiah 33:16).

Do you doubt whether God will fulfill His promise to you? Will the mountain of rock be carried away by a storm? Will the storehouse of heaven fail? Do you think that your heavenly Father, who knows your needs, will forget you? Not even a sparrow falls to the ground without your Father being aware of it, and the very hairs of your head are all numbered. (See Matthew 10:29-30.) Will you continue to mistrust and doubt Him? Many have been tried and tested until at last they have been driven, in sheer desperation, to exercise faith in God. The moment of their faith has been the instant of their deliverance. They have seen that God does keep His promises. Do not allow Satan to succeed in shaking your faith, and do not torment yourself by indulging those false thoughts of God any longer. It is not a small matter to doubt Jehovah. Remember, it is a *sin* in the highest degree. The angels never doubt Him and neither do the devils. We alone dishonor Him by unbelief and tarnish His honor by mistrust. God does not deserve to be suspected of a lack of care for His people. We have received many blessings of His love and kindness. It is inexcusable that we allow a doubt to remain within our heart. May we wage constant war against doubts of our God. They are the enemies to our peace and to His honor. With an unstaggering faith, let us believe that what He has promised, He will also perform. "Lord, I believe; help thou mine unbelief" (Mark 9:24).

"The eternal God is thy refuge" (Deuteronomy 33:27).

The word refuge may be translated "mansion" or "abiding-place." This gives the thought that God is our abode, our home. There is a fullness and sweetness in the metaphor, for dear to our heart is our home, although it may be the humblest cottage. Dearer still is our blessed God, in whom we live, move, and have our being. It is at home that we feel safe. We shut the world out and dwell in quiet security. So when we are with our God, we fear no evil. He is our shelter, our retreat, and our abiding refuge. It is at home we find rest after the fatigue and toil of the day. And so our hearts find rest in God, when, wearied with life's conflict, we turn to Him and our soul dwells at ease. So when we are with God, we can commune freely with Him, laying open all our hidden desires. If the secret of the Lord is with them that fear Him, the secrets of them that fear Him ought to be with their Lord. Home, too, is the place of our truest and purest happiness; and it is in God that our hearts find their deepest delight. We have joy in Him which far surpasses all other joy. It is also for home that we work and labor. The thought of it gives strength to bear the daily burden. We think of Him in the person of His dear Son, and a glimpse of the suffering face of the Redeemer constrains us to labor in His cause. We feel that we must work for we have brethren yet to be saved, and we have our Father's heart to make glad by bringing home His wandering sons. Happy are those who have the God of Jacob for their refuge!

November 10
Evening

"It is enough for the disciple that he be as his master" (Matthew 10:25).

No one will dispute this statement, for it would be wrong for the servant to be exalted above his Master. When our Lord was on earth, what treatment did He receive? "He is despised and rejected of men" (Isaiah 53:3). Outside the camp was His place; crossbearing was His occupation. Did the world give Him any comfort and rest? "Foxes have holes, and the birds of the air have nests; but the Son of man hath not where to lay his head" (Luke 9:58). This inhospitable country cast Him out and crucified Him. If you are a follower of Jesus and maintain a consistent, Christlike walk, you must expect that your spiritual life will come under the observation of men. They will treat you as they treated the Savior—they will despise you. Do not expect that the more holy and the more Christlike you are, the more respectfully people will act toward you. They did not prize the polished gem; how could they value the jewel in the rough? "If they have called the master of the house Beelzebub, how much more shall they call them of his household?" (Matthew 10:25). If we were more like Christ, we would be more hated by His enemies. It is a sad dishonor to a child of God to be the world's favorite. It is very dangerous to hear a wicked world clap its hands and shout, "Well done!" to the Christian. He should begin to look to his character and wonder what he has been doing wrong, when the unrighteous give him their approval. Let us be true to our Master and have no friendship with a blind and evil world which scorns and rejects Him. Far be it from us to seek a crown of honor where our Lord received a crown of thorns.

November 11
Morning

"Underneath are the everlasting arms" (Deuteronomy 33:27).

God—the eternal God—is our support at all times and especially when we are sinking in deep trouble. There are seasons when the Christian sinks very low in humiliation. Under a deep sense of his great sinfulness, he is humbled before God until he scarcely knows how to pray. He appears, in his own sight, so worthless. Child of God, remember that when you are at your lowest point, underneath you are the everlasting arms of the Lord. Sin may drag you low, but Christ's great atonement is still under all. You may have descended into deep distress, but you cannot have fallen so low that He cannot save you. If every earthly prop is cut away, what then? Still underneath you are the everlasting arms. You cannot fall so deep in distress and affliction but what the covenant of grace of an ever-faithful God will still encircle you. The Christian may be sinking under trouble from within through fierce conflict, but even then he cannot be brought so low as to be beyond the reach of the everlasting arms—they are underneath him. While thus sustained, all Satan's efforts to harm avail nothing. This assurance of support is a comfort to any weary but earnest worker in the service of God. It implies a promise of strength for each day, grace for each need, and power for each duty. And, further, when death comes, the promise will still hold good. When we stand in the midst of Jordan, we will be able to say with David, "I will fear no evil, for You are with me."

November 11
Evening

"He shall choose our inheritance for us"
(Psalm 47:4).

Believer, if your inheritance is a small one, you should be satisfied with your earthly portion. You may rest assured that it is the best for you. Perfect wisdom ordained your circumstances and selected for you the safest and best condition. Suppose a huge merchant ship must be brought up the river. In one part of the stream there is a sandbank. If someone asks, "Why does the captain steer through the deep part of the channel and deviate so much from a straight line?" his answer would be, "Because I would not get my vessel into harbor at all if I did not keep to the deep channel." Perhaps you would run aground and suffer shipwreck if your divine Captain did not steer you from the sandbank of affliction, where waves of trouble follow each other in quick succession. It may be that you are planted where you get little sunshine, but you are put there by the loving Gardener because only in that situation will you bring forth fruit. Had any other condition been better for you than the one in which you are, divine love would have put you there. You are placed by God in the most suitable circumstances. If you had to choose, you would soon cry, "Lord, choose my inheritance for me, for by my self-will I am pierced through with many sorrows." Be content with the things that you have, since the Lord has ordered all things for your good. Take up your own daily cross. It is the burden best suited for your shoulder and will prove most effective to make you perfect in every good work to the glory of God.

November 12
Morning

"The trial of your faith" (1 Peter 1:7).

Faith untried may be true faith, but it is sure to be little faith. It is likely to remain stunted as long as it is without trials. Faith never prospers as well as when all things are against her. Tempests are her trainers, and lightnings are her illuminators. When calm reigns on the sea, spread the sails as you will, the ship will not move to its harbor. But let the howling winds rush forth and rock the vessel until her deck is washed with waves and her mast sways under the pressure of the full and swelling sail. It is then that she makes headway toward her desired haven. No faith is so precious as that which lives and triumphs in adversity. You could not have believed your own weakness had you not been compelled to pass through the rivers. You would never have known God's strength had you not been supported amid the flood waters. Faith increases in solidity, assurance, and intensity the more it is exercised with tribulation. Faith is precious, and its trial is precious too. Do not let this discourage those who are young in faith. You will have trials enough without seeking them. The full portion will be measured out to you in due season. Meanwhile, if you cannot yet claim the result of long experience, thank God for what grace you have. Praise Him for that degree of holy confidence that you have attained. Walk according to that rule, and you will have more and more of the blessing of God until your faith will remove mountains and conquer impossibilities.

November 12
Evening

"And it came to pass in those days, that he went out into a mountain to pray, and continued all night in prayer to God" (Luke 6:12).

If anyone could have lived without prayer, it was our spotless, perfect Lord. Yet, no one was in supplication as often as He! His love for His Father was so great that He loved to be in constant communion with Him. His love for His people was so strong that He desired to be in constant intercession for them. The prayerfulness of Jesus is a lesson for us. The time He chose was admirable. It was evening, the hour of silence, when the crowd would not disturb Him. It was a time of inactivity when everyone but Jesus ceased to labor. While slumber made men forget their woes and cease coming to Him for relief, He interceded for them. While others found rest in sleep, He refreshed Himself with prayer. The place was also well selected. He was alone where none would intrude, and none could observe. Those dark and silent hills were a perfect prayer closet for the Son of God. Heaven and earth in midnight stillness heard the groans and sighs of the mysterious Being in whom both worlds were blended. The continuance of His pleadings is remarkable. The long night was not too long for Him. The cold wind did not chill His devotions. The grim darkness did not darken His faith or loneliness check His intercession. The occasion for this prayer is notable—it was after His enemies had been enraged. Prayer was His refuge and solace. He prayed before He chose the twelve apostles. Prayer was the herald of His new work. We should learn from Jesus to resort to special prayer when we are under trial or when we contemplate fresh endeavors for the Master's glory. Lord Jesus, teach us to pray.

November 13
Morning

"The branch cannot bear fruit of itself" (John 15:4).

How did you begin to bear fruit? It was when you came to Jesus and cast yourself on His great atonement and rested on His finished righteousness. Do you remember those early days? Have you declined since then? If you have, we charge you to remember that time of love. Repent and do your first works. Be involved in those activities which draw you nearest to Christ, because it is from Him that all your fruits proceed. Any holy exercise which will bring you to Him will help you to bear fruit. The sun is, no doubt, a great worker in creating fruit among the trees of the orchard; and Jesus is still more so among the trees of His garden of grace. When have you been the most fruitless? Has it not been when you lived farthest from the Lord Jesus Christ, when you slackened in prayer, when you departed from the simplicity of your faith, or when your graces engrossed your attention instead of your Lord? Have you forgotten where your strength dwells? We are taught, by past experience, that the more simply we depend on the grace of God in Christ and wait on the Holy Spirit, the more we will bring forth fruit. Trust Jesus for fruit as well as for life!

November 13
Evening

"Men ought always to pray" (Luke 18:1).

If *men* should always pray and not faint, much more should *Christian men* pray. Jesus sent His Church into the world on the same mission which He came, and this mission includes intercession. The Church is the world's priest. The door of grace is always open for her petitions, and they never return empty-handed. The veil of the temple was torn *for her,* the blood was sprinkled upon the altar *for her,* God constantly invites *her* to ask what she wills. Will she refuse the privilege which angels envy? She may go to her King at every hour. Will she allow the precious privilege to be unused? The Church always has need for prayer. There are always some in her midst who are falling into sin. There are lambs to be prayed for, that they may be carried in Christ's bosom; the strong, lest they grow presumptuous, and the weak, lest they despair. If we kept up prayer meetings twenty-four hours in the day, all the days in the year, we would never be without a special subject for supplication. Are we ever without the sick and the poor, the afflicted and the wavering? Are we ever without those who seek the conversion of relatives, the reclaiming of backsliders, or the salvation of the depraved? Congregations constantly gather, ministers preach, and millions of sinners lie dead in trespasses and sins. In a world full of idols, cruelties, and evil, if the Church does not pray, how will she excuse her neglect of the commission of her loving Lord? Let the Church be constant in supplication, and let every believer cast his mite of prayer into the treasury.

November 14
Morning

"I will cut off them that worship and that swear by the Lord, and that swear by Malcham" (Zephaniah 1:5).

Such persons thought themselves safe because they were with both parties. They went with the followers of Jehovah and bowed at the same time to Malcham. But duplicity is abominable with God. In the common matters of daily life, a double-minded man is despised, but in Christianity he is loathsome to the last degree. The penalty pronounced in the verse before us is terrible, but it is well-deserved. How could divine justice spare the sinner, who knows the right, approves it, professes to follow it, and all the while loves evil and gives it dominion in his heart? My soul, search yourself this morning and see whether you are guilty of double-dealing. You profess to be a follower of Jesus—do you truly love Him? Is your heart right with God? To have one foot on the land of truth and another on the sea of falsehood will involve a terrible fall and a total ruin. Christ will be all or nothing. God fills the whole universe; therefore, there is no room for another god. If He reigns in your heart, there will be no space for another reigning power. Do you rest alone on Jesus and live for Him alone? Is it your desire to do so? If so, blessed be the mighty grace which has led you to salvation. If not so, O Lord, pardon this sad offense.

November 14
Evening

"And Laban said, It must not be so done in our country, to give the younger before the first-born" (Genesis 29:26).

We do not excuse Laban for his dishonesty, but we can learn from the custom he quoted as his excuse. Some things must be taken in order. The second may be more lovely in our eyes, but the rule of the heavenly Kingdom must stand, and the elder must be married first. For instance, many men desire the beautiful Rachel of joy and peace, but they must first be wedded to the tender-eyed Leah of repentance. Everyone falls in love with happiness and would cheerfully serve many years to enjoy it, but according to the rule of the Lord's Kingdom, the Leah of true holiness must be loved by our soul before the Rachel of happiness can be attained. The cross must be carried before the crown can be worn. We must follow our Lord in His humiliation, or we will never rest with Him in glory. What is your response to this? Are you so vain as to hope to break through the heavenly rule? Do you hope for reward without labor or honor, without toil? Dismiss the idle expectation and be content to take the difficult things for the sake of the sweet love of Jesus, which will reward you for all. In a spirit of laboring and suffering, you will find that bitter things grow sweet and hard things become easy. Like Jacob, your years of service will seem like a few days because of your love for Jesus. When the hour of the wedding feast comes, all your toils will be as though they had never been—an hour with Jesus will make up for ages of pain and labor.

November 15
Morning

"The Lord's portion is his people" (Deuteronomy 32:9).

How are they His? By His own sovereign choice. He chose them and set His love on them. He did this altogether apart from any goodness in them at the time or any goodness which He foresaw in them. He had mercy on whom He would have mercy and ordained a chosen company unto eternal life; thus, they are His by His unconstrained election. They are not only His by choice but by purchase. He has bought and paid for them to the last cent. There can be no dispute about His title. The Lord's portion has been fully redeemed, not with corruptible things, as with silver and gold, but with the precious blood of the Lord Jesus Christ. There is no mortgage on His estate. There are no suits that can be raised by opposing claimants. The price was paid in open court, and the Church is the Lord's forever. See the blood-mark on all the chosen. It is invisible to the human eye but known to Christ, for the Lord knows them that are His. He forgets none of those whom He has redeemed from among men. He counts the sheep for whom He laid down His life and remembers well the Church for which He gave Himself. They are also His by conquest. What a battle He had in us before we were won! How long He laid siege to our hearts! We had barred our gates and fenced our walls against Him. But we have become the conquered captives of His omnipotent love. Thus chosen, purchased, and subdued, the rights of our divine Possessor are inalienable. We rejoice that we never can be our own. We desire, day by day, to do His will and to show forth His glory.

November 15
Evening

"Strengthen, O God, that which thou hast wrought for us" (Psalm 68:28).

Our wisdom, as well as our need, asks God continually to strengthen that which He has wrought in us. Because of neglect in this, many Christians blame themselves for trials and afflictions of spirit which arise from unbelief. Satan seeks to flood the garden of the heart and make it a scene of desolation. But many Christians leave the gates open and let in the dreadful deluge through carelessness and lack of prayer. We often forget that the Author of our faith must be the Preserver of it also. The lamp which was burning in the temple was never allowed to go out, but it had to be daily replenished with fresh oil. Likewise, our faith can only live by being sustained with the oil of grace, and we can only obtain this from God Himself. He who built the world upholds it, or it would fall in one tremendous crash. He who made us Christians must maintain us by His Spirit, or our ruin will be speedy and final. Let us go to our Lord evening by evening for the grace and strength we need. We have a strong argument to plead, for it is *His own work of grace* which we ask Him to strengthen. Do you think He will fail to protect and sustain His work? Let your faith take hold of His strength, and all the powers of darkness, led on by the master fiend of hell, cannot cast a shadow over your joy and peace. Why faint when you may be strong? Why suffer defeat when you may conquer? Take your wavering faith and drooping spirit to Him who can revive and replenish them.

November 16
Morning

"The Lord is my portion, saith my soul" (Lamentations 3:24).

It is not, "The Lord is *partly* my portion" or "The Lord is *in* my portion;" but He Himself makes up the sum total of my soul's inheritance. Within the circumference of that circle lies all that we possess or desire. The Lord is my portion, not His grace or His love or His covenant, but Jehovah Himself. He has chosen us for His portion, and we have chosen Him for ours. It is true that the Lord must first choose us, or else we would never choose Him for ourselves. The Lord is our all-sufficient portion. It is not easy to satisfy man's desires. But all that we can wish for is to be found in our divine portion, so that we ask, "Whom have I in heaven but thee? and there is none upon earth that I desire beside thee" (Psalm 73:25). Well may we delight ourselves in the Lord who makes us drink of the river of His pleasures. Our faith stretches its wings and mounts like an eagle into the heaven of divine love as its proper dwelling place. "The lines are fallen unto me in pleasant places; yea, I have a goodly heritage" (Psalm 16:6). Let us rejoice in the Lord always. Let us show to the world that we are a happy and blessed people, and thus induce them to exclaim, "We will go with you: for we have heard that God is with you" (Zechariah 8:23).

November 16
Evening

"Thine eyes shall see the king in his beauty" (Isaiah 33:17).

The more you know about Christ, the less will you be satisfied with superficial views of Him. The more deeply you study His work in the eternal covenant, His operation on your behalf as the eternal Surety, and the fullness of His grace which shines in all His offices, the more truly will you see the King in His beauty. Let your greatest desire be to see Jesus. Meditation and contemplation are often like windows of agate and gates of carbuncle, through which we behold the Redeemer. Meditation puts the telescope to the eye and enables us to see Jesus in a better way than we could have seen Him if we had lived in the days of His flesh. With more meditation, the beauty of the King would flash upon us with more resplendence. Beloved, we probably will have such a sight of our glorious King after we die. Many saints who were near death looked up from the stormy waters and saw Jesus walking on the waves of the sea. They heard Him say, "It is I, be not afraid." When the house begins to shake, and the clay falls away, we see Christ through the beams, and the sunlight of heaven comes streaming in. But if we want to see the King in His beauty face to face, we must go to heaven for the sight, or the King must come here in person. Oh, that He would come on the wings of the wind! He is our Husband, and we are widowed by His absence; He is our Brother dear and fair, and we are lonely without Him. Thick veils and clouds hang between our souls and their true life. When will the day break and the shadows flee away?

November 17
Morning

"To whom be glory forever. Amen" (Romans 11:36).

This should be the single desire of the Christian. All other wishes must be subservient to this one. The Christian may wish for prosperity in his business but only so far as it may help him to promote this—"To Him be glory forever." He may desire to attain more gifts and more graces, but it should only be for His glory. You are not acting as you should if you are moved by any other motive than a single eye to your Lord's glory. As a Christian, let this ambition fire your soul. Make God your only object. Depend on it. Where self begins, sorrow also begins. Let your desire for God's glory be a growing desire. You blessed Him in your youth, but do not be content with such praises as you gave Him then. Has God prospered you in business? Give Him more because He has given you more. Has God given you experience? Praise Him by stronger faith than you exercised at first. Is your knowledge growing? Then sing more sweetly. Do you enjoy happier times than you once had? Have you been restored from sickness, and has your sorrow been turned into peace and joy? Then give Him more music. Give honor to your great and gracious Lord by your own individual service and increasing holiness.

November 17
Evening

"He that cleaveth wood shall be endangered thereby" (Ecclesiastes 10:9).

Oppressors may have their way with poor and needy men as easily as they can split logs of wood; but they are in a dangerous business—a splinter from a tree has often killed the woodman. Jesus is persecuted in every injured saint, and He is mighty to avenge His beloved ones. Success in treading down the poor and needy is a thing to fear. If there is no danger to persecutors here, there will be great danger hereafter. There are also dangers connected with your calling and daily life of which you should be aware. These are not hazards by flood or by disease and sudden death, but perils of a spiritual sort. Your occupation may be as humble as log-splitting, and yet the devil can tempt you in it. You may be a domestic servant, a farm laborer, or a mechanic, and you may be screened from serious temptations. Yet, some secret sin may do you damage. Those who stay at home and do not mingle with the rough world may be endangered by their very seclusion. Pride may enter a poor man's heart; greed may reign in a pauper's bosom; uncleanness may venture into the quietest home; and anger, envy, and malice may push themselves into the most rural abode. Even in speaking a few words to a servant we may sin; a little purchase at a shop may be the first link in a chain of temptations; the mere looking out of a window may be the beginning of evil. O Lord, how exposed we are! How can we be secure? Only You are able to preserve us in such a world of evils. Spread Your wings over us, and we will cower beneath You and feel safe.

November 18
Morning

"A spring shut up, a fountain sealed" (Song of Solomon 4:12).

In this metaphor, which has reference to the inner life of a believer, the idea of *secrecy* is very plain. It is a spring shut up. There were springs in the Middle East over which an edifice was built so that none could reach them except those who knew the secret entrance. Such is the heart of a believer when it is renewed by grace. There is a mysterious life within which no human skill can touch. The Scripture includes not only secrecy but *separation*. It is not the common spring of which every passerby may drink. It is one kept and preserved from all others. It is a fountain bearing a particular mark—a king's royal seal—so that all can perceive that it is not a common fountain but a fountain owned by a proprietor. So it is with the spiritual life. The chosen of God were separated by God in the day of redemption to possess a life which others do not have. It is impossible for the redeemed to feel at home with the world or to delight in its pleasures. There is also the idea of *sacredness*. The spring shut up is preserved for the use of some special person. The Christian's heart is a spring kept for Jesus. Every Christian should feel that he has God's seal on him. He should be able to say like Paul, "From henceforth let no man trouble me, for I bear in my body the marks of the Lord Jesus" (Galatians 6:17).

November 18
Evening

"Thou art from everlasting" (Psalm 93:2).

Christ is everlasting. We may sing with David, "Thy throne, O God, is for ever and ever" (Psalm 45:6). Rejoice in Jesus Christ who is the same yesterday, today, and forever. (See Hebrews 13:8.) Jesus always *was.* The Babe born in Bethlehem was one with the Word, which was in the beginning, by whom all things were made. Christ revealed Himself to John on Patmos, "The Lord, which is, and which was, and which is to come" (Revelation 1:8). If He was not God from everlasting, we could not feel that He had any share in the eternal love which is the fountain of all covenant blessings. But since He was from all eternity with the Father, we trace the stream of divine love to Him along with His Father and the blessed Spirit. As our Lord always *was,* so also He *is* forever. Jesus is not dead. "He ever liveth to make intercession for them" (Hebrews 7:25). Turn to Him in all your times of need, for He is waiting to bless you. Moreover, Jesus our Lord ever *shall be.* If God blesses you with a long life, you will find that the Priest who filled the healing fount with His own blood lives to purge you from all iniquity. When your last battle remains to be fought, you will find that the hand of your conquering Captain has not grown feeble—the living Savior will cheer the dying saint. When you enter heaven, He will bear the dew of His youth. Through eternity, the Lord Jesus will remain the perennial spring of joy, life, and glory to His people. Draw the living waters from this sacred well! Jesus always was, He always is, and He always will be. All His attributes and all His might are combined in His willingness to bless, comfort, guard, and crown His chosen people.

November 19
Morning

"Avoid foolish questions" (Titus 3:9).

Our days are few and are far better spent in doing good than in disputing over matters which are of minor importance. Our churches suffer from petty wars over absurd points and unimportant questions. After everything has been said that can be said, neither party is any wiser. Therefore, the discussion no more promotes knowledge than love. Questions on points wherein Scripture is silent, on mysteries which belong to God alone, on prophecies of doubtful interpretation, and on mere modes of observing human ceremonies are all foolish; and wise men avoid them. Our business is neither to ask nor answer foolish questions, but to avoid them altogether. There are, however, some questions, which we must not avoid but fairly and honestly answer such as these: Do I believe in the Lord Jesus Christ? Am I renewed in the spirit of my mind? Am I walking, not after the flesh, but after the Spirit? Am I growing in grace? Does my conversation adorn the doctrine of God my Savior? Am I looking for the coming of the Lord and watching as a servant should do who expects his master? What more can I do for Jesus? Such inquiries as these urgently demand our attention. Let us be peacemakers and endeavor to lead others, both by our precept and example, to "avoid foolish questions."

November 19
Evening

"Oh that I knew where I might find him!" (Job 23:3).

In Job's severe affliction, he cried out to the Lord. The greatest desire of the troubled child of God is to see his Father's face. His first prayer is not, "Oh, that I might be healed of the disease," or even "Oh, that I might see my children restored from the grave, and my property returned!" The first and uppermost cry is, "Oh that I knew where I might find *Him,* who is my God! that I might come to His throne!" God's children run home when the storm comes. It is the heaven-born instinct of a redeemed soul to seek shelter from all adversity beneath the wings of Jehovah. *He whose refuge is God* could serve as the title of a true believer. A hypocrite resents the affliction and runs from the Master. He says with bitter pride, "I can handle my own problems!" Job's desire to commune with God was intensified by the failure of all other sources of consolation. He turned away from his miserable friends and looked up to the celestial throne, just as a traveler turns from his empty canteen and runs to the well. He bids farewell to earth-born hopes and cries, "Oh that I knew where I might find my God!" Nothing teaches us the preciousness of the Creator as when we learn the emptiness of everything else. Turning away with scorn from earth's hives where we find no honey but many sharp stings, we rejoice in Him whose faithful word is sweeter than honey. In every trouble we should first realize God's presence with us. If we can enjoy His smile, we can bear our daily cross with a willing heart.

November 20
Morning

"O Lord, thou hast pleaded the causes of my soul" (Lamentations 3:58).

Observe how positively the prophet speaks. He does not say, "I hope that God has pleaded the causes of my soul." He speaks of it as a matter of fact not to be disputed. Let us, by the aid of the gracious Comforter, shake off those doubts and fears which so often mar our peace and comfort. Notice how gratefully the prophet speaks, ascribing all the glory to God alone! There is not a word concerning himself or his own pleadings. He does not ascribe his deliverance in any measure to any man, much less to his own merit. But he says, "O Lord, *thou* hast pleaded the causes of my soul; *thou* hast redeemed my life." A grateful spirit should be cultivated by the Christian. Earth should be a temple filled with the songs of grateful saints, and every day should be a smoking censer filled with the sweet incense of thanksgiving. How joyful Jeremiah seems to be while he records the Lord's mercy! How triumphantly he lifts up the strain! He has been in the low dungeon and is the weeping prophet. We hear the voice of Jeremiah going up to heaven, "Thou hast pleaded the causes of my soul; thou hast redeemed my life." Children of God, seek after a vital experience of the Lord's lovingkindness. When you have it, speak positively of it, sing gratefully, and shout triumphantly.

November 20
Evening

"The conies are but a feeble folk, yet make they their houses in the rocks" (Proverbs 30:26).

Conscious of their own natural weakness, the conies, or rock badgers, resort to burrows in the rocks and are secure from their enemies. My heart, be willing to receive a lesson from these feeble folk. You are as weak and as exposed to peril as the timid cony; be just as wise to seek a shelter. My security is within the fortress of an unchangeable Jehovah, where His promises stand like giant walls of rock. Always hide in the protection of His glorious attributes, all of which are guarantees of safety for those who put their trust in Him. Long ago, when Satan and my sins pursued me, I fled to the cleft of the Rock, Christ Jesus, and in His pierced side I found a delightful resting place. My heart, run to Him anew tonight, whatever your present grief may be. Jesus feels for you; He will console you and help you. No king in his impregnable fortress is more secure than the cony in his rocky burrow. The master of ten thousand chariots is no better protected than the little dweller in the mountain's cleft. In Jesus, the weak are strong, and the defenseless are safe. They could not be stronger if they were giants or safer if they were in heaven. Faith gives men on earth the protection of the God of heaven. The conies cannot build a castle, but they use what is there already. I cannot make myself a refuge, but Jesus has provided it, His Father has given it, and His Spirit has revealed it. I enter it tonight, and I am safe from every foe.

November 21
Morning

"Grieve not the Holy Spirit" (Ephesians 4:30).

All that the believer has comes from Christ. Moreover, as all the blessings flow to you through the Holy Spirit, so also no good thing can come out of you apart from the sanctifying operation of the same Spirit. Even if the good seed is sown in you, it lies dormant until He works in you. Do you desire to speak for Jesus? How can you unless the Holy Spirit touches your tongue? Do you desire to pray? Alas! What dull work it is unless the Spirit makes intercession for you! Do you desire to subdue sin? Would you be holy? Would you imitate your Master? Do you desire to rise to superlative heights of spirituality? Are you wanting to be made, like the angels of God, full of zeal and ardor for the Master's cause? You cannot without the Spirit—"Without me ye can do nothing" (John 15:5). Branch of the vine, you can have no fruit without the sap! Child of God, you have no life within you apart from the life which God gives you through His Spirit! Then let us not grieve Him or provoke Him to anger by our sin. Let us not quench Him in one of His faintest motions in our soul. Be ready to obey every prompting of the Holy Spirit. Let us attempt nothing without Him. Let us depend on Him alone. May this be our prayer, "Open my heart and my whole being to Your incoming, and uphold me with Your free Spirit when I have received that Spirit in my inward parts."

*"Lazarus was one of them that sat at the table
with him"* (John 12:2).

He is to be envied. It was well to be Martha and
serve, but better to be Lazarus and commune.
There are times for each purpose, and each is
beautiful in its season, but none of the trees of the
garden yield such sweet clusters as the vine of
fellowship. To sit with Jesus, to hear His words, to
see His actions, and receive His smiles, was such a
blessing that it must have made Lazarus as happy
as the angels. When it has been our privilege to
feast with our Beloved in His banquet hall, we
would not have given half a sigh for all the kingdoms of the world. *He is to be imitated.* It would
have been a strange thing if Lazarus had not been
at the table where Jesus was, for Jesus raised him
from the dead. We, too, were once dead and like
Lazarus, stinking in the grave of sin. Jesus raised
us, and by His life we live. Can we be content to
live at a distance from Him? Do we fail to remember Him at His table, where He comes to feast with
His brethren? We must repent and do as He commanded us, for His slightest wish should be law to
us. To have lived without constant communion
with one of whom the Jews said, "Behold how he
loved him" (John 11:36) would have been dis-
graceful to Lazarus. Is it excusable in us whom
Jesus has loved with an everlasting love? To have
been cold to Him who wept over his lifeless
corpse would have displayed great ingratitude in
Lazarus. What does it show in us, over whom the
Savior has not only wept, but bled? Come brethren, let us return to our heavenly Bridegroom and
ask that we may have closer intimacy with Him.

"Israel served for a wife, and for a wife he kept sheep" (Hosea 12:12).

Jacob, while reasoning with Laban, describes his own toil: "This twenty years have I been with you. That which was torn of beasts I brought not unto you: I bare the loss of it; of my hand you did require it, whether stolen by day, or stolen by night. Thus I was: in the day the drought consumed me, and the frost by night; and my sleep departed from mine eyes" (Genesis 31:38). Even more toilsome than this was the life of our Savior here below. He watched over all His sheep until He gave as His last account, "Those that thou gavest me, I have kept, and none of them is lost" (John 17:12). His hair was wet with dew, and sleep departed from his eyes. He was in prayer all night, wrestling for His people. No shepherd sitting beneath the cold skies could ever utter such complaints as Jesus Christ might have, if He had chosen to do so, because of the sternness of His service in order to procure His spouse. It is sweet to dwell on the spiritual parallel of Laban having required all the sheep at Jacob's hand. If they were torn of beasts, Jacob must make it good. If any of them died, he must stand as surety for the whole. Was not the toil of Jesus for His Church the toil of one who was under suretyship obligations to bring every believing one safe to the hand of Him who had committed them to His charge? Look on toiling Jacob, and you see a representation of Him of whom we read, "He shall feed his flock like a shepherd" (Isaiah 40:11).

November 22
Evening

"The power of his resurrection" (Philippians 3:10).

The resurrection of Jesus is the cornerstone of the entire building of Christianity. It is the keystone of the arch of our salvation. It would take a volume to analyze all the streams of living water which flow from this one sacred source—the resurrection of our dear Lord and Savior Jesus Christ. But communing with the risen Savior by possessing a risen life and seeing Him leave the tomb by leaving the tomb of worldliness ourselves—this is even more precious. The doctrine is the basis of the experience, but as the flower is more lovely than the root, so is the experience of fellowship with the risen Savior more lovely than the doctrine itself. Believe that Christ rose from the dead, sing of it, and derive all the consolation which it is possible for you to extract from this well-documented and well-witnessed fact. Though you cannot see Him visibly, you can see Christ Jesus by the eye of faith. Though you may not touch Him, you are privileged to converse with Him and to know that He is risen, as you are raised in Him to newness of life. To know a crucified Savior who crucified all my sins is a high degree of knowledge. But to know a risen Savior who justified me, and to realize that He has given me new life by making me a new creature through His own newness of life is a noble experience. No one should be satisfied with anything less. May you "know him, and the power of his resurrection."

November 23
Morning

"Fellowship with him" (1 John 1:6).

When we were united by faith to Christ, we were brought into such complete fellowship with Him that we were made one with Him. His interests and our interests became mutual and identical. We have fellowship with Christ in His *love*. What He loves, we love. He loves the saints—so do we. He loves sinners—so do we. We have fellowship with Him in His *desires*. He desires the glory of God—we also labor for the same. He desires that the saints may be with Him where He is—we desire to be with Him there too. He desires to drive out sin—behold, we fight under His banner. He desires that His Father's name may be loved and adored by all His creatures—we pray daily, "Let Thy kingdom come, and Thy will be done on earth, even as it is in heaven." We have fellowship with Christ in His *sufferings*. We are not nailed to His cross to die a cruel death; but when He is reproached, we are reproached. We have fellowship with Him in His *labors*. We are to minister to men the Word of truth. Our meat and drink, like His, is to do the will of Him who has sent us and to finish His work. We also have fellowship with Christ in His *joys*. We are happy in His happiness, we rejoice in His exaltation. Have you ever tasted that joy, believer? There is no purer or more thrilling delight to be known this side of heaven than that of having Christ's joy fulfilled in us.

November 23
Evening

"Get thee up into the high mountain" (Isaiah 40:9).

Each believer should be thirsting for the living God and longing to see Him face to face. We should not be content to rest in the mists of the valley when the mountaintop awaits us. My soul thirsts to drink deeply of the cup which is reserved for those who reach the mountain's peak. How pure are the dews of the hills, how fresh is the mountain air, how rich the food of the mountain dwellers whose windows look into the New Jerusalem! Many saints are content to live like men in coal mines who do not see the sun. They eat dust like the serpent when they could taste the luscious meat of angels. They are content to wear the miner's garb when they could put on king's robes. Tears mar their faces when they could anoint them with celestial oil. Many believers weep in a dungeon when they could walk on the palace roof and view the beautiful land of Lebanon. Awaken, O believer, from your low condition! Cast away your laziness, coldness, or whatever interferes with your pure love for Christ, your soul's Husband. Make Him the source and the center of your soul's delight. What draws you into such foolishness that you remain in a pit when you may sit on a throne? Do not live in the lowlands of bondage now that a mountain of liberty is given to you. No longer be satisfied with earthly accomplishments, but press forward to heavenly things. Aspire to a higher, nobler, and fuller life. Upward to heaven! Nearer to God!

November 24
Morning

"The glorious Lord will be unto us a place of broad rivers and streams" (Isaiah 33:21).

Broad rivers and streams produce fertility and abundance in the land. Places near broad rivers are remarkable for the variety of their plants and their plentiful harvests. God is all this to His Church. Having God she has abundance. What can she ask for that He will not supply? "In the mountain shall the Lord of Hosts make unto all people a feast of fat things" (Isaiah 25:6). If you suffer any lack, it is your own fault. Broad rivers and streams also point to commerce. Our glorious Lord is to us a place of heavenly merchandise. Through our Redeemer we have commerce with the past. The wealth of Calvary, the treasures of the covenant, the riches of the ancient days of election, and the stores of eternity all come to us down the broad stream of our gracious Lord. We have commerce, too, with the future. What bounties and blessings come to us from the millennium! What visions we have of the days of heaven on earth! Through our glorious Lord we have commerce with angels. Better still, we have fellowship with the Infinite One. Broad rivers and streams are especially intended to set forth the idea of security. Rivers were a defense in the past. Oh, beloved, what a defense is God to His Church! The devil cannot cross this broad river of God. How he wishes he could turn the current. But fear not, for God abides immutably the same, and Satan cannot destroy us.

November 24
Evening

"Yet a little sleep, a little slumber, a little fold-ing of the hands to sleep: So shall thy poverty come as one that travelleth; and thy want as an armed man" (Proverbs 24:33-34).

The worst of sluggards only ask for a little slum-ber. They would be indignant if they were accused of total idleness. A little folding of the hands to sleep is all they crave, and they have a list of reasons to show that this indulgence is a very proper one. Yet, by these little rests, the day fades out, the time for labor is gone, and the field is overgrown with thorns. It is by little procrastina-tion that men ruin their souls. They have no inten-tion to delay for years—a few months will bring the more convenient time. Tomorrow they will attend to serious things. But like sands from an hourglass, time passes, life is wasted by drops, and seasons of grace are lost by little slumbers. May the Lord teach us this sacred wisdom, for other-wise a poverty of the worst sort awaits us—eternal poverty where we will beg for a mere drop of water in vain. Like a traveler steadily pursuing his journey, poverty overtakes the lazy, and ruin over-throws the undecided. Each hour brings the dreaded pursuer nearer. He does not pause by the way, for he is on his master's business and must not delay. As an armed man enters with authority and power, so want will come to the idle and death to the unrepentant. There will be no escape. Seek the Lord Jesus diligently before the solemn day dawns when it will be too late to plow and sow, too late to repent and believe. In harvest, it is useless to complain that the seed time was neglected. Faith and holy decision are available now. May we obtain them this night.

November 25
Morning

"To preach deliverance to the captives" (Luke 4:18).

None but Jesus can give deliverance to the captives. Real liberty comes from Him only. It is a liberty righteously bestowed for the Son, who is Heir of all things, has a right to make men free. It is a liberty which has been dearly purchased by His blood. He makes you free, but it is by His own bonds. You go clear, because He bore your burden for you. You are set at liberty, because He has suffered freely in your place. Jesus asks nothing of us as a preparation for this liberty. He finds us sitting in sackcloth and ashes and bids us put on the beautiful array of freedom. He saves us just as we are and without our help or merit. Satan may plot to enslave us, but if the Lord is on our side, whom will we fear? The world, with its temptations, may seek to ensnare us, but mightier is He who is for us than all they who are against us. Our own deceitful hearts may harass and annoy us, but He who has begun the good work in us will carry it on and perfect it to the end. If we are no more under the law, but free from its curse, let our liberty be practically exhibited in our serving God with gratitude and delight. "I am thy servant, and the son of thine handmaid: thou hast loosed my bonds" (Psalm 116:16). Lord, what will You have me to do?

November 25
Evening

"For he saith to Moses, I will have mercy on whom I will have mercy, and I will have compassion on whom I will have compassion" (Romans 9:15).

As the prerogative of life and death is vested in the monarch, so the Judge of all the earth has a right to spare or condemn the guilty. Men by their sins have forfeited all claim upon God. They deserve to perish for their sins, and if they all do so, they have no reason to complain. If the Lord steps in to save any, He may do so if the ends of justice are not thwarted. But if He decides it is best to allow the condemned to suffer the righteous sentence, none may accuse Him of unfairness. Foolish and impudent are all those discourses about the rights of men deserving consideration by the holy God. Ignorant, if not worse, are those contentions against discriminating grace which are rebellions of proud human nature against the crown and scepter of Jehovah. When we see our own wickedness and the justice of the divine verdict against sin, we no longer grumble at the truth that the Lord is not bound to save us. If He looks upon us, it will be His own free act of undeserved goodness, for which we shall forever bless His name. How can the redeemed sufficiently adore the grace of God? The Lord's will alone is glorified, and the very idea of human merit is cast out to everlasting contempt. There is no more humbling doctrine in Scripture than that of salvation by grace, none more deserving of our gratitude and, consequently, none more sanctifying. Believers should not be afraid of the grace of God, but adoringly rejoice in it.

November 26
Morning

"Whatosever thy hand findeth to do, do it with thy might" (Ecclesiastes 9:10).

Whatsoever thy hand findeth to do refers to works that are *possible*. There are many things which our *heart* finds to do which we will never do. We must not be content with forming schemes in our heart and talking about them. We must carry out "whatsoever our hand findeth to do." One good deed is worth more than a thousand brilliant theories. Let us not wait for large opportunities but do just the things we "find to do" day by day. We have no other time in which to live. The past is gone, and the future has not arrived. We never have any time but the *present*. Then do not wait until your experience has ripened into maturity before you attempt to serve God. Endeavor now to bring forth fruit. Do it *promptly*. Do not fritter away your life in thinking of what you intend to do tomorrow. No man ever served God by doing things tomorrow. We honor Christ by the things we do today. Whatever you do for Christ, do it with heart, soul, and strength. Where is the might of a Christian? It is not in himself, for he is perfect weakness. His might lies in the Lord of Hosts. Then let us seek His help. Let us proceed with prayer and faith. When we have done what our "hand findeth to do," let us wait on the Lord for His blessing.

November 26
Evening

"They shall rejoice, and shall see the plummet in the hand of Zerubbabel" (Zechariah 4:10).

Small things marked the beginning of the work in the hand of Zerubbabel. But no one could despise the small beginnings, for the Lord raised up one who would persevere until the headstone was ready to be brought forth with a shout of victory. Here is comfort for every believer in the Lord Jesus. The work of grace may be ever so small in its beginnings, but *the plummet is in good hands.* A Master Builder greater than Solomon has undertaken the raising of the heavenly temple, and He will not fail or be discouraged until the highest pinnacle is complete. If the plummet was in the hand of any human being, we could worry about the building. But the desire of the Lord will be accomplished by Jesus' hand. Had the walls been hurriedly built without proper planning and supervision, they might have deviated from the straight line. But the plummet was used by the chosen overseer. Jesus is always watching the construction of His spiritual temple, that it may be built securely and well. We like instant results, but Jesus prefers to use careful judgment. He will use the plummet, and that which is out of line must come down. This is what causes the failure of many flattering works and the overthrow of many a glittering testimony. It is not our responsibility to judge the Lord's Church since Jesus has a steady hand and a true eye and can use the plummet well. Rejoice that judgment is left to Him. *The plummet was in active use*—it was in the builder's hand. This gave a sure indication that he meant to push on the work to completion. O Lord Jesus, how glad we would be if we could see You at Your great work!

"Joshua, the high priest, standing before the angel of the Lord" (Zechariah 3:1).

In Joshua, the high priest, we see a picture of each and every child of God who has been drawn near by the blood of Christ and has been taught to minister in holy things. Jesus has made us priests and kings to God, and even here on earth we exercise the priesthood of consecrated living and hallowed service. But this high priest is said to be *"standing* before the angel of the Lord," that is, standing to minister. This should be the perpetual position of every true believer. Every place is now God's temple, and His people can as truly serve Him in their daily employments as in His house. They are to be always ministering, offering the spiritual sacrifice of prayer and praise and presenting themselves as a living sacrifice. Notice where Joshua stands to minister—it is before the angel of Jehovah. It is only through a mediator that we poor, defiled ones can ever become priests to God. I present what I have before the messenger, the angel of the covenant, the Lord Jesus; and through Him my prayers find acceptance wrapped up in His prayers. If I can bring Him nothing but my tears, He will put them with His own tears, for He once wept. If I can bring Him nothing but my groans and sighs, He will accept these as an acceptable sacrifice, for He once was broken in heart and sighed heavily in spirit. When I am standing in Him, I am accepted in the Beloved. See, then, the position of the Christian—"a priest—standing—before the angel of the Lord."

November 27
Evening

"The forgiveness of sins, according to the riches of his grace"(Ephesians 1:7).

Could there be a sweeter word in any language than that word *forgiveness,* when it is spoken in a guilty sinner's ear? Forever blessed is the dear light of pardon which shines into the condemned man's cell and gives the perishing a gleam of hope amid the midnight of despair. Can it be possible that my sin is forgiven forever? Hell is my destiny as a sinner—there is no possibility of escape while sin remains upon me. Can the load of guilt be lifted and the crimson stain removed? Jesus tells me that I may be righteous because of Him. The revelation of atoning love not only tells me that pardon is possible, but that it is secured to all who rest in Jesus. I believe in the atonement made by Jesus' blood, and, therefore, my sins are forever forgiven because of His substitutionary pains and death. My soul dedicates all her praise to Him who, because of His love, became my substitute and accomplished my redemption. What riches of grace does free forgiveness exhibit! Grace forgives all, forgives fully, forgives freely, and forgives forever! When I think of how great my sins were, how dear were the precious drops which cleansed me from them, and the gracious act which sealed my pardon, I am filled with wondering, worshipping affection. I bow before the throne which absolves me. I clasp the cross which delivers me. I serve the Incarnate God through whom I am a pardoned soul.

November 28
Morning

"For I rejoiced greatly when the brethren came and testified of the truth that is in thee, even as thou walkest in the truth" (3 John 3).

The truth was in Gaius, and Gaius walked in the truth. Truth must enter into the soul, penetrate and saturate it, or else it is of no value. Doctrines held as a matter of creed are like bread in the hand, which ministers no nourishment to the frame. But doctrine accepted by the heart is as food digested, which, by assimilation, sustains and builds up the body. In us truth must be a living force, an active energy, and an indwelling reality. If it is in us, we cannot part with it. A man may lose his garments or his limbs, but his inward parts are vital and cannot be torn away without absolute loss of life. A Christian can die, but he cannot deny the truth. Now, it is a rule of nature, that the inward affects the outward. When the truth is kindled within, its brightness soon beams forth in the outward life and conversation. It is said that the food of certain worms colors the cocoons of silk which they spin. The nutriment on which a man's inward nature lives colors every word and deed proceeding from him. To walk in the truth imports a life of integrity, holiness, faithfulness, and simplicity—the natural product of those principles of truth which the gospel teaches and the Spirit of God enables us to receive. Be it ours today, O gracious Spirit, to be ruled and governed by Your divine authority. May nothing false or sinful reign in our hearts, lest it extend its malignant influence to our daily walk among men.

November 28
Evening

"Seeking the wealth of his people" (Esther 10:3).

Mordecai was a true patriot. Since he was exalted to the highest position under King Ahasuerus, he used his influence to promote the prosperity of Israel. He was a type of Jesus, who, upon His throne of glory, seeks not His own, but uses His power for His people. Every Christian should be a Mordecai to the Church, striving according to his ability for its prosperity. Some are placed in positions of affluence and influence. Let them honor their Lord in the high places of the earth and testify for Jesus before great men. Others have something far better—close fellowship with the King of kings. Let them be sure to plead daily for the weak, the doubting, the tempted, and the comfortless. Believers may serve their Master greatly if they offer their talents for the general good and impart their wealth of heavenly learning to others by teaching them the things of God. The very least in the Body of Christ may at least *seek* the welfare of the people of God. His desire, if he can give no more, will be enough. It is both the most Christlike and the most happy life for a believer to cease living for himself. He who blesses others cannot fail to be blessed himself. On the other hand, to seek our own personal greatness is a wicked and unhappy way of life. Are you, to the best of your ability, seeking the wealth of the Church in your neighborhood? I trust that you are not hindering it by bitterness and scandal or weakening it by neglect. Friend, unite with the Lord's poor, bear their cross, and do all the good you can for them. You will not lose your reward.

"Thou shalt not go up and down as a tale-bearer among thy people. . . .thou shalt in any wise rebuke thy neighbor, and not suffer sin upon him" (Leviticus 19:16-17).

Tale bearing emits a threefold poison. It injures the teller, the hearer, and the person concerning whom the tale is told. Whether the report is true or false, we are by this precept of God's Word forbidden to spread it. The reputations of the Lord's people should be very precious in our sight, and we should be ashamed to help the devil dishonor the Church and the name of the Lord. Some tongues need a bridle rather than a spur. Many glory in pulling down their brethren, as if thereby they raised themselves. We ourselves may one day need forbearance and silence from our brethren, so let us render it cheerfully to those who require it now. Speak evil of no man. The Holy Spirit, however, permits us to censure sin and prescribes the way in which we are to do it. It must be done by rebuking our brother to his face, not by railing behind his back. This course is manly, brotherly, Christlike, and under God's blessing. Remember, hundreds have been saved from gross sin by the timely, wise, affectionate warnings of faithful ministers and brethren.

November 29
Evening

"Spices for anointing oil" (Exodus 35:8).

Much use was made of this anointing oil under the law, and that which it represents is of primary importance. The Holy Spirit, who anoints us for all holy service, is indispensable to us if we want to serve the Lord acceptably. Without His aid, our Christian services are a vain formality, and our inward experience is a dead philosophy. When our ministry is without anointing, how miserable it becomes! A holy anointing is the soul and life of the Christian experience, and its absence is the most grievous of all calamities. To go before the Lord without anointing is as though some common Levite thrust himself into the priest's office—his ministrations would have been sin rather than service. May we never attempt to minister without the sacred anointing. Choice spices were carefully compounded to form the anointing oil. This shows us the rich influences of the Holy Spirit. All good things are found in the divine Comforter. Matchless consolation, infallible instruction, spiritual energy, and divine sanctification all lie compounded with other excellent gifts in that sacred anointing oil of the Holy Spirit. It imparts a delightful fragrance to the character and person of the man or woman upon whom it is poured. Nothing like it can be found in all the treasuries of the rich or the secrets of the wise. It comes only from God, and it is freely given through Jesus Christ to every waiting soul.

November 30
Morning

"And Amaziah said to the man of God, But what shall we do for the hundred talents which I have given to the army of Israel? And the man of God answered, The Lord is able to give thee much more than this" (2 Chronicles 25:9).

This seemed to be a very important question to the king of Judah, and possibly it is of even more weight with the tried and tempted Christian. To lose money is at no time pleasant. "Why lose that which may be so useful to us? What will we do without it? Remember the children and our small income." All these things and a thousand more would tempt the Christian to put forth his hand to unrighteous gain or keep himself from carrying out his conscientious convictions when they involve serious loss. All men cannot view these matters in the light of faith; and even with the followers of Jesus, the doctrine of "we must live" has quite sufficient weight. *The Lord is able to give thee much more than this* is a very satisfactory answer to the anxious question. Our Father holds the purse strings; and what we lose for His sake, He can repay a thousandfold. If we obey His will, we may rest assured that He will provide for us. Saints know that a grain of heart's-ease is of more value than a ton of gold. God's smile in a dungeon is enough for a true heart, but His frown in a palace would be hell to a gracious spirit. Our treasure is above, where Christ sits at the right hand of God. Meanwhile, even now, the Lord makes the meek to inherit the earth, and no good thing does He withhold from them that walk uprightly.

November 30
Evening

"Michael and his angels fought against the dragon; and the dragon fought and his angels" (Revelation 12:7).

War always will rage between the two great kingdoms until one of them is destroyed. Peace between good and evil is an impossibility. The consideration of it would mean the triumph of the powers of darkness. Michael will always fight. His holy soul detests sin, and he will not endure it. Jesus will always be the dragon's foe, not in a quiet sense, but actively, vigorously, and with full determination to exterminate evil. All His servants, whether angels in heaven or messengers on earth, will and must fight. They are born to be warriors. At the cross they enter into covenant never to make a truce with evil. The duty of every soldier in the army of the Lord is daily, with all his heart, soul, and strength, to fight against the dragon. The dragon and his angels will not decline the battle. They use every available weapon in their relentless onslaughts. We are foolish to expect to serve God without opposition. The more zealous we are, the more sure we are to be assailed by the forces of hell. The Church may become slothful, but the restless spirit of her great antagonist never allows the war to pause. He hates the woman's seed and would gladly devour the Church if he could. War rages all around, and to dream of peace is dangerous and futile. Glory be to God, we know the outcome of the war! The great dragon will be cast out and forever destroyed, while Jesus and they who are with Him will receive the crown. Let us sharpen our sword and pray that the Holy Spirit will strengthen us for the conflict.

December 1
Morning

"Thou hast made summer and winter" (Psalm 74:17).

My soul, begin this wintry month with your God. The cold snows and the piercing winds all remind you that He keeps His covenant with day and night. You can be assured that He will also keep that glorious covenant which He has made with you in the person of Jesus Christ. He who is true to His Word in the revolutions of the seasons of this poor, sin-polluted world will not prove unfaithful in His dealings with His own well-beloved Son. Winter in the soul is by no means a comfortable season. If it is on you just now, it will be very painful to you. But there is this comfort, namely, that the Lord allows it. He is the great Winter King and rules in the realms of frost. Our circumstances come to us with wise design. Frosts kill noxious insects and put a stop to raging diseases. They break up the clods and sweeten the soil. Oh, that such good results would always follow our winters of affliction! How we prize the fire just now! How pleasant is its cheerful glow! Let us prize our Lord in the same manner, who is the constant source of warmth and comfort in every time of trouble. Let us draw near to Him and find joy and peace in believing. Let us wrap ourselves in the warm garments of His promises and go forth to labors which fit the season.

December 1
Evening

"Oh that men would praise the Lord for his goodness, and for his wonderful works to the children of men" (Psalm 107:8).

If we complained less and praised more, we would be happier, and God would be glorified. Let us daily praise God for *common blessings*—common, as we call them. Yet, they are so priceless that when deprived of them, we are ready to perish. Let us bless God for our eyes which behold the sun, for health and strength, for the bread we eat, and for the clothing we wear. Praise Him that we are not cast out among the hopeless or confined among the guilty. Thank Him for liberty, for friends, for family, and for comforts. Praise Him for everything which we receive from His bounteous hand, for we deserve little and yet are most generously endowed. The sweetest and the loudest note in our songs of praise should be of *redeeming love*. If we know what redemption means, let us not withhold our songs of thanksgiving. We have been lifted up from the depth of sin. We were led to the cross of Christ where our shackles of guilt were broken off. We are no longer slaves, but children of the living God. We can anticipate the time when we will be presented before the throne. Even now, by faith we wave the palm branch and wrap ourselves in the fair linen which is to be our everlasting array. Shall we not unceasingly give thanks to the Lord our Redeemer? Awake, you heirs of glory and cry with David, "Bless the Lord, O my soul: and all that is within me, bless his holy name" (Psalm 103:1).

December 2
Morning

"Thou art all fair, my love" (Song of Solomon 4:7).

The Lord's admiration of His Church is wonderful, and His description of her beauty is glowing. She is not merely fair, but *"all* fair." He views her in Himself, washed in His sin-atoning blood and clothed in His righteousness. He considers her to be full of comeliness and beauty. No wonder that such is the case, since it is but His own perfect excellency that He admires. The holiness, glory, and perfection of His Church are His own glorious garments on the back of His own well-beloved spouse. She is positively lovely and fair! She has actual merit! Her deformities of sin are removed. In addition, she has, through her Lord, obtained a meritorious righteousness. Believers have a positive righteousness given to them when they become "accepted in the Beloved" (Ephesians 1:6). The Church has a real worth and excellence which cannot be rivaled by all the nobility and royalty of the world. If Jesus could exchange His elect bride for all the queens and empresses of earth or even for the angels in heaven, He would not, for He puts her first and foremost—"fairest among women." One day, from the throne of His glory, He will avow the truth of this statement before the assembled universe. "Come, ye blessed of my Father" (Matthew 25:34) will be His solemn affirmation of the loveliness of His elect.

December 2
Evening

"Behold, all is vanity" (Ecclesiastes 1:14).

Nothing can satisfy the heart of a man except the Lord's love and presence. Solomon, the wisest of men, experimented with life for us all, and did for us what we must not dare to do for ourselves. Here is his testimony in his own words: "So I was great, and increased more than all that were before me in Jerusalem; also my wisdom remained with me. And whatsoever mine eyes desired I kept not from them, I withheld not my heart from any joy; for my heart rejoiced in all my labour: and this was my portion of all my labour. Then I looked on all the works that my hands had wrought, and on the labour that I had laboured to do: and, behold, all was vanity and vexation of spirit, and there was no profit under the sun" (Ecclesiastes 2:9-11). "Vanity of vanities; all is vanity" (Ecclesiastes 1:2). O favored king, is there nothing in all your wealth? Nothing in your glorious palaces? In all your music and dancing and wine and luxury, is there nothing? "Nothing," he replies, "but weariness of spirit." This was his verdict after he traveled the whole globe of pleasure. To embrace our Lord Jesus, dwell in His love, and be fully assured of union with Him—this is all in all. You do not need to try other life styles to see whether they are better than the Christian's. If you roam the world, you will see no sights like the Savior's face. If you could have all the comforts of life and if you lost your Savior, you would be wretched. But if you have Christ, then even if you rot in a dungeon, you would find it to be a paradise. If you live in obscurity or die from famine, you will be satisfied with favor and full of the goodness of the Lord.

December 3
Morning

"There is no spot in thee" (Song of Solomon 4:7).

Having pronounced His Church positively full of beauty, our Lord confirms His praise by a precious negative: "There is no spot in thee." It is as if the thought occurred to the Bridegroom that the world would insinuate that He had only mentioned her comely parts and had purposely omitted those features which were deformed or defiled. He sums up all by declaring her universally and entirely fair and utterly devoid of stain. If He had said there is no hideous scar, no horrible deformity, or no deadly ulcer, we might have marveled. But He testifies that she is free from the slightest spot. If He had but promised to remove all spots sooner or later, we would have had eternal reason for joy. But He speaks of it as already done. Oh, my soul, here is marrow and fatness for you. Eat your fill and be satisfied with royal dainties. Christ Jesus has no quarrel with His spouse. She often wanders from Him and grieves His Holy Spirit, but He does not allow her faults to affect His love. He sometimes chides, but it is always in the tenderest manner and with the kindest intentions. There is no remembrance of our follies. He does not cherish ill thoughts of us, but He pardons and loves us just as much after the offense as before it. Our precious Husband knows our silly hearts too well to take any offense at our ill manners.

December 3
Evening

"The Lord mighty in battle" (Psalm 24:8).

God is worthy of glory in the eyes of His people. He has worked great wonders for them, in them, and by them. *For them* the Lord Jesus triumphed over every foe, breaking all the weapons of the enemy in pieces by His finished work of obedience. By His triumphant resurrection and ascension He completely overturned the hopes of hell, leading captivity captive, making a show of our enemies openly, triumphing over them by His cross. Every arrow of guilt which Satan might have shot at us is broken, for who can accuse God's elect? The saved have reason to adore their Lord for His conquests *in them*. The arrows of their natural hatred are snapped and the weapons of their rebellion are broken. How glorious is Jesus when the will is subdued and sin dethroned! Our remaining corruptions will suffer an equally sure defeat, and every temptation, doubt, and fear will be destroyed. In the depths of our peaceful hearts, the name of Jesus is great beyond compare. We may securely look for victories *by us*. "We are more than conquerors through him that loved us" (Romans 8:37). We will cast down the powers of darkness which are in the world by our faith, zeal, and holiness. We will win sinners to Jesus, we will overturn false systems, we will convert nations for God is with us, and none can stand against us. This evening, let the Christian warrior chant the war song and prepare for tomorrow's fight—"Greater is he that is in you, than he that is in the world" (1 John 4:4).

December 4
Morning

"I have much people in this city" (Acts 18:10).

This should be a great encouragement to try to do good, since God has among the vilest of the vile those people who *must* be saved. When you take the Word to them, you do so because God has ordained you to be the messenger of life to their soul. They are as much redeemed by blood as the saints before the eternal throne. They are Christ's property; and yet, perhaps, they are still lovers of the tavern and haters of holiness. If Jesus Christ purchased them, He will have them. God is not unfaithful to forget the price which His Son has paid. He will not suffer His substitution to be in any case an ineffectual, dead thing. Tens of thousands of redeemed ones are not regenerated yet, but regenerated they must be. This is our comfort when we go forth to them with the quickening Word of God. "Neither pray I for these alone," said the great Intercessor, "but for them also which shall believe on me through their word" (John 17:20). Poor, ignorant souls, who know nothing about prayer for themselves, but Jesus prays for them. Their names are on His breastplate; and before long, they must bow their stubborn knee, breathing the penitential sigh before the throne of grace. When their moment comes, *they will obey,* for God will have His own. They must obey, for the Spirit is not to be withstood when He comes forth with fullness of power. "He shall see of the travail of his soul" (Isaiah 53:11).

December 4
Evening

"Even we ourselves groan within ourselves, waiting for the adoption, to wit, the redemption of our body" (Romans 8:23).

This groaning is universal among the saints. It is the sound of desire rather than of distress. We wait for the day when our entire manhood, in its trinity of spirit, soul, and body, will be set free from the last vestige of sin. We long to put off corruption, weakness, and dishonor and to wrap ourselves in incorruption, immortality, and glory which the Lord Jesus will give His people. We long for the manifestation of our adoption as the children of God. We groan, but it is *within ourselves*. It is not the hypocrite's groan, to make others believe we are saints because we are suffering. We keep our longings to our Lord alone. We are not to grumble like Jonah or Elijah when they said, "Let me die." We are not to whimper and sigh for the end of life because we are tired of work or because we wish to escape from our present sufferings. We are to groan for glorification, but we must wait patiently for it, knowing that the Lord's timing is best. Waiting implies being ready. We are to stand at the door expecting the Beloved to open it and take us away to Himself. This *groaning* is a *test*. You may judge a man by what he groans after. Some men groan after wealth. Some groan continually under the troubles of life. But the man who sighs after God and is uneasy until he is made like Christ is the blessed man. May God help us groan for the coming of the Lord and the resurrection which He will bring to us.

December 5
Morning

"Ask, and it shall be given you" (Matthew 7:7).

I know of a place in England where a ration of bread was served to every passerby who chose to ask for it. Whoever the traveler was, he only had to knock at the door of St. Cross Hospital, and there was a ration of bread for him. Jesus Christ so loves sinners that He has built the hospital of the cross. Whenever a sinner is hungry he has only to knock and have his needs supplied. Whenever a soul is black and filthy, he has but to go there and be washed. The fountain is always full, always effective. No sinner ever went into it and found that it could not wash away his stains. Sins which were scarlet and crimson have all disappeared, and the sinner has been made whiter than snow. Nothing that is good for him will be denied him. He will have all he needs as long as he lives; and he will have an eternal heritage of glorious treasure when he enters into the joy of his Lord. If all these things are to be had by merely knocking at mercy's door, O my soul, knock hard this morning, and ask large things of your generous Lord. Do not leave the throne of grace until all your needs have been spread before the Lord and by faith you have a comfortable prospect that they will all be supplied. No unbelief should hinder when Jesus promises.

December 5
Evening

"And the Lord shewed me four carpenters"
(Zechariah 1:20).

In the vision described in this chapter, the prophet saw four terrible horns. They were pushing this way and that, dashing down the strongest and the mightiest. The prophet asked, "What are these?" The answer was, "These are the horns which have scattered Judah" (Zechariah 1:21). He saw before him a representation of those powers which had oppressed the Church. There were four horns—the Church is attacked from all quarters. The prophet had good reason to feel dismayed; but suddenly there appeared before him *four carpenters*. These are the men whom God found to break those horns in pieces. *God will always find men for His work,* and He will find them *at the right time*. The prophet did not see the carpenters first when there was nothing to accomplish, but first the horns came and then the carpenters. Moreover, the Lord finds *enough men*. There were four horns, and there must be four workmen. God finds *the right men*. Not four men with pens to write or four architects to draw plans, but four carpenters to do rough work. When the horns grow troublesome, the carpenters will be found. You need not fret concerning the weakness of the Church. Apostles may come forth from unlikely places, and prophets arise from the thickest darkness of poverty. The Lord knows where to find His servants. He has a multitude of mighty men prepared to ambush, and at His word they will begin the battle. The battle is the Lord's, and He will be victorious. Let us remain faithful to Christ, and He, in the right time, will raise up for us a defense.

December 6
Morning

"As is the heavenly, such are they also that are heavenly" (1 Corinthians 15:48).

The head and members of the Body of Christ are of one nature. They are not like that monstrous image which Nebuchadnezzar saw in his dream. The head was of fine gold, but the belly and thighs were of brass, the legs were of iron, and the feet were part iron and part clay. Christ's mystical body is no absurd combination of opposites. The members were mortal, and therefore Jesus died. The glorified Head is immortal, and therefore the body is immortal too. The record stands: "Because I live, ye shall live also" (John 14:19). As is our loving Head, such is the body, and every member in particular. A chosen Head and chosen members; an accepted Head and accepted members; a living Head and living members. If the Head is pure gold, all the parts of the body are of pure gold also. Pause here, devout reader, and see if you can contemplate the infinite condescension of the Son of God in thus exalting your wretchedness into blessed union with His glory. In remembrance of mortality, you may say to corruption, "You are my father," and to the worm, "You are my sister." Yet, in Christ you are so honored that you can say to the Almighty, "Abba, Father," and to the Incarnate God, "You are my brother and my husband." Surely if relationships to ancient and noble families make men think highly of themselves, we have much more reason to glory above them all.

December 6
Evening

"Girt about the paps with a golden girdle" (Revelation 1:13).

"One like unto the Son of man" appeared to John on Patmos, and the beloved disciple noticed that He wore a girdle of gold. A *girdle,* for Jesus always stood ready for service. Now before the eternal throne, He continues His holy ministry, clothed as a priest in "the curious girdle of the ephod" (Exodus 28:8). We are blessed that He has not ceased to fulfill His work of love for us, since one of our best safeguards is that "He ever liveth to make intercession for them" (Hebrews 7:25). Jesus' garments are never loose as though His ministry was over. He diligently carries on the cause of His people. *A golden girdle* manifests the superiority of His service, the royalty of His person, the dignity of His Sonship, and the glory of His reward. No longer does He cry out in the dust, but He pleads with authority, a King as well as a Priest. Our Lord presents all His people with an example. This is not the time for lying down at ease—it is the season of service and warfare. We need to bind the girdle of truth more tightly around our loins. A heart that is not well braced with the truth of Jesus and with the fidelity of the Spirit will be easily entangled with the things of this life and caught in the snares of temptation. It is in vain that we possess the Scriptures unless we bind them around us like a girdle, surrounding our entire nature and keeping each part of our character in order. "Stand therefore, having your loins girt about with truth" (Ephesians 6:14).

December 7
Morning

"Base things of the world hath God chosen" (1 Corinthians 1:28).

Walk the streets by moonlight, and you will see sinners. Watch when the night is dark and the wind howling, and you will see sinners. Go to the jail and walk through the wards, and see men whom you would not like to meet at night. There are sinners there. Go where you will, you need not ransack the earth to find sinners, for they are common enough. You may find them in every street of every city, town, and village. It is for such that Jesus died. If you would find the grossest specimen of humanity, I would have hope for him yet, because Jesus Christ is come to seek and to save sinners. Electing love has selected some of the worst to be made the best. Worthless dross He transforms into pure gold. Redeeming love has set apart many of the worst of mankind to be the reward of the Savior's passion. Effectual grace calls forth many of the vilest of the vile to sit at the table of mercy. Therefore, let none despair. Reader, there is love looking out of Jesus' tearful eyes and love streaming from those bleeding wounds. By that faithful love, that strong love, that pure and abiding love, by the heart of the Savior's compassion, we urge you, do not turn away as though it were nothing to you. Believe on Him, and you will be saved. Trust your soul with Him, and He will bring you to His Father's right hand in glory everlasting.

December 7
Evening

"I am made all things to all men, that I might by all means save some" (1 Corinthians 9:22).

Paul's goal was not merely to instruct and to improve, but to save. Anything short of this would have disappointed him. He wanted men to be renewed in heart, forgiven, sanctified, *saved.* Has our Christian work been aimed at anything below this great point? What good will it be at the last great day to have taught and moralized men if they appear before God unsaved? Paul knew the ruin of man's natural state, and he did not try to educate him, but to save him. He saw men sinking to hell and did not talk of refining them, but of saving them from the wrath to come. To accomplish their salvation, he gave himself up with untiring zeal to preaching the gospel, warning and entreating men to be reconciled to God. His prayers and labors were incessant. To save souls was his consuming passion, his ambition, and his calling. He became a servant to all men, toiling for his race. If men received the gospel, he raised no questions about forms or ceremonies—the gospel was the one all-important business with him. If he saved some, he would be content. This was the crown for which he labored, the sole and sufficient reward of all his toil and self-denial. Have you and I lived to win souls at this noble rate? Are we possessed with the same all-absorbing desire? Jesus died for sinners; can we not live for them? Where is our love for Christ if we do not seek His honor in the salvation of men? Pray that the Lord would saturate us with an undying zeal for the souls of men!

December 8
Morning

"Thou hast a few names even in Sardis which have not defiled their garments; and they shall walk with me in white, for they are worthy" (Revelation 3:4).

We may understand this to refer to *justification*. That is, they will enjoy a constant sense of their own justification by faith. They will understand that the righteousness of Christ is imputed to them, and that they have all been washed and made whiter than the newly-fallen snow. Again, it refers to joy and gladness, for white robes were holiday attire among the Jews. They who have not defiled their garments will have their faces always bright. They will understand what Solomon meant when he said, "Go thy way, eat thy bread with joy, and drink thy wine with a merry heart; for God hath accepted thy works" (Ecclesiastes 9:7). He who is accepted of God will wear white garments of joy and gladness while he walks in sweet communion with the Lord Jesus. Why are there so many doubts, and so much misery and mourning? Is it because so many believers defile their garments with sin and lose the joy of their salvation and the comfortable fellowship of the Lord Jesus? Those who have not defiled their garments here will most certainly possess joys inconceivable, happiness beyond a dream, bliss which imagination knows not, and a blessedness which even the stretch of desire has not reached. In His sweet company they will drink of the living fountains of waters.

December 8
Evening

"Thou, O God, hast prepared of thy goodness for the poor" (Psalm 68:10).

God anticipates our needs. Out of the fullness which He has treasured up in Christ Jesus, He provides good things for the poor. You may trust Him to meet all of your needs, for He has foreknown every one of them. He can say of us in all conditions, "I knew that you would be in this situation." Suppose that a man goes on a journey across the desert. When he has made a day's hike and pitched his tent, he discovers that he has forgotten to bring many comforts and necessities. "Ah!" says he, "I did not foresee this. If I had this journey to do over again, I would bring these things with me which are so necessary to my comfort." But God knows all the requirements of His poor, wandering children, and when those needs occur, supplies are ready. "My grace is sufficient for thee" (2 Corinthians 12:9). "As thy days, so shall thy strength be" (Deuteronomy 33:25). Is your heart heavy this evening? God knew that it would be. You are poor and needy, but He has the exact blessing which you require. Plead the promise, believe it, and obtain its fulfillment. Do you feel that you were never so consciously sinful as you are now? Behold, the crimson fountain is still open, with all its former effectiveness to wash your sin away. You will never come to a place where Christ cannot help you. No trial will ever arrive in which Jesus Christ will not be equal to the emergency. Your history has all been foreknown and provided for in Jesus.

December 9
Morning

"Therefore will the Lord wait, that he may be gracious unto you" (Isaiah 30:18).

God often delays in answering prayer. We have several instances of this in sacred Scripture. Jacob did not get the blessing from the angel until near the dawn of day—he had to wrestle all night for it. The poor woman of Syrophenicia was answered not a word for a long while. Paul sought the Lord three times that "the thorn in the flesh" might be taken from him. He received no assurance that it would be taken away, but instead received a promise that God's grace would be sufficient for him. If you have been knocking at the gate of mercy and have received no answer, I will tell you why the mighty Maker has not opened the door and let you in. Our Father has reasons peculiar to Himself for keeping us waiting. Sometimes it is to show His power and His sovereignty so that men may know that Jehovah has a right to give or to withhold. More frequently the delay is for our profit. Perhaps you are kept waiting in order that your desires may be more fervent. You will prize the gift all the more because of its long tarrying. There may also be something in you that needs to be removed before the joy of the Lord is given. If your prayers are not immediately answered, they are certainly not forgotten. Your prayers are all filed in heaven. In a little while your prayers will be fulfilled to your satisfaction. Do not let despair make you silent. Continue in earnest supplication.

December 9
Evening

"My people shall dwell. . .in quiet resting places" (Isaiah 32:18).

Peace and rest do not belong to the unredeemed. They are the unique possession of the Lord's people. The God of Peace gives perfect peace to those whose hearts stay close to Him. When man was innocent, God gave him the flowery branches of Eden as his quiet resting places. How quickly sin destroyed the fair dwelling of innocence! In the day of wrath, when the flood swept away a guilty race, Noah's family was quietly secured in the resting place of the ark. It floated them from the condemned world into the new earth of the rainbow and the covenant, typifying Jesus, the ark of our salvation. Israel rested safely beneath the blood-sprinkled habitations of Egypt when the destroying angel killed the firstborn. In the wilderness, the shadow of the pillar of cloud and the water flowing from the rock gave the weary pilgrims sweet repose. At this hour, we rest in the promises of our faithful God, knowing that His words are full of truth and power. We rest in the doctrines of His Word which are consolation itself. We rest in the covenant of His grace which is a haven of delight. We are more highly favored than David in Adullam or Jonah beneath his gourd, for none can invade or destroy our shelter. Jesus is the quiet resting place of His people. When we draw near to Him in the breaking of bread, in the hearing of the Word, the searching of the Scriptures, prayer, or praise, we find that peace returns to our spirits.

December 10
Morning

"So shall we ever be with the Lord" (1 Thessalonians 4:17). Even the sweetest visits from Christ are brief and transitory. One moment our eyes see Him, and we rejoice with unspeakable joy, but in a little while our Beloved withdraws Himself from us. Oh, how sweet to think of the time when we will not behold Him at a distance but see Him face to face! He will no longer be as a wayfaring man tarrying but for a night, but He will eternally enfold us in the bosom of His glory! In heaven there will be no interruptions from care or sin; no weeping will dim our eyes. No earthly business will distract our happy thoughts. We will have nothing to hinder us from gazing forever on the Sun of Righteousness with unwearied eyes. Oh, if it is so sweet to see Him now and then, how sweet to gaze on that blessed face forever and never have a cloud rolling between and never have to turn one's eyes away to look on a world of weariness and woe! Blest day, when will you dawn? The joys of sense will leave us soon. If to die is to enter into uninterrupted communion with Jesus, then death is indeed gain, and the black drop is swallowed up in a sea of victory.

December 10
Evening

"Whose heart the Lord opened" (Acts 16:14).

Lydia's conversion was brought about by providential circumstances. She was a seller of purple in the city of Thyatira, but she was in Philippi just at the right time to hear Paul. Providence, which is the handmaid of grace, led her to the right spot. Grace was preparing her soul for the blessing. She did not know the Savior, but since she was Jewish, she knew many truths which were excellent stepping stones to a knowledge of Jesus. On the Sabbath she went where prayer was to be made, and there prayer was heard. God *may* bless us when we are not in His house, but we have greater reason to hope that He *will* when we are in communion with His saints. Observe the words, "Whose heart *the Lord* opened." She did not open her own heart. Her prayers did not do it, and Paul did not do it. The Lord Himself must open the heart to receive the things which bring us peace. He is the heart's Master because He is the heart's Maker. The first outward evidence of the opened heart was *obedience.* As soon as Lydia believed in Jesus, she was baptized. It is a sweet sign of a humble and broken heart when the child of God is willing to obey a command which is not essential to his salvation or forced upon him by a selfish fear of condemnation. Lydia's baptism was a simple act of obedience and of communion with her Master. The next evidence was *love,* manifesting itself in acts of grateful kindness to the apostles. Love for the saints has always been a mark of the true convert. Those who do nothing for Christ or His Church give poor evidence of an open heart. Lord, give me an open heart toward You.

December 11
Morning

"Faithful is he that calleth you, who also will do it" (1 Thessalonians 5:24).

Heaven is a place where we will never sin and where we will cease our constant watch against an indefatigable enemy. There will be no tempter to ensnare our feet. There the weary are at rest. Heaven is the "undefiled inheritance." It is the land of perfect holiness and complete security. But do not the saints even on earth sometimes taste the joys of blissful security? The doctrine of God's Word is that all who are in union with the Lamb are safe. Those who have committed their souls to the keeping of Christ will find Him a faithful and immutable preserver. Sustained by such a doctrine, we can enjoy security even on earth. Believer, let us often reflect with joy on the doctrine of the perseverance of the saints and honor the faithfulness of our God by a holy confidence in Him. May our God bring home to you a sense of your safety in Christ Jesus. May He assure you that your name is graven on His hand and whisper in your ear the promise, "Fear not, I am with thee." Look on Him, the great Surety of the covenant, as faithful and true, and, therefore, bound and engaged to present you, the weakest of the family, with all the chosen race before the throne of God. "Faithful is he that calleth you, who also will do it."

December 11
Evening

"Ye serve the Lord Christ" (Colossians 3:24).

To what choice group of officials was this word spoken? To kings, who proudly boast a divine right to rule? No—too often they serve themselves or Satan and forget God whose mercy permits them to wear their imitation majesty. Does Paul speak to those so-called "right reverend fathers in God," the bishops, or the venerable archdeacons? No, indeed; Paul knew nothing of these inventions of man. Not even to pastors and teachers or to the wealthy and esteemed among believers was this word spoken, but to servants and to slaves. Among the toiling multitudes, the journeymen, laborers, and the domestic servants, the apostle found some of the Lord's chosen. To them he said, "Whatsoever ye do, do it heartily, as to the Lord, and not unto men; Knowing that of the Lord ye shall receive the reward of the inheritance: for ye serve the Lord Christ" (Colossians 3:23-24). This saying ennobles the weary routine of earthly employments and sheds a halo around the most humble occupations. To wash feet may be servile, but to wash *His* feet is royal work. To untie the shoelace is a poor job, but to loose the great Master's shoe is a princely privilege. The shop, the barn, and the kitchen become temples when men and women do all to the glory of God! Divine service is not a thing of a few hours and a few places, but all life becomes holiness to the Lord. Every place and thing may be as consecrated as the tabernacle and its golden candlestick.

December 12
Morning

"His ways are everlasting" (Habakkuk 3:5).

What He has done at one time, He will do yet again. Man's ways are variable, but God's ways are everlasting and the result of wise deliberation. He orders all things according to the counsel of His own will. Human action is frequently the hasty result of passion or fear and is followed by regret and alteration. But nothing can take the Almighty by surprise. His ways are the outgrowth of an immutable character, and in them the fixed and settled attributes of God are clearly to be seen. Unless the Eternal One Himself can undergo change, His ways must remain forever the same. He is eternally just, gracious, faithful, wise, and tender. Humans act according to their nature. When their nature changes, their conduct varies also. But God's ways will remain everlastingly the same. The sun and moon stand still when Jehovah marches forth for the salvation of His people. Who can stay His hand or say to Him, "What are you doing?" But it is not might alone which gives stability. God's ways are the manifestations of the eternal principles of right and, therefore, can never pass away. Wrong breeds decay and involves ruin, but the true and good have about them a vitality which age cannot diminish. This morning let us go to our heavenly Father with confidence, remembering that Jesus Christ is the same yesterday, today, and forever.

December 12
Evening

"They have dealt treacherously against the Lord" (Hosea 5:7).

Believer, here is a sorrowful truth! You are the beloved of the Lord, redeemed by blood, called by grace, preserved in Christ Jesus, accepted in the Beloved, on your way to heaven. Yet, you have "dealt treacherously" with God, your best Friend; treacherously with Jesus, to whom you belong; treacherously with the Holy Spirit, by whom you have been quickened to eternal life! Do you remember your first love—the springtime of your spiritual life? Oh, how close you stayed to your Master then! You said, "My feet will never grow sluggish in the way of His service. I will not allow my heart to wander after other loves. In Him is every store of sweetness. I give all up for my Lord Jesus' sake." Has it been so? If conscience could speak, it will say, "He who promised so much has performed so little. Prayer has often been slighted—it is short, but not sweet; brief, but not fervent. Communion with Christ has been forgotten. Instead of a heavenly mind, there are carnal cares, worldly vanities, and thoughts of evil. Instead of service, there has been disobedience; instead of fervency, lukewarmness; instead of patience, complaining; instead of faith, confidence in an arm of flesh; and as a soldier of the cross there has been cowardice, disobedience, and desertion to a shameful degree." Let our penitent thoughts expel the sin which is surely in us. How shameful it is to be treacherous to Him who never forgets us, but who stands with our names engraved on His breastplate before the eternal throne!

December 13
Morning

"Salt, without prescribing how much" (Ezra 7:22).

Salt was used in every offering made by fire to the Lord. From its preserving and purifying properties, it was the grateful emblem of divine grace in the soul. When Artaxerxes gave salt to Ezra the priest, he set no limit to the quantity. We may be quite certain that when the King of kings distributes grace among His royal priesthood, the supply is not cut short by Him. Often we are restricted in ourselves but never in the Lord. He who chooses to gather much manna will find that he may have as much as he desires. There is no such famine in Jerusalem that the citizens should eat their bread by weight and drink their water by measure. "Ask what thou wilt, and it shall be given unto thee" (Mark 6:22). Parents need to lock up the candy jars, but there is no need to keep the salt shaker under lock and key, for few children will eat too greedily from that. A man may have too much money or too much honor, but he cannot have too much grace. More wealth brings more care, but more grace brings more joy. Abundance of the Spirit is fullness of joy. Believer, go to the throne for a large supply of heavenly salt.

December 13
Evening

"I will make thy windows of agates" (Isaiah 54:12).

The Church is symbolized by a building constructed by heavenly power and designed by divine skill. There must, therefore, be windows to let the light in and to allow the inhabitants to gaze outside. These windows are *precious* as agates. The ways in which the Church beholds her Lord, heaven, and spiritual truth in general should be held in highest esteem. *Faith* is one of these precious agate windows, but it is often so misty and clouded that we see only darkly and mistake much of what we do see. Yet, if we cannot gaze through windows of crystal and know Christ even as we are known by Him, it is a glorious thing to behold the lovely One through glass as hazy as the agate. *Experience* is another of these dim but precious windows, yielding a subdued religious light, in which we see the sufferings of the Man of Sorrows through our own afflictions. Our weak eyes could not bear windows of transparent glass to let in the Master's glory. But when they are dimmed with weeping, the beams of the Sun of Righteousness shine through the windows of agate with a soft radiance that is inexpressibly soothing to tempted souls. *Sanctification,* as it conforms us to our Lord, is another agate window. Only as we become heavenly can we comprehend heavenly things. The pure in heart see a pure God. Those who are like Jesus see Him as He is.

December 14
Morning

"They go from strength to strength" (Psalm 84:7).

There are various renderings of these words, but all of them contain the idea of progress. They grow stronger and stronger. Usually, if we are walking, we go from strength to weakness. We start fresh but before long the road becomes rough and the sun becomes hot. We must sit down to rest. But the Christian pilgrim, having obtained fresh supplies of grace, is as vigorous after years of toilsome travel and struggle as when he first set out. He may not be quite so elated and bouyant as he once was, but he is much stronger in all that constitutes real power. He may move slowly, but he moves more surely. Some gray-haired veterans have remained as firm and zealous in their grasp of truth as they were in their younger days; however, it must be confessed it is often otherwise. The love of many waxes cold, and iniquity abounds. But this is their own sin and not the fault of the promise: "The youths shall faint and be weary, and the young men shall utterly fall; but they that wait upon the Lord shall renew their strength; they shall mount up with wings as eagles; they shall run, and not be weary; and they shall walk, and not faint" (Isaiah 40:30-31). Fretful spirits sit down and trouble themselves about the future. "Alas," say they, "We go from affliction to affliction." Very true, you of little faith, but then you go from strength to strength also! You will never find a bundle of affliction which does not have sufficient grace bound up in the midst of it.

December 14
Evening

"I am crucified with Christ" (Galatians 2:20).

The Lord Jesus Christ acted as a great representative, and His death upon the cross was the death of all His people. Through Him, all His saints rendered to justice what was due and satisfied divine vengeance for all their sins. Paul delighted to think that as one of Christ's chosen people, he died upon the cross in Christ. He did more than believe this doctrinally—he accepted it confidently, resting his hope upon it. He believed that by virtue of Christ's death, he satisfied divine justice and found reconciliation with God. What a blessed thing it is when the soul can stretch itself upon the cross of Christ and feel, "I am dead. The law has slain me, and I am free from its power. In my Substitute, all that the law could do by way of condemnation has been executed upon me, for I am crucified with Christ." Paul not only believed in Christ's death and trusted in it. He actually felt its power which caused the crucifixion of his old corrupt nature. Every true Christian is a dead man to this world. Yet, while conscious of death to the world, he can exclaim with the apostle, "Nevertheless I live." He is fully alive to God. The Christian's life is a matchless riddle. No unbeliever can comprehend it; even the believer himself cannot understand it. Dead, yet alive! Crucified with Christ, and at the same time risen with Christ in newness of life! Union with the suffering, bleeding Savior, and death to the world and sin are blessed things.

December 15
Morning

"Orpah kissed her mother-in-law; but Ruth clave unto her" (Ruth 1:14).

Both of them had an affection for Naomi and, therefore, set out with her on her return to the land of Judah. But the hour of testing came. Naomi unselfishly set before each of them the trials which awaited them. If they cared for ease and comfort, she urged them to return to their Moabitish friends. At first both of them declared that they would cast in their lot with the Lord's people. But on further consideration, Orpah, with much grief and a respectful kiss, left her mother-in-law and went back to her idolatrous friends. Ruth, however, with all her heart, gave herself up to the God of her mother-in-law. It is one thing to love the ways of the Lord when all is fair and quite another to cleave to them under all discouragements and difficulties. Where do you stand? Is your heart fixed on Jesus? Have you counted the cost, and are you solemnly ready to suffer all worldly loss for the Master's sake? Worldly treasures are not to be compared with the glory to be revealed. Orpah is heard of no more. In glorious ease and idolatrous pleasure her life melts into the gloom of death. Ruth lives in history and in heaven, for grace has placed her in the noble line from which came the King of kings. Blessed among women will those be who for Christ's sake can renounce all.

December 15
Evening

"And lay thy foundations with sapphires" (Isaiah 54:11).

Foundations are out of sight, and as long as they are firm, they are usually unnoticed. But in Jehovah's work, everything is important. The deep foundations of the work of grace are as sapphires in their preciousness. No human mind is able to measure their glory. We build upon *the covenant of grace* which is firmer than concrete and as enduring as jewels. Sapphire foundations are eternal, and the covenant lasts throughout the lifetime of the Almighty. Another foundation is *the person of the Lord Jesus* which is clear, spotless, everlasting, and beautiful as the sapphire. It blends the deep blue of the earth's ever-rolling ocean and the azure of its all-embracing sky into our substance. Our Lord might have been compared to the ruby as He stood covered with His own blood, but now we see Him radiant with the soft blue of love abounding, deep, and eternal. Our hopes are built upon the *justice and the faithfulness of God,* which are clear and cloudless as the sapphire. The Lord Himself has laid the foundations of His people's hopes. Good works and ceremonies are not a foundation of sapphires, but of wood, hay, and stubble. They are not laid by God but by our own conceit. Foundations will all be tried before long. He who is built on sapphires may calmly face storm or fire, for he will withstand the test.

December 16
Morning

"Come unto me" (Matthew 11:28).

The cry of the Christian religion is the gentle word, "Come." The Jewish law harshly said, "Go, take heed to your steps as to the path in which you will walk. Break the commandments, and you will perish; keep them, and you will live." The law was a dispensation of terror which drove men before it like a whip. The gospel draws with bands of love. Jesus is the Good Shepherd going before His sheep, bidding them follow Him. He is always leading them onward with the sweet word, "Come." The law repels; the gospel attracts. The law shows the distance which there is between God and man; the gospel bridges that awful chasm and brings the sinner across it. From the first moment of your spiritual life until you are ushered into glory, the language of Christ to you will be "Come, come unto Me." As a mother puts out her finger to her little child and coaxes him to walk by saying, "Come," even so does Jesus. He will always be ahead of you, bidding you follow Him as the soldier follows his captain. He will always go before you to pave your way and clear your path, and you will hear His animating voice calling you after Him all through life. In the solemn hour of death His sweet words with which He ushers you into the heavenly world will be— "Come, ye blessed of my Father" (Matthew 25:34).

"Yea, thou heardest not; yea, thou knewest not; yea, from that time that thine ear was not opened" (Isaiah 48:8).

It is painful to remember that this accusation may be made against believers who often are *spiritually insensitive.* We murmur that *we* do not hear the voice of God as we should. There are gentle movements of the Holy Spirit in the soul which are ignored by us. There are whisperings of divine command and of heavenly love which are unobserved by our intellect. We have been *carelessly ignorant.* There are matters which we should have understood and corruptions which have made headway into our lives unnoticed. Sweet affections are blighted like flowers in the frost. Glimpses of the divine face might be perceived if we did not wall up the windows of our soul. But we have not known. We must adore the grace of God as we learn that all of our folly and ignorance was *foreknown by God.* Yet, He deals mercifully with us. Admire the marvelous sovereign grace which chose us in spite of all this! He who hung upon the cross foresaw us as unbelieving, backsliding, cold of heart, indifferent, careless, lax in prayer, and yet He said, "I am the Lord thy God, the Holy One of Israel, thy Savior. . . .Since thou wast precious in my sight, thou hast been honourable, and I have loved thee: therefore will I give men for thee, and people for thy life" (Isaiah 43:3-4).

December 17
Morning

"I remember thee" (Jeremiah 2:2).

Let us note that Christ delights to think on His Church and to look on her beauty. As the bird returns often to its nest and the wayfarer hastens to his home, so does the mind continually pursue the object of its choice. We cannot look too often on the face of our Lord Jesus. From all eternity, "His delights were with the sons of men" (Proverbs 8:31). His thoughts rolled to the time when His elect should be born into the world. He viewed them in His foreknowledge. David wrote, "In thy book all my members were written, which in continuance were fashioned, when as yet there was none of them" (Psalm 139:16). When the world was set on its pillars, He was there. On the plains of Mamre, by the brook of Jabbok, beneath the walls of Jericho, and in the fiery furnace of Babylon the Son of man visited His people. Because His soul delighted in them, He could not rest away from them. He had written their names on His hands and graven them on His side. As the breastplate containing the names of the tribes of Israel was the most brilliant ornament worn by the high priest, so the names of Christ's elect were His most precious jewels and glittered on His heart. He never ceases to remember us.

December 17
Evening

"I am the door: by me if any man enter in, he shall be saved, and shall go in and out, and find pasture" (John 10:9).

Jesus, the great I AM, is the entrance into the true Church and the way to God. He gives four choice privileges to the man who comes to God by Him. *He shall be saved.* None who take Jesus as the door of faith to their souls can be lost. Entrance through Jesus into peace is the guarantee of entrance by the same door into heaven. Jesus is the only door, an open door and a safe door. Blessed is he who rests all his hope of admission to glory upon the crucified Redeemer. *He shall go in.* He is privileged to go in among the divine family, sharing the children's bread, and participating in all their enjoyment. He will go in to the chambers of communion, to the banquets of love, to the treasures of the covenant, to the storehouses of the promises. He will go to the King of kings in the power of the Holy Spirit, and the secret of the Lord will be with him. *He shall go out.* This blessing is often forgotten. We go out into the world to labor and suffer, but what a joy it is to go in the name and power of Jesus! We are called to bear witness to the truth, to cheer the discouraged, to warn the careless, to win souls, and to glorify God. The Lord would have us proceed as His messengers in His name and strength. *He shall find pasture.* He who knows Jesus shall never want. Having made Jesus his all, he will find all in Jesus. His soul will be as a watered garden.

December 18
Morning

"Rend your heart, and not your garments" (Joel 2:13).

Garment-rending and other outward signs of religious emotion are easily manifested and are frequently hypocritical. But to feel true repentance is far more difficult and far less common. Men will attend to the most multiplied and minute ceremonial regulations that are pleasing to the flesh. But true faith is too humbling, too heart-searching, and too thorough for the tastes of carnal men. They prefer something more ostentatious, flimsy, and worldly. Eye and ear are pleased, self-conceit is fed, and self-righteousness is puffed up. But they are ultimately deceived, for in death and at the day of judgment, the soul needs something more substantial than ceremonies and rituals to lean on. Apart from vital godliness, all religion is utterly vain. Offered without a sincere heart, every form of worship is a sham and an impudent mockery of the majesty of heaven. Heart-rending is divinely wrought and solemnly felt. It is a secret grief which is personally experienced, not in mere form, but as a deep, soul-moving work of the Holy Spirit on the heart of each believer. The text commands us to rend our hearts, but they are naturally hard as marble. How, then, can this be done? We must take them to Calvary. A dying Savior's voice rent the rocks once, and it is as powerful now. O blessed Spirit, let us hear the death-cries of Jesus, and our hearts will be rent even as men rend their vestures in the day of lamentation.

December 18
Evening

"Be thou diligent to know the state of the flocks, and look well to thy herds" (Proverbs 27:23).

Every wise merchant will periodically update his accounts, examine his inventory, and discover whether his business is prospering or declining. Every man who is wise in the Kingdom of heaven will cry, "Search me, O God, and know my heart" (Psalm 139:23). He will frequently set apart time for self-examination to discover whether things are right between God and his soul. The God whom we worship is a great heart-searcher. Make a diligent investigation of your spiritual condition lest you come short of the promised rest. Let the oldest saint look well to the fundamentals of his faith for gray heads may cover wicked hearts. Do not let the young Christian despise the word of warning for the greenness of youth may be joined to the rottenness of hypocrisy. The enemy continues to sow tares among the wheat. It is not my aim to introduce doubts and fears into your mind; but I hope that the rough wind of self-examination may help to drive them away. It is only carnal security that we want to kill; not confidence, but fleshly confidence which we would overthrow; not peace, but false peace which we would destroy. The precious blood of Christ was not shed to make you a hypocrite, but so that sincere souls might show forth His praise.

December 19
Morning

"The lot is cast into the lap, but the whole disposing thereof is of the Lord" (Proverbs 16:33).

If the disposal of the lot is the Lord's, whose is the arrangement of our whole life? If the simple casting of a lot is guided by Him, how much more the events of our entire life—especially when we are told by our blessed Savior, "The very hairs of your head are all numbered" (Matthew 10:30). It would bring a holy calm over your mind, dear friend, if you were always to remember this. It would so relieve your mind from anxiety that you would be better able to walk in patience, quiet, and cheerfulness as a Christian should. When a man is anxious, he cannot pray with faith. When he is troubled about the world, he cannot serve his Master. His thoughts are of serving himself. "Seek ye first the kingdom of God, and his righteousness; and all these things shall be added unto you (Matthew 6:33). You are meddling with Christ's business and neglecting your own when you fret about your circumstances. Be wise, attend to obeying, and let Christ manage the providing. Come and survey your Father's storehouse, and ask whether He will let you starve while He has laid up so great an abundance in His garner. If He remembers even sparrows, will He forget one of the least of His poor children? "Cast thy burden upon the Lord, and he will sustain thee. He will never suffer the righteous to be moved" (Psalm 55:22).

December 19
Evening

"And there was no more sea" (Revelation 21:1).

We could hardly rejoice at the thought of losing the glorious old ocean. The new heavens and the new earth seem less attractive to our imagination if there is literally to be no great sea with its gleaming waves and sandy shores. A physical world without a sea would be an iron ring without the sapphire to make it precious. There must be a spiritual meaning here. In the new earth there will be no *division*. The sea separates nations and peoples from each other. To John on Patmos the deep waters were like prison walls, shutting him out from his brethren and his work. There will be no such barriers in the world to come. Leagues of rolling billows lie between us and many Christian brothers and sisters whom we prayerfully remember tonight. But in the next world, there will be unbroken fellowship for all the redeemed family. In this sense, there will be no more sea. The sea is the emblem of *change.*With its ebb and flows, its glassy smoothness and its mountainous billows, its gentle murmurs and its tumultuous roarings, it is never the same for long. Earth is constant only in her inconsistancy. But in the heavenly state all distressing change will be unknown along with all fear of storm to wreck our hopes and drown our joys. The sea of glass glows with a glory unbroken by a wave. No tempest howls along the peaceful shores of paradise. We will soon reach that happy land where separation, change, and storms will end! Jesus will take us there.

December 20
Morning

"Yea, I have loved thee with an everlasting love" (Jeremiah 31:3).

The Holy Spirit is often pleased to witness with our spirits of the love of Jesus. He takes of the things of Christ and reveals them to us. No voice is heard from the clouds, and no vision is seen in the night; but we have a testimony more sure than either of these. If an angel should fly from heaven and inform the saint personally of the Savior's love to him, the evidence would not be one bit more satisfactory than that which is borne in the heart by the Holy Spirit. Ask those of the Lord's people who have lived the nearest to the gates of heaven, and they will tell you that they have had seasons when the love of Christ toward them has been a fact so clear and sure that they could no more doubt it than they could question their own existence. Yes, beloved believer, you and I have had times of refreshing from the presence of the Lord, and then our faith has mounted to the height of assurance. We have had confidence to lean our heads on the bosom of our Lord, and we have no more questioned our Master's affection to us than John did when he rested there. Jesus has killed our doubts by the closeness of His embrace. His love has been sweeter than wine to our souls.

December 20
Evening

"Call the labourers, and give them their hire"
(Matthew 20:8).

God is a good employer. He pays His servants while they work as well as when they are finished. One of His payments is *an easy conscience.* If you have spoken faithfully of Jesus to one person today, you may go to bed happy in thinking, "I have this day shared the love of Jesus my Savior." There is a great comfort in doing something for Jesus. What a joy it is to place jewels in His crown and cause Him to see the results of His saving work! There is also great reward in watching the first buddings of conviction in a soul! You may say of that girl in the class, "She is tender of heart; I do hope that there is the Lord's work within." Or you may go home and pray over that boy who said something which made you think he must know more of divine truth than you had suspected. To be a soul-winner is the happiest thing in the world. With every soul you bring to Christ, you get a new heaven upon earth. But who can imagine the bliss which awaits us above? Oh, how sweet is that sentence, "Enter thou into the joy of thy Lord" (Matthew 25:21). Do you know what the joy of Christ is over a saved sinner? This is the same joy which we are to possess in heaven. When the heavens ring with "Well done, well done," you will share the reward. You have toiled with Him; you have suffered with Him; you will now reign with Him. You have sown with Him; you will reap with Him. Your face was covered with sweat like His, and your soul was grieved for the sins of men as His soul was. Now your face will be bright with heaven's splendor, and your soul will be filled with joy.

December 21
Morning

"Yet he hath made with me an everlasting covenant" (2 Samuel 23:5).

This covenant is divine in its origin. Oh, that great word—He! God, the everlasting Father, has positively made a covenant with you. Yes, God spoke the world into existence by a word. He, stooping from His majesty, takes hold of your hand and makes a covenant with you. The Prince of the kings of the earth, Shaddai, the Lord All-sufficient, the Jehovah of all ages, the everlasting Elohim— "He hath made with me an everlasting covenant." But notice, it is particular in its application. "Yet hath he made with *me* an everlasting covenant." Here lies the sweetness of it to each believer. It is nothing to me that He has made peace for the world; I want to know whether He has made peace for me! It is little that He has made a covenant; I want to know whether He has made a covenant with me. If God the Holy Spirit gives me this assurance, then His salvation is mine, His heart is mine, and He Himself is mine. An everlasting covenant means a covenant which had no beginning and which will never, never end. How sweet, amid all the uncertainties of life, to know that "the foundation of God standeth sure" (2 Timothy 2:19). How blessed to have God's own promise, "My covenant will I not break, nor alter the thing that is gone out of my lips" (Psalm 89:34).

"I clothed thee also with broidered work, and shod thee with badgers' skin, and I girded thee about with fine linen, and I covered thee with silk" (Ezekiel 16:10).

See the matchless generosity of the Lord's provision for His people's clothing. They are so arrayed that the divine skill produces an unrivaled *broidered work* in which every attribute takes its part and every divine beauty is revealed. There is no art like the art displayed in our salvation and no workmanship like that seen in the righteousness of the saints. Justification has fascinated brilliant minds in all ages of the Church, and it will be the theme of praise in eternity. Utility is mingled with durability in our shoes made *with badgers' skin*. This same animal skin covered the tabernacle and formed one of the finest and strongest leathers known. The righteousness which is of God by faith endures forever. He who wears this divine preparation will tread the desert safely and may even set his foot upon the lion and the snake. The purity and dignity of our holy vesture are displayed in *the fine linen*. When the Lord sanctifies His people, they are dressed as priests in pure white. Even in the Lord's eyes they are without spot. The royal apparel is delicate and rich as *silk*. No expense is spared, no beauty withheld, no daintiness denied. We are grateful for our beautiful clothing from our Father. Surely there is gratitude in our hearts and joy that is waiting to be expressed. Rejoice in His presence this evening.

December 22
Morning

"I will strengthen thee" (Isaiah 41:10).

God is able to do all things! Believer, until you can drain dry the ocean of omnipotence or break the towering mountains of almighty strength into pieces, you never need to fear. The strength of man will never be able to overcome the power of God. The same God who directs the earth in its orbit has promised to supply you with daily strength. While He is able to uphold the universe, do not think that He will prove unable to fulfill His own promises. Remember what He did in the former generations. Remember how He spoke, and it was done; how He commanded, and it stood fast. Will He that created the world grow weary? He hangs the world on nothing. Will He who does this be unable to support His children? Doesn't He hold the ocean in the hollow of His hand? How can He fail you? When He has put such a faithful promise as this on record, will you for a moment indulge the thought that He has outpromised Himself and gone beyond His power to fulfill? No! You must doubt no longer. O my God and my strength, I can believe that this promise will be fulfilled, for the boundless reservoir of Your grace can never be exhausted. The overflowing storehouse of Your strength can never be emptied by Your friends or pilfered by Your enemies.

December 22
Evening

"The spot of his children" (Deuteronomy 32:5).

What is the secret spot which distinguishes the child of God from the rest of the world? It would be presumptuous for us to decide this for ourselves. We are told concerning our Lord, "As many as received him, to them gave he power to become the sons of God, even to them that believed on his name" (John 1:12). If I have received Christ Jesus into my heart, I am a child of God. I believe on Jesus Christ's name—that is, simply from my heart I trust the crucified, but now exalted, Redeemer. I am a member of the family of the Most High. If I have this, I have the privilege to become a child of God. Our Lord Jesus puts it in another way. "My sheep hear my voice, and I know them, and they follow me" (John 10:27). Christ appears as a Shepherd to His own sheep. As soon as He appears, His sheep recognize Him—they trust Him, and they are prepared to follow Him. He knows them, and they know Him. There is a constant connection between them. Thus, the one mark, the sure mark, the infallible mark of regeneration and adoption is a hearty faith in the appointed Redeemer. Are you uncertain whether you bear the secret mark of God's children? Then do not let an hour pass without saying, "Search me, O God, and know my heart" (Psalm 139:23). Do not take matters concerning your eternal soul and its destiny lightly.

December 23
Morning

"Friend, go up higher" (Luke 14:10).

When the life of grace first begins in the soul, we do indeed draw near to God; but it is with fear and trembling. The soul, conscious of guilt and humbled thereby, is in awe over the solemnity of its position. It is cast to the earth by a sense of the grandeur of Jehovah, in whose presence it stands. But as the Christian grows in grace, his fear has all its terror taken out of it. He will never forget the solemnity of his position and will never lose that holy awe which must encompass a gracious man when he is in the presence of the God who can create or destroy. It becomes a holy reverence and no more an overshadowing dread. He is called up higher, to greater access to God in Christ Jesus. Then the man of God, walking amid the splendors of deity and veiling his face, will approach the throne reverently and bowed in spirit. Seeing there a God of love, of goodness, and of mercy he will realize the character of God rather than His absolute deity. He will see in God His goodness rather than His greatness. While prostrate before the glory of the Infinite God, the soul will be sustained by the refreshing consciousness of being in the presence of boundless mercy and infinite love and by the realization of acceptance in the Beloved. Thus the believer is bidden to come up higher and is enabled to exercise the privilege of rejoicing in God and drawing near to Him in holy confidence, saying, "Abba, Father."

December 23
Evening

"The night also is thine" (Psalm 74:16).

Lord, You do not abdicate Your throne when the sun goes down, nor do You leave us all through these long wintry nights to be the prey of evil. Your eyes watch us as the stars, and Your arms surround us as the constellations in the sky. All the influences of the moon are in Your hand. This is very sweet to me when I am lying awake through the midnight hours or tossing to and fro in anguish. The night of affliction is as much under the control of the Lord of Love as the bright summer days when all is bliss. Jesus is in the tempest. His love wraps the night around itself as a mantle. The eye of faith can see through the robe to the love within. From early evening to the break of day, the eternal Watcher observes His saints and overrules the shades and dews of midnight for His people's highest good. We hear the voice of Jehovah saying, "I form the light, and create darkness. . .I the Lord do all these things" (Isaiah 45:7). Gloomy seasons of spiritual indifference and sin are not exempted from the divine purpose. When the altars of truth are defiled and the ways of God forsaken, the Lord's servants weep with bitter sorrow. But they should not despair, for the darkest times are governed by the Lord, and they will soon come to their end. What may seem to be defeat to us may be victory to Him.

December 24
Morning

"For your sakes he became poor" (2 Corinthians 8:9).

The Lord Jesus Christ was eternally rich, glorious, and exalted; but "though he was rich, yet for your sakes He became poor." The rich saint cannot be true in his communion with his poor brethren unless he gives his substance to minister to their necessities. Likewise, it is impossible that our divine Lord could have had fellowship with us unless He had imparted to us of His own abounding wealth and had become poor to make us rich. Had He remained on His throne of glory, and had we continued in the ruins of the fall without receiving His salvation, communion would have been impossible on both sides. Our position by the fall, apart from the covenant of grace, made it as impossible for fallen man to communicate with God as it is for Belial to be in agreement with Christ. It was necessary that the righteous Savior give to His sinning brethren of His own perfection and that we, the poor guilty, should receive of His fullness grace for grace. Thus in giving and receiving, the one might descend from the heights, and the others ascend from the depths, and so be able to embrace each other in true and hearty fellowship. Jesus must clothe His people in His own garments, or He cannot admit them into His palace of glory. He must wash them in His own blood, or else they will be too defiled for the embrace of His fellowship. Believer, here is love! For *your sake* the Lord Jesus became poor, that He might lift you up into communion with Himself.

December 24
Evening

"The glory of the Lord shall be revealed, and all flesh shall see it together" (Isaiah 40:5).

We look forward to the happy day when the whole world will be converted to Christ. The gods of the heathen will be cast down and false religions will be exploded, never again to cast their deceitful rays upon the nations. Kings will bow before the Prince of Peace, and all nations will call their Redeemer blessed. Some give up all hope of this day ever appearing. They look upon the world as a vessel breaking up and going to pieces. We know that the world is one day to be burnt up, and afterward we look for new heavens and a new earth. We are not discouraged by the length of delays in Jesus' return. We are not disheartened by the long period during which He allows the Church to struggle with little success. We believe that God will never allow this world which has seen Christ's blood shed upon it to be always the devil's stronghold. Christ came to deliver this world from the detested powers of darkness. What a shout there will be when men and angels unite to cry, "Allelujah: for the Lord God omnipotent reigneth" (Revelation 19:6). What a satisfaction it will be in that day to have had a share in the fight and to have aided in winning the victory for our Lord! Happy are they who fight side by side with the Lord, doing battle in His name and by His strength! How unhappy are those on the side of evil. It is a losing side, and it is a war where all losses are lost forever. Whose side are you on?

December 25
Morning

"Behold, a virgin shall conceive, and bear a son, and shall call his name Immanuel" (Isaiah 7:14).

Jesus is Jehovah incarnate, our Lord and our God, and yet our brother and friend. Let us adore and admire Him. His miraculous conception was a thing unheard of before and unparalleled since. "The Lord hath created a new thing in the earth, A woman shall compass a man" (Jeremiah 31:22). The first promise ran thus: *"The seed of the woman,"* not the offspring of the man. Our Savior, although truly man, was, as to His human nature, the Holy One of God. By the power of the Holy Spirit, He was born of the virgin without the taint of original sin which pertains to all those who are born of the flesh. Every believer is a portrait of Christ. Let us joyfully remember our dear Redeemer's glorious birth. When did angels indulge in midnight songs, or did God ever hang a new star in the sky before? To whose cradle did rich and poor make so willing a pilgrimage and offer such hearty and unsought obligations? Earth may rejoice and men may cease their labor to celebrate "the great birthday" of Jesus. The golden name, Immanuel, is inexpressibly delightful. God with us in our nature, our sorrow, our lifework, our grave; and now we with Him, in resurrection, ascension, triumph, and second advent splendor. The babe of Bethlehem appears to be manifestly with us in weakness. Oh, for true spiritual fellowship with Immanuel all this day!

December 25
Evening

"And it was so, when the days of their feasting were gone about, that Job sent and sanctified them, and rose up early in the morning, and offered burnt offerings according to the number of them all: for Job said, It may be that my sons have sinned, and cursed God in their hearts. Thus did Job continually" (Job 1:5).

The early morning sacrifice of Job should be imitated by the believer for himself before he rests tonight. Amid the cheerfulness of household gatherings it is easy to slide into sinful levities and to forget our character as Christians. It should not be so. But our days of feasting are seldom days of sanctified enjoyment. They frequently degenerate into unholy mirth. There is joy that is as pure and sanctifying as though one bathed in the rivers of Eden. Holy gratitude should be just as purifying an emotion as grief. Unfortunately, the house of mourning often encourages spiritual growth more than the house of feasting. Believer, in what have you sinned today? Have you been forgetful of your high calling? Have you filled your conversation with idle words and loose speeches? Then confess the sin, and hurry to the sacrifice. The precious blood of the Lamb that was slain removes the guilt and purges away the defilement of the sins of ignorance and carelessness. This is the best ending of Christmas day—to wash anew in the cleansing fountain. Believer, come to this sacrifice every night. To live at the altar is the privilege of the royal priesthood. Sin, great as it is, is no reason for despair. If you draw near to Jesus and confess your faults, He will cleanse your conscience from dead works.

December 26
Morning

"The last Adam" (1 Corinthians 15:45).

Jesus is the head of His elect. In Adam every heir of flesh and blood has a personal interest because Adam is the covenant head and representative of the race. Every redeemed soul is one with the Lord since He is the Second Adam, the sponsor and substitute of the elect in the new covenant of love. The apostle Paul declares that Levi was in the loins of Abraham when Melchizedek met him. It is a certain truth that the believer was in Jesus Christ, the mediator, when in eternity the covenant settlements of grace were decreed, ratified, and made sure forever. Thus, whatever Christ has done, He has done for the whole body of His Church. We were crucified in Him and buried with Him. (See Colossians 2:10-13.) To make it still more wonderful, we are risen with Him and even ascended with Him to the seats on high. (See Ephesians 2:6.) It is thus that the Church has fulfilled the law and is accepted in the Beloved. It is thus that she is regarded with complacency by the just Jehovah, for He views her in Jesus and does not look on her as separate from her covenant head. As the anointed Redeemer of Israel, Christ Jesus has nothing distinct from His Church; but all that He has, He holds for her. All that the Second Adam is or does is ours as well as His, seeing that He is our representative. Here is the foundation of the covenant of grace.

December 26
Evening

"Lo, I am with you alway" (Matthew 28:20).

The Lord Jesus is in the midst of His Church. He is as surely with us now as He was with the disciples at the lake when they ate fish and bread with Him. Where Jesus is, *love becomes inflamed.* Of all the things in the world that can set the heart burning, there is nothing like the presence of Jesus! A glimpse of Him overwhelms us, and we are ready to say, "Turn away thine eyes from me, for they have overcome me" (Song of Solomon 6:5). Even the smell of the aloes, the myrrh, and the cassia which drop from His perfumed garments cause the sick and the faint to grow strong. A moment's leaning of the head upon that gracious bosom and a reception of His divine love into our poor, cold hearts causes us to glow with the fire of His love. If we know that Jesus is with us, we will throw ourselves into the Lord's service with all of our heart, soul, and strength. Therefore, the presence of Christ is to be desired above all things. His presence will be most realized by those who are most like Him. If you desire to see Christ, you must grow in conformity to Him. Bring yourself, by the power of the Spirit, into union with Christ's desires, motives, and plans of action, and you will be blessed with His company. His promise is as true as ever. He delights to be with us. If He does not come, it is because we hinder Him by our indifference. He will reveal Himself in answer to our earnest prayers and graciously be detained by our entreaties and tears. These are the golden chains which bind Jesus to His people.

December 27
Morning

"Can the rush grow up without mire?" (Job 8:11).

The rush plant is spongy and hollow and so is a hypocrite. There is no substance or stability in him. The rush plant is shaken to and fro in every wind, just as formalists yield to every influence. For this reason the rush is not broken by the tempest, neither are hypocrites troubled with persecution. Perhaps the text for this day may help me to try myself, whether I am a hypocrite or not. The rush by nature lives in water and owes its very existence to the mire and moisture wherein it has taken root. Let the mire become dry, and the rush withers very quickly. Its greenness is absolutely dependent on circumstances. Is this my case? Do I only serve God when I am in good company or when religion is profitable and respectable? Do I love the Lord only when temporal comforts are received from His hands? If so, I am a base hypocrite. Like the withering rush, I will perish when death deprives me of outward joys. But can I honestly assert that when bodily comforts have been few and my surroundings have been rather adverse to grace than helpful to it, I have still held fast my integrity? Then I have hope that there is genuine, vital godliness in me. A goodly man often grows best when his worldly circumstances decay. He who follows Christ for gain is a Judas. They who attend Him out of love are His own beloved ones. Lord, let me find my life in You and not in the mire of this world's favor or gain.

December 27
Evening

"And the Lord shall guide thee continually" (Isaiah 58:11).

"The Lord shall guide thee." Not an angel, but Jehovah will guide you. He said that an angel would go before His people to lead them through the wilderness. Moses said, "If thy presence go not with me, carry us not up hence" (Exodus 33:15). The Father Himself leads you through your earthly journey. You may not see the cloud or the fiery pillar, but Jehovah will never forsake you. Notice the word *shall*—"The Lord shall guide thee." How sure we can be that God will not forsake us! His precious *shalls* and *wills* are better than men's promises. "I will never leave thee, nor forsake thee" (Hebrews 13:5). We are not merely to be guided sometimes, but we have a perpetual Leader. We are to continually hear the guiding voice of the Great Shepherd. If we follow close beside Him, we will be led in the right way. If you have to change your position in life; if you have to emigrate to distant shores; if you are cast into poverty or suddenly promoted to a more responsible position; if you are thrown among strangers or cast among foes, do not fear, for "the Lord shall guide thee continually." There are no difficulties out of which you will not be delivered if you live near to God, and your heart is kept warm with holy love. Walk with God, and you cannot lose your way. You have infallible wisdom to direct you, unchanging love to comfort you, and eternal power to defend you.

December 28
Morning

"The life which I now live in the flesh, I live by the faith of the Son of God" (Galatians 2:20).

When the Lord in mercy passed by and saw us in our blood, He first of all said, "Live," because life is one of the absolutely essential things in spiritual matters. Until it is given, we are incapable of partaking in the things of the Kingdom. The life which grace confers on the saints at the moment of their quickening is none other than the life of Christ. Like the sap from the stem, faith runs into us, the branches, and establishes a living connection between our souls and Jesus. Faith is the grace which perceives this union, having proceeded from it as its firstfruit. Faith knows His excellence and worth, and no temptation can induce it to place its trust elsewhere. Christ Jesus is so delighted with this heavenly grace that He never ceases to strengthen and sustain faith by the loving embrace and all-sufficient support of His eternal arms. Here, then, is established a living, sensible, and delightful union which casts forth streams of love, confidence, sympathy, complacency, and joy, whereof both the bride and bridegroom love to drink. When the soul can evidently perceive this oneness between itself and Christ, the pulse may be felt as beating for both and the one blood as flowing through the veins of each. Then the heart is as near heaven as it can be while on earth and is prepared for the enjoyment of the most sublime and spiritual kind of fellowship.

December 28
Evening

"I came not to send peace, but a sword" (Matthew 10:34).

The Christian will be sure to make enemies. He will not set out to do this; but if to do what is right and to believe what is true causes him to lose every earthly friend, he will consider it a small loss. His great Friend in heaven will reveal Himself more graciously than ever. Your Master said, "I am come to set a man at variance against his father, and the daughter against her mother. . .And a man's foes shall be they of his own household" (Matthew 10:35-36). Christ is the great Peacemaker; but before peace, He brings war. Where the light enters, the darkness must leave. Where truth is, the lie must flee. If it remains, there will be a stern conflict for the truth cannot and will not lower its standard. If you live so as to stand the test of the final judgment, the world will not speak well of you. He who has the friendship of the world is an enemy to God. If you are true and faithful to the Most High, men will resent your unflinching fidelity since it is a testimony against their iniquities. Fearless of all consequences, you must do what is right. You will need the courage of a lion to pursue a course which will turn your best friend into your fiercest foe. But for the love of Jesus, you must be courageous. To risk your reputation and affection requires a degree of moral strength which only the Spirit of God can work in you. Do not turn your back like a coward. Follow boldly in your Master's steps, for He has traveled this rough way before you. A brief warfare and eternal rest is better than false peace and everlasting torment.

December 29
Morning

"Hitherto hath the Lord helped us" (1 Samuel 7:12).

The word "hitherto" seems like a hand pointing in the direction of the *past*. Twenty years or seventy years and hitherto the Lord has helped us! Through poverty or wealth, sickness or health, at home or abroad, and in trials or triumphs the Lord has helped us! We delight to look down a long avenue of trees. It is pleasing to gaze from end to end of the long vista. Even so look down the long aisles of your years, at the green boughs of mercy overhead and the strong pillars of lovingkindness and faithfulness which bear up your joys. But the word also points *forward*. For when a man gets up to a certain mark and writes "hitherto," he is not yet at the end. There is still a distance to be traveled. There are more trials, more joys; more temptations, more triumphs; more prayers, more answers; more toils, more strength; and more fights, more victories. Is it over now? No! There is more yet—awakening in Jesus' likeness, thrones, harps, songs, psalms, white raiment, the face of Jesus, the society of saints, the glory of God, the fullness of eternity, and he infinity of bliss. Be of good courage, believer. He who has helped you "hitherto" will help you on your journey all the way through.

December 29
Evening

"What think ye of Christ?" (Matthew 22:42).

The great test of your soul's condition is, *What do you think of Christ?* Is He to you "fairer than the children of men" (Psalm 45:2); "the chief among ten thousand" (Song of Solomon 5:10); the "altogether lovely" (Song of Solomon 5:16)? Measure your faith by this barometer: how highly esteemed is Christ in your heart? If you have thought little of Christ, if you have been content to live without His presence, if you have cared little for His honor, if you have neglected His laws, then your soul is sick—may God grant that it is not near death! But if the first thought of your spirit is, "How can I honor Jesus?"; if the daily desire of your soul has been, "Oh that I knew where I might find Him;" you may have a thousand difficulties and even be a babe in Christ, and yet you are perfectly safe, because you honor Jesus. Your rags disappear when you focus on *His* royal apparel. Your wounds, though they bleed in torrents, are small when you think of *His* wounds. Are they like glittering rubies in your esteem? What do you think of the King in His beauty? Does He have a glorious high throne in your heart? Would you be willing to die if you could add another trumpet to the melody which proclaims His praise? Then, you have a healthy spiritual life. Whatever you may think of yourself, if Christ is important to you, you will be with Him before long.

December 30
Morning

"Better is the end of a thing than the beginning thereof" (Ecclesiastes 7:8).

Look at our Lord and Master. In His beginning, He was despised and rejected of men; a man of sorrows and acquainted with grief. Do you see the end? He sits at His Father's right hand knowing His enemies will be made His footstool. "As he is, so are we also in this world" (1 John 4:17). You must bear the cross, or you will never wear the crown; you must wade through the mire, or you will never walk the golden pavement. Cheer up, then, poor Christian. "Better is the end of a thing than the beginning thereof." How contemptible is the appearance of a caterpillar. It is the beginning of a thing. Yet, later notice that insect with gorgeous wings and full of happiness and life; that is the end thereof. That caterpillar is like yourself, until you are wrapped up in the chrysalis of death. But when Christ appears you will be like Him, for you will see Him as He is. That rough-looking diamond is put on the wheel of the lapidary. He cuts it on all sides. It loses much—much that seemed costly to itself. That very diamond which was severely cut by the lapidary, now glitters in the king's crown. You may venture to compare yourself to such a diamond, for you are one of God's people; and this is the time of the cutting process. Let faith and patience have their perfect work, for in the day when the crown will be set on the head of the King Eternal, Immortal, Invisible, one ray of glory will stream from you. "They shall be mine," saith the Lord, "in the day when I make up my jewels" (Malachi 3:17).

December 30
Evening

"Knowest thou not that it will be bitterness in the latter end?" (2 Samuel 2:26).

Are you merely religious and not a true possessor of the faith that is in Christ Jesus? You regularly attend a place of worship. You go because others go, not because your heart is right with God. For the next twenty or thirty years, you will probably be permitted to go on as you do now—professing religion by an outward appearance, but having no heart in the matter. I must show you the deathbed of one like you. Let us gaze upon him gently. A clammy sweat is on his brow, and he wakes up crying, "O God, it is hard to die. Did you send for my minister?" "Yes, he is coming." The minister comes. "Sir, I fear that I am dying!" "Have you any hope?" "I cannot say that I have. I fear to stand before my God; oh! pray for me." The prayer is offered for him with sincere earnestness, and the way of salvation is for the ten-thousandth time put before him; but before he has grasped the rope, I see him sink into death. Where is the man now? It is written, "In hell he lift up his eyes, being in torments" (Luke 16:23). Why did he not lift up his eyes before? He was so accustomed to hearing the gospel that his soul slept under it. Let the Savior's own word reveal the suffering: "Father Abraham. . .send Lazarus, that he may dip the tip of his finger in water, and cool my tongue; for I am tormented in this flame" (Luke 16:24). There is a frightful meaning in those words. May you never have to experience Jehovah's wrath!

December 31
Morning

"In the last day, that great day of the feast, Jesus stood and cried, saying, If any man thirst, let him come unto me and drink" (John 7:37).

Patience had her perfect work in the Lord Jesus. Until the last day of the feast, He pleaded with the Jews. On this last day of the year, He pleads with us and waits to be gracious to us. Admirable is the long-suffering of the Savior in bearing with some of us year after year, notwithstanding our provocations, rebellions, and resistance of His Holy Spirit. Wonder of wonders that we are still in the land of mercy. He entreats us to be reconciled. How deep must be the love which makes the Lord weep over sinners. Surely at the call of such a cry our willing hearts will come. All that man needs to quench his soul's thirst is provided. Though the soul is utterly famished, Jesus can restore it. Proclamation is made, most freely, that every thirsty one is welcome. He bore our sins in His own body on the tree. Come now and drink, before the sun sets on the year's last day! A fool, a thief, a harlot can drink. Sinfulness of character is no bar to the invitation to believe in Jesus. The mouth of poverty is welcome to stoop down and take a deep drink of the flowing flood. Blistered, leprous, filthy lips may touch the stream of divine love. They cannot pollute it, but will themselves be purified. Jesus is the source of hope. Dear reader, hear the Redeemer's loving voice as He cries to each of us, "If any man thirst, let him come unto me and drink."

December 31
Evening

"The harvest is past, the summer is ended, and we are not saved" (Jeremiah 8:20).

Not saved! Is this your mournful plight? Warned of the judgment to come, called to escape for your life, and yet at this moment you are *not saved!* You know the way of salvation. You read it in the Bible, you hear it from the pulpit, it is explained to you by friends, and yet, you neglect it. You will be without excuse when the Lord judges the living and the dead. The Holy Spirit has placed His blessing upon the Word which has been preached to you. Times of refreshing have come from the divine Presence. Your summer and your harvest have past—and yet you are *not saved.* Years followed one another into eternity, and your last year will soon be here. Affliction and prosperity alike have failed to impress you. Tears and prayers and sermons have been wasted on your barren heart. Is it likely that you will continue on as you are until death forever bars the door of hope? The convenient time never has come for you yet; why should it ever come? Perhaps you will find no convenient time until you are in hell. Before another year begins, believe in Jesus who is able to save you. Consecrate the last hours of this year, and let it lead to a humble faith in Jesus. See to it that this year does not pass away leaving you with an unforgiven spirit. Believe *now* and live. "Escape for thy life; look not behind thee, neither stay thou in all the plain; escape to the mountain, lest thou be consumed" (Genesis 19:17).